Houghton Mifflin English

Grammar and Composition

Sixth Course

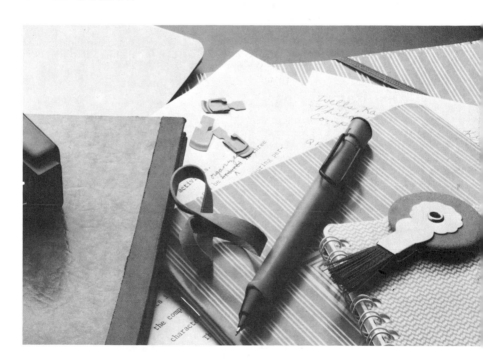

Houghton Mifflin Company • **Boston**

Atlanta   Dallas   Geneva, Illinois
Lawrenceville, New Jersey   Palo Alto   Toronto

Authors

Ann Cole Brown Former Lecturer in English composition and literature at Northern Virginia Community College in Alexandria, Virginia

Jeffrey Nilson Former teacher of English at the Wixon Middle School, South Dennis, Massachusetts, and independent computer software designer

Fran Weber Shaw Assistant Professor of English and Coordinator of the Writing Center at the University of Connecticut, Stamford

Richard A. Weldon Vice Principal, Associate Dean of Studies, and teacher of English at the Christian Brothers High School in Sacramento, California

Editorial Advisers

Edwin Newman Veteran broadcast journalist, author, and chairman of the Usage Panel of the *American Heritage Dictionary of the English Language*

Robert Cotton Vice Principal, Curriculum Director, and former chairman of the English Department at Servite High School in Anaheim, California

Consultant

Nancy C. Millett Professor of Language Arts Education at Wichita State University, Kansas, and co-author of *Houghton Mifflin English, K-8*

Special Contributors

Ernestine Sewell, University of Texas at Arlington

Luella M. Wolff, Washburn University, Topeka, Kansas

Acknowledgments

The Publisher gratefully acknowledges the cooperation of the National Council of Teachers of English for making available student writing from the Council's Achievement Awards in Writing Program.

(Acknowledgments continue on page 678.)

Copyright © 1986, 1984 by Houghton Mifflin Company

Printed in U.S.A.

ISBN: 0-395-38552-0

ABCDEFGHIJ-RM-943210/898765

Contents

Part Three Related Skills   612

The English Language

A Brief History

When the English language got its start about fifteen hundred years ago, it was spoken only by a few Germanic tribes living in England. Today, more than three hundred million people, or about one eighth of the world's population, speak English. But the English that we speak is a very different language from the English spoken fifteen hundred years ago. In fact, a speaker of modern English would be unable to understand a speaker of the earliest form of English. The changes that have taken place in the language as well as its status as an important world language are both the result of major cultural and social developments.

Beowulf, *an epic poem written in Old English about a Scandinavian hero, is considered to be the first great work of English literature. Like almost all Old English poetry, it uses a pattern of alliteration instead of rhyme.*

Importance of English

Today, English is the leading international language. More people may speak Chinese than English, but Chinese does not have the significance of English in international political, business, and cultural affairs. Nearly three hundred million people speak English as their native language, and more than one hundred fifty million others use it as a second language.

Most of the native speakers of English live in the United States, Canada, Great Britain, Ireland, Australia, New Zealand, and South Africa. Large numbers of people in India, Pakistan, and Bangladesh speak English almost as much as their native language. In addition, millions of business people, scientists, and government officials around the world use English in their work.

English is one of the six official languages of the United Nations and is an important language in international diplomacy. It is also widely used by scientists throughout the world to communicate the results of their research to colleagues in other nations.

Characteristics of English

Certain basic characteristics distinguish English from other languages. Among the more noteworthy are (1) the importance of word order, (2) the simplicity of inflections, (3) the difficulty of its spelling, and (4) its large vocabulary.

English relies primarily on the order of words in a sentence to indicate grammatical relationships. We can often recognize the function of a word by its position in a sentence. For example, in the sentence *John hit the ball,* we know that *ball* is the object and that it follows the verb. We cannot change the order of the words without changing the meaning of the sentence, as, for example, in the sentence *The ball hit John.* For this reason, word order in English is more regular and less flexible than in languages that indicate the function of a word by varying its form. These variable forms of a word are called inflections.

Inflections are used to indicate case, number, gender, voice, mood, and tense. In German, for example, the definite article is declined to indicate the case of the noun that it modifies. *Johann schlagte den Ball* is the German translation of *John hit the ball*. The article *den* is in the accusative (objective) case, thus indicating that *ball* is the direct object of the verb. As a result, the meaning would be the same if we wrote *Den Ball schlagte Johann.*

In English, only nouns, pronouns, and verbs are inflected, and most of those words have only a few inflections. For example, the verb *ride* has only five forms (*ride, rides, rode, riding, ridden*), while the corresponding German verb *reiten* has sixteen forms.

In English, unlike many other European languages, adjectives are uninflected. For example, the adjective *tall* is always spelled the same way no matter what noun it is modifying. In Spanish, however, the word for *tall* can be spelled *alto, alta, altos,* or *altas,* depending on the number and gender of the noun that it modifies.

An important characteristic of English is its flexibility of function for some words. For example, many words can be used as both nouns and verbs. We can "issue a plan" or "plan an issue"; "ruin a visit" or "visit a ruin"; and "clock the race" or "race the clock." Similarly, some words can be used as both nouns and adjectives. For example, on the side of a *mountain* we might see a *mountain* goat.

In such languages as Spanish and Italian, spelling is closely related to pronunciation. In English, however, spelling is difficult because there is not a one-to-one correspondence between the sounds of the language and their written forms. The same sound can be spelled various ways (*leaf, graph, laugh*), and the same combination of letters can represent a variety of sounds (*rough, through, though*).

With more than six hundred thousand words, English has the largest vocabulary of any language. Many of these words are technical terms used only by scientists or other specialists. Nevertheless, few languages can rival English in the richness of its vocabulary. The size of the vocabulary stems largely from the fact that, through most of its history, English has borrowed words freely from many other languages. English is also freer than most languages in its creation of new words by combining or modifying existing words.

Origins of English

Along with most of the languages spoken in Europe and western Asia, English belongs to the Indo-European family of languages. Linguists believe that all of these languages developed from Proto-Indo-European, a tongue spoken by nomadic groups in Europe more than five thousand years ago. No written records of Proto-Indo-European exist, but linguists have reconstructed the language by comparing all the languages that developed from it.

Over the centuries, Proto-Indo-European evolved into different dialects as its speakers resettled throughout parts of Europe. In northwestern Europe the dialect that was spoken formed the Germanic group of Indo-European languages. Scholars divide this group into East Germanic, North Germanic, and West Germanic. All the East Germanic languages are extinct. North Germanic includes Icelandic, Danish, Norwegian, and Swedish. English is classified as West Germanic, along with German and Dutch.

The Development of Old English

The history of the English language itself begins with the Angles, the Saxons, and the Jutes. These three groups lived near one another in what is now northern Germany and southern Denmark and spoke closely related dialects of West Germanic. After the Angles, Saxons, and Jutes invaded England in the A.D. 400s, their isolation from other Germanic speakers caused their language to become different from other varieties of West Germanic. We refer to this language as Old English or Anglo-Saxon.

The people who lived in England before the invasion of the Germanic tribes spoke a Celtic language. The Angles, Saxons, and Jutes drove these original inhabitants into Wales and established such complete domination over England that almost no words of Celtic origin dating from this period are found in English.

During the 600s and 700s, the Anglo-Saxon people were converted to Christianity. This event had great significance for Old English, because religious scribes, who knew Latin, began to use the Roman alphabet to write Old English. Thanks to these scribes, we have a wealth of written records in Old English. Because we know what sounds the letters of the Roman alphabet represented in Latin, we can also be fairly certain of how Old English was pronounced.

As time went on, Old English developed regional dialects of its own. The four main dialects—West Saxon, Kentish, Mercian, and Northumbrian—differed mostly in pronunciation. By the 900s, Wessex, the area south of the Thames between Cornwall and Kent where West Saxon was spoken, had become the political and cultural center of England. Thus, West Saxon became the dominant dialect and something of a standard national language. In fact, England became the first nation in Europe to have such a standard language for literature and official documents.

Most of the documents in Old English that have come down to us are written in West Saxon. These writings include a rich variety of literature as well as legal documents and inscriptions. The literature consists mostly of poetry and various forms of religious writing, including sermons and meditations.

The development of Old English was also influenced by invasions of Scandinavians during the 800s and again around 1000. A number of Scandinavian words were taken into the language, including most of the English words that begin with *sk,* such as *sky* and *skirt.* In addition, some English pronouns were replaced by Scandinavian pronouns, including the forerunners of *they, them,* and *their.*

Characteristics of Old English

In many ways Old English was more similar to Modern German than to Modern English. Like German, Old English had inflectional endings to show grammatical relationships of nouns and adjectives. Even the definite article was highly inflected; it had twelve different forms, depending on the case, gender, and number of the noun it was used with. Because of this system of inflections, word order in Old English was somewhat freer than in Modern English.

Also, as in German, nouns were of the masculine, feminine, or neuter gender, which determined the form of accompanying articles, adjectives, and pronouns. This gender had nothing to do with the actual gender of what the noun stood for. Thus, *joy* (*dream*) was masculine, shoulder (*eaxl*) was feminine, and *woman* (wif) was neuter.

The fact that Old English is essentially a foreign language for speakers of Modern English is clearly shown by the following lines from the masterpiece of Old English literature, the epic poem *Beowulf:*

> Nis þæt feor heonon
> milgemearces þæt se mere standeð,
> ofer þæm hongiað hrinde bearwas,
> wudu wyrtum fæst, wæter oferhelmað.

Notice that Old English used two letters not found in Modern English, þ (called thorn) and ð (called edh). Both letters represent the sound *th* as in the word *thorn*. In Modern English, the passage above reads:

> It is not far hence
> measured by miles that the mere stands;
> over it hang frost-covered groves;
> a wood made fast with roots, overshadows the water.

Despite the differences between Old English and Modern English, many of our most common words come directly from Old English. From the passage above, you can recognize *stand, over,* and *water.* Other examples include *being, father, house, life, mother, summer,* and *write.*

The Rise of Middle English

The conquest of England by the Normans from northwestern France in 1066 brought great changes to English culture and to the English language. The Normans were of Scandinavian ancestry, but they had adopted the French language and culture after conquering Normandy in the 800s. By 1100 Norman French had become the language of the dominant classes in England, and Old English as a standard language disappeared. English, in the form of its various dialects, became the language of peasants and workers and was for the most part an unwritten language.

The Normans ruled both England and Normandy in northwestern France until 1204, when France recaptured Normandy. With no territory on the continent, the Normans began to consider England their home and gradually started to use English rather than French. In the process, however, they introduced thousands of French words into the English vocabulary. This influx of French terms was especially great in certain categories, such as law and government (*court, judge, justice, parliament, council, tax, royal, prince, city, mayor, money*), military matters (*battle, siege, armor, fortress, assault*), and cooking (*sauce, boil, fry, roast*).

This borrowing of French words also helped open the door to a similar borrowing of words from other languages, especially Latin. French is a Romance language, which means that it developed from Latin. Furthermore, because Latin was the language of scholarship at the time, scholars naturally introduced many Latin words into English, including *educate, index,* and *library.*

During this period other important changes were taking place in English that had little to do with the influence of French. For the most part, these changes were continuations of trends that had begun during the last part of the Old English period. For example, English became a much less inflected language. Old English nouns had had inflections that consisted of final unstressed vowels. In Middle English, vowels in unstressed syllables began to be pronounced alike, and the significance of the inflections disappeared.

Similarly, grammatical gender also disappeared from English during this period. The gender of nouns could no longer be distinguished once inflections disappeared, and one definite article, *the,* replaced the masculine *se,* feminine *seo,* and neuter *thaet* of Old English. Thus, English speakers began to consider only actual gender in the use of pronouns. Males were referred to as *he,* females were referred to as *she,* and anything inanimate was referred to as *it.*

When English re-emerged as the official language of England, there were five main dialects: Northern, Southern, East Midland, West Midland, and Kentish. Since London had become the capital, its dialect—East Midland—became the standard, just as the speech of the political center of Anglo Saxon England—Wessex—had served as the standard dialect of Old English. East Midland became the prestigious dialect of Middle English because it was spoken not only at the royal court but also at the leading universities, Oxford and Cambridge.

The status of London English was further enhanced by the fact that it was the language in which the great Middle English author Geoffrey Chaucer wrote. The following passage from Chaucer's *The Canterbury Tales,* written in the late 1300s, shows that the language had taken a form that we can recognize as English:

> A Knyght ther was, and that a worthy man,
> That fro the tyme that he first bigan
> To riden out, he loved chivalrie,
> Trouthe and honor, fredom and curteisie.

Notice that the vocabulary is similar to Modern English, although the spelling is considerably different. This spelling reflects differences in pronunciation between Middle English and Modern English. The spelling in Middle English followed pronunciation closely. For example, all consonants were pronounced, including the *k* and the *gh* in *Knyght.* In addition, a final *e* was pronounced like the *a* in the Modern English word *sofa.*

The Emergence of Modern English

The transition from Middle English to Modern English took place during the period from 1350 to about 1550. The two forms of the language are distinguished primarily by major changes in the pronunciation of the long vowels that occurred during this period. Linguists refer to these changes collectively as the Great Vowel Shift. It was during this period, for example, that *a, e,* and *i* came to be pronounced as they are in the Modern English words *late, meet,* and *ride,* respectively. In Middle English these letters were pronounced much as we would pronounce *ah, ay,* and *ee.*

We can also trace the origin of the difficult spelling system of Modern English to this period. In 1476 William Caxton set up a press at Westminster and introduced printing into England. This event took place in the midst of the Great Vowel Shift, and Caxton chose to keep the spelling used by Middle English scribes rather than a spelling that followed the pronunciation of his day. Because Caxton's publications set the standard for spelling that later printers would follow, Modern English continued to resemble Middle English in its spelling even as it underwent great changes in pronunciation.

At the right is a sample page from Chapter One of The Game and Playe of Chess, *printed by William Caxton in 1480. Caxton's printer's mark, or signature (lower left), consisted of a monogram of the date 1474 and his initials.*

Caxton also unconsciously introduced at least one foreign element into English spelling. Caxton had spent much of his life in Holland and perhaps tended to confuse English spelling and Dutch spelling. He also hired Dutch printers because they were highly skilled. In any case, he and the Dutch printers introduced the Dutch form *gh* into words such as *ghost* and *ghoul*, which had formerly been spelled *gost* and *goul*.

Caxton's publications also marked the final establishment of the London dialect as the standard for literary works. Until this time, literature had continued to appear in each of the five major dialects of English. After Caxton, however, works of literature almost without exception were published in the standard language.

The vocabulary of English continued to expand dramatically during the 1400s and 1500s. The spread of the Renaissance to England in the 1500s brought a new interest in the works of Latin and Greek writers. Borrowing freely from Latin and Greek, Renaissance scholars introduced a multitude of new words into English. The language purists of the time were outraged at the introduction of what they called "inkhorn terms"—words such as *capacity, celebrate, fertile, native,* and *confidence.* But the borrowing from Latin and Greek, as well as from French and Italian, continued undiminished.

One result of all this borrowing was to give English a remarkable abundance of synonyms from a variety of sources. Consider, for example, *kingly,* which came from Old English, and *regal* and *royal,* both of which came from Latin by way of French. Some pairs of synonyms represent Latin words that came into English twice—once through French and again directly from Latin. Such pairs include *count* and *compute, frail* and *fragile,* and *sever* and *separate.*

In some cases, borrowing gave English two sets of words relating to the same objects. For example, *cow, calf,* and *pig* are all from Old English; but *beef, veal,* and *pork* are all from French. Similarly, the names of all the external parts of the body except *face* are Old English words, but many of the adjectives used to refer to those parts are of Latin origin. Examples include *mouth* and *oral, ear* and *aural,* and *eye* and *ocular.*

The Majority of English

The beauty and power of the language in the works of William Shakespeare, Christopher Marlowe, and other writers of the late 1500s and 1600s lent new prestige to the English language. The writers of this period considered the language alive and changing, and they experimented freely with vocabulary and sentence structure. Shakespeare himself borrowed words from other languages and apparently was the first writer to use such words as *dislocate, obscene,* and *premeditated.* Shakespeare also coined such phrases as *fair play* and *a foregone conclusion.*

The freedom that had characterized English in the 1500s and 1600s offended the scholars of the 1700s, who placed a high value on logic and order. Thus, they set about to impose rules and regularity on English but met with only qualified success.

Although Caxton had set the pattern for English spelling, considerable variation in spelling existed well into the 1600s. For example, the word *guest* was variously spelled *gest, geste, gueste, ghest,* and *ghestse.* Thus, there was concern over spelling, or orthography (literally, "right writing"), as it was called at the time. The first English dictionaries, which began to appear during the 1600s, listed and defined only what were considered difficult words.

The publication of Samuel Johnson's *Dictionary of the English Language* in 1755 was a landmark in the development of English. Johnson's dictionary established a standard correct spelling for each of its forty thousand entries. It also made abundant use of quotations from writers to illustrate the meaning and proper use of words.

The grammarians of the 1700s had a high regard for Latin, which they considered superior to English. They therefore based their grammars of English on Latin. These grammarians believed that English should be reduced to a system of rules. In fact, they originated most of the grammatical rules that we still apply today, such as those that ban the use of double negatives, regulate the use of *shall* and *will,* and prohibit the use of prepositions at the end of sentences.

These grammarians exerted considerable influence on the language because of the prestige of their position in society, but later linguists have questioned some of their judgments about the language. For example, the rule against double negatives was based on an analogy to mathematics and ignored the frequent use of double negatives in other languages as well as in the writings of many earlier masters of English, including Chaucer and Shakespeare. Nevertheless, the ideas of these grammarians became the rules that have governed English usage for more than two hundred years.

DICTIONARY

OF THE

ENGLISH LANGUAGE

IN WHICH

The WORDS are deduced from their ORIGINALS,

AND

ILLUSTRATED in their DIFFERENT SIGNIFICATIONS

BY

EXAMPLES from the best WRITERS

TO WHICH ARE PREFIXED,

A HISTORY of the LANGUAGE.

AND

AN ENGLISH GRAMMAR.

BY SAMUEL JOHNSON, A M

IN TWO VOLUMES

VOL. I.

Cum tabulis animum cenfori; fumet honeft.
Audebit quaecunque parum fplendoris habebunt.
Et fine pondere erunt, et honore indigna ferentur
Verba movere loco, quamvis invita recedant,
Et verfentur adhuc intra penetralia Veftae.
Obfcurata diu populo bonus eruet, atque
Proferet in lucem fpeciofa vocabula rerum,
Quae prifcis memorata Catonibus atque Cethegis,
Nunc fitus informis premit et deferta vetuftas.   Hor

LONDON

Printed by W STRAHAN,

For J. and P. KNAPTON, T. and T. LONGMAN; C. HITCH and L. HAWES;
A MILLAR, and R, and J. DODSLEY.

MDCCLV.

Samuel Johnson's achievements as a critic, writer and lexicographer earned him a place of honor in English literature. The sample on the right is the title page of Volume I of Johnson's dictionary, published in 1755.

The Spread of English

For the first thousand years of its history, the English language remained confined to a very small area of the world. In 1500 fewer than five million people spoke English, and all of them lived in the British Isles. In the 1500s, however, the British began a period of exploration and expansion that eventually carried the English language to North America, Africa, Asia, and Australia.

By 1700 the number of English speakers had reached nearly ten million, many of whom lived in North America. Although English speakers in America never lost contact with England, a variety of influences shaped American English into a distinct variety of the language.

As Great Britain became the leading world power in the 1800s, British colonists introduced English into Australia, India, and many parts of Africa. Local peoples and conditions also led to the development of distinct varieties of English in each of these areas. The native languages of these regions have also contributed to the vocabulary of English. From Australia came *kangaroo* and *boomerang,* and from India came *bungalow* and *verandah.*

The status of English as a world language received another boost with the emergence of the United States as a world power after World War II. The success of the American economic system has made English the language of international business. This economic power, coupled with the development of television and other means of mass communication, has brought American culture—and thus American English—to nearly every part of the world. Indeed, some countries have even felt the need to set up official policies to "protect" their own languages from the influence of English.

The Future

Because language is dynamic and living, English inevitably continues to change. Today we see that technology is constantly contributing new terms to our vocabulary—from *videodisc* and *byte* to *feedback* and *word processing.* In addition, the continuing immigration of Spanish speakers from Latin America is adding to the stock of Spanish words in the vocabulary of American English.

As for the future, we cannot predict the ways in which English will change. Nevertheless, we can be certain that it will continue to change along with economics, technology, and other aspects of culture. The English language has always demonstrated a capacity to assimilate the many influences that bear on it. This dynamic capacity keeps English the flexible, and thus powerful, tool for communication that it is.

The advent of the computer and word-processing equipment has changed the way English language is stored and retrieved. A writer can create a draft, revise it, and save it for future reference with minimal typing.

Assignments

Assignment 1
In your school or local library, locate a copy of Chaucer's *The Canterbury Tales* printed in Middle English. Select a passage of approximately ten lines and list all the words that are spelled differently from the corresponding words in Modern English. Describe any patterns that you find in the spelling of the Middle English words on your list and try to formulate a rule for one such pattern. Test the rule by trying to find other examples of it in a second passage.

Assignment 2
Make a list of ten words that you have encountered for the first time in your recent reading. Check the origin of each word in your dictionary. For any word that has Greek or Latin origins, give another familiar English word that has the same Greek or Latin root. For any word that is derived from Middle English, tell whether it comes from Old English or some other Germanic language.

Assignment 3
Using library resources, find a list of the most frequently used words in the English language. Trace the origins of the fifteen most frequently occurring nouns. Indicate which of the fifteen nouns have Middle English, Old English, and classical origins. Describe any patterns that you find in the nature of the words themselves, such as a group of words indicating family relationships or a group of words indicating physical surroundings.

Assignment 4
Prepare a short report on Samuel Johnson's influence on the spelling and grammar of Modern English. In your report explain why Johnson wanted to standardize the spelling and usage of English and discuss what degree of success he had. Cite some examples of current spellings and usage rules to support your case.

Assignment 5

A number of British scientists and inventors have given their surnames to the English language to identify the items or processes with which they were chiefly associated. Use library resources to determine the contributions of John Bowler, James Watt, Joseph Lister, and Henry Bessemer. Prepare a list of other famous individuals whose names have been assimilated into the language.

Assignment 6

Make a list of American English words that are commonly associated with a general class of objects, such as automobiles or clothing. Using encyclopedias, dictionaries, and other resources in your school or local library, determine the corresponding British term. For example, you might note the use of the terms *hood* and *bonnet* to describe the enclosure that covers an automobile engine.

Assignment 7

The legal profession contains many words that are derived from British and classical sources. Use a dictionary to trace the origins of such words as *bailiff, barrister, litigation, writ, sequester,* and *jury.* To this list add five other legal terms that you are familiar with and trace their origins. For any word that comes from Latin or Greek origins, name another familiar English word that is based on the same root word. For example, for the word *verdict,* you might point out the English words *veracity* and *dictum* as being also derived from the same Latin sources.

Assignment 8

Over the years there have been a number of movements to standardize the English language in spelling, pronunciation, and vocabulary. To date, no such attempt has been successful. Discuss whether such standardization, assuming that it is possible, would be a desirable or undesirable characteristic of the language. Give examples of the benefits that might be gained and the drawbacks that might be felt because of such standardization.

Part One

Grammar, Usage, and Mechanics

The units in Part One present a system of rules and guidelines that describe English grammar, usage, and mechanics. By applying the information presented in these units, you will be able to express your thoughts in sentences that are clear and precise. In the units on grammar and usage, for example, you will learn how to choose words correctly. You may refer to the unit on mechanics to check how to punctuate your sentences or how to prepare a final manuscript of your writing.

As you study the rules and guidelines presented in Part One, you will learn to express your thoughts in writing that is correct, interesting, and effective. You will have control of the language, which will be an advantage now and in your future work.

Grammar

Unit Preview

Expressing an idea on paper is one of the most essential tasks facing you as a writer. One effective way of expressing an idea is through analogy—that is, by comparing the idea to a process or an object that is familiar to the reader. However, to make the analogy clear to the reader, you need to understand parts of speech, sentence structure, and phrases and clauses.

For Analysis Both Paragraph A and Paragraph B develop analogies. Read them, asking yourself which paragraph makes the analogy clearer. On your paper, answer the questions that follow the two paragraphs.

PARAGRAPH A

(1) Most people have long-range goals, such as entering a certain career. (2) Working toward a long-range goal requires many organizing skills. (3) The Egyptians used organizing skills to build the pyramids four thousand years ago. (4) To attain a long-range goal, you need to plan and prepare. (5) The engineers who designed the pyramids planned how many levels each pyramid would have. (6) The building of the pyramids required the cooperation of thousands of people. (7) The attainment of long-range goals involves the cooperation of different people, such as employers, guidance counselors, teachers, parents, and friends. (8) Another requirement is the ability to develop short-range goals. (9) The Egyptians developed thousands of intermediate tasks and techniques that made possible the construction of the pyramids. (10) By following these steps, you will build a foundation for your aspirations. (11) The pyramids themselves are solid.

(1) Most people have long-range goals, such as entering a certain career. (2) Working toward a long-range goal requires many of the organizing skills that the Egyptians developed to build the pyramids four thousand years ago. (3) To attain a long-range goal, you need to plan and prepare, just as the engineers who designed the pyramids planned how many levels each pyramid would have. (4) As the building of the pyramids required the cooperation of thousands of people, so does the attainment of a long-range goal involve the cooperation of different people, such as employers, guidance counselors, teachers, parents, and friends. (5) Another requirement is the ability to develop short-range goals, which the Egyptians did by developing thousands of intermediate tasks and techniques that made possible the construction of the pyramids. (6) By following these steps, you will build a foundation for your aspirations that is as solid as the pyramids.

1. What analogy is developed in the two paragraphs?
2. Which two sentences from Paragraph A have been combined to form Sentence 3 of Paragraph B? Why have they been combined?
3. Which two sentences from Paragraph A have been combined to form Sentence 4 of Paragraph B? Why have they been combined?
4. In which paragraph is the analogy more clearly developed? Why?

One way to make an analogy clear to the reader is to use subordinate clauses. Most of the sentences in Paragraph B contain subordinate clauses that emphasize the similarities between building a pyramid and achieving long-range goals. In this unit you will study subordinate clauses and the other major aspects of grammar.

1.1   Parts of Speech

The eight parts of speech are nouns, pronouns, verbs, adjectives, adverbs, prepositions, conjunctions, and interjections.

1.1a   Nouns

A **noun** names a person, a place, a thing, or an idea.

PERSONS	operator	contestant	Louisa May Alcott
PLACES	kitchen	valley	Wyoming
THINGS	freighter	aardvark	oxygen
IDEAS	obsession	realism	quality

Dates and days of the week are also classified as nouns.

A.D. 1100   Tuesday   November 29, 1984

Common and Proper Nouns

A **common noun** names a class of people, places, things, or ideas. Do not capitalize a common noun unless it begins a sentence. A **proper noun** gives the name or title of a particular person, place, thing, or idea, and it always begins with a capital letter.

COMMON NOUN   A **speedway** is a race track for automobiles.

PROPER NOUN   The **Indianapolis Speedway** is the site of the Indianapolis 500.

Compound Nouns

A **compound noun** consists of two or more words used together to form a single noun. There are four kinds of compound nouns. One kind is formed by joining two or more words: *football*. A second kind consists of words joined by hyphens: *city-state*. A third kind consists of two words that are often used together: *sugar beet*. The fourth kind is a proper noun that consists of more than one word: *Missouri River*.

Collective Nouns

A **collective noun** refers to a *group* of people, places, things, or ideas.

A **swarm** of bees buzzed around us!
Phyllis has an **accumulation** of compositions that show her progress as a writer.

Concrete and Abstract Nouns

Concrete nouns refer to material things, to people, or to places. Some concrete nouns name things that you can perceive with your senses: *traffic, seasoning, barking.* Other concrete nouns name things that can be measured or perceived only with the aid of technical devices. Although you cannot see an atom, *atom* is a concrete noun because it names a material substance. In the following sentences, the nouns in boldface type are concrete.

In **polo** the **players** ride on **horseback** and hit a **ball** with a long-handled **mallet**.

You can tell that that is Denise's **car** because of the **noise** that it makes.

Penicillin, which was discovered by **Alexander Fleming** in **1929**, is actually a **mold** that combats disease-carrying **germs**. [Even though you cannot see, hear, smell, taste, or feel germs, they have a definite material existence.]

Abstract nouns name ideas, qualities, emotions, or attitudes.

Many critics consider the **conflict** between **integrity** and **power** to be the **theme** of *Macbeth*.

Disappointment was visible on the faces of the players, but the crowd, moved by the **intensity** of the team's **effort**, applauded loudly.

Galileo defended the **freedom** to pursue the **truth**.

Exercise 1   Kinds of Nouns

On your paper, rewrite each of the following sentences, replacing each blank with a noun. Use the kind of noun noted in parentheses. Underline the nouns that you use.

SAMPLE   A __?__ (*collective*) of people with whom Janet works plans to take a __?__ (*common*) together at __?__ (*proper; compound*) this summer.

ANSWER   A <u>group</u> of people with whom Janet works plans to take a <u>vacation</u> together at <u>Yellowstone National Park</u> this summer.

1. With __?__ (*abstract*), Paulette and __?__ (*proper*) watched the __?__ (*collective*) of puppies playing in the old barn.

2. When Frank rounded third base and slid into __?__ (*compound*), the __?__ (*collective*) cheered with __?__ (*abstract*).

3. Did you see that __?__ (*concrete*) fly over the __?__ (*common*) when we were on our way to __?__ (*proper*)?

4. A surge of __?__ (*abstract*) swept over me when __?__ (*proper*) gave me a __?__ (*common*) by __?__ (*proper*), my favorite author.

5. Monique noticed many __?__ (*concrete*) along the side of the __?__ (*common*) as she drove through __?__ (*proper; compound*).

6. A large __?__ (*collective*) of cattle plodded across the __?__ (*common*) while the ranchers, shouting with __?__ (*abstract*), urged them on.

7. In the __?__ (*compound*), Jessica and __?__ (*proper*) practiced on the trampoline, Ted went down the slide, and Roberta exercised on the __?__ (*common*).

8. Because __?__ (*abstract*) has intrigued me for some time, I will write a __?__ (*common*) about it after I have read several __?__ (*concrete*) on the subject.

9. When Paul saw the __?__ (*collective*) of letters in the __?__ (*concrete*), he smiled with __?__ (*abstract*).

10. We ate at __?__ (*proper*) last evening and had __?__ (*compound*) for dinner; then we bought a __?__ (*common*) of fresh fruit at the market.

Using Nouns Effectively

In writing, you usually need to use both concrete nouns and abstract nouns. Abstract nouns are necessary in most forms of writing. However, if you link them with details and examples that include concrete nouns, your writing will be clearer and more interesting.

Read the following paragraph from *Quite Early One Morning* by the Welsh writer Dylan Thomas. Notice how Thomas relies on concrete nouns to express his impressions and ideas. The concrete nouns are in italic type.

I was born in a large Welsh *town* at the beginning of the Great War—an ugly, lovely *town* (or so it was and is to me), crawling, sprawling by a long and splendid curving *shore* where truant *boys* and sandfield *boys* and old *men* from nowhere, beachcombed, idled and paddled, watched the dock-bound *ships* or the *ships* steaming away into wonder and *India*, magic and *China*, *countries* bright with *oranges* and loud with *lions;* threw *stones* into the *sea* for the barking outcast *dogs;* made *castles* and *forts* and *harbors* and *race tracks* in the *sand;* and on Saturday summer *afternoons* listened to the brass *band,* watched the *Punch and Judy,* or hung about on the fringes of the *crowd* to hear the fierce religious *speakers* who shouted at the *sea,* as though it were wicked and wrong to roll in and out like that, white-horsed and full of *fishes.*

Dylan Thomas, *Quite Early One Morning*

Dylan Thomas relies on concrete nouns to evoke certain feelings about childhood. *India, China, oranges,* and *lions* convey a sense of adventure and discovery. *Castles, forts, harbors,* and *race tracks* create a sense of the boys' imaginative play when they were young. Note that Thomas does not completely avoid abstract nouns; *wonder* and *magic* are both abstract.

In your own writing, use concrete nouns to make ideas and impressions more vivid and interesting.

Assignment Using Nouns Effectively On your paper, write the abstract nouns in each sentence of the following paragraph. Then, without altering the main idea, rewrite the paragraph so that it contains a greater number of concrete nouns. In your revision you may keep the abstract nouns that you consider necessary for clarity.

(1) The city is a study in contrasts. (2) At first, when you walk through it, you get a sense of power and permanence, but look more closely, and behind that permanence are signs of frailty. (3) From the top of one of the skyscrapers, the city seems to be a lesson in order. (4) Descend to street level, and that order turns to confusion. (5) Stand in the middle of the business section at noon, and you get a feeling of unity with others. (6) In the same section at midnight, you can feel the isolation. (7) In some places you see beauty; in others you see drabness. (8) A city exists in time, and it is always moving, always changing.

1.1b Pronouns

A **pronoun** is a word that is used in place of a noun. A pronoun identifies persons, places, things, or ideas without renaming them. The noun that a pronoun replaces is the **antecedent** of that pronoun.

There are seven kinds of pronouns: personal, demonstrative, reflexive, intensive, interrogative, relative, and indefinite.

Personal Pronouns

Personal pronouns require different forms to express person, number, and gender. **Person** refers to the relationship between the speaker or writer (first person), the individual or thing spoken to (second person), and the individual or thing spoken about (third person). The **number** of a personal pronoun indicates whether the antecedent is singular or plural. The **gender** of a personal pronoun indicates whether the antecedent is masculine, feminine, or neuter.

> *Tricia* and *Annette* will not soon forget Henrik Ibsen's *A Doll House,* for **it** was a relevant play to **them.** [*It* replaces *A Doll House,* and *them* replaces *Tricia* and *Annette.*]
>
> *Tourists* who went to Wisconsin last weekend were disappointed because **they** could not go snowmobiling. [*They* replaces *tourists.*]

Possessive Pronouns.   Possessive pronouns are personal pronouns that show ownership or belonging.

> The *packages* have arrived at the warehouse, and we can pick up **ours** at any time. [*Ours* replaces *packages.*]
>
> Is *Georgina* still looking for golf clubs? I think that the clubs in the corner of the basement are **hers.** [*Hers* refers to *Georgina.*]

The following chart shows the personal pronouns; the possessive pronouns are in parentheses.

	SINGULAR	PLURAL
FIRST PERSON	I, me (my, mine)	we, us (our, ours)
SECOND PERSON	you (your, yours)	you (your, yours)
THIRD PERSON	he, him (his)	they, them (their, theirs)
	she, her (her, hers)	
	it (its)	

Demonstrative Pronouns

Demonstrative pronouns specify the individual or the group that is being referred to. The demonstrative pronouns are *this, that, these,* and *those.*

This is a more interesting collection of photographs than **that.**

These are the clippers that I used to trim the hedge; **those** are too rusty to use.

Reflexive Pronouns

Reflexive pronouns indicate that people or things perform actions to, for, or on behalf of themselves. To form a reflexive pronoun, add the suffix *-self* or *-selves* to the personal pronoun.

FIRST PERSON	myself, ourselves
SECOND PERSON	yourself, yourselves
THIRD PERSON	himself, herself, itself, oneself, themselves

Pablo wrote **himself** notes so that he wouldn't forget his chores.

We set the alarm so that the *oven* will turn **itself** on at four o'clock.

Intensive Pronouns

Intensive pronouns are the same words as the reflexive pronouns, but they draw special attention to a person or a thing mentioned in the sentence. Intensive pronouns usually come immediately after the nouns or pronouns that they intensify.

We drove around the grounds of the estate but could not visit the *mansion* **itself**, which was locked. [The pronoun *itself* draws special attention to the word *mansion*.]

Following the play, the *playwright* **herself** appeared for a bow. [The pronoun, *herself*, draws special attention to the word *playwright*.]

Be sure to give the message to *Mrs. Burns* **herself**. [*Herself* draws special attention to *Mrs. Burns*.]

Interrogative Pronouns

Interrogative pronouns introduce questions. The most frequently used interrogative pronouns are *who, whom, which, what,* and *whose.*

Who will call the rest of the club members about the meeting tomorrow evening?

We can get tickets for two games next week. **Which** would you like to attend?

Whose is this glove that I just found in our closet?

Relative Pronouns

Relative pronouns introduce adjective clauses (*pages 59–60*), which modify nouns and pronouns. The relative pronouns are *who, whom, whose, which,* and *that.*

> On the way to their son's wedding, the Scotts had a *flat tire,* **which** they had to repair, and they were late for the ceremony. [*Flat tire* is the antecedent of *which.*]
>
> The *symphony* **that** we will hear this evening was composed by Gustav Mahler. [*Symphony* is the antecedent of *that.*]
>
> *Vincent Van Gogh,* **whose** paintings are now valuable, sold only one painting during his lifetime. [*Vincent Van Gogh* is the antecedent of *whose.*]

Indefinite Pronouns

Indefinite pronouns refer to people, places, or things in general. Often you can use these pronouns without antecedents. The following list contains commonly used indefinite pronouns:

all	either	most	other
another	enough	much	others
any	everybody	neither	plenty
anybody	everyone	nobody	several
anyone	everything	none	some
anything	few	no one	somebody
both	many	nothing	someone
each	more	one	something

> Cassie's ability as a diver certainly surprised **everyone**!
>
> When we went bowling last Saturday, there was practically **no one** else at the bowling alley.
>
> Are **all** of the members of the cast planning to attend the opening-night party backstage?

Exercise 2   Pronouns   On your paper, write the following sentences, replacing the blanks with suitable pronouns. Use the kind of pronoun indicated in parentheses. Underline the pronouns that you use.

SAMPLE   Larry, __?__ (*relative*) is always so critical of others for being late, was late __?__ (*intensive*) for the start of the game.

ANSWER   Larry, <u>who</u> is always so critical of others for being late, was late <u>himself</u> for the start of the game.

1. __?__ (*indefinite*) went to the church bazaar __?__ (*relative*) Barbara and I helped to organize.
2. With __?__ (*interrogative*) will he speak at the meetings that __?__ (*personal*) is attending?
3. __?__ (*personal*) are looking forward to staying with you during vacation, __?__ (*relative*) begins next week.
4. Is the bicycle __?__ (*relative*) is on the front sidewalk __?__ (*possessive*)?
5. __?__ (*indefinite*) turned their heads and watched in amazement as the celebrities __?__ (*intensive*) marched out the door.
6. __?__ (*personal*) sent in the form after the deadline, __?__ (*relative*) was well over a week ago.
7. __?__ (*interrogative*) did you do when you found __?__ (*reflexive*) without a ride home after work?
8. It was truly encouraging when the school principal __?__ (*intensive*) offered to work at the class car wash, __?__ (*relative*)__?__ (*personal*) had planned to make money for the prom.
9. Mr. Warren's car, __?__ (*relative*) had not been running well lately, disturbed __?__ (*indefinite*) with its loud noise as it entered the parking lot.
10. Of the work options __?__ (*relative*) the counselor described, Vanessa prefers __?__ (*demonstrative*) in which she can gain computer experience.

Assignment Using Pronouns in Writing The following paragraph needs pronouns in order to make it read more smoothly and less repetitiously. On your paper, rewrite the entire paragraph, replacing nouns with pronouns where suitable. Use any of the kinds of pronouns studied in this section. Underline the pronouns in your rewritten paragraph.

> Orson Welles has been an influential figure in both American radio and American motion pictures. Although Welles is known better as an actor and as a motion-picture director, Welles first established Welles in the public eye through radio broadcasting. In

1938, Welles produced a broadcast that described a fictional invasion of New Jersey by creatures from Mars. The broadcast by Welles was so realistic that scores of alarmed listeners phoned the local authorities of the listeners. After the sensation of the radio broadcast, Welles went to Hollywood to write, direct, and act in films of Welles's own. Welles made several films, including *Citizen Kane*. *Citizen Kane* was an immediate critical success. The next films by Welles, *The Magnificent Ambersons* and *Journey into Fear,* failed at the box office when the films were released, although critics admired both *The Magnificent Ambersons* and *Journey into Fear.* Since that time, Welles has acted in many films, but Welles has written and directed few. *The Lady from Shanghai, The Trial,* and *Falstaff* are the most notable of the later films that Welles directed. In spite of Welles's relatively few films, Welles has had an important and enduring impact on American films.

1.1c   Verbs

A **verb** is a word that expresses an action or a state of being. There are three kinds of verbs: action verbs, linking verbs, and auxiliary verbs.

Action Verbs

An **action verb** describes the behavior or action of someone or something. Action verbs may express physical actions or mental activities.

> The fire truck **raced** toward the scene of the fire. [*Raced* refers to a physical action.]
>
> A glacier **crawls** forward at a pace of only a few inches a year. [*Crawls* refers to a physical action.]
>
> Philip **memorizes** names and dates easily because he **concentrates** so well. [*Memorizes* and *concentrates* refer to mental activities.]
>
> The archeologist **believed** that the site contained some very interesting artifacts. [*Believed* refers to a mental activity.]

Linking Verbs

A **linking verb** connects a noun or a pronoun with a word or words that identify or describe the noun or pronoun. Many linking verbs are verbs of being, which you form from the word *be*.

Will Rogers **was** an American humorist of the 1920s and 1930s. [The word *humorist* identifies Will Rogers.]

The Wilkinsons **were** anxious about encountering heavy traffic on the way to the airport. [The word *anxious* describes the Wilkinsons.]

There are several linking verbs in addition to *be:*

appear	grow	seem	stay
become	look	smell	taste
feel	remain	sound	

The students standing on the corner **grew** impatient as they waited for the bus. [*Grew* links the descriptive word *impatient* to *students*.]

The howling of the coyote **sounds** rather distant. [*Sounds* links the descriptive word *distant* to *howling*.]

Some verbs can be either action verbs or linking verbs, depending on their use in a sentence.

ACTION   Lynette **felt** along the wall for the light switch.

LINKING   Although Ron studied late all week, he still **felt** energetic by the weekend.

Auxiliary Verbs

Sometimes a verb needs the help of another verb, called an **auxiliary verb** or a **helping verb.** The verb that it helps is called the **main verb.** Together, a main verb and an auxiliary verb form a **verb phrase.** A verb phrase may have more than one auxiliary verb. Common auxiliary verbs appear in the following list:

am, are, be, been, is, was, were	may, might
have, has, had	can, could
do, does, did	will, would
shall, should	must

In the following sentences, the auxiliary verbs are in italic type, and the main verbs are in boldface type. *Still* and *not* are not part of the verb phrase.

When Rhonda left, other cast members *were* still **rehearsing.**

The clerk at the warehouse *could* not *have been* wrong when she said that our package *had* **arrived**!

Will you *be* **waiting** for me at the entrance to the art institute?

Characteristics of Verbs

Verbs have several characteristics that you need to understand in order to use them correctly.

Transitive and Intransitive Verbs.   All action verbs are either transitive or intransitive. A verb is **transitive** when its action is directed toward someone or something, which is called the **object of the verb** (*pages 41 – 42*).

             verb   ┌────── obj. ──────┐
The Chinese **built** the Great Wall of China over a period of several hundred years. [*Great Wall* is the object of the verb, *built. Built* is transitive.]

                      verb   obj.   obj.
By using a timer, Mr. Allen **photographed** himself and his family. [*Himself* and *family* are the objects of the verb, *photographed. Photographed* is transitive.]

A verb is **intransitive** when the performer of the action does not direct that action toward someone or something. In other words, an intransitive verb does not have a receiver of the action. Some action verbs, such as *go,* are intransitive. All linking verbs are intransitive.

Although Bill **knew** about the surprise party ahead of time, he **acted** surprised. [The verbs *knew* and *acted* do not have objects. They are intransitive.]

The inn at the top of the mountain **seems** empty. [*Seems* is a linking verb. It is intransitive.]

Many verbs can be either transitive or intransitive, depending on whether there is a receiver of the action.

> verb   obj.
> TRANSITIVE   **Stop** Sheila because she forgot to take this letter to the mailbox. [The object of *stop* is *Sheila*.]
>
> INTRANSITIVE   The subway train approached the station and
> verb
> **stopped.** [*Stopped* has no object.]

Active and Passive Voice.   Verbs have active and passive voices to show whether the subject of the sentence performs or receives the action of the verb. If the verb is in the **active voice,** the subject performs the action. If the verb is in the **passive voice,** the subject receives the action. For a complete explanation of the active and passive voices, see Section 2.2c of Unit 2, "Usage."

Changes in Verb Form.   An important characteristic of the verb is that its form changes according to how it is used. A verb form changes in order to agree in person and number with its subject. A verb form also changes to express tense and mood. The basic forms of a verb are its **principal parts.** For an explanation of the rules governing changes in verb form, see Unit 2, "Usage."

Exercise 3   Verbs   Number your paper from 1 to 7. *Step 1:* Next to each number, write the verbs and verb phrases in that sentence in the following paragraph. There are twelve verbs and verb phrases. *Step 2:* Label each main verb *Action* or *Linking*. *Step 3:* Label each verb or verb phrase *Transitive* or *Intransitive*.

> SAMPLE   The League of Nations stirred people's hopes for permanent peace, but because the League was ineffective, disillusionment replaced those hopes.
>
> ANSWER   stirred—Action, Transitive; was—Linking, Intransitive; replaced—Action, Transitive

(1) The League of Nations was an international association of countries, and its goal was world peace. (2) After France, Great Britain, Italy, Japan, and the United States wrote a constitution for

the League in 1919, the League started operations in January 1920.
(3) Although President Woodrow Wilson of the United States was
the chief planner of the League, the United States did not join.
(4) The Senate disagreed with Wilson's terms for membership.
(5) In March 1920, the Senate rejected the treaty that would have
brought the United States into the League.   (6) Throughout the
1920s, people in the United States took less interest in foreign
affairs, and the country never joined the League.   (7) In April of
1946, the United Nations replaced the League of Nations.

Using Verbs Effectively

Verbs can make the difference between an ordinary piece of
writing and one that stirs the reader's imagination. For this reason,
good writers use verbs that tell *how* something happened. Consider
the verb *ran* and its synonym in the following example.

The dog **ran** across the field.

The dog **scampered** across the field.

When we read that a dog scampered, we form a definite image of how
the dog is moving.

The following paragraph is from the short story "The Lagoon"
by Joseph Conrad. Note how Conrad uses specific verbs to describe
the action. These verbs are in italic type.

The Malay only *grunted*, and went on looking fixedly at the
river. The [other] man *rested* his chin on his crossed arms and *gazed*
at the wake of the boat. At the end of the straight avenue of forests
cut by the intense glitter of the river, the sun *appeared* unclouded
and dazzling, poised low over water that *shone* smoothly like a band
of metal. The forests, somber and dull, *stood* motionless and silent
on each side of the broad stream. At the foot of big, towering trees,
trunkless nipa palms *rose* from the mud of the bank, in bunches of
leaves enormous and heavy, that *hung* unstirring over the brown
swirl of eddies. In the stillness of the air every tree, every leaf,
every bough, every tendril of creeper and every petal of minute
blossoms *seemed to have been bewitched* into an immobility perfect
and final.

Joseph Conrad, "The Lagoon"

With the verb *grunted,* Conrad tells us how the man sounded. The verb *gazed* suggests that the man was lost in thought. Later in the paragraph, the forests *stood,* the palms *rose,* and the leaves *hung.* All of these verbs make the forests seem alive. In your own writing, use verbs that show the reader *how* an action occurs.

Assignment   Using Verbs Effectively   The passage that follows contains ineffective verbs. On your paper, rewrite the passage so that the verbs are more effective. Underline all the verbs that you add to the paragraphs.

As Gina went slowly up the side of the mountain, she stopped and looked at the valley below. It was noon, and the sun was becoming warm. From this height the valley looked like the terrain of a board game.

Soon Gina was at the most difficult part of the climb. A thick mound of rock was on the side of the mountain directly above her. There was a narrow passage to the left, but she could not move through. She looked thoughtfully at the mound of rock. From her backpack she took a piton, or metal spike, through which she could put her rope. She placed the tip of the piton in a crevice and made it go into the rock until it was secure. Then she put her line through the loop at the other end of the piton and made it tight. She attached another piton to the side of the mountain to serve as an anchor and attached the line to it.

Gina took a deep breath and carefully went off the side of the mountain. Now only her line was between her and the valley below. From her pack she placed another piton in her hand. Almost immediately it was out of her fingers and was going to the rocks below. Unconsciously, she counted. When she was at ten, she heard the faint ping as the piton went against the rocks. A slight shiver went down her back. She placed another piton in her hand, put it into the rock, and went forward. A sudden breeze made her move backward and forward. Ever so cautiously, she made herself stop swinging. Painstakingly, she continued to put pitons into the rock and to creep around and up the mound of rock.

An hour later Gina was on top of the mound of rock, and there was a clear path to the top. For the first time that day, she could see the peak without obstruction, and its beauty made her stop walking. She took in the beauty and then moved quickly forward—without venturing to look back at the obstacle that had been in her way.

1.1d Adjectives

An **adjective** is a word that modifies a noun or a pronoun. To modify means to change; an adjective modifies a word by describing or limiting it. In some sentences, nouns and certain pronouns are used as adjectives. In such cases, consider them adjectives. Adjectives answer *Which? What kind?* or *How many?*

WHICH? The course focused on **Western** *civilization.* [Which civilization? *Western* civilization.]

WHAT KIND? The tennis player has an **unorthodox** *serve.* [What kind of serve? An *unorthodox* serve.]

HOW MANY? **Twenty thousand** *people* flocked to the amphitheater. [How many people? *Twenty thousand.*]

Articles. The most frequently used adjectives are the articles, *a, an,* and *the. A* and *an* are **indefinite articles** because they do not specify a particular person, place, thing, or idea. *The* is a **definite article** because it always specifies a particular person, place, thing, or idea.

INDEFINITE Tom took **a** large *supply* of food on his camping trip.

DEFINITE He ate nearly all of **the** *food* that he brought.

Placement of Adjectives

Adjectives usually appear directly before the nouns or pronouns that they modify. Sometimes, a comma separates adjectives from the words that they modify.

Just beyond the hill was a **beautiful** *valley* with **several small** *clusters* of houses.

Illogical and **vague**, the *speech* made the audience restless.

Adjectives may follow linking verbs and modify the subjects (*page 36*) of sentences.

The *staff* remained **loyal** throughout the long campaign, and the *candidate* was very **proud** of them. [*Remained* and *was* are linking verbs.]

Sometimes adjectives follow the words that they modify and are separated from them by commas.

Our team's offensive *line,* **large** but **mobile,** dominated our opponent's defense during the game.

Proper Adjectives

A **proper adjective** is an adjective formed from a proper noun. Proper adjectives are usually capitalized.

Last evening we heard a **Brahms** *symphony.*

The **New Orleans** *harbor* is one of the busiest harbors in the country.

To create many proper adjectives, you use the suffixes *-n, -an, -ian, -ese, -ish,* or *-al,* changing the spelling of the noun as needed.

PROPER NOUN	PROPER ADJECTIVE
Elizabeth	Elizabethan
Lebanon	Lebanese
Ireland	Irish
Albania	Albanian

Nouns Used as Adjectives

Some nouns function as adjectives without changing form, as in the following examples.

The office contained **mahogany** *paneling* and tables with **glass** *tops.*

The invention of the **jet** *airplane* has diminished the need for **passenger** *trains,* but **freight** *trains* have had an increase in business.

Possessive Nouns.   **Possessive nouns** are nouns that show possession or ownership; they function as adjectives because they modify nouns or pronouns. For rules on the spelling of singular possessives and plural possessives, see Unit 14, "Spelling Skills."

The **tunnel's** *lights* suddenly went out, plunging us into darkness.

Everyone admired the **actor's** *costumes.*

Pronouns Used as Adjectives

A pronoun functions as an adjective when it modifies a noun or a pronoun. Indefinite pronouns, demonstrative pronouns, interrogative pronouns, the relative pronoun *whose,* and the possessive pronouns in the following list may serve as adjectives.

	SINGULAR	PLURAL
FIRST PERSON	my	our
SECOND PERSON	your	your
THIRD PERSON	his, her, its	their

For **her** *class* in computers, Donna asked the neighbors whether she could use **their** *minicomputer.*

Your *guitar* seems to have lost **its** excellent *tone.* [Note that the possessive pronoun *its* is spelled without an apostrophe.]

The words in the preceding list are called *possessive pronouns* throughout this textbook, but some people call them *pronominal adjectives.* Use the term that your teacher prefers.

The following list contains examples of the other kinds of pronouns that can function as adjectives:

INDEFINITE	few, many, several, some
DEMONSTRATIVE	that, this, these, those
INTERROGATIVE	what, which, whose
RELATIVE	whose

Will the person **whose** *car* is blocking the entrance to the hospital please move it?

I would like to know **which** *newspaper* carried **that** *story* about the new amusement park, for **several** *friends* are interested in reading it.

Exercise 4 Adjectives Number your paper from 1 to 8. Next to each number, write the adjective or adjectives in that sentence in the following passage. Do not include articles. Next to each adjective, write the word or words that it modifies. You should list twenty-nine adjectives in all.

> **SAMPLE** In 1979 the United States launched *Voyager I* and *Voyager II,* space probes that produced fascinating pictures of our solar system.
>
> **ANSWER** space—probes; fascinating—pictures; our—system; solar—system.

(1) Perhaps the most dramatic pictures taken by *Voyager I* and *Voyager II* were of Jupiter and its four large moons, which were first discovered by Galileo. (2) Of the four Galilean moons, Io is the most interesting. (3) It is different from the others because it lacks surface ice and water in any identifiable form. (4) In addition, Io does not have impact craters, as the other moons do. (5) Orange and white, Io's surface colors are a result of sulfurous deposits. (6) Dark spots, fuzzy patches, and splotches of different colors are scattered over the outer layer of the moon. (7) The most startling feature is Io's volcanoes, the first active extraterrestrial volcanoes that we have observed in the solar system. (8) When these volcanoes erupt, they shoot bluish plumes of debris miles above the surface of Io.

Using Adjectives Effectively

Adjectives provide the means for creating a mood or a lasting impression of a person, a place, or a thing. To create mood, use adjectives that appeal to the senses. Examples of such adjectives include *white, black, gigantic, miniscule, tepid,* and *frigid*. However, you can also use adjectives that refer to emotional states and abstract qualities. *Innocent, angry, confusing,* and *hopeful* are examples of such adjectives.

The following passage is from the short story "The Fall of the House of Usher" by Edgar Allan Poe. Notice how Poe uses some adjectives that appeal to the senses and other adjectives that refer to emotional states and abstract qualities. Adjectives that contribute to the mood of the passage are in italic type.

> The room in which I found myself was very *large* and *lofty.* The windows were *long, narrow,* and *pointed,* and at so *vast* a distance from the *black oaken* floor as to be altogether *inaccessible* from within. *Feeble* gleams of *encrimsoned* light made their way through the *trellised* panes and served to render sufficiently *distinct* the more *prominent* objects around; the eye, however, struggled in vain to reach the *remoter* angles of the chamber, or the recesses of the *vaulted* and *fretted* ceiling. *Dark* draperies hung upon the walls. The *general* furniture was *profuse, comfortless, antique,* and *tattered.* Many books and *musical* instruments lay scattered about but failed to give any vitality to the scene. I felt that I breathed an atmosphere of sorrow. An air of *stern, deep,* and *irredeemable* gloom hung over and pervaded all.

Several of Poe's adjectives appeal to the senses: *large, lofty, vast, black, oaken, encrimsoned, trellised, vaulted,* and *dark.* On the other hand, *stern, deep,* and *irredeemable* refer to abstract qualities. The mood is one of gloom and decay.

In your writing, use adjectives that appeal to the senses and those that refer to emotional states or abstract qualities.

Assignment Adjectives in Writing The paragraph that follows needs adjectives to make it more descriptive. Rewrite the paragraph, using adjectives to make the setting more vivid. Underline the adjectives in your rewritten paragraph.

> Frank Smith has owned a shoe repair shop for years. Frank's shop is a reflection of his personality. Even before customers walk in, they can see bric-a-brac and paintings in the front window. Upon entering, most people notice the wood stove right away. The stove creates an atmosphere in the shop. Also setting the shop apart from

others are its antiques. In one corner is a cobbler's bench. A radio plays music. Another thing that permeates the shop is the smell of leather. Shelves of shoes line the walls. Shoes are arrayed in lines on the floor. On Frank's bench are shoes. Seated behind those shoes is the "shoe doctor" himself. With an expression on his face, he bends over a shoe and works on it. He wears a brown jacket. His fingers are brown from the shoe polish. He seems preoccupied. When a customer approaches him, his expression becomes different. It isn't hard to see why people bring their shoes to Frank for repairs.

1.1e Adverbs

Like adjectives, adverbs are modifiers. An **adverb** is a word that modifies a verb, an adjective, or another adverb. An adverb answers one of five questions about the word or phrase that it modifies: *How? When? Where? How often?* or *To what extent?*

HOW?	Tricia *raised* her arms **triumphantly** when she set a school record in the high jump.
WHEN?	The personnel manager *will see* you **now**.
WHERE?	We *called* **everywhere**, but no room is available for the conference.
HOW OFTEN?	**Sometimes** the smoke alarm *sounds* when something on the stove is burning.
TO WHAT EXTENT?	Jeanine is **rather** *doubtful* about getting a part-time job.

Adverbs such as *rather, really, certainly, indeed,* and *truly* are adverbs of extent and are used for emphasis.

Leonardo da Vinci was a **truly** *remarkable* man in both the breadth and the depth of his interests. [To what extent was Leonardo da Vinci remarkable? *Truly* remarkable.]

The words *not* and *never* are adverbs. They tell to what extent (*not at all*) and when (*never*).

Dennis *will* **not** *build* the kitchen cabinets himself because he *has* **never** *had* experience in carpentry.

Many sentences contain nouns that function as adverbs. Such adverbs usually tell when or where.

Yesterday our boss *informed* us that we have Saturday off.

Adverbs Used to Modify Verbs

Adverbs often modify verbs. An adverb does not have to appear next to the verb that it modifies. Notice the different positions of the adverbs *silently* and *slowly* in the following sentences.

BEGINNING   **Silently** and **slowly**, the tide *covered* the narrow strip of land.

MIDDLE   The tide **silently** and **slowly** *covered* the narrow strip of land.

END   The tide *covered* the strip of land **silently** and **slowly**.

Adverbs Used to Modify Adjectives

Adverbs may modify adjectives. An adverb usually comes directly before the adjective that it modifies.

In spite of its **very** *forbidding* title, the essay was **fairly** *easy* to read.

The Super Bowl drew an audience of **nearly** *one hundred million* viewers.

Adverbs Used to Modify Other Adverbs

Adverbs can modify other adverbs. Such adverbs usually precede the adverbs that they modify.

Rafael is popular because he listens so *well* to other people. [*So* emphasizes the fact that Rafael listens well.]

Although the footbridge over the ravine was considered safe, Ed

and Mark crossed it **quite** *slowly*.

Exercise 5 Adverbs Number your paper from 1 to 9. Next to each number, write the adverbs in that sentence in the following paragraph. Next to each adverb, write the verb, adjective, or adverb that it modifies. There are fifteen adverbs in the paragraph.

SAMPLE	Beekeeping is certainly a very special skill and is commonly practiced as an industry as well as a hobby.
ANSWER	certainly—is; very—special; commonly—is practiced

(1) As an industry, beekeeping has become quite popular in the United States, Canada, and Australia. (2) Farmers in those countries who care regularly for their bees can easily sell large amounts of honey and beeswax. (3) The bees pollinate the farmers' crops constantly. (4) Beekeepers usually provide standard hives that consist of several easily removable sections resembling drawers. (5) The bees can then simply build their honeycombs on frames inside the section.

(6) Other people view beekeeping as a hobby, and they study bees very closely in order to understand these fascinating insects. (7) These people often keep bees in a glass-walled hive, where the always bustling activity of the bees is easily seen. (8) Beginning beekeepers must always buy their bees. (9) A state inspector should carefully inspect the hive to see that it does not contain disease.

Assignment Adverbs in Writing The following paragraph needs adverbs to make it more descriptive. Rewrite the paragraph, adding adverbs. Underline the adverbs in your rewritten paragraph. For variety, use adverbs that modify verbs, adjectives, and other adverbs.

Ben had slept until the mooing of a calf brought him out of a deep sleep. He splashed water on his face and ate his breakfast from his old tin plate, which he balanced on a rock near the chuck wagon. To prepare for work, he pulled on his chaps to protect himself from cactus and sagebrush. It was the third straight month that he had ridden the trail, and he remembered what it was like to be in a city, dine in a restaurant, and talk to someone who was not a cowpoke about something that was not a cow. Ben walked to get his horse, which he trusted. If the herd of cattle stampeded, he had to trust his horse to lead the steers and protect them from harm. He tightened the saddle around the middle of the animal and lifted himself into the saddle. As Ben began to ride, his bad temper disappeared. Feeling the familiar motion of the horse beneath him, he watched as the sun rose over the horizon and illuminated the plains, which seemed to stretch around him. The sound of the cattle reminded him of an old song that he never tired of. With a slight movement that his horse understood, he raced to catch up with the other cowpokes.

1.1f Prepositions

A **preposition** is a word that expresses a relationship between a noun or a pronoun and another word in a sentence.

A special pilot **from** *shore* climbed **on** *board* and went **to** the *helm*. [The preposition *from* relates *shore* to *pilot*. The preposition *on* relates *board* to *climbed*. The preposition *to* relates *helm* to *went*.]

The following list contains frequently used prepositions:

along	beyond	off	to
among	by	on	toward
around	despite	onto	under
at	down	out	underneath
before	during	outside	until
behind	except	over	up
below	for	past	upon
beneath	from	since	with
beside	in	through	within
besides	near	till	without
between			

A **compound preposition** is a preposition that consists of more than one word.

When the Lansings got to the store, they bought two easy chairs **instead of** just *one.*

Frequently used compound prepositions are in the following list:

according to	in regard to
aside from	in spite of
as of	instead of
as well as	on account of
because of	out of
by means of	prior to
in addition to	with regard to
in front of	with respect to
in place of	

A preposition is usually followed by a noun or a pronoun, which is called the **object of the preposition.** Together, the preposition, the object, and the modifiers of that object form a **prepositional phrase.**

                         prep.
The referee called a charging foul **against the opposing team's**
      obj.
seven-foot-tall center. [The prepositional phrase consists of the preposition, *against;* the modifiers, *the, opposing, team's,* and *seven-foot-tall;* and the object, *center.*]

In some sentences, particularly interrogative sentences, the preposition follows the object.

obj.   prep.
Whom are you rooting **for** this weekend? [**Think:** *For whom* are you rooting this weekend?]

A prepositional phrase functions as an adjective if it modifies a noun or a pronoun. A prepositional phrase functions as an adverb if it modifies a verb, an adjective, or an adverb.

27

USED AS AN ADJECTIVE

The *road* **by the old mill** has a picnic *area* **for the residents.**

USED AS AN ADVERB

The defense attorney *looked* doubtfully **at the witness** and then

began her cross-examination **in a quiet but effective voice.**

Some words can function as prepositions or as adverbs, depending on their use in a sentence.

PREPOSITION   Larry saw Marilyn standing **outside the stadium.**

ADVERB   If you *venture* **outside** in the cold weather, wear a coat.

Exercise 6   Prepositional Phrases   On your paper, list the prepositional phrases in the following sentences. Underline the propositions once and the objects of the prepositions twice.

SAMPLE   The term *utopia,* which was first used by Thomas More, refers to any imaginary place with ideal political, social, and economic conditions.

ANSWER   by Thomas More; to any imaginary place; with ideal political, social, and economic conditions

1. Throughout history individuals have envisioned societies where people could live in harmony with one another and with nature.
2. Plato, a philosopher who lived in ancient Athens, wrote *The Republic,* which described his concept of the ideal society.
3. In Plato's perfect society, harmony would exist between the three classes: the philosopher kings, who would be responsible for government; the guardians, who would maintain order in the land; and the artisans, farmers, and merchants, who would supply material needs.
4. According to Plato all people in the society would find satisfaction in their roles, despite the divisions among the classes.
5. Since Plato's era many other people have been intrigued by the idea of utopian communities.

6. The Anabaptists, a Protestant group during the Reformation, believed that people could achieve moral perfection on the earth and established "holy communities" for the pursuit of such perfection.

7. In the late 1700s, many Europeans were concerned about the effects of industrialism; Robert Owen, a social reformer born in Wales, created a factory community where the interests of the workers were respected.

8. Among the reforms in Owen's community were shorter working hours for employees, clean housing, and schooling for the workers' children.

9. In 1888 Edward Bellamy, a writer born in Massachusetts, published *Looking Backward,* a novel about a socialist utopia; the popular novel sold one million copies in six languages within ten years.

10. Except for the Hutterian Brethren—a religious communal sect in South Dakota, Montana, and western Canada—few utopian communities exist in modern society.

1.1g   Conjunctions

A **conjunction** is a word that connects words or groups of words. In fact, the word *conjunction* literally means "the act of joining" or "combination." There are three kinds of conjunctions: coordinating conjunctions, correlative conjunctions, and subordinating conjunctions.

Coordinating Conjunctions

A **coordinating conjunction** connects individual words or groups of words that perform the same function in a sentence. The coordinating conjunctions are *and, but, for, nor, or,* and *yet.* A coordinating conjunction can connect words, phrases, or clauses. For a complete explanation of phrases and clauses, see Section 1.3 of this unit.

> The dolphin next to our boat *surfaced, jumped,* **and** *dived* as we watched. [connects words]
> The antique dealer, *hoping to find a bargain* **but** *not expecting to find one,* went to the auction. [connects phrases]
> *We may be a few minutes late for the picnic,* **for** *the road crews repairing the expressway have slowed traffic considerably.* [connects clauses]

Correlative Conjunctions

A **correlative conjunction** is a conjunction that consists of two or more words that function together. Like coordinating conjunctions, correlative conjunctions connect words that perform equal functions in a sentence. The following list contains correlative conjunctions:

both . . . and	not only . . . but (also)
either . . . or	whether . . . or
neither . . . nor	

Julian said that he had read **neither** *this novel* **nor** *that long poem* before. [connects words]

Not only *did we see a funny show at the club,* **but** *we* **also** *watched comedians doing improvisations after the regular show.* [connects clauses]

Subordinating Conjunctions

A **subordinating conjunction** introduces a subordinate clause (*page 59*), which is a clause that cannot stand by itself as a complete sentence. The subordinating conjunction connects the subordinate clause to an independent clause, which *can* stand by itself as a complete sentence.

```
   ┌──────sub. clause──────┐ ┌────── indep. clause──────────┐
```
As the months went by, the Smiths grew accustomed to their new home. [The subordinating conjunction, *as,* introduces the subordinating clause and connects the clause to the independent clause.]

Subordinating conjunctions usually express relationships of time, manner, cause, condition, comparison, or purpose.

TIME	after, as, as long as, as soon as, before, since, until, when, whenever, while
MANNER	as, as if, as though
CAUSE	because
CONDITION	although, as long as, even if, even though, if, provided that, though, unless, while

COMPARISON   as, than

PURPOSE   in order that, so that, that

Jerry has been practicing the drums constantly and plays

┌─────────────── sub. clause ───────────────┐
as though he has had a great deal of experience. [*As though* expresses manner.]

The stores are extremely crowded these days **unless** you go

┌───── sub. clause ─────┐
early on a Saturday morning. [*Unless* expresses condition.]

Conjunctive Adverbs

A **conjunctive adverb** is an adverb that functions somewhat
like a coordinating conjunction because it usually connects independent clauses (*page 58*). A semicolon precedes the conjunctive adverb,
and a comma usually follows it.

CONJUNCTIVE ADVERB

> An expert on career planning will speak in the auditorium on
> Friday; **furthermore,** he will answer your questions after the
> lecture.

COORDINATING CONJUNCTION

> An expert on career planning will speak in the auditorium on
> Friday, **and** he will answer your questions after the lecture.

The following list contains frequently used conjunctive adverbs:

also	furthermore	later	still
besides	however	moreover	then
consequently	indeed	nevertheless	therefore
finally	instead	otherwise	thus

Exercise 7   Conjunctions and Conjunctive Adverbs

Number your paper from 1 to 10. Next to each number, write a
coordinating conjunction, a subordinating conjunction, or a conjunctive adverb to replace the corresponding blank.

SAMPLE   __1__ scientists have been studying cryogenics, or extremely low temperatures, engineers can produce __2__ maintain low temperatures for a variety of uses.

ANSWER   1. Because; 2. and

The first industrial use of cryogenics was the production of liquid air, which is a source of liquid oxygen __1__ liquid nitrogen. __2__ the production of liquid oxygen became possible, it was used in certain types of aircraft __3__ spacecraft. __4__ the liquid oxygen was converted into gaseous form, crews could use it to breathe on long flights. Liquid oxygen has also proven to be quite versatile; __5__, it is used to manufacture synthetic gases __6__ to treat waste water.

__7__ the industrial uses of cryogenics have increased, the medical uses have increased even more rapidly. For instance, surgeons have more flexibility during operations __8__ cryogenics allows blood to be frozen __9__ preserved for a long time. With cryogenic techniques, internal organs can be frozen __10__ not harmed during surgery.

Assignment   Conjunctions and Conjunctive Adverbs

On your paper, rewrite the following paragraphs by using conjunctions and conjunctive adverbs whenever appropriate to connect ideas and to provide variety in your sentences. You may make other changes so that the passage reads more smoothly. Underline the conjunctions and the conjunctive adverbs that you use.

Margaret Mead was a psychological anthropologist. She was respected. She was controversial. Mead was born in Philadelphia, Pennsylvania, in 1901. She grew up in a liberal intellectual atmosphere. Her father was a professor. Her mother was a sociologist. Her mother was an early advocate of women's rights. Mead was a senior in college. She took a course in anthropology. She later said that this was the most influential event in her life. She decided to become an anthropologist. She became known as a tireless field investigator.

Margaret Mead's interests centered on several aspects of psychology and anthropology. She studied childhood and adolescence. She studied cultural change. She studied the contemporary national character. Her first field research was done in Samoa in 1925 and 1926. She went by herself. She studied the lives of adolescent girls. She went to New Guinea to study the young children. She wanted to test some of the psychological theories popular at that time. Twenty-five years later she returned to observe the changes. The children had become adults. In the late 1930s she did field research in Bali. There she pioneered the use of photography in the study of behavior and personality.

During her career she served on several United States government commissions. She was very involved in education. She taught in universities. She interpreted the lessons of anthropology to the general public. She was a curator at the American Museum of Natural History for most of her professional life. She was involved in programs concerned with mental health and technological change. Margaret Mead died in New York City on November 15, 1978. *Blackberry Winter* is her autobiography.

1.1h   Interjections

An **interjection** is an exclamatory word or phrase that can stand by itself, although it may also appear in a sentence. Many interjections express strong emotions. They are followed by exclamation marks.

Wow! That ball was really hit!

When an interjection appears within a sentence, you should set if off with a comma or commas.

So, you didn't find what you were looking for at the corner store.

My, these grapefruits are truly excellent!

Exercise 8   Interjections   On your paper, write an interjection that fits in each blank of the following paragraph. Use the interjections from the following list. Each interjection is used only once.

SAMPLE   __?__! Don't bump your head against the low ceiling.
ANSWER   Oops

of course	good grief	oh	whew
ouch	darn	well	alas

__1__, what a horrible day I had yesterday! First thing, I fell out of bed. __2__! It still hurts where I fell, if you want to know the truth. I went downstairs, and, __3__, there was absolutely nothing to eat for breakfast. I went back upstairs to get dressed. __4__! There were no clean shirts in the closet. I had no choice but to go back downstairs, get out the ironing board, and iron a shirt. Meanwhile, it had begun to rain, and by the time I went outside, we were having a regular thunderstorm. __5__! It was really coming down! __6__, as I drove to work, I got a flat tire. By the time I fixed it, I was completely waterlogged. __7__, the rest of my day didn't get much better, although I won't bore you with the details. I got home, ate dinner, and crept into bed two hours earlier than usual. __8__! It was a day that I would never want to relive!

Using Words Effectively

Write a character sketch of a fictional person. In the sketch, use nouns, verbs, adjectives, and adverbs that effectively reveal the character's personality traits. Try to show several sides to your character's personality. If appropriate, use the following list of common personality traits.

extroverted	optimistic	decisive
thoughtful	conscientious	reserved

1.2   Sentence Structure

1.2a   Four Sentence Purposes

A **sentence** is a group of words that has a subject and a predicate and that expresses a complete thought. It describes an action or states a condition of a person, a place, or a thing. There are four categories of sentences: declarative, interrogative, imperative, or exclamatory.

A **declarative sentence** makes a statement and ends with a period. An **interrogative sentence** asks a question and ends with a question mark. An **exclamatory sentence** shows strong feeling and ends with an exclamation point. An **imperative sentence** gives an order or makes a request. A mild command or request ends with a period, but a strong command or request ends with an exclamation point. Some imperative sentences take the form of questions but are actually mild commands or polite requests. Such sentences end with periods.

DECLARATIVE   Before reading the novel, Stephen read the preface.

INTERROGATIVE   Why did Napoleon lose the battle at Waterloo?

EXCLAMATORY   This traffic will make us miss our airplane!

IMPERATIVE   Lock the door on your way out.
Don't drink that sour milk!
Donna, will you please move your car.

Exercise 1 Sentence Purpose On your paper, write sentences in which you use the following groups of words, and add appropriate punctuation. Label each sentence *Declarative, Interrogative, Imperative,* or *Exclamatory.*

SAMPLE   would you look
ANSWER   Would you look to see whether the newspaper has come yet?—Interrogative

1. what a lucky person
2. waiting for a bus in the rain
3. don't forget
4. does the electronics store
5. the first signs of spring
6. from now on
7. talking to friends
8. is the company going to
9. twenty-five laps every day
10. a beautiful sight

1.2b   Subjects and Predicates

Simple Subjects

The **simple subject** is the noun or pronoun that names the person, place, thing, or idea that the sentence is about. The simple subject does not include modifiers. The complete subject (*page 37*) consists of the simple subject and its modifiers. In this book the term *subject* refers to the simple subject. In the following sentences, the simple subject is in boldface type.

> **Sigmund Freud** is considered one of the founders of modern psychiatry.
>
> The **last** of the artifacts that the archeologist discovered was the most interesting.
>
> Where will the **seminar** on computer education be held?

The simple subject of an imperative sentence is always *you*. Often, *you* is understood rather than stated.

> Be sure to study the chapter in your history book about Reconstruction. [**Think:** *You* be sure.]

Compound Subjects.   A **compound subject** is a simple subject that consists of two or more nouns or pronouns of equal rank. The term *compound subject* refers to a compound *simple* subject.

> A larger **dining room**, a **den**, and a big **closet** will be added to Mr. Grabowski's house. [*Dining room, den,* and *closet* form the compound subject.]

Simple Predicates

The **simple predicate** is the verb or verb phrase that describes the action or states the condition of the subject. The simple predicate does not include modifiers and words that complete the meaning of the verb. It also does not include the adverb *not* or *never*. The complete predicate (*page 38*) includes all such modifiers and complements (*page 41*). It also includes *not* or *never*. In this book the term *predicate* refers to the simple predicate. In the following sentences, the simple predicate is in boldface type.

> subj.　　　pred.
> For biology class each *student* **collected** samples of forty different kinds of leaves.

> subj.　 ┌── pred.──┐
> By this time tomorrow, our *family* **will have driven** through Sequoia National Park.

> pred.┌── subj.──┐pred.
> What **do** *social scientists* **view** as the major trends for cities in the next ten years?

Compound Predicates.　A **compound predicate** is a simple predicate that consists of two or more verbs or verb phrases of equal rank. The term *compound predicate* refers to a compound *simple* predicate.

> Julius Caesar **led** the Roman army in one conquest after another and **expanded** the Roman Empire all the way to Britain but **was assassinated** in 44 B.C. [*Led, expanded,* and *was assassinated* form the compound predicate.]

Complete Subjects and Complete Predicates

The **complete subject** consists of the simple subject and all the words that modify it or identify it.

> ┌────── complete subject ──────┐
> *Brown County,* **which is in the south-central part of Indiana,** is known for its art galleries. [*Brown County* is the simple subject.]

> ┌────── complete subject ──────┐
> **Remembered for his courage in battle,** *Chief Crazy Horse* actually had a quiet, unassuming manner. [*Chief Crazy Horse* is the simple subject.]

> ┌────── complete subject ──────┐
> *Harvard University,* **the oldest university in the United States, and** *Laval University,* **the oldest university in Canada,** were both founded to train people for the clergy. [Included in the complete subject is the compound simple subject, which appears in italic type.]

The **complete predicate** consists of the simple predicate and all the words that modify it or complete its meaning.

The Vikings, who came from Scandinavia, *made* raids on other

————————— complete predicate —————————
European countries from the eighth century through the eleventh century. [*Made* is the simple predicate.]

————————— complete predicate —————————
Film for your camera *can be bought* at the visitors' center at the zoo. [*Can be bought* is the simple predicate.]

————————— complete predicate —————————
Demographers *study* population trends and *predict* that the average age of people in the United States will rise. [Included in the complete predicate is the compound simple predicate, *study* and *predict*.]

Placement of Subjects and Predicates

Subjects and predicates may be arranged in a variety of ways in sentences. The placement of the subject and the predicate often depends on the purpose of the sentence. In the examples that follow, the complete subjects are underlined once and the complete predicates twice.

DECLARATIVE SENTENCES

Household utensils made of pewter, an alloy consisting primarily of tin, have been used since the fourteenth century. [The subject precedes the predicate.]

Here are the periodicals that you requested from the reference librarian. [The sentence has inverted word order; that is, the subject follows the predicate.]

Into the street rolled the tennis ball. [The sentence has inverted word order.]

Because they had been studying the ancient history of Britain, Sue and Paulette, who were on a tour, were particularly interested in seeing Stonehenge. [The subject is between the two parts of the predicate.]

INTERROGATIVE SENTENCE

How were you able to fix the plugged drain in the kitchen? [**Think:** You were able to fix.]

IMPERATIVE SENTENCE

> Try to finish painting the porch by this evening. [**Think:** *You* try to finish. The entire imperative sentence is the complete predicate because the subject, *you,* is understood.]

EXCLAMATORY SENTENCES

> The pictures that you took are beautiful!
> What a fascinating exhibit that was!

Exercise 2 Subjects and Predicates On your paper, write the following sentences. Underline the complete subjects once and the complete predicates twice. Write *subj.* over each simple subject and *pred.* over each simple predicate. If the subject is the understood *you,* write it in parentheses, underline it, and label it.

> **SAMPLE** Because the population of the world has been increasing so rapidly, the study of population trends has become an important science.
>
> **ANSWER** Because the population of the world has been
>
> increasing so rapidly, the study of population
>
> trends has become an important science.

1. The population of the world in the year 1650 was five hundred million.
2. Between 1650 and 1850, the world's population doubled.
3. During the 1800s, large numbers of people moved from the farms to the cities.
4. During the nineteenth century, the United States became home for the millions of Europeans who fled from the overcrowded conditions in their native countries.
5. In the past there was relatively little migration from the densely populated nations of Asia, which now accounts for three fifths of the world's population.
6. Will the rapid growth in population, now 2 percent a year, continue?
7. Because medical advances allow people to live longer, the birth rate exceeds the death rate in many countries.
8. Population experts expect continued growth and believe that the increasing population will put a strain on the world's resources, particularly food and energy.

9. The increased demands for food have been offset somewhat by the "Green Revolution," the rapid increase in food production aided by improved seeds and agricultural methods.

10. By the year 2015, the population of the world could reach eight billion people.

Exercise 3   Subjects and Predicates   In all of the following sentences, the subject precedes the predicate. *Step 1:* Rewrite the sentences so that they do not follow the subject-predicate pattern. To do so, invert the word order of the sentence, changing the sentence into a question or putting the subject between two parts of the predicate. *Step 2:* Draw one line under the complete subject and two lines under the complete predicate in your rewritten sentences.

> **SAMPLE**   The stepladder and the bucket of paint fell against the house.
>
> **ANSWER**   Against the house fell the stepladder and the bucket of paint.   **OR**
> Did the stepladder and the bucket of paint fall against the house?

1. The defendant, a middle-aged man in a business suit, appeared before the judge.

2. Mr. Hanson was stricken by Rocky Mountain spotted fever when the Hansons were traveling through the West.

3. Laura is taking a course in creativity because she wants to learn how to generate innovative ideas.

4. The emblem that you are holding in your hand is a keepsake from my grandmother.

5. The road that we are on winds through the Great Smoky Mountains.

6. The club that the Riveras belong to is going to do folk dances at the carnival tonight.

7. An important message for Norma has come by telegram.

8. Mrs. Lorenzo is covering her flowers so that they will not be harmed by tonight's freeze.

9. The neighbors gave us a wonderful sendoff before we started on our cross-country motoring trip!

10. You will find the Egyptian collection down the stairs and to your right.

1.2c   Complements

A **complement** is a word or a group of words that completes the meaning of a verb in a sentence or a clause (*page 58*). Complements are always part of the complete predicate.

> The oranges sent to us from Florida were **delicious**. [The oranges were *what*? Delicious. *Delicious* is a complement.]
>
> This afternoon Chet is chopping **wood** for the winter. [Chet is chopping *what*? Wood. *Wood* is a complement.]

If the preceding sentences did not have complements, their meaning would be incomplete.

> The oranges sent to us from Florida were [Were what?]
>
> Chet is chopping [Is chopping what?]

This section covers three types of complements: objects, objective complements, and subject complements.

Objects

Objects are nouns or pronouns that follow action verbs in the active voice (*Unit 2*). There are two kinds of objects: direct objects and indirect objects.

Direct Objects.   A **direct object** is a noun or a pronoun that follows an action verb in the active voice and receives the action of the verb. It answers the question *What?* or *Whom?* Verbs that take direct objects are called transitive verbs (*pages 14–15*). Modifiers are not part of the object.

D.O.
The Leggets *visited* the **aunt** of one of their friends. [Visited *whom*? Aunt.]

D.O.
The next-door neighbors *have* a small **tractor** for clearing the snow from the driveway. [Have *what*? Tractor.]

Indirect Objects. An **indirect object** is a noun or a pronoun that names the person or thing *to* whom or *for* whom an action is performed. An indirect object follows an action verb in the active voice. In most cases an indirect object is used with a direct object. The indirect object comes immediately after the verb and before the direct object.

The men's choir will sing us one more *song* to conclude the assembly. [**Think:** The choir will sing (*for*) us one more song.]

Will you bring me a *couple* of books from the library when you go there? [**Think:** Will you bring (*to*) me a couple of books?]

Compound Objects. Like subjects and predicates, objects may be compound. A compound object consists of two or more objects that complete the same predicate.

COMPOUND DIRECT OBJECT

Jerry read several **articles** and **books** about the presidency of James Monroe.

COMPOUND INDIRECT OBJECT

We will show **Maxine** and **Paulette** as many historical sites as we have time for.

Objective Complements

An **objective complement** is a noun or an adjective that follows a direct object and explains, identifies, or describes that object. Only certain verbs take an objective complement: *make, find, think, elect, choose, appoint, name, consider, call,* and synonyms of these verbs.

NOUN AS OBJECTIVE COMPLEMENT

The voters have elected *Alexandra Smith* **state senator**. [*State senator* is the objective complement of the verb phrase, *have elected*. It identifies the direct object, *Alexandra Smith*.]

ADJECTIVE AS OBJECTIVE COMPLEMENT

                  D.O.   O.C.
We considered the dancer's *performance* **brilliant**.
[*Brilliant* is the objective complement of the verb, *considered*.
It describes the direct object, *performance*.]

A sentence may have a compound objective complement,
which consists of two or more objective complements.

                          D.O.   O.C.
The board of trustees has appointed *Dan* the **director** of
                               O.C.
public information and the **coordinator** of the research department.
[The nouns *director* and *coordinator* are objective complements.]

Subject Complements

A **subject complement** is a word that comes after a linking
verb and identifies or describes the subject of a sentence or a clause
(*page 58*). Subject complements often follow forms of the verb *be*.
Other verbs that may take subject complements are in the following
list:

appear	look	sound
become	remain	stay
feel	seem	taste
grow	smell	

There are two kinds of subject complements: predicate nominatives and predicate adjectives.

Predicate Nominatives.   A **predicate nominative** is a noun or
a pronoun that follows a linking verb and identifies the subject of the
sentence. The root of the word *nominative* is *nominate,* which means
"to name." In a sense the predicate nominative renames the subject.

                                P.N.
During the coming year, *Ron* will remain a **volunteer** at the local
recycling center. [*Volunteer* identifies the subject, *Ron*.]

After Mrs. Sampson's expert training, *Butch* has become an
     P.N.
obedient **dog**. [*Dog* identifies the subject, *Butch*.]

┌────── P.N. ──────┐   P.N.
The *broadcast* will be either a **press conference** or a **speech**
by the governor. [The sentence has a compound predicate nominative, *press conference* and *speech*. Both identify *broadcast*.]

Predicate Adjectives.   A **predicate adjective** is an adjective
that follows a linking verb and modifies the subject of the sentence.

P.A.
The *sound* coming out of the speakers was rather **feeble**. [The
predicate adjective, *feeble*, modifies the subject, *sound*.]

P.A.
The *story* that I read last night was quite **difficult** to follow. [The
predicate adjective, *difficult*, modifies the subject, *story*.]

P.A.   P.A.
Harrison felt **refreshed** and **relaxed** after his month-long vacation.
[The sentence has a compound predicate adjective, *refreshed* and
relaxed.]

In some sentences the predicate adjective precedes the verb or
verb phrase.

P.A.
Lighthearted was the *play* that we saw at the theater. [The predicate
adjective, *lighthearted*, modifies the subject, *play*.]

Exercise 4   Complements   On your paper, write the words
and phrases that are in italic type in the following sentences. After
each word or phrase, write the label *Direct object, Indirect object,
Objective complement, Predicate nominative,* or *Predicate adjective.*

SAMPLE   Sir Winston Churchill, best remembered for his lead-
            ership during World War II, gave *Britain* six *decades*
            of service.

ANSWER   Britain—Indirect object; decades—Direct object

1. Winston Churchill experienced *setbacks* in his early life, but those
   setbacks did not prevent *him* from leading a distinguished life.
2. Churchill's childhood was *undistinguished,* for his teachers considered
   him the worst *student* in his class.

3. In addition, Churchill was *stubborn* and *high spirited,* and these personality traits alienated *adults.*

4. Churchill found a *direction* at the age of eighteen; at that time his father sent *him* to the Royal Military College at Sandhurst.

5. The school gave *Churchill* his first military *training,* and he became an excellent *student* of military tactics and fortifications.

6. After he had completed his education, Churchill sought *adventure,* and his experiences gave *him* the *opportunity* to become a war correspondent.

7. Churchill became a *member* of Parliament for the first time in 1900 and held several *positions* in the cabinet for the next ten years.

8. In 1911 the prime minister of Britain appointed *Churchill* first *lord* of the admiralty, but in 1915 Churchill resigned from that post after making a military decision that was disastrous.

9. Churchill saved his *reputation* by serving in several other posts toward the end of the war, and after the war he remained *active* in politics.

10. The years after World War I also gave *Churchill* the *time* to develop his writing ability, and he became an accomplished *historian.*

11. Later events gave *Churchill* yet another *opportunity* to serve his country, for in April of 1940 war broke out between Britain and Nazi Germany, and later that year he became the *Prime Minister.*

12. Churchill promised his fellow *Britons* "blood, toil, tears, and sweat"; he then led *England* to its finest hour, the defeat of the German air force over British soil.

13. In 1953 the Swedish Academy awarded *Winston Churchill* the *Nobel Prize* for literature, and in the same year Queen Elizabeth II made him a *peer.*

14. Those were not all the honors, for in 1963 the United States made *Winston Churchill* an honorary *citizen.*

Exercise 5   Complements   Next to each number that follows is a noun and a verb. *Step 1:* Using each noun as the subject and some form of each verb as the predicate, write a sentence that has one or more complements. Supply suitable modifiers for the subjects, the predicates, and the complements. *Step 2:* Label each complement that you write *D.O.* for direct object, *I.O.* for indirect object, *O.C.* for objective complement, *P.N.* for predicate nominative, or *P.A.* for predicate adjective.

SAMPLE	communication, is
ANSWER	P.A. Effective communication is necessary to the effective functioning of an organization.

1. explorer, find
2. golfer, hit
3. director, give
4. cabinet member, appoint
5. fox, appear

6. scientist, study
7. crowds, attend
8. sports writer, name
9. hawk, see
10. factory, become

Assignment   Complements   In descriptions of characters and settings, authors of stories and essays often use predicate nominatives and predicate adjectives to convey descriptive details and qualities. Find a fictional story or an essay that contains a descriptive passage. On your paper, write the predicate nominatives and predicate adjectives that appear in the passage. Label each one *P.N.* or *P.A.* Be sure to identify the selection that you use.

1.3   Phrases and Clauses

With phrases and clauses, you can have a variety of sentence structures in your writing. This section explains the functions of both phrases and clauses.

1.3a   Phrases

A **phrase** is a group of related words that functions as a single part of speech but lacks a subject, a predicate, or both. This section deals with three common kinds of phrases: prepositional phrases, appositive phrases, and verbal phrases.

Prepositional Phrases

A **prepositional phrase** consists of a preposition and its object, including any modifiers of that object. In the following sentences, the prepositional phrases are in boldface type.

prep.
An important challenge facing the United States **for the last**
obj.
two hundred years has been maintaining the proper balance
prep.   obj.   obj.
between the individual's rights and society's rights. [The second
prepositional phrase has a compound object of the preposition.]

obj.   prep.
Which person are you looking **for**? [**Think:** *For which person* are you
looking?]

Prepositional Phrases Used as Adjectives.   A prepositional
phrase that modifies a noun or a pronoun functions as an adjective.
Such a phrase is sometimes called an **adjective phrase.**

MODIFIES NOUN

The *man* **with the brown raincoat** will drive us downtown,

where we will find the *location* **of the meeting.**

MODIFIES PRONOUN

Several **of the students** have entered the chess tournament.

Prepositional Phrases Used as Adverbs.   A prepositional
phrase functions as an adverb if it modifies a verb, an adjective, or
another adverb. This kind of phrase is sometimes called an **adverb
phrase.**

MODIFIES VERB

The impressionist movement *spread* **from Europe** and influenced American artists in the early 1900s.

MODIFIES ADJECTIVE

The entire class was *curious* **about new energy sources.**

MODIFIES ADVERB

The tour guide led the visitors *down* **to the lowest deck.**

A prepositional phrase can modify the object in another prepositional phrase.

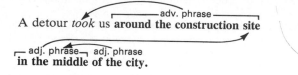

A detour *took* us **around the construction site**
in the middle of the city.

Appositive Phrases

An **appositive** is a noun or a pronoun placed near another noun or pronoun to explain it or identify it.

The senior class *president,* **Amy Jones,** has brought several new ideas into student government.

Will our supervisors show *us* **trainees** the best selling techniques?

Albert Schweitzer, **doctor, missionary,** and **philosopher,** will long be remembered for his humanitarian work in Africa. [The sentence has a compound appositive: *doctor, missionary,* and *philosopher.*]

Like an appositive, an **appositive phrase** explains or identifies a noun or a pronoun. It includes all the words or phrases that modify an appositive.

Colette's *hobby,* **nature and wildlife photography,** will probably lead to an interesting job.

We **listeners with questions** can talk to the professor after the lecture.

A year of fierce snowstorms and widespread drought, *1978* will long be remembered.

An **essential appositive** or an **essential appositive phrase** is an appositive that is necessary to the meaning of the sentence. This kind of appositive should not be separated from the rest of the sentence with a comma.

┌─────────────── appositive ───────────────┐
D. H. Lawrence's *short story* **"The Rocking-Horse Winner"** appears in numerous literature anthologies. [Lawrence wrote more than one story. The appositive is necessary to identify which story.]

A **nonessential appositive** or a **nonessential appositive phrase** is an appositive that is *not* necessary to the meaning of the sentence. Such an appositive should be separated from the rest of the sentence with a comma or commas.

┌─────────── appositive phrase ───────────┐
Lawrence also wrote *"The Fox,"* **a story that is widely read and studied.** [The appositive is not necessary to identify the story being discussed.]

Exercise 1 Prepositional and Appositive Phrases

Number your paper from 1 to 15. Next to each number, write a prepositional phrase or an appositive phrase to complete the sentence. Use the kind of phrase that is indicated.

SAMPLE   Frank put on his shoes, (1) _?_ (appositive phrase), and got his raincoat (2) _?_ (prepositional phrase).

ANSWER   1. a pair of brown loafers
2. from the closet

Frank, (1) _?_ (appositive phrase), left his house (2) _?_ (prepositional phrase) early this afternoon. As he walked (3) _?_ (prepositional phrase), he met his friend, (4) _?_ (appositive phrase), who was waiting (5) _?_ (prepositional phrase). They talked (6) _?_ (prepositional phrase) and continued together (7) _?_ (prepositional phrase). Frank and his friend passed the public library, (8) _?_ (appositive phrase), and turned the corner (9) _?_ (prepositional phrase). They, walked (10) _?_ (prepositional phrase) and finally arrived at the Shubert Theater, (11) _?_ (appositive phrase). They presented their tickets (12) _?_ (prepositional phrase) and climbed the stairs (13) _?_ (prepositional phrase). (14) _?_ (prepositional phrase), they were enthralled by *Hamlet,* (15) _?_ (appositive phrase).

Verbal Phrases

Verbals are verb forms that function as nouns, adjectives, or adverbs but retain some of the properties of verbs. For instance, they express action or being, and they may take complements. There are three kinds of verbals: participles, gerunds, and infinitives.

Participles.   A **participle** is a verb form that can function as an adjective while still keeping some of the properties of a verb. It expresses action or being, and it may take a complement.

> **Annoyed,** *Jane* kept driving around the block to find a **parking** *place.* [Both *annoyed* and *parking* are participles.]

There are two kind of participles: present participles and past participles. The present participle and the past participle are two of the four principal parts of a verb. For a complete explanation of the principal parts of verbs, see Section 2.2a of Unit 2.

Besides functioning as adjectives, present participles and past participles can form part of a verb phrase. When a participle functions as a verb, it is not a verbal. This section deals with present participles and past participles that function as adjectives. For an explanation of participles used as verbs, see Unit 2.

To form a present participle, add *-ing* to the infinitive form of a verb.

> Did you figure out a solution to that **puzzling** *problem?* [*Puzzling* is a present participle that consists of the verb *puzzle* and the ending *-ing.*]

To form a past participle, first determine whether the verb is regular or irregular (*Unit 2*).

1. *Regular verbs.* To form the past participle of a regular verb, add either *-d* or *-ed* to the infinitive form of the verb.

INFINITIVE	PAST PARTICIPLE
exhaust	exhausted

2. *Irregular verbs.* To form the past participle of an irregular verb, use a special form of the verb. See Section 2.2a of

Unit 2 for a list of past participles of commonly used irregular verbs.

INFINITIVE	PAST PARTICIPLE
freeze	frozen
tear	torn

A participle used as an adjective may have one or more auxiliary verbs. The auxiliary verb and the participle function as a unit to modify a noun or a pronoun.

Having been lost, *Jason* vowed never to drive in the city again without a map. [*Having* and *been* are the auxiliary verbs, and *lost* is the participle.]

Participial Phrases. A **participial phrase** consists of a participle and its modifiers and complements. The participial phrase functions as an adjective to modify a noun or a pronoun. Both present participles and past participles may be used to form participial phrases.

There is *Maria* **walking briskly to city hall.**

Disappointed by the cast's mediocre performance during dress rehearsal, the *director* emphasized the importance of concentration during a performance.

Having forgotten to send a birthday card, *Ed* sent a telegram to his brother.

Notice that in the preceding sentences, the participial phrases are near the words that they modify. For an explanation of the correct placement of participial phrases, see Unit 2.

Another kind of phrase that is formed with participles is the absolute phrase. An **absolute phrase** modifies the entire independent clause (*pages 58–59*) of the sentence; it does not have a direct grammatical connection with any single word in the independent clause. An absolute phrase contains both a participle and the noun or pronoun that is modified by the participle. Consequently, the phrase is "absolute," or complete within itself.

> **The flour having fallen from the top shelf of the pantry,** I had to spend half an hour cleaning the floor. [The absolute phrase modifies the entire independent clause by telling why I had to spend half an hour cleaning.]

Exercise 2 Participial Phrases On your paper, combine each of the following pairs of sentences by rewriting one sentence as a participial phrase. Underline the participial phrases in your rewritten sentences. You may change phrasing as necessary.

> **SAMPLE** Madeline's feature article was criticized for its poor organization. She worked until twelve o'clock that night to rewrite it.
>
> **ANSWER** Having been criticized for the poor organization of her feature article, Madeline worked until twelve o'clock that night to rewrite it.

1. Marita sent Julie a letter. Julie sent back a letter about her summer vacation.
2. Bill ran after Leslie's volley. He reached it and smashed the ball back to her side of the net.
3. The people were disappointed by the lack of snow this holiday season. They just stayed inside and watched television.
4. Amanda arrived late for the wedding. She sat down quietly in the last row of seats.
5. Cathy and Elizabeth walked down the street to the health food restaurant. The restaurant offers two dinners for the price of one before five o'clock.
6. Eugene visited his uncle during spring vacation. He took the train to St. Louis.
7. Fred was informed that he must appear as a witness in court on Monday. He told his employer that he would not be able to work that day.
8. A large crowd gathered to watch the man. He was attempting to walk a high wire.

9. Brenda was undecided about the next move to make in the chess game. She thoroughly examined each option before she decided to move the queen.
10. Vera had looked forward to reading the new novel. She was disappointed that it was so boring.

Gerunds

A **gerund** is a verbal that ends in *ing* and functions only as a noun. Although it functions as a noun, a gerund has some of the properties of a verb. It expresses action or being, and it may take a complement such as a direct object or an indirect object.

USED AS SUBJECT
According to doctors, **laughing** may be one way to treat certain kinds of illness.

USED AS DIRECT OBJECT
When you study, don't forget **skimming,** which allows you to review a great amount of material quickly.

USED AS INDIRECT OBJECT
Sue gave **skiing** high marks after her first try yesterday.

USED AS OBJECT OF PREPOSITION
To become an artist, one must first learn the fundamentals of **drawing**.

USED AS PREDICATE NOMINATIVE
A good way to gain exercise daily is **walking.**

USED AS APPOSITIVE
Most children's favorite pastime, **playing,** actually has great educational value.

Gerund Phrase. A **gerund phrase** consists of a gerund and its modifiers and complements.

┌──────gerund phrase ──────┐   ┌──────┐
The cheering of the crowd all but prevented us from **hearing**
┌──────────gerund phrase ──────────┐
the convention's main speaker.

Like gerunds, gerund phrases may perform all the functions of a noun.

USED AS SUBJECT

> **The marching of the band** made the ground tremble.

USED AS DIRECT OBJECT

> At this point in the hearings, the committee will avoid **debating specific policy proposals.**

USED AS INDIRECT OBJECT

> The city has given **developing new sources of revenue** the greatest importance this year.

USED AS OBJECT OF PREPOSITION

> The council has voted in favor of **setting aside additional land for public parks.**

USED AS PREDICATE NOMINATIVE

> One way to reduce grocery bills is **planting a garden of tomatoes, lettuce, beans, and cucumbers.**

USED AS APPOSITIVE

> Elaine's summer job, **selling sportswear in a department store,** will prove valuable in her career in merchandising.

Infinitives

An **infinitive** is a verbal that consists of the first principal part (*Section 2.2a of Unit 2*) of the verb. The word *to* usually, though not always, precedes the infinitive. An infinitive may function as a noun, an adjective, or an adverb. Like a participle and a gerund, an infinitive has some of the characteristics of a verb. It expresses action or being and may take a complement.

FUNCTIONS AS NOUN

> **To relax** is Greg's goal over spring vacation. [subject]
>
> Because the line for the movie was so long, we decided **to leave.** [direct object]
>
> The purpose of speech class is **to communicate.** [predicate nominative]

FUNCTIONS AS ADJECTIVE

> Phyllis has an excellent *ability* **to remember.** [What kind of ability? The ability *to remember*.]

FUNCTIONS AS ADVERB

> At the end of the play, the people *rose* **to applaud.** [Why did the people rise? They rose *to applaud*.]

> It looks to me as if the dog is too *lazy* **to run.** [To what extent is the dog lazy? It is too lazy *to run*.]

You may form an infinitive with one or more auxiliary verbs and a past participle. Such infinitives indicate the time of the action.

The *Super Bowl* **to have watched** was the 1969 game between the New York Jets and the Baltimore Colts.

The *route* **to be followed** is marked in red.

Infinitive Phrases.   An **infinitive phrase** consists of an infinitive and its modifiers and complements. An infinitive phrase can function as a noun, an adjective, or an adverb.

FUNCTIONS AS NOUN

> **To buy a birthday present** is my errand at noon.

FUNCTIONS AS ADJECTIVE

> The best *time* **to find bargains in the stores** is the last week of December. [Which time? The time *to find bargains in the stores*.]

FUNCTIONS AS ADVERB

> A crowd *gathered* **to watch the unveiling of the new sculpture.** [Why did a crowd gather? It gathered *to watch the unveiling of the new sculpture*.]

In some sentences an infinitive phrase may be used without the word *to*.

> Will you help me **put up the badminton net?** [**Think:** help me *to* put up the badminton net.]
>
> Silently, Peg's friends watched her **practice her figure skating.** [**Think:** watched her *to* practice her figure skating.]

Sometimes the infinitive has a subject. Together, the subject of the infinitive and the infinitive make up an **infinitive clause.** If the subject of the infinitive is a pronoun, that pronoun is in the objective case (*Section 2.4b of Unit 2*).

> ┌─────── infinitive clause ───────┐
> The gym teacher told **the class to run one more mile that day.** [*Class* is the subject of the infinitive.]
>
> ┌─────── infinitive clause ───────┐
> Sophie's aunt and uncle asked **her to pay them a visit when she passed through Cincinnati.**
>
> ┌─────── infinitive clause ───────┐
> Dale wants **us to start a collection of art objects from around the world.**

Exercise 3 Gerunds and Infinitives

On your paper, combine each of the following pairs of sentences by rewriting one sentence as a gerund phrase or an infinitive phrase. Use the kind of phrase indicated in parentheses. Underline the verbal phrases in your rewritten sentences.

> **SAMPLE** Mr. Harrison will plow part of the back yard for a garden. He will rent a small tractor. (infinitive phrase)
>
> **ANSWER** Mr. Harrison will rent a small tractor <u>to plow part of the back yard for a garden</u>.

1. Sheila raises German shepherd puppies. It is a rewarding and profitable project for her. (gerund phrase)

2. John plays golf every Saturday during the summer. He borrows his brother's golf clubs. (infinitive phrase)

3. Pedro built an oak desk. That was his final assignment for the year in industrial arts. (gerund phrase)

4. Kirsten sat in a quiet corner of the library all afternoon. She finished Jane Austen's *Pride and Prejudice*. (infinitive phrase)

5. As a reporter for the school newspaper, I met with the college president last month. We discussed the challenges of that position. (infinitive phrase)

6. Mary prepared to play a minuet for her piano recital. It took hours of practice. (gerund phrase)

7. Katrina knit the vest that she is wearing. She used wool yarn. (infinitive phrase)

8. I must collate these pages for the school yearbook by the last period today. Will you help me? (infinitive phrase)

9. Truck drivers spend long hours on the road and drive through all kinds of weather. If you don't mind those things, you should look further into becoming a truck driver. (gerund phrase)

10. Last Sunday our family drove around the countryside. We looked at the beautiful fall foliage. (infinitive phrase)

Exercise 4   Verbal Phrases   The sentences in the following paragraph are short, making the paragraph monotonous. On your paper, rewrite the paragraph to give the sentences more variety. Use participial phrases, gerund phrases, and infinitive phrases where appropriate. Underline the verbal phrases in your rewritten paragraph.

> **SAMPLE**   I was a new member of the debate team. I was
> particularly nervous during the few minutes before
> the start of the debate.
>
> **ANSWER**   <u>Being a new member of the debate team</u>, I was
> particularly nervous during the few minutes before
> the start of the debate.

I sat at the front of the auditorium. I held a white sheet of paper with a few tiny black marks scratched across it. I stared down at my own handwriting, but my notes were unrecognizable. I looked in front of me. I saw pencils and a glass of water on the table. I grew uncomfortable in my hard chair. I shifted my weight and wished that I could stand up. I waited for the opposing team. They would march in and sit behind the table on the other side of the lectern. They finally entered and sat down. They looked intelligent and informed. I stared at their confident faces. Doing so made me even more nervous, and I looked away. I kept my mind on the subject of the debate. I recalled my most important facts and ideas. The moderator then rose and walked toward the lectern. She would introduce the debate teams to the audience. The moderator finished her introduction. She sat down again. I took a deep breath. I hoped that the deep breath would control my nervousness. I walked to the lectern. I could feel a calmness come over me. I knew that I was in control, and I began. I spoke effortlessly, just like an experienced debater. I'd prepared my case thoroughly. The preparation had really paid off!

1.3b   Clauses

A **clause** is a group of related words that contains both a subject and a predicate. There are two kinds of clauses: independent clauses and subordinate clauses.

Independent Clauses

An **independent clause** can stand by itself as a sentence. The following sentence contains two independent clauses, which are in boldface type. Notice that each clause has a subject and a predicate and that each could be a separate sentence. In the following example, the subject is underlined once, and the predicate is underlined twice.

> **Our literary <u>club</u> <u>intended</u> to read *Dune,* by Frank Herbert, but <u>we</u> <u>chose</u> Ray Bradbury's *Fahrenheit 451* instead.**

A comma and the coordinating conjunction *but* join the clauses in the preceding sentence. *But* is not part of either clause. Rather, it coordinates, or connects, the independent clauses. The other coordinating conjunctions are *and, or, nor, for,* and *yet.*

You can also join independent clauses with either a semicolon or a semicolon and a conjunctive adverb (*page 31*).

> Career information has become increasingly critical to today's high school graduates; the guidance department is planning a series of workshops on careers this spring. [semicolon]

Career information has become increasingly critical to today's high school graduates; **therefore,** the guidance department is planning a series of workshops on careers this spring. [semicolon and conjunctive adverb]

Subordinate Clauses

A clause that cannot stand by itself is a **subordinate clause.** This kind of clause is sometimes called a **dependent clause.** In the following examples, the subjects are underlined once, and the predicates are underlined twice. However, the clauses cannot stand by themselves because they do not express complete thoughts.

Which is one of the vanishing species in the United States

While we are waiting for the car to be tuned up

Although the weather has been mild

Notice that the preceding subordinate clauses begin with the words *which, while,* and *although. Which* is a relative pronoun (*page 10*), and *while* and *although* are subordinating conjunctions (*pages 30–31*). Many subordinate clauses begin with either a relative pronoun or a subordinating conjunction. Such introductory words are part of the subordinate clause, and they join the subordinate clause to an independent clause.

┌────────── Indep. clause ──────────┐ ┌──────sub. clause ─────────┐
Most observers admire the bald eagle, **which** is one of the vanishing species in the United States.

┌────────── indep. clause ──────────┐ ┌──────sub. clause ─────┐
Why don't we walk around the shopping center **while** we are waiting for the car to be tuned up?

┌────────── sub. clause ──────────┐ ┌────── indep. clause ──────┐
Although the weather has been mild, forecasters are predicting a harsh winter.

Clauses Used as Adjectives.   A clause functions as an adjective if it modifies a noun or a pronoun. Such clauses are called

adjective clauses. Most adjective clauses begin with a relative pronoun: *that, which, who, whom,* and *whose.*

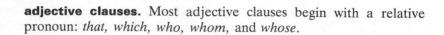

——— adj. clause ———

The policy *paper* **that** the candidate issued on city services has some worthwhile ideas. [*Which* paper? The paper *that the candidate issued on city services.*]

——— adj. clause ———

I can't remember the name of the *artist* **whose** paintings are being featured at the art institute. [*Which* artist? The artist *whose paintings are being featured at the art institute.*]

You may also begin adjective clauses with **relative adverbs.** Some of the relative adverbs are *after, before, since, when,* and *where.*

——— adj. clause ———

The *years* **since** the Wright brothers flew at Kittyhawk have brought enormous changes in people's lives. [*Which* years? The years *since the Wright brothers flew at Kittyhawk.*]

Sometimes the introductory word in an adjective clause is implied rather than stated.

——— adj. clause ———

The *bus* the commuters usually took to work was discontinued without any announcement. [**Think:** bus *that* the commuters usually took.]

Essential and Nonessential Clauses.   An adjective clause that is necessary to identify a noun or a pronoun is an **essential clause.** An essential clause is not separated from the rest of the sentence by commas.

ESSENTIAL CLAUSE

When our car broke down, we were lucky to find the only

——— adj. clause ———

service *station* **that** was open late at night. [The clause is essential in order to identify the station.]

A **nonessential clause** is an adjective clause that is not necessary to identify a noun or a pronoun. A nonessential clause is set off from the rest of the sentence by commas.

NONESSENTIAL CLAUSE

The morning classes were shortened because of the

———————————— adj. clause ————————————
assembly, **which** featured speeches by students running for student council. [The clause is nonessential because without it, the reader would still know which assembly is being discussed.]

Exercise 5   Adjective Clauses   On your paper, combine the following sets of sentences by writing one or more of the sentences as an adjective clause. Underline the adjective clauses in your rewritten sentences.

SAMPLE   Judo was developed in ancient Japan as a means of self-defense. It has grown rapidly as a sport and now has more than four hundred thousand participants in the United States.

ANSWER   Judo, which was developed in ancient Japan as a means of self-defense, has grown rapidly as a sport and now has more than four hundred thousand participants in the United States.

1. President Theodore Roosevelt was among the first people in the United States to learn judo. He was competent enough to earn a brown belt.
2. In the last one hundred years, judo has grown into an international sport. It was first included in the Olympic Games in 1964.
3. A person does not have to be big or strong to practice judo. In English the word means "the gentle way."
4. Instead of using brute strength, judo experts use timing and balance to protect themselves from their opponents. Opponents may weigh more and have more strength.
5. Judo teachers conduct their training in a gymnasium called a *dojo*. There, people take judo because it is good exercise and provides an excellent method of self-defense.

6. People participating in judo wear a special costume. The costume consists of a white jacket and pants and a belt in one of three colors.

7. According to the United States Judo Federation, the level of competence in judo is indicated by the colors of the belts. These belts are white for beginners, brown for intermediates, and black for experts.

8. In the first few sessions of a judo class, a student learns several exercises. These exercises train the student to fall without being hurt.

9. In later classes the student learns techniques in three areas. These areas include throwing, holding, and striking.

10. Judo competitors may appear in two types of contests, *kata* and *randori*. Both are supervised by a referee and scored by two judges.

Clauses Used as Adverbs.   A subordinate clause functions as an adverb when it modifies a verb, an adjective, or an adverb. Such clauses are called **adverb clauses.**

MODIFIES VERB

Newspapers *played* a large role in colonial America

—————————— adv. clause ——————————
because they supported and publicized the efforts of colonists protesting British rule.

MODIFIES ADJECTIVE

—————— adv. clause ——————
All of the neighbors were *sure* **that Mr. Wallace would recover completely from his illness.**

MODIFIES ADVERB

For her research paper, Evelyn went through the county

—————— adv. clause ——————
records more *thoroughly* **than anyone else had done before.**

An adverb clause always begins with a subordinating conjunction (*pages 30–31*), which is a word that shows the relationship between the subordinate clause and the independent clause. A list of frequently used subordinating conjunctions is on pages 30–31.

Adverb clauses tell *how, when, where, to what extent,* and *why.* In the following examples, the subordinating conjunctions are in boldface type.

HOW

Although nervous, Sharon *greeted* the

personnel director **as if** she were completely at ease.

WHEN

While the tide is coming in, you *should* not *stand* on those low rocks near the ocean.

WHERE

For lunch we *will meet* you **where** State and Madison streets intersect.

TO WHAT EXTENT

The tourists were so *eager* to see the Washington Monument **that** they walked to it before breakfast.

WHY

So that the restaurant can be sure of seating such a large party, you *should call* ahead of time for a reservation.

Elliptical Clauses. An elliptical clause is an adverb clause in which part of the clause is omitted. Even though the clause is incomplete, its meaning is clear; therefore, it is still classified as a clause.

You deserve more credit for the success of our fund-raising campaign **than I.** [**Think:** You deserve more credit than I *deserve. Than I* modifies *more.*]

While walking along the wharf, Larry *tripped* and *fell*. [**Think:** while
he was walking.]

Exercise 6 Adverb Clauses On your paper, combine each set
of sentences into one sentence. Do so by rewriting one or more of the
sentences as adverb clauses. You may change wording as necessary so
that the resulting sentence makes sense. Underline the adverb clauses
in your rewritten sentences.

> **SAMPLE** A committee of parents wants a new traffic light put
> up in front of the high school. Drivers will have an
> easier time entering the highway from the parking
> lot.
>
> **ANSWER** A committee of parents wants a new traffic light put
> up in front of the high school so that drivers will have
> an easier time entering the highway from the parking
> lot.

1. Luella spends three hours studying in the library every night. She
   hopes to make the honor roll this semester.
2. Kevin practices free throws every Saturday afternoon. He is already a
   member of the varsity basketball team.
3. We'll go skating later this afternoon. Barbara has an appointment with
   the ophthalmologist at one o'clock.
4. Joanne ordered the daisies for Mother's Day this afternoon. Her
   mother was shopping in the grocery store.
5. The Fletchers went tobogganing near Lake Tahoe last winter. More
   than ten feet of snow was on the ground.
6. Mrs. Sorenson has become very interested in business investing. She
   has signed up to take a course in investments.
7. Anne visited friends at a dairy farm in Vermont during Thanksgiving
   vacation. It was too expensive to fly home to Phoenix.
8. Mark crept quietly toward the deer and the fawn. He wanted to take
   photographs of them.
9. The officials in charge of the marathon were surprised. So many
   runners had qualified to run in the race!
10. The visitors lined up on the two-yard line of the home team. The
    crowd roared. The members of the visiting team could not hear their
    quarterback yell the signals.

Clauses Used as Nouns. Clauses that function as nouns in sentences are **noun clauses.** A noun clause may function as a subject, a predicate nominative, a direct object, an indirect object, an object of a preposition, or an appositive.

FUNCTIONS AS SUBJECT

┌────────────── noun clause ──────────────┐
Where the city should build a new library is the main item on the agenda at the city council meeting.

FUNCTIONS AS PREDICATE NOMINATIVE

                                    ┌── noun clause ──────────┐
The turning point of World War II was **when the Allied forces landed successfully on the shores of Normandy.**

FUNCTIONS AS DIRECT OBJECT

                                  ┌────────── noun clause ──────────┐
Research scientists are hoping **that the process of nuclear fusion will help to solve the world's energy problems in the twenty-first century.**

FUNCTIONS AS INDIRECT OBJECT

                      ┌────────── noun clause ──────────┐
Mr. Pritkin will give **whoever finds his pet poodle** a substantial reward.

FUNCTIONS AS OBJECT OF A PREPOSITION

The people in the train station are waiting for
┌────── noun clause ──────┐
whichever train arrives first.

FUNCTIONS AS APPOSITIVE

                              ┌── noun clause ──┐
It's after four-thirty, and the pranksters, **whoever they are,** are to return to my office at nine o'clock tomorrow morning.

You may introduce a noun clause with an interrogative pronoun, a subordinating conjunction, or the relative pronoun *whose.*

INTERROGATIVE PRONOUNS

who, whom, whose, which, what, whoever, whomever, whatever, whichever

SUBORDINATING CONJUNCTIONS
how, that, when, where, whether, why

RELATIVE PRONOUN
whose

Sometimes you may omit the introductory word in a noun clause.

┌─────────── noun clause ───────────┐
Has anyone told the reporters **they were the winners of several
awards for their documentaries this year?** [**Think:** informed *that* they
were the winners.]

Exercise 7   Noun Clauses   Complete the following sentences
by replacing the blank with a noun clause. The noun clause should
perform the sentence function indicated in the parentheses. Write the
entire sentence on your paper, and underline the noun clause.

SAMPLE   __?__ has been a subject of debate for at least twenty
years. (subject)

ANSWER   Whether the state should finance the construction of
a new community college in this area has been a
subject of debate for at least twenty years.

1. When we take the tour of the famous author's house, I hope __?__.
(direct object)
2. __?__ will be the national champion. (subject)
3. Brian guessed __?__. (direct object)
4. We are planning to buy a picnic table at __?__. (object of preposition)
5. Our partners for the project will be __?__. (predicate nominative)
6. When you walked through the tunnel, did you happen to see __?__?
(direct object)
7. __?__ certainly left our cabin remarkably neat and clean. (subject)
8. The hope of going on the archeological dig in the spring was __?__.
(predicate nominative)
9. Although she was busy herself, Margaret always helped __?__. (direct
object)
10. Even though she receives hundreds of letters every week, the actress
sends __?__ an autographed picture. (indirect object)

Assignment Clauses in Writing In the passage that follows, most of the sentences are short, making the passage repetitious. On your paper, rewrite the paragraph so that the sentences have more variety. Do so by using adjective clauses, adverb clauses, and noun clauses to combine sentences. Underline the clauses in your rewritten paragraphs.

> During the spring and fall of each year, nature creates its own light show. We call this show the aurora borealis, or the northern lights. The aurora is a multicolored glow. It seems to hover over the far northern horizon. Observers look in that direction on a clear night. They may see a glow. The glow is tinted green or red. Canadians have an excellent view of this natural light show. The northern lights have also been seen in the continental United States and even as far south as Mexico.
>
> Electrically charged particles from the sun hit the atmosphere of the earth. The aurora borealis results. The charged particles encounter friction. Their electrical charge changes. A glow results. The lights are actually more than seventy miles above the surface of the earth. They may appear in a variety of patterns. To the observer, these patterns look like arcs or rays in the sky. At times the sun has a great deal of sunspot activity. Then we can expect particularly vivid shows here on the earth. People view this natural phenomenon. They cannot fail to be impressed by its beauty.

1.3c Sentences Classified by Structure

Sentences are classified according to the number and kinds of clauses that they contain. The four kinds of sentences are simple, compound, complex, and compound-complex.

Simple Sentences. A sentence containing one independent clause and no subordinate clauses is a **simple sentence.** It may have any number of phrases, and it may have a compound subject, a compound predicate, or both. However, it does not have more than one clause.

> Fish, underwater plants, and coral were visible in the crystal blue water.
> Myra's car had a flat tire, forcing her off the road.

Compound Sentences.   A sentence consisting of two or more independent clauses is a **compound sentence.** A compound sentence never has a subordinate clause. The independent clauses are usually joined with a comma and one of the coordinating conjunctions: *and, but, nor, or, for,* or *yet.*

> ┌─────────── indep. clause ───────────┐ ┌────────
> Skydiving is an increasingly popular sport, **but** you should
> ┌─────────── indep. clause ───────────┐
> be in excellent physical shape to try it.

Independent clauses may also be joined with a semicolon or with a semicolon and a conjunctive adverb such as *nonetheless, consequently,* or *still (page 31).* A comma always follows the conjunctive adverb.

> ┌─────────── indep. clause ───────────┐ ┌───────
> A dirigible, a type of aircraft, is lighter than air; the first
> ┌─────── indep. clause ───────┐
> dirigible was built in 1884.

> ┌─────────────── indep. clause ───────────────┐
> During the 1800s a man named John Chapman traveled throughout
> the Ohio River valley and planted apple seeds;
> ┌─────────── indep. clause ───────────┐
> **consequently,** Chapman is known to us as Johnny Appleseed.

Complex Sentences

A sentence consisting of one independent clause and one or more subordinate clauses is a **complex sentence.**

> ┌─────────── sub. clause ───────────┐
> When herders in the mountains of Switzerland want to
> communicate to one another across long distances, they use a
> ┌──────── indep. clause ────────┐┌──── sub. clause ────┐
> twelve-foot-long instrument that is called an alpenhorn.

> ┌─────────── sub. clause ───────────┐
> Paris's Arc de Triomphe, which commemorates Napoleon's victories,
> ┌─────────── sub. clause ───────────┐
> was not completed until 1836 even though it was started in 1806.
> [The sentence contains one independent clause: *Paris's Arc de Triomphe was not completed until 1836.* That clause contains a subordinate clause: *which commemorates Napoleon's victories.*]

Compound-Complex Sentences. A sentence consisting of two or more independent clauses and one or more subordinate clauses is a **compound-complex sentence.**

```
┌──────────────────── sub. clause ────────────────────┐
When the first synthetic fiber, rayon, was developed in 1884,
┌──────────────────── indep. clause ──────────────────┐
the way was opened for the development of modern textiles,
┌──────────────────── indep. clause ──────────────────┐
and these textiles have revolutionized the clothing industry.
```

```
┌──────────────────── sub. clause ────────────────────┐
Since commercial television became popular in the 1950s,
┌──────────────── indep. clause ────────────────┐        ┌──────
the major networks have dominated the programming, but recent
```
┌──────────────────── sub. clause ────────────────────┐
developments, which include cable television and public television,
may change the structure of the industry. [The second independent clause, *recent developments may change the structure of the industry,* is interrupted by the subordinate clause *which include cable television and public television.*]

Exercise 8 Sentence Classification Each numbered item contains a set of sentences. Rewrite each set, combining the sentences into one sentence. Label each sentence that you write *Simple, Compound, Complex,* or *Compound-complex.*

> **SAMPLE** Experts have made a prediction. The small computer will allow many people to work at home to develop and sell computer software.
>
> **ANSWER** Experts have predicted that the small computer will allow many people to work at home to develop and sell computer software.—Complex

1. Marcia loves all water sports. She especially enjoys swimming for the school team. The team travels all over the state for meets.
2. Roberto has never seen the Grand Canyon. He is planning a vacation there.
3. We were in Washington, D.C., last summer. We visited the Library of Congress. The library was founded in 1800 to provide members of Congress with reference and research assistance.

4. New England whalers were successful in the early 1800s. The United States was the world's foremost whaling country at that time. The wealth originating from that industry helped boost the foreign trade of the United States.

5. Morris is a die-hard Dodgers fan. He considers himself an expert on baseball. He was too busy this summer to go to a game.

6. John Singleton Copley is considered the finest colonial American portrait painter. The Boston native studied in London in his later years. He remained in London for the rest of his life.

7. Virginia and I met some bird watchers. We were at the wildlife refuge on Saturday. They let us use their binoculars to look at the bald eagle. They had spotted it.

8. *Nicholas Nickleby* was recently adapted for television. It was one of Charles Dickens's early novels. The television version effectively dramatized the author's biting criticism of the private-school system in nineteenth-century England.

9. I am going to be outside in cold weather. I always try to wear wool clothing. Wool is a natural fiber. The fiber insulates well.

10. One of the basic tenets of economics is the inverse relationship between inflation and unemployment. The unemployment rate declines. The rate of inflation tends to increase.

1.3d   Writing Complete Sentences

A **complete sentence** is a group of words that has at least one subject and one predicate and that expresses a complete thought. You should use complete sentences in your writing. Two common errors in writing are the use of sentence fragments and run-on sentences. In this section you will learn how to recognize and correct both kinds of errors.

Avoiding Sentence Fragments

A **sentence fragment** is a group of words that lacks a subject or a predicate or does not express a complete thought.

COMPLETE SENTENCE
> Harriet planned to pick up the reupholstered chair on her way home.

FRAGMENT

Harriet planned. **To pick up the reupholstered chair on her way home.** [The second group of words lacks a subject and a predicate.]

FRAGMENT

Harriet, planning to pick up the reupholstered chair on her way home. [The group of words lacks a predicate.]

If the sentence fragment is a phrase, you can correct it by combining the fragment with a related sentence.

FRAGMENT

During lunch today. I would like to talk about the plans for the panel discussion.

COMPLETE SENTENCE

```
┌── prepositional ──┐
│      phrase       │
```
During lunch today I would like to talk about the plans for the panel discussion.

FRAGMENT

The zoo has acquired an anaconda. **A large snake native to South America.**

COMPLETE SENTENCE

```
                              ┌── appositive phrase ──┐
```
The zoo has acquired an anaconda, **a large snake native to South America.**

FRAGMENT

To buy an old car and rebuild the engine. That is what Al has decided to do.

COMPLETE SENTENCE

```
          ┌──────────── infinitive phrase ────────────┐
```
Al has decided **to buy an old car and rebuild the engine.**

FRAGMENT

I think that I saw Uncle Bill. **Waiting in line at the concession stand.**

COMPLETE SENTENCE

┌─────── participial phrase ───────
I think that I saw Uncle Bill **waiting in line at the concession stand.**

FRAGMENT

Paddling upstream in a canoe. That requires a great expenditure of energy.

COMPLETE SENTENCE

┌─────── gerund phrase ───────┐
Paddling upstream in a canoe requires a great expenditure of energy.

If the sentence fragment is a subordinate clause used without an independent clause, you can also correct it by combining the fragment with a related sentence.

FRAGMENT

The entire group has decided to go to Palomar Park. **Which is featuring carnival rides at half price over the weekend.**

COMPLETE SENTENCE

┌───────
The entire group has decided to go to Palomar Park, **which**

──────────────────── subordinate clause ────────────────────┐
is featuring carnival rides at half price over the weekend.

FRAGMENT

Before you apply to all those colleges. You should give more thought to your career goals.

COMPLETE SENTENCE

┌─────── subordinate clause ───────┐
Before you apply to all those colleges, you should give more thought to your career goals.

Some sentence fragments require additions or rewording to make them complete sentences.

FRAGMENT

The ocean, sparkling under the noonday sun.

COMPLETE SENTENCE

The ocean sparkled under the noonday sun.

FRAGMENT
> The metric system, which is becoming more widely used in the United States.

COMPLETE SENTENCE
> The metric system is becoming more widely used in the United States.

Exercise 9 Eliminating Fragments The following passage contains numerous sentence fragments. On your paper, rewrite both paragraphs, eliminating all the sentence fragments.

SAMPLE Without water, no living thing can live on the earth, yet most people take water for granted. Until they are deprived of its benefits.

ANSWER Without water, no living thing can live on the earth, yet most people take water for granted until they are deprived of its benefits.

More than three hundred million cubic miles. That's how much water covers our planet. However, 97 percent being salty. Which leaves 3 percent fresh water. Three quarters of that fresh water is in ice caps. And in glaciers. Sixteen thousand gallons. That's how much water the average person drinks in a lifetime. Each person, using seventy gallons a day. Although the world's demand for water has more than doubled since 1960. There is still a sufficient supply to take care of humanity's needs. However, regular water shortages in certain parts of the world. Because the pattern of rainfall throughout the world is uneven. For instance, four hundred inches of rain a year in some parts of India, but no rain for several years in other parts of the world.

We can understand the effects of water shortages. When we read about the long droughts in the southwestern United States during the 1930s. When that region came to be known as the Dust Bowl. Today, many communities have devised inventive ways. To conserve water. One of the most effective being to treat sewage water and use it to water lawns and to form lakes. In spite of such efforts. There is still a great deal of waste. For instance, leaks from faucets and water pipes. Add up to 20 percent of the amount of water that a city uses. Leaks that rob the city of Chicago of one hundred fifty million gallons of water every day.

Avoiding Run-on Sentences

A **run-on sentence** consists of two or more separate sentences written as one sentence. In some run-on sentences, only a comma separates the two sentences; in others there is no punctuation at all.

RUN-ON	Radio and television announcers have warned people not to look at the sun during the eclipse tomorrow, doing so could result in blindness. [A comma by itself cannot connect two independent clauses.]
RUN-ON	Radio and television announcers have warned people not to look at the sun during the eclipse tomorrow doing so could result in blindness. [The sentences are run together without punctuation or a conjunction.]
CORRECT	Radio and television announcers have warned people not to look at the sun during the eclipse tomorrow, for doing so could result in blindness. [A comma and the coordinating conjunction *for* connect the two clauses.]

There are several ways to correct run-on sentences. Read the following run-on sentence. Then study the five ways in which you can correct that sentence.

RUN-ON SENTENCE   The bridge over the river is closed, a ferry will take you to the other side.

1. Separate the run-on sentence into two or more sentences.

    CORRECT   The bridge over the river is closed. **A** ferry will take you to the other side.

2. Join the independent clauses with a comma and a coordinating conjunction (*page 29*).

    CORRECT   The bridge over the river is closed, **but** a ferry will take you to the other side.

3. Join the independent clauses with a semicolon.

    CORRECT   The bridge over the river is closed; a ferry will take you to the other side.

4. Turn one of the independent clauses into a subordinate clause, and add a subordinating conjunction (*pages 30–31*) or a relative pronoun (*page 10*).

CORRECT   **Because** the bridge over the river is closed, a ferry will take you to the other side.

5. Join the independent clauses with a semicolon and a conjunctive adverb such as *also, thus,* or *however* (*page 31*).

CORRECT   The bridge over the river is closed; **however,** a ferry will take you to the other side.

Exercise 10   Eliminating Run-on Sentences   The following passage contains numerous run-on sentences. On your paper, rewrite the paragraphs, correcting all the run-ons.

SAMPLE   The maps of ancient peoples were by no means accurate, they provide us with a vivid record of humanity's gradually increasing knowledge of geography.

ANSWER   The maps of ancient peoples were by no means accurate, but they provide us with a vivid record of humanity's gradually increasing knowledge of geography.

The oldest map that we know about dates back about 4300 years to ancient Babylonia, it shows an estate surrounded by mountains. As in so many other endeavors, the Greeks were ahead of their time in map making for their maps showed the world as round rather than flat, the Greeks also developed a system of longitude and latitude for identifying locations. The Romans were excellent administrators and military strategists, therefore, it is no surprise that they made worthy road maps and military maps. The most famous map maker of ancient times was Claudius Ptolemy of Alexandria, Egypt, he created a comprehensive map of the world and maps of the regions that were known to ancient travelers.

In the 1300s and the 1400s, European explorers began venturing into unknown parts of the world, consequently, they developed charts and maps to assist those who followed them. Most ships on voyages of exploration carried chart makers and these experts made maps of coasts, islands, bays, and other geographical features that were discovered. One such map maker was the most famous explorer of all, Christopher Columbus, Martin Waldseemüller, a German who in 1507 first used the name *America* on a map, was another.

America was a completely unknown territory to Europeans, indeed, one of the greatest challenges facing explorers in the New World was charting the lands, rivers, and mountains that they encountered. The task was monumental but Lewis and Clark, John C. Frémont, and Zebulon Pike all made maps these maps helped gold seekers in the California Gold Rush of 1849. The maps of these explorers were not completely accurate, however, they were the basis for the truly accurate maps that the United States government began to develop in about 1875.

Assignment   Run-on Sentences and Fragments   On your paper, rewrite the following paragraph, correcting all the run-on sentences and the sentence fragments.

George Mason, the Virginian statesman who influenced Thomas Jefferson. He once wrote, "The freedom of the press is one of the great bulwarks of liberty, and can never be restrained but by despotic governments." The shapers of the Constitution took Mason's words seriously for they made freedom of the press the First Amendment in the Bill of Rights. However, it has not always been widely accepted. That people should have the right to publish what they think without pressure from the government or from private citizens and organizations. For example, during the Middle Ages, before the idea of individual rights was generally acknowledged. Governments required printers to obtain licenses before publishing material and the state closely regulated the content of books and newspapers. Philosophers gradually popularized the idea of a "marketplace of ideas." Which meant that the free exchange of ideas led to a better-informed citizenry and to a more responsive government. In the American colonies, the turning point for freedom of the press came in 1735 with the trial of newspaper publisher John Peter Zenger, Zenger had published articles criticizing British rule but a jury found him innocent of libel, or publishing statements that injure someone's reputation.

Even though freedom of the press is an accepted ideal in the United States. The practice of this right sometimes causes extremely difficult dilemmas. For instance, most journalists would probably agree that the press should not publish libelous material, however, what constitutes libel has been a source of disagreement between the press and the courts. A controversy also surrounding the interpretation of national security. This was an issue during World War II. When Congress made it illegal to publish material that might hinder the war effort. During the 1960s a major controversy arose over gag orders, these are orders from a judge to the press not to print disclosures. Making it impossible for defendants to receive fair trials. The freedom of the press will continue to be the source of controversy in the future for interpreting the limits of such a freedom is never a black-and-white affair. Often the way it is under a democratic form of government.

Phrases and Clauses

The preview for this unit shows the importance of subordinate clauses in making an analogy clear. With adjective clauses, adverb clauses, and noun clauses, you can emphasize the similarities between the two parts of an analogy. Using one of the following topics or a topic of your own, write one or two paragraphs in which you use an analogy to make a process clear to your reader. In your paragraphs be sure to use subordinate clauses. Underline the clauses that you write.

1. Making decisions
2. Gaining the cooperation of others
3. Making friends
4. Listening to other people
5. Taking part in an artistic activity

Unit Practice

Practice 1

A. Parts of Speech (*pages 3–34*)   On your paper, write the words that are in italic type in the following sentences. Next to each word or phrase, write the label *Noun, Pronoun, Verb, Adjective, Adverb, Preposition, Conjunction,* or *Interjection.*

1. While riding in the train to San Antonio, Max got along *very* well with the man sitting next to him.
2. The fence *that* Anthony helped his father build twenty years ago is still in excellent shape.
3. All of the people at the picnic formed a *cluster* around the campfire in order to stay warm.
4. Do you know which fence the horse jumped *over* when it escaped from the corral?
5. The *trained* dolphins delighted the adults in the audience as much as the children.
6. The students were curious to see *what* the outcome of the experiment would be.
7. As the twins became older, they *grew* distant from each other and developed separate interests.
8. During the *Johnson* administration, Congress passed several laws that guaranteed civil rights.
9. *According to* Betty's friend Stacy, the bicycle path along the river has been maintained well throughout the summer.
10. People have enjoyed Uncle Rich's stories *as long as* I can remember.
11. *Must* you really *drive* into town during this blizzard?
12. Lynette approached the lectern with confidence, for she felt *extremely* well prepared to give her speech to the class.
13. *Well,* I never expected to redecorate the living room so quickly!
14. The official put the *three-inch-thick* pile of papers before him on the desk and prepared to go through it.
15. *Carefully,* the supervisor inspected the foundation of the building to make sure that the cement had been poured properly.
16. Rumors swept through the science community that Atlantis *itself* had been discovered by a team of divers.
17. Any athletic equipment that is *ours* must be removed from lockers by three o'clock this afternoon.

18. We have *not* been able to accept all the people who are interested in the French cooking class.

19. Because the snow was so wet and heavy, the Lesters helped to clean the snow off their *neighbors' bushes*.

20. *Not only* did the seniors produce a literary magazine with excellent content, *but* they *also* illustrated it well.

21. Samantha was surprised to find that the trees were sprouting buds in March; *usually* buds did not appear until April.

22. Even as a youngster, when he loved animals, Woody *considered* a career as a veterinarian.

23. According to many ancient philosophers, the emotion that causes the most division among people is *jealousy*.

24. The captain ordered all deck hands to appear for the *lifeboat* drill.

25. When the pioneers traveled *overland* to the West, they faced the dangers of disease and bad weather.

B. Sentence Structure (*pages 34–46*)   On your paper, write the words that are in italic type in the following sentences. Then write the correct label for each word or phrase: *Simple subject, Simple predicate, Complete subject, Complete predicate, Direct object, Indirect object, Objective complement, Predicate nominative,* or *Predicate adjective.*

26. Last week the environmental group appointed Mrs. Jenkins *chairperson* of the committee on legislative relations.

27. As we walked around the lake, we *saw* several turtles sunning themselves on logs and boulders.

28. *Most political cartoons* include caricature, in which the cartoonist exaggerates some characteristics in order to achieve a satirical effect.

29. My niece made *me* a lovely blue and yellow patchwork quilt for my birthday.

30. In 1932, just five years after Lindbergh's historic transatlantic flight, Amelia Earhart became the first *woman* to pilot a plane across the Atlantic.

31. My *brother* Arturo always stops to feed the swans by the pond.

32. The *Taj Mahal,* a tomb built for the wife of a seventeenth-century Indian ruler, took twenty-one years to build.

(Continue on the next page.)

33. The Lincoln High School marching band's half-time show was *outstanding*.
34. Loons, aquatic birds that often make their homes near isolated lakes in northern states, *can be distinguished by their unusual cry*.
35. Ryan promised to take *all* of us water-skiing next Saturday.
36. Our Explorer troop *is planning* a canoe trip in Florida's Ocala National Forest.
37. Rembrandt, who painted about one hundred self-portraits throughout his career, was the most influential *artist* from the Netherlands.
38. Driving through western Pennsylvania just after sunrise, we saw a doe and her *fawn* at the edge of a meadow.
39. The Hudson River School painters in the nineteenth century portrayed the *beauty* and grandeur of America's untamed wilderness.
40. Although she has played the game for only a year, Ann's strategy on the soccer field is *flawless*.

C. Phrases and Clauses (pages 46–77)

C. Phrases and Clauses (*pages 46–77*)   On your paper, write the phrases and clauses that are in italic type in the following sentences. Then write the correct label for each phrase or clause: *Prepositional phrase, Appositive phrase, Participial phrase, Gerund phrase, Infinitive phrase, Independent clause, Adjective clause, Adverb clause,* or *Noun clause.*

41. Andrea stood *before the department store window* admiring the beautiful silk dress.
42. *Whenever my family goes out for dinner,* my six-year-old brother, Mark, always orders chicken.
43. The hearing *on environmental issues* will be held tomorrow.
44. Eleanor Roosevelt, *who was a niece of one President and the wife of another,* earned fame for her humanitarian work.
45. Sarah, *who has the best batting average on the team,* can't play because of a sprained thumb.
46. *Whoever supervises chemistry labs* should instruct students in the proper precautions while working with acid.
47. *Circling the globe in Friendship 7,* John Glenn became the first American to orbit the earth on February 20, 1962.
48. Just after dawn we went out on the beach *to collect shells during low tide.*

49. *The bicycle trails on Cape Cod are beautiful,* but they are often crowded during peak periods of the summer vacation.
50. Historians sometimes ponder how the country would have fared *if President Kennedy had not been assassinated.*
51. *Since she has been away at college,* Cindy and I have exchanged letters, but we have seen each other only occasionally.
52. Our company may have an opening *for a certified public accountant* like you.
53. After their annual concert, the Monroe High School orchestra held a reception for friends and relatives *who had attended the performance.*
54. This novel, *published last year,* has been praised as the writer's finest.
55. Jessica must leave home before eight o'clock every morning *to catch the bus at the corner.*

Practice 2

On your paper, rewrite the following paragraph to eliminate all fragments and run-on sentences.

A bright object appears suddenly in the sky the object makes a trail and disappears just as suddenly. Although we call the light a shooting star, it is actually a meteor. A piece of metal or rock that enters the atmosphere of the earth. Friction with the atmosphere. That is what makes the meteor glow so brightly. Some meteors burn up completely in the atmosphere others hit the earth's surface, the latter are called meteorites. Approximately two hundred million meteors, which add about one thousand tons to the weight of Earth. These meteors enter the atmosphere every day. Sometimes meteors appear in a group. Which we call a meteor shower. The brightest meteor shower in recorded history was the Leonid shower of November 13, 1833, the same shower can be seen every November as it makes its orbit around the sun. A meteorite makes a crater. When it hits the surface of the earth. One giant crater in the United States, the Great Meteor Crater of Arizona. It was created fifty thousand years ago scientists believe, this crater is 4150 feet across and 570 feet deep. Some craters being several miles wide. It is difficult. To imagine the impact that such a meteorite must have made as it hit the earth.

Unit Tests

Test 1

A. Parts of Speech (*pages 3–34*)   On your paper, write the words that are in italic type in the following sentences. Next to each word or phrase, write the label *Noun, Pronoun, Verb, Adjective, Adverb, Preposition, Conjunction,* or *Interjection.*

1. I know that the task of cleaning this basement seems *herculean,* but perhaps if you get an early start, you can finish by noon.
2. The aircraft mechanics placed blocks of wood in front of and in back of the tires *so that* the airplane would not roll.
3. Although the man was chopping wood a half mile away on the other side of the lake, he *sounded* much closer than that.
4. Why are there *never* any envelopes around here when I need one?
5. *Oh,* you'd better check the air pressure in the tires before we drive to the mountains tomorrow.
6. Hundreds of people stood outside for more than four hours to buy tickets for the opera *in spite of* the bad weather.
7. If you use the binoculars, you can see a *bevy* of larks flying in the distance.
8. The father asked the children to play *downstairs* so that he could concentrate on his reading upstairs.
9. An atmosphere of tension pervaded the packed stadium, but the players *themselves* seemed relaxed and confident.
10. When your family went to Williamsburg, Virginia, last summer for vacation, what hotel or motel did you stay *in*?
11. While looking through the newspaper, Clair saw an advertisement for a sale on fine *leather* shoes at Goodson's Department Store.
12. The parade officials are meeting in order to decide *who* will be the grand marshal.
13. Carla could not find her necklace *anywhere,* but Barbara called and said that it was at her house.
14. The west side of Mt. Everest *has* never *been scaled* successfully during the winter.
15. The advertising executives decided that *either* radio *or* television would be an effective medium on which to advertise the new product.
16. Our history teacher, Mrs. Jorgenson, makes a persuasive argument

that discussions of current *issues* are more enlightening when the participants are well informed.

17. The Hendersons took the elevator to the top of the Empire State Building but could not see *very* far because of the haze.

18. One of the *museum's* favorite attractions is the model of a coal mine.

19. Did you hear the name of the person *whom* the announcer just named as winner of the door prize?

20. Auguste Rodin, a French sculptor of the nineteenth century, created a famous sculpture of a man who sits and *reflects*.

21. The cross-country skis in the shed are *mine,* but you are certainly welcome to use them while you are visiting us.

22. The film about the Air Force during World War II featured many exciting sequences, but I *feel* that the film was somewhat long.

23. We should pack a lunch for the *seven-hour-long* trip on the car ferry.

24. Small ships are not the only ones that use this harbor; *sometimes* we see large ocean-going ships as well.

25. The journalism teacher told the class that a questioning *attitude* is the mark of a good reporter.

B. Sentence Structure (*pages 34–46*)

On your paper, write the words that are in italic type in the following sentences. Then write the correct label for each word or phrase: *Simple subject, Simple predicate, Complete subject, Complete predicate, Direct object, Indirect object, Objective complement, Predicate nominative,* or *Predicate adjective.*

26. *The meeting of the Union Pacific from the east and the Central Pacific from the west in 1869* marked the completion of America's first transcontinental railroad.

27. When Scott called home to wish his mother a happy birthday, the *time* was eleven o'clock in North Carolina but only eight o'clock in Orgeon.

28. At the medical school graduation ceremony, the members of the graduating class *pledged to uphold the Hippocratic oath, named for the ancient Greek healer, Hippocrates.*

29. To John Locke, the seventeenth-century British philosopher, the human mind resembles a blank *slate* at birth.

(Continue on the next page.)

30. Be sure to visit the 110-story *Sears Tower* during your stay in Chicago.

31. When I took a course in French literature, I found the novels by Victor Hugo *fascinating.*

32. Like his Imperial Hotel in Tokyo, which survived the earthquake of 1923, Frank Lloyd Wright's designs were innovative and *functional.*

33. By the end of today's art class, these newspaper and magazine clippings will become a *collage.*

34. The basketball circled the *hoop* several times and finally fell through, scoring the winning *point.*

35. *Leaves* of the bay laurel tree were used to make wreaths for heroes and victors in ancient Greece and Rome.

36. In 1981 President Ronald Reagan named Sandra Day O'Connor a *justice* of the United States Supreme Court.

37. After nearly every rugby game, Phil is bruised and *muddy.*

38. With a population of fifty-five hundred animals, the San Diego Zoo *must have* a representative of nearly every species.

39. Will you buy *Derek* and *Ginger* tickets for the Saturday-night performance of the musical?

40. The opinions expressed on the editorial pages of the newspaper could affect the *outcome* of this year's gubernatorial race.

C. Phrases and Clauses (pages 46–77)   On your paper, write the phrases and clauses that are in italic type in the following sentences. Then write the correct label for each phrase or clause: *Prepositional phrase, Appositive phrase, Participial phrase, Gerund phrase, Infinitive phrase, Independent clause, Adjective clause, Adverb clause,* or *Noun clause.*

41. As we walked *through the covered bridge,* we could hear the old wooden joints creak and groan.

42. Renee worked on her calculus assignment all evening, but she still did not understand the new concept well enough *to complete all the problems.*

43. The father, *beaming with pride,* snapped photograph after photograph as his daughter crossed the stage to receive her diploma.

44. Gilbert Stuart's "Athenaeum" portrait of George Washington, *which is unfinished,* is probably the best known portrait by an American painter.

45. Will you patch my jeans, *the pair with the hole in the knee?*

46. *Almost every state has a two-house legislature,* but Nebraska, with its one-house legislative body, is an exception.

47. *Although Cheryl loves seafood,* she must avoid shellfish; she's allergic to lobster, clams, and crab.

48. The coach told Marybeth *how she could improve her jump shot.*

49. *Walking quickly,* Anthony made it to his dental appointment on time.

50. An important step in making maple syrup is *boiling the sap from the maple tree.*

51. Things just haven't been the same *since Rachel moved away.*

52. *Whoever is elected as head of the city council* will have a time-comsuming job.

53. Ulysses S. Grant was elected President in 1868 *after his success* as a Union general during the Civil War.

54. After Bart broke his arm playing football, he could not write and was forced *to record his class lectures on cassettes.*

55. *After the movie* we all went out for hamburgers.

Test 2

On your paper, rewrite the following paragraph to eliminate all fragments and run-on sentences.

One of the first leaders of the women's rights movement in the United States. That is who Elizabeth Cady Stanton was. She was born in 1815 in Johnstown, New York, she attended the Troy Female Seminary. Women's rights and abolition of slavery, being two issues that interested her. In fact, she married a leader of the abolition movement. Henry B. Stanton. She met Lucretia Mott, another leader of the women's rights movement, together they organized the first convention for women's rights. Which was held in Seneca Falls, New York, in 1848, for that convention Stanton wrote the Declaration of Sentiments, which stated that "all men and women are created equal." The National Woman Suffrage Association. It was an organization founded in 1869 by Stanton and Susan B. Anthony. To push for a constitutional amendment giving women the vote. Women did not accomplish this goal during Stanton's lifetime they did attain it in 1920 with the passage of the Nineteenth Amendment. Elizabeth Cady Stanton. She will long be remembered for her role in the women's rights movement.

Usage

Unit Preview

By following certain accepted standards of English usage, you will enhance your ability to communicate clearly, thereby increasing the impact of whatever you want to say or write.

For Analysis The following paragraph has been adapted from Chapter 1 of Charles Dickens's *A Tale of Two Cities*. As you read this intentionally altered version, try to find the errors in usage.

> They were the better of times, they were the more worser of times, it were the age of wisdom, it were the responsibility age, it was the foolishness age, it is the belief epoch, it is the incredulity epoch, it is the Light season, it were the season for Darkness, it were the spring of hope, it were the despair of winter, we did have everything before us, us didn't have nothing before us, we was all going direct to Heaven, we was all going direct the other way—in short, the period were so far just like the present period, that some of your noisiest authorities insisted on its be received, for good or evil, in the superlative only degree of comparison.

Now read the paragraph the way Dickens wrote it, and compare the two versions.

> It was the best of times, it was the worst of times, it was the age of wisdom, it was the age of foolishness, it was the epoch of belief, it was the epoch of incredulity, it was the season of Light, it was the season of Darkness, it was the spring of hope, it was the winter of despair, we had everything before us, we had nothing before us, we were all going direct to Heaven, we were all going direct the other way—in short,

the period was so far like the present period, that some of its noisiest authorities insisted on its being received, for good or for evil, in the superlative degree of comparison only.

Answer the following questions based on your comparison of the two paragraphs.

1. What standards of usage have been ignored in the first paragraph?
2. How does the switch from *they* to *it* affect the first version?
3. What is the difference in meaning between *despair of winter* and *winter of despair*?
4. What is wrong with the following phrases: *the more worser of times; it were*; and *didn't have nothing*?
5. How does the change in location of *only* affect the meaning of the last phrase in the two paragraphs?
6. Which paragraph is easier to understand?

In answering these questions, you have dealt with several usage problems that can affect the clarity and meaning of your speaking and writing. You have seen how adherence to accepted English usage makes Dickens's writing understandable, interesting, and even powerful. In this unit, you will study usage problems like those in the altered paragraph and learn ways to avoid them in your own communications.

2.1 The Scope of Usage

The English language is dynamic. It embraces usage ranging from that found in particular occupations or professions (jargon) to that used in particular locales or by particular ethnic groups (dialect); from that used in everyday conversation (colloquial) to that used only on important occasions (ceremonial); from that used only in the past (archaic or obsolete) to that used briefly by cliques or by certain age groups (slang). Moreover, the English language is constantly changing. Words and idioms (unit expressions, such as *to make believe*) that are now slang may be considered part of formal usage in the future. Other language that we use today may in time be obsolete.

To communicate effectively, we must learn to recognize levels of English usage and to use them appropriately. The way we speak and write says much about us. Using language appropriately is somewhat like dressing appropriately: rightly or wrongly, we are judged by our use of language just as we are by the style of our clothing.

Levels of Usage

Formal English.   Formal English is the standard English that is used for serious occasions or writing. It is composed of the words, expressions, grammar, and standards of usage found in formal essays, research papers, scholarly writing, literary criticism, and speeches made on significant or solemn occasions. The sentences used in formal English are often long and precisely structured, sometimes employing parallelism and repetition for rhetorical effect. Formal English uses extensive vocabulary, few contractions, and almost no slang.

Informal English.   Informal English is the standard English used in almost all conversation and broadcasting and in many newspapers, magazines, books, letters, and nonceremonial speeches. It is characterized by the sentence variety and length typical of conversation, by vocabulary understood and used in conversation, and by more relaxed standards of usage than those of formal English. Informal English includes contractions, colloquialisms, and slang.

Nonstandard English.   Nonstandard English is composed of words, expressions, and grammatical constructions that are not generally accepted as correct English, although they may sometimes be accepted in certain geographic areas or by certain groups of people. Nonstandard English should not normally be used to communicate with a general audience.

Jargon and Occupational Language

Jargon often refers to the special words used by people in a particular field of work or activity. Computer programmers use jargon; so do baseball players. Such **occupational language** can be an efficient, precise means of communication for specialists. When specialists write or speak to a wider audience, however, they must adjust their language, being careful not to bewilder the reader or listener. At its worst, jargon can be inflated and pretentious: "The position afforded much interface, impacting on management objectives."

Avoiding Redundancy and Verbosity

Redundancy is the practice of saying or writing the same thing in several different ways to no purpose; it usually occurs because of carelessness or ignorance. **Verbosity,** or wordiness, is the practice of saying something in the most complicated way possible.

To eliminate redundancy and verbosity, use concrete words. Never avoid a short, simple word just because it is common; use specific verbs, such as *grumbling* instead of *talking*; and repeat an idea in a phrase or a sentence only when the idea is made clearer by the repetition. For more help in avoiding redundancy and verbosity, see Section 6.5 in Unit 6, "Revising."

Exercise   The Scope of Usage   On your paper, rewrite each of the following sentences in clear, informal English, removing jargon, redundancy, and verbosity.

1. It has been a good month saleswise, even though the net profit shows only a moderate increase over last month, which, when compared with our expectations for the new year as a whole, is disappointing.
2. It is understood that the aforementioned landowner shall lease all rights to the property, except for the rights of access outlined in the preceding paragraph, to the party of the second part, herewith referred to as Mr. Peters, for the sum of two hundred dollars per month.
3. We hope to involve ourselves in the implementation, as well as the execution, of the proposal to have installed for the well-being of those members of the community whose needs will most clearly be met by such a move, the new street light on the corner of Maple and Vine streets.
4. The gray-green color of the hospital walls, so commonplace yet so inexplicable, only served to exacerbate my already almost overwhelming sensation of nausea.

5. I am resolved, without further discussion, debate, or argument, to consider most thoroughly, if not to meditate upon, the idea, or notion, of requiring each and every member of this class, not excepting anyone, to remain following the conclusion of school if you do not immediately and forthwith cease your unnecessary, rude, impolite, and irrelevant talk.

Assignment   Eliminating Jargon   Jargon and inflated language appear frequently in printed matter, in broadcasts, and in business communications. Find and write down at least five actual examples of such usage from various sources. Then rewrite each example, using more precise, understandable language.

2.2   Correct Use of Verbs

Your ability to communicate increases dramatically with your ability to use verbs correctly. By changing the form of a verb, you can express its tense, the number and the person of its subject, its voice, and its mood.

2.2a   Principal Parts of Verbs

The four **principal parts** of a verb, the basic forms of a verb, are the infinitive, the present participle, the past, and the past participle. By using these forms alone or with auxiliary verbs, you can express the various tenses of a verb.

The infinitive and the present participle are formed in the same way for all verbs. The **infinitive** is the basic verb form that appears in the dictionary. The word *to* usually precedes the infinitive in a sentence; in some sentences, however, the word *to* is understood but not stated.

INFINITIVE   Five miles is a long way *to* **walk** in the cold. Raising money for charity, however, will make us all **walk** willingly.

The **present participle** is always a combination of the infinitive and -*ing*; it is used in a sentence with a form of the verb *be* as an auxiliary verb.

PRESENT
PARTICIPLE   Jenny *is* **walking** to prove to herself that she can.

Regular Verbs

Verbs are considered regular or irregular depending on how their past and past participle forms are constructed. You form the **past** and the **past participle** of any regular verb by adding -*d* or -*ed* to the infinitive. In a sentence, the past participle takes a form of the verb *have* as an auxiliary verb.

PAST   Margaret **walked** ten miles every week to get ready for the big day.

PAST
PARTICIPLE   We *have* **walked** several miles a week to get ready.

Here are the principal parts of two regular verbs. The auxiliary verbs in parentheses remind you that the correct form of the verb *be* is used with the present participle and the correct form of the verb *have* is used with the past participle.

INFINITIVE	PRESENT PARTICIPLE	PAST	PAST PARTICIPLE
offer	(is) offering	offered	(has) offered
contribute	(is) contributing	contributed	(has) contributed

Irregular Verbs

Irregular verbs are considered irregular because they do not follow the standard rules for forming their past and past participle. Like regular verbs, however, they do use a form of the auxiliary verb *be* with the present participle and a form of the auxiliary verb *have* with the past participle. The sentences on the following page show the correct use of the principal parts of the irregular verb *drink*.

INFINITIVE   You can lead a horse to water, but you can't make it **drink.**

PRESENT
PARTICIPLE   The horse *is* **drinking** the water now.

PAST   The horse **drank** the water when we moved away from its trough.

PAST
PARTICIPLE   The horse *has* **drunk** all of the water.

Although no standard rules govern the formation of the past and the past participle of irregular verbs, you should have little trouble mastering their usage. You have probably already developed a good sense of what is correct by what sounds correct. Memorize the principal parts of verbs that you use frequently, and consult your dictionary for those that you do not use as often. The following list contains many common irregular verbs and should serve as a useful reference.

INFINITIVE	PRESENT PARTICIPLE	PAST	PAST PARTICIPLE
be	(is) being	was	(has) been
become	(is) becoming	became	(has) become
begin	(is) beginning	began	(has) begun
bite	(is) biting	bit	(has) bitten
blow	(is) blowing	blew	(has) blown
burst	(is) bursting	burst	(has) burst
catch	(is) catching	caught	(has) caught
choose	(is) choosing	chose	(has) chosen
come	(is) coming	came	(has) come
dive	(is) diving	dived, dove	(has) dived
do	(is) doing	did	(has) done
draw	(is) drawing	drew	(has) drawn
drive	(is) driving	drove	(has) driven
eat	(is) eating	ate	(has) eaten
fall	(is) falling	fell	(has) fallen
find	(is) finding	found	(has) found
fling	(is) flinging	flung	(has) flung
fly	(is) flying	flew	(has) flown
get	(is) getting	got	(has) gotten
give	(is) giving	gave	(has) given

go	(is) going	went	(has) gone
grow	(is) growing	grew	(has) grown
have	(is) having	had	(has) had
know	(is) knowing	knew	(has) known
lay	(is) laying	laid	(has) laid
lead	(is) leading	led	(has) led
leave	(is) leaving	left	(has) left
lie	(is) lying	lay	(has) lain
lose	(is) losing	lost	(has) lost
ride	(is) riding	rode	(has) ridden
ring	(is) ringing	rang	(has) rung
rise	(is) rising	rose	(has) risen
say	(is) saying	said	(has) said
set	(is) setting	set	(has) set
sit	(is) sitting	sat	(has) sat
speak	(is) speaking	spoke	(has) spoken
swear	(is) swearing	swore	(has) sworn
swim	(is) swimming	swam	(has) swum
tear	(is) tearing	tore	(has) torn
tell	(is) telling	told	(has) told
throw	(is) throwing	threw	(has) thrown
wear	(is) wearing	wore	(has) worn
write	(is) writing	wrote	(has) written

Exercise 1   Principal Parts of Verbs   On your paper, write the form of the verb in parentheses that correctly completes each sentence. Do not use auxiliary verbs other than those already given in the sentences.

SAMPLE   Are you __?__ to join us for the walkathon? (*go*)

ANSWER   going

1. Have you __?__ behind in your studies? (*be*)
2. The guide __?__ the frightened couple to safety. (*lead*)
3. The doorbell had __?__ several times before anyone inside __?__ it. (*ring, know*)
4. They are __?__ to the newspaper to express their opinions. (*write*)
5. The team __?__ all it could, but it __?__ the game anyway. (*do, lose*)
6. Alicia has __?__ repeatedly that she dislikes crowds. (*say*)
7. Joshua __?__ a new life and __?__ the old one behind. (*choose, leave*)

8. The motorist __?__ fifty miles before he __?__ a restaurant. (*drive, find*)
9. Claudette had __?__ her promise, but she __?__ to regret her decision. (*give, come*)
10. I __?__ an unusual experience when I __?__ to Europe. (*have, fly*)

2.2b   Verb Tense

You use the various forms of a verb to show whether an action or a condition takes place in the present, took place in the past, or will take place in the future. The forms of a verb that express time are called **tenses.** To form tenses, you combine the principal parts with auxiliary verbs. The six English tenses are present, past, future, present perfect, past perfect, and future perfect.

To **conjugate** a verb is to list all of the forms for its six tenses. The **conjugation of a verb** also shows how the verb forms change for the first person, the second person, and the third person and for the singular and the plural.

Conjugation of the Regular Verb *Walk*

Singular	Plural

Present Tense

I walk	we walk
you walk	you walk
he/she/it walks	they walk

Past Tense

I walked	we walked
you walked	you walked
he/she/it walked	they walked

Future Tense

I will (shall) walk	we will (shall) walk
you will walk	you will walk
he/she/it will walk	they will walk

Present Perfect Tense

I have walked	we have walked
you have walked	you have walked
he/she/it has walked	they have walked

Past Perfect Tense

I had walked
you had walked
he/she/it had walked

we had walked
you had walked
they had walked

Future Perfect Tense

I will (shall) have walked
you will have walked
he/she/it will have walked

we will (shall) have walked
you will have walked
they will have walked

The Six Tenses of Verbs

Present Tense.   To form the present tense of a verb, use its infinitive. To form the third-person singular, you usually add -*s* or -*es* to the infinitive.

Rule   Use the present tense to show an action that takes place now, to show an action that is repeated regularly, or to show a condition that is true at any time.

We **walk** four miles to school.

We **walk** every day to increase our endurance.

We found that walking **is** good exercise. [**Think**: Walking is *always* good exercise.]

Rule   Use the present tense in statements about literary works or other works of art.

A Tale of Two Cities **is** one of Charles Dickens's most intriguing novels. Its hero **confronts** a difficult choice.

Rule   Use the present tense occasionally to describe past events with special immediacy. When the present tense is used for this effect, it is called the **historical present.**

In World War I, the English **see** London damaged severely.

In informal communication, you can use the present tense to describe future action if you include a word or a phrase that clearly indicates that the action will occur in the future.

We **walk** in the walkathon *next Monday*.

Past Tense.   To form the past tense of a regular verb, add *-d* or *-ed* to the infinitive. To avoid confusion, memorize the principal parts of irregular verbs.

Rule   Use the past tense to express action that occurred in the past and was completed entirely in the past.

> We **walked** home from the theater last night.

Future Tense.   To form the future tense, combine *will* or *shall* with the infinitive form of the main verb.

Rule   Use the future tense to describe action that will occur in the future.

> We **will walk** in the walkathon next Monday.

Present Perfect Tense.   To form the present perfect tense, use *has* or *have* with the past participle of the main verb.

Rule   Use the present perfect tense to describe action that was completed either in the recent past or at an indefinite time in the past.

> We **have** just **walked** farther than we have ever walked before.

Past Perfect Tense.   To form the past perfect tense, use *had* with the past participle of the main verb.

Rule   Use the past perfect tense to describe an action that was completed by a certain time in the past or before another action was completed.

> past perf.   past
> We **had walked** the required distance before we **realized** that we could have stopped to rest.

Future Perfect Tense.   To form the future perfect tense, use *will have* or *shall have* with the past participle of the main verb.

Rule   Use the future perfect tense to describe a future action that will be completed before another future action will be completed.

> We **will have walked** ten miles before the rest of our group begins.

Tenses of Infinitives and Participles

Infinitives (*page 54*) and participles (*page 50*) have two tenses: the present and the perfect.

	INFINITIVE	PARTICIPLE
PRESENT	to walk	walking
PERFECT	to have walked	having walked

Rule Use infinitives and participles in the present tense to express action that occurs at the same time as that of the main verb.

PRESENT

$\overset{\text{inf.}}{\text{I wanted to walk}}$ by myself.

$\overset{\text{part.}}{\textbf{Walking}}$ alone, I saw a flock of geese.

Rule Use infinitives and participles in the perfect tense to express action that takes place before the action of the main verb.

PERFECT

$\overset{\text{inf.}}{\textbf{To have walked}}$ in the walkathon made me feel good.

$\overset{\text{part.}}{\textbf{Having walked}}$ by myself most of the way, I gladly joined my friends for the final mile.

Exercise 2   Verb Tense   On your paper, write the following sentences, correcting all errors in verb tense. Underline the corrected verb forms. If a sentence has no errors, write *Correct*.

SAMPLE   The apples arrive four hours after I made all the preparations.

ANSWER   The apples <u>arrived</u> four hours after I <u>had made</u> all the preparations.

1. Mrs. MacGrady based her comment on the adage that a penny saved was a penny earned.
2. By the time the apples come in, I will boil the cherries for three hours.
3. Being here all morning, they finally saw four truckloads of apples arrive just after noon.

4. I will make four pots of applesauce by the time the store closes.
5. Having eaten the apples while I work is part of the fun of making applesauce.
6. The family hired Jed Lawrence to help because he had worked for ten years in an orchard.
7. After we counted all the jars, we saw that we surpassed last year's total by 20 percent.
8. To have avoided all the work, Helen and Sally stayed back in the house.
9. Next year my mother and father will harvest apples for thirty-nine years.
10. Having thought Jed was out of town, Mary was surprised to see him at the store.

The Progressive and Emphatic Forms

The Progressive Form.   To form the progressive, use the appropriate tense of the verb *be* with the present participle of the main verb.

Rule   Use the progressive form of a verb to describe continuing action.

PRESENT PROGRESSIVE
> We **are walking** to raise money for charity.

PAST PROGRESSIVE
> We **were walking** near the coast.

FUTURE PROGRESSIVE
> We **will be walking** for the next two hours.

PRESENT PERFECT PROGRESSIVE
> We **have been walking** for two hours.

PAST PERFECT PROGRESSIVE
> We **had been walking** for two hours when we met the rest of our group.

FUTURE PERFECT PROGRESSIVE
> We **will have been walking** for two hours by the time the main group starts.

When communicating informally, you can use the present progressive tense to express future action. Be sure to include a word or a phrase that indicates the future.

We **are walking** in the walkathon *next Monday*.

The Emphatic Form. To use the emphatic form, use the present or the past tense of the verb *do* with the infinitive form of the main verb.

Rule Use the emphatic form to add emphasis or force to the present and past tenses of a verb.

PRESENT EMPHATIC We **do walk** every day when the weather is good.

PAST EMPHATIC We **did walk** before the snow began to accumulate.

Modals. Modals are the auxiliary verbs *can, could, do, did, may, might, must, shall, will,* and *would*. These auxiliary verbs are used with main verbs to add emphasis to a sentence or to provide shades of meaning.

Rule Use *can* (present tense) and *could* (past tense) to express ability to perform the action of the main verb.

We **can** call home if we need to.
We **could** have *taken* the car yesterday, but not today.

Rule Use *do* (present tense) and *did* (past tense) to make negative statements and to ask questions.

We **do** not *walk* more than four miles without resting.
Did you *walk* farther today than you did yesterday?

Rule Use *may* to mean "have permission to" or to express a possibility.

His uncle said we **may** *go* now.
We **may** *be* late if we do not hurry.

Rule Use *might,* the past tense of *may,* to express a possibility that is somewhat less likely than one expressed by *may.*

There is always a chance that the exam **might** *be cancelled.*

Rule Use *must* to convey the idea that the action of the main verb is required or to suggest a possible explanation.

We **must** *return* immediately.
We **must** *be* thoughtless to ask for such a favor.

Rule Use *should,* the past tense of *shall,* to suggest that something ought to happen or that, although something ought to happen, it may not.

We **should** *call* home right now. [**Think:** We ought to call.]
We **should** *be* home right now. [**Think:** We should be, but we aren't.]

Rule Use *would,* the past tense of *will,* to express actions that were repeated in the past or to show that you disapproved of an action in the past.

In the winter we **would** *drive* to school every day. [repeated action]
We were always late. Well, we **would** *leave* everything until the last minute! [disapproval]

Exercise 3 Progressive and Emphatic Forms On your paper, write a sentence with each of the following verbs, using the form of the verb indicated in parentheses.

SAMPLE   volunteer (present perfect progressive)
ANSWER   I have been volunteering my time to the hospital for three years.

1. make (present emphatic)
2. offer (future progressive)
3. buy (past perfect progressive)
4. may (auxiliary showing future possibility)
5. may (auxiliary showing future permission)

6. relax (present progressive)
7. manufacture (past emphatic as a question)
8. can (auxiliary in the past tense expressing possibility)
9. snow (past progressive)
10. publish (future perfect progressive)

Sequence of Tenses

In most sentences, you use verbs that are in the same tense because the time periods described are the same. In some situations, however, you need to use verbs in different tenses to show a difference in time. You can show this difference in time effectively by changing not only the forms of the verbs but also the relationship of one verb to another.

Consistency of Tenses.   When two or more actions take place at the same time, you should use verbs that are in the same tense, particularly when you write compound sentences and sentences with compound predicates. Also, remember to use the same verb tense throughout a paragraph unless the meaning of the paragraph requires that you shift tense.

Rule Use verbs in the same tense to describe actions occurring at the same time.

	past	pres.
INCORRECT	Hugh **held** the clutch in, while the rest of us **push** the car.	

	past	past
CORRECT	Hugh **held** the clutch in, while the rest of us **pushed** the car.	

Shifts in Tense.   If you need to show a shift from one time period to another, be sure to indicate accurately the relationships between the tenses. By changing forms and tenses, you can express precisely the time sequence that is required.

Rule If two actions occurred at different times in the past, use the past perfect tense for the earlier action and the past tense for the later one. To emphasize the closeness in time of two events, however, use the past tense for both.

earlier   later
past perf.   past

I **had waited** in line for hours before I **bought** my ticket. [actions that occurred at different times in the past]

earlier   later
past   past

We **traveled** for many miles and **reached** the coast by dark. [past actions that were close in time]

Rule If two actions occur in the present but one began in the past, use the present perfect tense for the earlier action and the present tense for the later one.

earlier   later
pres. perf.   pres.

Because she **has been making** calls all afternoon, Meg **feels** a sense of accomplishment.

Rule If two actions will occur in the future, use the future perfect tense for the action that will take place earlier and the future tense for the action that will occur later.

earlier
future perf.

Because we **will have been working** on this project for several weeks

later
future

before its deadline, we **will want** to finish it correctly.

Exercise 4 Correct Use of Tense On your paper, write a sentence for each set of actions indicated. Underline the verbs. If you wish, you may write your sentences about a single situation, such as a dramatic performance, an athletic contest, or a historical event.

SAMPLE Three actions occurring in the present

ANSWER A drama critic <u>attends</u> a performance, <u>evaluates</u> the production, and <u>writes</u> a review.

1. Two actions occurring at the same time in the past
2. Two actions occurring in the future, one before the other

3. Two actions occurring at the same time in the present
4. Two actions occurring at the same time in the future
5. Two actions occurring in the past, one before the other
6. Two actions occurring in the present, one beginning in the past
7. An action occurring in the past and an action occurring in the present
8. An action occurring in the present and an action occurring in the future

2.2c   Active Voice and Passive Voice

A verb is in the **active voice** when the subject performs the action of the verb. The active voice is generally a more direct and effective way of expressing action.

The *audience* **applauded** the orchestra's encore.

A verb is in the **passive voice** when the subject receives the action of the verb. Use the passive voice only when you want to emphasize the receiver of the action, or when the person or thing performing the action is unknown, or occasionally when there is no other way to write the sentence. Overuse of the passive voice quickly becomes tedious and weakens your writing.

Rule   To form the passive voice, use a form of the verb *be* and the past participle of the main verb.

The orchestra's *encore* **was applauded** by the audience.

Only transitive verbs (*page 14*) can be used in the passive voice. Intransitive verbs (*page 14*) cannot be in the passive voice because they do not take objects. When a verb in the active voice is changed to the passive voice, its direct object becomes the subject of the sentence, and the subject becomes the object of a preposition.

	subj. verb D.O.
ACTIVE	The symphony *orchestra* **played** a Beethoven sonata.

	subj. verb
PASSIVE	A Beethoven *sonata* **was played** by the symphony
	obj. of prep.
	orchestra.

When you shift a transitive verb that has both a direct object and an indirect object to the passive voice, either object can become the subject. The other object, however, remains as the complement of the verb. An object that remains as a complement in a passive construction is called a **retained object.**

ACTIVE
subj. verb I.O.   D.O.
His friends **gave** Bill a surprise party.

PASSIVE
subj.   verb   D.O.
Bill **was given** a surprise party by his friends.

PASSIVE
retained
subj.   verb   object
A surprise party **was given** Bill by his friends.

Rule   Avoid shifting from the active voice to the passive voice when describing a series of events.

INCORRECT
active   passive
The stable manager **fed** the horses, **was reminded**
active
to change the straw in their stalls, and **gave** them fresh water.

CORRECT
active   active
The stable manager **fed** the horses, **remembered** to
active
change the straw in their stalls, and **gave** them fresh water.

Exercise 5   Active and Passive Voice   On your paper, write each verb in the following sentences and label it *Active* or *Passive*. If an active verb cannot be changed to the passive voice, write *Intransitive.*

SAMPLE   This play seems to be a comedy.
ANSWER   seems—Active—Intransitive

1. Jane Austen wrote many novels about courtship and marriage, but she remained single herself.
2. Jonathan Swift's *Gulliver's Travels* satirizes humanity in a memorable way.
3. In 1926 Agatha Christie disappeared, and a cross-country search for her was conducted.

4. John Milton lost his sight but still produced poetry of great beauty.
5. Some of Maggie Tulliver's experiences in *The Mill on the Floss* were borrowed from the life of the author, George Eliot.
6. Mary Shelley wrote the classic *Frankenstein* when she was in her early twenties.
7. Charles Dickens's books were first published in serial form.
8. The popular musical *My Fair Lady* is based on George Bernard Shaw's play *Pygmalion*.

2.2d   Mood

In addition to tense and voice, verbs also express mood. Although you use the indicative mood more frequently, the effective use of the imperative mood and the subjunctive mood will enhance your writing.

The Indicative and the Imperative Moods

Rule   Use the indicative mood to make a statement of fact or to ask a question.

> Thunder often **frightens** small children.
> **Did** you **remember** the license plate number?

Rule   Use the imperative mood to make a request or to give a command.

In the imperative mood, the subject of the sentence is often understood rather than stated. Use of the imperative mood adds directness and emphasis to your writing.

> **Consider** taking the train the next time you travel.
> **Take** all your belongings when you leave.

The Subjunctive Mood

Of the three moods, the subjunctive mood is the most infrequently used in conversation and in informal writing. It is primarily used in formal communications, especially in diplomatic statements and in parliamentary procedure. You also use the subjunctive mood, however, to make doubtful, wishful, or conditional statements; to express something that is contrary to fact; or to ask, insist, order, request, or propose in a respectful manner.

You can use verbs in the subjunctive mood in the present tense and in the past tense.

PRESENT SUBJUNCTIVE   If the truth **be** known, I am to be congratulated.

PAST SUBJUNCTIVE   If the truth **were** known, I should have been congratulated.

The most commonly used verb in the subjunctive mood is the verb *be,* used as a linking verb or as an auxiliary verb. Study the differences between the indicative mood and the subjunctive mood in this partial conjugation of the verb *be.*

	INDICATIVE		SUBJUNCTIVE	
PRESENT	I am	we are	(if) I be	(if) we be
	you are	you are	(if) you be	(if) you be
	he is	they are	(if) he be	(if) they be
PAST	I was	we were	(if) I were	(if) we were
	you were	you were	(if) you were	(if) you were
	he was	they were	(if) he were	(if) they were

Rule   Use *be* for the present subjunctive of the verb *be* regardless of its subject.

Mrs. Penwell asks that her children **be** friendly to their neighbors.

Rule   Use *were* for the past subjunctive of the verb *be* regardless of its subject.

If Rudy **were** a better actor, we wouldn't have known that he forgot a line.

Rule   To form the present subjunctive of verbs other than *be,* use the infinitive form of the verb regardless of its subject.

Professor Art insists that the class **listen** attentively.

Rule To form the past subjunctive of verbs other than *be,* use *had* as an auxiliary verb with the past participle of the main verb.

If I **had seen** her, I would have invited her too.

Had I **known,** I would have told you sooner.

Rule To express something that is not true or that you doubt will ever be true, use a verb in the subjunctive mood in a clause that begins with *if, as if, as though,* or *that.*

Notice that something that is contrary to fact is often expressed as a wish or a condition.

Because this has been such a long day, I wish *that* I **were** home. [I am not at home.]

If I **were** you, I would ask Diane before I borrowed her book. [I cannot be you; this statement is contrary to fact.]

Rule Use the subjunctive mood in clauses that begin with *that* and that follow verbs that (1) make requests, such as *ask, prefer,* and *request*; that (2) make demands, such as *demand, determine, insist, order,* and *require*; and that (3) make proposals, such as *move, propose, recommend,* and *suggest.*

These clauses often appear in formal usage, particularly in standard expressions used in parliamentary procedures.

Morris recommended that the session **be postponed.**

Exercise 6 Mood On your paper, write each verb or verb phrase in italics. Then label each one *Indicative, Imperative,* or *Subjunctive.*

SAMPLE If I *were* you, I *would follow* her example.

ANSWER were—Subjunctive; would follow—Indicative

1. *Hitch* your wagon to a star.
2. Edgar Allan Poe and Nathaniel Hawthorne *made* major contributions to the development of the American short story.
3. Ms. Zimmerman *insisted* that the student *submit* an outline before proceeding with his term paper on Henry James.

4. *Did* you *know* which film is an adaptation of a novel by Theodore Dreiser?

5. If I *were* a faster reader, I *would finish* this book before the end of the term.

6. Before Bill *runs* in the marathon, it *is* necessary that he *be* mentally alert and physically fit.

7. *Give* examples of Dickens's method of social protest in two of his novels.

8. *Would* you please *lend* me your copy of Elizabeth Barrett Browning's poems?

9. Mr. Guiness *suggested* that the class *attend* a local production of a Shakespearean play.

10. I *was delighted* when Denise *asked* that I *read* her original short story.

Assignment 1   Active and Passive Voice   On your paper, write a paragraph in which you narrate a brief incident. You may invent a situation, describe a personal experience, or tell about a historical event. Use verbs in the passive voice whenever possible. Then rewrite your paragraph, changing verbs to the active voice. Finally, write a brief statement explaining which paragraph is more effective.

Assignment 2   Mood   On your paper, write a paragraph explaining to a friend how to do or make something. Use verbs in the indicative mood throughout your paragraph. Then rewrite your paragraph as a set of directions, changing verbs to the imperative mood whenever possible. Finally, write a brief statement explaining which paragraph is more effective and why.

2.3   Subject-Verb Agreement

2.3a   Singular and Plural Subjects and Verbs

Rule   A subject and its verb must agree in number.

You can change the forms of nouns, pronouns, and verbs to express number. If the subject is singular, the form of the verb should be singular. If the subject is plural, the form of the verb should be plural.

SINGULAR	*Peter* **lives** in Ottawa, near my sister's house.
PLURAL	Those three *people* **live** near the capital.

Verb Phrases. For a verb phrase to agree with its subject, the auxiliary verb must agree in number with the subject.

	verb phrase
SINGULAR	*Marianne* **has taken** dancing lessons.
	verb phrase
PLURAL	*Marianne and I* **have taken** dancing lessons.

Intervening Words and Phrases. Sometimes words and phrases come between a subject and its verb. Such intervening words or phrases do not change the number of the subject, and, as always, the verb must agree in number with the subject. Be sure to make the verb agree in number with the subject of the sentence, not with some word in the intervening phrase.

SINGULAR	The *director,* a newcomer to the world of movies, **was** not conscious of the producer's concerns. [**Think:** director **was.**]
PLURAL	The *spectators* waiting outside the theater **were becoming** restless. [**Think:** spectators **were.**]

Exercise 1 Subject-Verb Agreement   On your paper, write the verb form in each sentence that agrees in number with the subject of the sentence. Label each verb or verb phrase *Singular* or *Plural*.

SAMPLE	The woman who lives next door to the Smiths (is moving, are moving) next week.
ANSWER	is moving—Singular

1. Arthur's friends (is swimming, are swimming) for the school team.
2. Ted's refusal to do the dishes (was, were) responsible for his having to stay home tonight.
3. Halloween, one of my favorite holidays, (is, are) on Sunday this year.
4. The tools in the tool chest (is rusting, are rusting) away.

5. The curators of the museum (distributes, distribute) information to all interested community groups.
6. Steven, one of the animal trainers, also (wants, want) to be a veterinarian.
7. Janice, one of the interns, (has written, have written) to her representative in Washington, D.C.
8. The campaign officials who are working for the governor (travels, travel) all over the state.
9. Most creatures in the forest (is, are) wary of loud noises.
10. The winners of the contest (has been notified, have been notified).

2.3b   Determining the Number of the Subject

In some sentences, you may find it troublesome to determine the number of the subject. To avoid confusion, pay special attention to the following types of subjects.

Compound Subjects

A **compound subject** (*page 36*) is composed of two or more subjects that are connected by *and, or, nor, either . . . or,* or *neither . . . nor.* A compound subject may take a singular or a plural verb, depending on (1) which conjunction is used and (2) whether the words in the compound subject are singular or plural.

Rule   Use a plural verb with most compound subjects connected by *and.*

PLURAL   The *Prime Minister and the President* **were** to attend the meeting.

Rule   Use a singular verb with a compound subject that refers to one person or one thing or to something that is generally considered as a unit—that is, plural in form but singular in meaning.

SINGULAR   This year's most popular *author and lecturer* **is addressing** our class tomorrow. [The author and lecturer are the same person.]

Rule Use a singular verb with a compound subject that is composed of singular nouns or pronouns connected by *or* or *nor.*

SINGULAR   Either my *aunt or* my *uncle* **likes** to read poetry.

Rule Use a plural verb with a compound subject that is composed of plural nouns or pronouns connected by *or* or *nor.*

PLURAL   Neither the farmer's *goats nor* his *sheep* **have been sold.**

Rule When a compound subject is composed of a singular subject and a plural subject connected by *or* or *nor,* use a verb that agrees in number with the subject that is closer to the verb in the sentence.

SINGULAR
pl.   ┌─ sing.─┐
Neither the *musicians* nor the *conductor* **is** on stage.

PLURAL
sing.   ┌─pl.─┐
Neither the team *manager* nor the *players* **agree** on the terms of the contract.

In following this rule, you may discover that some sentences sound awkward. In that case, rephrase the sentence.

The *musicians* **are** not on stage, and neither **is** the *conductor.*

Rule When the subject is both affirmative and negative, use a verb form that agrees in number with the affirmative part of the subject.

pl.   sing.   pl.
My *brothers, not I,* **are planning** to travel this summer.

Indefinite Pronouns as Subjects

Indefinite pronouns (*page 10*) are pronouns that refer to people or things in general. Some indefinite pronouns are always singular and, therefore, always take singular verbs. The following are examples of singular indefinite pronouns:

anybody	everybody	nobody	other
anyone	everyone	no one	somebody
anything	everything	nothing	someone
each	much	one	something
either	neither		

SINGULAR   Almost *everybody* **watches** television sometime.

Some indefinite pronouns are always plural and, therefore, always take plural verbs. The most common are *both, few, many,* and *several.*

PLURAL   *Many* **go** jogging in the park on Saturday morning.

The indefinite pronouns *all, any, enough, more, most, none, plenty,* and *some* may be singular or plural, depending upon their antecedents (*page 7*).

SINGULAR   *All* of the music presented that day **was** enjoyable.
[The indefinite pronoun refers to music; it is singular and takes the singular verb *was.*]

PLURAL   All of the band's members **have** exceptional talent.
[*All* refers to members; it is plural and takes the plural verb *have.*]

Sometimes an indefinite pronoun refers to a word that is understood rather than stated.

Even though *many* had gone, *most* **were** still at the party when we arrived. [The listener or reader would know that the pronouns refer to guests.]

Collective Nouns as Subjects

A **collective noun** (*page 4*) is a word that names a group of people or a collection of objects that is singular in form and may be either singular or plural in meaning. Examples include *committee, crowd, fleet, jury,* and *team.*

Rule If a collective noun refers to a group as a whole, use a singular verb.

SINGULAR   The *crowd* **wants** action. [The crowd is thought of as a whole.]

Rule If a collective noun refers to individual members or parts of a group, use a plural verb.

PLURAL   The *cast* **know** themselves well. [The members of the cast are acting as individuals.]

Nouns with Plural Form

Nouns such as *economics, mathematics, measles,* and *news* are plural in form but singular in meaning. Although they end in *s,* they refer to a single thing or to a unit and, therefore, take a singular verb. (Notice that removing the *s* does not make a singular noun.)

SINGULAR   *Aeronautics* **is** a subject that I have never studied.

Other nouns, such as *clothes, congratulations, pliers,* and *scissors,* end in *s* but take a plural verb, even though they refer to one thing.

PLURAL   Your garden *shears* **are** on the workbench.

Some nouns, such as *athletics, dramatics,* and *politics,* end in *s* but may be singular or plural, depending on their meaning in the sentence. Use your dictionary to find out whether a noun that ends in *s* takes a singular or a plural verb.

SINGULAR   In her lecture she told us that *dramatics* **is** her avocation.

PLURAL   His *dramatics* **are** often ignored by his friends.

Titles and Names as Subjects

Titles of individual books, stories, plays, movies, television programs, musical compositions, and magazines take the singular form of the verb, even though the titles may contain plural words.

The name of a country or of an organization also takes a singular verb when it refers to an entire country or group. (See Unit 3, "Mechanics," for rules regarding capitalization and underlining, or italics, for titles.)

SINGULAR   Hemingway's *A Farewell to Arms* **was made** into a movie.

SINGULAR   The *United Nations* often **sends** peacekeeping forces into troubled areas.

Words of Amount and Time

Rule   Use singular verbs with words and phrases that refer to single units: fractions, measurements, amounts of money, weights, volumes, or intervals of time when the interval refers to a specific unit.

SINGULAR   *One hundred yards* **is** the length of a football field.

Rule   Use a plural verb when the amount or the time is considered to be a number of separate units.

PLURAL   *Five quarters* **are** all that you need to do the laundry.

When you use *the number* or *the variety* as a subject, you usually use a singular verb. When you use *a number* or *a variety* as a subject, you usually use a plural verb.

SINGULAR   *The variety* of plants at the garden shop **is** amazing.

PLURAL   *A variety* of plants **are** for sale at the garden shop.

Exercise 2   Subject-Verb Agreement   On your paper, write the verb that correctly completes each sentence.

SAMPLE   A number of different insects, such as crickets and grasshoppers, (use, uses) leaping as a means of escape from enemies.

ANSWER   use

1. Neither Toronto nor Vancouver (is, are) as large as Montreal.
2. Gloves, sweaters, and ties (was, were) on sale at Garvin's today.

3. The entire committee (was, were) invited to attend the reception.
4. The bookstore and the libraries nearby (provide, provides) many hours of pleasure for John and his daughter.
5. Nobody (is, are) able to solve all the world's problems.
6. Homemade bread and milk (has, have) always been my uncle's favorite snack.
7. The team (was, were) debating the strategy that they would use for the game on Saturday.
8. Although the community (has, have) expressed its support, the school committee (has, have) voted against providing funds to build a new auditorium.
9. (Has, Have) the League of Nations been a topic of discussion yet?
10. Bacon, lettuce, and tomato (is, are) a popular combination for a sandwich.

2.3c   Problems in Agreement

Inverted Word Order.   In some sentences, especially questions or sentences beginning with *Here* or *There,* you may have difficulty locating the subject because the verb comes before the subject. By mentally rearranging the sentence in its normal subject-verb order, you can find the subject and make the verb agree with it in number.

SINGULAR	Near the building **was** a public park. [**Think**: park **was.**]
PLURAL	There **are** many ideas to be explored. [**Think**: ideas **are.**]
SINGULAR	**Is** Uncle George or Aunt Susan meeting us at the restaurant? [**Think**: Aunt Susan **is.**]
PLURAL	Here **are** the coat and the shirt that you ordered. [**Think**: the coat and the shirt **are.**]

Sentences with Predicate Nominatives.   Using a predicate nominative (*page 43*) can confuse subject-verb agreement when the subject and the predicate nominative differ in number.

Rule   Use a verb that agrees in number with the subject, not with the predicate nominative.

INCORRECT   *Violets* **is** one of her favorite flowers.

   subj.   P.N.
CORRECT   Violets **are** one of her favorite flowers. [plural subject; singular predicate nominative]

Agreement in Adjective Clauses.   When a relative pronoun, such as *who, which,* or *that,* is the subject of an adjective clause (*page 60*), decide whether the verb of the adjective clause should be singular or plural by finding the antecedent (*page 7*) of the relative pronoun.

Rule   The verb of an adjective clause and the antecedent of the relative pronoun must agree in number.

SINGULAR   Willie Mays, who **was** one of baseball's greatest center fielders, used to make spectacular catches. [*Who* refers to *Willie Mays,* the singular subject.]

PLURAL   People who **do** a job well seem to feel better about themselves. [*Who* refers to *People,* the plural subject.]

Rule   When an adjective clause follows the term *one of those,* use a plural verb in the clause.

PLURAL   Yesterday's assignment is *one of those* that **are meant** to be a challenge.

Every and Many a.   As adjectives, *every* and *many a* (or *many an*) emphasize separateness when they modify subjects. *Every teacher* means "every single teacher," not "all teachers"; *many a teacher* means that each teacher is separate from all the other teachers.

Rule   Use a singular verb with a single subject or a compound subject modified by *every, many a,* or *many an.*

Every teacher and student **wants** to be at the meeting.
Many a teacher **corrects** papers every night.

Exercise 3 Subject-Verb Agreement   On your paper, write the verb form that correctly completes each sentence.

> **SAMPLE**   Many an intriguing sight (awaits, await) the observant visitor to Los Angeles.
>
> **ANSWER**   awaits

1. Near the congested downtown area (stands, stand) the Victorian houses of Carroll Avenue.
2. Their ornate architecture and their gingerbread-style trimmings are what (makes, make) them attractive to photographers.
3. Not many years ago, houses on Carroll Avenue (was, were) one of the great undiscovered treasures in local real estate.
4. Restoring an old house is one of those activities that (appeals, appeal) to many people.
5. By now, there (is, are) rarely a house for sale in the neighborhood, and property values, like those throughout the country, (has, have) soared.
6. Not far from Carroll Avenue (is, are) other examples of the city's architectural heritage.
7. The Bradbury Building and the Oviatt Building, both specimens of the city's nineteenth-century skyline, (has, have) been restored as office buildings that (houses, house) twentieth-century businesses.
8. Much of the architecture in Los Angeles (seems, seem) to reveal attempts to disguise a building's function.
9. One of the most startling sights (is, are) a building that (looks, look) like a huge ship.
10. Designed in the style of California's early Spanish missions (is, are) Union Station.
11. A number of people (has, have) commented that one of the more recently built hotels (resembles, resemble) a cappuccino machine.
12. Plenty of variety in architecture, both serious and whimsical, (represents, represent) the complexity of this vast city's history.

Assignment Subject-Verb Agreement   On your paper, write ten interesting sentences, using one of the following phrases to begin each sentence. Be certain that subjects and verbs agree. Underline each verb that you provide.

SAMPLE	Neither the manager nor the cashier
ANSWER	Neither the manager nor the cashier <u>has</u> any idea when the store <u>will be</u> open tomorrow.

1. The restless crowd
2. Either Jim or Joan
3. Mother's scissors
4. School athletics
5. Every parent

6. The children next door who
7. One of those friends who
8. Foreign languages and mathematics
9. There
10. Someone

Subject-Verb Agreement

In writing a letter to a friend, you want to recommend a novel, a play, or a film that you have recently read or seen. Choose a work that has several characters to discuss, and describe them and their actions both individually and as a group. Include a brief statement telling why you recommend the work to your friend. Revise your paragraphs, making sure that subjects and verbs in your sentences agree in number.

2.4   Correct Use of Pronouns

2.4a   Pronoun Antecedents

All pronouns, whether they are personal (*page 8*), indefinite (*page 10*), relative (*page 10*), reflexive (*page 9*), or intensive (*page 9*), must agree with their antecedents in number, gender, and person (*page 8*).

Agreement in Number

Rule Use a singular pronoun to refer to or to replace a singlular antecedent; use a plural pronoun to refer to or to replace a plural antecedent.

SINGULAR

I, me, my, mine
you, your, yours
he, him, his
she, her, hers
it, its

PLURAL

we, us, our, ours
you, your, yours
they, them, their, theirs

SINGULAR *Jack* said that **he** would take **his** car.

PLURAL Jack's *friends* said that **they** would take **their** cars.

Rule Use a plural pronoun to refer to or to replace two or more singular antecedents joined by *and*; use a singular pronoun to refer to or to replace two or more singular antecedents joined by *or* or *nor*.

Jack and Rick went to hear **their** favorite singer.

Neither Jack nor Rick wanted to drive **his** car.

Indefinite Pronouns as Antecedents. The following indefinite pronouns are singular in meaning. Use singular pronouns to refer to or to replace them.

anybody	everybody	nobody	other
anyone	everyone	no one	somebody
anything	everything	nothing	someone
each	much	one	something
either	neither		

SINGULAR *Each* of the women paid for **her** own ticket.

In sentences where the intended meaning of a singular indefinite pronoun is plural, use a plural pronoun to refer to or to replace the antecedent. For example, it is not sensible to use a singular pronoun in the following sentence.

UNCLEAR   When *everybody* arrived at the theater, **he or she** bought a ticket and went inside.

Because the antecedent *everybody* really means *all* and not *each person individually,* you should use a plural pronoun or, preferably, rewrite the sentence to avoid the awkward construction.

CLEAR   When *everybody* arrived at the theater, **they** bought tickets and went inside.

BETTER   When *all* of the people arrived at the theater, **they** bought tickets and went inside.

Some indefinite pronouns, such as *several, both, few,* and *many,* are plural in meaning; use plural pronouns to refer to or to replace them.

PLURAL   *Several* of the students made **their** own lunches.

Some indefinite pronouns, such as *all, any, enough, more, most, none, plenty,* and *some,* can be either singular or plural. Use either singular or plural pronouns to refer to or to replace them, depending on the meaning of the sentence.

SINGULAR   *All* of the color in the painting had lost **its** vibrancy. [*All* refers to *color,* which is singular; *its* refers to *all.*]

PLURAL   All of the books need to have **their** bindings replaced. [*All* refers to *books,* which is plural; *their* refers to *all.*]

Collective Nouns as Antecedents.   When an antecedent is a collective noun (*page 4*), you must first determine whether the collective noun is singular or plural in meaning. If it is singular, use a singular pronoun to refer to or to replace it; if it is plural, use a plural pronoun to refer to it.

SINGULAR   The ad hoc *committee* voted to change **its** meeting time. [The meeting time is for the entire committee as a unit.]

PLURAL   The ad hoc *committee* voted to increase **their** salaries. [The committee voted for individual salaries.]

Agreement in Gender

The gender (*page 8*) of a noun or a pronoun is either masculine, feminine, or neuter. The masculine pronouns are *he, him,* and *his;* the feminine pronouns are *she, her,* and *hers;* and the neuter pronouns, those refering to neither masculine nor feminine antecedents, are *it* and *its.*

Rule Use a pronoun that agrees in gender with its antecedent.

MASCULINE   *Martin Luther King* motivated **his** followers to take action.

FEMININE   *Flannery O'Connor* based **her** stories on **her** own experience.

NEUTER   A *ship* has to have **its** keel scraped annually.

Sometimes it is unclear whether the gender of a singular antecedent is masculine or feminine. If a neuter pronoun will not work, you can use the phrase *his or her* to show that the antecedent could be either masculine or feminine. This construction, however, is often awkward. If possible, rewrite the sentence so that the antecedent and all words that refer to it or replace it are plural. Sometimes you can repeat the noun that is the antecedent.

AWKWARD   A *lawyer* has a confidential relationship with **his or her** clients.

BETTER   *Lawyers* have confidential relationships with **their** clients.

Agreement in Person

Pronouns are in either the first person, the second person, or the third person (*page 8*).

121

Rule   Use a pronoun that agrees in person with its antecedent.

FIRST PERSON   *I* will graduate from high school before **my** brother does.

SECOND PERSON   Will *you* graduate from high school before **your** brother does?

THIRD PERSON   *Harriet* will graduate from high school before **her** brother does.

When the indefinite pronoun *one* is an antecedent, use a third-person singular pronoun to refer to it or to replace it, or repeat the indefinite pronoun.

One often feels that **he or she** is under a microscope during exam time.

One often feels that **one** is under a microscope during exam time.

Note: In general, do not use *he* to represent both *he* and *she*. You should either repeat the noun or pronoun that is the antecedent or rewrite the sentence to make both the antecedent and the pronoun plural.

Agreement of Reflexive and Intensive Pronouns

Reflexive and intensive pronouns (*page 9*), formed by adding either *-self* or *-selves* to personal pronouns, must also agree with their antecedents in number, gender, and person. Reflexive and intensive pronouns are always used with antecedents; do not use them alone to replace a noun or a personal pronoun.

INCORRECT   For the first time, Robert and I are filing income tax forms by themselves.

INCORRECT   For the first time, Robert and myself are filing income tax forms.

CORRECT   For the first time, Robert and I are filing income tax
reflexive
forms by **ourselves.**

(For more information on correct usage of reflexive and intensive pronouns, see the Usage Notes on pages 152, 156, and 160.)

Exercise 1   Pronoun Antecedents   On your paper, write the pronoun that correctly refers to the antecedent in each sentence. Make sure that each pronoun and its antecedent agree in number, gender, and person.

> **SAMPLE**   When everyone saw Meg, __?__ shouted, "Surprise!"
>
> **ANSWER**   they

1. One of the goals of the program is for each worker to establish __?__ own production goals.
2. She is a dancer who knows when __?__ is performing well.
3. Everyone needs time for __?__ own interests.
4. This is one of those rainstorms that last for days; I wonder when __?__ will let up.
5. The school committee discussed __?__ proposals for the agenda.
6. Neither of the other organizations has written __?__ agenda.
7. No one on the board has been willing to change __?__ vote.
8. Neither Sarah nor Jessica has __?__ umbrella with __?__.
9. Does Melissa __?__ know any games that __?__ might teach Karen?
10. June and Nathan have learned to tie __?__ shoelaces by __?__.

2.4b   Pronoun Case

To show the grammatical use of a pronoun in a sentence, you change its form, or **case.** The three cases are nominative, objective, and possessive.

	SINGULAR	PLURAL
NOMINATIVE CASE	I	we
	you	you
	he, she, it	they
OBJECTIVE CASE	me	us
	you	you
	him, her, it	them
POSSESSIVE CASE*	my, mine	our, ours
	your, yours	your, yours
	his, her, hers, its	their, theirs

*The pronouns *my, your, his, her, its, our,* and *their* are sometimes called pronominal adjectives (*page 20*).

Pronouns in the Nominative Case ━━━━━━

Rule   Use the nominative case when a pronoun acts as a subject (*page 36*), as a predicate nominative (*page 43*), or as an appositive to a subject or to a predicate nominative (*page 48*).

SUBJECT

I would like to speak to Rosalie, please.

PREDICATE NOMINATIVE

This is **she**. To whom am I speaking?

APPOSITIVE TO A SUBJECT

Your *friends*, **Sandy and I,** would like you to go to the game with us. [**Think:** Sandy and I would like.]

APPOSITIVE TO A PREDICATE NOMINATIVE

We are the *friends*, **Sandy and I,** who helped you with your science project. [**Think:** We are Sandy and I.]

Pronouns in the Objective Case ━━━━━━

Rule   Use the objective case when a pronoun acts as a direct object (*page 41*), as an indirect object (*page 42*), as an objective complement (*page 42*), as an object of a preposition (*page 46*), as a subject of an infinitive clause (*page 56*), as an appositive to a direct or an indirect object (*page 48*), or as an appositive to an object of a preposition (*page 48*).

DIRECT OBJECT

Mara met **her** just before school began.

INDIRECT OBJECT

She lent **her** a notebook for her first class.

OBJECT OF A PREPOSITION

Nancy gave it back to **her** after her class.

SUBJECT OF AN INFINITIVE CLAUSE

Mr. Mitchell told **them** to see him after school.

OBJECT OF AN INFINITIVE CLAUSE
> Mara wanted to ask **him** why he wanted to see them.

APPOSITIVE TO A DIRECT OBJECT
> She liked her *friends,* **Mara and her.**

APPOSITIVE TO AN INDIRECT OBJECT
> She told *them,* **Mara and her,** the whole story.

APPOSITIVE TO AN OBJECT OF A PREPOSITION
> Mr. Mitchell wanted to read over their papers with both of
> *them,* **Mara and her.**

Pronouns in the Possessive Case

Possessive pronouns show to whom or to what something belongs. They do not include apostrophes.

Rule Use the possessive pronouns *mine, yours, his, hers, its, ours,* and *theirs* to refer to or to replace nouns.

You can use these possessive pronouns in the same way that you would use nouns: as subjects, predicate nominatives, direct or indirect objects, objects of prepositions, or appositives.

SUBJECT
> **Hers** is the short story that won first place.

PREDICATE NOMINATIVE
> The second-place short story is **his.**

DIRECT OBJECT
> After thinking about the plot for a long time, Kathleen wrote
> **hers** in two hours.

INDIRECT OBJECT
> Carl gave **hers** a rave review.

OBJECT OF A PREPOSITION
> We should really find a publisher for **theirs.**

APPOSITIVE
> A publisher has requested that both *stories,* **hers** and **his,** be
> submitted at once.

Rule Use the possessive pronouns* *my, your, his, her, its, our,* and *their* to modify nouns.

Will you visit *your* grandparents this summer?

Rule Use a possessive pronoun to modify a gerund.

Gerunds (*page 53*) are *-ing* forms of verbs that are used as nouns. Because they function as nouns, use the possessive forms of nouns and pronouns to modify them.

Your visiting your grandparents will be a great pleasure for them. [*Your* is used instead of *you* because it is the *visiting—your visiting* —that will be a great pleasure for them.]

Compound Constructions with Pronouns

It is sometimes troublesome to choose the correct case for pronouns in compound constructions, such as compound subjects or compound objects of a preposition. To determine which case you should use, say the sentence to yourself, leaving out the conjunction and the noun or the other pronoun in the compound construction. When you have determined how the pronoun functions by itself, you can decide whether to use the nominative case or the objective case.

Thomas and **they** are responsible for the decorations. [**Think:** *They* are responsible for the decorations.]

Between you and **me,** I think David deserved to win. [Because *you* and *me* are compound objects of the preposition *between,* use a pronoun in the objective case, *me.*]

Exercise 2 Pronoun Case On your paper, write the correct pronoun for each sentence; then indicate how the pronoun is used in the sentence.

SAMPLE   In recent months, I have not seen (she, her) very much.

ANSWER   her—Direct object

*These possessive pronouns are sometimes called pronominal adjectives (*page 20*).

1. Tony will drive his cousins and (we, us) to the theater.
2. (We, Us) will see that nothing is taken from the museum without permission.
3. Although (she, her) looks younger, Caroline is actually older.
4. The three contestants, the twins and (I, me), took our places at the starting line.
5. Answering the door, we discovered that it was (he, him).
6. (You, Your) moving to another town will make it difficult for (we, us) to practice together.
7. I never expected to find (he, him) here with the children.
8. Will you see (him, he) or (she, her) after the rehearsal?
9. Let us give (he, him) a surprise party.
10. Did you realize when you met them that it was (them, they)?

Who and *Whom*

You can use the forms of the word *who* either as interrogative pronouns (*page 9*) or as relative pronouns (*page 10*). As is true of other pronouns, the way that you use the pronoun determines which case or form of the word you should choose. *Who* and *whoever* are in the nominative case; *whom* and *whomever* are in the objective case; *whose* is in the possessive case.

Who and Whom as Interrogative Pronouns. *Who* and *whom* are interrogative pronouns when they introduce questions. To determine whether to use *who* (the nominative case) or *whom* (the objective case), simply turn the question into a statement.

Rule Use *who* when an interrogative pronoun acts as a subject or as a predicate nominative. Use *whom* when an interrogative pronoun acts either as an object of a verb or as an object of a preposition.

NOMINATIVE   **Who** is singing the lead in *Madama Butterfly*? [*Who* is the subject of the verb *is singing.*]

OBJECTIVE   To **whom** did you speak when you telephoned the White House today? [*Whom* is the object of the preposition *to.*]

If the interrogative pronoun *who* or *whom* is followed by an interrupting phrase, such as *do you feel,* you can mentally rearrange the sentence to determine the use of the pronoun in the sentence and which form of the pronoun to use.

> **Who** do you feel will best fill the position of vice-president? [**Think:** Who will best fill the position? *Who* is the subject.]

In informal writing and in conversation, *who* is often used to ask a question, regardless of whether the nominative or the objective case is needed. In formal usage, however, you should follow the rules for using the nominative case, *who,* and the objective case, *whom.*

> INFORMAL   **Who** do you plan to go with to the movie?
>
> FORMAL   With **whom** will you attend the plenary session next week?

Who and *Whom* as Relative Pronouns.

When forms of the word *who* introduce subordinate clauses (*page 59*), they are relative pronouns. Choose the form of the word to use by its use in the subordinate clause, *not* by its use in the main clause.

Rule Use *who* or *whoever* when a relative pronoun is the subject of the subordinate clause; use *whom* or *whomever* when a relative pronoun is an object within the subordinate clause.

> The new teacher, **who** has been here only a week, has made many friends among the students and faculty. [*Who* is the subject of the clause *who has been here only a week.*]
>
> My mother, **whom** many people respect, was honored at a testimonial dinner. [*Whom* is the direct object of *respect.*]

Exercise 3 *Who* and *Whom* On your paper, write the pronoun that is correct in formal usage. Also, indicate how the pronoun is used in the sentence.

> SAMPLE   About (who, whom) was that story written?
>
> ANSWER   whom—Object of the preposition <u>about</u>

1. (Who, Whom) wants to buy my bicycle helmet for twenty dollars?
2. Even though I don't know (who, whom) you gave my old clothes to, I wish that you had asked my permission first.
3. Jackie, (who, whom) was elected student council president last month, announced today that her family is moving.
4. (Who, Whom) noticed where I misplaced my glasses?
5. My father, (who, whom) I respect even though I don't always agree with him, feels more strongly than I about the conservation of natural resources.
6. Jason's aunt, (who, whom) is almost ninety years old, lives with him and his family.
7. The students did not know (who, whom) their new mathematics teacher would be.
8. Nobody saw (who, whom) placed the chair on top of the flagpole.
9. Patricia, (who, whom) I saw just yesterday, is leaving today for a cross-country bicycle trip.
10. It was John Donne (who, whom) wrote, "Ask not for (who, whom) the bell tolls; it tolls for thee."

Pronouns in Appositive Phrases

The pronouns *we* and *us* are often used in appositive phrases, such as *we engineers* or *us pilots*. Because an appositive explains or renames the word with which it is in apposition, you must first determine how the appositive phrase is used in the sentence. If the phrase is a subject or a predicate nominative, use the nominative case of the pronoun; if the phrase is an object, use the objective case.

To determine which case to use, say the sentence to yourself without the noun in the appositive phrase.

NOMINATIVE   **We engineers** attended the computer conference in Los Angeles last April. [**Think:** We attended. Because *we* and *engineers* are subjects, *we* is in the nominative case.]

OBJECTIVE   The refresher course for **us pilots** will be given again in the spring. [**Think:** The refresher course for **us.** Because *us* and *pilots* are objects of the preposition *for,* *us* is in the objective case.]

Pronouns in Comparisons

In some comparisons using *than* or *as,* part of the phrase or clause is not stated, but merely implied. To choose the correct pronoun, mentally supply the missing words to determine how the pronoun is used. Because the case of the pronoun used in an incomplete comparison can alter your intended meaning, make your choice carefully. In the following examples, notice the change in meaning according to the choice of pronoun.

NOMINATIVE   I will walk as far with you as **she.** [**Think:** as far as she will walk. Use the nominative-case pronoun because *she* is the subject of the implied clause, *she will walk with you.*]

OBJECTIVE   I will walk as far with you as **her.** [**Think:** as far with you as with her. Use the objective-case pronoun, *her,* because the intended meaning makes *her* the object of the implied preposition *with.*]

Exercise 4   Other Uses of Pronoun Case On your paper, write the correct pronoun for each of the following sentences.

SAMPLE   The coach really lectured (we, us) players.
ANSWER   us

1. (We, Us) performers will need to be ready by Wednesday.
2. I wish that I were more coordinated than (he, him).
3. If Jane had listened to (we, us) swimmers, she would have known that the lake was too shallow for competitive swimming.
4. Will you arrive home sooner than (I, me)?
5. Mrs. Berstein asked (we, us) neighbors to water her lawn while she was away.
6. The crate was a great deal heavier than (they, them) thought.
7. The crate was a great deal heavier than (they, them).
8. Mary's mother gave (we, us) band members a ride to the concert.
9. Do you think my present made her as happy as (I, me)?
10. The broken axle on the train car made the journey rather uncomfortable for (we, us) passengers.

2.4c   Correct Pronoun Reference

To avoid confusing your listeners or readers, be certain that the pronouns you use refer clearly to their antecedents. If you find an unclear reference, rephrase the sentence.

Rule Avoid using a pronoun that could refer to more than one antecedent.

UNCLEAR	Jerry picked Bill to be on his team because he knows the game well. [Who knows the game well? The antecedent of *he* is unclear.]
CLEAR	Jerry picked Bill to be on his team because Bill knows the game well.

Rule Avoid using the pronoun *it, they, you,* or *your* without a clear antecedent in formal usage.

The following example shows how you can usually replace the pronoun with a noun to eliminate confusion.

UNCLEAR	I forgot my umbrella and my flashlight. When I thought about it, I laughed. [What is *it*? The pronoun has no clear antecedent.]
CLEAR	I forgot my umbrella and my flashlight. When I thought about my forgetfulness, I laughed.

Rule Do not use the pronoun *your* in place of an article (*a, an,* or *the*) if possession is not involved.

AVOID	Many of your gymnasts have been training for years.
USE	Many gymnasts have been training for years.

Rule Avoid using *which, it, this,* and *that* to refer to ideas that are not clearly stated.

The following example demonstrates how you can avoid making such general references.

GENERAL   We went to every game in the series, but we didn't see anyone hit a home run, which was quite disappointing. [The pronoun *which* has no clear antecedent; instead, *which* refers generally to an idea in the previous sentence.]

CLEAR   We went to every game in the series, but we were quite disappointed because we didn't see anyone hit a home run.

Exercise 5   Pronoun Reference

On your paper, rewrite the following sentences, making certain that all pronoun references are clear and accurate. If a sentence is correct, write *Correct*.

SAMPLE   I was locked out of my house with a bottle of milk in my hand when it started to pour.

ANSWER   I was locked out of my house with a bottle of milk in my hand when the rain started.

1. Arabella is devoted to nature, and she once became very angry with a woman because she saw her littering her garden.
2. Examination of the Table of Contents of Shakespeare's First Folio shows that when *Timon of Athens* first appeared it replaced *Troilus and Cressida*.
3. Although there are a great many pre-Columbian metal objects in museums and private collections, we know relatively little about the techniques or implements that they employed in its manufacture.
4. Like Antwerp's, New York's rise from provincial capital to cosmopolitan center demonstrates its historical connections between the development of trade and the flowering of culture and art.
5. It is characteristic of organizations that they are not immortal; they may not seem it, but they flourish and then die just as a living organism does.
6. For all its immense intellectual vigor, the James family was one beset by personal calamities and disorders.
7. Billy told Eli, Jake, and Steve that he shouldn't have done it.
8. The day was bright, my family was close by, and the food was delicious, which I will never forget.
9. Good training techniques are essential to the development of fine race horses because without them, any competitive edge would be lost.

10. Until Napoleon's dreams of an empire led him into the land of the pharaohs, knowledge of Egypt's past was as obscure as the hieroglyphics on its stone facades.

Assignment 1 Pronoun Usage   On your paper, list the eleven pronouns from the passage and classify each according to type and to its use in the sentence.

> With malice toward none, with charity for all, with firmness in the right, as God gives us to see the right, let us strive on to finish the work we are in, to bind up the nation's wounds, to care for him who shall have borne the battle, and for his widow and orphans; to do all which may achieve and cherish a just and lasting peace among ourselves and with all nations.

> *From Abraham Lincoln's*
> *"Second Inaugural Address"*

Assignment 2 Pronoun Usage   On your paper, rewrite each of the following sentences, using personal pronouns to replace the nouns in italics. Underline the pronouns that you supply. Be certain that the person, number, and case are correct.

> **SAMPLE**   *The bouquet* is a gift for *the neighbors*.
> **ANSWER**   It is a gift for them.

1. *Victoria Woodhull* was the first woman to be nominated for the presidency of the United States.
2. I expected *a reply* from *Celeste* yesterday.
3. Several of *the players* received injuries during the game. *The players* had to be given medical attention.
4. *O. Henry* wrote *short stories* while serving a prison term for embezzlement.
5. *Charles and Tina* consider *Mr. O'Hara* their best teacher.
6. *Barbara* gave *Thomas* a watch for his birthday.
7. *The winning essay* was *Claudia's*.
8. *Mrs. Torres* told the babysitter to make *Margaret* a sandwich.
9. Whose book did *Ed* borrow, *Judy's* or *Robert's*?
10. No one can bring *Joan* happiness but *Joan*.

2.5   Correct Use of Modifiers

2.5a   Comparison of Modifiers

By using different forms of adjectives and adverbs, you can compare two or more persons or things. The three degrees of comparison are positive, comparative, and superlative.

The Three Degrees of Comparison

You use a modifier in the **positive degree** to assign some quality to a person, a thing, an action, or an idea. You use a modifier in the **comparative degree** to compare a person, a thing, an action, or an idea with another one. You use a modifier in the **superlative degree** to compare a person, a thing, an action, or an idea with at least two others.

	ADJECTIVES
POSITIVE	That line is **long.**
COMPARATIVE	That line is **longer** than the one for the other movie.
SUPERLATIVE	That line is the **longest** one that I have ever seen.

	ADVERBS
POSITIVE	Roger behaves **maturely.**
COMPARATIVE	Roger behaves **more maturely** than Eric.
SUPERLATIVE	Of all the students, Roger behaves the **most maturely.**

Using Comparisons Correctly

Rule   Add the suffix -er to form the comparative and the suffix -est to form the superlative of modifiers with one or two syllables.

In some cases, to form the comparative modifier correctly, you must drop a final e, double a final consonant, or change a final y to i before adding the suffix. (See Unit 14, "Spelling Skills.")

short, shorter, shortest
funny, funnier, funniest

Rule Use *more* to show the comparative degree and *most* to show the superlative degree in three instances: with all three-syllable words, with two-syllable words that would otherwise be difficult to pronounce, and with adverbs ending in *ly.*

> serious, more serious, most serious
> dreadful, more dreadful, most dreadful
> restfully, more restfully, most restfully

Rule Use *less* and *least* to form the comparative and superlative degrees of comparisons showing less.

> humorous, less humorous, least humorous
> hopeful, less hopeful, least hopeful
> ambitiously, less ambitiously, least ambitiously

Remember, also, that some modifiers are irregular and do not form comparisons in a standard way. You should memorize them to be able to use them correctly.

bad, worse, worst	little, less, least
far, farther, farthest	many, more, most
far, further, furthest	much, more, most
good, better, best	well, better, best
ill, worse, worst	

Rule Avoid double comparisons. Use either the word *more* or *most* or else the appropriate suffix; do not combine the two.

INCORRECT   Jim is **more funnier** than anyone else in the group.

CORRECT   Jim is **funnier** than anyone else in the group.

Rule Avoid incomplete comparisons by clearly indicating the things being compared.

When you compare one member of a group with the rest of the group, you can avoid being unclear or misleading by using the comparative degree and the word *other* or *else.*

UNCLEAR   Richard plays the oboe better than anyone in the
class. [This sentence says either that Richard plays

the oboe better than anyone in the class, including himself, or that Richard plays the oboe better than anyone in a class of which he is not a part.]

CLEAR   Richard can play the oboe better than anyone **else** in the class. [Richard is the best oboe player in **his** class.]

Rule Use the words *as . . . as* or *as . . . as . . . than* to complete a compound comparison.

A **compound comparison** really makes two statements by using both the positive and the comparative degrees of a modifier. The positive degree shows that the things being compared are at least equal or similar; the comparative degree shows that they may, in fact, be different. Because you would still have a complete sentence if you removed the second, or parenthetical, part of the comparison, use commas to set off the parenthetical part from the rest of the sentence.

Being on time to my 8:00 A.M. class is **as** difficult **as**, if not more difficult **than,** being on time to my 7:00 A.M. class.

Being on time to my 8:00 A.M. class is **as** difficult **as** being on time to my 7:00 A.M. class, if not more difficult.

Rule Avoid making comparisons that are illogical because of missing or faulty elements or because no comparison can be made.

To avoid having your reader or listener misunderstand your meaning, rephrase the comparison to include all of the important words.

ILLOGICAL   Sarah writes computer programs that are as complicated as Francine. [Computer programs cannot be compared to Francine. Sarah can write programs; she cannot write Francine.]

LOGICAL   Sarah writes computer programs that are as complicated as Francine's. [**Think:** Sarah's programs are as complicated as Francine's programs.]

Certain adjectives, such as *perfect, unique, dead, round, full,* and *empty,* do not have a comparative or superlative degree because they express an absolute condition. Because logically nothing can be "more perfect" or "more empty," use the forms *more nearly* or *most nearly* when you use these words in comparisons.

Jim's plate was the most nearly empty at the end of the meal.

Exercise 1 Correct Use of Comparisons On your paper, write the correct form of the modifier given in parentheses. Identify the degree of comparison of each correct modifier.

> **SAMPLE**   Of my two goldfish, Fred was the (deader, more nearly dead) when I returned from vacation.
>
> **ANSWER**   more nearly dead—Comparative

1. *Mutiny on the Bounty* is one of the (more engrossing, most engrossing) novels that I have ever read.
2. Your solution is good, but his is (better, best).
3. Which comedy in the double feature is (funnier, funniest)?
4. Of the four faces carved on Mount Rushmore, the one that seems (less lifelike, least lifelike) is Theodore Roosevelt's.
5. Is Chaucer or Milton the (more difficult, most difficult) writer to understand?
6. That was the (worse, worst) résumé that the employment counselor had ever received.
7. Which sport do you find (livelier, liveliest): tennis, volleyball, or handball?
8. Who is the (more tragic, most tragic) of the three heroines: Madame Bovary, Anna Karenina, or Tess of the D'Urbervilles?
9. Does a liquid quart or a liter have the (greater, greatest) volume?
10. I am not certain which is the (shorter, shortest) book: *Ethan Frome, The Pearl,* or *Of Mice and Men.*

2.5b Placement of Phrases and Clauses

Rule Place modifying phrases and clauses as close as possible to the words that they modify.

Misplacement of phrases and clauses can create unclear and unintentionally humorous sentences. To avoid misplacing modifiers, identify the word to be modified and place the modifying phrase or clause as close as possible to that word, while retaining your intended meaning.

UNCLEAR	Mrs. Santos decided to support the referendum, persuaded by the editorial. [The phrase *persuaded by the editorial* appears to be modifying *referendum,* thereby distorting the meaning of the sentence.]
CLEAR	Mrs. Santos, persuaded by the editorial, decided to support the referendum.
CLEAR	Persuaded by the editorial, Mrs. Santos decided to support the referendum.

Notice in the following example that improper placement of the modifying phrase can alter the meaning of the sentence. As you revise your sentences, check to be certain that your intended meaning is still clear.

UNCLEAR	Strolling by the lake, a family of ducks walked in front of me. [Who was strolling by the lake?]
CLEAR	Strolling by the lake, I noticed a family of ducks in front of me. [Meaning: I was strolling by the lake when I noticed the ducks in front of me.]
CLEAR	In front of me, I noticed a family of ducks strolling by the lake. [Meaning: The ducks were strolling by the lake.]

Rule   To avoid dangling modifiers, provide an antecedent for every modifying phrase or clause to modify.

A **dangling modifier** is a modifying phrase or clause that does not clearly or logically modify any word in the sentence; a dangling modifier can make a sentence unclear or unintentionally humorous.

UNCLEAR	Before going home, the door must be locked. [Who is going home?]
CLEAR	Before going home, you must lock the door. [The adverb phrase *before going home* now modifies the verb phrase *must lock.*]

You can also correct a dangling phrase by changing the phrase to a subordinate clause.

CLEAR   Before you go home, the door must be locked.

In current usage some dangling modifiers have become accepted as part of idiomatic expressions. These are usually such present and past participles as *allowing for, based on, considering, concerning, failing, generally speaking, granting, judging, owing to,* and so forth.

Judging from the cover, the magazine is about computers.

According to available information, the scholarship committee won't be meeting until July.

You can determine whether an expression is acceptable even though it may seem to be a dangling modifier by asking yourself these questions: "Does the reader expect a word for the phrase to modify, or is the phrase or clause common enough to be considered an idiom? Is the meaning of the sentence clear?"

Exercise 2   Placement of Modifiers   On your paper, rewrite each of the following sentences, eliminating all misplaced or dangling modifiers.

SAMPLE   Obsessed with locating the sunken treasure, the ocean floor was scoured.

ANSWER   Obsessed with locating the sunken treasure, the divers scoured the ocean floor.

1. Being newcomers to the community, the one-way streets confused the Bryants.
2. Brad watched the parade riding his bicycle.
3. Roasted over charcoal, we particularly like corn on the cob.
4. After being sequestered in the jury room for ten hours, the need for food was felt by the jury.
5. Having practiced the role for a month, the prospect of an audition no longer alarmed Lucille.
6. As guests in their home, the Coopers urged us to use their station wagon freely.

7. While chatting with his former teacher recently, the subject of careers was raised.
8. After attending college and law school for seven consecutive years, a break in the academic routine was welcomed.
9. Watching the movie intently, the screen suddenly went blank.
10. Upon receiving the defective record, it was immediately returned to the mail-order house.

Assignment   Use of Modifiers   On your paper, write sentences using each of the following phrases correctly.

> **SAMPLE**   through the thick fog
>
> **ANSWER**   The encouraging sight of the lighthouse beacon appeared through the thick fog.

1. made of a gritty substance
2. more accurately
3. in spite of repeated warnings
4. examining the beaker
5. at the age of eighteen
6. speaking in a stentorian voice
7. as miraculous
8. according to the theory of
9. most obedient
10. acting petulant
11. misinterpreting their intentions
12. feigning ignorance
13. as outspoken
14. less productive
15. if not sooner

Using Modifiers

You can convey a great deal of information and atmosphere in just a few sentences by using concrete modifiers. Write a one-paragraph description of a scene that you witnessed in the past week. Limit your paragraph to the number of details you would have perceived if you had observed this scene for only one minute. Make your description detailed and interesting by using colorful phrases and clauses as modifiers. Include at least one comparison. Check over your paragraph to be sure that you have placed modifiers correctly.

2.6   Usage Notes

The following pages contain an alphabetical list of words and phrases that often present usage problems. Each entry describes correct usage, and most entries include examples. Cross-references help you to locate related information.

a lot, alot   *A lot* means "a great number or amount" and is always two words; avoid using *a lot* in formal usage. *Alot* is not a word.

a while, awhile   *While* is a noun and can be preceded by *for a* or *in a* to make a prepositional phrase. *Awhile* is an adverb; do not use *for* or *in* before *awhile.*

> We have been here for **a while.**
> We have been here **awhile.**

accept, except   *Accept* is a verb that means "to agree" or "to receive." *Except* is a preposition that means "leaving out" or "but."

> We did not want to **accept** the expensive gift.
> Beth has taken every art course offered by the school, **except** the course on silk screening.

adapt, adopt   *Adapt* means "to change or adjust" or "to make more suitable." *Adopt* means "to take or accept."

> Since he had always lived in a warm climate, it took Jeremy several months to **adapt** to our cold climate.
> The Macintosh family has decided to **adopt** a child.

advice, advise   *Advice* is a noun that means "helpful suggestion or opinion." *Advise* is a verb that means "to give or offer counsel."

> My accountant **advised** me to file my income tax forms on time. Unfortunately, I did not follow that **advice.**

affect, effect   *Affect* is a verb that means "to influence." *Effect* can be a verb that means "to bring about or achieve" or a noun that means "result."

> Because our town was not directly **affected** by the flood, we could offer refuge to several families who were forced out.
>
> The severe storm **effected** a change in our travel plans. [verb meaning "brought about"]
>
> The **effects** of the flood were less extreme than we had thought. [noun meaning "results"]

ain't   *Ain't* is nonstandard. Do not use it.

all ready, already   *All ready* functions as a compound adjective that means "entirely ready" or "prepared." *Already* is an adverb that means "before some specified time" or "previously." Do not confuse the two.

> Are you **all ready** to begin the test?
>
> I can't believe that you've **already** finished that typing!

all right, alright   *All right* means "satisfactory," "unhurt," "correct," or "yes, very well." *Alright* is an incorrect spelling; do not use it.

> Because we were so late, we telephoned Uncle Jack to let him know that we were **all right.**
>
> **All right,** who has a better suggestion?

all the farther, as far as   *All the farther* should not be used for *as far as*.

> Two miles is **as far as** I will run today. [not *all the farther*]

all together, altogether   *All together* means "in a group." *Altogether* means "completely" or "thoroughly."

> We bought tickets **all together** because no one wanted to be responsible for choosing the seats.
>
> They are **altogether** too late to be considered.

almost, most   Do not confuse the adverb *almost* with the adjective *most.*

> adj.   adv.
> **Most** people sleep **almost** eight hours.

although, though   Both of these conjunctions mean "in spite of the fact." In conversation, *though* can be used as an adverb to mean "however." Avoid this usage in written English.

> David goes to the gym to exercise, **although** (*or* **though**) the track season is months away. [conjunction]
>
> He didn't mind going to a basketball game, **though,** when his friends were going. [adverb]

among, between   Use *among* for comparisons involving groups of persons or things. Use *between* when only two items are being considered at a time.

> Only one **among** all the race car drivers would win.
>
> Can you tell the difference **between** a jonquil and a daffodil?

amount, number   Use *amount* with a noun that names something that can be measured or weighed. Use *number* to refer to things that can be counted.

> A large **amount** of snow fell last night.
>
> A large **number** of snowstorms are expected next winter.

and/or   *And/or* means "either *and* or *or.*" It is confusing and should be avoided.

anxious, eager   Both words can mean "strongly desirous," but you should use *anxious* to suggest concern or worry.

> Abigail was **anxious** to get to work before the storm broke.

any more, anymore   These terms are not interchangeable. The phrase *any more* describes quantity; *any* is an adverb modifying the adjective *more*. *Anymore* is an adverb meaning "at present" or "from now on."

> Is there **any more** traffic on the bridge than there is in the tunnel?
>
> I don't drive to work **anymore.**

anywhere, everywhere, nowhere   Do not use in a plural form: *anywheres, everywheres, nowheres.*

appraise, apprise   *Appraise* means "to evaluate"; *apprise* means "to inform."

> Having **appraised** the old desk, the antique dealer **apprised** its owner that it was worth one thousand dollars.

apt, liable, likely   In informal usage, these words are often used interchangeably. In formal usage, only *apt* and *likely* are interchangeable, meaning "tending to" or "inclined to be." Use *liable* to suggest the probability of a harmful, unfortunate, or negative event or to show exposure to legal action.

> Robert is **apt** to be unpleasant when he first awakens in the morning.
>
> Mark is **liable** to strain a muscle during the game if he doesn't start practicing more regularly.
>
> Barbara was **liable** for damages when her daughter accidentally knocked over a carton of glassware in the department store.

as, like   In formal usage, *like* is most often used as a preposition to introduce a prepositional phrase. *As* is most often used as a conjunction to introduce a subordinate clause.

> Margot thinks **like** her father. [prepositional phrase]
>
> Margot thinks **as** her father does. [subordinate clause]

In informal usage, *like* is sometimes used as a conjunction. Avoid using *like* as a conjunction in formal usage in place of *as, as if,* or *as though.*

| AVOID | The hikers felt **like** they had walked twenty miles. |
| USE | The hikers felt **as if** they had walked twenty miles. |

as far as, all the farther   See *all the farther, as far as.*

author   Do not use *author* as a verb. Books are written, not authored.

bad, badly   *Bad* is always an adjective, and *badly* is always an adverb. Use *bad* following a linking verb.

> You have a **bad** cold. Are you feeling **bad?**
> The foundation **badly** needs repairs.

because, on account of   *On account of* means "because of" or "due to." The phrase functions as a preposition and takes an object. Do not use *on account of* instead of *because* to introduce a subordinate clause.

> The flights to Chicago were cancelled **on account of** snow.
> I am going to be quiet now **because** I have talked enough in this meeting. [not *on account of*]

being as, being as how, being that   Do not use these expressions for *since* or *because.*

> **Since** he had broken his arm, Harvey could not help us lift the cartons. [not *Being as*]
> **Because** he couldn't help lift the cartons, Harvey volunteered to get us all cold juice. [not *Being that*]

beside, besides   *Beside* means "next to." *Besides* means "in addition to."

> I parked the car **beside** our neighbor's truck.
> **Besides** a truck, our neighbor owns a station wagon.

between, among   See *among, between.*

between you and me Never use the nominative case *I* as the object of a preposition. *Between* is a preposition.

> The discussion is **between you and me.** [not *between you and I]*

borrow, lend, loan A person *borrows from* and *lends to* another person. *Loan* is a noun meaning "that which is lent" or "the act of lending." You may also use *loan* as a verb, but *lend* is preferred.

> Michael **borrowed** a book from Louise. [verb]
>
> Louise **lent** (*or* **loaned**) Michael a book. [verb]
>
> The **loan** of the book helped Michael to complete his homework assignment. [noun]

both, either, neither When used to modify compound elements, place *both, either,* and *neither* just before the compound construction. The elements in the compound construction should be parallel or similar in form.

> INCORRECT Nelson intends **both** to study business and engineering.
>
> CORRECT Nelson intends to study **both** *business* and *engineering.*

bring, take Use *bring* when you mean "to carry to." Use *take* when you mean "to carry away."

> **Bring** your swimming suit with you when you come to the party.
>
> Remember, **take** your swimming suit with you when you go to the party.

bust, busted Do not use these words as verbs to substitute for *break* or *burst.* The verbs *bust* and *busted* are nonstandard.

> That little girl's balloon just burst. [not *busted*]

can, may See "Modals," page 99.

cannot (can't) help but In standard English, use *cannot (can't) help* followed by a gerund.

> Madeline **can't help** *wishing* that her brother could attend her graduation. [not *can't help but wish*]

can't hardly, can't scarcely Avoid these terms; they are double negatives.

> That insect is so tiny that I **can hardly** see it without a magnifying glass. [not *can't hardly*]

compare to, compare with Use *compare to* when pointing out similarities; use *compare with* when pointing out similarities and differences.

> In that metaphor the bright yellow flowers are **compared to** sunshine.
>
> **Compared with** a tornado, this is a minor windstorm.

consensus of opinion Because consensus means "group or collective opinion," this phrase is redundant. Use only the word *consensus*.

credible, creditable, credulous *Credible* means "believable" or "worthy of belief." *Creditable* means "worthy of commendation." *Credulous* applies always to people and means "willing to believe" or "gullible."

> It was a **credible** story; we did not need to force ourselves to become involved in the plot.
>
> The movie director did a **creditable** job; the movie won three awards.
>
> Rick is a **credulous** young man; he thought that the science fiction about robots running the Pentagon was true.

data is, data are *Data* is the plural form of the Latin *datum*. In formal English it should be followed by a plural verb. In informal English a singular verb may be used.

differ from, differ with   Things (or persons) *differ from* each other if they are physically dissimilar. When persons *differ with* each other, they are in disagreement.

> Children **differ from** adults.
> I **differ with** Hank about the need for a new stadium.

different from, different than   Use *different from*. Use the idiom *different than* only to introduce a subordinate clause.

> My ideas are **different from** hers. [not *different than*]
> My ideas are **different than** *hers are*.

disinterested, uninterested   *Disinterested* implies a lack of self-interest; it is synonymous with *unbiased* or *impartial*. *Uninterested* implies a lack of any interest.

> Although I am **disinterested** in which party wins the court case, I am not **uninterested** in the principles of law that are being challenged by the case.

double negative   A double negative is the use of two negatives where one is sufficient. Avoid using *not* or contractions with *-n't* with words such as *no, none, never,* and *nothing.* (See also *can't hardly, can't scarcely.*)

> Sometimes I feel that I **don't** have **any** friends.

double subject   Do not use a noun and a pronoun together as a single subject.

> INCORRECT   My **friend she** helped me with the dishes.
>
> CORRECT   My **friend** helped me with the dishes.
>
> CORRECT   **She** helped me with the dishes.

each and every   *Each and every* is redundant. Use either *each* or *every.*

eager, anxious   See *anxious, eager.*

effect, affect   See *affect, effect.*

e.g., i.e.   *E.g.* stands for the Latin words *exempli gratia,* meaning roughly "an example for free." *E.g.* means "for example" in English. *I.e.* stands for the Latin words *id est,* meaning "that is," and should be used to cite an equivalent. Use both sparingly.

either, both, neither   See *both, either, neither.*

eminent, imminent   *Eminent* means "prominent" or "outstanding in some way." *Imminent* means "about to occur."

> We were fortunate that the **eminent** historian agreed to visit our school.
> The heavy, dark clouds indicated that a storm was **imminent.**

et al.   This is a Latin abbreviation for *et alii* and means "and others" (persons, not things). It is used most often in footnotes to refer to other members of a team of authors.

etc.   This Latin abbreviation for *et cetera* means "and other things," "and so forth." Avoid using *etc.* in formal writing; use *and so forth* instead. Do not use *and etc.*; it is redundant.

every day, everyday   *Every day* means "each day." *Everyday* is an adjective meaning "ordinary."

> I am supposed to check the mail **every day.**
> **Jim wore his everyday** clothes to work.

every one, everyone   *Every one* refers to each person or thing in a group and is usually followed by *of. Everyone* means "everybody, every person."

> **Every one** of us went home after the picnic.
> **Everyone** went home after the picnic.

everywhere, anywhere, nowhere   See *anywhere, everywhere, nowhere.*

except, accept   See *accept, except*.

explicit, implicit   These adjectives are antonyms. *Explicit* refers to something that is directly stated. *Implicit* refers to something that is not directly stated.

> Patty was **explicit** in her description of the swearing-in ceremonies.
>
> Betty's feelings about her mother were **implicit** in her willingness to help her in any way she could.

famous, noted, notorious   *Famous* means "renowned or celebrated." *Noted* means "celebrated." *Notorious* means "known widely and regarded unfavorably."

> The **famous** (*or* **noted**) economist predicted that inflation would continue.
>
> The **notorious** prankster was finally caught and punished.

farther, further   These two words are not interchangeable. *Farther* means "more distant in space." *Further* means "more distant in time or degree, additional."

> Bill swam **farther** than Tom did.
>
> The **further** you investigate this story, the more confused the facts seem to be.
>
> Conway **further** discussed his ideas about pedestrian safety.

fewer, less   Use *fewer* to refer to things that you can count individually. Use *less* to refer to quantities that you cannot count and to amounts of time, money, or distance when the amount is a single quantity.

> There were **fewer** requests for help this week than last week.
>
> I have **less** trouble with number concepts than he does.
>
> I have **less** than three dollars in my pocket.

figuratively, literally   *Figuratively* and *literally* are antonyms. An expression that uses a metaphor to represent a fact is figurative; an expression that states a fact is literal.

Felix was speaking **figuratively** when he said, "It's raining cats and dogs out there." What he meant **literally** is that it was raining heavily.

first, firstly; second, secondly   Use *first* and *second,* not *firstly* and *secondly* to mean "in the first (or second) place."

> **First,** put the flowers into a vase. [not *Firstly*]

formally, formerly   These two words sometimes sound alike but have distinct spellings and meanings. *Formally* means "in a formal or official manner." *Formerly* means "previously" or "at an earlier time."

> Beth spoke **formally** to the audience.
> He **formerly** was a doctor.

former, latter   Of two things or persons named sequentially, the first is the former; the second is the latter.

> Betsy and Peter will come to dinner tonight. The **former** [Betsy] may be half an hour late, but the **latter** [Peter] will be on time.

further, farther   See *farther, further.*

good, well   *Good* is an adjective. *Well* can be an adverb or a predicate adjective meaning "satisfactory" or "in good health." The opposite of feeling sick is feeling *well.*

> Fuller is a **good** writer.
> Oliver teaches **well.**
> Are you feeling **well?**

got, have   *Got* is the past tense of the verb *get.* It means "obtained." Avoid using *got* with or in place of *have.* Also avoid using *don't got* in place of *don't have.*

> I **have** to pick up Freddy this afternoon. [not *I got to*]
> I **don't have** any other errands. [not *I don't got*]

had ought, hadn't ought   Avoid using *had* and *hadn't* with *ought.* Instead, use *ought,* which is usually followed by the preposition *to.*

> Lewis **ought** to be ready for the concert. [not *had ought*]
> He **ought** not to miss any rehearsal. [not *hadn't ought*]

half a   Use *a half* or *half a(n).* Do not use *a half a(n).*

> Will drove by about **a half** hour ago. [not *a half an hour*]

hanged, hung   *Hanged* and *hung* are alternative forms of the past tense and past participle of the verb *to hang.* Use *hanged* when referring to death by hanging. Use *hung* in all other cases.

> The Scarlet Pimpernel was **hanged** at dawn.
> They **hung** plants on the porch.

have, got   See *got, have.*

have, of   *Have* and *of* sound similar in rapid speech, but they are different parts of speech. *Have* is a verb; *of* is a preposition. Be careful to say and write *have* when completing a verb phrase, especially after the helping verbs *should, would,* and *could. Of* is not a verb.

> We **should have** visited him earlier. [not *should of*]

hisself, theirselves   *Hisself* and *theirselves* are both nonstandard forms. Do not use them. *Himself* and *themselves* are the correct forms for reflexive and intensive pronouns.

hung, hanged   See *hanged, hung.*

i.e., e.g.   See *e.g., i.e.*

imminent, eminent   See *eminent, imminent.*

implicit, explicit   See *explicit, implicit.*

imply, infer *Imply* means "to hint at" or "to suggest." *Infer* means "to reach a conclusion based on evidence or deduction." These words are not interchangeable.

> I **implied** in my remarks that the council should approve the plans to build a new school.
>
> I **inferred** from the applause that followed my remarks that the audience supported my suggestion.

in, into Use *in* to mean "within" and *into* to suggest movement toward the inside from the outside.

> Ruth walked **into** the store to buy supplies for the camping trip.
>
> While she was **in** the store, she found the lantern that she wanted.

individual, person Use *individual* to distinguish one person from a larger group. Do not use *individual* generally in place of *person*.

> **Persons** in the hospital should be treated as **individuals.**

ingenious, ingenuous *Ingenious* means "clever"; *ingenuous* means "naive."

> The **ingenious** child was always trying to invent questions that we couldn't answer.
>
> The newcomer was so **ingenuous** that we had to explain even the most basic things to him.

irregardless, regardless Do not use *irregardless*; it is nonstandard. Use *regardless* instead.

> We will call you when we arrive, **regardless** of the time.

its, it's *Its* is a possessive pronoun; *it's* is the contraction for *it is*.

> The bear was standing on **its** hind legs, ready to attack.
>
> **It's** a nice day, so leave your heavy jacket at home.

judicial, judicious *Judicial* means "of or pertaining to a court of law." *Judicious* means "having or showing good judgment."

> The **judicial** proceeding was scheduled to take four days.
> Jeremy's use of money is **judicious;** he is able to save even though his salary is rather small.

just exactly This phrase is redundant. Use either *just* or *exactly*.

> It's **just** thirty-five feet from my desk to yours.
> It's **exactly** thirty-five feet.

kind of, sort of In most writing do not use these colloquial forms to mean "somewhat." See also *these kinds, this kind*.

> The casserole is **rather** tasty. [not *kind of* or *sort of*]

latter, former See *former, latter*.

lay, lie *Lay* is a transitive verb that means "to put or to place something somewhere." It always takes a direct object. *Lie* is an intransitive verb that means "to be in or to assume a reclining position." It does not take a direct object. (See page 93 for the principal parts of these irregular verbs.)

> **Lay** the placemats on the table before you **lie** down to rest.

learn, teach Do not use these words interchangeably. To *learn* is "to receive knowledge" or "to acquire knowledge." *Teach* means "to give knowledge."

> Maureen will **learn** to play the flute quickly if you will **teach** her.

leave, let *Leave* means "to go away" or "to abandon." *Let* means "to permit" or "to allow."

> Will you **let** me **leave** with them on the train tomorrow?

lend, borrow, loan See *borrow, lend, loan*.

less, fewer See *fewer, less*.

liable, apt, likely   See *apt, liable, likely.*

lie, lay   See *lay, lie.*

like, as   See *as, like.*

likely, apt, liable   See *apt, liable, likely.*

likewise   Likewise is an adverb that means "similarly." Do not use it as a conjunction to mean "and" or "together with."

> Her cheerfulness, **together with** her intelligence, made her the perfect candidate for the job. [not *likewise*]

literally, figuratively   See *figuratively, literally.*

loan, borrow, lend   See *borrow, lend, loan.*

many, much   Use the adjective *many* to describe things that you can count (pencils, people). Use the adjective *much* to describe things that you cannot count (gas, truth, strength). When used as indefinite pronouns, *much* is singular and *many* is plural.

> **Many** responded to our requests for volunteers.
> **Much** was expected, but little gained.

may, can   See *can, may.*

may, might   See "Modals," page 99.

may be, maybe   In the term *may be, may* is an auxiliary that indicates possibility. (See "Modals," page 99.) The adverb *maybe* means "perhaps."

> Donna **may be** able to attend the planning session.
> **Maybe** Donna will attend the planning session.

more than one   This phrase, although plural in meaning, takes a singular verb.

> **More than one** child *has* the flu.

most, almost   See *almost, most.*

much, many   See *many, much.*

myself, yourself   Do not use a reflexive pronoun in place of *I, me,* or *you.*

INCORRECT	My brother and **myself** enjoy sightseeing together.
CORRECT	My brother and **I** enjoy sightseeing together.

neither, both, either   See *both, either, neither.*

nohow, noway   *Nohow* and *noway* are nonstandard. Avoid using them. You can, however, use *no way* correctly as two words.

INCORRECT	**Noway** can we finish on time.
CORRECT	There is **no way** that we can finish on time.

noted, notorious, famous   See *famous, noted, notorious.*

nothing like, nowhere near   In formal English, use *nothing like* to mean "not at all like"; use *nowhere near* to mean "not anywhere near."

This movie is **nothing like** the one that we saw last Saturday. [formal]

The studio is **nowhere near** my house. [formal]

That book was **nowhere near** as suspenseful as I had thought it would be. [informal]

nowhere, anywhere, everywhere   See *anywhere, everywhere, nowhere.*

of, have   See *have, of.*

off, off of   *Of* is unnecessary. Do not use *off* or *off of* in place of *from.*

We lifted the chair **off** the carpet so that we could vacuum. [not *off of*]

Larry got that idea **from** his brother. [not *off*]

only   To avoid confusion, place *only* before the element that it modifies. The placement of *only* can dramatically affect the meaning of your sentence.

> **Only** Dale gave him a watch.
> Dale **only** gave him a watch.
> Dale gave **only** him a watch.
> Dale gave him **only** a watch.

on to, onto   In the phrase *on to, on* is an adverb and *to* is a preposition. *Onto* is a preposition that means "to a position on" or "upon."

> When we leave Denver, we will go **on to** Phoenix.
> He got **onto** the train in Denver.

outside, outside of   Use *outside of* only when *outside* is a noun and *of* is a preposition.

> Will you wait **outside** the room for a minute? [not *outside of*]
> The **outside of** the box has been damaged in shipping.

passed, past   *Passed* is the past tense of the verb *to pass,* which means "to move on or ahead, to proceed." *Past* is an adjective that means "no longer current," "over," or "before the present"; a noun that means "a time earlier than the present"; an adverb that means "so as to go beyond"; and a preposition that means "beyond, after."

> Jocelyn **passed** us without even waving. [verb]
> Don't let **past** events bother you now. [adjective]
> Margaret likes to study the **past.** [noun]
> Harrison drove **past** in a cloud of dust. [adverb]
> It is **past** the time for the concert to begin. [preposition]

people, persons   Use *persons* when referring to a relatively small, specific group. Use *people* when referring to a large group in a collective sense.

> Ten **persons** (*or* **people**) were winners in the contest.
> Some **people** who are very pessimistic always expect to fail. [not *persons*]

persecute, prosecute   To *persecute* people is to harass or otherwise mistreat them. To *prosecute* is to bring a court action.

> The bullies **persecuted** the small children in the neighborhood.
> The store owners **prosecuted** the alleged shoplifter.

person, individual   See *individual, person.*

precede, proceed   *Precede* means "to exist or come before in time." *Proceed* means "to go forward or onward."

> Tim and Willy **proceeded** with the job, wishing that Max and Sam, who had **preceded** them in the use of the carpentry shop, had sharpened the saws.

provided, providing   In formal usage use *provided* as a conjunction meaning "on the condition that" or "if."

> I will call you tomorrow **provided that** I don't see you this evening. [not *providing*]

raise, rise   *Raise* is a regular transitive verb that means "to lift"; it always takes a direct object. *Rise* is an irregular intransitive verb that means "to move upward." See page 93 for the principal parts of the irregular verb *rise.*

> Adele **raised** her feet from the table when her mother scowled at her.
> The moon **rises** early in the afternoon.

real, really   *Real* is an adjective; *really* is an adverb.

> It is **really** fortunate that you found your wallet. [not *real*]
> That is a **real** surprise!

reason is because, reason is that   *Reason is because* is redundant. Use *reason is that* or simply *because.*

> INCORRECT   The **reason** that I am late **is because** I missed my bus.

> CORRECT   The **reason** that I am late **is that** I missed my bus.

refer back   *Refer back* is redundant. Use just *refer.*

> I **refer** to our discussion of this morning. [not *refer back*]

regardless, irregardless   See *irregardless, regardless.*

regretful, regrettable   *Regretful* means "full of sorrow or regret." *Regrettable* means "deserving regret or sorrow."

> Mark was **regretful** over the decision to close the theater.
> Closing the theater was a **regrettable** decision.

respectfully, respectively   *Respectfully* means "showing respect or esteem." *Respectively* means "each in the order indicated."

> Bob and Linda always spoke **respectfully** to their grandmother.
> The librarian discussed the issue with Nate and Louise **respectively.**

rise, raise   See *raise, rise.*

said, says, goes, went   *Said* is the past tense of the verb *say; says* is a present-tense form. Do not use *says* for *said.* Also, do not use *goes* or *went* for *said.*

> Gary called and **said,** "Do you have a tent for the camping trip, or are you going to rent one?" [not *says* or *goes*]

second, secondly; first, firstly   See *first, firstly; second, secondly.*

seldom ever   *Seldom ever* is redundant. Use only *seldom.*

-self, -selves   The suffix *-self* is singular; *-selves* is plural. Be sure to use the correct suffix to form a reflexive pronoun.

SINGULAR   *myself, yourself, himself, herself*

PLURAL   *ourselves, yourselves, themselves*

set, sit   *Set* is a transitive verb that means "to place something." *Sit* is an intransitive verb that means "to rest in an upright position"; *sit* does not take a direct object.

Sit down next to the door, please.

Set your books on the floor next to you.

slow, slowly   *Slow* is an adjective that can be used as an adverb in informal speech, especially in commands or for emphasis. *Slowly* is an adverb; it is preferred in formal usage.

Our waiter is very **slow**. [predicate adjective]

He is walking **slowly** from table to table. [adverb]

Do you think that someone told him to walk **slow**? [adverb; informal]

so, so that   Both can be used to mean "in order that." However, use *so* only in informal speech or writing. *So* is also used as an explanatory or superlative qualifier of adjectives and adverbs.

Tilson went early **so that** he would be sure to get tickets for the nine-o'clock show. [or informally, *so*]

The six-year-old was **so** excited about the circus that she could not sleep.

some time, sometime, sometimes   When you use two words, *some* is an adjective modifying *time*. *Sometime* can be an adverb that means "at an indefinite time," or it can be an adjective that means "occasional." *Sometimes* is an adverb that means "occasionally, now and then."

adj.   noun
He needs **some time** to be alone.

adv.
I would like to go to Peru **sometime**.

adj.
Evan is a **sometime** musician.

adv.
Sometimes I like to go away by myself.

sort of, kind of   See *kind of, sort of.*

supposed to, used to   *Supposed to* means "expected to" or "required to." *Used to* means "accustomed to, familiar with." Be sure to spell *supposed* and *used* with a final -*d.*

> You were **supposed to** take the children shopping with you. [not *suppose to*]
> They are quite **used to** you now. [not *use to*]

sure, surely   *Sure* is an adjective meaning "certain" or "dependable." *Surely* is an adverb meaning "certainly, without doubt."

> Rob was **sure** that the dog was in the house.
> The dog will **surely** return by morning.

take, bring   See *bring, take.*

teach, learn   See *learn, teach.*

than, then   Use *than* as a conjunction in a comparison. Use *then* as an adverb to show a sequence of time or events. Do not use either one as a conjunction between two independent clauses.

> The play was, in my opinion, truer to the book **than** the movie was.
> If we get home in time, **then** you may watch television.

that, which, who   Use *that* as a relative pronoun to introduce essential clauses (*page 60*) that refer to things or to collective nouns referring to people. Because it introduces an essential clause, do not use a comma before *that.*

> The cat **that** was crying at our door has just run away again.

Use *which* as a relative pronoun to introduce nonessential clauses (*page 61*) that refer to things or to groups of persons. Always use a comma before *which* when it introduces a nonessential clause.

> This book, **which** is one that I received for my birthday, is extremely interesting.

Use *who* or *whom* as a relative pronoun to introduce essential and nonessential clauses that refer to persons. Use a comma before *who* or *whom* when it introduces a nonessential clause.

> The girl **who** won that prize is Cathy's sister.
> Nadia, **who** goes to the same school as I do, is a clerk in this store.

that there, this here   Do not use either construction. Use only *this* or *that*.

> Where do you want **this** chair moved? [not *this here*]

theirselves, hisself   See *hisself, theirselves.*

then, than   See *than, then.*

these kinds, this kind   Use *this* or *that* to modify the singular nouns *kind, sort,* and *type.* Use *these* and *those* to modify the plural nouns *kinds, sorts,* and *types.* Use the singular form of these nouns when the object of the preposition is singular; use the plural form when the object of the preposition is plural.

> This **kind of** *book* is easy to read. [sing.]
> These **kinds of** *books* are more difficult. [pl.]

though, although   See *although, though.*

till, until   Both words are acceptable. *Until* is preferred as the first word in a sentence. Do not use *til* or *'til.*

> **Until** I have my homework finished, I cannot leave the library.

toward, towards Both mean "in the direction of" or "approaching," but *toward* is preferred. *Towards* is the British form.

try and, try to Use *try to* instead of *try and*.

> Please **try to** be on time. [not *try and*]

uninterested, disinterested See *disinterested, uninterested.*

used to, supposed to See *supposed to, used to.*

very Use *very* only sparingly. Overuse diminishes its effect.

way, ways Do not use *ways* when referring to distance.

> You have only a short **way** to go to reach the supermarket. [not *ways*]

well, good See *good, well.*

where . . . at Do not use *at* after *where*.

> **Where** is that discount store located? [not *Where is it at?*]

which, that, who See *that, which, who.*

who, whom See pages 127-128.

-wise Avoid using *-wise* on the end of a word to mean "with reference to" or "concerning."

> AVOID **Weatherwise,** it is a pleasant week.
>
> USE The weather has been pleasant this week.

would have Do not use *would have* instead of *had* in clauses that begin with *if*.

> If he **had** let me know, I would have gone with him to the hospital. [not *if he would have*]

yourself, myself See *myself, yourself.*

Unit Practice

Practice 1

A. The Scope of Usage (*pages 87–90*) On your paper, identify each sentence as an example of *Formal English, Informal English, Nonstandard English,* or *Occupational language.*

1. The present governor of Indiana won't run in next year's primary race, but he's interested in a higher office.
2. After Chuck finished reconciling the books, he was sure that the debits balanced the credits in the general ledger.
3. If you're finished reading that photo magazine, I'd like to borrow it.
4. Why doesn't youse set in this here shade before you takes off?
5. In turbulent times a spirit of cooperation grows; at this particular juncture, let us work together.

B. Correct Use of Verbs (*pages 90–108*) On your paper, copy each sentence, replacing each blank with the correct verb or verb phrase. Use a form of the infinitive that is given in parentheses.

6. __?__ all of the proposals fairly and without any personal bias. (*judge*)
7. Mr. Penny requests that the landscaping crew __?__ thoroughly. (*trim*)
8. Finally the vending machine in the lobby __?__ properly because the worn parts have been replaced. (*operate*)
9. Marc used to be forgetful; he often __?__ his gloves in odd places. (*leave*)
10. The interviewer asked that I __?__ my transcript and test scores with me. (*bring*)
11. By the time Tim and Laurie finish the cottage, they __?__ for three days. (*paint*)
12. Right now the store aisles __?__ with bargain items and eager shoppers. (*crowd*)
13. Having completed debate over the document, John Hancock __?__ the Declaration of Independence. (*sign*)
14. By next month they __?__ whole sentences in German for some time, and they will present a short dialogue. (*speak*)
15. Yesterday a professional storyteller dramatically __?__ the audience a local legend. (*tell*)

C. Subject-Verb Agreement (*pages 108–118*) On your paper, write the verb that correctly completes each sentence.

16. Mason, a fan of silent films, (have, has) tickets for the film festival.
17. Neither Burt nor Cathleen (were standing, was standing) close enough to the microscope.
18. Nobody (want, wants) the building facade to be remodeled, yet the present structure is cracked and worn.
19. Preparing for the long voyage, the crew (cleans, clean) the deck, the cabins, and the equipment.
20. *Romeo and Juliet* still (gives, give) pleasure to audiences today.
21. Gymnastics (demands, demand) discipline and strength.
22. Either the workers or the supervisor (take, takes) the night shift occasionally.
23. Plenty of the participants (answers, answer) the political poll as honestly as possible.
24. Near the plaza and the frescoes on the old city wall, merchants (sells, sell) their wares.
25. My aunt is one of the people who (owns, own) this florist shop.

D. Correct Use of Pronouns (*pages 118–133*) On your paper, rewrite each sentence, correcting all errors in the use of pronouns.

26. Him traveling by ship across the Atlantic has given him all sorts of interesting tales to relate.
27. When the band members play well, his or her fans always cheer appreciatively.
28. Whom do you imagine actually discovered that continent first?
29. Depend on your colleagues, Betsy and I, to help you meet your deadline.
30. Anyone on the trail might get lost, but not if they had adequate instructions.
31. Martin's brothers are as likely to become veterinarians as him.
32. Let we specialists polish and refinish the surface of that marble monument.
33. Bold headlines proclaimed it; everyone was excited by the news about the scientific advance.

(Continue on the next page.)

34. Your car manufacturers recommend that spark plugs be replaced periodically.
35. My brother and myself will take a vacation when we finish our summer jobs.

E. Correct Use of Modifiers (*pages 134–141*)   On your paper, rewrite each sentence, correcting all errors in the use of modifiers.

36. Of all the county's delegates, Gina was the younger.
37. Don's career is as rewarding as his friends.
38. I attended an art history lecture, curious about Renaissance painting.
39. Barry has a more smooth running stride than his cousin Sid.
40. My fitness routine is as strenuous if not more strenuous than his.
41. What is the most far distance that you have hiked?
42. Cacti are more abundant in the desert than any plants.
43. After leaving a profession, finding a new career is challenging.
44. I enjoy physics more than calculus, although physics is hardest.
45. Of all the states, Wyoming was less populated in 1970.

Practice 2

Rewrite the following passage, correcting all errors in usage.

Sagarmatha National Park receives many adventurous visitors yearly. In order to reach the park, everyone climb more than twenty thousand feet. Sir Edmund Hillary, the famous climber, first suggested that a park is built on the summit of Mount Everest in Nepal. With the aid of New Zealand advisers, the 480-square-mile park is established in 1976. This park may be considered more unique than any other park because it includes the three most highest mountains in the world. Among the park's other features are 120 species of birds, and musk deer, yaks, and snow leopards attracting thousands of visitors. Sherpas, who are the native people of the region, live here and manage the park itself. The reason for selecting this unusual site was conservation. Scarce forests has been endangered by an increasing demand for firewood. Supporters of this park hope that its efforts to plant trees and to enforce conservation measures will preserve the area.

Unit Tests

Test 1

A. The Scope of Usage (*pages 87–90*)   On your paper, identify each sentence as an example of *Formal English, Informal English, Nonstandard English,* or *Occupational language.*

1. "Why doesn't you guys just clam up?" shouted someone in the crowd.
2. So many students signed up for the computer course that the school had to buy more equipment.
3. The sea represents liberation; water imagery consistently illustrates the dominant theme of the novel.
4. A subpoena has been served; if the witness fails to appear, the court will issue a bench warrant.
5. This committee has devoted an inordinate amount of time to trivialities; let us turn our attention to more significant matters.

B. Correct Use of Verbs (*pages 90–108*)   On your paper, copy each sentence, replacing each blank with the correct verb or verb phrase. Use a form of the infinitive that is given in parentheses.

6. Get plenty of rest because tomorrow you __?__ in the fields. (*work*)
7. A glass beaker __?__ when it fell from the laboratory shelf. (*crack*)
8. The workers were informed that they __?__ the production target sooner than expected. (*achieve*)
9. Ivan __?__ unable to get to last night's play rehearsal on time because of the rush-hour traffic. (*be*)
10. The townspeople gathered quickly when the meeting bell __?__ yesterday. (*ring*)
11. Fortunately, we __?__ a makeshift shelter just before the rain started. (*construct*)
12. If I __?__ in charge, I would have sent detailed instructions along with the original plans. (*be*)
13. Although my brother __?__ heavy cartons all morning, he is not tired yet. (*lift*)
14. When Gino arrived at the information desk, a welcoming committee __?__ there. (*wait*)
15. The moderator asked that the panel __?__. (*proceed*)

(Continue on the next page.)

C. Subject-Verb Agreement (*pages 108–118*)   On your paper, write the verb that correctly completes each sentence.

16. Twilight and dusk (is, are) two terms associated with sunset.
17. Loretta, not they, (contributes, contribute) most to the success of the production.
18. On weekends the children in the neighborhood (like, likes) to watch my brother, who is rebuilding a car engine.
19. The ailment is one of those that (resist, resists) easy diagnosis.
20. Either mangoes or papayas (arrives, arrive) periodically at the fruit stand.
21. On the windowsill (grow, grows) a variety of herbs in containers.
22. Few (decides, decide) at first glance; many customers need time to compare and to test the products.
23. Of all the unusual items, bongo drums (were, was) his favorite gift.
24. Neither Doug nor his sisters, (practices, practice) every day; however, they are all dedicated musicians.
25. Because his parents' company (has, have) again been relocated, Darryl has moved twice in the past year.

D. Correct Use of Pronouns (*pages 118-133*)   On your paper, rewrite each sentence, correcting all errors in the use of pronouns.

26. Most of the village changed after architects and contruction workers together restored them.
27. I eagerly read the letter from Lucy; at this moment she is most likely exclaiming over the news in theirs.
28. One usually benefits when it works patiently to attain a goal.
29. Dr. Sudbury instructed we dental students with a high degree of professionalism.
30. Donna and Suzanne went to the box office, and she purchased tickets as her birthday surprise for Dominic.
31. Mrs. Santos told Phyllis to remember to bring a book to read while she waits for the plane.
32. Responsibility for scheduling rests with yourself.
33. When one does an excellent job, they deserve some recognition.
34. Its owners were amused by the loyalty of the beagle that trotted behind Lila and I.
35. Who did Gerry invite to speak at the ground-breaking ceremony?

E. Correct Use of Modifiers (*pages 134–141*)   On your paper, rewrite each sentence, correcting all errors in the use of modifiers.

36. When mending fences, posts are carefully measured.
37. The view from the porch was as peaceful as the garden.
38. Incandescent light is more dependable than any form of illumination.
39. This auction is as crowded if not more crowded than the last one.
40. Maya changes a tire faster than anyone in the driver's training class.
41. None are more braver than the members of that mountaineering club.
42. Greenland is larger than any island in the world.
43. Mr. Fiedler hurried out the revolving door rushing to an appointment.
44. *Odd Facts* is the most unique program on television.
45. Fortunately, Deb feels more well today than she felt yesterday.

Test 2

Rewrite the following passage, correcting all errors in usage.

Are your name Baxter, Bailey, Hill, or Wood? Then perhaps your ancestors was employed as bakers or as bailiffs, or one lived near a hill or a forest. In the past people do not always have last names. One might have identified themselves adequately with just a first name. The population began to require last names as it increased. Although last names become fashionable in some countries, they were not employed universally until the 1700s. In the fifteenth century, Henry V ordered that occupations and dwellings are listed on formal papers. Because of his order, many last names used today be derived from jobs and surroundings. Since your members of royalty usually inherited its names, other people eventually followed this trend. Surnames has continued to change, especially in the United States, due to the pioneers and the immigrants whom misspelled or Anglicized their last names.

Unit 3

Mechanics

Unit Preview

When you speak, you use pauses and vocal inflections to help convey meaning to your listeners. When you write, you use **mechanics**—capitalization, punctuation, italics, and numbers —to convey meaning to your readers.

For Analysis Read the following passage from *David Copperfield*, and try to answer the questions about it. You may have some difficulty, because it lacks the mechanics of capitalization and punctuation.

> well ill tell you what said mr barkis praps you might be writin to her I shall certainly write to her i rejoined ah he said slowly turning his eyes towards me well if you was writin to her praps youd recollect to say that barkis was willin would you that barkis is willing i repeated innocently is that all the message yees he said considering yees barkis is willin

1. How many speakers are there in the passage?
2. What is the first speaker's name?
3. What is the message the first speaker wants to send?
4. How many separate quotations are there; that is, how often does one person stop speaking and another begin?
5. How many contractions are there in the passage?

Now read the same passage with the mechanics correctly in place.

> "Well, I'll tell you what," said Mr. Barkis. "P'raps you might be writin' to her?"

"I shall certainly write to her," I rejoined.

"Ah!" he said, slowly turning his eyes towards me. "Well! If you was writin' to her, p'raps you'd recollect to say that Barkis was willin'; would you?"

"That Barkis is willing," I repeated, innocently. "Is that all the message?"

"Ye—es," he said, considering. "Ye—es. Barkis is willin'."

Charles Dickens, *David Copperfield*

You can see that quotation marks, commas, dashes, and other mechanical devices clarify and enliven this passage. By using the rules of mechanics that you will learn about in this unit, you can make your own writing clear and interesting.

3.1 Capitalization

Capital letters are most frequently used to indicate the beginning of a sentence or to show that a word is a proper noun (*page 4*).

3.1a Capitalization in Sentences

Rule Capitalize the first word of a sentence and the first word of a direct quotation that is a complete sentence.

Creatures that normally roam the woods at night are called nocturnal animals.

Marcie said, "**Aerial** photographs of the affected region would be extremely helpful."

Begin the second part of an interrupted quotation with a capital letter if it is a new sentence; otherwise use a lower-case letter.

"The bobsled team has just come around the final curve!" he announced excitedly. "**A** new record has been set on this course."

"That leaky pipe can be repaired," said Mr. Hobbes, "**if** I replace the worn section with a new piece."

Rule   Capitalize the first word of each line of a poem.

> **Fair** daffodils, we weep to see
> **You** haste away so soon;
> **As** yet the early-rising sun
> **Has** not attained his noon.

> Robert Herrick, "To Daffodils"

Many modern poets do not capitalize the first word of each line of poetry. When you copy a poem, follow the style of the poet.

> **beauty** is a shell
> **from** the sea
> **where** she rules triumphant

> William Carlos Williams, "Song"

3.1b   Proper Nouns

Rule   Capitalize the names and initials of people. If a last name begins with *Mc, O',* or *St.,* capitalize the next letter as well. If a last name begins with *Mac, de, D', la, le, van,* or *von,* use capitalization according to individual family preference.

> J. **O'**Shea   Hernando **de** Soto   Robert **La** Follette

Family-Relationship Words. Capitalize a word that shows family relationship if it is part of a particular person's name or if it is used in place of a particular person's name. Usually, if a word is preceded by a possessive pronoun (*page 8*), or if it is used as a general term, it is not capitalized.

> Grandfather Hosmer   Aunt Jeanne   Cousin Rita

> Harriet told **Mother** that she would be late for dinner this evening.
> Karen hoped that **Uncle Frank** would visit in September.
> Her **brother** said that he wished he had a new car.

Personal and Official Titles. Capitalize a personal or official title or its abbreviation when it is used as a name in direct address (*page 182*) or precedes a person's name.

Capitalize the names and abbreviations of academic degrees or honors that follow a person's name. Capitalize the abbreviations *Sr.* and *Jr.*

Dean Simpson	**Superintendent** Rossi
Eleanor Brock, **M.D.**	**Governor** Ralston
David Oleson, **Jr.**	Roberta Myers, **Ph.D.**

Yes, **Senator,** the report has been delivered.
I told the **senator** that the report had been delivered.

Do not capitalize a title that follows or substitutes for a person's name unless it is the title of a head of national government. Do not capitalize prepositions, conjunctions, and articles that are part of titles unless they begin a sentence.

TITLE BEFORE NAME	TITLE FOLLOWING NAME
Professor Fischer	Walter Fischer, **professor**
President Wilson	Woodrow Wilson, **President**

The **President** will address the nation at four o'clock this afternoon.

Gods of Mythology. Capitalize the names of gods of mythology, but do not capitalize the word *god* when it refers to one of them.

Myths about the ancient Egyptian **god Osiris** portray the process of cyclic renewal.

Rule Capitalize the names of particular places, such as continents, countries, cities, parks, and rivers.

Bering Strait	Erie Avenue	Iceland	Ohio
Cooper River	Fairmont Park	Kalamazoo	Paraguay

Compass Points. Capitalize compass points that refer to specific geographic regions. Do not capitalize compass points that simply indicate directions or general regions.

We spent our vacation in the **Southwest** last fall.
They traveled **west,** then **northwest** to reach their destination.

Heavenly Bodies. Capitalize the names of planets, stars, and constellations. Do not capitalize *sun* and *moon.* Capitalize *Earth* when referring to the planet, but do not capitalize *earth* when it is preceded by the word *the.*

Andromeda   Neptune   Sirius   Aquarius

Photographs of **Earth** taken from satellites in space revealed many cloud formations above the planet's surface.

The path of **the earth** around the sun is called **the earth**'s orbit.

Rule Capitalize the names of nationalities, peoples, and languages.

Asian   Melanesian   Finnish
Brazilian   Hopi   Latin

Rule Capitalize the names of days, months, holidays, and special events. Do not capitalize the name of a season unless it is part of a proper noun.

Tuesday   August   spring
Winter Carnival   Memorial Day   winter

Rule Capitalize the names of historical events and periods. Capitalize the names of awards and documents.

the Middle Ages   the Treaty of Versailles
the Emancipation Proclamation   the Nobel Prize

Rule Capitalize the first, the last, and all other important words in the titles of books, newspapers, poems, television programs, musical works, paintings, and so forth. (See also pages 190, 202.) Capitalize a conjunction, an article, or a preposition only when it is the first or the last word in a title or when a conjunction or a preposition has five or more letters.

"**The** Corn Grows **Up**"   *A Man **Without** a Country*
"Singing **in the** Rain"   *For Whom the Bell Tolls*

Rule Capitalize the names of school subjects that are languages or that are followed by a course number. Capitalize proper adjectives in the names of school subjects.

Latin	science	French literature
Biology II	history	American history

Rule Capitalize the names of structures and the names of organizations, such as businesses, religions, government bodies, clubs, and schools. Capitalize a word such as *school* or *club* only when it is part of a proper noun.

Abbot Hall		House of Representatives
Taoism		Gordon's Bookstore
the Museum of Fine Arts		The Chess Association
the Broadcasters' **Club**	BUT	a broadcasters' **club**
Essex **College**	BUT	an agricultural **college**

Rule Capitalize trade names. Do not capitalize a common noun that follows a trade name.

Tree-Ripe fruit juice   Lyle lamps

Rule Capitalize names of trains, ships, airplanes, rockets, and spacecraft. (See also page 202.)

the *Lake Shore Limited*   *Viking II*

3.1c Other Uses of Capitalization

Rule Capitalize most proper adjectives (*page 19*). Use a lower-case letter for a proper adjective that is in common usage.

Queen Anne's lace   **Persian** cat   **Gordian** knot
BUT   oxford shoes

If you are not sure whether to capitalize a proper adjective, consult your dictionary.

Rule Capitalize both letters in the abbreviations *A.D.*, *B.C.*, *A.M.*, and *P.M.* Write *A.D.* before the date; write *B.C.* following the date.

1120 B.C.   A.D. 1970   4:30 P.M.

Rule   Capitalize both letters in the two-letter Postal Service abbreviations of state names.

Use Postal Service abbreviations only in addresses that include the ZIP code; do not use them in formal writing.

Minnesota **MN** 55411   Rhode Island **RI** 02915

Exercise   Capitalization   On your paper, rewrite each sentence, using capitalization correctly. Use your dictionary if you need help.

> **SAMPLE**   the drama club meets in Massell hall at 4:30 p.m.
> **ANSWER**   The Drama Club meets in Massell Hall at 4:30 P.M.

1. cellophane, which was first made in france, was invented by jacques edwin brandenberger, a swiss chemist.
2. "have you ever taken a train ride along the coastal route?" asked roy. "the *silver meteor* passes through the southern states."
3. i warmed my hands over the franklin stove after a long walk near mt. katahdin, in maine.
4. this new advertising campaign for glow-ever lightbulbs is certainly eye-catching!
5. for their research on the structure of crystals, sir william henry bragg and his son shared the 1915 nobel prize for physics.
6. one winter the explorers meriwether lewis and william clark camped in oregon; fort clatsop national memorial now marks the site.
7. newton's bookstore has everything in stock from thomas hardy's *the mayor of casterbridge* to a futuristic novel about society on the planet pluto.
8. mrs. weatherby's great-niece plays the viola in the plainfield symphony orchestra, and she will take part in a recital this sunday at 2:00 p.m.
9. would you repeat that humorous remark that the writer h. l. mencken made many years ago in *the american mercury* magazine?
10. john donne, a poet of the seventeenth century, wrote these lines in the poem "song":

> o how feeble is man's power,
>   that if good fortune fall,
> cannot add another hour,
>   nor a lost hour recall!

Assignment Capitalization Choose a country that you would like to know more about. Using appropriate reference books (*pages 485–488*), gather information about the country. What is the capital city? What is the main language spoken? What are some geographical points of interest such as lakes, rivers, and mountain ranges? What countries border the country? What sites, buildings, or landmarks are well known? What historical events are associated with the country? When you have gathered several facts, write a paragraph about the country using capitalization correctly.

Capital Letters

You have recently visited a historical site that has especially interested you and a friend for a long time. Because your friend was unable to make the trip, you have decided to write a brief but detailed description of the site and its attractions. The site may be real or imaginary, but be sure to include details in your description. Describe the structures, monuments, artifacts, or documents that you saw. Use proper nouns when appropriate. Tell about an important event associated with the site, giving names, dates, and other important information. Using direct quotations, summarize a brief conversation with another visitor about what impressed each of you at the site. When you have completed your description, check to see that you have followed the rules of capitalization.

3.2   Punctuation

Punctuation marks show when to stop, when to pause, and when to pay special attention to a particular part of a sentence. By using punctuation correctly, you help your readers understand what you have written.

3.2a   Periods, Question Marks, and Exclamation Points

The Period

Rule   Use a period at the end of a declarative sentence, a mild command, or a polite suggestion.

> A rook is a bird that closely resembles a crow.
> Soon the stage lights will dim, and the production will begin.
> Wait here until the traffic stops.
> Dorothea, would you please lower the volume of the television.

Rule   Use a period after most standard abbreviations, including initials that are used as part of a person's name or title.

Do not use periods after abbreviations for most units of weight, units of measure, or for chemical elements. Use the abbreviation *in.* for *inch* to show that you are not writing the preposition *in.*

Do not use periods when the abbreviation of a company or an organization is in all capital letters or when you are writing Postal Service abbreviations of state names.

USE PERIODS	DO NOT USE PERIODS
Capt. Mario Venditto	**min**—minute
Julia **S.** Drake, **R.N.**	**Kr**—Krypton
Dec.—December	**gal**—gallon
Rte.—route	**AZ**—Arizona
Co.—company	**FAA**—Federal Aviation Administration
Miss.—Mississippi	

Do not confuse standard two-letter state abbreviations (which require periods) with Postal Service abbreviations (which require no periods).

USE PERIODS	DO NOT USE PERIODS
Preston, **Ga.** [no ZIP code]	Rhine, **GA** 31077
Cascade, **Ky.** [no ZIP code]	Clark, **KY** 41011

Rule When a period in an abbreviation precedes a question mark or an exclamation point in a sentence, use both marks of punctuation.

> When is it correct to use *Dr.*?

Note: Avoid using abbreviations in formal writing. Spell out words instead.

The Question Mark

Rule Use a question mark at the end of an interrogative sentence.

> Has Del applied for the summer internship?
> Were those old watches appraised at the jewelry store?

Rule Use a question mark after a question that is not a complete sentence.

> The date? December 30.

Rule Use a question mark to express a doubt about what comes before it.

> Josiah Clark (1762?–1809) made furniture that is sturdy and usable even today.

The Exclamation Point

Rule Use an exclamation point at the end of a sentence that expresses strong feeling or a forceful command or after a strong interjection or other exclamatory expression.

> He nearly escaped!
> Don't miss the total eclipse!
> Congratulations! You are the new assistant.
> Wait! Never leave a campfire burning!

Exercise 1   End Punctuation and Abbreviations   On your paper, write each sentence and supply the correct punctuation.

SAMPLE	Leave the premises at once
ANSWER	Leave the premises at once!

1. Wait That flashlight needs new batteries
2. The postcard mailed from San Antonio, Texas, had a picture of La Villita, a restoration of a small city
3. The architect said, "That house is the best example of the Colonial period in this region"
4. Oh Don't forget the symbol for iron, Fe, in the equation
5. Mrs. Knudson, will you please repeat the last statistic
6. At last, Gerald has completed his Ph D
7. Copy the list of ingredients
8. The newspaper gave a full account of the latest NATO meeting
9. Give me your answer this minute
10. A J Foyt has won numerous auto racing championships

3.2b   Commas

Commas in Series

Rule   Use commas to separate three or more words, phrases, or clauses in a series. Use a comma after each item except the last.

> Donna bought **potting soil, marigold seeds,** and **fertilizer** at the plant store.
>
> The campers **climbed the mountain, selected a campsite,** and **pitched their tents** for the night.
>
> In preparation for the play, **Bert rehearsed his lines, Carla checked the props,** and **Florence tested the sound system.**

Do not use commas to separate items in a series if all of them are joined by conjunctions.

> Did you decide to go swimming **or** fishing **or** boating last weekend?

Do not use commas to separate pairs of nouns that are thought of as a single item or as a unit.

> ┌─── unit ───┐
> For breakfast we ordered juice, cereal, **bacon and eggs,** and milk.

Commas After Introductory Expressions

Rule Use a comma to show a pause after an introductory word or phrase.

Prepositional Phrases. Use a comma after an introductory prepositional phrase (*pages 46–47*) of four or more words.

> **After the management seminar,** the participants handed in their reports.

Participial Phrases. Use a comma after an introductory participial phrase (*pages 51–52*).

> **Wondering if she had missed her appointment,** Carol raced to the elevator.

Adverb Clauses. Use a comma after an introductory adverb clause (*pages 62–63*) regardless of its length.

> **Before she left,** Sandra watered the plants.

Interjections. Use a comma to separate *yes, no,* and other interjections, such as *oh* and *well,* from the rest of the sentence.

> **Yes,** Sheila is eligible for the athletic scholarship.
> **No,** I will not be able to go bowling tomorrow evening.
> **Oh,** here are some hand-lettered greeting cards for sale.
> **Well,** the harvest next year may be more bountiful.

Modifiers. Use commas to separate two or more adjectives that modify the same noun. Do not use commas if the adjectives form a compound with the noun (*page 4*).

To determine whether to use a comma, ask yourself whether the sentence would sound right if you reversed the adjectives or if you put *and* between them. If it sounds natural, use a comma or commas. If it does not, do not use commas. Do not use a comma between the last adjective and the noun that it modifies.

NATURAL	Meri manages a successful, innovative business. [comma: *successful* and *innovative* each modify business.]
NATURAL	Meri manages an innovative, successful business.
NATURAL	They listened avidly to the first radio broadcast. [no comma: It is the *radio broadcast* that is first; *radio broadcast* is a compound.]
UNNATURAL	They listened avidly to the radio first broadcast.
UNNATURAL	They listened avidly to the first and radio broadcast.

Commas to Separate Sentence Parts

Rule   Use a comma to separate sentence parts that might otherwise be read together in a confusing manner.

Later, former senators will gather for a formal group photograph.

Whenever **possible, alternatives** should be researched.

Repeated Words. Use a comma to separate most words that are repeated.

What little food there **was, was** shared by all.

Rewrite sentences to avoid repeating words whenever possible.

Rule   Use a comma before a coordinating conjunction (*pages 30–31*) that joins the independent clauses of a compound sentence (*page 68*).

Josie never saw a meteor shower, **but** she viewed the Great Meteor Crater in Arizona.

Deliver this message immediately, **and** call Mr. Hutchinson before tomorrow morning.

Rule   Use a comma or a pair of commas to set off words of direct address and parenthetical expressions within a sentence.

Frank, please do not forget the maps.

Her evaluations of the play have, **after all,** been positive.

Rule Use a comma or a pair of commas to set off nonessential appositives (*page 49*). Do not set off essential appositives (*pages 48–49*).

Treat an abbreviated title or a degree following a name as a nonessential appositive.

NONESSENTIAL

Karen's brother, **Steve,** will meet her at the airport tonight. [Karen has only one brother.]

Jules Verne, **the author of** *Twenty Thousand Leagues Under the Sea,* was one of the first writers of science fiction.

Wilma Sarkin, **D.D.S.,** will be the guest speaker this afternoon.

ESSENTIAL

My cousin Tony moved from Boston to Los Angeles fifteen years ago. [I have more than one cousin.]

The American novelist Nathaniel Hawthorne wrote about the duality of human nature. [There is more than one American novelist.]

Julie's cat Tiny Tim purred contentedly. [Julie has more than one cat.]

Rule Use a comma or a pair of commas to set off a nonessential phrase or a nonessential clause (*page 60*) from the rest of the sentence. Do not set off an essential phrase or an essential clause (*page 61*).

NONESSENTIAL

The students, **who found the new material difficult,** met in study groups after school. [All of the students found the new material difficult.]

Every week I shop at the same store, **where I often see people whom I know.**

ESSENTIAL

The students who found the new material difficult met in study groups after school. [Only the students who found the new material difficult met in study groups.]

Every week I shop at the store that is nearest to my home.

Rule Use commas before and after the year when it is used with the month and the day. Do not use commas when only the month and the year are given.

> Joanne moved into her new apartment on **July 7, 1983,** and she plans to stay there until she graduates from college.
> Stuart visited Boston in **May 1979.**

Rule Use commas before and after the name of a state, province, or country when it is used with the name of a city. Do not use commas between a state and its ZIP code.

> Arlene lives in **Lincoln, Wisconsin,** with her brother and sister-in-law.
> Craig carefully wrote the following address on the package: John Saxon, 100 South Street, Waltham, **MA 02154.**

Rule Use a comma after the greeting, or salutation, of a social letter and after the complimentary close of any letter.

> Dear Roseann,   Sincerely yours,   Yours truly,

Exercise 2   Commas On your paper, rewrite the following sentences, using commas where necessary.

> **SAMPLE**   Yes Norma does plan to play softball next year.
> **ANSWER**   Yes, Norma does plan to play softball next year.

1. Lyndon B. Johnson was a United States representative a senator and the Vice President before he became President.
2. Sam borrowed the library book he read the first chapter and he copied some information for his research.
3. Ms. Slade a noted historian lectured about the events leading up to the Civil War the war itself and the Reconstruction.
4. We can try either Indonesian Chinese or Vietnamese cuisine in this city.
5. After his death in 1792 the naval hero John Paul Jones was buried in the chapel at the United States Naval Academy.
6. The Dobson family has purchased a new time-saving lawnmower.
7. Whatever caused it it had a disruptive effect on the whole community.

8. The outcome of their experiment unfortunately was rather disappointing.
9. Signing the contract in the presence of a witness the partners were ready to begin their business venture.
10. The architect who won the prize for the best design received the award on June 11 1975 at a small ceremony.

3.2c Semicolons

Semicolons are used to connect independent clauses and to clarify meaning in sentences that contain a number of commas.

Rule Use a semicolon to connect independent clauses.

Without a Coordinating Conjunction. Use a semicolon in a compound sentence to connect closely related independent clauses that are *not* joined by a coordinating conjunction.

> Many times we prepared to turn back; swift rapids nearly tipped the canoes.

With a Conjunctive Adverb, or an Explanatory Expression. Use a semicolon to connect independent clauses that are joined by a conjunctive adverb (*page 31*) or an explanatory expression. Use a comma after the conjunctive adverb or after the explanatory expression.

> The members of the diving team were excited about being in the state finals; **however,** each member seemed calm when the event began.
> Hal really enjoyed his trip to Canada; **in fact,** he said that it was the best trip he had ever taken.

Rule Use a semicolon to clarify meaning in a sentence that contains several commas.

Independent Clauses. Use a semicolon to clarify and separate independent clauses that have several commas within them, even when a coordinating conjunction is used.

I have studied the works of Ralph Waldo Emerson, a neighbor of one of my ancestors; and I would also like to study the works of Henry David Thoreau, Louisa May Alcott, and Bronson Alcott.

Items in a Series. Use semicolons to separate items in a series if those items have internal commas. The semicolons make clear how many items are in the series.

UNCLEAR	The main characters are Walter, a talented but unrecognized young artist, Pamela, a dedicated art student, Will, a famous art critic, and Harriet, a patron of the arts. [four or seven characters?]
CLEAR	The main characters are Walter, a talented but unrecognized young artist; Pamela, a dedicated art student; Will, a famous art critic; and Harriet, a patron of the arts. [four characters]

Exercise 3 Semicolons On your paper, write each sentence, adding semicolons where they are needed. You may need to replace commas with semicolons to make a sentence clearer.

SAMPLE	She had already seen the movie therefore, she stayed at home.
ANSWER	She had already seen the movie; therefore, she stayed at home.

1. Rhode Island is the smallest state in the country it measures forty-eight miles north to south and thirty-seven miles east to west.
2. The poinsettia grows outdoors in southern states, but, because of its vibrant red and green coloring, it is also a popular indoor plant during the winter months in cold climates.
3. Neptune was the god of the sea in Roman mythology he resembled the Greek sea god Poseidon.
4. Edgar Allan Poe published "The Raven" in 1845 as a result, the poem brought him great recognition, and it is still read widely today.
5. Sara had been expecting an important call all afternoon therefore she dashed to the telephone and picked up the receiver after the first ring.
6. The most valuable players on Gainesville High School's varsity baseball team include Greg Hillman, the catcher, Chuck Ruggeroli, the shortstop, and Frank Fletcher, an outfielder.
7. This train stops at Riverview, Oakland, and Raymond, but it does not stop at Marston.

8. The view from the top of the skyscraper was unclear, however, we could see the tugboats in the harbor as they pushed the ocean liner out to sea.

9. Cheryl wanted to go blackberry-picking at a local farm however, when she arrived, she found that the berries were not ripe.

10. The merchandise arrived on Friday, the last possible day the store was able to have the sale, and, although they had little time to browse, the customers were quite pleased.

3.2d Colons

Rule Use a colon to introduce an explanatory phrase or a statement or a list of items that completes a sentence. The part of a sentence before a list may contain a demonstrative word such as *these* or *those* or an expression such as *the following* or *as follows*.

> The disappointing news was reported to the waiting crowd: **the building would have to be torn down.**
> New legislation will affect the following cities: **Frankfort, Louisville, and Bowling Green.**
> Of the marsupials, he was able to study these: **kangaroos, koalas, and opossums.**

Do *not* use a colon to introduce a list that immediately follows a verb or a preposition.

> The graphic design **includes** triangles, parallelograms, and circles. [not *includes:*]
> What products are made **in** Venezuela, Bolivia, and Brazil? [not *in:*]

Rule Use a colon to separate two independent clauses when the second clause explains or completes the first sentence.

> I think I know why I have read that book three times: I have the same outlook on life that the main character has.

Rule Use a colon to separate the hour and minutes in an expression of time, the chapter and verse in a Biblical reference, the title and subtitle of a book, and the volume and page number of a book or magazine reference.

3:22 P.M.   *Wheels and Wagons: Early Transportation*
Genesis 12:2   *Mountaineering Monthly* 6:72

Rule   Use a colon after the salutation of a business letter.

Dear Mr. Statler: Dear Ms. Fortuna:

Rule   Use a colon to introduce a direct quotation.

Dr. Doneski began her presentation with these words: "I feel honored to be speaking to such a distinguished group."

Exercise 4   Colons   Some of the sentences that follow need colons. On your paper, write the sentences, supplying colons where needed. If a sentence is correct as it is, write *Correct*.

SAMPLE   The artist bought the following supplies charcoal, an
            easel, and a sketch pad.

ANSWER   The artist bought the following supplies: charcoal, an
            easel, and a sketch pad.

1. Marge went to the post office with an armful of materials to mail letters, parcels, and postcards.
2. Because the sidewalks were slick after the storm, Virginia gave the following advice to her students "Watch out for icy patches."
3. In order to get to the gym in time for the 800 P.M. tip-off, we will have to leave by 715 P.M.
4. John Paul Jones's response to the British commander's demand for surrender is famous "I have not yet begun to fight."
5. Mr. Perry referred to an article about geological exploration in *Scientific American* 245 2.
6. A golfer might use the following clubs woods, irons, and a putter.
7. For my course in traditions of Western literature, I read Genesis 2 15.
8. Before moving to her new home, Barbara read an informative book entitled *Florida Ponce de Leon to the Present.*
9. Dear Mr. Saunders
        Thank you very much for your helpful letter that suggests people to contact in the area, information to include with my application, and possible employment opportunities in the Midwest.

10. The group arrived equipped with hoes, rakes, shovels, plant food, and a watering can.

3.2e   Quotation Marks

Rule   Use quotation marks to show that you are writing the exact words that someone said, thought, or wrote. Use quotation marks at both the beginning and the end of the quotation.

Do not use quotation marks around an **indirect quotation:** a retelling, in the writer's words, of what another person said, thought, or wrote.

> Eliza asked, "**May** I borrow this tape recorder?"
> Vic said, "**The** opera *The Magic Flute* was on the radio last night, and I really enjoyed listening to it."
> Vic said that he thoroughly enjoyed listening to *The Magic Flute* on the radio last night. [indirect quotation]

Dialogue. When you are writing dialogue, begin a new paragraph and use a separate set of quotation marks each time the speaker changes.

> "**Did** you check the source of your information?" Dale asked.
> "**Of** course," replied Irene. "I always double-check information concerning a controversial subject."

Brief Quotations. If you are writing a brief quotation that continues for more than one paragraph, use opening quotation marks at the beginning of each paragraph, but use end quotation marks only at the end of the last paragraph.

> "**No**, he had never written about Paris. Not the Paris that he cared about. But what about the rest that he had never **written?** [no quotation marks]
>
> "**What** about the ranch and the silvered gray of the sage brush, the quick, clear water in the irrigation ditches, and the heavy green of the **alfalfa.**"
>
> Ernest Hemingway, "The Snows of Kilimanjaro"

Long Quotations. When you are copying a quotation of five or more lines, set it off from the rest of your paper by indenting it five spaces from the left and right margins. Single-space the quotation if you are typing. Do *not* use quotation marks with a quotation that is set off in this way.

Rule Use quotation marks to set off the title of a short story, an article, an essay, a short poem, or a song.

Use quotation marks to set off the title of any piece that forms part of a larger work such as the following: a single television show that is part of a series, a chapter of a book, a section of a newspaper, or a feature in a magazine. (See also page 202.)

> Miguel will recite Browning's poem **"My Last Duchess."**
>
> Please rehearse **"The Impossible Dream,"** the second song in the show.
>
> The sixth and final episode, entitled **"Today's Environment,"** was informative.
>
> Luke always reads the **"Hints for Hikers"** column in *Wilderness* magazine.

Rule Use quotation marks to call attention to the special nature of such words as nicknames used with a person's full name, technical terms, and odd expressions.

> Colonel Edwin E. **"Buzz"** Aldrin, Jr., participated in the historic moon-landing mission.
>
> The bottom of a hydroplane is designed so that the boat **"planes"** on the surface of the water.

Note: The preceding rule is for informal usage only. Avoid such usage in formal writing if possible.

Rule Use quotation marks to set off a word that defines another word.

> I use the word *calculating* to mean **"shrewd."**

Other Punctuation with Quotation Marks. The following rules will help you to determine where and how to use single quotation marks, commas, periods, colons, semicolons, question marks, and exclamation points with quotation marks.

Rule Use single quotation marks around a quotation or a title that occurs within a longer quoted passage.

> "Watch the episode called **'The Industrial Revolution'** at eight o'clock tonight," said Mr. Creiger.

Rule Place a comma or a period inside closing quotation marks.

> "Return one day and visit," suggested our guide, "for I have enjoyed showing you some of the spectacular sights this city has to offer."

Rule Place a semicolon or a colon outside closing quotation marks.

> Grady reported, "The dam is close to overflowing"; consequently, safety measures were taken immediately.
>
> Now I remember why I carefully read the article "How to Improve Your Memory": I didn't want to forget any of the details.

Rule Place a question mark or an exclamation point inside the closing quotation marks if it applies only to the material quoted. If the entire sentence is a question or an exclamation, place the question mark or exclamation point outside the closing quotation marks. If both the quotation and the sentence require a question mark or an exclamation point, put the end mark inside the closing quotation marks.

> Loren wondered, "Did I miss the appointment?" [The quotation itself is a question.]
>
> Did Alicia say, "I think that I will buy a digital watch"? [The entire sentence, not the quotation, is a question.]
>
> How did you answer the question "What is your job experience?" [Both the quotation and the sentence are questions.]

Exercise 5 Quotation Marks On your paper, write correctly the sentences that need single or double quotation marks. Be sure to use capitalization, other punctuation, and paragraphing correctly. If a sentence needs no quotation marks, write *Correct* on your paper.

| **SAMPLE** | Why did they leave asked Larry. |
| **ANSWER** | "Why did they leave?" asked Larry. |

1. Kenny watched the production of the episode The Eisenhower Era for the television series *News Watch*.
2. Do you know the lyrics to the song Give My Regards to Broadway? asked Mr. Rodgers.
3. The great Charlie Bird Parker was noted for playing the alto saxophone.
4. Grace wondered where the next exposition would be held.
5. Golf originated in Scotland Peter said in the twelfth century.
6. Marianne said to her friend Lise, We should be arriving at the most scenic point of the park very shortly.
7. Scholars have searched for years to find the actual urn described in John Keats's poem Ode on a Grecian Urn.
8. How does sleet differ from hail? asked Warren. Although sleet and hail are formed in nearly the same way, sleet occurs only in the winter, replied Mrs. Hartwick.
9. When Lenore said, Pack these items, she gave us a helpful list for travel in Europe.
10. The artist explained that *intaglio* means engraving.

3.2f   The Apostrophe

Possessives

Rule   Use an apostrophe to show possession.

Singular and Plural Nouns. Use an apostrophe and an *s* (*'s*) to form the possessive of a singular noun or a plural noun that does not end in *s*.

| the bear's cubs | the people's choice |
| Keats's poetry | the sheep's grazing land |

Plural Nouns Ending in s. Use an apostrophe alone to form the possessive of a plural noun that ends in *s*.

| the settlers' land | the Elks' convention |
| the Davises' house | the petitioners' plea |

Do not add an apostrophe or *'s* to **possessive personal pronouns:** *mine, yours, his, hers, its, ours, theirs.* They already show ownership.

The house is finally **ours**!
Isn't that jacket **his**?

Compound Nouns. Change the last word of a compound noun (*page 4*) to the possessive form.

the passer-**by's** comment
the bell**boys'** uniforms

Joint Ownership. Use the possessive form of only the last person's name when a thing is jointly owned. Use the possessive form of each name when two or more people each possess separate items.

Richard Rodgers and Oscar Hammerstein**'s** musicals
Wallace Stevens**'s** and T.S. Eliot**'s** poetry

Expressions Ending in s. Use an apostrophe alone to form the possessive of most expressions that end in *s* or the sound of *s*.

for goodness**'** sake   three years**'** work

Ancient Classical Names Ending in s. Use an apostrophe alone to form the possessive of ancient classical names that end in *s*.

Socrates**'** dialogues   Hippocrates**'** oath

Contractions

Rule Use an apostrophe to replace letters or numbers that have been left out in a contraction.

I **can't** lift these barrels by myself.
They'll be ready to leave in less than an hour.
Were the clothing styles of the **'20s** quite different?

Plural Forms

Rule Use an apostrophe and an *s* (*'s*) to form the plural of letters, numbers, symbols, and words that you are referring to as words or symbols.

Use italics (underlining) correctly in forming plurals with apostrophes. Do not underline the *'s*.

There are three *s*'s in *dissatisfied*.
The vote received twenty-five *yea*'s and three *nay*'s.
She told him to mind his *p*'s and *q*'s.

Note: The plurals of abbreviations that do not include periods are formed by adding just *-s*.

There are several **PTAs** in our school district.

BUT The **PTA**'s on the poster were faded. [Referring to the letters, not to the organization.]

Although names of years are written with numerals, they also usually function as words and should be treated as such.

My grandmother told stories about growing up in New England in the early **1900s.**

BUT The *1983*'s were blurred in Chapter 2 and Chapter 17. [Referring to the numerals, not to the year.]

Exercise 6   Apostrophes   On your paper, write correctly the sentences that need apostrophes. If a sentence needs no apostrophes, write *Correct*.

SAMPLE   Phylliss bike is in the repair shop.
ANSWER   Phyllis's bike is in the repair shop.

1. The mens track teams at the University of Southern California held state championships throughout the 1960s.
2. How many *ss* and *is* are there in *Mississippi*?
3. Lewis and Clarks expedition to the Pacific Ocean strengthened the claims of the United States to the northwestern territory.
4. The Gianellis collie wound his chain around the chestnut tree in their back yard.
5. Saddle shoes reached their height of popularity during the 1950s.
6. The class vote was tied with sixteen *yes*s and sixteen *no*s.

7. Stephen told the other attorneys that his view of the case was the same as theirs.

8. Stephanies science-fair project on solar energy won two prizes: a blue ribbon and the Best of Show award.

9. The *s* key sticks on both Chriss and Ellens electric typewriters.

10. "Weve done it! Weve scaled the mountain!" exclaimed Ryan as we reached the top of Pine Peak.

3.2g   Hyphens, Dashes, and Ellipsis Points

The Hyphen

Rule   Use a hyphen to divide a word at the end of a line.

Do not divide a word of one syllable, such as *washed* or *grieve*. Do not divide any word so that one letter stands by itself.

Always divide a word between its syllables and in such a way that the reader will not be confused about its meaning or pronunciation.

INCORRECT	Marsha went to the bank Friday and **cash-ed** her paycheck. [*Cashed* is a word of one syllable.]
CORRECT	Marsha went to the bank Friday and **cashed** her paycheck.
INCORRECT	During Jan's vacation trip, the weather was **a-greeable** and the accommodations were satisfactory. [The letter *a* stands by itself.]
CORRECT	During Jan's vacation trip the weather was **agree-able** and the accomodations were satisfactory.

Prefixes and Suffixes. Divide a word with a prefix only after the prefix. Divide a word with a suffix only before the suffix.

Paula and Frank told me that they attended an important **inter-national** conference last week.

The only way to open the lock is to turn the dial in a **clock-wise** direction.

Compound Words. For a compound word that is written as one word, divide it only between the base words. Divide a hyphenated compound word at the hyphen.

> If we work quickly, we will be able to finish everything **some-time** in February.
>
> He described his trip to the mountains during the storm as a **hair-raising** experience.

Rule Use a hyphen after the prefixes *all-*, *ex-*, and *self-*. Use a hyphen to separate any prefix from a proper noun or adjective.

all-purpose	**Neo-**Platonism	BUT	**neo**phyte
ex-president	**pre-**Alexandrian	BUT	**pre**view
self-assured	**intra-**Asian	BUT	**intra**state

Note: Do not use a hyphen between most other prefixes and their root words.

> **en**title   **pre**determine   **sub**standard

Rule Use a hyphen after the prefix of a word that is spelled the same as another word but has a different origin and meaning (a homograph).

> re-collect   re-count   re-form
> recollect   recount   reform

Rule Use a hyphen after the prefix of a word when the last letter of the prefix is a vowel and is the same as the first letter of the base word.

> de-**e**scalate   pre-**e**minent   re-**e**ducate

Rule Hyphenate a compound adjective when it precedes the noun that it modifies, but not when it follows it. Do not hyphenate a compound adjective when its first word is an adverb that ends in *-ly.*

> Kate admires this **well-written** column.
>
> This column that Kate admires is **well written.**

The moderator introduced **up-to-date** issues.

The issues that the moderator introduced were **up to date**.

A **barely moving** train slowed to a complete stop in order to avoid an obstruction on the tracks.

Fractions. Hyphenate a fraction that is used as a modifier. Do not hyphenate a fraction that is used as a noun.

MODIFIER   The soup was **two-thirds** water.

NOUN   **One third** of the soup was vegetables.

Rule Use a hyphen to separate compound numbers from *twenty-one* through *ninety-nine*.

forty-nine   seventy-three

BUT   five hundred   ninety thousand

The Dash

Rule Use a dash to show an interruption in a thought or in a statement. Use a second dash to end the interruption if the sentence continues.

"If we can just—"; suddenly he had another idea.

Someone—**I think it's Barbara**—will bring the table decorations.

Appositives and Parenthetical Expressions. Use dashes when appositives or parenthetical expressions have internal commas.

We will need some equipment—**I think that a tent, sleeping bags, backpacks, and cooking utensils will do**—before we can plan an overnight camping trip.

Several colors—**orange, green, and violet, for example**—are made up of combinations of other colors.

In typing, use two hyphens to represent a dash. Do not type a single hyphen to stand for a dash.

Note: Avoid the overuse of dashes in formal writing.

Ellipsis Points

Rule   Use **ellipsis points,** a set of three spaced periods (. . .), to indicate an omission or a pause in written or quoted material.

> A little neglect may breed great mischief . . . for want of a nail the shoe was lost; for want of a shoe the horse was lost; and for want of a horse the rider was lost.
>
> Benjamin Franklin, *Poor Richard's Almanac*

Other Punctuation Marks. If what precedes the ellipsis points is part of a complete sentence, use a period followed by three ellipsis points (. . . .). If what precedes the ellipsis points is not part of a complete sentence, use only the three ellipsis points leaving a space before the first point (. . .). If what precedes the ellipsis points is part of a complete sentence ending with a question mark or an exclamation point, retain that mark before the three ellipsis points.

ORIGINAL PASSAGE

> None of them knew the colour of the sky. Their eyes glanced level, and were fastened upon the waves that swept toward them. These waves were of the hue of slate, save for the tops, which were of foaming white, and all of the men knew the colours of the sea. The horizon narrowed and widened, and dipped and rose, and at all times its edge was jagged with waves that seemed thrust up in points like rocks.
>
> Stephen Crane, "The Open Boat"

ABRIDGED PASSAGE

> None of them knew the colour of the sky. Their eyes . . . were fastened upon the waves. . . . These waves were of the hue of slate, . . . and all the men knew the colours of the sea. The horizon narrowed and widened, . . . and at all times its edge was jagged with waves. . . .

Sentences and Paragraphs. Use a line of periods to indicate the omission of a stanza of poetry or of an entire paragraph from written material.

Exercise 7 Hyphens, Dashes, Ellipsis Points On your paper, copy the following sentences. Add hyphens, dashes, and ellipsis points where necessary.

> **SAMPLE** Sharon likes to study pre Columbian art.
>
> **ANSWER** Sharon likes to study pre-Columbian art.

1. Muriel was obviously self conscious as she practiced her speech.
2. Please take that package if you haven't already done so to the post office this afternoon.
3. Steven wrote down the beginning of the Preamble to the Constitution of the United States: "We the People of the United States, in order to form a more perfect Union."
4. The grocery bill for one week amounted to forty three dollars.
5. I found *Robinson Crusoe* so fascinating that I read 175 pages in a single evening one third of Defoe's novel!
6. Joanne spent most of Saturday shopping for a new all weather coat.
7. The application form was three quarters essay questions and one quarter statistical information.
8. Someone I think it was your brother telephoned while you were at the meeting.
9. The rarely shown film received good reviews for its accurate portrayal of pre Victorian life.
10. The dusty carriage slowed to a stop, and when the travel weary passengers stepped out, they were delighted to view a many hued rainbow.

3.2h   Parentheses and Brackets

Parentheses

Rule Use parentheses to enclose material that is not basic to the meaning of the sentence.

> Kathleen requested information from the FEC (**Federal Election Commission**) about the campaign funds of the congressional candidates in her district.
> Senator Blake (**Utah**) will serve on the committee.
> The cardinal (**sometimes called the redbird**) is the state bird of Illinois.

Other Punctuation with Parentheses. Place commas, semicolons and colons outside parentheses. Place periods outside parentheses unless the parenthetical material is a separate sentence beginning with a capital letter; then place the period inside the parentheses. Place question marks and exclamation points inside the parentheses if they are part of the parenthetical material; otherwise place them outside the parentheses.

Brackets

Rule Use brackets to enclose explanations, or comments that are inserted in a quotation, but that are not part of the quotation.

> The tour guide said, "It [the Great Salt Lake] is four to five times as salty as the ocean."

Use brackets to enclose parenthetical information that is part of the material already in parentheses.

> Over a dozen oil companies are bidding for the rights to drill in the Atlantic Ocean off the New Jersey shore. (Today's newspaper also contains an article on the environmental risks of off-shore drilling [see p. 56].)

Other Punctuation with Brackets. The only punctuation marks used with brackets are those within the bracketed material.

Exercise 8 Parentheses and Brackets On your paper, write the following sentences, using parentheses and brackets correctly.

SAMPLE	I recognized Chuck he was wearing his cowboy hat the moment he walked through the door.
ANSWER	I recognized Chuck (he was wearing his cowboy hat) the moment he walked through the door.

1. Old Faithful it received its name in 1870 erupts continuously four minutes out of every sixty-five.
2. Thomas Jefferson relied on elements of classical European architecture when he designed Monticello Charlottesville, Virginia.

3. Barbara Sorenson '72 attended law school after graduation and is now legal advisor to the public utilities commission in Clark County.

4. The term *psychology* is derived from the Greek words *psyche* "soul" and *logos* "word."

5. The textbook described a case of ornithophobia fear of birds and listed several other interesting studies.

6. Nathaniel Hawthorne wrote *The House of the Seven Gables* 1851, a riveting tale about descendants of the Pyncheon family.

7. The pamphlet gives the following information: "The population of Virginia City, Nevada, see photograph and caption below the most famous ghost town in the United States, dwindled from a high of 23,000 people 1876 to the current 450 permanent residents."

8. Our physics class was taught by a substitute Mr. DuPont had left a complete set of instructions for a whole week.

9. The explorer's memoirs included this account: "Several times during our trek through the Canadian wilderness, our party was forced to portage carry canoes."

10. One of the biographies was about the British bacteriologist Sir Alexander Fleming, who was awarded the Nobel Prize 1945 for his work.

Assignment Punctuation Write a paragraph that states an opinion that you would like your readers to accept. (See the first two pages of Unit 8, "Persuasive Writing.") First, write your paragraph omitting all punctuation marks except periods. Read the paragraph as written. Does it effectively convey what you want to say? Is it convincing enough to influence your readers? Then rewrite the paragraph, using additional punctuation correctly.

3.3   Using Italics and Numbers in Writing

3.3a   Italics

In printed material, certain words and symbols are set in italic type (*slanted letters like these*). In handwriting and typing, you should underline such words and symbols according to the following rules.

Rule Italicize (underline) the names or titles of books, book-length poems, newspapers, magazines, periodicals, plays, movies, television series, paintings, trains, ships, aircraft, and so forth.

Italicize (underline) an article (*a, an, the*) that comes before a title only if it is part of the title. (See also page 190.)

> *The Portrait of a Lady*　　　　*Paradise Lost*
> *Casablanca*　　　　　　　　　*Apollo 11*

Rule Italicize (underline) letters, numbers, symbols, and words when you are referring to them as words or symbols.

> I marked a *21* in the last column to complete the store's inventory.
> Ryan noticed that *occasionally* was misspelled in the caption.

Rule Italicize (underline) words from other languages if those words are not commonly used in English. Do not italicize foreign place names or currency.

> 　　　A spontaneous shout of appreciation followed the singer's solo, the *pièce de résistance* of the evening.
>
> BUT　Paula spent the day at the Musée de Louvre. This new restaurant has a standard à la carte menu. [À la carte is commonly used in English.]

Italicize (underline) a word or phrase that you wish to emphasize. Avoid overuse of this device.

> "After *hours* of work," reported the excited archaelogist, "we finally found evidence of a structure."

Exercise 1   Italics On your paper, copy the following sentences, underlining (italicizing) wherever necessary.

> SAMPLE　　This account describes the fate of the passenger ship Lusitania.
>
> ANSWER　　This account describes the fate of the passenger ship Lusitania.

1. The 1927 Warner Brothers production of The Jazz Singer, which included a speaking role by Al Jolson, brought an end to the era of silent films.
2. "Homogenize should be divided between the g and the e," announced the typist.
3. Did you read the article about the Dodgers in this morning's Los Angeles Times?
4. Maureen spells her surname, MacDonald, with a capital M and a capital D: MacDonald.
5. Louis yelled "Au revoir!" to his friends as he ran to catch the airport bus.
6. Virgil drew upon the works of the Greek poet Homer as he composed the Aeneid, his epic on the founding of Rome.
7. Was Renoir's Oarsman at Chatou on exhibit when you visited the National Gallery of Art?
8. Lou methodically wrote in the $'s next to each number on the club's record of annual dues that had been paid.
9. Everyone laughed at the list of faux pas described in the nineteenth-century handbook of social etiquette.
10. Stuart has resolved to write his e's more legibly so they will not look like c's.

3.3b   Using Numbers in Writing

Rule Spell out numbers of one hundred or less. Spell out numbers that are rounded to hundreds and that can be written in two words or less.

> Ferdinand Magellan's expedition from Spain began with **five** ships, yet only **three** of them continued the trip to the Pacific Ocean.
> Were there nearly **one thousand** boxes of hats delivered yesterday?

BUT   Nina collected **1250** postcards from around the world.

Note: Do not mix numerals and words when writing two or more numbers in the same category.

| INCORRECT | **Two hundred** general practitioners and **350** specialists attended the convention on May 29. |
| CORRECT | **Two hundred** general practitioners and **three hundred fifty** specialists attended the convention on May 29. [Words are used to describe the numbers of people in attendance; numerals are used in the dates.] |

Rule   Spell out any number that begins a sentence, or rewrite the sentence.

The word *and* is unnecessary in writing numbers except those numbers between *one hundred* and *one hundred and ten*, and so forth.

INCORRECT	**106** guardrails will be placed along that steep incline.
CORRECT	**One hundred and six** guardrails will be placed along that steep incline.
CORRECT	Along that steep incline, **106** guardrails will be placed.

Ordinal numbers. Spell out ordinal numbers (first, second, third, and so forth) in your writing. You may write the day of the month as an ordinal number preceding the month, but the month followed by an Arabic numeral is the preferred form.

fifth day	June 8
seventh grade	eighth of June

Compound numbers. Hyphenate compound numbers from *twenty-one* through *ninety-nine*.

thirty-two	eighty-six	ninety-three

Spell out cardinal numbers (one, two, three, and so forth) that occur in a compound with nouns or adjectives.

five-dollar tickets	twenty-pound turkey

Rule   Spell out an expression of time unless it is a specific time using A.M. or P.M. Use numerals and A.M. or P.M. in all technical writing.

Ruth usually leaves her apartment around **eight o'clock.**

BUT   My computer printout was finished at **3:51 A.M.**

Rule Use numerals to express dates, street numbers, room numbers, apartment numbers, telephone numbers, page numbers, and percentages. Spell out the word *percent*.

July 16, 1925   pages 56–101
122 San Gabriel Avenue   10 percent

Dates. When you write a date, do not add -*st, -nd, -rd,* or -*th* to the numeral.

INCORRECT   May 5th, 1971   October 2nd

CORRECT   May 5, 1971   October 2

Exercise 2 Numbers in Writing On your paper, write the following sentences, correcting any errors in the writing of numbers.

SAMPLE   The gas stove is not working in Apartment Twelve.
ANSWER   The gas stove is not working in Apartment 12.

1. The human foot has 26 bones, including 7 ankle bones, 5 instep bones, and 14 toe bones.
2. 105 members of the Tacoma chapter of the Audubon Society were present at the meeting held on Thursday, March 3rd.
3. Marcie sold 200 bumper stickers during the campaign to raise funds for the recreation center.
4. The Garcías packed one hundred and three boxes before they were ready to move to their house at seventy two Crescent Drive.
5. Did you know that the average watermelon is ninety three % water?
6. In 1909 Robert Peary reached the North Pole on the 6th of April; he was the first person to make this journey.
7. We observed and took notes on the chimpanzee's behavior for 2 hours until the building closed at 4 o'clock.
8. Remember to bring your 2 dollar coupon when we meet for dinner at 6 o'clock.

9. Only 10% of the two hundred and ninety seven applicants sent all of the necessary forms to Sacramento by the April 15th deadline.

10. The article about F. Scott Fitzgerald is 5 pages long; it runs from page 87 to page 91.

Assignment 1   Italics   Write a paragraph about one of the three topics listed. Include in your passage as many of the following as you reasonably can: titles, foreign words, words used emphatically, letters, numbers, and symbols. Check your paragraph for correct underlining (italicizing).

1. A trip that you have taken or would like to take
2. An exciting sports event that you recently attended
3. The works of a well-known author or a well-known musician

Assignment 2   Numbers in Writing   Find information about one of the planets in our solar system. Your information should answer some of the following questions:

1. What is the distance of the planet from the sun?
2. How long does it take the planet to make one revolution around the sun?
3. What is the size of the planet?
4. Does the planet have any satellites? If so, how many does it have?

Write a short paragraph about the planet, using numbers correctly.

Using Mechanics

You are planning to teach a continuing education course in a subject that you know very well. You have been asked to write a brief description of the course for a brochure that will be mailed to members of your community. In your description give your prospective students the following information: course title, time and place, and starting and ending dates. Then describe your own background, education, and degrees in the subject area, including any awards or special recognition that you have received. Then describe the course itself. Highlight aspects that you think will be particularly appealing to prospective students. Suggest books or articles to be read as background material, and list all of the reading that will be required for the course. As you write your description, make sure that you correctly use mechanics: capitalization, punctuation, underlining (italicizing), and numbers.

3.4   Preparing Your Manuscript

3.4a   Proofreading Symbols

The following symbols are commonly used to identify and correct errors in composition. Use them when you revise and proofread your writing.

∧	insert something	lost her *balance* walking on stilts
#	space	bought a red#balloon
¶	begin new paragraph	last of the heroes. ¶ In the next century
∼	transpose letter or words	this fabﬁrc ⁀made has⁀
ℓ	delete	a mountaintop ~~top~~ retreat

(Continue on the next page.)

◯ close up letters	I am happ◯y to introduce
.... let it stand (under something crossed out)	consisted of a ~~large~~ percentage
≡ capitalize	the Department of agriculture ≡
/ make lower case	Marlene gazed at the /portrait.

3.4b   Manuscript Form

Handwritten Manuscripts

Paper.   Write on standard-size paper (8½ by 10 inches or 8½ by 11 inches). Write on one side only.

Ink.   Use black or blue ink.

Margins.   Leave margins of 1½ inches at the left side and 1 inch at the right side. The left margin must be even.

Title.   Write the title, if any, in the center of the top line. Skip at least one line between the title and the first paragraph. Do not put quotation marks around the title.

Indentation.   Indent the first line of every paragraph about 1 inch.

Typewritten Manuscripts

Paper.   Use standard-size white typing paper (8½ by 11 inches). Double space, and use only one side of the paper.

Ribbon.   Use a black typewriter ribbon.

Margins.   Leave margins of 1½ inches at the left side and 1 inch at the right side. The left margin must be even. On all pages except the title page, place the first line at least 1 inch below the top of the page. Leave a margin of 1 inch at the bottom of all pages.

Title.   Center the title about 2 inches below the top of the page. Do not put quotation marks around the title. Begin the first paragraph four lines below the title.

Indentation.   Indent the first line of every paragraph five spaces.

Labeling and Numbering Pages

Unless your teacher gives you other instructions, write your name, the subject, and the date (in that order) in the upper-right corner of the first page. On every page except the first page, put the page number in the upper-right corner. Use Arabic numerals.

If your paper consists of more than one page, attach the pages at the upper-left corner with a staple or a paper clip.

Unit Practice

Practice 1

A. Capitalization (*pages 171–177*)   On your paper, rewrite each of the following sentences, supplying the appropriate capitalization.

1. the meteor never reached earth, according to the account in *science news*.
2. when uncle kenneth decided to clean and repair the old boat, all of his nephews and nieces were willing to help him.
3. historians cite tremendous progress in commerce, science, and the arts during the renaissance.
4. one of the most popular courses, ceramics II, is being offered again this semester at the community center.
5. "oh, no!" exclaimed coach o'leary. "we have only three minutes remaining on the clock."
6. A new restaurant that will open next wednesday features polynesian cuisine.
7. in order to reach san diego, turn southwest on the expressway and head south for several miles.
8. the *broadway limited* leaves new york at 2:10 p.m., and it is scheduled to arrive in chicago at 9:15 a.m.
9. the original bill of rights can be viewed in the national archives building in washington, d.c.
10. send this sample copy of the *williamette gazette* to 125 gurney street, wilmington, de 19899.

B. Punctuation (*pages 177–201*)   On your paper, rewrite each of the following sentences, supplying the appropriate punctuation.

11. Comments about this years proposed budget appear in *Congressional News* pages 60 62
12. On the large white chart Betsy please add the symbol *Ni* where the element nickel is written said Mrs. Stewart
13. Speaking at a recent meeting of the EEC European Economic Community a representative began a speech as follows The climate for exports this quarter was generally good
14. One of the meanings of the word *extract* is concentration for example plants and herbs yield flavored extracts used in cooking

15. Dear Aunt Loretta
    Yes Im anxious to see you
    I'll arrive at 3 30 PM on Tuesday
16. Doreen wanted to see the play however she was not able to get reasonably priced tickets
17. Kyle enjoyed reading the biographical sketch of Lawrence Yogi Berra
18. Her brother in laws performance of September Song received a good review in *Songfest* 12 81
19. Dawn read three chapters Our Constitution The Supreme Court and Political Parties in a book about government
20. The honored guests at the celebration were Dora Graham a fashion designer Burt Chester a reporter and Evelyn DuBarry a physicist

C. Italics and Numbers in Writing (*pages 201–207*)   On your paper, rewrite each of the following sentences, underlining the words that should be italicized and correcting all errors in the use of numbers in writing.

21. According to the sports page of the Baltimore Sun, your favorite team lost by 23 points.
22. On November 12th each voter will mark an x on a paper ballot.
23. Ray and Jamie will be late for the seven-thirty P.M. showing of the classic film Mutiny on the Bounty.
24. The words For Sale were written on a sign that the owner of the sailboat Belle Isle had attached to its mast.
25. Almost 3000 ticketholders crowded the auditorium on the 2nd day of the concert tour.
26. On page two hundred sixty-eight of the detective novel, the modus operandi of the clever sleuth was clearly described.
27. Were there actually four hundred twenty-two participants in the dance marathon that was held on June 27th, 1952?
28. 25 members of the French Club will meet at thirty-seven Hillcrest Avenue at two o'clock on Friday.
29. Gilbert and Sullivan's musical The Mikado will be presented on April 14th and 15th.
30. Del told me to look for the office building with the 34 written over the door; it is the only 30-story building on the block.

(Continue on the next page.)

Practice 2

Rewrite the following passage, supplying the appropriate capitalization, punctuation, and italics (underlining), and correcting the use of numbers in writing.

one of the worlds largest art collections is housed in paris france the louvre situated on the northern bank of the river seine has 8 miles of galleries 275,000 pieces of art are estimated to be within the museums one hundred forty rooms the louvre noted for its gothic and renaissance architecture was built by king philip II in the 13th century to be used as a fortress eventually french kings used the louvre as a palace today the museum provides space for the following government offices an art school and museum offices when the private art collections of kings were exhibited in 1793 the louvre became the 1st public art museum visitors to the louvre may view the well known painting mona lisa and the sculpture winged victory of samothrace among the priceless artwork

Unit Tests

Test 1

A. Capitalization (*pages 171–177*) On your paper, rewrite each of the following sentences, supplying the appropriate capitalization.

1. last january the drama club of murphreyville organized an actors' workshop.
2. please purchase a pair of sew-right embroidery scissors at nelson's sewing goods store.
3. arlene, a student teacher, enjoyed preparing lessons for her trigonometry class.
4. the orders were secretly delivered to captain james d. colwell, jr.
5. has astrid returned from a year-long stay at the university in helsinki, finland?
6. Doris asked, "where does the armadillo usually live?"
7. carl copied these lines from "the woodspurge," by dante gabriel rossetti:

> my eyes, wide open, had the run
> of some ten weeds to fix upon;
> among these few, out of the sun,
> the woodspurge flowered, three cups in one.

8. "one of the playwrights who intrigue me," said brett, "is thornton wilder, the author of *our town*."
9. is that an authentic indian arrowhead?
10. the largest planet, named for the god in roman mythology, is jupiter.

B. Punctuation (*pages 177–201*) On your paper, write each of the following sentences, supplying appropriate punctuation.

11. When a glacier melts it forms the following lakes moraines and drumlins
12. The mechanic said to the concerned car owner Don't worry about it well take care of it today
13. Did you watch Roosevelts Youth the first episode of the series asked Stella
14. Don is reading *Crossing the Bering Strait A Personal History* his interest is in nonfiction books

(Continue on the next page.)

15. Robins and Juless projects for the weekend include the following to move the sofa to the other side of the room and to address a package to Powder Springs Ga

16. How much does that wooden rocker if it is for sale cost

17. Auguste Comte a French philosopher coined the term *sociology*

18. Oh dear exclaimed Dr. Peterson Bandages gauze and tongue depressors must be ordered immediately

19. Lets ask tonights lecturer who spoke so enthusiastically at last years banquet if she is available to speak again next year

20. Did Brady read the following comment by the theater reviewer This is an all star cast

C. Italics and Numbers in Writing (*pages 201–207*)   On your paper, rewrite each of the following sentences, underlining the words that should be italicized and correcting all errors in the use of numbers in writing.

21. This month's edition of Vacation Guide lists the 3 most popular resort towns in the United States.

22. When Greg looked at the neon sign in the store window, the M seemed to flicker.

23. 102 interested guests arrived at approximately 8:30 to view the newly acquired objets d'art.

24. A record-breaking train run was achieved when the Jersey Arrow reached a speed of nearly 100 miles per hour.

25. Before the rain began, Jim O'Dell worked steadily, and he was able to harvest 15% of the wheat crop.

26. From a group of two thousand two hundred designs, the executive advertising committee selected Claudia's submission.

27. Gerald and Pam completed the laboratory research project at exactly eight forty-three A.M.

28. When Loren was in the 10th grade, he attended a performance of Bizet's opera Carmen at the Metropolitan Opera House.

29. This new alarm system effectively gives a piercing 30 second warning.

30. Remember to include a $ when you write down the figures in the taxable income column of the form.

Test 2

Rewrite the following passage, supplying the appropriate capitalization, punctuation, and italics (underlining), and correcting the use of numbers in writing.

each autumn approximately 30 writers from all over the world gather to lecture to write to exchange ideas and to view american life where do writers from such diverse countries as ethiopia trinidad and tobago ireland and hungary meet these novelists poets and playwrights congegrate in iowa city iowa prominent foreign writers are invited to the international writing program at the university of iowa the program which was founded by paul engle and is currently directed by hualing nieh engle began on june 9th 1967 the task of creating an esprit de corps or a feeling of harmony among people from so many different cultures is difficult however it is accomplished by a well trained staff an example of this cooperative spirit is the collaboration on translations between american and foreign writers the engles were honored in 1976 when they were nominated for a nobel peace prize by participants in the international writing program

Part Two

Composition

In your work in the future as well as in your assignments now, you will need to present your thoughts to others in essays, reports, and letters. To communicate your ideas clearly in writing, you must develop them thoughtfully and present them in a logical order. In Part Two, you will learn and practice techniques for generating, organizing, and presenting your ideas in effective writing.

Units 4 through 6 explain the process of writing in three steps: prewriting, writing, and revising. Units 7 and 8 provide strategies for writing for a specific purpose: explaining, describing, narrating, or persuading. Units 9 through 13 present the special techniques required for writing essays, research papers, technical reports, and business correspondence.

Unit 4

Prewriting

Unit Preview

To become a good writer, you need to understand the steps in the writing process, learning and practicing them one step at a time. For whatever you are writing, you follow a three-step process: prewriting, writing a draft, and revising.

Prewriting is the planning, exploration, and preparation that you do before you write a first draft. At this stage, you gather ideas for writing, explore them from different angles, and finally focus them by deciding on topics and by identifying a purpose and an audience for your writing. If you work thoroughly at the prewriting stage, you will greatly simplify the actual writing stage.

The following are some prewriting notes on the subject of television.

Used for recreation, education, information

My favorite shows are old movies and documentaries.

Some children spend more time watching TV than attending school.

Cable TV one of fastest growing areas in television industry

CATV transmits programs via cable rather than airwaves.

Most TV shows sponsored by advertisers

How is public TV supported?

TV signals transmitted by relay towers or underground wires

Satellites used in cable TV transmission. How?

Phosphor dots used in color TV

New developments: television-telephones, video disks, large-screen TV, computer hookups to TVs

How was television developed?

How is television programming determined?

What kinds of jobs are available in the TV field?

How are people affected by many hours of watching television?

For Analysis   Reread the prewriting notes, and follow these directions.

1. Write two additional questions that you could ask to find out more about television.
2. List two writing topics that come to mind when you look at these prewriting notes about television.
3. Copy the notes that would be useful if you were planning to write about cable television.

In following these directions, you began to practice the process of prewriting. In this unit you will learn techniques for prewriting. You will find ideas for writing, develop these ideas, and focus your prewriting notes for specific assignments.

4.1   Finding Ideas for Writing

When you write, one of your first tasks is finding something to write about. Prewriting activities will help you to discover ideas for writing and will provide you with a rich collection of source material for later writing assignments. Your goal at this point is simply to record a substantial number of possible subjects in a reasonably orderly way. You will choose a few of these subjects to develop later.

4.1a   Keeping a Writer's Notebook

A good way to assemble ideas for writing is to keep a writer's notebook, in which you record interesting information that you have read, seen, or heard. A writer's notebook is similar to an artist's sketchbook. It is a personal, often spontaneous, record of ideas, thoughts, observations, and experiences. You may record entries in any form that makes sense to you: single words, phrases, lists, sentences, and symbols. Each entry should contain enough information to refresh your memory when you reread it. Along with each entry, you may want to add a question, a related idea, or a possible subject to write about.

The following strategies and examples demonstrate some methods for starting a writer's notebook.

Strategies

1. *Compile a list of your interests, activities, hobbies, talents, and ambitions.* Include notes for each entry.

EXAMPLES	NOTES
Photography	How is a disk camera different from a single-lens reflex camera?
Swimming	Nervous about next week's meet
Debating Club	Paralegal careers— educational requirements? First appointment of woman to Supreme Court How is logic learned?
Hang gliding	Ms. Johnston's hobby (Talk to her) Safety equipment required?

2. *List or briefly record some memorable experiences.* You may include facts, feelings, causes, outcomes, or whatever seems most important to you.

EXAMPLE	NOTES
Saw volcano erupt last summer	Changes in Earth's crust—explanations? Feelings of awe, wonder, fear; relate feelings to myths about natural phenomena

3. *Record problems or issues that interest you.*

EXAMPLES	NOTES
River is polluted (again!).	Why aren't antipollution laws more strictly enforced? Whose interests are served?
School dress code	Seems reasonable; helpful to students—explain

4. *Record anything that you observe, think, or do and want to remember.*

EXAMPLES	NOTES
Saw migrating birds flying in V-formation	Scientific reasons Metaphor for society?
Shook hands with governor	Origin of custom? Dates, reasons

5. *Clip and save pictures, cartoons, and advertisements.*

EXAMPLES	NOTES
Advertisement for kitchen appliance	What kitchen appliances are really necessary? Effect on energy consumption
Political cartoon	Why is dove symbol of peace? Other symbols for peace

6. *React to what you read.* Take notes on subjects or ideas that you would like to learn more about. Include your opinions about what you read.

EXAMPLES	NOTES
A billboard advertisement for suntan lotion	Medical reports on overexposure to sunlight
Newspaper report on immunization program for children	What diseases have been almost eradicated through immunization? Roosevelt had polio—courage to live with disability

Thoreau's *Walden:* "Our life is frittered away by detail . . . Simplicity, simplicity, simplicity!"

My life is growing more complicated. How can I simplify it?

7. *Record your significant viewing and listening experiences.* Radio and television programs, movies, exhibits, performances, and everyday conversations are potential sources of ideas for writing. Think about the ideas that you encounter, and note your responses to those ideas.

EXAMPLES	NOTES
Television documentary about runaways	Common problem. What agencies provide shelter and counseling?
Lecture about Picasso's life and work	Find out about artists who may have influenced his work.

Exercise 1 Prewriting: Writer's Notebook Choose one item from each group below. In your notebook, make a specific entry; then make at least two notes for each entry.

SAMPLE A situation in which you were not assertive

ANSWER New record was defective. Store would not exchange it, so I bought another copy.

Notes: What was intimidating about clerk's manner, words?

"Press" a record—meaning?

1. a. A hobby that, if you pursue it, could lead to a career
   b. An interest that requires some scientific knowledge
   c. A team sport that you play or enjoy watching
2. a. An experience that challenged you to behave maturely
   b. A situation in which you declined a friend's offer of help
   c. An expedition that turned out very differently from what you had anticipated
3. a. An issue that cannot be broached without arousing strong emotions
   b. A political event of current national or international significance
   c. A problem that your school handles well

4. a. An observation of a natural phenomenon
   b. A thought that occurred to you in response to an everyday experience
   c. A series of unlikely coincidences

5. a. A political cartoon that makes a strong point about a national issue
   b. An advertisement for a product that could be harmful to health
   c. A picture that indicates a sentimental attitude toward children

Exercise 2 Prewriting: Writer's Notebook From the list below, choose five items that interest you. Make an entry for each in your notebook. Record any related thoughts, feelings, or ideas that occur to you.

1. Business ethics
2. Chemical research
3. Comedy routines
4. Electronic games
5. Food chains
6. Greek mythology
7. Japanese art
8. Mathematics
9. Medical careers
10. Holiday customs
11. Pet training
12. Political campaigns
13. Stage design
14. Television broadcasting
15. Utility companies
16. Air pollution

Exercise 3 Prewriting: Writer's Notebook Make an entry in your notebook for five of the items that follow. Give a specific example; then record your responses, thoughts, and ideas.

SAMPLE   An interview with a movie actor

ANSWER   Interview with Colin Scott. Wants to play a fish next
             —how could that be staged? His kind of humor is
             bizarre—what other kinds of humor are there?

1. A novel in which the main character does not conform in some way
2. A paragraph from a textbook, magazine, or newspaper
3. A conversation that you had with a child
4. A comic strip or cartoon that deals with some human weakness
5. A situation comedy that conveys a serious message
6. A concert, dance performance, or song to which you had a strong response
7. A ceremony you have witnessed that marks a passage from one stage of life to another

8. A discussion or debate in which you participated
9. A newspaper or television editorial on an issue that you consider important
10. A comment by a political leader
11. A letter that you have received or written
12. A novel or an article that deals with some past era

4.1b   Analyzing and Interpreting Information

Another way to find ideas for writing is to analyze and interpret what you read, see, and hear. As you analyze and interpret, you attempt to go beyond the words, events, and sounds in order to understand them in a way that was not immediately obvious. From your new understanding, you may find ideas for writing.

The following questions will help you to begin analyzing and interpreting information. Not every question will apply to every kind of material, and you will probably think of other questions as you work.

1. Which statements can be proved, and which cannot?
2. Does the work seem to indicate that the author (or painter, dancer, and so on) has a particular point of view or feeling about an issue? What evidence in the work indicates a point of view?
3. Is the work meant to entertain, to persuade, or to inform?
4. How do the ideas presented relate to each other and to my own experience?
5. What are the major ideas and feelings in the work?
6. Can these ideas and feelings be expressed in another way or through another medium?
7. Can I make a general statement based on this information?
8. What examples can I think of that use this information?
9. What predictions can I make from this information?
10. To what trends in events or current thinking does this work point?

For example, suppose that you read the following:

The amount of money available for federally supported student loans will be reduced by 50 percent next year.

The maximum allowable family income for students eligible for these loans has been lowered by 20 percent to $20,000 a year.

Many major colleges and universities will be raising their tuition rates by at least 20 percent for the next year.

Using the list of questions to analyze these facts, you might write the following notes.

1. Fewer students whose family income is between $20,000 and $25,000 a year will be able to attend college.
2. Alternatives: work-study programs, other kinds of loans, deferred tuition-payment plans
3. Will colleges lower admission requirements because fewer students can afford to attend?

The following example is a newspaper article that lends itself to interpretation.

Dairy farmers in this area face bleak economic prospects for the next year. The problem, ironically, is that their cows are producing too much milk. Because the demand for milk has not kept pace with increased production, prices are down fifteen cents per hundred pounds of milk from this time last year.

As one farmer explains, "The price of milk has gone down, but our expenses for feed, equipment, transportation, and land rental have gone up. If I sell off part of my herd now, I won't be able to replace it later when the price of milk and cows goes up."

There is no doubt that many smaller farmers will go out of business before the year is over, and the problem is, for the moment, insolvable.

Using the list of questions to interpret the information in the paragraph, you might write the following notes.

1. Milk prices down, but is problem really insolvable?
2. Supply and demand affect price—true in other industries?
3. If some cows are sold, fewer cows will be producing milk, and prices will probably rise again.

Exercise 4   Prewriting: Using Information   Read the newspaper article that follows. On a sheet of paper, analyze and interpret the article. Write three possible writing subjects that you think of as you work.

> A recent survey of graduating students in two city high schools revealed that students' scores on college entrance examinations and students' plans for the future are determined by the particular school that they have attended.
>
> At Meadowbrook High School, it was found that 30 percent of the 350 graduating students plan to attend four-year colleges, 40 percent will attend two-year colleges, 10 percent will seek vocational training, and 20 percent will look for jobs. Students at Blue Ridge, on the other hand, will most likely pursue vocational training (70 percent). Another 20 percent will look for jobs, while only 10 percent of the graduating class of 250 will attend college.
>
> Scores on college entrance examinations varied significantly, with scores of students at Meadowbrook averaging 150 points higher than students at Blue Ridge. It is clear that this discrepancy in scores indicates a lack of college preparatory classes at Blue Ridge.

Assignment 1   Prewriting   Keep a log of your television and movie viewing for one week. Make at least one note for each show. At the end of the week, classify the shows (comedy, talk show, documentary, drama, and so on) and analyze each group.

Assignment 2   Prewriting   Clip several factual articles from a newspaper or a magazine, and put them into your writer's notebook. Analyze each article according to the questions on page 224. Write at least three statements about each article, based on these questions or others that you think of. Write down one possible writing idea about each article that develops from this preliminary analysis and interpretation.

Assignment 3   Prewriting   Keep your writer's notebook with you for three days. In it, jot down interesting bits of conversation, quotations from any materials that you read, thoughts that occur to you, and observations about yourself, other people, or events.

Continuing Assignment Prewriting Select three items. from your writer's notebook. One should be based on factual information; the second should be based on a personal experience, an observation, or an idea from your analysis and interpretation of what you read, see, and hear; the third should be a subject about which you would like to learn more. Write each item on a separate page in your notebook. Later you will develop these items into possible writing subjects.

Assignment Checklist

Check your assignments for the following points:

    ✔ 1. Did you accurately record information in your notebook?
    ✔ 2. Did you analyze and interpret the information?
    ✔ 3. In the Continuing Assignment, did you choose one factual item, one based on a personal experience or an idea, and one new subject?

4.2   Developing Your Ideas

In your writer's notebook, you will accumulate an extensive file of ideas for writing. Each item in your writer's notebook is a subject that you can develop through a process of expansion or amplification. By making lists and by exploring your ideas from many angles, you can expand your notes into a variety of writing subjects. Your goal is to produce a large amount of material from which you can later select specific topics.

4.2a Making Lists

To begin, choose a subject and write down everything that you know or want to find out about it. You may include opinions, hypotheses, terminology related to the subject, questions, and facts that you have learned through research. Next, let your mind wander, and write down any related facts, experiences, or impressions that you associate with the subject. Some of your notes will overlap, some may be irrelevant, and some may contradict one another. Do not be concerned at this point; just try to write down as many ideas as you can.

Suppose, for example, that you have chosen the subject of photography. Your list might look like the following:

Types of cameras—range finder, single-lens reflex, twin-lens reflex, studio

Camera obscura invented by ancient Greeks

Zoom lens good for sports, wildlife subjects

Crime detection; police photograph scene; fingerprints

F-stop? Aperture? Depth of field?

Louis Daguerre, daguerreotype (mid-1800s)

Light meters (reflected light, incident light)

Minor White (book with his photos at library)

Photos screened for printing in newspapers, books

Color photography—when invented?

Developing film (process); darkroom, enlarger

Exercise 1   Prewriting: Making Lists   On your paper, make a list of at least ten notes for each of five of the following subjects. You may consult reference books.

SAMPLE	Printing
ANSWER	Visited newspaper printing plant
	Phototypesetting uses computers.
	Chinese invented movable type in 11th century
	Lithography process
	Type faces (roman and italic)
	Incunabula—books printed before 1500
	Franklin's *Poor Richard's Almanac* (printing and American Revolution)
	Letterpress vs. offset printing
	Compositors
	Word processing

1. Driving
2. Ecology
3. Filmmaking
4. Freedom of the press
5. Industry

6. Physics
7. Popular music
8. Senior citizens
9. Supply and demand
10. Wildlife refuges

4.2b   Exploring Your Subject

By making lists, you have begun to explore the ramifications of your writing ideas. Your goal now is to generate additional detailed information in a systematic way. The following list of general questions is· designed to help you explore many aspects of your subject. Not all of these questions will be useful for every subject. When exploring your subject, use those questions that apply and that will produce useful information.

1. What are the characteristics of my subject?
2. What is the history of my subject?
3. What are recent developments in my subject and trends for the future?
4. What important people, books, and other resources are connected with my subject?
5. What terms or definitions are related to my subject?
6. What processes are involved in my subject?
7. What comparisons can I make within my subject or between my subject and another?
8. Can I develop an analogy related to my subject?
9. What contrasts or opposites are within my subject?
10. What causes and effects are involved with my subject?
11. What problems and issues are connected with my subject?
12. What are my experiences with my subject?

As you work, you may think of other questions that will help you to explore your subject.

By using some of the preceding questions to explore the subject of photography, you might write the following notes.

History: camera obscura—ancient Greeks; daguerreotype developed 1830-1840; calotype (silver chloride), 1841; wet-plate photography, 1850s; dry-plate, 1870s; roll film, 1885 (Eastman)

Processes: developing latent image on film (developer, stop bath, fixer) to produce negative from exposed film

Comparison: similar to realistic painting—two-dimensional image from one point of view

Analogy: Film is to a photographer what canvas is to an artist.

Cause and effect: overexposing film leads to prints with too much light

Problems, issues: copyright laws for photographs; how does amateur photographer sell pictures?

Personal experience: Picture album in attic includes some daguerreotypes; I've set up my own darkroom.

Exercise 2   Prewriting: Exploring Ideas   On your paper, explore five of the following subjects by giving the information requested. You may consult reference books.

SAMPLE   Plants: two terms; a process; two problems

ANSWER   *Terms: epiphytes*—plants that get nutrients from air; *photochrome*—a light-sensitive pigment that acts as an enzyme in plants

Process: photosynthesis—green plants convert carbon dioxide, water, and sunlight into glucose and oxygen

Problems: irrigating deserts to produce food; air pollution affects amount of sunlight available to plants

1. Pollution: two causes and two effects; an analogy; a personal experience
2. Postal system: history; a reference book; a comparison
3. Advertising: two issues; an effect; two terms
4. Lasers: two characteristics; two recent developments; a process
5. Abstract painting: a contrast; a definition; two important artists
6. United Nations: history; a cause and an effect; two issues
7. Television: two future trends; two processes; two personal experiences
8. Sports: two terms; two reference books or other resources; a contrast
9. Pottery: history; a process; two definitions
10. Patriotism: two characteristics; an analogy; an effect

Exercise 3   Prewriting: Exploring Ideas   On your paper, explore five of the following subjects. For each subject use as many of the questions on page 229 as you find appropriate.

1. Cable television
2. Comic books
3. Contemporary crafts
4. Food additives
5. Popular bands

6. Newspaper publishing
7. Sports legends
8. Unemployment
9. Whaling
10. Higher education

Assignment 1   Prewriting   Imagine that you are going to interview a famous person who lived more than a hundred years ago. Write the person's name; then make a list of facts and ideas about the person and the time period in which he or she lived. Use the questions on page 229 to develop a list of possible interview topics and questions.

Assignment 2   Prewriting   Assume that you have been asked to write a research paper for your science class. Choose two science-related subjects, and develop them by making lists and exploring ideas.

Assignment 3   Prewriting   Develop the subject of the Federal Reserve System, exploring at least three of the following areas: definition, comparison, contrast, cause, effect, and problems.

Assignment 4   Prewriting   Select one aspect of contemporary society that interests you. Some possible subjects are effects of television, business conglomerates, international finance, magazine advertising, food processing, city management. Develop the subject using the techniques presented in this unit.

Continuing Assignment   In the Continuing Assignment on page 227, you chose three items of interest. Develop these items by making lists and exploring ideas. Choose exploration techniques appropriate to each item. Save your notes.

Assignment Checklist

Check your assignments for the following points:

✔ 1. In Assignment 1, did your list reflect the life and times of your subject?

✔ 2. In Assignment 2, did you explore two scientific subjects?

✔ 3. In Assignments 3 and 4, did you fully explore your subjects?

✔ 4. In the Continuing Assignment, did you develop each subject as fully as possible?

4.3   Focusing Ideas

As you develop subjects, you will accumulate a vast amount of material for writing. However, you are not yet ready to write. First you must focus and refine this material for use in specific writing assignments. In focusing it, you will determine a topic for your writing and identify your purpose and your audience.

Finding Topics

A **topic** is a specific aspect of a subject; it must be broad enough to provide sufficient material for your assignment and, at the same time, narrow enough to be appropriate for a coherent, well-developed piece of writing. The following procedure will help you to focus on a topic.

Procedure

1. *Review your prewriting notes on a subject. Jot down topic ideas that emerge.* Consider your analyses and interpretations, your lists, and the notes that you made when exploring subjects.

2. *Look for logical groupings of information.* You might find many notes on the history of a subject, on the causes and effects involved in a particular process, or on a specific contrast or comparison.

3. *Conduct a preliminary exploration of one or more topics that occur to you.* Review your notes to find related

material. Develop the topic. Ask yourself whether you have too little or too much information for a specific assignment. For example, the topic "History of photography" might be too broad for a five-page research paper; a suitable topic might be "Nineteenth-century cameras."

Determining Your Purpose

Your **purpose** in writing is what you intend to accomplish with a particular paragraph, essay, letter, or research paper. The following list gives several common purposes for writing and a topic that would be appropriate for each.

PURPOSE	TOPIC
To inform or explain	New developments in photography
To entertain	How I set up a darkroom by trial and error
To describe	Effects of solarization on printing photographs
To persuade	Photography contests should not require nonwinning entrants to relinquish rights to their photos.
To narrate	How I took my best photograph

Audience

Your **audience** is the group of readers for whom your writing is intended. Identifying your audience will help you to select an appropriate topic and relevant supporting material, to choose a purpose for your writing, and to determine what style of writing you should use. To understand the interests of your audience, ask yourself the following questions:

1. How much does the audience know about the topic?
2. What else might the audience want to know?
3. Might the audience have strong ideas or opinions about the topic?
4. Would a formal or informal writing style (*Unit 9*) be more effective with this audience?

Once you have identified your topic, your purpose, and your audience, you may need to repeat some of the prewriting techniques in this unit. As you work on a writing assignment, you will do additional prewriting in the form of organizing information, making outlines, and doing research. Each subsequent composition unit in this book will give you further practice in prewriting for specific kinds of writing.

Exercise   Prewriting: Focusing Ideas   On your paper, answer the four questions that follow these prewriting notes on the subject of glass.

> Made mostly of silica (sand)
>
> Mirror of Palomar Observatory's Hale telescope is 200 inches in diameter.
>
> Sodium carbonate and silica form water glass (dissolves in water).
>
> Pittsburgh—glass-making center of United States in 1800s
>
> Botanical glass models at Harvard University Museum, Cambridge, Mass.
>
> First glass manufactured in ancient Egypt about 1500 B.C.
>
> Stained glass, a popular craft
>
> *History:* Glass-blowing invented in Phoenicia in 1st century B.C.; Romans used window glass, 1st century A.D.; glass-making revived in Europe mid-12th century; Venice—glass capital of Europe in 16th century
>
> *Important people:* Henry William Stiegel, glass factory in Pa., 1763; Michael J. Owens invented bottle-making machine, 1903; J. H. Lubbers, machine for blowing glass mechanically
>
> *Manufacturing processes:* rolling, casting, pressing, floating
>
> *Causes and effects:* flux added to silica causes it to melt at lower temp.; boron oxide added to make heat-resistant glass
>
> *Personal experiences:* cutting glass bottles to make cups and vases; broke window accidentally and replaced pane

1. What are three possible topics suggested by these notes?
2. State a purpose for each of the three topics.
3. For what audience would each topic be appropriate?
4. Write the notes that you would use if you were writing about "How glass is manufactured."

Assignment 1   Prewriting   Choose a subject from your writer's notebook and develop it. From your notes identify two possible writing topics. Indicate a purpose for writing and an audience for each topic.

Assignment 2   Prewriting   Assume that you have been assigned a five-page research paper in a science class. Review the material that you have developed in your writer's notebook for Assignment 2 on page 231. Select two possible topics from your notes. For each topic, list the relevant information that you have collected; then list several questions that will require further research.

Assignment 3   Prewriting   Write down an idea that occurred to you in response to a book that you read or a movie that you saw recently. Develop the idea; then define a topic for a three-page essay, and identify a purpose and an audience.

Continuing Assignment   In the Continuing Assignment on page 231, you developed three subjects. Now focus your prewriting notes, and identify at least three possible writing topics. Indicate a purpose and an audience for each.

Assignment Checklist

Check your assignments for the following points:

   ✔ 1. In Assignment 1, did you develop your subject fully enough to find two possible writing topics?

   ✔ 2. In Assignment 2, did you choose topics that could be adequately treated in a five-page report?

   ✔ 3. In Assignment 3, did you develop the idea sufficiently to identify a topic, a purpose, and an audience?

   ✔ 4. In the Continuing Assignment, did you identify a purpose and an audience for each topic?

Going Places: Plans for an Article

Situation: You are writing a feature article for the "Going Places" column in the travel supplement to the Sunday newspaper. The editor has suggested that you compare travel today with travel at the turn of the century. As you begin prewriting, keep in mind the following information.

Writer:　you as a feature writer

Audience:　readers of the Sunday supplement

Topic:　travel today and travel eighty years ago

Purpose:　to develop and focus your ideas for an article

Directions:　To develop ideas, follow these steps.

Step 1. On a separate sheet of paper, copy and fill in the chart on the facing page. For each category, list ideas and associations, and write down questions of interest.

Step 2. Review your completed chart, and jot down ideas that emerge. Group related ideas.

Step 3. Choose a specific topic that you want to use for your article. Be sure that you include a comparison between then (conditions eighty years ago) and now (conditions today).

Step 4. State the purpose of your proposed article. Answer these questions: How much will readers of the Sunday supplement know about my topic? What else might they want to know?

Step 5. List key ideas that you need to research. Write down where you might find additional information about your topic.

Step 6. Write a proposed title for your article.

	TRAVEL THEN (80 years ago)	TRAVEL NOW
LAND TRAVEL		
Types of vehicles		
People involved		
Advantages		
Disadvantages		
Costs		
Problems or issues		
Questions		
SEA TRAVEL		
Types of vehicles		
People involved		
Advantages		
Disadvantages		
Costs		
Problems or issues		
Questions		
AIR AND SPACE TRAVEL		
Types of vehicles		
People involved		
Advantages		
Disadvantages		
Costs		
Problems or issues		
Questions		

Unit Assignments

Assignment 1 Choose a memorable experience that relates to the subject of friendship. Make a list that includes facts and impressions related to the subject. Develop the subject further by using whatever exploration techniques are appropriate.

Assignment 2 Assume that you have been asked to write a two-page essay on the necessity for promptness. Your audience is junior high school students in your community. Develop the subject with particular emphasis on making comparisons, discussing causes and effects, and stating problems or issues related to the subject. Be sure to keep your audience in mind as you develop your subject.

Assignment 3 Choose a newspaper article that interests you. Assume that you will write a letter to the editor of the newspaper in which the article appeared. Analyze the article, and develop your findings by making lists and exploring the ideas. Then state a topic for your letter, identify a purpose for writing, and describe your audience.

Assignment 4 Choose a subject related to one of your school courses. Develop and explore the subject. State two possible topics that emerge from your work. For each, identify a purpose for writing and an audience.

Assignment 5 Assume that you have been asked to make a market-survey questionnaire for a product that you have seen advertised. Develop information about the product by making lists and exploring ideas. Make a preliminary list of ten questions that might be included in the questionnaire.

Assignment 6 Think about an issue that is currently in the news. Using this issue as your subject, develop ideas about it. Then focus your notes; decide on a topic, a purpose for writing, and a possible audience for your topic.

Assignment 7 Choose an annual award, prize, or medal that interests you (Nobel Prize, Pulitzer Prize, Newbery Medal, Caldecott Medal, Academy Award, Grammy Award, and so forth). Imagine that you have been asked to interview a winner of that award for your school newspaper. Prepare a list of questions to ask that person. As you develop your list, keep in mind the readers of your school newspaper.

Assignment 8 You are planning to write about the advantages and disadvantages of daylight-saving time. Develop the subject with particular emphasis on causes and effects, problems and issues, and personal experiences related to the subject.

Unit Tests

Test 1

A. Number your paper from 1 to 5. Next to each number, write *True* if the sentence is true and *False* if it is false.

1. A writer's notebook is organized by topic.
2. Analyzing and interpreting information is one part of the prewriting process.
3. After you have identified a topic, a purpose for writing, and an audience, you may have to do further research.
4. Your reactions to the world around you may provide writing ideas.
5. Knowledge of your audience is important in selecting a topic.

B. Number your paper from 6 to 10. Next to each number, write the letter of the term that correctly completes each sentence. You will use all but one of the terms.

a. focusing   d. analogy

b. writer's notebook   e. topic

c. prewriting   f. analyzing

6. When you ask what the author's point of view is, you are __?__ a piece of writing.
7. You are __?__ your ideas for writing when you identify a topic, an audience, and a purpose.
8. A good place to record your notes and ideas for writing is your __?__.
9. Finding a(n) __?__ is one way to explore an idea in prewriting.
10. A(n) __?__ is a particular aspect of a subject.

C. Number your paper from 11 to 15. Next to each number, write the letter of the item that correctly answers the question.

11. Which one of the following is *not* a good way to expand your prewriting notes?
    a. Look for causes and effects in your subject.
    b. Do research on the history of your subject.
    c. Organize your notes.
    d. List terms and definitions relevant to the subject.

240

12. Which one of the following is the least productive way to develop the subject of education?
    a. Record your own school experiences.
    b. Watch a TV documentary about high school students.
    c. Read a magazine article about the health of children.
    d. Talk to teachers about their jobs.

13. Which one of the following is *not* a purpose for writing a paper about electricity?
    a. To explain how hydroelectric plants work
    b. To list questions about utility companies
    c. To persuade the public to conserve electrical energy
    d. To explain city codes for wiring in public buildings

14. Which one of the following is *not* a good way to find ideas for writing?
    a. To watch television and go to the movies
    b. To record personal observations and ideas
    c. To decide on a formal or an informal writing style
    d. To analyze and interpret what you have read and seen

15. Which one of the following should you *not* do when you are developing a subject by making a list?
    a. Note words relevant to the subject whose definitions you do not know.
    b. Carefully organize your list.
    c. Record hypotheses that you have about the subject.
    d. Ask questions that you will answer later.

Test 2

Choose one of the Unit Assignments or one that your teacher suggests. Complete the assignment and hand it in to your teacher.

Writing Paragraphs

Unit Preview

A **paragraph** is a group of sentences that develops an idea in an orderly way. As you read the following paragraph, notice its structure and organization. Note how the choice and arrangement of details support the idea that is stated in the first sentence, the topic sentence.

(1) Japan was already an important manufacturing nation when the first visitors from western Europe arrived in 1543. (2) The European visitors observed that Japan manufactured many more kinds of paper than were available anywhere else. (3) For example, the Japanese had invented thin, disposable tissue paper. (4) The Japanese also showed little interest in European iron and steel because their own were superior. (5) In fact, Japan had long been a manufacturer of high-quality metal weapons. (6) A modern film has documented the remarkable strength of a fifteenth-century Japanese sword by showing it cut through a thick piece of metal. (7) Clearly, Japan was not a country hungering for technological gifts from the European visitors.

Notice that the paragraph is organized clearly. That is, each sentence leads logically to the next. In good paragraphs, transitional words and phrases such as *then, more important, for example,* and *however* help to emphasize the logical connections between sentences.

For Analysis On your paper, answer the following questions about the preceding paragraph.

1. What idea is stated in the first sentence?
2. What goods manufactured in Japan are mentioned to support the idea in the first sentence?
3. What is the relationship of Sentence 3 to Sentence 2? How is that relationship emphasized in Sentence 3?
4. Does the concluding sentence restate the idea of the first sentence, or does it present a final comment on that idea?

In answering questions about this paragraph, you have been able to observe the structure and organization of all paragraphs. In this unit you will practice organizing and writing paragraphs.

5.1 Developing Paragraphs

5.1a Selecting and Limiting a Topic

If you are free to choose a topic, select one that you find interesting and feel will be interesting to your audience. To write well about a topic, you should be familiar with it or be prepared to do research to learn about it.

Once you have a general topic, limit it so that you can cover it fully in a paragraph. You can limit a topic by narrowing it to just one aspect, one example, or one time period. For example, you could narrow the general topic "Buildings" to the limited topic "Protecting buildings from earthquakes" or "A skyscraper designed by Frank Lloyd Wright." You could narrow the general topic "Careers" to the limited topic "Careers for women in the eighteenth century" or "The benefits of career counseling."

If you need help in limiting a topic, list details about the general topic as you think of them. For example, the following is a list of details related to the general topic "The theater."

1. The director selects a performer for each part in a play.
2. In a theater-in-the-round, members of the audience sit on all sides of the stage.

3. Making sure that the costumes and sets are coordinated is a task of the director.
4. In a community theater, members of a community put on plays in their spare time.
5. The director and the playwright work together to rewrite ineffective parts of plays.
6. Many cities have acting companies that employ professional performers.
7. High schools often have drama clubs that put on plays.
8. Coaching the performers during rehearsals is one of the duties of a director.
9. The director makes sure that the audience can clearly see and hear the performers.
10. Members of the audience sit on three sides of an open stage.

In the preceding list, Details 1, 3, 5, 8, and 9 are related because they all explain the duties of a director. Similarly, Details 2 and 10 are related because they describe types of stages, and Details 4, 6, and 7 are related because they concern types of acting groups. You could use any one of the three groups of details as the basis of a limited topic. Using the largest group would be best because it contains more information for developing a paragraph. This choice would narrow the general topic "The theater" to the limited topic "The duties of a director."

Exercise 1 Prewriting: Limiting Topics Write two limited topics for each of the following general topics. If necessary, list details to help you limit the general topic.

SAMPLE	Books
ANSWER	The invention of the printing press
	How *All the King's Men* influenced me

1. Inventions
2. Films
3. Transportation
4. Science
5. Cities

6. Politics
7. Friendship
8. The environment
9. Art
10. Sports

5.1b   Writing a Topic Sentence

A **topic sentence** states the main idea of a paragraph. In it you tell the reader what information to expect in the paragraph and how the details in the paragraph are related. The topic sentence also helps you to focus on the main idea, to avoid adding ideas that are not related to the topic.

An effective topic sentence is specific. It states clearly what the details in the paragraph have in common. A topic sentence is too general if it suggests that you will discuss more than you actually do. A topic sentence is too narrow if it suggests that you will discuss less than you actually do.

The following details for a paragraph about the American painter Albert Pinkham Ryder need to be united by a topic sentence.

> In contrast to the brilliant colors of his contemporaries, Ryder's tones were dark and somber, suitable to the gloomy moods that he was expressing.
>
> In his effort to express moods, Ryder applied layer upon layer of paint.
>
> Even though Ryder's drawing is regarded as technically deficient, all design elements in a Ryder picture are harmonious because they work together to express one mood.

The following statements are suggestions for a topic sentence to unite the preceding details.

> A. Technique can be used to express mood in a painting.
> B. Ryder did not demonstrate technical skill.
> C. Ryder's technique developed from his need to express certain moods.

Sentence A is too general. The preceding details reveal how Ryder used technique to express mood, not how artists in general use technique to express mood. Sentence B is too narrow. The details discuss more than Ryder's lack of technical skill. Sentence C is an effective topic sentence because it focuses on the same idea that the details do: the relationship between Ryder's technique and the moods that he wanted to express.

Exercise 2   Prewriting: Topic Sentences   On your paper, write a topic sentence for each of the following groups of details. Make sure that each topic sentence states clearly what the details have in common.

1. a. People's lungs supply their blood with oxygen and remove impurities from the blood.
    b. Impurities are removed from the blood by the kidneys.
    c. Kidneys regulate the water and salt content of the blood.
    d. Nutrients are supplied to the blood by the liver and intestines.
2. a. Sea pens, relatives of jellyfish, hide in the sand during the day.
    b. Humans' body temperatures drop approximately two degrees at night.
    c. During the day, deep-sea creatures move closer to the surface of the water.
    d. Many leaves and flowers open during the day and close at night.

5.1c   Developing the Body of a Paragraph

When you write the **body,** or main part, of a paragraph, present statements that will help your audience to understand your topic. You may also provide a concluding sentence that ties together all of your statements.

Writing Supporting Sentences

You need to support your topic with details. **Supporting sentences** provide the specific details that explain or illustrate your topic.

The most common types of supporting sentences contain facts, examples, and reasons. A **fact** is something that can be proved to be true. Statements of fact include statistical, historical, and technical information. For example, "Seventy percent of company employees attended the exercise program" is a statement of fact. Some facts can be used as examples. An **example** is something that is representative of a larger group. The following statement presents an example: "Ellie Burns was one of the workers who attended the exercise program during the lunch hour." A **reason** is presented in a statement that explains or proves something. For example, this statement provides a reason: "The on-the-job exercise program is beneficial because it makes the employees healthier and more productive."

In most paragraphs, you will use more than one kind of supporting sentence. The notes in the margin of the following paragraph show how facts and examples can be combined in a paragraph.

Model

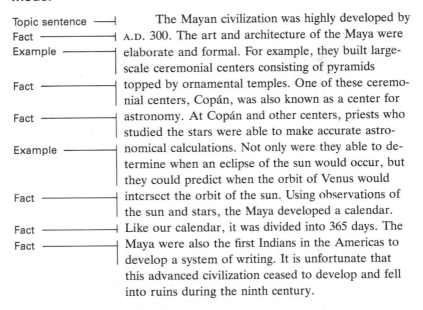

Topic sentence ——| The Mayan civilization was highly developed by
Fact ——————| A.D. 300. The art and architecture of the Maya were
Example ————| elaborate and formal. For example, they built large-
                scale ceremonial centers consisting of pyramids
Fact ————————| topped by ornamental temples. One of these ceremo-
                nial centers, Copán, was also known as a center for
Fact ————————| astronomy. At Copán and other centers, priests who
                studied the stars were able to make accurate astro-
Example ————| nomical calculations. Not only were they able to de-
                termine when an eclipse of the sun would occur, but
                they could predict when the orbit of Venus would
Fact ————————| intersect the orbit of the sun. Using observations of
                the sun and stars, the Maya developed a calendar.
Fact ————————| Like our calendar, it was divided into 365 days. The
Fact ————————| Maya were also the first Indians in the Americas to
                develop a system of writing. It is unfortunate that
                this advanced civilization ceased to develop and fell
                into ruins during the ninth century.

Exercise 3 Prewriting: Supporting Sentences On your paper, write the numbers of the five statements that provide the best support for the following topic sentence. After each number, write whether the statement presents a fact, an example, or a reason.

Topic sentence: The southeastern states are no longer the largest producers of cotton in the United States.

1. Southeastern farmers now find it profitable to grow fruits and vegetables as market crops.
2. Cotton is used to make many types of clothing.

3. Mining, lumbering, and manufacturing have developed in the southeastern states in this century.
4. Cottonseed oil is used in many food products.
5. Cotton growing has been moving to western states.
6. Texas now produces the largest cotton crop.
7. The cotton gin, invented in 1793, speeded the separation of cotton seed from fiber.
8. Of the old cotton states, only Mississippi is still a top producer.
9. Bales of cotton are transported across the country in trucks.
10. Most all of the cotton grown in the United States is harvested by machines.

Exercise 4   Prewriting: Supporting Details   Copy the following three topic sentences on your paper. Under each one, list the letters of the supporting details that develop it.

Topic sentences:
1. Many methods are used to predict the weather.
2. Some situations cause changes in our climate.
3. For more than forty years, scientists have been experimenting with methods to increase the rainfall in certain areas.

Supporting details:

a. The eruption of volcanoes can cause cooler weather by creating clouds of ash that block the sun's rays.

b. Today silver iodide, which resembles table salt, is shot into clouds to create rain.

c. Satellite pictures of storms around the world help meteorologists to predict the weather.

d. Carbon dioxide exhaust from cars and factories encircles the earth and traps heat, making the climate warmer.

e. In 1946 scientists shot ice crystals into clouds to produce rain.

f. To determine what the weather will be, meteorologists study data from balloons sent into the upper atmosphere every twelve hours.

g. Sometimes modern rainmakers drop silver nitrate into clouds from a plane.

h. Air pollution from factories heats the air and causes an increase in precipitation in the immediate area.

i. Examining weather records from past years can help scientists to predict weather for the current year.

j. Meteorologists read data from instruments that record changes in temperature, humidity, and air pressure.

Position of the Topic Sentence

Usually you place the topic sentence at the beginning of a paragraph and follow it with supporting sentences. Then your reader knows immediately what you will discuss in the paragraph. You may, however, place the topic sentence in the middle or at the end of a paragraph. In this way, you can build up to the topic sentence for emphasis, for clarity, or for surprise.

In the following example, the topic sentence, which is in italic type, appears in the middle of the paragraph.

Model

When you push against a wall, a door, or a heavy piece of furniture, you put stress on your muscles. *That stress is the basis of a valuable and easy form of exercise, called isometric exercise.* In isometric exercise, there is little movement; all benefit comes from exerting pressure against an immovable object. It is a valuable form of exercise because it not only tones muscles by forcing them to contract but also increases their strength by overloading them. It is an easy form of exercise because it takes only a few minutes each day and requires no special equipment.

By giving an example before presenting the topic sentence, the writer helps the reader to understand the topic sentence.

The Implied Topic Sentence

Not every paragraph needs a topic sentence. The topic idea may be implied rather than stated directly. If your supporting sentences clearly present your topic idea, you do not have to include a topic sentence in the paragraph. A narrative paragraph that is part of a sequence of paragraphs about the same topic frequently has the implied topic sentence "This is what happened next."

The topic idea of the following paragraph is implied.

Model

> In early spring the grass is light green when you look with the wind, and dark green when you look toward the wind. In summer the grasses take on a reddish-brown hue and by autumn they show purple and copper tints that contrast with the red, gray, white, and silvery tones of tall dropseed, switchgrass, squirreltail, and Indian grass.
>
> David F. Costello, *The Prairie World*

The implied topic sentence of the preceding paragraph is "As the seasons change, so do the colors of the grass." All of the supporting sentences work together to convey that idea.

Exercise 5   Prewriting: Topic Sentences   On your paper, write the topic sentence or implied topic sentence of each of the following paragraphs. Write *Implied* after each topic sentence that is not actually expressed.

PARAGRAPH 1

> The race in 1492 was to create the first shipping lane to Asia. The Portuguese expeditions had always sailed east, around the southern tip of Africa. Columbus decided to head due west, across open ocean, a scheme that was feasible only thanks to a recent invention—the magnetic ship's compass. Until then ships had stayed close to the great land masses even for the longest voyages. Likewise, it was only after an invention of the 1940s and early 1950s, the high-speed electronic computer, that NASA would even consider propelling astronauts out of the earth's orbit and toward the moon.
>
> Tom Wolfe, "Columbus and the Moon"

PARAGRAPH 2

> The air not only moves horizontally; it rises and sinks, and in so doing, it affects the state of the sky. Descending air has the effect of inhibiting cloud formation, while ascending air, if it rises enough, causes clouds. Sometimes there are weak upward air motions over large regions and, as a result, cloud layers cover the entire sky. At

other times, particularly in the summer, violent updrafts and down-drafts accompany the formation of thunderstorms. The variable air motions over small distances account for the turbulence experienced by planes flying through thunderstorms.

Louis J. Battan, *Fundamentals of Meteorology*

PARAGRAPH 3

In the young conch, the shell is simply twisted spiral upon spiral. Only in adulthood does the animal produce its dramatic flared lip, and then the shell stops enlarging and continues to lay down material in the lip area alone. Thus the older a conch gets—biologists believe they live for about six years—the thicker and heavier is its shell. The conch's lopsided shell—the flaring lip develops only on one side—may be a result of the lack of mantle tissue on the other side of the conch's body, or just a clever adaptation that allows the conch more security, the ability to wedge itself more easily in the sand in turbulent water.

Carrol Fleming,
"The Snail That's Too Good for Its Own Good"

Exercise 6 Writing: Position of the Topic Sentence

Using the following topic sentence and details, write supporting sentences about what you could have seen in a chaparral, a dense area of shrubs and small trees. Place the topic sentence in an effective place in the middle of the paragraph. Save your paper.

Topic sentence: When I entered the chaparral, I discovered that it was composed of two worlds: one above and one below the branches of the shrubs.

Supporting Details:
1. Visited the chaparral in California in the foothills around Los Angeles
2. From a distance, the chaparral looked all green.
3. The shrubs were green only on top.
4. Yellow and blue flowers only on top too
5. Dark twisted branches down to the ground
6. No plants in underbrush
7. Mice and rabbits in underbrush

Writing a Concluding Sentence ▬▬▬▬▬▬

A **concluding sentence** helps your reader to recall or to understand more clearly the point of a paragraph. For example, when you write a long paragraph containing many facts, you can remind your reader of what the facts show by writing a concluding sentence that restates the topic sentence or summarizes the supporting statements. On the other hand, you can help your reader to understand a topic by writing a concluding sentence that offers a final comment. That final comment may be a logical conclusion, a personal impression, a question, or a recommendation for a course of action.

Sometimes a paragraph does not need a concluding sentence because the last supporting detail ties together the ideas of the paragraph. Paragraphs that are part of a larger composition very often are complete without a concluding sentence.

The following paragraph has a concluding sentence in which the writer makes a comment about the topic.

Model

> In the town of St. Malo on the coast of Brittany, the French government has begun a daring experiment to launch every French household into the computer age. The townspeople are receiving free computer terminals provided by the state-run telephone company. The French call the idea *telematique,* and it is putting computing power in the hands of people in their homes. The initial reason for distributing the electronic terminals is to replace the telephone book; therefore, the terminals are, for the moment, used just for locating telephone numbers. In the future they can be linked to electronic mail, computerized shopping, and a host of other computerized information networks.
>
> WGBH Boston, "Les Smart Cards"

The topic sentence and the supporting sentences of the paragraph explain what has already been done by the French government. In the concluding sentence, the writer speculates about the future.

Exercise 7   Prewriting/Writing: Concluding Sentences

On your paper, write the type of concluding sentence that is used in the following paragraph—one that restates the topic sentence or one that offers a final comment. Then write a different concluding sentence of the type that is not used.

> In the United States, billions of dollars are spent each year on advertising. Most large companies that market their retail products nationally advertise on television. Why is television so popular? First, advertisers often prefer television to newspapers and magazines because commercials have a captive audience. Most viewers do not leave the room or change the channel when a commercial interrupts a program. Second, although the cost of advertising on television is higher than it is for advertising in newspapers or magazines, more than a million people may watch a program, and consequently, the television advertiser pays less per person exposed to the advertising. Finally, the television advertiser hopes to become identified with the program that it interrupts, thus capturing the loyalty of the viewers of that program. For these three reasons, most national advertising is done on television.

Exercise 8 Writing: Concluding Sentences On your paper, write a concluding sentence that restates the topic sentence to complete the paragraph that you wrote for Exercise 6 on page 251.

Assignment 1 Prewriting/Writing Choose one of the limited topics that you listed for Exercise 1 on page 244. Write a topic sentence for the limited topic, and list details that support it. Using the topic sentence and details, write a paragraph. Place the topic sentence at the beginning of the paragraph, and write a concluding sentence that summarizes the paragraph.

Assignment 2 Prewriting/Writing Choose a limited topic from the general topic "The arts." Write a topic sentence for the limited topic, and list some details that support it. Using the topic sentence and details, write a paragraph. Arrange your sentences so that the topic sentence in the middle of the paragraph, and write a concluding sentence that provides a final comment on your topic.

Assignment 3   Writing   From the paragraphs that you have written for previous exercises in this section, select one with a topic sentence. Rewrite the paragraph so that it has an implied topic sentence. Change the wording of the sentences in the paragraph so that the topic idea is clear even though there is no topic sentence.

Assignment Checklist

Check your paragraphs for the following points:

    ✔ 1. Did you limit your topic so that it could be covered fully in a paragraph?

    ✔ 2. In Assignments 1 and 2, did you write a specific topic sentence and place it in the appropriate place?

    ✔ 3. Did you write supporting sentences that fully develop the topic?

    ✔ 4. Did you write an effective concluding sentence?

    ✔ 5. In Assignment 3, did you rewrite the supporting sentences so that your main idea is clear to your reader?

    ✔ 6. Did you check your paragraphs for correct grammar, usage, spelling, and punctuation?

5.2   Organizing Paragraphs

To express your ideas clearly, you must write a paragraph that is coherent. In a **coherent** paragraph, ideas are organized in a logical way. Each sentence in a paragraph should lead to the next, and transitional words and phrases should emphasize the relationship between the sentences. All details in the supporting sentences should relate to the topic.

When you organize the ideas in your paragraph, follow these guidelines.

Strategies

    1. *Introduce your topic* before discussing it at length.

    2. *Precede an example with a general statement about the idea that the example illustrates.*

3. *Discuss a series of items in the same order that you used to introduce them.*

4. *Define any obscure or technical words or ideas* when you first use them and before you move to a new idea.

If you use the preceding guidelines and the following methods for organization, you will be able to write coherent paragraphs.

5.2a   Chronological Order

When you use **chronological order** in a paragraph, you arrange events in the order in which they occur. Use chronological order to tell a story, to explain a process, or to recount a historical event. In a paragraph arranged in chronological order, the sequence of events should be indicated by dates and time-related transitional words or phrases such as the following: *after, at first, before, in the beginning, next, then,* and *when.*

The writer of the following paragraph uses time-related transitional words to show chronological order. Those words are in italic type.

Model

Before a bill becomes law in the United States, it must go through a complicated process. *First,* the bill must be introduced to one of the houses of Congress, either the Senate or the House of Representatives. *Then* the bill is assigned to a committee that specializes in bills about one specific subject, such as transportation or education. *Next,* the committee studies the bill and decides whether to recommend the bill as it is, to recommend the bill with changes, or to stop the bill from going any further. If the bill is recommended, the members of the Senate or the House of Representatives discuss the bill and *then* vote on it. The bill passes if a majority of the members vote for it. *After* the bill passes in one house, it must follow the same procedure in the other house of Congress. If the members of the two houses do not agree on the same form of the bill, members from both houses meet in a conference committee to work out their disagreements. *Finally,* the bill must be signed by the

President. If the President does not sign it, the bill may still become law if two-thirds of the members of both houses vote to overrule the President. Because the process is so complicated, some bills take months to become law.

Exercise 1   Writing: Chronological Order   On your paper, write the numbers of the following supporting details in chronological order. Then write a chronologically arranged paragraph, using the topic sentence and at least four of the details. Include dates and at least three transitional words or phrases. You may change the wording of the supporting details when you write the paragraph.

Topic sentence: For most of her adult life, Frances Perkins tried to improve working conditions in the United States.

Supporting details:

1. In 1933 became secretary of labor for President Roosevelt; first woman cabinet member; helped to draft labor legislation and to build the Department of Labor; held post until 1945
2. In 1910 took volunteer job as secretary of the Consumers' League in New York City, where she worked to eliminate bad working conditions in bakeries
3. Became professor at Cornell University's School of Industrial and Labor Relations in 1957 when she was seventy-seven
4. Appointed member of the United States Civil Service Commission by President Truman in 1945 and held the position until 1953
5. In 1912 became director of investigation for New York state's Factory Investigating Commission and helped to identify employers who jeopardized the health of their workers
6. As member of the New York State Industrial Commission in 1918, settled strikes and helped to pass a law reducing the work week from fifty-four to forty-eight hours

5.2b   Spatial Order

When you use **spatial order** in a paragraph, you arrange the details about an object or a scene according to their location in space. To write a clear paragraph, you must choose a specific spatial order to describe an item or a scene. The most common spatial arrangements are bottom to top, side to side, and foreground to background. Emphasize the order that you choose by using spatial transitional words or phrases such as the following: *above, behind, beside, inside, next to, over, to the side of,* and *under.*

The writer of the following paragraph uses transitional words to emphasize the top-to-bottom spatial order of the details. Those words are in italic type.

Model

Because the new subway line near my house was constructed in a large ditch, I could see all of the features that are now hidden under tons of dirt. *At the top* of the enormous ditch, I could see layers of pavement from times when the road was resurfaced. *Under* the pavement were the cobblestones from the original street. *Below* the cobblestones were smooth concrete walls that covered the sides of the ditch. *Halfway down* one wall, I saw a partly finished stairway, which now carries passengers to and from the street. *At the mud-filled bottom* of the pit, I could see two rectangular concrete tunnels, one for subway traffic in each direction. Now, every time that I walk down the stairs into the subway tunnel, I remember how different it looked when it was under construction.

Exercise 2   Writing: Spatial Order   Write a paragraph using the following topic sentence and supporting details. Arrange the details in left-to-right spatial order. You may change the wording of the supporting details, but be sure to use at least three transitional words or phrases in the paragraph.

Topic sentence: When I first saw my neighbor's home computer, I was surprised because all of its components were small enough to fit together on a table top.

Supporting details:
1. On the left side of the processing unit, a row of red flashing lights that show how fast it is working
2. In the center of the table, a one-foot-square disk drive with two slots for disks
3. On the right side of the table, the computer itself
4. Dark green background with light green letters on terminal screen
5. Disks are used to store information for the computer

6. The processing unit is a blue metal box that is three feet wide and eight inches tall.

7. On the left side of the table, a terminal with a screen to enter and display data and a keyboard like that of a typewriter

8. On the right side of the processing unit, red and blue switches that control it

5.2c   Order of Importance

When you use **order of importance** in a paragraph, you arrange details according to their significance or value. This order is particularly useful for arranging a series of reasons, causes, effects, or accomplishments. You may begin with the most important detail and end with the least important item. It is usually more effective, however, to begin with the least important item and build to the most important item. You can emphasize the order that you choose by using transitional words and phrases such as the following: *finally, first, least important, more important,* and *best of all.*

In the following paragraph the writer proceeds from the least important purpose to the most important purpose. The transitional words and phrases that emphasize that progression are in italic type.

Model

Researchers at the Beltsville Agricultural Center near Washington, D.C., are working with satellite photographs of fields of crops. The photographs may be used for several purposes. *First,* by monitoring the color of the fields as seen from above, researchers can tell how effective various watering and fertilizing schedules are. *More important,* the photographs can help researchers to predict what crop yields will be. With that information, experts can set prices in advance and arrange to make up shortages and sell surplus crops. *Most important,* the photographs can be used to save crops. From aerial views researchers can detect sooner and more clearly any problems created by drought and insect infestation. In this way, these conditions can be corrected before the crops are lost. Before long, farmers throughout the country will benefit from the research with satellite photographs.

Exercise 3 Writing: Order of Importance Using the following topic sentence, its supporting details, and the further explanations of the details, write a paragraph that is organized from the least important to the most important detail. Include at least three transitional words or phrases in the paragraph. You may change the wording of the details when you write the paragraph.

Topic sentence: Paramedics, trained medical assistants, can perform many medical tasks.

Supporting details:
1. Provide medical education that doctors do not have time to give; for example, can teach patients how to plan a good diet or how to diagnose simple problems
2. Provide medical care for all but most serious cases when doctors are not available; for example, can provide care in remote areas or at scene of accident
3. Work with doctors to provide routine care, freeing doctors for tasks requiring more specialized knowledge; for example, can take medical history, give physical exam, do laboratory work, and provide physical therapy

5.2d Classification

When you use **classification** in a paragraph, you arrange the details in various categories according to a single principle. This order is especially useful when you want to analyze a larger whole by breaking it into smaller, distinct sections. For example, you might discuss a zoological phylum by dividing it into the classes it comprises, or you might discuss the methods of generating electricity by sorting them according to the power source. When you use classification, you may arrange the details in some order of rank—for example, the extent to which they are common or are important. By using such transitional words and phrases as *one kind, another kind,* and *a third type,* you can emphasize the order that you chose.

The writer of the following paragraph uses four categories, which are arranged in a time order.

Model

      Nowhere are differences in human nature better illustrated than in people's habits of punctuality. When they must be at a certain place at a certain time, people seem to fall into one of four categories. One category is the Early Arrivals. They are the people you see at a bus terminal, standing in front of the ticket window before it is open, three hours before their bus is scheduled to leave. Another category is the compulsive On the Dots. Usually promptness is a virtue, but the On the Dots are punctual to an extreme. On the Dots are the people you see arriving at a dance on the stroke of nine, when the custodian is turning on the lights and the band members are taking the instruments out of their cases. The Late Bloomers, on the other hand, are the people who startle their host by arriving for dinner as he is serving the dessert course. At that, the Late Bloomers are more punctual than the No Shows, the least reliable group of people, well known to long-suffering airline personnel. Early Arrival, On the Dot, Late Bloomer, No Show—does one of these names describe you?

Exercise 4   Writing: Classification   Write a paragraph in which you use the following topic sentence and organize the supporting details by classification. Present the details in a logical order, using transitional words and phrases to make the progression of thought clear. Sometimes you will want to combine two details in one sentence.

Topic sentence:
All fabrics are made from one or more of the three basic types of fibers.

Supporting details:
1. Fibers from plants
2. Fibers from animals
3. Synthetic fibers
4. Plant fibers sometimes called *cellulose fibers*
5. Animal fibers sometimes called *protein fibers*
6. Silk and wool fibers come from animals.
7. Cotton and linen fibers come from plants.
8. Cotton and linen are cool.
9. Synthetic fibers manufactured from chemical elements

10. Nylon and polyester: synthetic fibers
11. Wool the warmest fiber
12. Most synthetic fibers are strong.

5.2e   Comparison and Contrast

When you develop a paragraph by **comparison,** you point out the similarities between two items. When you develop a paragraph by **contrast,** you point out the differences between two items. You may combine the two methods in one paragraph to show your readers how an unfamiliar item is both similar to and different from an item with which they are familiar. You can also combine comparison and contrast to provide your readers with information about two unfamiliar objects. Your paragraph will be clearer if you emphasize the comparison and contrast by using transitional words and phrases such as *however, in contrast,* and *similarly,* and the comparative and superlative forms of adjectives (*page 134*).

When you compare or contrast two items, follow one of two plans. You may use a balanced style by presenting all of the information about one item and then all of the corresponding information about the other item. Alternatively, you may decide to present one point about the first item, give the similar or contrasting information about the second item, and then move on to a new point, repeating the pattern to form a point-by-point comparison. Whichever strategy you use, make sure that you discuss the same points for each item and that you present them in the same order.

The writer of the following paragraph contrasts two items using the point-by-point method. The words that emphasize the contrast are in italic type.

Model

Although some people prefer to see a stage play rather than a film when they have the chance, *both* plays and films have their good points. Seeing the performers in person makes the dialogue and action of a play *more* convincing and exciting than those of a film. The action of a play, however, is limited to the stage. It may be hard to imagine the stage as a beach or a crowded street. *In contrast,* the action of a film can move from a real beach to a real city street. In addition, a film can emphasize an emotion or an idea by focusing on one face or object. Playgoers lose that advantage *but* gain the advantage of being able to focus on the performer or object that interests them most. Thus, although films and plays do have important *differences,* neither of them is *better* than the other.

Exercise 5   Writing: Comparison and Contrast   On your paper, use the following topic sentence and lists of information to write a paragraph organized by comparison and contrast. Use the point-by-point method of comparison and contrast, and include words to emphasize the comparisons and contrasts. Make sure that you consider the same points about each group.

Topic sentence: Two ways of life—that of the farmer and that of the nomad—are common in the rural areas of southwest Asia.

Farmers:
Raise grain and fruit
Live on seacoasts and in river valleys
Make up seventy percent of the population
Live in small mud houses in villages
Rent their land from landlords
Eat their own products: grain, dates, olives
Live with extended families—that is, with several generations of their families

Nomads:
Eat what they produce: cheese, meat, milk
Herd camels, goats, sheep
Live in tents made from animal skins
Live with extended families
Live in and near deserts
Wear clothing made from the fur and skin of animals

5.2f   Analogy

When you develop a paragraph by **analogy,** you make an extended comparison between a familiar item and a less familiar item. Your purpose is usually to teach your readers about the less familiar item. The items should not be similar in all ways. They should, however, be similar in at least one important way. As in a paragraph developed by comparison, you may present the similarities for each item in a block, or you may alternate between corresponding points for each item.

In the following paragraph, the writer provides an interesting way to view the unfamiliar subject of interviewing for a job by comparing it with the more familiar subject of acting in a play.

Model

As I left my first job interview, I realized that interviewing for a job is like playing a role in a drama. Before you interview, you know the role that you are expected to play: secretary, salesperson, or computer programmer, for example. You prepare for the interview by reviewing the skills and knowledge that you need to play the part well. After rehearsing the part, you enter the interview; you are onstage. You must show the interviewer—the audience—how convincingly you can play the role. Just as an actor has to overcome stage fright to play a part well, you have to overcome your nervousness in order to show that you can do the job well. Once the performance is over, you wait for the reviews from the interviewer. If the reviews are excellent, you will probably get the job.

Exercise 6   Writing: Analogy   Use the following information to write a paragraph that presents an analogy between speed reading and driving quickly through the countryside. Use at least two similarities from the following lists, but do not include unrelated points.

Speed reading:
Useful when you need to digest large amounts of information
Not useful for complex, dense works
Taught in classes throughout the country
Does not allow you to enjoy word choice or sentence structures
Allows you to cover material quickly—two thousand words per minute
Used by many students

Driving quickly through countryside:
Allows you to cover ground quickly—fifty-five miles per hour
Not as safe as driving more slowly
Not possible on small, winding roads
Useful when you need to travel far
Most common to drive slowly through country
Does not allow you to gaze at scenery

5.2g   Cause and Effect

When you develop a paragraph by **cause and effect,** you explain how one event or situation necessarily results in another. The cause brings about the effect. The effect is the result of the cause. The following list provides examples of causes and their effects.

CAUSES	EFFECTS
Warm air meeting cold air	Fog
Earth spinning on its axis	Change from day to night
Invention of power looms	Increased production of fabric

In developing a paragraph by cause and effect, be sure that the one event is a cause of another and not merely something that preceded it in time. For example, chills may precede a cold, but they do not cause it. A virus causes a cold. Also, make sure that one event is the direct cause of another and not merely a reason that explains its occurrence. For example, the existence of mines in New South Wales, Australia, was a reason for building many factories there, but it did not cause the factories to be built. You can demonstrate that an event or situation is a cause by explaining the process by which it produces an effect.

A cause may have more than one effect, and an effect may have more than one cause. Therefore, in writing a cause-and-effect paragraph, be sure to discuss all causes or effects, or at least mention that there are multiple causes or effects. Also, causes and effects can work like a chain reaction: an effect of one cause may become the cause of other effects. For example, plant disease caused the failure of the potato crop in Ireland in 1845. That effect in turn caused famine among the Irish people, who relied upon potatoes for most of their nourishment.

When you organize a paragraph by cause and effect, you may present a cause first and then examine its effects, or you may present an effect and then analyze its causes. Whichever method you choose, make sure that you clearly distinguish the causes from the effects. One way to do that is by using words and phrases such as *as a result, because, causes, consequently, creates, effect, produces, reason, results, therefore,* and *why.*

In the following paragraph, the writer states an effect—the noise that a house makes—and then explains the causes. The words that indicate causes or effects are in italic type.

Model

> Squeaks and creaks are not generally a matter for the police. They are most likely the sounds of your house settling down for the night. During the day the house heats up. The materials in the house expand when they are heated. After dark the house cools off, and the materials in the house shrink. The *results* of this expanding and shrinking are heard as pops and creaks and squeaks. The *reason* you hear them only late at night is that in most houses the noises from the activity of the day drown them out. Also, maybe late at night you are listening a little harder for strange noises. If you listen, you may notice that your house *makes* strange noises all day long. Some houses *make* such regular noises that you can tell the time of day by the sound of expansion and shrinking—the creaks act like a clock.

> Linda Allison, *The Wild Inside*

Exercise 7 Writing: Cause and Effect Write a paragraph using the following effect and its causes. Begin with the effect and then present the causes. Include a topic sentence and use words that emphasize the cause-and-effect relationship.

Effect: Soil becoming unsuitable for growing crops

Causes:
1. Growing plants for years without using fertilizer depletes the nutrients necessary for growing more crops.
2. Using too much fertilizer destroys soil's ability to produce nutrients.
3. Pesticides destroy bacteria that help to produce necessary nutrients.
4. Harmful chemicals buried nearby may leak into farmland.
5. High winds and rains can erode the topsoil in which plants grow.

Assignment 1 Prewriting/Writing Make a list of events that occur when a tornado forms, or list devices that have been developed to aid the blind. Organize your list in chronological order. Using the list, write a paragraph. Use transitional words to emphasize the chronological order of the paragraph.

Assignment 2   Prewriting/Writing   Make a list of details about a room in which you spend a lot of time. For example, you could list details about a gym, your room at home, or a library. Arranging the details in spatial order, write a paragraph that describes the room. Use transitional words.

Assignment 3   Prewriting/Writing   List reasons for learning how to play a musical instrument, how to program a computer, how to drive, or how to type. Order the reasons according to their importance, moving from least to most important. Using the list, write a paragraph that explains why someone should learn that skill. Use transitional words to indicate which reasons are the most important.

Assignment 4   Prewriting / Writing   Think of the last time you went to a large store, and try to classify the shoppers you saw. Write a light-hearted paragraph in which you discuss at least three types of shoppers. Give each group a name, and arrange the groups in a logical order, using transitional words for clarity. Begin with a topic sentence, and end with a sentence that brings the paragraph to a definite conclusion.

Assignment 5   Prewriting/Writing   Write a paragraph that contrasts a place as it seemed to you five or more years ago with the same place as it seems to you today. Before you write, make lists of details about the place at each time. When you write, present all of the information about the place at the earlier time and then all of the information about the place as it is now. In your concluding sentence, present a general comment about how the place has changed.

Assignment 6   Prewriting/Writing   Write a paragraph that presents an analogy between a certain type of athlete and a certain type of animal. Before writing, list the characteristics that the athlete and the animal share. Alternate between the two subjects as you present their similarities.

Assignment 7   Prewriting/Writing   Do research to find the causes of the mudpots in Yellowstone National Park. List details about the causes on your paper, and use the list to write a paragraph organized by cause and effect. Begin with the effect and then discuss the causes. Use transitional words to help the reader to understand the cause-and-effect relationship.

Assignment Checklist

Check your assignments for the following points:

✔ 1. Does each paragraph have a precise topic idea, relevant supporting sentences, and a concluding sentence if one is necessary?

✔ 2. In Assignment 1, did you list details in chronological order?

✔ 3. In Assignment 2, did you present the details as they appear from side to side, top to bottom, or front to back?

✔ 4. In Assignment 3, did you begin with the least important reasons and progress to the most important reasons?

✔ 5. In Assignment 4, did you arrange the groups in a logical order and use transitional words to make clear the progression from group to group?

✔ 6. In Assignment 5, did you present all of the information about the place at the earlier time before presenting the contrasting information about the place at the later time?

✔ 7. In Assignment 6, did your analogy include one or two striking characteristics shared by the athlete and the animal?

✔ 8. In Assignment 7, did you move from the effect to the cause?

✔ 9. Did you use suitable transitional words to make clear the organization of your paragraphs?

✔ 10. Did you check your paragraphs for correct grammar, usage, spelling, and punctuation?

5.3 Combining Methods of Organization

Sometimes a paragraph will be most clear to your reader if you combine two methods of organization. For example, when you develop a paragraph by presenting an analogy between two items, you can arrange the similarities in the order of their importance. Similarly, when you develop a paragraph by cause and effect, you can present the effects in chronological order.

The writer of the following paragraph contrasts two types of spaceships. The points of the contrast are arranged in chronological order.

Model

> Compare a Lightsail with an ordinary rocket. A one-ton rocket could push a cargo pod weighing more than a ton to a kilometer per second in a few minutes. A one-ton sail (more than a mile wide) would take all day to reach the same speed with the same cargo. But the next day the rocket would coast, drained of fuel, while the sail would add another kilometer per second to its speed. Accelerating just over one thousandth as fast as a falling brick, it would pass twenty times the speed of sound (in air) in less than a week. . . . Rockets beat sails at giving swift kicks, but in the long haul they run out of gas and then can only coast along.
>
> Eric Drexler,
> "Sailing Through Space on Sunlight"

The writer of the model paragraph presents a point about a rocket's first day in space and then the contrasting point about a Lightsail's first day in space. Next, the writer presents a point about the rocket's following days in space and then the contrasting point about the Lightsail's following days in space. The paragraph ends with a concluding sentence that summarizes the difference between the two types of spaceships.

Exercise 1   Prewriting: Methods of Organization   Read the following list of details. One of the items is an effect, and the others are its causes. On your paper, write the number of the effect first. Then list the numbers of the causes in chronological order.

1. From 1700 on, travelers brought plants, such as the palm from Madagascar, that grew faster than native plants and crowded them out.
2. Dutch settlers arrived in 1638 and exported most of the local ebony trees.
3. Many of the native plants and animals on the island of Mauritius are almost extinct.
4. Recently, escaped pet birds have taken over the territories of native birds.

5. In the 1500s Spanish and Portuguese sailors released pigs and pet monkeys, which have become established and have eaten enormous numbers of local plants and bird eggs.
6. French settlers arrived in 1715 and removed most remaining forests to make room for farms.

Exercise 2 Writing: Methods of Organization Using the information that you organized in Exercise 1, write a paragraph. You may change the wording of the details as you write.

Assignment Prewriting/Writing Each of the following topics can be developed in a paragraph with more than one method of organization. Select one of the topics and then list several supporting details for it. Do research to find additional details. Then organize the details according to the methods indicated next to the topic. Write your paragraph.

1. Differences between the civil service system and the spoils system in United States politics: comparison and contrast, order of importance
2. Effects of latitude on the climate: cause and effect, spatial order
3. Effects of pollution on a lake: cause and effect, chronological order
4. Differences between broadleaf and needleleaf trees: comparison and contrast, spatial order

Assignment Checklist

Check your assignment for the following points:

 ✔ 1. Did you list enough supporting details to develop your topic adequately?
 ✔ 2. Did you combine two methods of development in your paragraph?
 ✔ 3. Did you use transitional words and phrases to make clear the methods of development that you used?
 ✔ 4. Did you check your paragraph for correct grammar, usage, spelling, and punctuation?

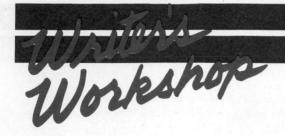

Student Success Survey: Writing a Paragraph

Situation: The editors of the community newspaper, *News and Views,* plan to run a weekly column about the reasons that students succeed in a wide variety of activities. To gather information for the column, they published a request that all students write paragraphs explaining what abilities and skills help them to succeed at various activities. As you write your paragraph, you will keep in mind the following information:

Writer: you as a student who reads *News and Views*

Audience: editors and readers of *News and Views*

Topic: the abilities and skills that help you to succeed at a particular activity

Purpose: to explain the reasons for your success

Directions: To write your paragraph, follow these steps:

Step 1. Read the editors' request for paragraphs that appears on the facing page. Then decide which activity you will write about.

Step 2. List all skills and abilities that help you to succeed in the activity. Ask yourself the following questions: What helps me to do well? What training or background do I have for the activity?

Step 3. Select three or four reasons that seem most important and arrange them in the order of their significance, from least to most important.

Step 4. Using your list, write a paragraph. Include transitional words and phrases that emphasize the order of importance. In your concluding sentence, present a word of advice to others who would like to succeed in the activity.

STUDENT SUCCESS STORIES

A Survey Sponsored by *News and Views*

Please submit one paragraph that explains the reasons for your success at one of your favorite activities. The results of our survey will be presented in a series of weekly columns. We would like information about your success in an activity such as one of the following:

Playing a musical instrument

Writing stories, essays, poems, or songs

Participating in a sport

Working with small children

Organizing events

Acting in or doing backstage work for a play

Explaining something to others

Taking photographs

Getting support for school events

Repairing cars

Working at a part-time job

Doing volunteer work

Participating in a club

Working with animals

Collecting a particular type of item

Unit Assignments

Assignment 1   Write a paragraph about one topic from the following list. Use chronological order to organize the paragraph, and include transitional words and time-related words to make that order clear to your readers. Place your topic sentence at the beginning of the paragraph. Write for an audience of adults who are not familiar with the topic.

1. Distilling water
2. The history of newspapers in the United States
3. How a Presidential candidate is nominated at a convention
4. Training for a certain career

Assignment 2   In a paragraph, compare and contrast hydroponics (farming in water) with farming in soil. Define all difficult or technical terms so that your readers clearly understand your topic. Use an implied topic sentence, and make sure that all of the sentences are clearly related to the topic idea.

Assignment 3   Choose a person whom you admire. Write a paragraph about that person's accomplishments, listing them in chronological order. Then write another paragraph, listing the accomplishments in the order of their importance. In each paragraph, use transitional words to indicate the order that you chose. Write for an audience of your friends.

Assignment 4   Write a paragraph in which you explain one of the following groups of effects. Organize the effects in that group from least to most important. Place your topic sentence somewhere other than at the beginning. Write a concluding sentence that presents your comment on the topic.

1. The effects of people on a forest or other natural setting
2. The effects of surface tension on liquids
3. The effects of excessive salt in the diet

Assignment 5   Write a paragraph in which you compare and contrast two lakes or rivers, two bridges, or two pieces of sculpture.

Organize the details of the comparison in spatial order, and use transitional words that emphasize the order that you choose.

Assignment 6 Choose a recent political event that interests you. Write a paragraph in which you either discuss the causes and effects of the event or present the actions of the event in chronological order. Use transitional words to emphasize the order that you choose.

Assignment 7 Write a paragraph in which you compare and contrast two works of art by the same artist. Use the point-by-point comparison strategy, and arrange those points in spatial order. Place your topic sentence somewhere other than at the beginning of the paragraph, and conclude with a sentence that summarizes the paragraph.

Assignment 8 Write a paragraph in which you explain the different types of musical instruments in a band or orchestra. Use classification to arrange the supporting details, and include examples. Use transitional words and phrases to give your paragraph clarity.

Revising Your Assignments

For help in revising a paragraph, consult the Checklist for Revision on the last page of this book.

Unit Tests

Test 1

A. Number your paper from 1 to 5. Next to each number, write *True* if the sentence is true or *False* if it is false.

1. You should limit a topic by choosing to write about just one aspect of it, one example of it, or one time period in it.
2. A good topic sentence should indicate that you will discuss more than you actually do.
3. Supporting sentences provide the details that explain or illustrate your topic.
4. A fact may be used as a reason or as an example.
5. You may not combine chronological order and cause and effect in the same paragraph.

B. Number your paper from 6 to 10. Next to each number, write the letter of the item that correctly completes the sentence. You will use all but one of the items.

a. concluding sentence   d. fact
b. paragraph   e. topic sentence
c. analogy   f. transitional word

6. A(n) __?__ is a group of sentences that develops an idea in an orderly way.
7. A(n) __?__ states the main idea of a paragraph.
8. A(n) __?__ helps the reader to recall or to understand more clearly the point of a paragraph.
9. A(n) __?__ emphasizes the logical order of a paragraph.
10. A(n) __?__ is an extended comparison between a familiar item and a less familiar item.

C. Number your paper from 11 to 15. Read the following passage. Next to each number, write the letter of the item that correctly answers the question.

> (1) Worms in the Waitomo Caves in New Zealand glow in the dark, and their lights attract the insects that they eat. (2) Like these glowworms from New Zealand, most cave-dwelling animals

are specially suited to their dark environment. (3) For example, crayfish that live in caves have longer legs and antennae than crayfish that live in light areas. (4) Their longer appendages help them to find food by enabling them to reach farther. (5) One type of cave-dwelling fish has ridges on its head. (6) The ridges help the fish to detect the movement of its prey in the water. (7) Another type of fish has an exceptionally large head and big fins that cause it to bump into its prey more often than a fish with a smaller head and normal fins would. (8) These special characteristics help the cave animals to survive in their dark world.

11. Which of the following is the topic sentence for the paragraph?
    a. Sentence 1   c. Sentence 3
    b. Sentence 2   d. Sentence 8

12. Which of the following describes Sentence 1?
    a. Topic sentence   c. Concluding sentence
    b. Supporting sentence   d. Transitional sentence

13. Which of the following is contained in Sentence 3?
    a. A comparison   c. An analogy
    b. A contrast   d. A cause

14. Which of the following describes Sentence 5?
    a. An example   c. A cause
    b. A reason   d. A comparison

15. Which of the following contains a transitional word?
    a. Sentence 3   c. Sentence 5
    b. Sentence 4   d. Sentence 8

Test 2

Choose one of the Unit Assignments. Write the assignment as directed and hand it in to your teacher.

Unit 6

Revising

Unit Preview

When you have completed a first draft, you are ready for the last phase of the writing process: revision. **Revision** entails rethinking your work, reorganizing and rewriting it so that your finished paragraph expresses your thoughts in a clear and effective manner.

The following paragraph is a writer's first draft. As you read the draft, consider how you might improve it.

(1) There are differences in the height of tides. (2) The positions of the sun and the moon and the shapes of the coastlines cause the variations. (3) When the sun and the moon line up, their gravitational forces pull together, causing the tides to rise. (4) When they do not line up and, therefore, pull in different directions, the tides are lower. (5) The size and the shape of coastlines have almost as great an effect on the height of tides. (6) For example, because of the fact that the Bay of Fundy in eastern Canada is shaped like a funnel, the level of the tides there has risen as much as fifty feet in height. (7) The tides are irregular. (8) Scientists who analyze the data about the sun, the moon, and the coastlines can predict the height of each tide.

For Analysis Answer the following questions about the writer's first-draft paragraph.

1. The topic sentence, Sentence 1, should be more specific to emphasize the purpose of the paragraph. Which of the following revisions would be a better topic sentence?
   a. Ocean tides vary at different times and in different places.
   b. Ocean tides, the periodic rising and falling of water levels, vary in height from week to week and from area to area.

2. Which sentence could be improved by making it concise?

    a. Sentence 3   b. Sentence 6

3. How can Sentences 7 and 8 be combined? Write one effective sentence that includes the information contained in both sentences.

In answering these questions, you made decisions about revising. As you gain experience in writing and revising, you will develop methods that work well for you. This unit will give you both an approach to revising and techniques for revising.

6.1 Revising: Coherence and Clarity

To be understandable, a paragraph must be coherent. In a coherent paragraph, the supporting information is unified by its close relationship to the topic sentence and by its appropriateness for the audience. The paragraph is developed and organized according to a plan that makes clear the relationships among the ideas. Furthermore, a coherent paragraph is consistent in the way that it presents the material.

6.1a Unity and Order

Unity

A paragraph has **unity** when all of the information in it directly relates to the topic. To unify your paragraph, you must make clear your purpose in writing about your topic and develop your paragraph fully with related information.

Use the following strategies to examine your writing for unity.

Strategies

1. *Be sure that your paragraph has a topic sentence* that makes clear the topic and the purpose of your paragraph.

2. *Make sure that the supporting sentences contain only information that directly relates to the topic.* Remove irrelevant information or rewrite it so that it fits the topic.

3. *Be sure that your paragraph is completely developed.* Include enough explanation (facts, examples, and reasons) so that your reader completely understands your point. If you require more information, do the necessary research to find it.

4. *If you have used a concluding sentence, be sure that it adds to the paragraph* by restating the topic or offering a final comment on the topic.

Order

An important requirement in any piece of writing is order. An effective sequence of sentences helps to unfold your ideas to your readers and to show the relationships between the ideas.

The following strategies will help you to present your ideas in a logical and effective order.

Strategies

1. *Introduce your topic before treating it in any detail.* Similarly, define an issue or a problem before offering solutions to it.

2. *Define obscure words or ideas before repeating them.*

3. *Discuss a series of items in the order in which you introduced them.*

4. *Give an example only after you have stated the general idea that the example illustrates.*

5. *Organize your ideas according to an appropriate order:* chronological order, spatial order, or order of importance.

6. *Use a method of development that is appropriate for your purpose:* classification, comparison and contrast, analogy, or cause and effect.

Transitional Words and Expressions. To emphasize the order used in your paragraph, use transitional words and expressions (*pages 254–260*), which make clear the connections between the ideas and help the paragraph flow smoothly from one sentence to another.

Exercise 1 Revising: Unity The following paragraphs are insufficiently developed. On your paper, revise each paragraph to create unity. Be sure that the topic sentence clarifies the purpose of the paragraph. Add facts and examples to support the topic. Remove or rewrite any details that are not closely related.

1.   I attended the Senior Stunt Night. The acrobatic dancing was great. The jazz chorus never sounded better. The life-sized puppets were especially clever. The teachers' skit was hilarious. I'm glad that I saw the show. It ran late.

2.   Stories are valuable for many reasons. Stories can be in books, in movies, or on television. A well-told story can almost always captivate us with the lure of "what comes next." Stories also tell us about people. In the simplest sense, stories describe problems and tell how people deal with them. The imaginary characters who move through the pages of a story can often teach us about real people.

Exercise 2 Revising: Unity and Order On your paper, revise the following paragraph. Add or remove information as necessary to unify the paragraph. Present the supporting information logically and effectively. Insert transitional words and expressions and adjust wording as necessary.

      The city of Venice was built in the fifth century. It was a clean, beautiful city. Twentieth-century industrial development is causing the city to deteriorate. The canals were deepened so that tankers could use them to reach the factories. The increased water flow in the deeper canals caused the erosion of seawalls and building foundations. The factories created air pollution, which caused the deterioration of statues and the outsides of buildings, just as pollution has damaged the Acropolis in Greece. More than twenty thousand artesian wells were built to supply water to the industries and to the people employed in them. Removing water from the wells caused the lagoon bed to fall and created a threat to all of the buildings in Venice. Now experts have halted the sinking of the lagoon bed, and they are working hard to save the beautiful old city.

6.1b   Consistency

Consistency in your writing is a further requirement for coherence. When you revise, be sure that you have been consistent in the tense (*page 101*), voice (*page 104*), and mood (*page 105*) of verbs; the person of pronouns (*pages 121–122*); and the tone in which you discuss the topic. Although shifts are occasionally appropriate, unnecessary shifts can make your writing awkward and confusing.

The following strategies will help you to revise for consistency.

Strategies

1. *Use the same verb tense, either within sentences or between them, unless there is a change in the time in which the actions occur.*

   INCONSISTENT

   The first paragraph of the story *establishes* the place and time through its detailed description of the carnival. In the second paragraph, the central event of the story *occurred*. [Tense shifts from present to past.]

   REVISED

   The first paragraph of the story *establishes* the place and time through its detailed description of the carnival. In the second paragraph, the central event of the story *occurs*. [Present tense used consistently.]

2. *Do not switch unnecessarily between the active voice and the passive voice.* Be aware that a change in the voice of the verb also causes a change in the subject and, thus, a change in the focus or emphasis. The active voice is generally preferable.

   INCONSISTENT

   The triumphant pitcher *received* a generous offer from the ball club, but a contract *has* not yet *been signed* by him for next year. [Voice shifts from active to passive; subject changes from *pitcher* to *contract*.]

REVISED

> The triumphant pitcher *received* a generous offer from the ball club, but he *has* not yet *signed* a contract for next year. [Active voice used consistently; subject is the same.]

3. *Be consistent in the mood of the verb (pages 105–107).* Do not shift unnecessarily from the indicative mood to the subjunctive mood, for example, or from the subjunctive mood to the imperative mood.

INCONSISTENT

> The personnel department requires that the editorial applicant *write* a paragraph and *takes* a proofreading test. [Mood shifts from subjunctive to indicative.]

REVISED

> The personnel department requires that the editorial applicant *write* a paragraph and *take* a proofreading test. [Subjunctive mood used consistently.]

INCONSISTENT

> First *take* the test, and then you *will worry* about the essay. [Mood shifts from imperative to indicative.]

REVISED

> First *take* the test, and then *worry* about the essay. [Imperative mood used consistently.]

4. *Be consistent in your use of pronouns.* Do not make needless shifts from the third person (*she, he, one, it,* and nouns) to the second person (*you*) or the first person (*I*).

INCONSISTENT

> Although a beginning *skater* should not become preoccupied with the danger of falling, *you* should exercise some caution. [Shifts from third person to second person.]

REVISED

> Although a beginning *skater* should not become preoccupied with the danger of falling, *he* or *she* should exercise caution. [Third person used consistently.]

REVISED

> Although *you* should not become preoccupied with the danger of falling, *you* should exercise some caution. [Second person used consistently.]

5. *Be consistent in the tone, or attitude, that you convey about your topic.* Establish a tone that is suitable for your topic and your audience. For instance, do not change from critical to sympathetic, or from sympathetic to sarcastic. Maintain a degree of formality that suits the tone.

INCONSISTENT

> Although it is generally known that Benjamin Franklin once conducted an experiment by flying a kite during a storm, I'll bet that you don't know what got Ben started on that experiment. It was a glass jar, known as a Leyden jar. [Tone shifts from serious to casual.]

REVISED

> Although it is generally known that Benjamin Franklin once conducted an experiment by flying a kite during a storm, few people realize that the experiment was prompted by an invention called the Leyden jar. [Serious tone used consistently.]

Exercise 3   Revising: Consistency   On your paper, revise the following paragraph to make it consistent in tense, voice, mood, person, and tone.

Although mosquitoes are found even in the Arctic, they are relatively rare in cold or dry parts of the world. When you are relaxing by a lake at five o'clock on a lazy summer afternoon, however, one may have abundant reason to doubt that statement. Mosquitoes seemed to be everywhere, at least everywhere that you were. The following facts may give you some perspective, if not any relief. Most other insects are not interested in you; you are sought out only by the mosquito. There are more than twenty-five hundred species of mosquitoes, but only a few of them will ever bite anyone. Of the species that do bite, only the females will request that you supply her with nourishment. When the next attack comes, be grateful that the invading troops are a squad of mosquitoes and not an army of spiders, and then you will want to start slapping away.

Assignment Revising On your paper, revise the following paragraph for coherence and clarity. Make sure that your revised paragraph is unified, well organized, and consistent.

> Serendipity is the capacity for making a fortunate discovery by accident, often while keeping your eyes peeled for something else. Horace Walpole, an eighteenth-century English writer, created the term in honor of the many accidental discoveries of the main characters in the fairy tale "The Three Princes of Serendip." Walpole also wrote *The Castle of Otranto.* Serendipity has been responsible for many important discoveries. Christopher Columbus lands in America by accident when he is searching for gold in the Indies. A really wild discovery about the value of penicillium mold is made by Sir Alexander Fleming by accident. He noticed that some of the mold in his laboratory had accidentally killed all of the bacteria that it touched. If you discover your grandfather's diary while you are cleaning the attic, that is serendipity. In addition, serendipity often plays a part in everyday life. Although serendipity is never expected, it always is welcome.

Assignment Checklist

Check your assignment for the following points:

✔ 1. Did you state the topic clearly and develop it fully?
✔ 2. Did you remove or rewrite unrelated information?
✔ 3. Did you organize the supporting information in an order that will make sense to a reader?
✔ 4. Did you supply transitional expressions where necessary?
✔ 5. Did you maintain consistency in the tense, voice, and mood of the verbs, in the person of the pronouns, and in the tone?

6.2 Revising: Combining Sentences

Combining some sentences to establish the desired relationships between the ideas in them will make your sentences more effective and will contribute to the coherence of your paragraph. Furthermore, you often can express more information in a single sentence.

SEPARATE SENTENCES

>The architect was in favor of the proposal. She could not find time for the Fieldstone project.

SINGLE SENTENCE

>The architect was in favor of the proposal, but she could not find time for the Fieldstone project. [contrast relationship]

You can often combine sentences in more than one way. Sometimes a different combination can express very nearly the same relationship.

REVISED SENTENCE

>Although the architect was in favor of the proposal, she could not find time for the Fieldstone project. [contrast relationship]

At other times a different combination expresses a different relationship, changing the meaning of the sentence.

REVISED SENTENCE

>The architect was in favor of the proposal because she could not find time for the Fieldstone project. [cause relationship]

As you examine your sentences, see whether you can improve some of them by combining them. Make sure that the combination you choose expresses the correct relationship. The following strategies provide guidelines for combining sentences.

Strategies

1. *Coordinate sentences.* Coordination is the joining of similar or equal parts into pairs or series. To coordinate sentences, join them with coordinating or correlative conjunctions (*page 30*) or conjunctive adverbs (*page 31*). You may also use a semicolon without a conjunction. When you coordinate sentences, you form a compound sentence.

   TWO SENTENCES

   >Representative Rea had voted against the original highway bill. He was in favor of the revised version.

REVISED SENTENCE

Representative Rea had voted against the original highway bill, **but** he was in favor of the revised version. [Sentences coordinated with comma and conjunction *but*.]

REVISED SENTENCE

Representative Rea had voted against the original highway bill; **however,** he was in favor of the revised version. [Sentences coordinated with semicolon and conjunctive adverb *however*.]

REVISED SENTENCE

Representative Rea had voted against the original highway bill; he was in favor of the revised version. [Sentences coordinated with semicolon.]

2. *Subordinate some sentences by converting them to subordinate clauses (pages 59–66).* Put the less important (subordinate) ideas in adjective, adverb, or noun clauses. Use the appropriate relative pronouns (*page 10*) or subordinating conjunctions (*pages 30–31*). When you join a subordinate clause with an independent clause, you form a complex sentence.

TWO SENTENCES

The front door opened directly into the living room. It was used only by guests.

REVISED SENTENCE WITH ADJECTIVE CLAUSE

The front door, *which opened directly into the living room,* was used only by guests. [Subordinate idea becomes adjective clause modifying *door*.]

TWO SENTENCES

The front door opened and closed just as easily as the back door. Hardly anyone used the front door.

REVISED SENTENCE WITH ADVERB CLAUSE

Although the front door opened and closed just as easily as the back door, hardly anyone used it. [Subordinate idea becomes adverb clause modifying *used*.]

TWO SENTENCES

> Carl Sandburg was not only a famous poet but also a biographer of Abraham Lincoln. Only a few in the class knew that.

REVISED SENTENCE WITH NOUN CLAUSE

> Only a few in the class knew *that Carl Sandburg was not only a famous poet but also a biographer of Abraham Lincoln.* [Clause becomes object of verb *knew* in revised sentence.]

3. *Subordinate some sentences by converting them to phrases.* You may use participial phrases (*page 51*), appositive phrases (*page 48*), absolute phrases (*page 52*), gerund phrases (*pages 53–54*), and infinitive phrases (*pages 55–56*).

TWO SENTENCES

> Sheila was awakened by a loud whirring noise. She ran to the window.

REVISED SENTENCE WITH PARTICIPIAL PHRASE

> *Awakened by a loud whirring noise,* Sheila ran to the window. [Subordinate idea becomes participial phrase modifying *Sheila.*]

TWO SENTENCES

> Antoine Cartier visited our restaurant last night. He is one of the world's foremost writers on food.

REVISED SENTENCE WITH APPOSITIVE PHRASE

> Antoine Cartier, *one of the world's foremost writers on food,* visited our restaurant last night. [Predicate nominative becomes appositive identifying *Antoine Cartier.*]

TWO SENTENCES

> Its streets were bedecked with cheerful yellow jonquils and forsythia. The town seemed to be greeting spring.

REVISED SENTENCE WITH ABSOLUTE PHRASE

> *Its streets bedecked with cheerful yellow jonquils and forsythia,* the town seemed to be greeting spring. [Subordinate idea becomes absolute phrase.]

TWO SENTENCES
> Carmen watched the world darken during the eclipse. It was an eerie but thrilling experience for her.

REVISED SENTENCE WITH GERUND PHRASE
> *Watching the world darken during the eclipse* was an eerie but thrilling experience for Carmen. [Activity of original sentence changed to gerund which replaces *it* as subject.]

TWO SENTENCES
> They wanted to avoid rush-hour traffic. They would leave early.

REVISED SENTENCE WITH INFINITIVE PHRASE
> They would leave early *to avoid rush-hour traffic.* [Subordinate idea becomes infinitive.]

Exercise 1 Revising: Combining Sentences On your paper, combine each of the following groups of sentences into one sentence. Coordinate or subordinate as indicated in parentheses. You may adjust the wording of the revised sentence.

SAMPLE An exciting variety typifies New York City. Variety is found in its food as well as in its inhabitants. Therefore, one can dine in almost any national style. (adverb clause; adjective clause)

ANSWER Because the exciting variety that typifies New York City is found in its food as well as in its inhabitants, one can dine in almost any national style.

1. Both native New Yorkers and visitors to the city enjoy eating different kinds of food. That is obvious from the vast number and varied kinds of restaurants. These restaurants thrive there. (noun clause; adjective clause)
2. Just about every cuisine has developed its own version of meat or vegetables. These are wrapped in dough. Just about every version, therefore, can be found somewhere in New York. (adverb clause; participial phrase)
3. Pita from the Middle East is a flat bread with a pocket. The pocket is good for many kinds of sandwich fillings. (adjective clause) tive clause)

4. You remain in a Middle Eastern mood. You fill your pita with a fried mass of chickpeas and spices. This is known as falafel. (participial phrase; participial phrase)

5. You want to try Greek cuisine. You stuff the pita with souvlaki. Souvlaki is meat. The meat has been cooked slowly on a skewer. (adverb clause; appositive phrase; participial phrase)

6. You know that samosa came to New York from India. Samosa is a turnover. It is filled with meat or vegetables or both. You are not surprised. You learn the following. The dish is highly spiced. (participial phrase; appositive phrase; participial phrase; infinitive phrase; noun clause)

7. In France you can put a filling in a folded pancake. Doing so produces a crêpe. In Eastern Europe you can put a filling in a folded pancake. Doing so produces a blintz. (gerund phrase; compound sentence; gerund phrase)

8. Mexico has not only given us the taco, but it has also contributed the enchilada. The taco is a toasted tortilla. The tortilla is stuffed with ground meat or chicken and covered with chopped tomato, onion, cheese, and lettuce. The enchilada is similar except that the tortilla is soft and the cheese is melted. (adjective clause; participial phrase; adjective clause)

9. Tacos, enchiladas, and empañadas come from the Caribbean, Mexico, and South America. They are often prepared with sauces. The sauces range in spiciness from fiery to explosive. (adjective clause; participial phrase)

10. Novices should taste these foods with care. They retain sensation in their mouths. The novices wish that. (adverb clause; infinitive phrase)

Exercise 2   Revising: Combining Sentences   On your paper, write a paragraph based on each of the following sets of sentences. Combine the sentences appropriately, using coordination and subordination. You may adjust the wording as necessary to produce a clear and smooth paragraph.

1. United States Forest Service experts can minimize the danger of avalanches.
   They try to predict and prevent avalanches.
   Predicting avalanches requires careful observation.

These avalanche experts observe the temperature, the wind velocity, the rate of snowfall, the water content in the snow, and the type of snow crystals.

Certain weather conditions lead to avalanches.

These conditions exist just before an avalanche occurs.

They observe all of the warning signs.

They can, with confidence, predict an avalanche.

Sometimes only some of the warning signs are present.

The experts cannot make a prediction with certainty.

2. Preventing avalanches is easier than predicting them.

Forest Service experts confirm that.

The experts use explosives.

They set off several small avalanches.

These small avalanches relieve the tension.

The tension otherwise would result in a dangerous avalanche.

Forest Service experts want to learn enough.

They want to prevent 90 percent of the avalanches.

They will improve their accuracy.

Damage from avalanches will be reduced greatly.

Assignment   Revising   On your paper, revise the following paragraph. Combine sentences as necessary to make clear the relationships between the ideas in the sentences.

People speak different languages. They conduct business, scientific, and diplomatic meetings. They must talk with one another. Therefore, there is a need for an international language. An international language is one that can be spoken by people from all nations. In the Middle Ages, Latin was an international language in Western Europe. Few people speak Latin now. L. L. Zamenhof wanted to fill the need for a universal language. He was a Polish physician and linguist. He developed Esperanto in 1887. He tried to make the language easy to learn. He used words that are similar in many languages. He gave all nouns and all verbs consistent forms. Esperanto is now used in almost ninety countries. In addition, government agencies of some countries publish books and brochures about their countries in Esperanto. Nineteen radio stations broadcast programs in the language. All things are considered. Esperanto has proved valuable in international relationships.

Assignment Checklist

Check your assignment for the following points:

✔ 1. Did you coordinate some ideas of equal importance in compound sentences?
✔ 2. Did you subordinate ideas of less importance by placing them in subordinate clauses or in phrases?

6.3   Revising Sentences for Variety

Vary the structure and length of the sentences in your paragraph. Variety in your sentences helps to establish a flow of ideas and a rhythm that makes your writing more interesting. Include different sentence elements (subordinate clauses, participial phrases, appositives, and so forth) from one sentence to the next. Make sure that your paragraph contains a mixture of simple, compound, and complex sentences. Try occasionally to express a declarative remark in the form of an interrogative or imperative sentence.

REPETITIVE STRUCTURE AND LENGTH

Jupiter is a planet of many mysteries. The Great Red Spot is perhaps its most unusual feature. The spot has been calculated as being eight thousand miles wide and twenty-five thousand miles long. Its actual size is subject to change. The spot's color also seems to change. It is red sometimes, pink sometimes, and gray sometimes. The spot rotates more slowly than its surroundings. It therefore cannot be a part of the planet's surface. Astronomers know a great deal about what the spot is *not*. The exact nature of the spot still baffles them.

VARIED STRUCTURE AND LENGTH

Jupiter is a planet of many mysteries. Perhaps its most unusual feature is the Great Red Spot. Although its actual size is subject to change, the spot has been calculated as being eight thousand miles wide and twenty-five thousand miles long. The spot's color seems subject to change, too, appearing sometimes red, sometimes pink, and sometimes gray. The spot rotates more slowly than its surroundings; it cannot, therefore, be part of the planet's surface. Indeed, astronomers know a great deal about what the spot is *not*. But what exactly *is* it?

The following strategies will help you to revise your sentences for variety.

Strategies

1. *Vary the structure and length of your sentences by using coordination and subordination (pages 284–287).* Often you can say essentially the same thing in more than one way. Choose the way that best expresses your intended meaning and fits well with the surrounding sentences. The following sentences state basically the same idea in a variety of ways.

   > The attorney had directed the firm for twenty years and was now retiring to raise horses. [simple sentence with compound predicate]
   >
   > Having directed the firm for twenty years, the attorney was now retiring to raise horses. [simple sentence with verbal phrase]
   >
   > The attorney who had directed the firm for twenty years was now retiring to raise horses. [complex sentence]
   >
   > The attorney who had directed the firm for twenty years was now retiring, for he wanted to raise horses. [compound-complex sentence]

2. *Begin some sentences with a modifier rather than with the subject.* If you place a modifier at the beginning of a sentence, be sure that the modifier is still close to the word that it modifies so that there is no confusion in meaning.

   ADVERB
   > *Surprisingly,* the tulip did not originate in Holland but in Turkey.

   PREPOSITIONAL PHRASE
   > *With flowers in window boxes, on streets, in stores, and in lapels,* the city seems to be built of flowers.

   PARTICIPIAL PHRASE
   > *Determined to retain its serenity,* Haarlem prohibits cars in its central areas.

INFINITIVE PHRASE

> *To meet the demand for tulips,* Haarlem residents'
> devote much of their time to raising them.

ABSOLUTE PHRASE

> *Their colors exploding like a fireworks display,* these
> tulips attract sightseers from all over the world.

ADVERB CLAUSE

> *As if Haarlem were not already blessed with recogni-*
> *tion,* it also has a museum devoted to the works of
> the seventeenth-century painter Franz Hals.

3. *Invert the normal word order of the sentence (page 38).*

> Among the guests were the governor and several of his
> aides.

Exercise   Revising: Variety   On your paper, combine each of
the following sets of sentences into one sentence, coordinating and
subordinating ideas appropriately. Change wording as necessary, but
do not alter the original meaning. Then revise your sentence to vary
its structure or its beginning.

SAMPLE	Community gardens are fast becoming a popular use for vacant public land. The gardens are appearing everywhere on patches of land. This land has been given to the public. The land must be cultivated.
ANSWER	Community gardens, fast becoming a popular use for vacant public land, are appearing everywhere on patches of land given to the public to be cultivated.
	Community gardens are fast becoming a popular use for public land, for they are appearing everywhere on patches of land given to the public to be cultivated.

1. The gardens are thriving in cities and suburbs. People can be in touch with nature. They can also eat well at the same time.

2. Spring comes. The sun is higher in the sky. You notice a crop of bent backs. The backs sprout in the vacant lots of the city. The bent backs sprout on rooftop gardens of apartment houses. They sprout on conservation land in the suburbs.

3. The bent backs belong to the community gardeners. The gardeners are preparing the inhospitable soil of the city. They may be preparing soil that is carried in to rooftops. Alternatively, they may be preparing the more receptive ground of suburban land. The ground will nourish a variety of vegetables.

4. They spend their days planting, weeding, and watering. The reason is that the home-grown vegetables taste so much better. They are picked and eaten fresh. They seem to be different species from the supermarket varieties.

5. Perhaps just as important as the quality of the vegetables is the satisfaction. This satisfaction comes from having grown them.

6. The community garden in the suburb or the city offers people a chance. They can feel somewhat self-sufficient in an urban society.

Assignment Revising On your paper, revise the following passage to include sentences of different structures and lengths. You may combine some sentences, and you may move some modifiers to the beginnings. You do not need to change every sentence.

It was not so very long ago. The term *recycling* conjured up images of scouts. They were collecting newspapers. Recycling is being recognized as an economic and environmental necessity today. It is becoming big business, furthermore. Factories buy old newspaper, and they make more newspaper. Factories also transform glass, aluminum cans, and scrap metal into usable items.

Scrap collection for reuse or resale is not new. Civilization has produced scrap for a long time. Recycling in some form has probably existed nearly as long. People born sixty or seventy years ago certainly remember an earlier time. At that time little was thrown away. Ashes became soap. Old clothes became patchwork quilts. Bottles were returned. They became new bottles. Organized recycling reached its height during World War II. No self-respecting citizens would throw away newspapers. They would not throw away a piece of metal. They would not think of it. We have become adept at many things since that time. We have, perhaps, become adept at waste-making most of all.

The last few years have brought a heightened awareness. There are serious problems being generated along with the prodigious amounts of trash. Problems arise from where to put the trash. Problems also arise from how to pay for putting it there. There are also problems resulting from shortages in energy and materials. Recycling is a way to start reducing these problems. It reduces the amount of trash.

Assignment Checklist

Check your assignment for the following points:

✔ 1. Did you coordinate and subordinate sentences to vary the structures and the lengths?
✔ 2. Did you vary the beginnings of some sentences?
✔ 3. Did you leave unchanged the structure and length of some sentences?

6.4   Revising Sentences for Parallel Structure

When you revise your sentences, make sure that you use parallel structure where necessary. A sentence has **parallel structure** when similar parts of it are written in the same grammatical form. That is, the conjunctions *and, or, than* and the correlative conjunctions *not only . . . but (also)* and *either . . . or* and *neither . . . nor* must join two or more adjectives, phrases, clauses, or other structures of the same type.

The parallel parts are in italic type in the following sentences:

In gas consumption *what the car dealer claimed* and *how the car performed* were surprisingly close. [The parts joined by *and* are both noun clauses.]

Chester has tried *roller-skating, ice-skating,* and *riding a bicycle,* but he still prefers *jogging* for exercise. [The direct objects are all gerunds or gerund phrases.]

Many times, sentences with faults in parallel structure can be corrected in more than one way.

NOT PARALLEL

A good chair, a good book, and listening to good music are all that Clarisse needs to be content.

REVISED

> *A good chair, a good book,* and *good music* are all that
> Clarisse needs to be content.

REVISED

> *Sitting in a good chair, reading a good book,* and *listening to
> good music* are all that Clarisse needs to be content.

You must use parallel structure with correlative conjunctions;
that is, you must follow each part of the correlative conjunction with
the same type of structure. Be sure that you place the two parts of the
conjunction immediately before the parallel parts.

NOT PARALLEL

> As a rule, European trains run *not only* **frequently** *but also*
> **run** on time. [*Not only* precedes an adverb; *but also* precedes
> a verb.]

REVISED

> As a rule, European trains *not only* **run** frequently *but also*
> **run** on time. [Both *not only* and *but also* precede verbs.]

If you omit an article, a preposition, a pronoun, or the word *to*
in an infinitive from one part of a parallel structure, then you must
omit that word from every occurrence of that structure. Similarly, if
you include such a word in a parallel structure, you must include it
each time you use that structure.

NOT PARALLEL

> He hoped that the price would be reasonable, the delivery
> would be prompt, and that the products would work.

REVISED

> He hoped that the price would be reasonable, the delivery
> would be prompt, and the products would work.

RLVISED

> He hoped that the price would be reasonable, that the deliv-
> ery would be prompt, and that the products would work.

Exercise 1   Revising: Parallel Structure   On your paper,
revise the following sentences to give them parallel structure.

SAMPLE   Mr. Marlowe did not like to fly kites, walk on jetties, or playing checkers.

ANSWER   Mr. Marlowe did not like to fly kites, walk on jetties, or play checkers.

1. On that typewriter you can either use a regular fabric ribbon or a carbon film ribbon.
2. The audience was composed of people who had positions at the bank, people who were enrolled in training programs there, and whoever was interested in a bank job.
3. Almost everyone thought Jonathan to be wise, Elena to be witty, and that Howard was both.
4. For her trip Ms. Russo plans to buy a pair of reflecting sunglasses, large sun hat, and a big, bright beach towel.
5. Georgette was pleased with both the atmosphere of the restaurant and how the food tasted.
6. To type well, to take shorthand, and knowing basic bookkeeping techniques were the major requirements for the job.
7. In Carmel, California, the visitor not only finds a charming, flower-bedecked town but also a breath-taking view of the Pacific.
8. Amazingly, not only could the cat roll over on command but also come when called.
9. The photographer caught her subjects working at their jobs, competing in a sport, or when they were just relaxing in their homes.
10. Detective McLeod suspects that the butler is guilty and he will confess.

Exercise 2   Revising: Parallel Structure   On your paper, rewrite each group of sentences as one sentence with parallel structure.

SAMPLE   Delighted with the new product, the research staff supported the decision to expand production. The sales force agreed. Both staffs were convinced that the product would sell well.

ANSWER   Delighted with the new product and convinced that it would sell well, both the sales force and the research staff supported the decision to expand production.

1. Appearing unconcerned, Lester Reilly walked out of his office. He was actually concentrating on the challenge before him. He strode determinedly down the corridor to the meeting room.

2. Appearing at a press conference was not a new experience for him. Announcing a new product was also not new for Reilly, founder of Reilly Technology, Inc. He was president of the firm as well.

3. Although Reilly did not dislike speaking to the press, he much preferred to work alone in the laboratory. He did not mind appearing on television occasionally. However, he preferred to discuss his research with the younger scientists.

4. Nonetheless, Reilly realized the importance of public relations activities. He always made sure to smile as he entered the board room. He entered the conference room the same way.

5. Thinking of how little he had started out with made him smile. At the same time, he was thinking of how much he had accomplished in twenty years.

Assignment   Revising   Revise the following paragraph so that the sentences have parallel structure where necessary.

> Computers can solve mathematical problems both more accurately and do them more quickly than people. However, scientists still are trying to program computers to master certain tasks and skills that so far have required human intelligence. These tasks include understanding language, to learn from experience, and program themselves. For tasks such as these, computers cannot be programmed with step-by-step instructions as they are programmed to solve mathematical problems. Instead, scientists must program them with general strategies, similar to the thinking skills and patterns of human beings. Then the scientists test the computers' success in responding to questions or in how they write new programs. The computers pass the tests if either their answers make sense or are similar to those that a person could give. Some computers can perform one specific type of task very well, but so far no computer has been programmed to do as well as people do in all tasks.

Assignment Checklist

Check your assignment for the following points:

✔ 1. Did you make parallel the parts of sentences that serve similar functions?

✔ 2. Did you place correlative conjunctions immediately before the parallel sentence parts?

✔ 3. Did you either repeat or omit introductory words in each part of a parallel structure?

6.5 Revising Sentences for Conciseness

6.5a Eliminating Wordiness

Concise writing is effective writing. Conciseness is not necessarily the use of the fewest possible words; it is the use of only words that are needed. Wordiness, which is the use of more words than necessary, weakens your writing. By using only necessary words and by using shorter constructions, you can often improve the clarity and power of your writing. The following strategies will guide you in revising your writing for conciseness.

Strategies

1. *Do not mistake flowery expressions and pretentious words for good writing.* Good writing is usually clear, simple, and direct.

   WORDY
   > Being desirous of remaining sanguine in the face of a seemingly omnipotent adversary, the chess player centralized his concentrative powers on the chessboard.

   REVISED
   > Wanting to remain optimistic in the face of a powerful opponent, the chess player focused his attention on the chessboard.

2. *Use direct expressions* unless you have a good reason to use less direct ones. Here are examples of indirect expressions, together with concise replacements.

WORDY	CONCISE
reading resource room	library
institution of higher learning	university
medical facility	hospital
musical group	band, orchestra
a person in the arts	artist
a person in physics	physicist
the members of our family	our family
has the capability of	is able to, can
make the purchase of	buy
functioning in the capacity of	working as

3. *Eliminate certain fixed expressions that provide nothing but padding.* Substitute more concise expressions or eliminate the expressions altogether.

WORDY	CONCISE
in point of fact	in fact
at the present time	now
at this point in time	now
in this day and time	now
each and every	each, every
due to the fact that	because
to make a long story short	in short
in and of itself	in itself

4. *Use the active voice* to make your sentences more direct and forceful. Whenever possible, rewrite passive constructions, especially those that begin with *It is* or *There is*.

WORDY

It has been decided by us that we will study Chinese.

REVISED

We have decided to study Chinese.

WORDY

There is a striking pair of cardinals that is living in our oak tree.

REVISED

A striking pair of cardinals is living in our oak tree.

5. *Avoid redundancy.* Redundancy is needless repetition. Deliberate repetition can be effective, as in parallel structure. Careless repetition, on the other hand, can rob your sentences of clarity and conciseness. In any sentence do not use several words that are alike in meaning, and do not use a word that is part of the meaning of another word.

REDUNDANT

The tiny little kitten charmed everyone but Tony.
[*Tiny* and *little* mean the same thing.]

REVISED

The tiny kitten charmed everyone but Tony.

REDUNDANT

The leopard retreated back from the fire. [The meaning of *back* is contained in *retreated*.]

REVISED

The leopard retreated from the fire.

The following are additional examples of redundant expressions. In your writing you should omit the words in italic type.

race *speedily*	audible *to the ear*
prefer *best*	*true* fact
return *back*	each *separate* thing
mix *together*	*predicted* forecast
extend *further*	*necessary* requirement
cooperate *together*	8:00 P.M. *at night*
heavy *in weight*	close location *nearby*
red *in color*	sunset *in the west*
tall *in height*	wear a hat *on your head*

6. *Reduce clauses to phrases and phrases to words* if you can do so without significantly affecting the meaning. Reduction is not always appropriate, but it can be an effective way to make your sentences concise and direct.

CLAUSE TO VERB PHRASE

Ms. Sanchez closed the door, but *she didn't lock it.*
Ms. Sanchez closed the door but *didn't lock it.*

CLAUSE TO PARTICIPIAL PHRASE

> *Because the caterpillars ate heartily,* they left only skeletons of the leaves.

> *Eating heartily,* the caterpillars left only skeletons of the leaves.

> The trees, *which have been strengthened by years of good care,* are surviving.

> The trees, *strengthened by years of good care,* are surviving.

CLAUSE TO GERUND PHRASE

> *Before the veterinarian examined the German shepherd,* she patted the dog.

> *Before examining the German shepherd,* the veterinarian patted the dog.

CLAUSE TO INFINITIVE PHRASE

> Because he had a tight schedule *that he had to follow,* Mr. Liu always hurried through lunch.

> Because he had a tight schedule *to follow,* Mr. Liu always hurried through lunch.

CLAUSE TO PREPOSITIONAL PHRASE

> *After only a few minutes had passed,* Carla put down the book.

> *After only a few minutes,* Carla put down the book.

CLAUSE TO APPOSITIVE PHRASE

> Henriette Wyeth, *who is the sister of the painter Andrew Wyeth,* is also an accomplished artist.

> Henriette Wyeth, *the sister of the painter Andrew Wyeth,* is also an accomplished artist.

CLAUSE TO WORD

> The chair *that is broken* belonged to my Aunt Sadie.

> The *broken* chair belonged to my Aunt Sadie.

> *It is obvious* that her taste in furniture was quite different from mine.

> *Obviously,* her taste in furniture was quite different from mine.

PHRASE TO WORD

> Preston always had trouble opening the door *to the garage*.
>
> Preston always had trouble opening the *garage* door.

Exercise 1   Revising: Conciseness   On your paper, revise the following sentences to make them concise.

SAMPLE	While it is certainly a true fact that journeys to distant parts can be edifying and also recreational, it happens also to be true that engaging in preparations for such pilgrimages can be an exhausting experience.
ANSWER	While long trips can be educational and fun, preparing for them can be exhausting.

1. In the midst of the making of preparations for the journey on which she was due to embark the following morning at 6:00 A.M., Heather Hillman came to the realization that she had neglected to make the purchase of an implement with which to perform dental hygiene.

2. This particular incident seemed to Heather to be just another incident in a long succession of disastrous catastrophes that had occurred one after another since the time when her plans for the trip had first been formulated by her.

3. In point of fact, there had been no single moment in the period during the past month at which preparations had seemed to be proceeding with any degree of smoothness whatsoever.

4. The first unfortunate event that occurred had been that the original dates first established for the trip had undergone an alteration as a result of action by the charter service.

5. At that point in time, it was considered by Heather that she might perhaps precipitate a change of plans with respect to the trip that she was planning.

6. The next occurrence that followed was that it came to Heather's attention that her deposit of money had been misplaced somewhere by the person functioning in the capacity of travel-arrangement coordinator, who, it would seem, neglected to make due written record of the receipt of such deposit.

7. Perhaps it is possible that in and of themselves such things as these would not have caused Heather to experience any significant degree of misery, but the fact is that the catastrophes kept continuing on for Heather.

8. As far as Michele is concerned, she happens to believe that Heather is to be admired for her tenacious persistence and for her resilient buoyancy.

9. Just on this very day, as Heather was collecting her possessions together that she intended to place in her suitcase, a triple tragedy occurred simultaneously when three things went wrong all at the same time: the timekeeping mechanism became inoperative in the bedroom, the appliance that cleansed the laundry malfunctioned in the basement under the house, and, in addition, the canine became ill in the living room.

10. To make a long story short, after putting her hat on her head and her gloves on her hands, Heather descended down the stairs carrying her suitcases in her hands only to discover with her own eyes that a heavy precipitation of snow had been coming down from the sky continuously for the last few hours of time.

6.5b Revising Sentences That Lack Coherence and Clarity

Sentences that include too many ideas may lack coherence as well as conciseness. In such sentences the important ideas become obscured and the relationships between ideas unclear. When revising, rewrite long, overloaded sentences as direct, concise statements. Use the following strategies to revise sentences that lack coherence.

Strategies

1. *Divide the sentence into two or more sentences.* Put the main ideas in independent clauses and the less important ideas in subordinate clauses and phrases.

2. *Subordinate some ideas that have been coordinated.* Subordination is often more precise than coordination. Use subordinate elements to avoid overusing the common coordinating words *and* and *but.*

3. *Eliminate unnecessary words and details.*

    NOT COHERENT

    The strange childishness of Emily Dickinson intrigues Derek and so does her reclusiveness, and so he has chosen her poetry as the subject of his essay, because he wonders why she spent her life as she did, and he cannot imagine how she could feel so much when she lived so little, but perhaps an intense study of her work will shed some light on these matters.

REVISED

Because the strange childishness and reclusiveness of Emily Dickinson intrigue Derek, he has chosen her poetry as the subject of his essay. Perhaps an intense study of her work will shed some light on why she spent her life as she did and on how she could feel so much when she lived so little.

Exercise 2   Revising: Conciseness   On your paper, revise the following sentences, which lack coherence. Divide each one into two or more shorter sentences and make other necessary changes.

SAMPLE   Athough the trip to Greece that Mr. and Mrs. Puopolo are considering taking offers round-trip air transportation and first-class hotel rooms, and it also provides baggage handling, transfers to and from the hotels, and tours of the famous sights, as well as of the countryside, they have not yet decided whether to go because of the fact that the dates coincide with tax time, and that time is the busiest time of year in their office.

ANSWER   The trip to Greece that Mr. and Mrs. Puopolo are considering taking offers not only round-trip air transportation and first-class hotel rooms, but also baggage handling, transfers to and from the hotels, and tours of the famous sights. They have not yet decided whether to go, however, because the dates coincide with tax time, the busiest time of year in their office.

1. During the years of the late 1400s, as the two existing royal houses of Britain, the House of York, which had adopted the pure white rose as its representative emblem, and the House of Lancaster, which had become identified with the crimson rose, clashed over the possession of the English monarchy, their battles became known as the Wars of the Roses.

2. It had been suggested by Mrs. Nelson, her chemistry instructor, that Rosa, who was desirous of a summer job, apply to the Parks and Recreation Department for the position of lifeguard at the local swimming pool, which involved not only watching swimmers during the afternoon and early evening hours, but also giving swimming lessons to young children starting each and every weekday morning at 9:00 A.M.

3. Frances Perkins had become the first woman member of the Cabinet in 1933 when President Franklin Roosevelt appointed her to be Secretary of Labor in which post she served until 1945.

4. One of the first bicycles, which was called a *Draisine,* was invented in the early nineteenth century, in 1816, by Baron Karl von Drais of Germany, who created a wooden scooterlike vehicle with a steering bar connected to the front wheel.

5. Dan, who had learned to type when he took a typing course during his high school years, found typing a very useful skill when he attended an institution of higher learning and he was assigned papers and lab reports, and even now, at the present time, since he has become a sports reporter for the city newspaper.

6. The Anglins, who are our neighbors, drove in their car part way up the mountain one bright Saturday and parked, and then they continued together on foot to the top of Mount Charleston, where they had an outdoor picnic lunch and enjoyed the beautiful day until the sun began to set in the west at 5:00 P.M. in the afternoon.

7. Though the nineteenth century was, as a whole, an age of architectural revival, the English architect Sir Joseph Paxton created a brand-new style and employed recently developed industrial materials, such as wrought iron and glass, and new techniques when he designed the Crystal Palace in London in the year 1851 for the Exhibition of the Industry of All Nations, which attracted over six million visitors.

8. The plane was packed with business executives from all across the entire country flying to the annual hardware convention, which was held in Seattle every single year during the month of June.

9. In Tennessee Williams's play *The Glass Menagerie*, Laura, the sister of the narrator, Tom Wingfield, who recalls his past in St. Louis to form the substance of this memory play, lives in a fantasy world centering on her collection of tiny, miniature glass animals.

10. Pierre L'Enfant, a French engineer who was hired by George Washington, who made the Capitol the center of Washington and who established the city's broad streets that radiate out from the Capitol, created the plan for the city of Washington, D.C.

Assignment Revising   On your paper, revise the following paragraph to make it concise and direct.

Caricature is the art of satirical portraiture, and it is not new, for it was used by the ancient Assyrians, Egyptians, Greeks, and Romans hundreds of years ago. In modern times today, with the easy and widespread availability of printed materials, caricature has become a popular form of satire, because many well-known famous personalities are more readily identified with caricatures than with serious paintings or photographs, although this is not always a fact that pleases the subject, because a clever caricaturist going after a vulnerable victim can be like an assassin attacking with a sharp eye and a sharp pen. Although caricaturists search for the most minute idiosyncrasy of their subject, and then they exploit it, transforming an eyebrow, a lower lip, an earlobe, or a lock of hair into a personality, the person in the arts must take care not to overdo too much the exaggeration, for while an effective caricature must be outrageous and witty, it must also be instantly recognizable. Because of the fact that, with only a bold line here and a sharp angle there, some of the finest drawings need only a few strokes of the pen, the formula for fine caricature seems to be a mysterious mixture of abbreviation and exaggeration.

Assignment Checklist

Check your assignment for the following points:

✔ 1. Did you eliminate wordiness by using simple, direct, and clear expressions?
✔ 2. Did you eliminate redundant words and expressions?
✔ 3. Did you reduce clauses and phrases where appropriate?
✔ 4. Did you divide and adjust sentences that lack coherence?

6.6   Revising for Emphasis

Effective writing highlights the important ideas. Think carefully about the ideas that you want to stress and the effect that you want them to have. Then, in your writing, emphasize the important details by using emphatic positions and emphatic structures. The following strategies will help you to emphasize ideas in your writing.

Strategies

1. *Use the strong positions in a sentence.* The strong positions are the beginning and the end. Reserve these places for important ideas. Place your most important ideas at the end, for that is the most emphatic position of all. Weak ideas at the end or at the beginning make your sentences weak.

WEAK	He discovered that he had one too many pearls when he counted them. [weak idea at end]
EMPHATIC	When he counted the pearls, he discovered that he had one too many. [important idea at end]
WEAK	After a trying day, Margaret was relieved to be home from the office. [weak idea at end]
EMPHATIC	After a trying day at the office, Margaret was relieved to be home. [strong idea at end]

2. *Use periodic sentences.* Periodic sentences take advantage of the emphatic position at the end of the sentence. In a **periodic sentence,** you build up details to a climax, where you finally state the main idea. The suspense created gives the main idea added force. Like any dramatic technique, periodic sentences should not be overused.

   PERIODIC SENTENCES

   > With the score tied, the bases loaded, and two out, Merrill confidently stepped up to bat.

   > Tiptoeing carefully to avoid the creaky places, the candle cupped in his hand to direct the glow, Marshall neared the gaping doorway.

3. *Write balanced sentences.* Balanced sentences emphasize parallel ideas, particularly contrasting ideas. In a balanced sentence, you use parallel structure to convey the effect of equal but different.

   BALANCED SENTENCES

   > We come not to bury Caesar, but to praise him.
   > William Shakespeare, *Julius Caesar*

. . . ask not what your country can do for you; ask what you can do for your country.

> John F. Kennedy, Inaugural address

Just as autumn follows summer, so does football follow baseball.

4. *Subordinate less important ideas.* Stress the more important ideas by putting them in independent clauses. You can change the emphasis and therefore the cue to the reader, according to which idea you subordinate.

> Chester Malcolm, *who is a computer scientist,* is giving the seminar.
>
> Chester Malcolm, *who is giving the seminar,* is a computer scientist.

5. *Repeat key words and phrases or key ideas.* Pointless repetition is wordy, but deliberate repetition can be powerful and emphatic.

> . . . government of the people, by the people, and for the people shall not perish from the earth.
>
> Abraham Lincoln, Address at Gettysburg

John was a good man, an honest man, a hard-working man, but not a cautious man.

6. *Use voice effectively.* The active voice is generally more forceful than the passive.

WEAK PASSIVE

> A strange sound was detected by Kristin. [passive]

MORE EMPHATIC

> Kristin detected a strange sound. [active]

When the focus is on the receiver rather than on the performer of the action, or when the performer is not specified, the passive voice can be more emphatic than the active voice.

WEAK ACTIVE

> The group elected Sheridan president.

EMPHATIC PASSIVE

> Sheridan was elected president.

WEAK ACTIVE
> Someone returned the book yesterday.

EMPHATIC PASSIVE
> The book was returned yesterday.

7. *Change sentence length.* You can capture your reader's attention with a short sentence that follows or precedes a group of longer sentences.

> The furniture had been polished till it shone, and the floors looked too clean to be stepped on. Not a trace could be seen of a newspaper or a carelessly tossed magazine or a pen set down and forgotten. The house was ready.

Exercise   Revising: Emphasis   On your paper, revise each sentence or group of sentences to improve the emphasis. You may separate the sentences or combine them.

SAMPLE	The plant seemed to shrivel after a day or two.
ANSWER	After a day or two, the plant seemed to shrivel.

1. Less interest has been shown in the hero's movie adventures than has been manifested in his real-life activities.
2. Because the garage has repaired Ms. Casazza's car, she can drive us to the softball game.
3. Mr. Stewart was determined not to drive. He bicycled all the way to the construction site.
4. The chair was being sat in by Albert Whittingill.
5. It was embarrassingly obvious that Mr. Schoenberg had little knowledge of the problem from his comments.
6. The sun shone all day because Vanessa, dressed in an uncomfortable plastic raincoat, had prepared for a torrent, her old boat moccasins flapping on her feet, a plastic hat crushed into her purse, and an umbrella on her arm.
7. No one will be allowed to enter the studio until the recording session has been completed.
8. The rolling landscape shone after the rain, the air felt cleansed and pure, and our nostrils were touched with the scent of new spring growth. It was really true that at last we were home.
9. Mr. Pomorsky was not angry at Ida. He was not angry at the taxi driver. He felt little fury at the reporter. He was angry at himself.

10. Jeremy's ostensible purpose in attending the conference was to learn what was new in the field. The real reason that he was there, however, was to discover what jobs might be available to him.

Assignment   Revising   On your paper, revise the following paragraph to emphasize important ideas.

> Not many generations ago, every neighborhood had its grocery store, its drugstore, its shoemaker, its bank, and its ice-cream parlor. Then, as technology advanced, the smaller stores were driven out of business by large firms, and automobiles allowed people to move out of the neighborhoods. Small businesses became outdated as people chose the security offered by large corporations over the insecurities of their own businesses. Now the small business is making a comeback, however. People are going out on their own once more because they have become frustrated by the impersonality, the rules, and the procedures common in many large companies. The corner variety store is making a reappearance, and other, more novel, enterprises are being launched to meet the needs of our changing society. Because many of those novice entrepreneurs are often youthful and lacking in experience and financial resources, they rely on imagination and on hard work. Obviously, becoming your own employer is once again becoming fashionable.

Assignment Checklist

Check your assignment for the following points:

- ✔ 1. Did you put important ideas in strong positions in sentences?
- ✔ 2. Did you subordinate less important ideas?
- ✔ 3. Did you use balanced sentences and periodic sentences where appropriate?
- ✔ 4. Did you use either the active or the passive voice for the proper emphasis?
- ✔ 5. Did you occasionally change sentence length for emphasis?

6.7   Revising and Proofreading

Completing Your Revision

Proofreading, the last stage in the revision process, is the checking of a piece of writing for correct grammar, usage, spelling, and punctuation. If you are unsure about the correctness of a word or a sentence structure, assume that it is incorrect. Then look up the information in this book or in some other reference book.

You may use the proofreading symbols shown on pages 207–208. After you have completed your revision, you can type or write your finished copy.

An Example of Revising and Proofreading

Here is a first draft of a paragraph. To the left of the draft are notes indicating where revision is needed. After you have read the draft and the notes, read the revised version that follows it, reviewing one by one the changes that were made.

FIRST DRAFT

Emphasis missed	The string instruments have their giant bass
Wordy	fiddle. There are bass horns too. The low bass horns,
	which are the horns known as tubas, play the low
Emphasis missed	horn notes in a band or orchestra. People do not take
Relationship unclear	this brass giant seriously as an instrument. It has coils
	and a shiny bell-shaped top. "I am a tuba player"
Punctuation error	does not usually elicit the same admiration as I am a
Not coherent	violinist" or "I am a guitarist," and the outlandish
Relationship unclear	appearance of the tuba is partly to blame for this.
Inconsistent tense	The tuba's bell provides a fine place. Pepper and
Not parallel	flour were tossed in, which started the band sneezing,
Sentence out of order	and the audience would laugh too. Comedians took advantage of the unwieldy size of the tuba to create a medley of sight gags. The tuba player in a marching band hardly had the snap and dash of the trumpeter. Then, too, the relentless oom-pah-pah that is the only music many people associate with the tuba does
Capitalization error	not conjure up images of Ballet Dancers or angels. Nevertheless, the tuba seems to be gaining new respect at last. It is gaining respect in jazz as well as in pop and classical music. People do not regard it as a
Variety needed	joke. The tuba is viewed as a serious instrument more and more, for it is the bass of the horns.

REVISED VERSION

Balanced sentence

Concise

Ideas subordinated

Punctuation corrected

Sentence divided

Tense consistent

Sentence moved

Transition

Idea subordinated

Parallel structure

Tense consistent

Capitalization corrected

Sentences combined

Adverbs to beginning

Idea subordinated

Just as the string instruments have their giant bass fiddle, the horns have their bass horns. The bass horns, known as tubas, play the low horn notes in a band or orchestra. This brass giant, with its coils and shiny bell-shaped top, is not always taken seriously as an instrument. "I am a tuba player" does not usually elicit the same admiration as "I am a violinist" or "I am a guitarist." The outlandish appearance of the tuba is partly to blame. Comedians take advantage of its unwieldy size to create a medley of sight gags. The tuba's bell, for example, provides a fine place in which to toss pepper or flour, which starts the band sneezing and the audience laughing. The tuba player in a marching band hardly has the snap and dash of the trumpeter. Then, too, the relentless oom-pah-pah that is the only music most people associate with a tuba does not conjure up images of ballet dancers or angels. Nevertheless, the tuba seems to be gaining new respect at last, in jazz as well as in popular and classical music. More and more, the tuba is being viewed not as a joke but as a serious instrument, the bass of the horns.

Exercise   Revising: The Paragraph   On your paper, revise and proofread the following passage. Use the notes as a guide.

Not parallel

Wordy

Emphasis missed

Wordy

Person inconsistent

Wordy

Relationship unclear

Emphasis missed

One of the world's fastest sports takes place not on a race track but an ice-covered rink. The fact that ice hockey is played with such fast speed makes it an exciting game to watch, and it is an entertaining game too. The skaters flash quickly across the ice. Using wooden hockey sticks, you try to send the puck, a hard rubber disk, past the other team's goalie into their net. The puck is often slammed so hard that it streaks across the ice at a rate of more than 160 kilometers an hour. The game was developed in Canada, in the 1850s. The basic idea probably came from field hockey. Students at Montreal's McGill

University drew up the first formal rules in the 1870s, and by the 1890s the game had become widespread. The hockey players of those days who played a game that was far slower and played less roughly than the game of today, did not need the protective padding and helmets that now prevent so many injuries. The faster more violent game that we know now is a popular sport in many countries of the world. Like soccer, it attracts millions of fans too.

Punctuation error

Not parallel

Punctuation error

Wordy

Irrelevant detail

Assignment   Revising   On your paper, revise and proofread the following passage.

Ragtime is a kind of music. It is obviously not a time to collect rags. It sets off a lively highly syncopated melody against a strongly rhythmic accompaniment. The melody can be thought of as teasing the accompaniment, and so the name may come from the slang use of *rag,* meaning "to tease. His "Maple Leaf Rag" was the first piece of ragtime. It is the case that people have applied the term to early types of jazz, true ragtime first originated in the very early years of the century with the piano playing of Scott Joplin.

The popularity of rags ends temporarily with Joplin's death in 1917, but it is renewed again in the 1970s, and there was a recording then of an album of Joplin's rags and the making of a movie, *The Sting.* The movie was based on the period and used Joplin's music. Joplin's "The entertainer" then became a great hit. That happened more than five decades after his death. His folk opera *Treemonisha,* which no one would produce in his lifetime, was performed, and his *Collected Works* sold thousands and thousands of copies.

Assignment Checklist

Check your assignment for the following points:

✔ 1. Did you place ideas in the most effective order for coherence?
✔ 2. Did you combine some sentences to make clear the relationships between the ideas?
✔ 3. Did you make the tense, voice, person, and tone consistent?
✔ 4. Did you make the passage direct and concise?
✔ 5. Did you give sentences parallel structure where necessary?
✔ 6. Did you emphasize important details?
✔ 7. Did you proofread for correct grammar, usage, spelling, and punctuation?

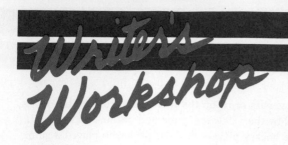

Computers: What They Do, Why We Need Them

Situation: One issue of *Sunday Magazine* in your newspaper is featuring computers. As a new assistant editor, you have been asked to revise an article that has been submitted as a brief overview of the uses of computers. The magazine editor has reviewed the article and given you notes to improve the emphasis and coherence of the article. As you work on the article, keep in mind the following information.

Writer: you as assistant editor
Audience: readers of *Sunday Magazine*
Topic: uses of computers
Purpose: to revise an article for coherence and appropriate emphasis

Directions: To revise the first draft, follow these steps.

Step 1. Read the first draft of the article on the facing page. Then read the editor's notes on page 316.

Step 2. Revise the article, sentence by sentence, according to the notes. Rewrite the sentences on a separate sheet of paper. Be sure to follow all the instructions for each sentence.

Step 3. Proofread your revised article. Make sure that your sentences flow smoothly and contain no errors in grammar, spelling, or punctuation.

Uses of Computers

(1) The new technology is fast becoming an integral part of the business world. *(2)* How computers and computer languages work, what computers do, and why we need them are what interest people today. *(3)* You might think of a computer as a worker capable of three tasks, any of which it can perform easily. *(4)* Computers can process data, be a controller, and a designer. *(5)* As designers, computers can engineer and "test" bridges for resistance to earthquakes and wind. *(6)* A computer can even design a piece of music and play it back. *(7)* Computers are processors of information and they can handle large volumes of material with accuracy and speed. *(8)* It can transform basic information into more useful information according to instructions. *(9)* Computers are used to store, analyze, and process information for banks, hospitals, educational institutions, and when we do business. *(10)* Colleges are being helped by computers that keep track of students applying, enrolling, and transferring. *(11)* Computers can take on such problems as regulating the flow of the traffic out of the school parking lot. *(12)* Computers as controllers are used in small airports without control towers. *(13)* There they monitor wind speed and direction, and, via radio, indicate to pilots the proper runway for landing. *(14)* Computers help us live, and these are just some of the ways we use them.

Notes for revision

<u>Sentence</u>

1 Omit this sentence. The information is not
   directly related to the limited topic.

2 Need stronger topic sentence. Write a question
   that limits the topic to what computers do and
   why we need them. Remove unnecessary words.

3 Emphasize the strong idea ("three tasks") by
   having it at the end of the sentence. Omit
   unnecessary information.

4 Make items parallel (three nouns in series).

5, 6 Discuss the items in the order used to introduce
      them. Place Sentences 5 and 6 before Sentence
      14 so that supporting details follow the order
      introduced in Sentence 4.

7 Begin sentence with "As processors of
   information" to emphasize the order of ideas in
   the paragraph. Make <u>computers</u> the subject of
   the sentence.

8 Use third person plural pronoun as the subject.
   The pronoun must agree with the word <u>computers</u>
   in the preceding sentence.

9 Insert introductory transitional phrase to
   introduce examples. Make last item in series
   parallel with other items.

10 Use the active voice for emphasis.

11 To emphasize a key idea in the paragraph, repeat
    the word <u>controller;</u> begin with the transitional
    phrase "As controllers."

12, 13 Combine Sentences 12 and 13. Use the
        prepositional phrase in 12 to begin the new
        sentence. Use <u>computers</u> as the subject of the
        sentence. Note: Follow with sentences 5 and 6
        here.

14 For a strong conclusion, put the important idea
    ("help us live") at the end of the sentence.

Unit Assignments

Assignment 1   Select a paragraph that you have written for a previous assignment. Use the information in this unit to revise your paragraph. Then proofread it and make a finished copy.

Assignment 2   In your school or local newspaper, find an article or a letter that you think can be improved. Use the information in this unit to improve it. Then proofread your revised version. Submit the original with your revised version.

Assignment 3   Find a piece of writing that is wordy or overwritten. You might look at editorials, copies of speeches or lectures, or campaign literature. Revise the writing to make it direct, concise, and forceful.

Assignment 4   Write a paragraph on a serious or controversial topic. Your purposes are to inform and to express your opinion. Establish a serious tone. Revise your paragraph, concentrating especially on the tone. Proofread your revised version before submitting it.

Assignment 5   *Step 1:* Write a paragraph about your plans for the next five years. Address it to an audience of your classmates. *Step 2:* Rewrite your paragraph on another sheet of paper, making necessary changes to adapt it for use with an application for college or for a job. *Step 3:* Revise each paragraph, concentrating especially on correct emphasis. Proofread your revised versions before submitting them.

Revising Your Assignments

For help in revising your writing, consult the Checklist for Revision on the last page of this book.

Unit Tests

Test 1

A. Number your paper from 1 to 5. Next to each number, write the letter of the term that correctly completes the sentence. You will use all but one of the items.

a. coherence   d. emphasis
b. periodic sentence   e. conciseness
c. revising   f. consistency

1. __?__ is reorganizing and rewriting your work so that it expresses your thoughts in a clear and effective manner.
2. A sentence has proper __?__ when it highlights the important ideas.
3. A paragraph has __?__ when it has been developed and organized to make clear the relationship among the ideas.
4. __?__ is the use of only words that are necessary.
5. In a __?__, you build up details to a climax, where you finally state the main idea.

B. Number your paper from 6 to 10. Next to each number, write the letter of the item that correctly answers each question about the following paragraph.

(1) The skills needed for a career in business are becoming more complex, and competition for jobs in business is increasing. (2) Therefore, high school students are preparing for careers in business. (3) They take courses in accounting and typing. (4) The Junior Achievement organization was founded in 1919 by a paper manufacturer, and many students who want to get actual business experience join it. (5) The members from the same community form their own company. (6) They not only plan the company and sell stock but also they market a service or a product. (7) For example, some groups operate cleaning services, and other groups make and sell radios. (8) Because of advances in technology, a radio can be as small as a watch. (9) Running the companies is an exciting, challenging way for each and every member to achieve the desired goal of learning business skills that will be useful in the business world.

6. Which sentence should be removed to unify the paragraph?

   a. Sentence 2   c. Sentence 7
   b. Sentence 5   d. Sentence 8

7. Which of the following is the best revision of Sentences 2 and 3?

   a. Therefore, high school students are preparing for careers in business, and they take courses in accounting and typing.
   b. Therefore, high school students are preparing for careers in business by taking courses in accounting and typing.
   c. Therefore, high school students are preparing for careers in business in order to take courses in accounting and typing.

8. Which of the following is the strongest revision of Sentence 4?

   a. Students who want to get actual business experience join the Junior Achievement organization, which was founded in 1919 by a paper manufacturer.
   b. In 1919 a paper manufacturer founded the Junior Achievement organization, which many students who want to get actual business experience join.
   c. Because the Junior Achievement organization was founded in 1919, many students who want to get actual business experience join it.

9. Which one of the following revisions gives Sentence 6 parallel structure?

   a. Not only do they plan the company and sell stock but also market a service or a product.
   b. They plan the company and sell stock as well as marketing a service or a product.
   c. They not only plan the company and sell stock but also market a service or a product.

10. Which of the following sentences is wordy?

   a. Sentence 1   c. Sentence 7
   b. Sentence 5   d. Sentence 9

Test 2

Choose one of the Unit Assignments or one suggested by your teacher. Write and revise the assignment as directed and submit it to your teacher.

Three Modes
of Writing

Unit Preview

Whenever you write, you use one of four **modes,** or forms, of writing: exposition, description, narration, or persuasion. Your purpose in writing determines which mode you use. If your purpose is to inform or explain, you use exposition. If your purpose is to convey an impression of a person, a place, or an object, you use description. For the purpose of telling a story, you use narration. To convince your reader that your opinion is correct, you use persuasion. In this unit you will study the first three modes. Persuasion is presented separately in Unit 8.

Each of the following passages illustrates one of the three modes of writing that are covered in this unit.

Exposition

When most people write letters or make grocery lists, they do not realize that a complicated process was used to produce the paper they are using. There are four major steps in the process of making paper: cutting wood into chips, cooking the chips into pulp, treating the pulp, and drying and pressing the pulp into paper.

Description

Kay breezed into the kitchen with her arms full of packages. All I could see over the packages was her round, smiling face surrounded by her curly, orange-red hair. Although she was short and plump, she moved with the grace of a gymnast. When she put down her load, I could see the yellow of her dress, the brightest color in the room. Then, her green eyes shining, she made me guess what she had purchased in town.

Narration   My friend Hal and I arrived at the base of Mt. Snow at two o'clock one Saturday afternoon in October. Looking up at the bottom half of the mountain, we chose the trail that we would follow on our hike to the top. It was a broad, grassy trail dotted with large rocks. We slowly made our way up the first part of the trail, stopping frequently to enjoy the view. By the time the sun had set, we regretted the time that we had spent just relaxing.

For Analysis   On your paper, answer the following questions about the preceding paragraphs.

1. What is the writer's purpose in the first paragraph?
2. What general impression of Kay is created in the descriptive paragraph?
3. What setting and characters are introduced in the narrative paragraph?
4. What does the writer of the third paragraph hint will happen later in the narrative?

In analyzing the passages of exposition, description, and narration, you have considered some important features of the three modes of writing. In this unit you will learn how to write clear explanations, vivid descriptions, and lively narratives. As you write, you will follow the three steps of the writing process: prewriting, writing, and revising.

7.1   Considering Your Purpose and Audience

Your purpose for writing may be to explain, to describe, or to narrate. For example, you may want to explain how land is surveyed or what services public libraries provide. On the other hand, you may wish to describe the sounds and appearance of your old manual typewriter or the stillness and fresh smells of a garden after a rainstorm. You may wish to tell a story about your first day in a new home or about Robert E. Peary's journey to the North Pole. When you begin to write, you must make sure that every sentence helps to accomplish your purpose.

Sometimes you can combine modes in your writing. For example, in a narrative you may include descriptions of the major characters, the setting, and important objects in the story. Also, you may make an expository composition clearer and more interesting by using a short narrative to introduce your explanation.

You should direct your writing to anyone who might be interested in your topic. When you write for a general audience, you may have to explain details that you would not have to explain to someone who is familiar with your topic.

Some of your writing will be directed to a specialized audience. When it is, you should include and emphasize details of particular interest to that audience. For example, if you were writing a description of a scene for members of a camera club, you might include details about lighting and shadows that would be important to a photographer.

The purpose of the following expository paragraph is to explain why traveling by train in Mexico is enjoyable.

Model

> If you are a train buff or simply prefer to see the countryside through which you are traveling rather than the center line of a highway, Mexico is the place for you. Mexico has fifteen thousand miles of railroad lines connecting its mountains, coasts, and jungles. You need only get to a station on time; after that, put your watch in your pocket and relax. You may not get to your destination exactly at the appointed hour, but you'll have a marvelous time looking out the window, eating food, and enjoying the comfort of the ride.
>
> Stephen Birnbaum, *Mexico 1982*

The writer of the paragraph addresses a specialized audience, people who enjoy traveling by train. He tells these people why they would enjoy a trip in Mexico.

Exercise 1 Prewriting: Purpose On your paper, write whether the purpose of each of the following topics is to explain, to describe, or to narrate.

    SAMPLE   How an insulated container keeps foot hot
    ANSWER   To explain

1. The physical appearance of the space shuttle
2. Ways to prepare for a secretarial job
3. Looking for my first job
4. How computers control subway cars
5. How a childhood friend looked
6. Highway sounds
7. My first driving lesson
8. How my community will have changed by the year 2050
9. The seashore at dawn
10. The game that we almost won

Exercise 2 Prewriting: Audience On your paper, write one or two sentences that describe the audience to whom the following narrative paragraph seems to be directed.

     I was excited by my family's move to Key West, Florida, because it would give me the opportunity to explore Florida's coral reefs, which are large offshore colonies of coral animals. On our first free day after unpacking, my brother and I decided to investigate the reefs near the shore. Because we would not be going into deep water, we used only snorkels, short breathing tubes that extend from divers' mouths to the surface of the water.

Assignment 1 Prewriting Choose a topic that is related to a job, a craft, or a sport that interests you. On your paper, list the topic, a purpose for writing, and an audience for the topic. Then, keeping your purpose and audience in mind, list details that you could use to develop the topic in a single paragraph.

Assignment 2 Writing/Revising Using the topic, the purpose, the audience, and the list of details that you developed in

Assignment 1, write a paragraph. When your paragraph is complete, reread your work as if you were the intended audience. Make any changes that would help you to understand the paragraph. Then proofread the paragraph.

Assignment Checklist

Check your writing assignments for the following points:

✔ 1. Did you include only details that help to accomplish your purpose?
✔ 2. If you have a specialized audience, did you emphasize details of special interest to it?
✔ 3. Did you proofread your work for correct grammar, usage, spelling, and punctuation?

7.2   Expository Writing

7.2a   Writing an Expository Composition

Your purpose in **expository writing** is, as you have already learned, to explain something to your reader or to inform your reader about something. For example, you can tell your reader how a printing press works, what causes a glacier to form, or what a copyright is.

Selecting and Limiting a Topic

In a short expository composition, write on a topic that you can cover fully in no more than five to seven paragraphs. A detailed discussion of a limited topic is better than an incomplete discussion of a general topic. Whether you choose your own topic or use one that has been assigned, limit it by choosing a single aspect of it to write about.

For example, the general topic "Energy" can be limited to the topic "How automatic thermostats can save fuel." The general topic "Movies" can be narrowed to the manageable topic "Why musicals became popular in the 1930s."

Exercise 1   Prewriting: Selecting a Topic   For each of the following general topics, write on your paper a limited topic that could be developed in a short expository composition.

1. Foreign countries
2. Magazines
3. Machines
4. Agriculture
5. Medical professions

6. Radio
7. Driving
8. Tests
9. Banking
10. Community organizations

Planning an Explanation

Your explanation will be clear to your reader if you plan it carefully before you start to write. The following strategies will help you to plan your composition.

Strategies

1. *List the information that you want to include in your explanation.* If you are not familiar with the topic, you may need to do research on it before completing the list.

2. *Review your list.* Add any important points that you may have forgotten to list, and eliminate any unnecessary information.

3. *Organize the information in a logical way.* For a composition that explains how something works or how to do something, use chronological order (*page 255*). For a composition that explains the causes or effects of something, use chronological order or order of importance (*page 258*). When you organize points in order of importance, you usually move from the least important detail to the most important detail. In any case, use one method of organization consistently throughout your composition.

4. *Analyze the information to see whether you can divide it into two or more groups.* If you can, you should place each group of related points in a separate paragraph when you write your composition.

Writing an Explanation

When you have completed your plan, you will use it as a guide for writing your explanation. The following strategies will help you to write a clear explanation.

Strategies

1. *Include a topic sentence in each paragraph.* Although a topic sentence usually is placed at the beginning of a paragraph, you may place it wherever it is most effective. The topic sentence of the first paragraph should present the topic of the entire explanation.

2. *Use transitional words to emphasize the relationships among your ideas.* Use such words and phrases as *first, for example, most important,* and *therefore* to move from one sentence or paragraph to the next.

3. *Define all terms that may be unfamiliar to your reader.* For example, if you are explaining what types of bank accounts exist, you probably will have to define the term *time deposit.*

4. *Write a concluding sentence.* Your last sentence should let your reader know that the explanation has come to an end. A concluding sentence may summarize what you have explained, or it may comment on the explanation.

The following paragraphs explain to the reader what tasks and skills are associated with being a legal assistant. The transitional words are printed in italic type.

Model

Overall
topic sentence

People who have the skills and training to be legal assistants are almost assured of finding challenging jobs. The demand for legal assistants has been increasing yearly because it has become apparent that there are not enough lawyers to do all of the legal work that exists. Legal assistants help lawyers by doing a wide range of tasks. *For example,* they interview clients, prepare simple contracts and documents, and do research for major cases.

Topic sentence for second paragraph

Traits in order of importance

People who hope to be legal assistants should possess several traits. *First,* they should be interested in working with people and in helping people to solve problems. *Next,* they should be concerned with accuracy; that is, they should be willing to work carefully and to check their work to eliminate errors. *In addition,* they should be able to keep track of small details.

Topic sentence for third paragraph

Concluding sentence

People who have the traits needed to be good legal assistants also need training. Some law firms provide on-the-job training. Most firms, *however,* want applicants to have completed at least a two-year training program at a junior college. In such a program, students learn how to do research and legal writing, and they take introductory law courses. *Once* the students have completed the program, they are ready for jobs as legal assistants.

The writer has divided the preceding explanation into three paragraphs: one paragraph about the duties, one paragraph about the traits needed, and one paragraph about the training needed. Each paragraph has its own topic sentence, and the topic sentence of the first paragraph serves as the topic sentence for the entire explanation. The concluding sentence summarizes the explanation.

Exercise 2 Writing/Revising: Exposition Write an expository paragraph that explains the causes of static. The following notes contain all of the information that you will need for the composition. Organize the notes before you begin to write, arranging the three causes in order from least to most frequent. When your first draft is complete, revise the paragraph.

Magnetic storms are a result of increased sunspot activity.

Lightning usually causes static.

Occasionally, magnetic storms cause static.

Motors or electrical appliances may cause static.

Static is the crashing or popping noise heard on radios or television sets.

It is difficult to eliminate static; therefore, people must endure it.

Appliances that have rotating motors, such as hair dryers, are especially likely to cause static.

Lightning travels from clouds to earth, where it interferes with the transmission of radio and television signals.

7.2b   Writing a Review

A **review** is a type of expository writing in which you evaluate a book, a play, a film, or a television program. A review is more than a summary of the work or a statement of whether you like or dislike the work. It explains the meaning of the work and the techniques that are used to present that meaning. In a review you provide examples from the work to support the statements that you make about the meaning and techniques.

You should include five kinds of information in your review. Usually, you present the information in the order suggested here, but you may rearrange the order of information if necessary.

Introduction.   Begin a book review by mentioning the author and title of the book and by identifying the book as a particular type of literature: a novel or a historical account, for example. Begin a play review by identifying the author, the title, and the type of play: a serious drama or a light musical, for example. For a television or film review, give the title and the type of work: a documentary or a comedy, for example. You may also include the name of the director, particularly if he or she is well known. In the introduction to a review of a play, a film, or a television program, you may also mention the names of the important performers.

Brief Description.   Describe the work in no more than a few sentences so that your reader has an overview of it. Identify the essential characters, the setting, and the situation. For example, you might describe the play *Pygmalion* by George Bernard Shaw in this way: "In *Pygmalion* Shaw presents a professor of phonetics who changes the life of a poor flower girl by teaching her a new way of speaking."

The Central Idea.   Present the central idea, the intended meaning of the work. The central idea is not the same as the plot, or "what happens." For example, the plot of Shakespeare's *Macbeth* concerns a man who fights all those who challenge his power. The central idea of *Macbeth*, however, concerns the corrupting forces that accompany blind ambition.

Evaluation.   In the evaluation section of a review, analyze how successfully the central idea of the work has been presented to the audience. In reviewing a book, for example, judge the effectiveness of the author's writing and the plot. In reviewing a film, judge the effectiveness of the script, the directing, and the acting. In addition, discuss any aspect of the work that is particularly important, such as the use of symbolism, the set design, or the cinematography. Referring to specific details will make your evaluation clearer.

The following passage is the evaluation from a film review.

Model

> Without a doubt *Citizen Kane* is a true work of art. The consolidation of new techniques and processes in it show that Orson Welles is a genius. The film is a prime example of how visual effects can be used to enhance the overall effect of the drama.
>
> The film contains many symbols if the viewer is skilled enough to catch them. Lighting plays a key role in communicating the symbolism. Through the use of shadows, the makers of the film are conveying hidden messages and subtleties. For example, contrasting lighting is used to show the contrasts within Kane. Darkness is used to show despair and possible death.
>
> In addition to the unusual lighting effects, many camera angles are skillfully employed. The argument on the staircase between Kane and the political boss is viewed from a low angle. By looking up at them, the viewer sees more clearly the power of the two men in conflict.
>
> The audience is also kept involved through the unraveling of the mystery of "Rosebud," Kane's last word before his death. The dramatic impact is great when the viewer finally discovers its meaning. The solution of the puzzle ties together the loose ends and helps the audience to understand the type of person that Kane was.

(Adapted)
Ruel Tolman, Fayetteville-Manlius High School
Manlius, New York

Notice that the writer analyzes how lighting, camera, and dramatic techniques contribute to the effectiveness of the film. The evaluation is particularly strong because the writer provides an example to illustrate each point.

Conclusion.   In your conclusion present your final comment on what you feel the work achieves. State that comment briefly. The following passage concludes a review of the novel *The Rise and Fall of Silas Lapham* by William Dean Howells.

Model

> Silas is a universal character who represents in some ways every person who goes through life trying to reach maturity and happiness. Each time that one reads Howells's masterpiece, one will find something new and interesting about self and life.
>
> *Kelleryn Wood, Deering High School*
> *Portland, Maine*

In this conclusion the writer summarizes what Silas represents in the novel. She also explains why the novel is important and how a person can benefit from reading the novel more than once.

Exercise 3 Prewriting: The Review   Each of the following numbered passages represents one of the five categories of information that appear in a review: introduction, brief description, central idea, evaluation, and conclusion. Number your paper from 1 to 5. Next to each number, write the category of the passage.

1. The film *The Bicycle Thief* follows the actions of a father and son who try to get a bicycle for another man who needs it in order to work.
2. These are the elements in Lewis's critique of society that made the deepest impression on me. *Babbitt* is the profile of a trap—a trap to be avoided at all costs.

> *Nancy Hammond, Asheboro High School*
> *Asheboro, North Carolina*

3. *Wuthering Heights* is a novel written by Emily Brontë in nineteenth-century England.
4. Some of the actors were miscast, or they played their parts poorly. The actor playing Lysander was an example of miscasting. Because he

was much smaller than the actor playing Demetrius, the credibility of their "evenly-matched" scuffles was stretched. . . . In another instance, Titania recited her lines with such a lack of vitality that the hilarity of the scene was lost.

Jerry Deck, Santa Cruz High School
Santa Cruz, California

5. All of the characters and events in *Bleak House* are presented as a criticism of two groups of people. Dickens satirizes lawyers who conduct cases that devour all of the money and time of some people. He also attacks people who merely pretend to help the poor.

Assignment 1   Prewriting/Writing/Revising   Think of a situation that you would like to explain to your reader. For example, you could explain what problems are caused by an inadequate bus system, how renovations to a theater have made attending plays more enjoyable, or how tax laws affect people in your town. Do whatever research is necessary to find information on the topic. Then write your explanation, making sure that each group of related points is placed in its own paragraph. Using the Assignment Checklist that follows, revise your explanation.

Assignment 2   Writing/Revising   Select a book, a play, a film, or a television program to be the subject of a review. Write a review, presenting information about the work as well as your reaction to the work. Be sure to include all five parts of a review. Then revise your review.

Assignment Checklist

Check your expository composition for the following points:

   ✔ 1. Did you select a topic that is limited enough so that you can explain it thoroughly?
   ✔ 2. Did you present the points in your explanation in a logical order?
   ✔ 3. Did you place each group of related points in its own paragraph?
   ✔ 4. Did you include a topic sentence in each paragraph?
   ✔ 5. Did you use transitional words?

   ✔ 6. Did you write a concluding sentence for your explanation?
   ✔ 7. Did you proofread your explanation for correct grammar, usage, spelling, and punctuation?

Check your review for the following points:

   ✔ 8. Did you write an introduction in which you mention the author and title of the work and identify the type of work?
   ✔ 9. Did you provide a brief description of the work?
   ✔ 10. Did you explain the central idea of the work?
   ✔ 11. Did you evaluate the effectiveness of the techniques used to convey the central idea?
   ✔ 12. In the conclusion did you present your final comment on what the work achieves?
   ✔ 13. Did you proofread your review for correct grammar, usage, spelling, and punctuation?

7.3   Descriptive Writing

In **descriptive writing** your purpose is to communicate to your reader your impression of a person, a place, or an object. If you combine careful observation with descriptive techniques that help you to choose the most effective words, you can create a vivid impression for your reader.

7.3a   Selecting Sensory Details

Sensory details are the characteristics that you perceive with your senses of sight, hearing, touch, taste, and smell. You will create a sharp impression of a person, a place, or an object if your description includes not only details that you see but also details that you perceive with your other senses. For example, if you describe your room on a cold morning, you can include details about the white, lacy patterns formed by the frost that you see on your window. You can also include details about the harsh scraping of snowplows that you hear on the street outside your window, the shocking chill of the floorboards that you feel under your feet, and the fresh smell of the cold air that stings the inside of your nose.

Begin by making a list of as many sensory details about your subject as possible. Then, as you continue to plan your description, select only the most important details to include in your writing. Choose the details that show your subject as unique and that help to create a sharp, unified impression of your subject.

The writer of the following description presents details that make the kitchen unusual. All of the details, which come from the senses of smell and sight, work together to show how comfortable and lived-in the kitchen is.

Model

> As I enter the spacious kitchen, the familiar smell greets me. It is a combination of the kitchen and hall linoleum floors, the gas heating coming from the musty basement, and dinner baking in the oven. The old woodburning stove is at the kitchen's end. It is white porcelain with a black top and a fat smokestack that travels up to the high ceiling. The pantry, next to the stove, is an indentation in the wall filled with a sink, a counter, glass-paned cupboards, and a cooler, which is a room that keeps everything cold—not as much as a refrigerator, but cool enough so that food does not get moldy. In the middle of the room stands the immense kitchen table, surrounded by gray plastic chairs that slide easily over the yellow and blue linoleum. The kitchen is the most-used room in the house.

> *Deborah Eisenstein, Mira Costa High School*
> *Manhattan Beach, California*

In addition to choosing details that create a unified impression of a subject, you may choose details that create a **mood,** a certain emotional response in the reader. For example, when you describe a house in your neighborhood, you can convey the impression that it is run-down and abandoned. As you convey that impression, you could create a sad mood by emphasizing how unfortunate it is that no one repairs the crumbling porch that once was a gathering place for the family. On the other hand, you could create an eerie mood by emphasizing how frightening the creaking doors and broken windows seem.

The writer of the following description of stars creates a mood of wonder by reciting the list of their strange names and by mentioning their mythological connections.

Model

On a cool, clear night in the late winter, I stepped out on the back porch and turned off the lights. As I looked up at the clear sky, I began to see, one by one, the many stars of the winter sky sinking slowly in the west. Betelgeuse, Bellatrix, Rigel, Procyon—these were the stars whose names and histories I had spent so much time learning. As I looked up, I saw not just points of light of varying color and brightness, but whole groupings. Orion, the mighty hunter of the sky, was battling the great bull Taurus, whose baleful red eye, Aldebaran, stared fiercely down at me. The dogs of Orion followed at his heels, with the great star Sirius glowing like a jewel on the collar of the greater dog. Lepus, the hare, scampered out from under the feet of Orion.

Mark Looper, Saint Charles High School
St. Charles, Missouri

Exercise 1   Prewriting: Sensory Details   On your paper, list five of the following items. For each item write at least three precise sensory details. Use all five senses to think of the details.

SAMPLE	A street in winter
ANSWER	Crunch of snow under people's feet
	Smell of wood smoke from chimneys
	Piles of dirty snow on the side of the streets

1. A swamp
2. A chalkboard
3. A courtroom
4. An ear of corn
5. A washing machine
6. A train or a subway car
7. A tree in spring
8. A boat
9. A sandwich

7.3b   Using Descriptive Techniques

Effective Words

By choosing your words carefully, you can make your descriptive writing vivid and interesting. Use specific nouns and strong verbs to help your reader create a strong mental picture of your subject. For example, in the sentence "The building has many windows," *building* is not a specific noun. Either *house* or *skyscraper* would give the reader more information. Similarly, in the sentence "He got a book," *got* is not a strong verb. Either *found* or *bought* would be a stronger verb to describe the action in the sentence.

In your descriptive writing, you will also use modifiers: adjectives, adverbs, and participles. A modifier may be a phrase, such as "running down the hall," as well as a single word. If you find yourself using worn-out modifiers, use your dictionary or a dictionary of synonyms to find more interesting replacements.

When you select descriptive words, you must consider not only their **denotative meanings,** the dictionary definitions, but also their **connotative meanings,** the emotions or ideas that are associated with the words. Two words with nearly the same denotation may have different connotations. For example, *to bargain* and *to negotiate* have nearly the same denotation: "to try to reach agreement." Their connotations, however, are different. The word *bargain* usually refers to trying to reach an agreement about the cost of products or services. The word *negotiate*, however, usually refers to trying to reach an agreement in a dispute, on a contract, or on an international issue.

In the following paragraph, the writer uses effective language to create a scene for the reader.

Model

Turning and looking west, I was immediately struck by the simple beauty of the little town, its geometric, whitewashed houses gleaming in the hot, bright sun. The town was perched atop a hill directly underneath the jagged peaks of the coastal range. An old road wound its way up the hillside and into the town, and faraway little cars hurled like juggernauts around the steep, sharp curves.

Dan Staley, Woodrow Wilson High School
Long Beach, California

In the paragraph, the noun *peaks* is more specific than *tops* would have been because it tells the reader that the mountaintops are pointed, not rounded. The vivid modifier *jagged* further emphasizes their sharpness. *Perched* is a stronger verb than *located* would have been; it makes the town's position seem precarious.

Similes and Metaphors

Using similes and metaphors is another way to make your descriptions effective. In a **simile** you make a direct comparison between two unlike things that share one striking characteristic. A simile always contains the word *like* or *as* to emphasize the comparison. A **metaphor** is an implied comparison that does not contain the word *like* or *as*. In a metaphor you describe your subject as if it actually is the thing to which you are comparing it.

The following description of a leopard contains both a simile and a mctaphor.

Model

He turned his head our way, the long white whiskers spreading out from his face *like two thick fans,* gave us an uneasy look, and *poured slowly head first off the log and down into some bushes.*

Evelyn Ames, *A Glimpse of Eden*

In the simile, *like* is used in the comparison between the whiskers and fans. In the metaphor, the leopard is described as a thick liquid that pours from the log.

Overused metaphors and similes like "as sly as a fox" are called **clichés.** You should avoid using them because they will not seem fresh and interesting to your reader.

Overwriting

A carefully chosen modifier or an appropriate simile or metaphor will make your writing clear and interesting. A long series of modifiers or several similes in a row, however, will make your writing confusing. In addition, a simile or a metaphor that is forced or farfetched will not be effective. The following sentence contains these problems; it is overwritten.

OVERWRITTEN   The long, winding, narrow river coiled through the town like a snake, a jump rope dropped by a child, a strand of hair.

The sentence contains too many modifiers for *river* and too many similes. The more effective sentence that follows contains only one simile.

EFFECTIVE   The narrow river wound its way through the town like a snake slithering through the grass.

When you write a description, use modifiers, similes, and metaphors sparingly and effectively, as in the second example.

Exercise 2 Writing: Effective Words   On your paper, rewrite the following sentences. Replace words that do not create a sharp impression, and add modifiers where they would be effective. Use specific nouns, strong verbs, and vivid modifiers.

SAMPLE   The person put wood on the fire.
ANSWER   The camper tossed pieces of kindling on the smoldering fire.

1. The food was good.
2. The man sat in the comfortable chair.
3. The animal was in front of the building.
4. The vehicle stopped at the traffic signal.
5. The person was happy to get the message from another person.
6. The machines made a loud noise.
7. The people went to the famous place.
8. The person returned from a long trip.
9. The big rain changed the ground.
10. The shelf held many jars.

Exercise 3 Writing: Similes and Metaphors   Choose three of the following items. Write a descriptive sentence about each object. Include a simile or a metaphor in the sentence, and label the sentence *Simile* or *Metaphor*.

SAMPLE   Waves
ANSWER   From a distance, the white caps of the waves looked like sea gulls flying over the blue water.—Simile

1. A telephone
2. A rocking chair
3. The smell of dinner
4. A teapot
5. A desk
6. A pond

7.3c   Organizing and Writing a Description

To make your description of a person, a place, or an object interesting, you must organize it well and write it clearly. The following steps will help you to organize and write your description.

Strategies

1. *Include a topic sentence* that introduces the person, the place, or the object and that, if possible, states your general impression of the subject.

2. *Use chronological order, spatial order, or order of importance to present your sensory details (page 332).* Use one order consistently throughout your description.

3. *Use transitional words and phrases,* such as *next, in the middle,* and *most important,* to emphasize the order of your description.

4. *Place each group of related details in a separate paragraph.* For example, if you were using spatial order to describe a two-story building, you could place all of the details about the first story in one paragraph and all of the details about the second story in another paragraph.

5. *Conclude with a sentence that restates your general impression or in some other way indicates the end of your description.*

In the following paragraph, the writer arranges the details in spatial order.

Model

We lighted our lamps in our miner's helmets and started downward into the cave. The entrance hall was filled with boulders, piled together like children's marbles. We stepped from one to another, descending deeper and deeper into the earth. The vast mouth of the cave diminished behind us until it looked no bigger than a rathole. Then it vanished completely. We began feeling our way down a great slope in complete darkness except for the puddles of light from our headlamps.

Daniel P. Mannix, "Bat Quest"

The words *downward, descending, deeper and deeper, behind,* and *down* emphasize the spatial order of the passage. Notice the effective simile in the second sentence of the passage.

Exercise 4 Writing: Organizing Details Using the following topic sentence and details, write a brief description of Pam. Present the details of her changing appearance in chronological order. As you write, you may change the wording of the details.

Topic sentence: At each point on our hike last Saturday, my friend Pam's appearance reflected how tired she was.

Details:
One hour later, cheeks becoming red and hair falling in face
By the end of the trip, limping because of blister on right heel
As we started going up steep, rocky trail, walked briskly and swung arms
Three hours later, slowing her pace and dragging her feet in dirt on the trail
In beginning, dark hair neatly tied back
Near end of the trail, dirt smudges on face where she wiped it with her hand

Assignment 1 Writing/Revising Write a description of the most comfortable room in which you often spend time. Include sensory details that create a mood of nostalgia or pleasure. Arrange the details in spatial order or in order of importance. Using the Assignment Checklist that follows, revise your description.

Assignment 2 Writing/Revising Write a description of someone working at a job that you would like to have. Include sensory details about any uniform or safety equipment that the person wears at work. Organize the details of your description in order of importance, beginning with the most striking characteristic and moving to the less striking characteristics. Then revise your description.

Assignment 3   Writing/Revising   Write a description of an object that you have had for a long time. Using chronological order, present sensory details to show how the object has changed over time. If possible, use a metaphor or a simile to make the description of the object more vivid. Before you make a final copy of your description, revise it.

Assignment Checklist

Check your assignments for the following points:

✔ 1. Did you include sensory details that show the uniqueness of the person, place, or object that you described?
✔ 2. Did you use specific nouns, strong verbs, and vivid modifiers?
✔ 3. Did you use a simile or a metaphor?
✔ 4. Did you use words with appropriate connotations?
✔ 5. Did you include a topic sentence that introduces your subject?
✔ 6. Did you present your sensory details in a logical order?
✔ 7. If your description contains many details, did you place each group of related details in a paragraph of its own?
✔ 8. Did you proofread your description for correct grammar, usage, spelling, and punctuation?

7.4   Narrative Writing

Narrative writing presents a story, either nonfictional or fictional. Nonfictional narratives include biographical and autobiographical writings. Fictional narratives include all short stories and novels.

7.4a   Planning a Narrative

You should plan a narrative carefully before you begin to write. First choose a topic; then list and organize details about the topic.

Choosing a Topic

The first step in planning a narrative is choosing an event to narrate. Choose an event that is short enough for you to present completely in two to eight pages.

If you choose to narrate a true event, you will write about real actions and the people who performed them. If you choose to narrate a fictional event, you will invent the actions, the characters, or both. Fictional actions and characters may be based on your experiences or the experiences of others, which you narrate as fiction by changing details as you wish. For example, if you see someone trying out for a part in a community play, you may imagine what it would be like to try out for a part in a Broadway play. You may also imagine another incident in the life of the character in the play.

Organizing a Narrative

The next step in planning your narrative is listing the actions that you wish to narrate. List the actions in chronological order and include a conflict, a climax, and a conclusion.

Conflict. The actions of a narrative center on a **conflict,** a situation or a problem that must be resolved at the end. The conflict may occur between two people, between a person and a force of nature, or within the mind and feelings of one person. For example, a conflict may occur between a person who wants to build a store on a piece of land and a person who wants to turn the land into a park.

Climax. The conflict in a narrative is greatest at the **climax,** or high point. For example, in a story about the conflict that is mentioned in the preceding paragraph, the climax may occur when the two people meet to argue their cases in front of the city zoning board.

Conclusion. The actions in a narrative lead from the climax to the **conclusion,** in which the conflict usually is resolved. In the story about the use of the land, the resolution of the conflict may come when the two people and the members of the zoning board agree that a store may be built if a small community park is built in front of it.

Exercise 1   Prewriting: Organizing a Narrative   On your paper, describe a conflict, a climax, and a conclusion that could develop in each of the following situations.

> SAMPLE   Amy wants to be a newspaper reporter.
>
> ANSWER   *Conflict:* Amy wants to learn how to write newspaper articles, but no school in her community teaches journalism.
>
> *Climax:* Amy applies for a job with a newspaper in a nearby town and is turned down because she has no experience.
>
> *Conclusion:* She decides to save her money so that she can go to a town where journalism is taught.

1. A bicyclist has twenty hilly miles to travel before reaching home.
2. A new task needs to be performed in an office.
3. A city has a water shortage.
4. Jeff has money to buy either a new coat or a new radio.
5. Two friends support different political candidates.

7.4b   Writing a Narrative

When you begin to write a narrative, consider which point of view you will use, how you will start your narrative, how you will present your characters, and how you will use description.

Establishing a Point of View

You can write a narrative from a first-person or a third-person point of view. When you write a narrative using a **first-person point of view,** you are the "I" who presents the actions. You write as a participant in the action. When you write a narrative using a **third-person point of view,** you usually do not write as a participant in the action, and you refer to the characters as *he, she,* and *they* when you do not use their names.

Use the first person when you write autobiographical narratives and the third person when you write biographical narratives. You can use either the first person or the third person when you write fictional narratives.

The following examples illustrate the difference between first-person and third-person narration.

FIRST-PERSON NARRATION

> Usually I am nervous about speaking to a large group of people, but I was so excited about my new plan for the cafeteria that I spoke to the assembly without any fear.

THIRD-PERSON NARRATION

> Usually she is nervous about speaking to a large group of people, but she was so excited about her new plan for the cafeteria that she spoke to the assembly without any fear.

The first-person point of view and the third-person point of view may be either omniscient or limited. If your point of view is **omniscient,** or all-seeing, you may reveal what all of your characters are thinking and doing at all times, even when they are far away or alone. If your point of view is **limited,** you may reveal what other characters are thinking only when they express their thoughts, and you may reveal what they are doing only if they are in sight. Of course, you may speculate about what they are thinking or doing. When you write a narrative, the characters and events will help you to decide whether your point of view should be omniscient or limited. For example, if your narrative contains many characters in different places at the same time, using an omniscient point of view might make their activities clearer to the reader.

Maintain one point of view throughout your narrative. If you begin your narrative in the first person, use that form consistently. Similarly, if you begin a narrative in the third person, use the pronoun *I* only in direct quotations.

Exercise 2   Writing: Point of View   The following paragraph is written in the third person. On your paper, rewrite the passage, changing the point of view from the third person to the first person.

> For years, Craig had heard about his grandmother's trips to an antique auction on the first Monday of each month. Last month she finally asked him to accompany her to the auction. He went, imagining that the auction would be conducted quietly in a wood-paneled room richly furnished with valuable antiques. When they drove up to the auction building, he was surprised to see a one-story cement

warehouse. Inside, he saw an enormous room filled with people sitting on rows of metal folding chairs. Bidders called out loudly from their seats to claim large, torn cardboard boxes. When he went to the front of the room to get the boxes of items that his grandmother bought, he discovered that the boxes were filled mainly with old toys and broken dishes. Before they left, he and his grandmother sorted through the boxes to pick out the real antiques for her store. The rest he took back to the auctioneers. On the way home, he thought about how the experience had been far different from what he had expected.

Beginning a Narrative

The beginning of your narrative should indicate to your reader what will appear in the rest of the story. To do that, establish the point of view that you will use. Present the **setting**—the time and location of the actions—and introduce the important characters. When possible, suggest the conflict that will develop in the story. Present all of the information in an interesting way so that your reader will want to read further in your story.

The following paragraph is a strong beginning for a narrative.

Model

On the first Thursday of last March, I waited on a folding chair in a dingy hallway above the music store as I had waited every Thursday for the past three years. Soon the bulky shape of Mr. Bednarek appeared in the doorway of a room down the hall, and he called me in as usual to start my weekly classical guitar lesson. This Thursday, however, he did not ask me to start plucking exercises right away. Instead he began to explain how my playing had improved in the past six months. Then he said that, in order to get any better, I would have to get a new guitar. I was stunned. I did not see how I could manage to earn money for a new guitar.

The writer decided to use the first person to tell the story. The setting of the action is presented clearly, and the two main characters of the narrative are introduced. Finally, the writer indicates that the conflict will concern finding a way to earn money for a new guitar.

Creating Characters

Because they perform most of the actions, the characters are an especially important part of a narrative. By describing your characters clearly, explaining their motivations, and presenting their dialogue, you can make your narrative come to life for your reader.

Description.   To help your reader form a mental picture of your characters, describe them precisely. Describe their physical characteristics: how tall they are, how heavy they are, and what colors their eyes and hair are. Emphasize their outstanding or unusual features. In addition, describe the clothing that the characters are wearing and their expressions and movements. Use details about appearance to reveal the personalities of the characters.

Motivation.   Explain what situations and feelings motivate your characters, or cause them to act as they do. For example, if a character suddenly changes jobs, you should explain why. Did some event make her unhappy with her old job? Did she finally get the job that she had wanted for years?

Dialogue.   Present not only the appearance and motivations of your characters but also their conversations. You can present conversation indirectly, by summarizing what the characters say, or directly, by giving their exact words. **Dialogue**—the exact words of your characters—is more interesting to your reader than indirect reporting of conversations; therefore, use dialogue unless the conversation of the characters would be too long.

Dialogue can reveal the personalities, ages, and geographical backgrounds of your characters. Because spoken language is more informal than written language, dialogue often will be less formal than the rest of your narration. It may even contain slang, contractions, or sentence fragments (*page 70*).

In a narrative, you can use dialogue instead of just explaining events and feelings. Rather than writing "Nick was worried" or "Angela was brave," you can use dialogue to show more vividly that he was worried or that she was brave. In presenting the words of your characters, you will need to add explanatory details, such as "Kim stated calmly," to tell which character is speaking and how he or she is speaking.

When you write dialogue, follow the rules for punctuating and making paragraph divisions that are presented on pages 189–190.

In the following dialogue, the writer presents the exact words of two young people. He also uses explanatory details such as "I answered" and "she exclaimed in astonishment." Notice the punctuation and paragraphing of the passage.

Model

"I was visiting Madge Reagan . . . ," she explained. . . . "Where were you?"

"Oh, I was at work," I answered.

"At work?" she exclaimed in astonishment. "Till this hour?"

"I have to work from eight to seven," I said modestly.

"But aren't they terrible hours?" she said.

"Ah, I'm only filling in time," I explained lightly. "I don't expect to be there long."

Frank O'Connor, "The Duke's Children"

The writer uses dialogue to reveal the personalities of the speakers. The girl seems friendly and concerned. The narrator is also friendly, but he is defensive about the long hours that he has to work.

Personality.   You may reveal the personalities of your characters with their actions as well as with their words. For example, a football player who claims not to care about doing well in a game may, nevertheless, practice hard before every game. In that case, the character's actions reveal more about his feelings than his words do. In addition, you may include direct comments about the personality of a character. For example, you may write, "Even when he tried to be stern, James could not hide his good humor."

Using Description

As you have learned, you can bring your characters to life by describing them for your reader. You can also use description to make the settings, the objects, and the actions in your narrative more interesting for your reader.

The following passage from a narrative contains effective description.

Model

> I sat on the front porch of the old makeshift cabin in the evening mountain air. A cool, dry breeze carried off the nimble, plucking sounds of my banjo with the hollow thuds and squeaks of the rocking chair on the wooden porch. Gradually, these sounds faded, and my attention drifted to some car lights on a neighboring mountain. Because of the great distance, the cars seemed to move along slowly in complete silence. Below, lights of the town shone without a sound while the wind whispered occasionally through the pines around me.
>
> *Eric Heywood, Mount Vernon High School*
> *Mount Vernon, Iowa*

Effective modifiers such as *cool* and *plucking* describe the breeze and the noise of the banjo. Carefully chosen nouns and verbs such as *thuds* and *whispered* describe the noise of the rocking chair and the wind.

Developing the Action

As you write your narrative, present the actions in chronological order, as they appear on your list. Place each group of related actions in a paragraph of its own. Introduce the conflict and present the actions leading up to the climax. Then resolve the conflict in your conclusion. Your conclusion may come soon after the climax.

Finishing Your Narrative

When your draft is complete, revise it. Then select a brief title that indicates the central issue or conflict but that does not reveal too much about the actual events of the narrative.

Exercise 3 Writing/Revising: Dialogue The following paragraph contains information for a dialogue. Rewrite the passage using dialogue. Use explanatory details where they are necessary. Use punctuation and paragraphing as needed, and revise your dialogue before making a final copy.

One hot day last August, I was visiting my cousin Sheryl in Wisconsin. I complained that it was too hot to do anything. Sheryl said that she knew a way to cool off. I asked her what her idea was. She suggested that we go tubing. I said that I did not know what tubing is. She said that tubing is floating down a river while sitting in an inner tube. She said that we could go down the river that is one mile from her house. I said that I was not sure that I could stay in the inner tube. She said that it would be easy and fun. Reluctantly, I said that I would go. Then we went into the garage to get inner tubes for our trip down the river.

Exercise 4   Writing: Beginning a Narrative   Use some or all of the following information in a passage that could serve as a beginning of a first-person narrative. In your beginning you should introduce the setting and the characters and establish the conflict.

1. One-day trip to Bear Island
2. On island: small towns and country roads
3. Most of day uneventful
4. Drove to ferry
5. Took ferry to island
6. Took bicycles aboard ferry
7. Two-hour ferry ride
8. Rode around island all day
9. Dusk came
10. Real adventure began on way home
11. Went with friends Gene and Maryann
12. Went one Saturday last October

Assignment 1   Writing/Revising   Write a narrative about an event that you want to share with a reader. For example, you could write about an event in which you performed well under pressure or an event in which you were adventurous. Write your narrative so that it has a strong beginning, a climax, and a conclusion. Use the first-person point of view. Then, using the Assignment Checklist that follows, revise your narrative.

Assignment 2 Writing/Revising Imagine how one person acted in a historical event that interests you. Write a fictional narrative about that person's role in the event. Invent the character's actions and words as necessary. Write from the third-person, omniscient point of view. Use correct punctuation and paragraphing for dialogue. When your draft is complete, revise your narrative.

Assignment Checklist

Check your assignments for the following points:

✔ 1. Did you present the actions of your narrative in chronological order?

✔ 2. Did you place each group of related actions in its own paragraph?

✔ 3. Did you use one point of view consistently?

✔ 4. Did you introduce the main characters and the setting early in your narrative?

✔ 5. Did you develop a conflict in your narrative?

✔ 6. Did you present the actions leading to the climax?

✔ 7. Did you resolve the conflict in your conclusion?

✔ 8. Did you use description and dialogue to develop characters?

✔ 9. Did you make clear what motivates your characters?

✔ 10. Did you proofread your narrative for correct grammar, usage, spelling, and punctuation?

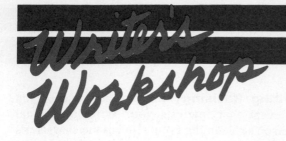

Interesting Places:
Writing Descriptive and Narrative Paragraphs

Situation: The producer of the television series *Interesting Places* has decided to feature in an upcoming show the historic town hall in your community. As a research assistant for the series, you have been asked to provide two paragraphs of background information. In one paragraph you will describe the town hall, and in the other you will narrate its history. You will work from a photograph of the building and a list of notes that you have made from historical records. As you plan and write your paragraphs, you will keep in mind the following information.

Writer: you as a research assistant for *Interesting Places*
Audience: viewers of *Interesting Places*
Topic: the historic town hall
Purpose: to describe the building and to narrate its history

Directions: To plan and write your paragraphs, follow these steps.

> *Step 1.* List sensory details about the striking features of the town hall in the photograph on the facing page. Arrange the details in spatial order. Then review your list to make sure that all of the details work together to create a unified impression of the building.

> *Step 2.* Using your list of details, write a descriptive paragraph. Use vivid and specific words to make your

(Continue on page 352.)

Notes on the History of the Old Town Hall

1973 — total restoration completed, including the
addition of a Hall of Flags in the main
lobby

1821 — built as private residence of Josiah Clark,
a local merchant

1982 — cited by United States Landmark Commission
as a place of historical interest

1870 to 1940 — town meetings held there

1840 — purchased from Clark's daughter by
the town and used as a schoolhouse

1870 — designated as the town hall

The Clark family moved to another estate.

Now contains exhibits of prints, furniture,
paintings, rare books, and old
documents, which attract hundreds of
visitors each year

1940 — fire that partially destroyed upper story

1951 — became a museum with a collection
of journals and town records

description clear and interesting to your audience.

Step 3. Read your historical notes on the facing page. List the facts that you will use in your paragraph. Then arrange the facts in chronological order.

Step 4. Using your list of facts, write a paragraph about the history of the town hall. Use transitional words to emphasize the chronological order of the paragraph.

Step 5. Review your paragraphs. Check them for errors, and revise them if necessary.

Unit Assignments

Assignment 1   Select a process to explain to a friend. For example, you could explain how a jet engine works or how to find a job. Do whatever research is necessary to find information on your topic. Then write your explanation, defining all terms that your friend may not know. When your draft is complete, revise the explanation.

Assignment 2   Write a review of a film that you would like your friends to see. Include the five parts of a review and make sure that you provide information about the techniques used in the film as well as your evaluation of the film. Then revise your review.

Assignment 3   Recall a person whom you have seen recently who was clearly happy, angry, or tired. Write a description of that person. Include sensory details about the person's general appearance and specific details that show how the person was feeling. Organize your description by spatial order or by order of importance, and use vivid language. Finally, revise your description.

Assignment 4   Write a nonfictional narrative about an event in which you depended on a friend for help or in which someone depended on you. Present the actions in chronological order and place each group of related actions in a paragraph of its own.

Assignment 5   Write a fictional narrative about a person who visits an unfamiliar community or about a person who tries to change something in his or her own community. Base the characters and the setting of your narrative on real people and a real place. Use vivid description and write from a limited third-person point of view. Then revise your narrative.

Revising Your Assignments

For help in revising expository, descriptive, or narrative writing, consult the Checklist for Revision on the last page of this book.

Unit Tests

Test 1

A. Number your paper from 1 to 5. Next to each number, write *True* if the sentence is true or *False* if it is false.

1. When you write for a specialized audience, include details that are of particular interest to that audience.
2. In a review provide a detailed description for people who are not familiar with the work.
3. In a description you should present details from only one sense.
4. A metaphor is an implied comparison that does not contain *like* or *as*.
5. The conflict in a narrative may occur within the mind and feelings of one person.

B. Number your paper from 6 to 10. Next to each number, write the letter of the item that correctly completes the sentence. You will not use one of the terms.

    a. review   d. limited

    b. omniscient   e. expository writing

    c. mood   f. sensory details

6. In __?__ your purpose is to explain something to your reader or to inform your reader about something.
7. A(n) __?__ explains the meaning of a work and the techniques that are used to present that meaning.
8. __?__ are those characteristics that you perceive with your senses of sight, hearing, touch, taste, and smell.
9. When you create a(n) __?__ in a description, you create a certain emotional response in your audience.
10. In a narrative written from the __?__ point of view, you may reveal what the characters are thinking and doing at all times.

C. Number your paper from 11 to 15. Next to each number, write the letter of the item that correctly answers the question.

11. Which of the following is a transitional phrase that emphasizes spatial order?

    a. Later that day   c. Most important

    b. For example   d. In the middle

12. Which of the following is a limited topic for the subject "Spaceships"?
   a. The invention of airplanes
   b. Navigation equipment in early spacecraft
   c. How astronauts train on Earth
   d. Qualifications for becoming an astronaut

13. Which of the following should *not* be introduced at the beginning of a narrative?
   a. Characters   b. Setting   c. Climax   d. Conflict

14. Which of the following contains the most vivid description?
   a. Making loud noises, the bird flew over the boat.
   b. The sea gull flew over the fishing boat.
   c. Screeching loudly, the sea gull circled the fishing boat.
   d. The sea gull circled the boat.

15. Which of the following is from a third-person narrative?
   a. "My guitar needs new strings," Sandy explained to the salesperson.
   b. "Erin ran in the race yesterday," I explained.
   c. I saw Jeff at the park this morning.
   d. Last week we visited our friends in Austin, Texas.

Test 2

Choose one of the Unit Assignments. Write the assignment as directed and hand it in to your teacher.

*Persuasive
Writing*

Unit Preview

Your purpose in **persuasive writing** is to get other people to accept an idea. The idea is your topic. The other people are your audience, the readers whom you hope to influence. The following paragraph is an example of persuasive writing.

(1) Career-education courses should be part of the high school curriculum. (2) Such courses acquaint students with the various careers open to them, with the requirements and advantages of each, and with the needs of the job market. (3) Too often, high school graduates find themselves unprepared to decide what to do after graduation. (4) As a result, some graduates make poor choices of colleges or training programs and eventually hold jobs that they do not like. (5) Graduates who have had career-education courses, however, can make informed choices about satisfying careers. (6) Furthermore, graduates who make wise career choices contribute more fully to society. (7) The result is that career education benefits society as well as the student.

For Analysis   Reread the paragraph and then, on your paper, follow these directions.

1. Copy the number of the sentence stating the opinion that the writer wants the audience to accept.
2. Explain the purpose of Sentence 2.
3. List the numbers of the sentences in which the writer gives reasons that support the opinion expressed in Sentence 1.
4. Explain the purpose of Sentence 7.

In analyzing the paragraph, you thought about the main challenge of persuasive writing: getting an audience to accept an idea and perhaps to take some sort of action. This unit will give you some insight into the art of persuasion. It will also explain techniques that you can use in writing a persuasive paragraph or composition. As you learn to write persuasively, you will follow the three steps of the writing process: prewriting, writing, and revising.

8.1 Selecting a Topic

8.1a Recognizing Opinions

Your topic in persuasive writing is an opinion that you want readers to accept. An **opinion** is the statement of a view that is not shared by everyone. Opinions differ from facts in that opinions are subject to disagreement but facts are not. The following statements are examples of opinions and facts.

OPINIONS	FACTS
Spanish is a beautiful language.	Spanish is a Romance language.
The United States should always strive to be a land of opportunity for immigrants.	France gave the Statue of Liberty to the United States in 1884.
The world's greatest spectator sport is American professional football.	The footballs used by the National Football League are made of leather.

It is precisely because they are subject to disagreement that opinions make suitable topics for persuasive writing. There are four types of opinions that you can use.

EXPLANATION
Political anarchy was the real cause of the fall of the Roman Empire.

EVALUATION

> The new film *Revenge of the Catpeople* is almost entirely without merit.

PREDICTION

> There will be a breakthrough in cancer research within the next ten years.

ADVICE ("SHOULD" STATEMENTS)

> Congress should revise the law on minimum wages.

Exercise 1   Prewriting: Opinions and Facts   Two statements are made about each of the five subjects that follow. On your paper, write *Opinion* next to the letter of any statement that is subject to disagreement. Write *Fact* next to the letter of any statement that either is clearly true or can easily be shown to be true.

1. a. Motorcycles are a fuel-efficient means of transportation.
   b. Motorcycles should be banned because they make too much noise.
2. a. Hospital care will soon be so expensive that few people will be able to afford it.
   b. Hospital care is better in the United States than it is abroad.
3. a. Water is made up of two parts hydrogen and one part oxygen.
   b. Water boils at 100° C.
4. a. Students in junior high school usually have poor study habits.
   b. Students in junior high school are too young to start dating.
5. a. Farmers in the United States are among the world's leaders in food production.
   b. Farmers in the United States have been reckless in their use of water for irrigating arid regions.

8.1b   Selecting an Opinion as a Writing Topic

Before you begin writing about an opinion, consider whether it is a suitable topic for persuasion. Keep in mind three points when you choose a writing topic.

> 1. *An opinion suitable for persuasive writing is based on more than personal preference.* You cannot expect readers to accept opinions based only on your individual tastes.

UNSUITABLE
> Colonial architecture is more attractive than Victorian architecture.

2. *An opinion suitable for persuasive writing is based on a logical idea rather than on a feeling or a hunch.* You cannot convince readers that an opinion is correct if it is based only on intuition or guesswork.

UNSUITABLE
> I have a feeling that people will support the club's blood-donor drive.

3. *An opinion suitable for persuasive writing is specific and clear.* You cannot persuade readers to accept an opinion that they find vague or general.

UNSUITABLE
> Soccer is better than hockey.

The following opinions would make suitable topics for persuasive writing.

SUITABLE Our trial system would be more efficient if juries were made up of eight people rather than twelve.
No government should spend more in a year than it takes in.

These two opinions are suitable for the following reasons: (1) They do not simply state personal preferences. (2) They are based on logical ideas, not on feelings or hunches. (3) They are specific and clear.

Exercise 2   Prewriting: Suitable Topics   On your paper, write *Suitable* or *Unsuitable* to indicate whether each of the following opinions is an acceptable topic for persuasive writing. Each time you classify a topic as *Unsuitable*, specify *Personal preference, Hunch,* or *Vague*.

1. Green is a more relaxing color than blue.

2. Something tells me that science fiction movies are going to be the wave of the future.

3. Civil service tests are unfair.

4. Every driver should take a course on how to make basic automobile repairs.

5. There is no real craftsmanship these days.

6. Swimming in the ocean is more fun than swimming in a pool.

7. Colorado is the most beautiful state in the country.

8. The value of automobile safety devices must be weighed against how much they cost consumers.

9. The private ownership of property is a citizen's most important right.

10. Automobile imports are a problem.

8.1c Suiting Your Topic to Your Audience

When you select a topic for persuasive writing, you usually have a certain audience in mind. Before proceeding with the topic, weigh your audience's likely reaction to it. Ask yourself two questions.

1. *Is my audience already likely to agree with the opinion?* If so, select another opinion that some of your readers will disagree with. Of the two topics that follow, the second is better because some persuasion would be needed to convince the audience of its merit.

   AUDIENCE
   > A consumer group

   POOR TOPIC
   > Grocery shoppers have a right to know the ingredients of the items that they purchase.

   BETTER TOPIC
   > Grocery-store items should be given a health-quality rating based on their ingredients.

2. *Is my audience likely to oppose the opinion very strongly?* If so, you would be setting yourself an impossible task. Unless you hold your opinion so strongly that you do not want to

modify it, or unless you enjoy defending an unpopular view, consider selecting another opinion that your audience could more readily be persuaded to accept. Of the two topics that follow, the second is better than the first because readers are more likely to be persuaded to accept it.

AUDIENCE
    Scientists

POOR TOPIC
    Modern science is entirely to blame for the existence of the devastating weapons that threaten the world.

BETTER TOPIC
    Modern science is partly responsible for the existence of the devastating weapons that threaten the world.

Exercise 3   Prewriting: Audience   For each of the following opinions, an audience is listed. On your paper, write *Suitable* if the opinion would make a suitable writing topic for that audience; write *Unsuitable* if it would not. If the opinion is unsuitable, explain why.

1. *Opinion:* Union workers provide the best labor available on the market. *Audience:* Union members
2. *Opinion:* The city rent commission should put a ceiling on the amount of rent that landlords may charge. *Audience:* Renters
3. *Opinion:* Physical-fitness courses are a luxury that most high schools can do without. *Audience:* High school administrators
4. *Opinion:* Home owners should not try to sell their homes without the help of a real estate agent. *Audience:* Home owners
5. *Opinion:* The government should censor the political articles of newspapers during times of national crisis. *Audience:* Journalists

Assignment 1   Prewriting/Writing   Write eight opinions of your own that some of your classmates are likely to disagree with. The opinions should be on a wide variety of subjects. Write two explanations, two evaluations, two predictions, and two statements that advise. Label each opinion.

Assignment 2   Prewriting   Select four of the opinions that you wrote for Assignment 1, and copy them on a separate sheet of paper. Conduct a poll of at least ten classmates to find out whether they agree or disagree with each opinion. (Some students may neither agree nor disagree.) Based on the results of your poll, rank the four opinions from the least controversial to the most controversial.

Continuing Assignment   Prewriting/Writing   *Step 1:* Select and record on your paper an opinion that would make a good topic for a persuasive composition of at least four paragraphs. If you wish, choose from among the opinions that you used in Assignments 1 and 2. *Step 2:* Identify the audience for whom you will write the composition. You may wish to choose one of the following: parents or guardians, teachers, classmates, teen-agers in general, a specific interest group (such as sports fans), or government representatives. Save your paper.

Check your writing assignments for the following points:

 ✔ 1. Did you write opinions that are subject to disagreement?
 ✔ 2. Did you write opinions that explain, evaluate, predict, or advise?
 ✔ 3. Did you base your opinions on logical ideas rather than on feelings or personal preferences?
 ✔ 4. Did you make your statements of opinion clear and specific?
 ✔ 5. Did you take into account the probable reactions of your audience?

8.2   Using Facts

Once you know your topic and audience, you must devise an effective way of persuading that audience to accept your opinion. As a writer, you have a variety of persuasive tools at your disposal: the use of language that is forceful and moving; the flow and the strength of your sentences; the use of clear images and effective comparisons; the tone that you convey—your sincerity, fairness, and enthusiasm. Even more important than your use of language is your use of sound reasoning to support your opinion.

A persuasive paragraph is a series of logically connected statements. It consists mainly of a position statement and supporting sentences. The **position statement** is the opinion that you want your audience to accept. The **supporting sentences** are the facts and opinions that provide **evidence,** or reasons, for your position. Study the following example.

POSITION STATEMENT

The city should mark off bicycle lanes on major streets.

SUPPORTING SENTENCES

More people in the city are using bikes for transportation.

Auto traffic is heavy on major streets.

The number of bike-car accidents is increasing.

On streets with bicycle lanes, bike-car accidents are very unusual.

8.2a   Recognizing Facts

To write persuasively, you must present evidence that readers consider reliable. Facts are the most reliable evidence that you can offer your audience.

A **fact** is something that is known to be true or that can be shown to be true by observation, measurement, or research. Study the types of verification suggested for the factual statements below.

FACT	METHOD OF VERIFICATION
Calligraphy is the art of fine handwriting.	Look up *calligraphy* in a dictionary.
Aristotle was the tutor of Alexander the Great.	Look up Aristotle or Alexander the Great in an encyclopedia.
Jane's portrait was done with luminous paints.	Examine the portrait in the dark to see whether it glows.
The winner of the 100-meter dash in the 1900 Olympic games was Francis Jervis.	Consult an almanac.
The whole equals the sum of its parts.	No verification necessary. The truth of the statement is universally accepted.

The facts that you have just examined illustrate the various kinds of factual statements. The first statement is a definition; the second is the statement of something that happened. The third is an observation, and the fourth is a statistic. The fifth is a truth so well known that it needs no verification. If necessary, however, it could be verified in a geometry textbook.

Exercise 1   Prewriting: Facts   Study the position statement and supporting sentences that follow. On your paper, write the numbers of the supporting sentences that express facts. Next to each number, indicate a reliable way of verifying the fact.

Position statement: The United States Senate is right to limit the freedom of its members to filibuster.

1. To filibuster is to use lengthy speeches or other means to delay or prevent a vote on a bill under consideration.
2. In 1975 the Senate ruled that debate on an issue can be ended by the vote of three fifths of the Senate membership.
3. Without such a policy, a stubborn senator or a small group can exercise unfair influence.
4. Before the ruling, filibusters lasting as long as seventy-five days were not unheard of.
5. Since the ruling, the Senate has functioned much more smoothly and efficiently.

8.2b   Using Facts as Evidence

Facts make very convincing evidence. In the following paragraph, the writer uses four logically related factual statements to support the position stated at the beginning.

Model

Fact ——————— Astronauts have little or no chance of traveling out among the stars in the foreseeable future. The brightest star in the sky, and one of the nearest, is Sirius, located in the constellation Canis Major. Sirius

Fact ──────────── is approximately 8.7 light years, or 51 trillion miles,
Fact ──────────── away from Earth. The fastest speed astronauts have
ever traveled is slightly less than 25,000 miles per
Fact ──────────── hour. Even assuming that a ship capable of maintaining that top speed could be designed, it would take
the passengers more than 230,000 years to reach their
destination!

In gathering factual evidence to support your position, keep in mind the following points.

Strategies

1. *Use facts as evidence only if they help to show the correctness of your position.* In the paragraph about travel to the stars, for example, each fact supports the idea that such travel will be impossible in the foreseeable future. On the other hand, a fact such as "Sirius is known as the Dog Star" would not qualify as evidence. Although the fact relates to the topic, it does not support the position statement.

2. *Do not confuse statements of fact with statements that combine fact and opinion.* Study the following sentences.

   FACT AND OPINION COMBINED
   > Mr. Kahn feels that new employees in a company should start at the bottom and work their way up.
   >
   > The referees insisted on enforcing every one of the silly rules.

   In the first sentence, it is a fact that Mr. Kahn feels the way he does. *What* he feels, on the other hand, is an opinion. Most of the second sentence is a factual report about the referees. The word *silly,* however, presents an evaluation and therefore expresses an opinion.

3. *Indicate the source of your facts if you are presenting unusual evidence.* You may do so by including the source as part of your persuasive paragraph or composition, or you may choose to give the source in a footnote. (See Section 11.5a in Unit 11, "Writing a Research Paper.")

If you keep in mind the guidelines that you have just read, you will choose facts that form strong evidence for your opinion. You will then have a good chance of persuading your audience to accept your position.

Exercise 2   Prewriting: Facts as Evidence   Study the position statement and list of factual statements that follow. On your paper, write the numbers of those factual statements that provide genuine evidence for the position.

Position statement: Tackle football in high schools and colleges is a somewhat risky sport.

1. Every year more than a million high school and college students compete in football.
2. One out of every five high school and college players incurs some type of injury during a season.
3. In spite of the high rate of injury, football draws more spectators than any other sport that schools offer.
4. Eight percent of students hurt playing football suffer a major injury such as a fracture or severe concussion.
5. At some big-name universities, millions of dollars are spent annually on the football program.
6. Broken bones and joint injuries occur more frequently in football than in any other college or high school sport.

Exercise 3   Prewriting: Combination Statements   All of the supporting sentences below the following position statement combine fact and opinion. On your paper, copy those words in each supporting sentence that express opinion rather than fact.

Position statement: Perhaps the most accomplished actor of modern times is Katharine Hepburn.

1. Hepburn made her theatrical debut in *The Czarina* in 1928, and she has been one of our most talented actresses ever since.
2. In 1939 she won the New York Film Critics Award for her exciting performance as Tracy Lord in *The Philadelphia Story*.
3. She has starred in dozens of first-rate plays and movies, and in none of them has she ever given a mediocre performance.

4. Hepburn has won more Academy Awards for acting (four) than any other actor, and deservedly so.
5. Many of her fans think that her role opposite Humphrey Bogart in *The African Queen* in 1952 was her best performance.
6. Hepburn's superlative acting career has spanned more than half a century; in that time she has set new standards of excellence for the entire acting profession.

Assignment Writing Write a position statement about a major event currently in the news. Then make a list of at least five factual statements that support the position. Obtain your facts from newspapers, magazines, and television news shows. Underneath each fact, give its source.

Continuing Assignment Prewriting/Writing Take out the paper on which you wrote the opinion that you will develop in a persuasive composition (*page 362*). The opinion will be your position statement. After doing any needed research, list at least eight facts that support your position. Save your paper.

Check your assignments for the following points:

✔ 1. Did you write a position statement that expresses an opinion clearly?
✔ 2. Did you write supporting sentences that are entirely factual?
✔ 3. Did you write supporting sentences that relate directly to your position?

8.3 Using Other Types of Evidence

Although facts are the best support for a position, opinions can also be useful as evidence. Among the opinions that you can use effectively as evidence are the opinions of experts, opinions based on common experience, and opinions arrived at through reasoning.

8.3a   Opinions of Experts

An expert is a person with a high degree of skill or knowledge in a certain area. Readers usually value the opinion of an expert. The writer of the following persuasive paragraph uses the opinion of an expert as evidence.

Model

> Pesticides are not always an effective means of controlling insects. As the biologist Rachel Carson states in her famous book *Silent Spring,* "insects possess an effective counterweapon (resistance) to aggressive chemical attack. . . . However rapidly technology may invent new uses for insecticides and new ways of applying them, it is likely to find the insects keeping a lap ahead." The main problem, according to Carson, is that pesticides cause insects to develop immunities, thereby making the insects harder to destroy. As a consequence, pesticide users find themselves on a never-ending quest to discover progressively more potent chemicals.

When using an expert's opinion as evidence, give your readers specific information about the expert. In the paragraph on insecticides, for example, the writer identifies the expert, mentions her occupation, gives a quotation from one of her books, and then summarizes her views.

Keep two more points in mind when you use expert opinion as evidence.

Strategies

1. *Do not try to use the opinion of an expert as proof of your position.* That is, use the opinion as evidence for your position, but do not suggest that the opinion proves the position. An expert can be wrong. It is not uncommon for experts in the same field to hold opposing opinions on a subject. Clearly, they cannot all be correct.

2. *Cite the opinion of an expert only if it is in the area of his or her expertise.* Experts often voice opinions on subjects that are outside their specialized area of knowledge. Such opinions are no more reliable than anyone else's.

Exercise 1 Prewriting: Expert Opinion Each position statement is followed by a list of three persons. Identify the person in the list who would best qualify as an expert on the subject of the position statement.

1. More should be done to protect football players from injury. (An orthopedic surgeon, a lawyer, a physical education instructor)
2. The exploration of outer space is well worth its cost. (A politician, an astronomer, a stockbroker)
3. Inflation encourages people to spend, not to save, their money. (A store manager, an economist, a consumer advocate)
4. A state should not enact laws that violate a person's constitutional rights. (A Supreme Court justice, a historian, a governor)
5. *Citizen Kane* is one of the ten greatest movies ever made. (A film critic, a movie star, a theater owner)

8.3b Opinions Based on Common Experience

Opinions based on common experience often make effective evidence. The term *common experience* refers to experiences that most people have had or have observed. Readers generally value the evidence of experience, for it is knowledge that they themselves have gained firsthand or that they can verify in their own lives. The evidence given in the following persuasive paragraph consists of opinions that are based on common experience.

Model

As a rule, you should avoid cramming before an examination. If you are like most people, you have crammed for an exam at one time or another. What kind of results did you achieve? Quite possibly you were not as alert during the test as you normally are because your late-night efforts at studying left you feeling tired and sluggish. Also, while answering the questions, you probably found it difficult to keep information straight and to recall details. Worst of all, within twenty-four hours of the exam you most likely forgot nearly everything you learned while cramming. A moderate amount of last-minute preparation can be helpful before an examination. Trying to cram several months' worth of study into a single night, however, is usually a self-defeating task.

Arguing on the basis of experience is effective only if you show your audience *how* the experience supports your position. In the paragraph on cramming, the writer explains the ways in which cramming affects most people.

Keep in mind these additional points when you use common experience as evidence.

Strategies

1. *Make sure that your opinions reflect the actual experiences of your audience.* You cannot expect readers to agree with you on the basis of experiences that they have never had. For example, if your readers have never done any scientific research, the opinion "Scientific research is often tedious" will not be useful as evidence.

2. *Avoid overgeneralizing from your experience.* If you have had considerable experience with a certain type of activity, for example, you may feel confident in stating a general opinion about that activity. It is risky, however, to make a general statement based on very little experience.

Exercise 2   Writing: Common Experience   Write an opinion on each of the following topics. The opinion must be one that you think most people would agree with on the basis of their experience.

1. The value of patience
2. The main problem with gossip
3. The true meaning of friendship
4. The best way to get ahead in life
5. The value of getting work experience as early as possible

8.3c   Opinions Based on Reasoning

Opinions based on reasoning are yet another type of evidence that you can use to support a position. **Reasoning** is the process of drawing conclusions from statements that you know or believe to be true. A persuasive passage that is based on reasoning says, in effect, "This position is correct because it follows from these other statements." The writer of the following persuasive paragraph supports the position statement by using opinions based on reasoning.

Model

People who abuse the rights of others forfeit their own rights. For instance, you can hardly complain about the loud music coming from your neighbor's house at 2:00 A.M. if you have been guilty of the same offense. By ignoring your neighbor's right to peace and quiet, you have given your neighbor license to ignore *your* right to peace and quiet. What is it that entitles you to a particular right in the first place? If it is the fact that you are a citizen, then you must acknowledge that all other citizens possess the right too. If it is the fact that you are a human being, then you must grant the right to every human being. Thus, in claiming a right for yourself, you also grant it to your neighbor. What is more to the point, in denying a right to your neighbor, you also deny it to yourself.

To argue effectively by using reasoning, present your thoughts to readers in step-by-step fashion. Each step in your reasoning process must move readers logically toward the opinion expressed in your position statement.

Keep in mind these additional points when you use reasoning as evidence.

Strategies

1. *Be sure to include all major steps in your reasoning process.* Reasoning is like building a house. If you leave out an important beam, the entire structure may collapse.

2. *Do not support an opinion with other opinions that are even more questionable than the first one.* It does little good, for example, to claim that one statement logically follows from another if readers think that the first one is false. As far as possible, show that your opinions follow from other very reliable opinions—or better yet, from facts.

Exercise 3   Writing: Reasoning   The blank in each of the following persuasive passages indicates a step that has been left out of the writer's sequence of reasoning. In each passage supply a sentence that would make the reasoning complete.

1. For a system of government to serve the people effectively, citizens must have the authority to elect and to remove government leaders. __?__. Thus, dictatorship is not an effective form of government.

2. Sid should not be appointed treasurer of the club. The club treasurer should be good at math. __?__. Although Sid does well in math, he has had no experience whatsoever in handling large sums of money.

3. Geometry is one of the most valuable subjects that a school can offer. A major goal of education is to teach students how to think logically. __?__.

4. Judge Taylor should disqualify herself from hearing the Smith-Hernandez case. __?__. A judge should maintain strict neutrality in a trial. A judge may not be able to remain neutral if a trial involves a relative.

5. The winner of the decathlon in the Olympic games deserves to be considered one of the world's finest athletes. Athletic excellence consists in being able to perform a great number of physical activities well. __?__.

Assignment 1   Writing   *Step 1:* Write a position statement that you are prepared to support with an expert's opinion. *Step 2:* Underneath the position statement, identify the expert and state his or her qualifications. *Step 3:* Copy at least one quotation that expresses the expert's support of your position. Identify the source of the quotation.

Assignment 2   Writing   *Step 1:* Select one of the following subjects and copy it on your paper. *Step 2:* Write a brief paragraph describing the experiences that you have had with the subject. *Step 3:* Write a position statement that is based on the experiences that you described. *Step 4:* State whether you think that most people would agree with the position on the basis of *their* experience.

1. Waiting in line
2. Following a diet
3. Taking an important test
4. Learning a new skill

Assignment 3 Writing *Step 1:* Write a position statement that can be supported by reasoning. *Step 2:* Give the main reason that you think the position is correct. This reason should be a statement of opinion. *Step 3:* Give a second reason that justifies the first reason. The second reason should be a statement of fact.

Continuing Assignment Prewriting/Writing To the list of supporting facts that you wrote for the Continuing Assignment on page 367, add at least three more pieces of evidence for your position. Your new evidence should consist of experts' opinions, opinions based on common experience, or opinions arrived at through reasoning. Make sure that each piece of evidence directly supports your position. Save your paper.

Assignment Checklist

Check your assignments for the following points:

- ✔ 1. Did you write position statements that are clearly expressed?
- ✔ 2. Did you provide evidence that consists of experts' opinions, opinions based on common experience, or opinions arrived at through reasoning?

8.4 Organizing and Writing an Argument

The impact that your persuasive paragraph or composition has on readers depends finally on how well you write it. You must organize the parts of your paragraph or composition so that the progression of thought is clear. Occasionally you will need to provide additional information for clarity and completeness.

The logically connected statements in a persuasive paragraph or composition form an **argument.** An argument usually includes four parts, two of which you have already studied. A full argument contains (1) a position statement, (2) clarifying remarks, (3) supporting sentences, and (4) concluding sentences. In this section you will study each of the four parts of an argument in turn. You will also learn how to expand your information into a persuasive composition when you have too many ideas for one paragraph.

8.4a   Writing a Position Statement

In persuasive writing you can almost always state your position in one sentence. When you write a single paragraph, your position statement is your topic sentence. Place it at the beginning so that your audience knows from the outset what you want to show. When you write a composition, state your position in the first paragraph wherever it seems most appropriate.

To express your position effectively, follow these guidelines.

Strategies

1. *Phrase your position as a statement, not as a question.* If you phrase your position as a question, your audience may not be able to decide whether you are for or against the idea or action being discussed.

   NOT EFFECTIVE

   > Why should people be forced to retire because they have reached a certain age?

   EFFECTIVE

   > People should not be forced to retire because they have reached a certain age.

2. *Limit your position statement to one opinion.* Different opinions about a subject require separate supporting sentences.

   NOT EFFECTIVE

   > We need more effective rent-control laws; in addition, the existing rent-control laws should be enforced more strictly.

   EFFECTIVE

   > We need more effective rent-control laws.

   EFFECTIVE

   > The present rent-control laws should be enforced more strictly.

3. *Avoid using biased wording in your position statement.* Such wording weakens your argument.

NOT EFFECTIVE

The unfair parking regulations for the downtown area should be changed.

EFFECTIVE

The parking regulations for the downtown area should be changed.

Exercise 1   Revising: Position Statements   Indicate which of the following comments most accurately describes each position statement. On your paper, write the letter of the appropriate comment next to the number of the statement. Then rewrite the statement to make it effective.

   a. Position statement is phrased as a question rather than as a statement.

   b. Position statement expresses two opinions.

   c. Position statement contains biased wording.

1. Has the time come to re-evaluate the way in which business and labor negotiate contracts?
2. Our lazy, irresponsible officers do not deserve re-election.
3. What about curbing some of the travel expenses of our elected representatives?
4. Congress should reject the ill-conceived proposal for pollution control submitted by radical Representative Phillip Crosby.
5. Maintaining our natural resources is in the interest of all citizens, and so is preserving our national heritage.

8.4b   Writing Clarifying Remarks

Having stated your position, you should provide any information that your audience may need in order to understand the issue involved or your position on it. In a paragraph your **clarifying remarks** will be no more than one or two sentences. In a composition you may devote most of the first paragraph to clarifying your position statement.

There are at least four ways in which you can clarify a position statement.

Strategies

1. *Clarify by defining or explaining a key term.*

POSITION STATEMENT

The spoils system detracts from the integrity of our democratic electoral process.

CLARIFYING REMARK

The spoils system is the postelection practice of giving public offices to supporters of the winning candidates.

2. *Clarify by qualifying or limiting the position statement.*

POSITION STATEMENT

The United States should provide economic assistance to some of the developing countries.

CLARIFYING REMARK

By "assistance" I do not mean unconditional grants but, rather, long-term, low-interest loans that would enable these countries to stand on their own.

3. *Clarify by providing background information.*

POSITION STATEMENT

The rapid-transit plan currently under study by the Transportation Board should be approved without delay.

CLARIFYING REMARK

The plan was first proposed two years ago but was held up because of changes in the city's zoning laws.

4. *Clarify by giving an example or a specific application of the position statement.*

POSITION STATEMENT

Our local library should launch a fund-raising program to improve its facilities.

CLARIFYING REMARK

For example, donations should be sought so that carrels for private study can be built.

Exercise 2 Writing: Clarifying Remarks Select one position statement from each of the following pairs. On your paper, write a sentence or two providing the type of clarification specified. You may need to use a dictionary, an encyclopedia, or another reference work.

1. a. Canada's most critical environmental problem is acid rain.
   b. In today's world, colonialism as an active policy of major governments should be discouraged.
   Clarification: Define or explain a key term.

2. a. Most families would probably get to know one another better if they stopped watching television.
   b. Thrift is as worthwhile a quality today as it was when Benjamin Franklin wrote about it.
   Clarification: Qualify or limit the position statement.

3. a. The Twenty-Sixth Amendment has proved to be a wise addition to the law of the land.
   b. The British Museum should return the famed Elgin Marbles to Greece.
   Clarification: Provide helpful background information.

4. a. Prompt action is needed if we are to save some of our endangered species from extinction.
   b. National holidays ought to be celebrated on the days on which they occur, not on the nearest Monday.
   Clarification: Give an example or specific application.

8.4c   Writing Supporting Sentences

Once you have stated your position and clarified it, you are ready to present your supporting evidence. In a persuasive paragraph, you express each point of evidence in one or two supporting sentences. In a persuasive composition, you may write an entire paragraph about a single point of evidence or several related points.

Alternatively, you may write a paragraph about each stage of your reasoning process. The order to use in organizing your supporting sentences depends on how they relate to one another.

Presenting Reasons

In some arguments your evidence will consist of three or more independent reasons that support your position. These reasons may have little to do with one another. If your reasons are of equal importance, the order in which you present them does not matter. Quite often, however, you can arrange independent reasons in the order of least to most important, as the writer of the following persuasive paragraph has.

Model

(1) Position statement	(1) The softball team should play its games at Lincoln Field rather than at school. (2) For one
(2) First reason	thing, Lincoln Field is more attractive than the school
(3) Second reason	field. (3) Then, too, the pitcher's mound and base paths of the school field are designed for hardball, but Lincoln Field has a genuine softball diamond.
(4) Third reason	(4) More important, the Lincoln Field bleachers seat two hundred more spectators than the school bleach-
(5) Fourth reason	ers do. (5) Finally, Lincoln Field is available on more afternoons than the school field.

Exercise 3   Writing: Reasons   Each of the following pairs of sentences consists of a position statement and one supporting sentence. Copy the pairs of sentences on your paper. Underneath each supporting sentence, write two more supporting sentences that are different from the first one and are also independent of each other. Number the three sentences to indicate the order of their importance, making Number 1 the least important. Save your paper.

1. *Position statement:* If you have never learned to swim, you definitely should consider taking swimming lessons.
   Supporting sentence: Swimming is an excellent form of exercise because it stretches arm, leg, back, and stomach muscles.

2. *Position statement:* If the opportunities are available, a student should develop a working acquaintance with computers.

Supporting sentence: The lack of a firsthand knowledge of computers may prevent a young person from obtaining a desirable job.

3. *Position statement:* Students ought to think about possible careers as early as their sophomore year.
   Supporting sentence: In this way they have plenty of time to take the courses that they need.

Presenting a Chain of Reasoning

Sometimes your evidence will consist not of independent reasons grouped together but, rather, of thoughts that form a **chain of reasoning.** In a chain of reasoning, the ideas are interrelated; each statement is connected to the next one, with the position statement representing the final link in the chain. To build a chain of reasoning, you must be able to arrange your supporting sentences in their logical sequence. Study the order of the links in the chain of reasoning given in the following argument.

Model

(1) Position
statement
(final link)

(2) First link

(3) Second link

(4) Third link

(5) Fourth link

(1) The startling idea that the great continents have drifted like logs in a pond was scoffed at for many years, but recently a great deal of evidence has been found to support it. (2) It is known that when certain kinds of rocks are formed, either by settling sediment or cooling lava, magnetic particles in them behave like compass needles, lining up with the earth's magnetic field, which for fundamental reasons tends to point north and south. (3) This happened in ancient rocks too, and if they had stayed in the same position since their formation, their magnetism would still point north and south. (4) In some cases it does, but many ancient rocks have been found with fossil magnetism pointing in other directions. (5) This is taken to indicate that they have shifted position since they were formed.

Carl Sagan and Jonathan Leonard, *Planets*

Notice how the fourth link in the argument leads into the position stated at the beginning.

Exercise 4 Prewriting: Chain of Reasoning After the following position statement are five supporting sentences that could be organized into a chain of reasoning. On your paper, copy the supporting sentences, arranging them in a logical sequence.

Position statement: In democratic decision-making, the majority should always consider the feelings of the minority.

1. If the feelings of the minority are completely ignored now, what is likely to be the minority's attitude when it comes into power?
2. Today's minority may well become tomorrow's majority.
3. It is only prudent, therefore, that the majority treat the minority as it would wish to be treated itself.
4. History shows us that no single party or group stays in power forever.
5. In all probability it will do just what the former majority did.

Arguing by Rebuttal

In some arguments you may present your opponents' position and evidence that supports it, and then show what is wrong with that evidence by offering insights overlooked by the opposition. The evidence that refutes opposing evidence is called a **rebuttal.** In an argument that contains a rebuttal, order your supporting sentences in either of two ways: (1) by presenting all of your opponents' points first and then your own or (2) by alternating individual points. The writer of the following persuasive paragraph uses the first type of rebuttal.

Model

(1) Position statement

(2) Clarifying remark

(3)(4) Evidence supporting opponents' position

(1) For the average high school student, the most desirable program is study of the liberal arts. (2) A liberal arts education is a program of academic courses, as distinguished from a technical or vocational program. (3) There are those who say that a liberal arts education is impractical, because it does not train students to perform any particular job. (4) The students' time, they say, would be more profitably spent

(5)(6)(7)
Rebuttal:
evidence
countering
opponents'
evidence

in learning a trade or in acquiring other marketable skills. (5) These assertions are somewhat short-sighted, however. (6) Though it is true that a liberal arts education does not prepare students for a particular job, it is equally true that people with wide educational backgrounds find it easier to adapt to changing opportunities in the job market. (7) Furthermore, the knowledge that students gain through a liberal arts education often enables them to bring fresh insights and approaches to the workplaces that they ultimately enter.

In this section you have considered three kinds of supporting sentences: independent reasons, a chain of reasoning, and rebuttal. In a persuasive paragraph, you generally use only one kind of supporting sentence. In a persuasive composition, you may use two or three types, placing them in separate paragraphs, each with a strong topic sentence.

Exercise 5 Writing: Rebuttals The following sentences begin five arguments. Select three and copy them on your paper. Under each one write two or more objections that you could use as a rebuttal in an argument of your own. Save your paper for later use.

1. Watching movies is a more enjoyable pastime than reading books, because films maintain a faster pace, involve the audience to a greater extent, and require little effort on the part of the viewer.
2. Organized sports have no place in school. Taxpayers support schools so that young people can receive an education, not so that they can play games or prepare to become professional athletes.
3. Teen-agers should be charged more for their automobile insurance than adults. After all, teen-agers as a group are high-risk drivers.
4. It is no longer necessary for people to learn mathematics. In today's world all basic computations can be performed quite simply on convenient, inexpensive calculators.
5. Politics is not a promising field for a conscientious person to enter. There are too many possibilities for corruption.

8.4d Writing Concluding Sentences

To strengthen your argument, end it with a formal conclusion. You can write an effective conclusion for a paragraph in one or two sentences. In a composition you may need a whole paragraph to conclude your argument. There are three main ways to conclude an argument.

Strategies

1. *Conclude your argument by restating the position statement in different words.* Here is how you could restate the position statement of the model paragraph on liberal arts education (*page 380*).

   POSITION STATEMENT

   > For the average high school student, the most desirable program is study of the liberal arts.

   RESTATEMENT

   > Clearly, the varied nature of a liberal arts education makes it ideal for most students.

2. *Conclude your argument by recommending an action based on the position statement.*

   RECOMMENDATION

   > Students should avail themselves of the varied program of study that a liberal arts education offers.

3. *Conclude your argument by stating a personal judgment that is based on your position statement.*

   PERSONAL JUDGMENT

   > The complexity of today's world makes the wide educational experience of a liberal arts program more valuable than ever.

You must always base your conclusion on what you have said in your persuasive paragraph or composition.

Exercise 6 Writing: Concluding Sentences Write two concluding sentences for the model paragraph on Lincoln Field (*page 378*). Label each of your sentences *Restatement, Recommendation,* or *Personal judgment.*

Assignment 1 Writing Write a persuasive paragraph, using one position statement and three of the supporting sentences from Exercise 3 on page 378. If necessary, include a clarifying remark. Arrange your supporting sentences in order of increasing importance. Conclude your paragraph by expressing the position statement in different words.

Assignment 2 Writing Write a persuasive paragraph, using one set of the rebuttal sentences that you developed for Exercise 5 on page 381. Begin by stating and clarifying your own position (the position opposing the one taken in the argument presented in Exercise 5). Remember that you will need to present the opposing point of view and reasons for it in order to show why you hold a different position. Write a concluding sentence that recommends an action based on your position statement.

Assignment 3 Writing Write a persuasive composition in which you argue for or against (1) altering Social Security legislation or (2) offshore drilling for oil and gas. *Step 1:* Place your position statement and clarifying remarks in the first paragraph. *Step 2:* Group related supporting sentences and place each group in a separate paragraph. *Step 3:* Put your concluding sentences in a final paragraph.

Continuing Assignment Writing Using the material that you compiled in the Continuing Assignments on pages 362, 367, and 373, write a persuasive composition of at least four paragraphs. *Step 1:* State your position in the first paragraph. Use the remainder of the paragraph for clarifying remarks. *Step 2:* Organize your evidence into two or more paragraphs. Present different types of supporting sentences, such as independent reasons or rebuttal, in separate paragraphs. *Step 3:* Write a concluding paragraph in which you (1) express your position statement in different words, (2) recommend an action, or (3) state a personal judgment based on the position statement. Save your paper.

Assignment Checklist

Check your assignments for the following points:

✔ 1. Did you write clear position statements?
✔ 2. Did you write clarifying remarks that will help your readers to understand your argument?
✔ 3. Did you present your evidence in a well-organized series of supporting sentences?
✔ 4. Did you write conclusions that re-express the position statement, recommend an action, or offer a personal judgment?
✔ 5. In a persuasive composition of more than one paragraph, did you group the sentences in a logical, effective way?
✔ 6. Did you proofread your work for correct grammar, usage, spelling, and punctuation?

8.5   Revising Your Argument

Revision is especially important in persuasive writing because the success of an argument can depend on a single statement. As you revise your first draft, concentrate on moderation and logical development.

8.5a   Revising for Moderation

You often hear opinions expressed as sweeping statements that pertain to entire classes of people, objects, or actions. The following opinions represent sweeping statements.

Everyone should follow a daily exercise routine.
All scientists are dedicated to their work.

Usually it is a mistake to make a sweeping statement, because a single exception can disprove it. For instance, if your readers know just one person who has been forbidden by a doctor to exercise and just one scientist who lacks dedication, they will reject both of the preceding statements. A moderate statement, such as "Many scientists are dedicated to their work," is easier to support with evidence. In persuasive writing, both your position statement and your supporting sentences should be moderate. The following strategies will help you to turn sweeping statements into moderate statements.

Strategies

1. *Replace superlatives,* modifiers that end in *-est* or that are preceded by the words *most, best, least,* or *worst.* In their place, you can use the positive forms of the modifiers. For example, you can replace *most efficient* with *efficient.* Alternatively, you can insert a phrase such as *one of the* before the superlative. The following statements show how you can alter superlatives.

   SWEEPING STATEMENT
   > The electronic-parts industry is the most competitive business today.

   MODERATE STATEMENTS
   > The electronic-parts industry is a competitive business today.
   > The electronic-parts industry is one of the most competitive businesses today.

2. *Replace other absolute terms to limit sweeping statements.* Such words as *all, always, anytime, completely, constantly, every, everyone, invariably, never, no,* and *none* often appear in sweeping statements. To limit such statements, use instead such words and phrases as *many, most, often, usually, sometimes, frequently, in most cases, for the most part, some, rarely,* and *few.* The following example shows how sweeping statements can be limited.

   SWEEPING STATEMENT
   > Projects that are rushed *never* turn out well.

   MODERATE STATEMENT
   > Projects that are rushed *often* do not turn out well.

3. *Add modifiers to limit sweeping statements.* For example, the sweeping statement "Basketball players are good long-distance runners" implies "*All* basketball players are good long-distance runners." To limit a sweeping statement, add a suitable modifier, such as *some* or *many*. "Some basketball players are good long-distance runners" is a moderate statement.

When you revise a persuasive paragraph or a persuasive composition, you may have to use one or more of these techniques for making your statements more moderate.

Exercise 1   Revising: Moderation   On your paper, list the number of each sentence that makes a sweeping statement. Next to the number, rewrite the sentence to make it a moderate statement of opinion.

1. Choosing a career is always a difficult process.
2. Drilling for oil is the least imaginative solution to our long-range energy problems.
3. The test for my driver's license was difficult but fair.
4. The most famous romance of the ancient world was that of Julius Caesar and Cleopatra.
5. Swimming is the best exercise for toning your muscles.
6. The publicity committee has presented an effective plan for advertising the banquet.
7. Going to a museum is the only way to learn about art.
8. Emily Dickinson was one of America's greatest poets.
9. Babe Didrikson Zaharias was an extremely gifted athlete.
10. Every adult wants to have a full-time job.

8.5b   Revising for Logical Development

Effective Evidence

Review your argument to make sure that you have presented effective evidence in your supporting sentences. Each piece of evidence must clearly support your position statement. Eliminate any unrelated evidence that would only distract your reader's attention from your position. Also, be sure that your evidence is complete. Add any important pieces of evidence that are missing.

The following argument is not effective because it contains unrelated evidence and because it lacks important evidence.

INEFFECTIVE ARGUMENT

Position statement

Evidence

Unrelated information

> Most people in the United States like the work that they do. They have a favorable attitude toward the positions that they hold. Most people would not change their occupations even if they were given a chance to start over. In addition, most people would not move to other parts of the country if they could. Because only a few people in the United States find serious fault with their jobs, the work climate in this country is favorable.

The information about people's preference for the area in which they currently live distracts the reader's attention from the remarks about people's satisfaction with their work. Also, because the writer does not present strong evidence to support the claim that people are happy with their jobs, the argument seems weak. The following revised argument is more effective.

EFFECTIVE ARGUMENT

Position statement

Important evidence added

Unrelated evidence removed

> Most people in the United States like the work that they do. A recent poll shows that four out of every five people have a favorable attitude toward their jobs. Forty-nine percent of those polled indicated that they were "highly satisfied" with their employment; another 46 percent said that they were "satisfied" with what they do. Only 5 percent said that they were "not satisfied" with their jobs. The poll also revealed that most people would not change their occupations if they were given a chance to start over. Because relatively few people in the United States find serious fault with their jobs, the work climate in this country is favorable.

The revised argument is more effective because it contains no unrelated information and because the evidence in it is complete.

Exercise 2 Revising: Evidence Some sentences in each of the following lists give evidence for the position statement. Other sentences are unrelated to the position statement. On your paper, label each sentence *Evidence* or *Unrelated*.

1. *Position statement:* Most people do not spend enough of their leisure time reading.
   a. Reading is the favorite activity of some people.
   b. Reading ranks far behind watching television and participating in sports as a popular activity.
   c. Reading is first taught in kindergarten or in first grade.
   d. Three out of four people in the United States do not read even one book each year.
   e. Reading for pleasure helps a person to develop skills that are valuable for many types of work.

2. *Position statement:* More people should use seatbelts and shoulder harnesses when they ride in cars.
   a. Only 20 percent of the people in the United States use seatbelts.
   b. Seatbelts and shoulder harnesses fasten in a number of ways.
   c. Safety experts believe that twelve to fourteen thousand people could be saved each year if everyone used seatbelts and shoulder harnesses.
   d. New cars must be equipped with safety devices.
   e. Only 15 percent of the people in the United States use both seatbelts and shoulder harnesses.

Avoiding Fallacies

As the final step in revising your argument, you must eliminate **fallacies,** or unsound reasoning. A reader who detects a fallacy in your argument probably will not be persuaded to accept your position. Among the fallacies that you should avoid are the following six types.

Begging the Question. If you take for granted the point that you should be proving, you beg the question. That is, you fail to provide evidence to support your position and, instead, treat your position as evidence. In the following passage, the writer begs the question.

BEGGING THE QUESTION

> Laurie Monson should receive this year's Academy Award for best documentary. Without a doubt, her film on Mt. Everest was the best documentary this year.

Examination of the argument reveals that the writer has not offered any evidence to support the position but has simply restated the position. To argue effectively, the writer would need to establish, with evidence, the specific elements of the documentary that make it the best one of the year.

False Assumption.   An argument is also faulty if you make a false assumption and then make a prediction or draw a conclusion based on that assumption. For example, you could reason, "There is a large amount of extra money in the city budget; therefore, the city can afford to pay for an arts center." If there really is a large amount of extra money in the city budget, then the reasoning is sound. If the budget does not contain the extra money, however, the argument contains a false assumption, an assumption that is not in accord with the facts.

False Association Between a Cause and an Effect.   In many arguments you examine the cause of an effect or the effect of a cause. In doing so, you must demonstrate that a cause-and-effect relationship actually exists. You make a false association between a cause and an effect if you conclude that because one event occurs after another event, the first event must be the cause of the second event. In the following passage, the writer does not demonstrate a cause-and-effect relationship.

FALSE ASSOCIATION

> A work crew dug a foundation for a new building next to the store. Then a crack appeared in the south wall of the store. The crack must have been caused by the construction work on the foundation.

The writer ignores the possibility that other events or situations may have caused the crack in the wall. For example, the wall may have cracked because it was old or made of poor-quality plaster or because the ground beneath it settled.

False Choice.   In an argument you often present solutions to a problem. Presenting two solutions and stating that either one or the other must be accepted is sound if there are only two solutions to the problem. You present a false choice, however, if you indicate that there are only two solutions to a problem that really has more than two solutions. In the following passage, the writer presents only two solutions although there are more.

FALSE CHOICE

> Something must be done to conserve gasoline. Either we must raise the gasoline tax to discourage drivers from buying gasoline, or we must use coupons to ration gas.

The writer ignores other possibilities, such as drivers' voluntary conservation of gas or regulations permitting drivers to buy gas only during limited hours.

False Analogy.   Arguing by analogy is attempting to make a point about something by comparing it to a similar item. You make a false analogy if you compare two items in an area in which they are not truly similar. The writer of the following passage makes a false comparison.

FALSE ANALOGY

> The food that we eat, like the air that we breathe, is vital to our survival. No one would think of charging for the air that we breathe. The same ought to be true of food.

The analogy is false because although air and food are both necessary for human existence, they are different in an important way. No one works and spends money to produce the air that we breathe, but farmers must do both while producing food. The dissimilar points of comparison make the argument faulty.

Argument from Character.   In an argument you may decide to evaluate the opinion of an expert on your topic. Such an opinion should be judged by its content, not by the character or experience of the expert. In the following passage, the writer makes a statement about the motivation of an expert.

ARGUMENT FROM CHARACTER

> Senator Farnsworth claims that the job-training program will be successful. His opinion cannot be trusted because he is simply seeking the youth vote in the next election.

Senator Farnsworth may or may not be seeking the youth vote. Whether he is or not has nothing to do with the validity of his statement about the job-training program. The only way to determine the value of his position is to examine the position itself.

Exercise 3 Prewriting: Fallacies On your paper, evaluate each group of sentences by writing *Fallacy* or *No fallacy*. Then identify each fallacy as *Begging the question, False assumption, False association, False choice, False analogy,* or *Argument from character*.

1. It never snows in Minnesota. Therefore, towns in Minnesota need not include money for snow removal in their yearly budgets.
2. Riding on a Ferris wheel and parachuting produce similar sensations. You need no special training to ride a Ferris wheel; therefore, you need no special training to go parachuting.
3. Next month we voters will be asked to approve the mayor's parking plan. Because the plan has worked well in four nearby communities of the same size, we should try it in our community.
4. The newspaper advertising campaign for Figel's department store was a success. Business increased after the advertisements were run, and 45 percent of the customers said that they were shopping at Figel's because of the advertisements.
5. I have not received the package that Paula mailed to me two weeks ago. Either she addressed the package incorrectly, or the package has been lost in the mail.
6. Our building superintendent claims that the carpet in the halls does not need to be replaced. His opinion cannot be trusted because the rugs in his apartment are in terrible condition.
7. You are not truly educated unless you have learned a second language. Being able to speak a second language is a sure sign that you are well educated.
8. You will have a particularly enjoyable visit in a foreign country if you know the language. You will be able to ask for exactly what you need, and you will be able to travel to areas where people do not speak your language.

9. The new Congress deserves credit for the recent improvement in the country's economy. Before the new senators and representatives took office, both inflation and unemployment were high. Now both are down to their lowest levels in years.

10. When I arrived at the station on time, the train was not there. Either it had left early, or it was late in arriving.

Exercise 4   Revising: Fallacies   On your paper, rewrite the following groups of sentences in order to eliminate the fallacies in them. You may have to add evidence or facts so that each group of sentences presents effective evidence.

1. A controversial solution to the problem of unemployment has been suggested by Miles Everett, a noted economist and author. However, his solution cannot be taken seriously because he is just trying to increase sales of his most recent book.

2. Last year scientists experimented with cloud seeding in our region. This spring we were plagued by hail and rainstorms. It is obvious that the cloud seeding caused our violent weather this year.

3. All young children should have easy access to play areas. Either more public land must be turned into playgrounds, or communities should provide transportation to existing playgrounds.

4. Marathon runners, much like tennis players, must practice and train. Because both athletic pursuits require some discipline and skill, the same training and practice regimens should be followed for them.

5. Wood sculptors should use ebony in order to create stunning works of art. Ebony is a beautiful type of wood to use in sculpture.

Assignment   Revising   Rewrite the following paragraph. Revise it by making sweeping statements more moderate, by removing unrelated evidence, and by correcting unsound reasoning.

Computer science is the most valuable field of study that anyone can explore in school or college. First, if you learn about computers, you will definitely get a job. Computers are being used in increasingly more companies, and employers need people to build, program, and operate them. Gene Gifford, a computer analyst, claims that the number of computer-related jobs will more than double in the next ten years. He should know because he accurately predicted who would win this year's World Series. Also, computers will become more common in people's homes because more people will have computers in their homes. You will need to know how to operate a computer in order to live in a modern home. You also may have to adjust to such inventions as solar heating. Either you will learn about computers or you will not be able to cope with the future.

Continuing Assignment Revising Revise the persuasive composition that you wrote for the Continuing Assignment on page 383. Concentrate on moderation, effectiveness, and sound reasoning.

Assignment Checklist

Check your assignments for the following points:

✔ 1. Did you revise sweeping statements to make them moderate?
✔ 2. Did you eliminate points that do not relate to your position statement?
✔ 3. Did you add any important pieces of evidence that were missing from your argument?
✔ 4. Did you eliminate fallacies from your argument?
✔ 5. Did you proofread your argument for correct grammar, usage, spelling, and punctuation?

Writer's Workshop

Help Wanted: A Persuasive Notice for a Bulletin Board

Situation: As committee head of Students for a Youth Center, you have asked about the possibility of using the basement of City Hall for a youth center. In a letter, shown on the facing page, city administrators have agreed to allow students to use the basement, on the condition that the students clear everything out of the basement and clean it thoroughly. The secretary of your committee has typed some notes about reasons for having the center and also about details of the clean-up work. You want to write a notice for the school bulletin board that will persuade students to volunteer their time. As you write the notice, you will keep in mind the following information.

Writer: you as the project coordinator

Audience: fellow students

Topic: the work needed for the proposed youth center

Purpose: to persuade students to help with the project

Directions: To plan and write your notice, follow these steps.

   Step 1. Read the letter and the notes on the following pages.

   Step 2. On a sheet of paper, organize relevant information from the letter and from the sheet of notes. Arrange the information in two categories: (1) what is offered and (2) what is needed.

   Step 3. Consider your audience, fellow students who may not want to give up their Saturday to work. Make a list of reasons that explain why it would be in their interest to participate in this project.

(Continue on page 396.)

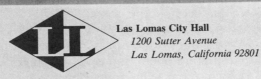

Las Lomas City Hall
1200 Sutter Avenue
Las Lomas, California 92801

March 12, 19___

To Students for a Youth Center:

The City Council has considered your request for a youth center to be housed in the basement of City Hall. Although we are not certain how many young people in the neighborhood will use the center, we are willing to donate the space rather than see it go unused.

At present, however, the basement is filled with the accumulated rubble of fifty years and needs to be cleared out and cleaned thoroughly. Cosmo Carting Company has agreed to dispose of the material once it has been removed from the building. Neither they nor we have the time or staff to clear out the basement. The work will have to be done by the students themselves on a Saturday in order not to interfere with the regular operation of city departments. When your group is ready to begin the work, we suggest that you call Ms. Jane Hardy at City Hall, who will give you keys and show you around the basement.

Sincerely,

Thomas Kane

Thomas Kane
City Council Secretary

Notes of the Students for a Youth Center Committee:

—Room is jammed with discarded furniture and filing cabinets that are no longer usable.

—Room is also full of papers, pamphlets, and other trash.

—Room must be cleared, swept.

—Floors and walls must be washed.

—Once removed from basement, trash must be placed neatly on curb.

—The clearing and cleaning work can be done in one day, this Saturday, March 30.

—For one day's work, we can begin a permanent center that young people will use for many years.

—Basement has its own entrance.

(continued on the next page)

Step 4. Write a position statement.

Step 5. Write the introductory paragraph of your three-paragraph notice. Begin with a sentence or a question that will engage your readers' attention. Use *you* and *we* to set the tone; for example, "We have been offered . . ." or "Wouldn't you like . . . ?" Explain the situation briefly and include your position statement.

Step 6. In the second paragraph, stress the long-term benefits (you might quote the opinion of an expert) and the small amount of work required. Try to meet possible objections (Example: students have home responsibilities and jobs).

Step 7. In the final paragraph, make a strong restatement of your position and conclude with a recommendation for action.

Step 8. Reread your draft and revise it. To do so, ask yourself these questions: Did I state my position clearly? Did I present my reasons logically and convincingly? Did I write a strong conclusion?

Step 9. Make a final copy of the notice.

—Brooms, rags, buckets, mops, cleaning supplies will be provided by City Hall maintenance crew.

—Get key from Ms. Hardy.

—Remind volunteers to bring lunch.

—Bring radio? People like to work to music.

—Organize volunteers into crews for light and heavy work.

—At least fifteen students are needed.

—Work will take the whole day.

—Interior designer Roberta Thompson says, "It's a large, open space that can accommodate a number of activities at the same time."

—Student Council President Leslie Higgins says, "We could hold meetings, dances, craft fairs, and dramatic productions. The space is perfect."

                              Pat Halsey, secretary

Unit Assignments

Assignment 1 Write a persuasive paragraph on the effectiveness of a consumer organization, a club, or a service organization that you know about. Give examples to support your position, and present your strongest evidence last. Revise your argument to eliminate errors in reasoning.

Assignment 2 Write a persuasive paragraph in which you present the benefits of learning a certain skill or participating in a certain sport. Write for an audience of your friends. Use more than one type of evidence to support your position.

Assignment 3 Select an issue relating to the type of work that you would like to do or the type of work that someone in your family does. Write a persuasive paragraph that expresses your position on that issue. Direct your argument to people who are unfamiliar with the type of work that you are discussing.

Assignment 4 Write a persuasive composition about a sport with which you are familiar. In your position statement, make a prediction about the future of the sport or the future of a particular team or player. Provide facts to support your opinion and, if possible, include the opinion of an expert on the sport.

Assignment 5 In the editorial section of a newspaper, find a letter to the editor that expresses an opinion with which you disagree. Write a persuasive composition directed to the writer of the letter. Explain not only why you hold your position but also what you think is wrong with the author's argument.

Assignment 6 Take a position on the issue of returnable bottles and cans. Write a persuasive paragraph or composition about your topic. Follow your position statement with clarifying remarks. After presenting your evidence, conclude by restating your position or by recommending some particular action.

Revising Your Assignments

For help in revising a persuasive paragraph or composition, consult the Checklist for Revision on the last page of this book.

Unit Tests

Test 1

A. Number your paper from 1 to 5. Next to each number, write *True* if the sentence is true or *False* is it is false.

1. Facts make suitable topics for persuasive writing because they are not subject to disagreement.
2. An opinion suitable as a topic for persuasive writing may be based on a personal preference.
3. Supporting sentences present evidence, or reasons, for your position.
4. You must explain the source of any unusual facts in your argument.
5. You may include one or two pieces of unrelated evidence in your argument if you make them brief.

B. Number your paper from 6 to 10. Next to each number, write the letter of the term that correctly completes the sentence. You will use all but one of the terms.

     a. opinion   d. fallacy

     b. reasoning   e. position statement

     c. rebuttal   f. clarifying remarks

6. A(n) __?__ is the statement of a view that is not shared by everyone.
7. A(n) __?__ presents the opinion that you would like your audience to accept.
8. __?__ is the process of drawing conclusions from statements that you know or believe to be true.
9. A(n) __?__ is the evidence that you use to refute opposing evidence.
10. A(n) __?__ is a piece of unsound reasoning.

C. Number your paper from 11 to 15. Next to each number, write the letter of the item that correctly answers the question.

11. Which of the following opinions is suitable for persuasive writing?
    a. Walking along the lakefront is more enjoyable than shopping.
    b. I just know that a corporation or a developer will buy the land along the lakefront.
    c. We should limit the number of businesses that can be built along the lakefront.
    d. Should we protect the lakefront?

12. Which of the following statements contains both an opinion and a fact?
    a. Three candidates have entered this year's mayoral race.
    b. Because the company was established one hundred years ago, it is the best in its field.
    c. Electric cars cause less pollution than cars with gasoline engines do.
    d. Broiling food is more healthful than baking it.

13. Which of the following would be the best person to provide an expert opinion about how safe an appliance is?
    a. Someone who uses the appliance often
    b. Someone who sells the appliance
    c. Someone who designed another appliance
    d. Someone who tests appliances

14. Which of the following is *not* a way to clarify a position statement?
    a. Recommend an action
    b. Define or explain a key term
    c. Provide background information
    d. Give an example or a specific application

15. Which of the following does *not* contain a fallacy?
    a. Because no building in New York City is more than two stories high, the city's fire department does not need trucks with ladders that can reach higher floors.
    b. Because I have found several errors in the first part of the mayor's budget, I do not trust the rest of the figures.
    c. Either you take a long trip during a vacation or you stay home and do nothing.
    d. I do not support Dana Helm's recommendation to the school board because she has never been nice to me.

Test 2

Choose one of the Unit Assignments. Write the assignment as directed and hand it in to your teacher.

Unit 9

Writing an Essay

Unit Preview

When you write an **essay,** you present an idea, an observation, an opinion, or an event to your audience. Your essay may be expository, descriptive, narrative, or persuasive. If necessary, you may read about your topic before you plan and write your essay, but you should present your own ideas in the essay.

The topics of essays vary widely, but the form does not. Every essay has an introductory paragraph that presents the topic, body paragraphs that develop the topic, and a concluding paragraph that summarizes or presents a final idea about the topic. The tone of an essay can range from serious to light, and the style of an essay can range from formal to informal.

The following paragraph is the introductory paragraph of an essay.

> The baseball stories that one sees on the evening news today are grim reminders of the sorry state that major league baseball is in. The headlines in today's sports pages shout out more depressing news about the faltering game—multi-millionaire players threatening to strike for more money, ticket prices soaring in order to pay the huge payroll of these prima donnas of the summer. It is disheartening to think back to a time when baseball was fun and innocent, a time when players were heroes who played for the love of the game, not for the sky-rocketing profits that can be made in baseball today.

> *Thomas Scott Busbee, Druid Hills High School*
> *Decatur, Georgia*

400

For Analysis On your paper, answer the following questions about the preceding paragraph.

1. What is the topic of the essay?
2. What is the writer's purpose?
3. What information would you expect the writer to present in the following paragraphs?
4. Is the tone of the paragraph serious or light?

In analyzing the topic, the purpose, and the tone of one essay, you have prepared yourself for selecting a topic, a purpose, and a tone for the essay that you will prepare as you read this unit. As you work on your essay, you will follow the three steps of the writing process: prewriting, writing, and revising.

9.1   Selecting and Limiting a Topic

Selecting a Topic

Choose the topic for your essay carefully; select one that interests you. You are likely to write a clear and interesting essay if you enjoy your topic. Your ideas for essay topics will probably come from two sources: your own experiences and your observations of the world around you. Although your essay may include information that you have found in your reading, the main ideas in your essay should be your own. A composition based mostly on information found by reading is a research paper, which is considered in Unit 11.

If you cannot think of a topic easily, ask yourself the following questions. The answers to these questions can help you to choose a writing topic.

1. What do I know most about?
   Possible answer: Computers
2. What do I care about that might interest a reader?
   Possible answer: Working on the school newspaper

3. What have I seen or experienced that I would like to present to a reader?
   Possible answer: Sailing on the ocean

4. Which of my experiences has given me an idea of the kind of future that I would like to have?
   Possible answer: My summer job as a camp counselor

5. Who have been the most important people in my life?
   Possible answer: My music teacher

6. What issues and situations do I feel strongly about?
   Possible answer: The energy shortage

7. What is important in life?
   Possible answer: Good nutrition

Limiting a Topic

When you have chosen a topic, decide whether you can develop it fully in two to six pages. If you cannot, your topic is too general. You should limit a general topic to make it more specific.

The following examples show how four of the general topics that were found by answering the preceding questions can be limited.

> *General topic:* Computers
>
> *Limited topic:* The first time that I operated a computer by myself
>
> *General topic:* Working on the school newspaper
>
> *Limited topic:* How working on a school newspaper taught me to organize my time
>
> *General topic:* Sailing on the ocean
>
> *Limited topic:* The sights, sounds, and smells of the ocean
>
> *General topic:* Good nutrition
>
> *Limited topic:* People in the United States should eat more vegetables and grains

Identifying a Writing Purpose

You can develop your topic by exposition, description, narration, or persuasion. That is, your purpose may be to explain; to present sensory details about a person, a place, or an object; to tell about an experience; or to persuade someone that your opinion on an issue is correct. You may combine more than one purpose in an essay. For example, you may include description of people and places in a narrative essay. Most successful essays, however, contain a principal, or main, writing purpose.

When you decide on a limited topic, you usually determine the purpose for writing at the same time. Study the following examples of limited topics and principal writing purposes that may be associated with them.

> *Limited topic:* The first time that I operated a computer by myself
> *Purpose:* To narrate

> *Limited topic:* What I learned about organizing my time while working on a school newspaper
> *Purpose:* To explain

> *Limited topic:* The sights, sounds, and smells of the ocean
> *Purpose:* To describe

> *Limited topic:* People in the United States should eat more vegetables and grains.
> *Purpose:* To persuade

A writing purpose helps to focus an essay. As you develop your essay, keep in mind that every sentence must help to carry out your principal writing purpose.

Exercise 1 Prewriting: Essay Topics Read the following list of topics. For each topic write *Suitable* if it is suitable for an essay or *Unsuitable* if it is not.

1. What I would like to be doing fifteen years from now
2. The history of choral music
3. The techniques that geologists use to locate new water supplies
4. What I learned on a one-week bicycle trip
5. The first time that I gave a speech
6. The first environmental legislation in the United States
7. The early development of modern dance

8. How to make money by doing typing
9. The effects of weightlessness on humans
10. The beauty of the Catskill Mountains

Exercise 2   Prewriting: Limiting Topics   Read the following list of general topics. On your paper, write a limited topic and a principal writing purpose for each general topic.

> **SAMPLE**   Rivers
>
> **ANSWER**   Limited topic: How I learned to canoe through rapids in a river
>
> Purpose: To narrate

1. Films
2. Architecture
3. How the world could be improved
4. Travel
5. Saving money

6. Machines
7. Wildlife
8. Loyalty
9. Businesses
10. Art

Assignment   Prewriting   List four essay topics that interest you. Then limit each topic so that it could be developed fully in two to six pages. Write the four limited topics and a principal writing purpose for each limited topic.

Continuing   Assignment   Prewriting   List five topics that you would enjoy writing about in an essay of two to six pages. Limit the topics as needed and list the limited topics on your paper. List a principal writing purpose for each limited topic. Then put a check mark beside the topic that interests you most. Save your paper.

Assignment Checklist

Check your assignments for the following points:

   ✔ 1. Did you choose essay topics to which you can bring your own experience?
   ✔ 2. Did you limit your topics so that they can be developed fully in two to six pages?
   ✔ 3. Did you list a principal writing purpose for each topic?

9.2 Determining Your Audience, Tone, and Style

You must determine the audience for which you are writing as well as the purpose of your writing. Then you can adopt a tone and a style that are appropriate for your audience and purpose.

9.2a   Identifying the Audience

In most essays you should address a general audience of anyone who might be interested in your topic. At times, however, you may write for a special audience, such as an employer or the admissions committee of a college. As you write, address the special interests of that audience. For example, if you are writing an essay for your local consumer interest group, the members probably will be interested in details about businesses in your community rather than facts about businesses in some distant town.

The following introductory paragraph of an essay illustrates how a writer can choose details and language to appeal to a particular audience.

Model

>   I have long thought that there is no atmosphere quite like that of a concert hall before a performance. Beyond the apron of the stage, a hum comes from the stream of people that floods the doors outside the auditorium and trickles in past unobtrusive blue-uniformed ushers. This persistent sound, however, is barely audible to those on stage. Here, there is murmuring, laughter. I smile a little when I hear an edge of nervousness in the voice of one of the music students as he anticipates his first performance. My smile is sympathetic: I have played in this orchestra for almost two years now, and yet my heart still pounds with nervousness when I join the crowd on stage.

>   *Becky MacDougall, Burris Laboratory High School*
>   *Muncie, Indiana*

The writer addresses an audience of people who have never waited on stage for a performance to begin. She tells her audience how the concert hall seems to the people on stage and how the performers feel.

Exercise 1   Prewriting: Audience   The following paragraph begins an essay. On your paper, write one or two sentences to describe the audience that the writer of the following paragraph is addressing.

> Down in the southern hemisphere, off the coast of Ecuador, lies a place that has been called a biologist's paradise. Its name is Galápagos, a group of small islands yet untouched by people's destructive forces and teeming with unique animal life. My father, a biology teacher, for years had the dream of visiting the Galápagos. On August 2 last year, this dream became a reality.
>
> *Andrea Easter, Newark High School*
> *Newark, Ohio*

9.2b   Selecting the Tone

Tone is the attitude that a writer conveys about a topic and an audience. Audience, purpose, and tone must work together. In the paragraph about the concert hall (*page 405*), the purpose is to describe performers' feelings when they are on stage before a performance, and the tone is suitably nostalgic and affectionate.

You may choose from a wide variety of tones: serious, ironic, affectionate, critical, nostalgic, humorous, persuasive, and many more. Whatever tone you choose must be appropriate for your subject.

Your tone is affected by the point of view (*pages 342–343*) that you choose. You create a personal tone, a close relationship with the reader, by using a first-person point of view. In contrast, you create a more distant tone by using a third-person point of view. The distant tone emphasizes the subject rather than your personality. No matter which tone you select, use one tone consistently throughout your essay to avoid confusing your audience.

Exercise 2 Prewriting: Tone Each of the following paragraphs is from an essay. For each paragraph, write one or two sentences that describe the tone and the point of view.

PARAGRAPH 1

The town had a peculiar, enchanting atmosphere. Depending on which street one was on, it would seem now like a typical timeless Spanish village, now like an international artists' colony. Mingling among the veiled, black-garbed old Spanish widows were English writers and French artists and a number of drifters of dubious nationality. Walking down the cobblestoned alleys between rows of tall whitewashed houses, one could see a dark old Spanish store selling nothing but bread and milk located directly across from a small French café. These contrasts made the town fascinating.

Dan Staley, Woodrow Wilson High School
Long Beach, California

PARAGRAPH 2

At one time, I thought that my cow and I had an understanding: I would be nice to her, and she would be nice to me. Maybe I should have written a contract with her. Her name was Rose (Indian Creek Fargo Rose, if one bothered to read her registration papers). Last fall I was preparing her for the cattle show at the state fair when she decided to breach our agreement.

Todd Nichols, Saluda High School
Saluda, South Carolina

PARAGRAPH 3

I find jigsaw puzzles challenging. Although a large number of my acquaintances look upon this pastime as a form of boredom, I fully enjoy tinkering with the hundreds of small pieces, turning them this way and that in an attempt to make a box full of precut chaos into a lovely Alpine scene. Perhaps the most satisfying part of constructing jigsaw puzzles is that single instant of enlightenment when the right piece fits in the right place and you know just where the rest of those temperamental pieces should go. Short, squatty pieces splotched with yellow magically click together to form an elegant patch of jonquils; uncooperative bearers of blue and scarlet bands interlock to form a July twilight.

Christine Andresen, Central High School
St. Joseph, Missouri

9.2c   Considering the Style

Style in writing is the unique way in which a person expresses his or her ideas in words. Your style is a result of choices made—consciously or unconsciously—as you write. You choose particular words and arrange them in a particular order. Since style is the cumulative result of many choices, it is something that you can control by making the choices purposefully.

Diction

Diction, the choice of words to express your thoughts, is one aspect of style. In choosing any word, consider its **connotations**, the ideas associated with the word, as well as its **denotations**, or its literal meanings. Consider the different connotations of *shy* and *aloof,* for example. Although both are used to describe a person who is reserved, *shy* suggests timidity and bashfulness, and *aloof* suggests snobbery and condescension. Choose your words carefully because a word with unsuitable connotations can ruin the effectiveness of a sentence or a paragraph.

The level of your diction—its degree of formality—should be consistent throughout an essay. You may choose among three levels of diction.

Casual.   This level of diction contains contractions, words labeled by a dictionary as informal or colloquial (such as *beat* meaning "tired"), and slang. Because casual diction resembles informal speech, it is appropriate only for writing letters to friends or for writing dialogue in a narrative.

Informal.   Most writing is informal. This level of diction contains both simple and complex words. It includes only a few contractions, little slang, and only a few words labeled by a dictionary as informal or colloquial. As a rule, you should use such words in informal writing only when no other words convey the meaning as well.

Formal.   This level of diction contains many words that are more common in writing than in speech. The vocabulary is large. Formal diction includes no words that are labeled by a dictionary as informal or colloquial, no slang, and only a few contractions. You should use formal diction for research papers, literary essays and other serious essays, some business reports, and some persuasive writing.

When you use formal diction, do not allow your language to become unnecessarily or artificially formal. Stilted language is always inappropriate. Choose the most precise word, not the biggest word, to express an idea. Direct, unaffected language is appropriate even in the most formal situations. Overwritten, stilted language not only seems awkward and even comical but also is difficult for the reader to understand.

In your school writing assignments, you should aim for a level of diction in the range between formal and informal. By including or omitting contractions and colloquial phrases, you can adjust the formality to suit a particular writing situation.

Sentence Length and Complexity

The length and complexity of your sentence structure, the other part of your writing style, should vary according to the formality of your writing. Generally, informal writing calls for short and medium-length sentences that may be simple, compound, or complex (*pages 67–69*). In the following example, the simplicity of the sentences suits the simple personal experience that is described.

Model

> The sun shines warmly on my back. I bend over and place yet another seed in the rich, brown soil. Wiggling my toes in the moist and cool earth reminds me of many other times that I have done this. I feel secure, knowing that this is one thing that doesn't change. No matter how many times I do this, I feel a sense of purpose.

> *Judy Gunn, Dublin High School*
> *Dublin, Georgia*

In contrast, a more formal style is created by longer sentences that are mainly compound or complex. The following paragraph is written in a formal style.

Model

> It is important for parents to monitor the commercials as well as the programs that their children watch. The underlying messages that are communicated in the commercials should be analyzed and discussed with even young children who watch television. Because these messages imply certain things about how we judge ourselves and others, it is essential that children be made aware of them.

The length and complexity of the sentences in the preceding paragraph contribute to its formal style. Although the language is formal, it is not stilted or overwritten. You will find that the shifts from brief to lengthy sentences and from simple to intricate ones will occur almost naturally when you begin to write about a topic that you treat formally.

Exercise 3   Prewriting: Style   On your paper, write *Casual, Informal,* or *Formal* to identify the style of each of the following passages. Then for each paragraph write a sentence to explain why you chose the answer.

PARAGRAPH 1

> Let Canada become not a melting pot, but a massive synergism. Canadians must strive to attain an ideal balance between an undesirable homogenization and an equally unwanted separation of the ethnic groups in Canada. The differing cultures must be respected, but no culture must dominate or overshadow another. In a multicultural society, the contrasting lifestyles should be preserved rather than changed to conform to a single monotonous pattern of behavior. Human beings are not and cannot be made into a uniform species.

> *(Adapted)*
> *Suzanne Dowse, Park View Education Centre*
> *Bridgewater, Nova Scotia*

PARAGRAPH 2

> In rhythm, rhyme, and general structure, poetry and songs share characteristics. However, a songwriter works with what may be called an advantage over the poet—music. You may doubt my use of the word *advantage* because song melodies aren't always the

easiest thing to write. An experienced songwriter, however, knows
how to combine words and music to create a mood within the
listener.

Darla Lundy, North High School
Torrance, California

Exercise 4   Writing: Tone   Write three sentences about politics
or business. Make one sentence serious, one humorous, and one
sarcastic. Then rewrite each of the sentences using another tone. You
may have to make changes in point of view to emphasize the changes
in tone.

Exercise 5   Revising: Style   Rewrite the following casual passage so that it is informal. You will have to make changes in the level
of diction, in the sentence length, and in the sentence structure.

> I think that all cars should be kicked off Main Street. That
> way, shoppers could hang out in the street. Cars just hassle shoppers
> and smell up the air anyway. It wouldn't be a big deal for drivers to
> park on another street and walk a couple of blocks to a store. Then
> downtown wouldn't be a bad place for everyone. And people would
> think that it was neat to buy stuff there. That would really make the
> store owners happy. The city could even fork over money to make a
> park in the middle of the street.

Assignment 1   Prewriting/Writing   Select one of the following topics and its accompanying audiences. Write two separate
paragraphs on the topic, one for the first audience and one for the
second audience. Both paragraphs should include almost the same
information, but they should differ in the way in which the information is presented to each audience.

1. Why you liked or disliked an event that you attended recently
   Audience A: others who attended the event
   Audience B: people who did not attend the event

2. A new law or rule
   Audience A: those who are affected by the law or rule
   Audience B: those who are not affected by the law or rule

3. A perfect means of entertaining out-of-town guests
   Audience A: people interested in outdoor activities
   Audience B: people interested in indoor activities

Assignment 2   Prewriting/Writing   Write two separate paragraphs on one of the following topics. One paragraph should have a serious tone, and the other should have a light tone.

1. Preparing a nutritious breakfast
2. Returning defective merchandise to a store
3. Curing a cold
4. Making the most of a vacation

Assignment 3   Prewriting/Writing   Using an informal style, write a paragraph on one of the following topics. Then rewrite the paragraph using a formal style. For each paragraph, use appropriate diction, sentence length, and sentence structure.

1. An adventure that you had with a friend
2. Competition for a role, a position, or an office
3. A simple change that would improve your school
4. The qualities that a leader should possess

Continuing Assignment   Prewriting   Take out the paper on which you listed your essay topic and its writing purpose for the Continuing Assignment on page 404. Add the following information to your paper.

1. The audience to which the essay is directed
2. The tone that is appropriate for that audience, for your topic, and for your purpose
3. The point of view that you plan to use in the essay
4. The level of diction that you plan to use in the essay

Assignment Checklist

Check your assignments for the following points:

   ✔ 1. Did you address your audience?

2. Did you choose a tone and a point of view that are appropriate for the topic, purpose, and audience?
3. Did you consider the style: the level of diction and the length and structure of your sentences?
4. Did you proofread your writing for correct grammar, usage, spelling, and punctuation?

9.3 Planning Your Essay

Before you begin to write, you must plan your essay carefully. You must analyze your topic to determine the clearest and most interesting way to present it to your reader.

9.3a Listing and Organizing the Ideas

First, list ideas that are related to your topic. You may use either phrases or complete sentences to express your ideas. Then review your list to choose which ideas you will include in your essay. Eliminate any ideas that are not directly related to your topic.

Next, organize the ideas on your list. Begin by dividing them into main ideas and supporting details, which are ideas that further explain a main idea. Then arrange the groups of main ideas and their supporting details in a logical order. Your topic and purpose will help you to choose an order. You may use one or more of the following organizations, just as you do when you organize the details of a single paragraph.

Chronological Order. When you use chronological order, you present details or events in the order in which they occurred. This is the usual organization of a narrative essay.

Spatial Order. When you use spatial order, you present details or objects in the order in which you see them—top to bottom, side to side, or front to back. This order is often used in a descriptive essay.

Order of Importance. When you use order of importance, you usually list the least important ideas first and progress to the most important ideas. Sometimes, however, you can present the most

413

important idea first for special emphasis. This order works well for listing the points of an expository or persuasive essay.

Other Methods of Organization.   You also may write an essay in which you compare and contrast aspects of a topic or in which you explain causes or effects.

1. *Comparison and Contrast.* When you use comparison and contrast, you make clear the similarities and differences between two subjects. For example, you might compare and contrast the way that you think about an issue and the way that the governor thinks about the same issue. You might discuss the similarities in one paragraph and the differences in another paragraph, or you might discuss one point at a time, noting how the items are similar and different in regard to each point. With either method, you could further arrange the similarities and differences in the order of their importance.

2. *Causes or Effects.* When you use a cause-or-effect pattern of development, you explain the causes or the effects of an event or a situation. For example, you could discuss the causes of a low voter-turnout for a particular election. You could use chronological order by listing the effects in the order in which they occurred, or you could use order of importance by listing the least important effect first and then progressing to the most important effect.

Exercise 1   Prewriting: Choosing Details   Read the following topic and list of details. On your paper, write the numbers of the details that are relevant to the topic. Then arrange the relevant details in chronological order.

Topic: Starting my own house-painting business

Details:

1. By the end of July, many people had called to ask if I could do painting jobs for them.
2. Our neighbor needed her basement painted, and I offered to do it.

3. After I finished the basement, word spread throughout the neighborhood about the good job that I had done.
4. House painting is an art, not just a job.
5. In the middle of June, I was looking for a summer job.
6. Paint must be applied to a house when the weather is dry and moderately warm.
7. When I could not find a job by the beginning of July, my father suggested thinking of services that the neighbors might use.
8. By mid-August I was working every day, ten hours a day.

9.3b   Writing a Thesis Statement

Once you have organized your main ideas and supporting details, you need to write a **thesis statement,** the statement in the first paragraph that presents the topic and purpose of your essay. Because the thesis statement tells your reader what you will discuss in the essay, it must be precise. The following example shows how to improve a vague thesis statement by making it precise.

VAGUE THESIS STATEMENT
    Playing in a band taught me a lot.

PRECISE THESIS STATEMENT
    Playing in a band taught me the importance of cooperation.

In addition to helping your reader by making the subject and direction of your essay clear from the beginning, a thesis statement also helps you to focus the essay, making it easier to plan and write.

When you plan an essay, you may formulate a preliminary thesis statement early in the prewriting process. You can use it as a guide when you list your ideas. Then, when you are preparing your outline or writing your introductory paragraph, you can write the final version of the thesis statement.

Exercise 2   Prewriting: Thesis Statements   Rate each of the following thesis statements by writing *Precise* or *Vague* on your paper. If a thesis statement is vague, revise it to be more precise.

SAMPLE	Going camping can be rough.
ANSWER	Vague—Although I planned carefully, my first camping trip was a disaster.

1. Visiting my grandparents last summer gave me an opportunity to learn about my family history.
2. My town contains some unusual and interesting places.
3. Part-time jobs can be interesting.
4. All citizens should spend five hours each month doing volunteer work for the community.
5. Brothers and sisters can teach one another many important things.

9.3c   Outlining the Essay

The last step in planning your essay is preparing an outline to use as a guide when you write the essay. An outline shows the sequence of ideas in your essay and their importance.

The most common type of outline is a **topic outline.** In a topic outline the main ideas become main headings, and the supporting details become subheadings. You do not write either type of heading in complete sentences. Place Roman numerals at the beginning of main headings and capital letters at the beginning of subheadings. Use the Roman numeral *I* for the introduction and the last Roman numeral for the conclusion. Also, use at least two subheadings for each main heading that you wish to explain further. See Section 11.4 in Unit 11 for a sample topic outline and for more information about outlining.

A **sentence outline** is similar to a topic outline except that the headings are written in complete sentences. Often a **rough outline,** a simple list of main points, is sufficient for a short essay, particularly a narrative or descriptive essay. In all types of outlines, you usually write the thesis statement at the top of the page.

Exercise 3   Prewriting: Outlining   Prepare a topic outline by arranging the following subheadings under the main headings that have been provided. Under each main heading you may vary the order of the subheadings as you wish. The finished outline should include all of the headings.

Thesis statement: You can change your home and your habits in order to save money on your heating bill.

Main headings:
Introduction
Improving efficiency of old materials
Installing new equipment
Changing your habits
Conclusion

Subheadings:
Turning down thermostat at night
Filling in cracks around doors and windows
Installing quilted window shades
Increasing amount of insulation on attic floor
Buying an energy-saving thermostat
Turning down heat when you leave your home
Installing a wood-burning or coal-burning stove
Dressing warmly to be comfortable at lower temperaures

Assignment   Prewriting   List ideas for a brief essay about something that you learned from a friend. Choose the ideas that you wish to use in your essay. Divide your ideas into main ideas and supporting details and then arrange them in a logical order. Write an appropriate thesis statement. Finally, prepare an outline for the essay. You will use the outline as the basis for a brief practice essay that you will write as you study the remaining sections of this unit. Save your paper.

Continuing Assignment   Prewriting   List ideas for the essay topic that you analyzed for the Continuing Assignments on pages 404 and 412. Divide the ideas into main ideas and supporting details, and arrange them in a logical order. Then write a thesis statement. Using the list of ideas, prepare an outline for the main essay that you will write as you study this unit. Save your paper.

Assignment Checklist

Check your assignments for the following points:

   ✔ 1. Did you list ideas that are related to your topic?
   ✔ 2. Did you divide your ideas into main ideas and supporting details?
   ✔ 3. Did you arrange your ideas in a logical order?
   ✔ 4. Did you write a thesis statement that expresses precisely the topic and purpose of your essay?
   ✔ 5. Did you prepare an outline showing the order in which your ideas will appear in your essay?
   ✔ 6. Did you place your thesis statement at the top of your outline?

9.4   Writing Your First Draft

When you have planned your essay, you are ready to write your first draft. As you write the draft, present your ideas in the same order in which they appear in your outline. As you write, do not spend a long time searching for the best word or sentence structure because you will do that when you revise the draft.

9.4a   Writing the Introductory Paragraph

Although an introduction is brief, it is important because it creates your reader's first impression. A reader who is bored or confused by an introductory paragraph will not want to read further in the essay. In your introduction, you should accomplish the following goals.

Strategies

    1. *Establish the topic and purpose of your essay.* In your thesis statement, present your topic clearly and indicate what your principal writing purpose is. You may place your thesis statement anywhere in the introductory paragraph; however, the end of the paragraph is the usual place for it.

2. *Establish the tone of your essay.* Choose a tone that suits your topic, your purpose, and your audience. Make sure that you will be able to maintain that tone throughout the essay. Begin to use the point of view that you will use throughout the essay.

3. *Capture your reader's interest.* You can capture a reader's interest in several ways. For example, you can use a quotation or an example, or you can raise a question that you will answer in the body of the essay. Alternatively, you can simply preview the essay by briefly suggesting the main points. If you are narrating a personal experience, you can create interest by making it clear that the experience was unusual, humorous, or important to you.

The following paragraph is the introductory paragraph of a narrative essay.

Model

> The four of us were standing, sitting, and crouching in a darkened hall on the lowest level of Canby High School at eight-thirty in the morning. We were waiting our turns to compete in our first-ever speech tournament. Sometime in the next twenty minutes, all of us would be obliged to speak for a maximum of five minutes on a topic chosen from two subjects, having roughly ten seconds to prepare for the ordeal.

> *Philip Bornkamp, Sunset High School*
> *Beaverton, Oregon*

The writer interests the reader by briefly suggesting what will happen in the rest of the essay. The writer also captures the reader's interest by stating how intimidating the experience was.

Exercise 1　Writing: The Introductory Paragraph　Write an introductory paragraph based on the following thesis statement and the main headings of the following outline. Use a serious tone and the third-person point of view.

Thesis statement: The city should allow a movie theater to open in the old Franklin Street bank building.

I. Introduction
II. Need for evening entertainment in the community
III. Benefits for nearby restaurants and stores
IV. Conclusion

9.4b   Writing the Body Paragraphs

In the body paragraphs, the main part of the essay, you develop the topic that you have presented in the introductory paragraph. You must write and organize the sentences so that they present your topic clearly and systematically.

Following the Outline

As you write the body paragraphs, follow your outline. Decide how much attention you will give to each main heading of the outline. In most essays, you can include in a single paragraph all of the information about a main heading and its subheadings. If a main heading has many subheadings, however, you may need to devote two or three paragraphs to that main heading. The idea of the main heading usually is expressed in the topic sentence of the paragraph that first mentions it.

Transitional Devices

Each sentence in your essay should flow smoothly from the preceding sentence. In addition, the opening sentence of a paragraph should indicate how that paragraph is related to the preceding paragraph. To achieve coherence in your essay, use the following transitional techniques.

Strategies

1. *Repeat a key word or phrase from the previous sentence or paragraph.*

2. *Use a pronoun to refer to a person or an idea in the previous sentence.*

3. *Use transitional words and phrases such as* first, next, then, *and* most important.

The following passage is a body paragraph from an essay in which the writer analyzes the changes in the appearance of cars. Notice how the writer uses transitional devices.

Model

Consumers' desires to save money and fuel have also affected the look of American automobiles. For example, they are smaller than earlier models because smaller cars consume less gasoline. In addition, the shape of cars has been changed to increase their aerodynamic efficiency, enabling them to use less fuel. Even though the cars are small, their designers tried to create a feeling of spaciousness in them. For example, the trunk space of many cars was decreased or eliminated to allow more space for seats and more space between seats.

The writer repeats the word *smaller* to emphasize the major change in the cars and uses the pronouns *their* and *them* to refer to the cars. The writer also uses transitional words such as *for example* and *in addition* to emphasize the flow of the sentences.

Exercise 2   Writing: Body Paragraphs   Write two body paragraphs based on the following thesis statement and outline. Use transitional devices to indicate the flow of the ideas in the paragraphs.

Thesis statement: Whenever I have the time, I prefer to make a long journey by bus rather than by plane or car.

    I. Introduction
   II. Able to see more
      A. Can go almost anywhere by bus
      B. Can see areas when traveling through them
      C. Can get off bus to spend time in interesting places
  III. Able to relax during long, slow journey
      A. Can talk with others on the bus
      B. Can catch up on reading
      C. Can nap throughout the ride
  IV. Conclusion

9.4c   Writing the Concluding Paragraph

Your concluding paragraph should make your essay seem complete and should help your reader to understand the full meaning of your essay. Write a concluding paragraph that accomplishes these tasks by using one or more of the following methods.

1. *Summary*. Present a summary of the main points that you made in the body of the essay. If you return to the main ideas that you have presented in the introduction, approach the idea from the larger perspective offered in the body of the essay.
2. *Final Idea*. Present a final idea that is closely related to your topic.
3. *Personal Reaction*. Present your reaction to the topic of your essay. In an essay about a personal experience, you can make clear what the experience meant to you.
4. *Suggested Solution*. Suggest a solution to the problem or issue that you discussed in your essay. Your solution may ask your audience to take some kind of action.

Some descriptive and narrative essays do not need a concluding paragraph because the descriptions or recounted experiences are complete in themselves. In those essays, the final point of a description or the final incident of an experience may serve as a conclusion.

The following paragraph is the concluding paragraph of an essay about the writer's experience as a violinist in a quartet.

Model

We played the quartet smoothly and confidently, each drawing strength from the others. At times one of us rose above the rest, carrying the melody and being borne aloft by the support of the others. Even before the performance ended, I felt an enormous sense of completion. I suspect that we all did. Each person had made the sacrifice of individualism but had emerged with greater strength and meaning as an inseparable part of a miniature musical community.

Jonathan Rosen, New Rochelle High School
New Rochelle, New York

The writer ends the essay with his personal reaction to playing in the quartet. He also adds a final idea about what the members of the quartet gained by sacrificing individuality.

Exercise 3   Prewriting: Concluding Paragraphs   On your paper, write *Summary, Final idea, Personal reaction,* or *Suggested solution* to describe the method used in each of the following concluding paragraphs.

PARAGRAPH 1

As I stood there for so long just watching the stars, I realized what I truly want to do. The stars helped to show me my interest in science and space. True, I may never live near Alpha Centauri, but I may live in a space colony on the moon, and I fully intend to.

Robert Hurt, Western Guilford High School
Greensboro, North Carolina

PARAGRAPH 2

Thus, only the legislature can ensure that the Highland Forest will be preserved. All voters in the county should send their senators and representatives letters and telegrams urging them to pass the necessary conservation legislation. With the help of everyone, we can save one of the last wildlife areas in the state.

PARAGRAPH 3

Thus, the varied types of work and the large number of positions that are now available make computer science one of the most rapidly expanding fields. There are many opportunities for people who are willing to acquire the training that is required.

Exercise 4   Prewriting: The Essay   Read the following brief essay about a personal experience. Then write the answers to the following questions.

1. What is the thesis statement?
2. What is the tone?
3. What is the principal writing purpose of the essay? Does the writer include other purposes for writing?
4. How does the writer conclude the essay?

I have always loved the seashore. I love its variability: it's loud and then quiet; it's still and then very much alive. Last summer in a moment of stillness at the seashore, I made a special discovery.

I was standing at the water's edge on a fresh July morning. It was early, not yet six o'clock, and I was all alone on the expanse of sand and seashells. As I looked over the water towards the eastern horizon, I saw a few crimson streaks stretching towards me as the sun began to crawl out from under the sea. I stood for a moment, listening and seeing and feeling, lost in introspection. I felt somehow related to the ocean, to the sun, to the earth beneath my sandals.

In that fleeting, quiet moment, I knew that humans were as much a part of nature as the sand dollar and the sea gull. Everyone learns this in elementary school biology. Yet, as I stood there, I felt its truth for the first time.

(Adapted)
Kendra Sisserson, Rockledge High School
Rockledge, Florida

Assignment   Writing   Take out the paper on which you wrote a thesis statement an and outline for your practice essay about something that you learned from a friend (*page 417*). Write the first draft of the essay. In your introductory paragraph, try to capture the interest of your audience. Follow your outline as you write the body paragraphs, and conclude the essay with a summary, a final idea, a personal reaction, or a possible solution. Save your paper.

Continuing Assignment   Writing   Write the first draft of the main essay that you planned and outlined for the Continuing Assignment on page 418. Follow your outline and, as you write, keep in mind your thesis statement, your principal writing purpose, and your audience. Save your paper.

Assignment Checklist

Check your assignments for the following points:

✔ 1. Did you write an introductory paragraph that includes a thesis statement, establishes the tone of your essay, and introduces the topic in an interesting way?

✔ 2. Did you write body paragraphs that fully develop the ideas in the order in which they appear on your outline?

✔ 3. Did you write a concluding paragraph that makes clear the meaning of your essay?

✔ 4. Did you use transitional devices to emphasize the order of your essay?

9.5 Revising and Finishing Your Essay

Once you have completed the first draft of your essay, you will probably need to revise it. When you revise an essay, you do far more than correcting spelling and punctuation errors. You look at your essay as a reader would so that you can see whether the main ideas are presented clearly. You also review your word choice and sentence structure. That is, you reconsider and improve both the content and the style of your essay.

If possible, wait a day or two before you revise your essay so that you will have a fresh outlook. Then it will be easier to be critical of your own writing.

Reviewing the Content

To make sure that your ideas are presented clearly and completely, review your essay for the following points.

Strategies

1. *Introductory Paragraph.* Make sure that your topic is established clearly in the thesis statement and that your introduction indicates your purpose and will capture the interest of the audience that you are addressing.

2. *Body Paragraphs.* Check for coherence. Be sure that your ideas are arranged logically and that transitional words and phrases are used to indicate that order.

3. *Concluding Paragraph.* Review your conclusion to make sure that it will help your reader to understand your main idea.

4. *Unity*. Make sure that the idea presented in the thesis statement is developed throughout the essay (*pages 277–278*). Remove or rewrite sentences that have little or nothing to do with the topic.

5. *Completeness*. Check to see whether there are any passages that need additional details or examples. If there are, add material to existing sentences or add new sentences.

Reviewing the Style

The next step in revising your essay is reviewing the way in which you expressed your ideas. Make sure that your tone is consistent throughout the essay and that you have maintained a single point of view. Then use the following methods to improve your style.

Strategies

1. *Check the length and complexity of your sentences*. Rewrite sentences that are so complicated that your reader may not understand their meaning. A long sentence can often be divided into two or more effective sentences. Also, revise any sections that contain several short sentences close together: such sentences can often be combined (*pages 283–287*).

2. *Check your level of diction*. Make sure that you have used a consistent level of diction throughout your essay and that the level of diction is appropriate for your topic, your purpose, and your audience.

3. *Examine your word choice*. Replace any words that do not have appropriate denotations and connotations.

Proofreading

As the final step in revising your essay, proofread it for errors. First, check your essay for correct grammar and usage. For example, be sure that all of your verbs agree with their subjects. Then, check your essay for correct punctuation, capitalization, and spelling. For example, make sure that your essay contains no sentences that are joined by commas rather than semicolons or colons and that all proper nouns are capitalized.

Choosing a Title

When you have revised the first draft of your essay, select a title for it. Your title should indicate the topic of your essay, and it should be interesting to your reader. For example, as a title for the essay about the speech contest that is introduced on page 421, the title "Speech Contest" would not be interesting. The title "Quick Thinking" would arouse the curiosity of the reader and also indicate the skill that the writer needed to do well in the contest. A title should not be so unusual, however, that it sounds odd.

Preparing the Finished Paper

After you have revised your essay, prepare the finished paper. On pages 208–209 you will find guidelines for preparing a final manuscript. Use them, making any changes that your teacher suggests. As you copy the essay, remember that accuracy and neatness will make your essay easier to read and will make a positive impression on your reader. Proofread your finished essay to correct any errors made in copying.

Exercise **Revising: The Essay** Rewrite the following brief essay. Revise it for content by removing any details that are not directly related to the thesis statement. Revise it for style by (1) making the point of view consistent, (2) revising diction that is not consistent with the rest of the essay, (3) replacing incorrect words, (4) dividing sentences that are too long, and (5) combining short, choppy sentences.

> For years I had wondered what I would do when I completed high school. Last fall I attended career-counseling sessions at school and read books containing job descriptions. None of the jobs, how-

ever, seemed right for one, and I remained condensed. Then suddenly, when I was doing a favor for my mother, my confusion cleared.

My father works for a company that makes film and photographic paper. My mother runs a sales company out of her house. When one becomes very busy, she neglects to keep her books, to update her inventory, and to do her filing. When I looked in her office one Saturday last month, papers were scattered across tables and chairs, and I asked her if I could help her to get organized again, and she gave me permanence, and I went to work.

Hours later, I realized that I had been enjoying myself so much that I had worked past my usual lunch time. My brother often does that when he is reading a book. In fact, I got such a kick out of messing around with my mother's records and files that I decided I should try a career in business. This fall I plan to enroll in business school. I will learn more. I will discover what aspect of business interests me most.

Assignment   Revising   Revise the first draft of the practice essay that you completed for the Assignment on page 424. Revise both the content and the style of the essay. Then prepare a final copy of the essay and proofread it.

Continuing Assignment   Revising   Revise the first draft of the main essay that you have been writing for the Continuing Assignments throughout the unit. Revise both the content and the style. Copy or type the finished paper and then proofread it.

Assignment Checklist

Check your assignments for the following points:

✔ 1. Did you revise your introductory paragraph to make it more interesting and to introduce your topic and your purpose more clearly?

✔ 2. Did you revise your concluding paragraph to make the end of your essay more effective?

✔ 3. Did you add details where needed and remove sentences that were not related to your topic?

✔ 4. Did you make revisions to improve the coherence of your essay?

✔ 5. Did you revise your sentences to make their length and structure appropriate for your topic and purpose?

✔ 6. Did you revise your sentences so that their level of diction is consistent throughout the essay?

✔ 7. Did you replace any words that had inappropriate denotations or connotations?

✔ 8. Did you revise your essay to make its tone and point of view consistent?

✔ 9. Did you proofread your final draft for correct grammar, usage, spelling, and punctuation?

✔ 10. Did you choose a suitable title?

✔ 11. Did you prepare a final copy and proofread it?

Qualifications for a Job: Writing an Essay

Situation: You are a twenty-year-old looking for a new job. In last Sunday's newspaper, you saw an interesting advertisement for a job as a management trainee at a department store. To apply for the job, you must write a short essay explaining why you are qualified for the position. As you plan and write your essay, you will keep in mind the following information.

Writer: you as a twenty-year-old applying for a new job

Audience: the personnel director of a department store

Topic: your qualifications for the job

Purpose: to explain your qualifications in an essay of no more than three hundred words

Directions: To plan and write your essay, follow these steps:

Step 1. Read the advertisement on the facing page. Then read the personal history inventory that you made recently to prepare you for seeking a new job.

Step 2. Write a thesis statement that indicates your topic and your purpose. You may want to begin, "I believe that I am well qualified for the management trainee program at Emerson's because. . . ."

Step 3. Prepare an outline for your essay. Plan to write three body paragraphs; each will develop one of the sections of your personal inventory.

Step 4. Write your essay. Include a strong opening statement, and write a concluding paragraph in which you summarize your main points or present a final idea.

Management Trainee

Join the management team at Emerson's and enjoy the challenge of management in our friendly, fast-growing department store. We offer good salaries, fringe benefits, a bonus plan, and excellent opportunities for advancement.

Several management trainee positions are available for highly-motivated individuals who are able to work well with people. Communications skills are essential. Trainees must have good high school records and a minimum of two years' work experience.

Qualified applicants should send a brief essay explaining why they belong in Emerson's management trainee program. Write to Philip Otero, Personnel Director, Emerson's, 565 Piedra Street.

Personal Inventory

Education
—Graduated from Jefferson High School two years ago with a 3.0 average
—Favorite subjects were English, history, and computer programming
—Currently enrolled in the evening business program at Franklin Community College; presently taking courses in marketing and accounting

Employment History
—During last two years of high school, worked in the Reliable Pharmacy; eventually given some responsibility for ordering stock
—For two summers worked at the Community Daycare Center teaching swimming and gymnastics
—For past two years, worked for Anderson's Furniture Store full-time; assistant to the buyer of patio and outdoor furniture

Interests and Achievements
—Was in charge of advertising for my high school yearbook
—Was elected to Student Council in twelfth grade
—Was member of the swim team and the gymnastics team in high school; won several events
—Play clarinet in local band

431

Unit Assignments

Assignment 1 Write two separate paragraphs about coping with the weather or about being disorganized. The first paragraph should be serious in tone and directed to a general audience. The second paragraph should be humorous in tone and directed to any particular audience that you wish. At the top of your paper, identify the audience that you have selected. In each paragraph, include details that are suited to the audience that you are addressing.

Assignment 2 Write a brief essay in which you present your view of the role that television should play in people's lives or your view of the ways that people can improve television programming. Address a specific audience; in your introductory paragraph try to capture the attention of that audience; Present a summary or a personal reaction in your concluding paragraph.

Assignment 3 Write a brief essay in which you tell your reader about an experience that helped you to decide what you would like to do in the future. Address an audience of your friends, and choose a tone, a level of diction, and sentence structures that are appropriate for your audience and purpose.

Assignment 4 Write a brief essay that explains the benefits of having a part-time job or of learning to do a task such as carpentry, sewing, or auto repair. Arrange the benefits from least to most important, and use transitional devices that contribute to the coherence of the essay.

Assignment 5 Write an essay in which you try to persuade your audience to accept a change that you would like to see made in your community or throughout the country. Address an audience that would be affected by the change and choose a level of diction that would appeal to that audience. In your concluding paragraph, present the action that you would like your audience to take.

Assigment 6 Write a brief essay in which you explain the benefits of participating in a team sport. Address an audience that does not participate in team sports. Use a light tone, and try to capture the attention of your audience in the introductory paragraph.

Assignment 7 Write a brief essay in which you tell your audience about a challenge that you faced successfully. For example, you could tell about hiking to the top of a mountain or learning a foreign language well enough to converse with native speakers. Present the details of the challenge in chronological order, and use transitional devices that emphasize that order. Present a personal reaction in your concluding paragraph.

Assignment 8 Write an essay in which you try to persuade your audience that voting is an important responsibility of every citizen, Write for readers who are eligible to vote but have never voted. Use a serious tone and the third-person point of view. Present a summary of your important points in the concluding paragraph.

Revising Your Assignments

For help in revising your essays, consult the Checklist for Revision on the last page of this book.

Unit Tests

Test 1

A.   Number your paper from 1 to 5. Next to each number, write *True* if the sentence is true or *False* if it is false.

1. The tone of an essay must always be serious.
2. Although you may combine more than one purpose in an essay, you should have a principal writing purpose for each essay.
3. Always address a general audience whenever you write an essay.
4. Your thesis statement must be the first sentence in the introductory paragraph.
5. Your concluding paragraph may present a summary, a final idea, a personal reaction, or a suggested solution.

B.   Number your paper from 6 to 10. Next to each number, write the letter of the item that correctly completes the sentence. You will use all but one of the items.

    a. style   d. denotations

    b. connotations   e. thesis statement

    c. tone   f. essay

6. In a(n) _?_ you present your experiences or your observations of the world around you.
7. _?_ is the attitude that a writer conveys about a topic and an audience.
8. _?_ is the unique way in which a person expresses his or her ideas in words.
9. _?_ are the ideas associated with a word.
10. A(n) _?_ presents the topic of your essay.

C.   Number your paper from 11 to 15. Next to each number, write the letter of the item that correctly answers the question.

11. Which of the following has a formal level of diction?
    a. Concerned about halting inflation, the economists debated about the new policies for several hours.
    b. She slaved over her work so that it wouldn't be a pain during the weekend.

  c. Rushing to beat the crowds to the beach, we took off without our lunch.

  d. If he can't leave right away, he doesn't want to go at all.

12. Which of the following is a suitable topic for an essay?
  a. The history of the income tax in the United States
  b. Why I think that the tax laws should be changed
  c. The difference between progressive and proportional income taxes
  d. How tax returns are processed

13. Which of the following is a precise thesis statement?
  a. Someone is doing something about pollution in our country.
  b. Camping is fun.
  c. I understood my grandparents better when I visited Finland, their native land.
  d. Sometimes when I travel, I see beautiful scenes and interesting people.

14. Which of the following is *not* a transitional device?
  a. Using sentences of appropriate length and complexity
  b. Repeating a key word from a previous sentence or paragraph
  c. Using a word or a phrase such as *first* or *more important* that emphasizes the order of the essay
  d. Using a pronoun to refer to a person or an idea in the previous sentence

15. Which of the following contains no incorrect words?
  a. The politician's speech perspired us to join his campaign.
  b. After school on Thursdays, I insist a veterinarian with her work.
  c. I believe that good commotional skills are important in all jobs.
  d. Before building a wall, a bricklayer makes careful measurements.

Test 2

  Choose one of the Unit Assignments. Write the assignment as directed and hand it in to your teacher.

Writing
About Literature

Unit Preview

Writing about literature can greatly enhance your appreciation of what you read. It helps you to read sensitively, to focus on the author's meaning, and to be aware of the writer's techniques. In an essay about literature, you do not simply report what happens in a work; instead, you present an interpretation of one aspect of the work. You may explain how an author develops the theme of a short story or how a poet uses imagery. In a literary essay, you must present evidence from the work to support your interpretation.

The following paragraphs begin a literary essay.

Theodore Dreiser's novel *Sister Carrie,* written in the era of literary realism, depicts a naive, small-town girl adapting to life in a metropolis. Through the actions and ambitions of the various characters in the novel, Dreiser comments on many facets of life and society as a whole. His view of people's concern for money is especially pervasive and is one of the underlying themes in the novel. Dreiser shows that the preoccupation with money can ultimately cause one to lead an unhappy life or, more often, cause one to lead a dissatisfied life.

The first characters whom Dreiser uses to illustrate this point are Minnie and Sven Hanson, the two people with whom Carrie lives upon moving to Chicago. Although the Hansons do not have an excessive desire for wealth, they tend to be extremely frugal. Almost immediately upon moving in, Carrie senses that there is "disapproval of the doing of those things which involve the expenditure of money" (34). The Hansons rarely, if ever, spend money on entertainment or pleasure, and thus they lead a very routine, tedious existence. To emphasize the boredom of the Hansons' lives, Dreiser contrasts the dull routine of Minnie and Sven with the eager anticipation of Carrie, who has just moved to a lively urban area. . . .

Paul Langer, Glenbrook South High School
Glenview, Illinois

For Analysis Reread the paragraphs from the essay about *Sister Carrie*. Then, on your paper, write the answers to the following questions.

1. In which sentence does the writer introduce the aspect of the novel that he will analyze? In which sentence does he state the main idea that he will develop in the essay?
2. What is the writer's first point in the body of the essay?
3. What evidence does he give to support this point?
4. What do you think the rest of the second paragraph will be about?

By analyzing two paragraphs from an essay about *Sister Carrie,* you have begun to explore the techniques of writing about literature. In this unit, you will learn what to look for when you read a literary work, how to choose a suitable topic, and how to gather evidence from the work to support your ideas. Then you will learn how to plan and write a literary essay. As you write your essay, you will follow the three steps of the writing process: prewriting, writing, and revising.

10.1 The Nature of the Literary Essay

Purpose and Audience

Purpose. When you write a literary essay, your purposes are to analyze, to interpret, and, perhaps, to evaluate the work. A literary essay may also be called a critical essay, an interpretive essay, a literary analysis, or a literary paper. Whatever its name, the literary essay is entirely different from a report that recounts an author's life, discusses a literary period, or summarizes the plot of a novel. When you write a literary essay, you must demonstrate that you have thought about what you have read. You must base your interpretation on the details, ideas, and characters presented by the author. In a literary essay, you will do one or more of the following:

1. Explore the theme, or central meaning, of the work.
2. Explore a technique that the author uses to develop that meaning.
3. Make some judgment about the quality and the impact of the work.

Audience.   When you write a literary essay, address an audience that includes anyone who might be interested in your view of the work that you discuss. Assume that most of your readers have read the work, but provide enough information to refresh their memories.

Tone, Point of View, and Tense

When you write a literary essay, you must observe certain conventions. The appropriate tone, point of view, and tense are illustrated in the following excerpt.

Model

Human beings have always known fear. Some fears are acquired. They stem from childhood experiences, such as falling from a tree or nearly drowning. But other fears—fears of the unknown or of darkness—seem to be inborn. These primeval instincts are universal—almost a genetic curse. After all, what child is not afraid of the dark? Two poems recount the terror of the unknown. Both Hart Crane's "Fear" and Rudyard Kipling's "Song of the Little Hunter" illustrate humanity's attempts to come to grips with their fears.

The attempt to conquer fear is illustrated by the striking differences between these two similar poems. In "Fear" the reader is pacified by a brilliant fire and a pleasant meal. In "Song of the Little Hunter," it seems that no danger lurks because no warning is found. . . .

James Bauerschmidt, Caro High School
Caro, Michigan

Tone. The tone of any writing is the attitude that the author conveys about the topic and the audience. (For more information about tone, see page 406.) The tone of a literary essay should be serious, in keeping with your approach to the work that you are discussing. The preceding excerpt is rather formal, appropriate for a serious discussion of a serious subject.

Point of View. Use the third-person point of view (*page 358*) in a literary essay. It is not correct to write in the first person, as in "I believe . . ." or "It is my opinion. . . ." The excerpt illustrates how using the third person avoids a repetitious use of the pronoun *I*. Using the third person also keeps the focus of your essay on the author and the work.

Tense. Use the present tense when you refer to the characters, the actions, or the author's techniques or subject matter. For example, you might write, "Two poems *recount* the terror of the unknown."

Exercise 1 Prewriting: The Literary Essay Decide whether each of the following sentences is more appropriate for a literary essay or for a report. On your paper, write *Literary essay* or *Report* after the number of each sentence.

1. *Beowulf,* the famous epic poem, was composed more than 1200 years ago by an unknown British author.
2. William Shakespeare's Macbeth shows himself to be a true tragic hero by the greatness of his emotional depth and his moral potential.
   Brian Henry Cheu, Aragon High School
   San Mateo, California
3. The traits of the three main characters in *Faust,* by Johann Wolfgang von Goethe, and *The Scarlet Letter,* by Nathaniel Hawthorne, are strikingly similar.
4. Samuel Taylor Coleridge wrote "The Rime of the Ancient Mariner" in 1798.
5. Daniel Defoe, in *Robinson Crusoe,* was one of the first British writers to create characters who spoke realistic dialogue.

Exercise 2 Revising: Tone The tone of the following passage is not appropriate for a literary essay. On your paper, write an improved version.

Geoffrey Chaucer wrote something called *The Canterbury Tales*. He wrote it in a language with funny spellings called Middle English, the way folks wrote and talked in England in the fourteenth century. The story is pretty good. It's about a bunch of people who go together on a pilgrimage from London to visit the shrine of the famous English martyr Thomas à Becket at Canterbury. They tell these stories on the way.

Assignment Revising The following passage fails to observe two conventions of the literary essay. Identify the problems; then, on your paper, revise the passage.

I think that in *Gulliver's Travels* Jonathan Swift criticized the real world in which he lived. I read Book IV, which is about the land of the Houyhnhnms, thoughtful horselike creatures, and the Yahoos, their slaves, who were senseless beasts that looked like humans. It seemed to me that Swift was rejecting both extremes of behavior.

Continuing Assignment Prewriting Begin to read a literary work of your own choice or one that is assigned by your teacher. You will be writing about it as you study this unit.

Assignment Checklist

Check your revising assignment for the following points:

  ✔ 1. Did you rewrite the passage from an appropriate point of view?

  ✔ 2. Did you use the most appropriate tense in your revision?

10.2 Preparing to Write a Literary Essay

Getting ready to write a literary essay will require almost as much of your attention as the writing itself. First, you will have to read much more carefully than when you read solely for pleasure. Then, as you choose a topic, you will also have to form your interpretation of it. Finally, you will want to find specific incidents or statements from the work that support the interpretation.

Reading the Work Carefully

If you know in advance that you will be writing an essay about a literary work, keep the essay in mind as you read. If you are asked to write about a work that you have already read, reread the work thoughtfully. As you read, ask yourself the following questions. In your literature course, you have probably studied most of the concepts that appear in the questions.

QUESTIONS TO ASK ABOUT A WORK OF FICTION

What is the main plot of the work?

Who are the central characters?

From what point of view is the story told—first person, or third person? Is the point of view omniscient or limited?

What is the setting? Does the work have a certain atmosphere or mood?

What is the central conflict?

What is the climax?

How is the conflict resolved?

What is the theme, or main idea, of the work?

What is distinctive about the author's style?

The reading of poetry raises special questions, such as the ones that follow. Later in this unit, beginning on page 464, you will find a special section on writing an explication, or explanation, of a poem.

QUESTIONS TO ASK ABOUT A POEM

On a literal level, what is the situation in the poem?

Is there a persona (speaker) in the poem? What can you deduce about the persona? Does the speaker have a reaction to the situation?

What images does the poem contain? Does one or more of the images seem to be a symbol—that is, does it stand for something larger than itself?

Is the poem written in a particular form, such as an ode or a sonnet?

What patterns of sound—such as rhyme, alliteration, assonance, rhythm, or meter—does the poem contain? Does the pattern of sound help to convey the meaning?

What figurative language—such as metaphors, similes, and personification—does the poem contain? How does the figurative language help to convey the meaning?

What is the tone of the poem?

Does the poem suggest anything beyond the literal situation? What is the theme of the poem?

Choosing a Topic and an Approach

If your teacher does not assign a topic, take the time to choose your own topic carefully. It should develop logically and naturally from your reactions to the work. You will probably want to choose one of the following approaches to a literary work.

1. *Interpreting the meaning of the work.* By providing evidence from the work, you can explain how the theme is developed. For example, *Gulliver's Travels,* by Jonathan Swift, can be understood on two levels: as a fantasy of adventure and as a social and political satire.

2. *Analyzing a character.* Another approach is showing how a character is changed by his or her experiences—that is, how the character matures or develops. For example, you can explain how Jerry, in Doris Lessing's "The Tunnel," matures as a result of his experience.

3. *Analyzing a technique.* You can also investigate an aspect of the writer's craft, such as symbolism, imagery, poetic sound, characterization, or creation of setting. For example, you can explain how Dylan Thomas, in "Do not go gentle into that good night," effectively and movingly uses the verse form called the villanelle.

4. *Comparing an element in two works.* Another approach is to compare the same element in two works. For example, you can discuss how Shakespeare, in his sonnet "That time of year thou mayst in me behold," and Christina Rossetti, in her poem "Song," express different views of the immortality of love. You can also compare two characters in a single work or in two works.

Writing a Preliminary Thesis Statement

Writing a preliminary thesis statement—the statement of what you intend to prove in your essay—will help you to focus your attention as you search for evidence to support it. If you can find evidence to support your interpretation, the statement will become the main idea, and the final thesis statement, of your literary essay. If you cannot find sufficient evidence, you must be willing to revise or abandon that thesis statement.

A thesis statement should be precise and clear. The following are examples of suitable topics and preliminary thesis statements for literary essays.

TOPIC

>The theme of "The Eve of St. Agnes," by John Keats

PRELIMINARY THESIS STATEMENT

>Keats highlights the uncertainty of first love by filling "The Eve of St. Agnes" with contrasts.

TOPIC

>The use of poetic sound in "The Lake Isle of Innisfree," by William Butler Yeats

PRELIMINARY THESIS STATEMENT

>In "The Lake Isle of Innisfree," Yeats's use of poetic sound helps to convey the sense of peace that the speaker hopes to find in this ideal place.

TOPIC

>The theme of "Rappaccini's Daughter," by Nathaniel Hawthorne

PRELIMINARY THESIS STATEMENT

>The main theme of "Rappaccini's Daughter" is that when human beings, in their cleverness, tamper with nature, the result is disastrous.

Exercise Prewriting: Thesis Statements Number your paper from 1 to 5. After each number write *Appropriate* if the corresponding sentence is appropriate as the thesis statement for a literary essay. Write *Not appropriate* if it is not acceptable as a thesis statement.

1. *The Stranger,* by Albert Camus, does not indicate that there is a divine meaning and goal in life, but it does show that there is a harmony and a freedom in life that each individual can attain.

    Nancy Woodruff, Prospect High School
    Mount Prospect, Illinois

2. Although Alexander Pope was plagued by poor health all his life, he devoted his enormous energies to his literary career and lived to be fifty-six years old.

3. In *Billy Budd* Melville considers the reaction of society to the conflict between good and evil.

4. Herman Melville's "Bartleby the Scrivener" is narrated by the Wall Street lawyer who is Bartleby's employer.

5. Some of the most famous words in Middle English are the opening lines of the Prologue to *The Canterbury Tales,* by Geoffrey Chaucer.

Assignment   Prewriting   Reread a short story or a poem that you enjoy. Ask yourself questions about the work in order to choose an essay topic. Then write the topic and a preliminary thesis statement. Save your paper for use in an assignment on page 461.

Continuing Assignment   Prewriting   If you have not already done so, finish reading the work that you started for the Continuing Assignment on page 440. Select a topic for a literary essay of three to five pages. Write a preliminary thesis statement. Save it for later use.

Assignment Checklist

Check your assignments for the following points:

   ✔ 1. Did you limit your topic to one element of the work?
   ✔ 2. Did you choose a topic that interprets this element of the work?
   ✔ 3. Did you write a preliminary thesis statement that summarizes your interpretation in one sentence?

10.3 Taking Notes

Now you can begin to test your interpretation. Reread the work for any details that can be used to support your preliminary thesis statement. For example, if your topic is the poet's use of sound in "The Lake Isle of Innisfree," look carefully at the rhythm and the letter sounds in the words of the poem.

Gathering Evidence from the Work

Take notes on the details that you find. Perhaps the simplest way to take notes is to use three-by-five-inch or four-by-six-inch note cards, placing one piece of evidence on each card (so that you can easily rearrange them for outlining). Each note card should include a subject heading at the top and, at the bottom, the number of the page on which the evidence appears in the work. When you take notes, record only the essential details of a passage. You need not write in complete sentences or connect one point with another, as the notes on the following excerpt from Doris Lessing's "A Sunrise on the Veld" show.

PASSAGE FROM "A SUNRISE ON THE VELD"

Suddenly it all rose in him: it was unbearable. He leapt up into the air, shouting and yelling wild, unrecognizable noises. Then he began to run, not carefully, as he had before, but madly, like a wild thing. He was clean crazy, yelling mad with the joy of living and a superfluity of youth. He rushed down the vlei under a tumult of crimson and gold, while all the birds of the world sang about him. He ran in great leaping strides, and shouted as he ran, feeling his body rise into the crisp rushing air and fall back surely onto sure feet; and thought briefly, not believing that such a thing could happen to him, that he could break his ankle any moment, in this thick tangled grass. He cleared bushes like a duiker, leapt over rocks; and finally came to a dead stop at a place where the ground fell abruptly away below him to the river. It had been a two-mile-long dash through waist-high growth, and he was breathing hoarsely and could no longer sing. But he poised on a rock and looked down at stretches of water that gleamed through stooping trees, and thought suddenly, I am fifteen! Fifteen! The words came new to

him; so that he kept repeating them wonderingly, with swelling
excitement; and he felt the years of his life with his hands, as if he
were counting marbles, each one hard and separate and compact,
each one a wonderful shining thing. That was what he was: fifteen
years of this rich soil, and this slow-moving water, and air that smelt
like a challenge whether it was warm and sultry at noon, or as brisk
as cold water, like it was now.

NOTES ON PASSAGE

Boy's feeling of exuberant freedom
Leaps, then shouts
Rushes down vlei for two miles
Sits on rock and thinks of his age
Repeats "Fifteen" wonderingly, excitedly
Rejoices at the years that have constituted his life
pp. 122–123

There are three special types of notes: direct quotation, paraphrase, and summary.

Direct quotation.   If you find a particularly memorable statement or description, copy it exactly as it appears in the work and
enclose it in quotation marks. The following example is from Jane
Austen's *Pride and Prejudice*.

Elizabeth's response to Darcy
"From the very beginning, from the first moment I may almost say,
of my acquaintance with you, your manners impressing me with the
fullest belief of your arrogance, your conceit, and your selfish dis-
dain of the feelings of others, were such as to form that ground-
work of disapprobation, on which succeeding events have built so
immoveable a dislike; and I had not known you a month before I
felt that you were the last man in the world whom I could ever be
prevailed on to marry."
p. 145

Paraphrase.   A **paraphrase** is the expression of an author's idea
in your own words. A paraphrase may be almost as long as the
original passage, but it allows you to write in your own words in order

to avoid too long or too frequent direct quotations. A paraphrase must be written in complete sentences. The quotation in the preceding example is paraphrased here.

Elizabeth's response to Darcy

Elizabeth asserts that from the beginning she has considered Mr. Darcy arrogant, conceited, and disdainful. Events increased her disapproval and dislike to the extent that a month after meeting him, Elizabeth knew that Mr. Darcy was the last man on earth she would ever wish to marry.

p. 145

Summary. A **summary,** like a paraphrase, is the expression of the author's ideas in your own words. It, too, is written in complete sentences. However, in a summary, the author's narration and dialogue are condensed to essential details. In the following example, the passage from Lessing's "A Sunrise on the Veld" (*pages 445–446*) is summarized in three sentences.

Boy's feeling of exuberant freedom

Leaping, shouting, the boy rushes down the vlei for two miles. Sitting on a rock, he thinks of his age and repeats "Fifteen" wonderingly, excitedly. He rejoices at the years that have constituted his life.

pp. 122–123

Using Secondary Sources

Secondary sources are books or essays written by scholars who specialize in interpreting literature. This kind of information can be helpful in presenting you with other views of the work that you will discuss. However, a secondary source should not be regarded as a replacement for your own reading and interpretation of the work. In fact, many teachers prefer an interpretation to be based solely on a student's own reactions to a work. If you do use secondary sources, you can treat an idea or a quotation from the work as an additional piece of evidence to support your thesis statement.

When reading secondary sources, take notes just as you would for the work itself. At the top right of each note card, place the author's last name, so that you will know the work from which the information came. For each source, be sure to fill out a separate bibliography card that lists the author, title, publisher, and place and date of publication. (See Section 11.2b in Unit 11.) You will need this information when you write footnotes and a bibliography.

Exercise 1   Prewriting: Evidence   Read the following preliminary thesis statement and its accompanying evidence. On your paper, list the numbers of the sentences that support the thesis statement.

Thesis statement: Unlike ghosts in other Shakespearean plays, the ghost in *Hamlet* is important to the development of the drama.

1. Hamlet is the Prince of Denmark.
2. The ghost's words lead to Hamlet's actions against Claudius.
3. Hamlet is distressed that his mother has married so soon after his father's death.
4. People of Shakespeare's time believed wholeheartedly in ghosts.
5. To Hamlet the ghost reveals that Claudius is the murderer.
6. The ghost gives Hamlet the duty of avenging his murder.
7. This Shakespearean ghost speaks eloquently.
8. Hamlet hates Claudius.

Exercise 2   Prewriting: Note Taking   Read the following passage from pages 1385–1386 of a secondary source about James Joyce. Without quoting, take notes on this background information as if you were going to use the notes for a literary essay. Give your notes a heading.

> Joyce's almost life-long exile from his native Ireland has something paradoxical about it. No writer has ever been more soaked in Dublin, its atmosphere, its history, its topography; in spite of doing most of his writing in Trieste, Zurich, and Paris, he wrote only and always about Dublin. He devised ways of expanding his accounts of Dublin, however, so that they became microcosms, small-scale models, of all human life, of all history and all geography. Indeed, that was his life's work: to write about Dublin in such a way that he was writing about all of human experience.
>
> M. H. Abrams

Exercise 3 Prewriting: Paraphrase   Reread the passage in Exercise 2 and write a paraphrase that you could use in a literary essay.

Assignment Prewriting   At the library find a secondary source about the author or the work that you have been reading for your literary essay. Read it and take notes on information that you could use to support your thesis statement.

Continuing Assignment Prewriting   Reread the work that you will discuss in your essay. Take notes on evidence to support your preliminary thesis statement. Save them for later use.

Assignment Checklist

Check your assignments for the following points:

✔ 1. Did you take careful notes as you gathered evidence?
✔ 2. Did you place quotation marks around the direct quotations on the note cards?
✔ 3. Did you include subject headings and page numbers on all note cards?
✔ 4. When you used a secondary source, did you record, on a separate card, the publication information needed for foot-notes and a bibliography?

10.4 Organizing Your Ideas

Revising the Preliminary Thesis Statement

After studying a literary work, you will often find that your first impression of it has changed to some degree. Before you begin to organize your notes, look critically at your preliminary thesis statement. Does your evidence support it? Is the statement clear and concise? Revise the preliminary thesis statement if necessary.

Outlining the Essay

Prepare an outline of your essay so that you will have a logical plan for presenting your ideas and supporting evidence. The process of outlining and writing a literary essay will be illustrated by a student essay that analyzes the theme of Nathaniel Hawthorne's short story "Rappaccini's Daughter." This model typifies the kind of literary essay that is based entirely on the original work, with no interpretations from secondary sources. In the essay the writer develops three points to support a thesis statement about the disaster that results when people tamper with nature. The points are presented in the order in which they appear in the story.

1. Rappaccini has tampered with nature in his garden.
2. Beatrice is like the beautiful but poisonous plants.
3. The love of Giovanni and Beatrice is not allowed to grow naturally.

These three points become the three main headings, indicated by Roman numerals, in a sentence outline of the essay. Supporting evidence for each main heading is listed under it as subheadings, indicated by capital letters. The introductory and concluding paragraphs are identified by Roman numerals but do not need to be outlined. (For information about other kinds of outlines, see Section 11.4 in Unit 11.)

Thesis statement: The main theme of "Rappaccini's Daughter" is that when human beings, in their assumed cleverness, tamper with nature, the result is disastrous.

   I. Introduction
  II. Rappaccini has tampered with nature in his garden.
     A. Beautiful plants are poisonous.
     B. Medicines made from these plants have harmed patients.
     C. Rappaccini has enough knowledge to influence nature but not enough knowledge to avoid mistakes.
     D. Only the water in the fountain has not been harmed by Rappaccini.
 III. Beatrice is like the beautiful but poisonous plants—in particular, like the flowering shrub.

    A. They share a common essence of poisonous beauty.
    B. The shrub must be cared for by Beatrice alone.
    C. Her very touch sears Giovanni's hand; it is evidence of her power.
    D. Neither she nor the shrub is naturally evil; both have been corrupted by Rappaccini.
  IV. The love of Giovanni and Beatrice is not allowed to grow naturally.
    A. Beatrice loves Giovanni sincerely.
    B. He loves her beauty but cannot surrender his heart because he does not trust her.
    C. When Giovanni discovers the poisonous powers that Beatrice has given him, he accuses Beatrice of poisoning him.
    D. As a result, their love is destroyed and Beatrice dies.
   V. Conclusion

To prepare the outline of your essay, assemble your note cards and follow these steps.

Strategies

1. *Sort your note cards into several groups according to their subject headings.* Each group will form one main heading of the outline.

2. *Place the main-heading groups in a logical order.* Use order of importance or chronological order (in this case, following the order of the work)—whichever will enable you to present your evidence most clearly.

3. *Within the main-heading groups, choose the cards that will form the subheadings of the outline.* Select only those cards that provide strong evidence for your points. Put the other cards aside.

4. *Arrange the cards for the subheadings in a logical order.* Your purpose is to make your discussion of each point easy to follow.

5. *Write the main headings and subheadings in outline form.* Place the thesis statement at the top of the outline. Add headings for the introduction and conclusion.

If your note cards contain a great deal of supporting information, you may wish to use a third order of headings. This order consists of numbered sentences or phrases. The sample outline requires only two orders of headings.

Exercise   Prewriting: Outlining   Use the following list of headings and subheadings to prepare an outline for a paper supporting the thesis statement that is given. You will have to determine which items on the list are headings and which are subheadings. There is no one correct order for the main headings or for the subheadings under each heading.

> *Thesis statement:* In "Neighbor Rosicky," Willa Cather effectively uses techniques of characterization to create a realistic portrait of the main character.
>
> Rosicky's actions
> Rosicky's special gift for loving
> "To be a landless man was to be . . . a slave . . . to be nothing."
> Other characters' observations of Rosicky
> Refuses to sell cream because children can use extra nourishment
> Conclusion
> Rosicky's family happy to care for him
> Big cities "built you in from the earth itself, cemented you away from any contact with the ground."
> Arranges for his daughter-in-law to get to town more often
> Introduction
> Rosicky's attitudes

Assignment   Outlining   The first three paragraphs of a literary essay follow. Copy its thesis statement and write a sentence outline of the passage. The introduction should form the first main heading, and each of the other paragraphs should form another main heading and its accompanying subheadings.

> John Steinbeck's novel *The Pearl* is set against the vivid backdrop of the California Gulf region. To create this setting, Steinbeck relies largely on descriptions of the wildlife of the area. Ants in

particular appear frequently, and Steinbeck goes into great detail about seemingly unimportant episodes in their existence. Despite their apparent insignificance, these episodes actually play an important role, expressing some of the story's more subtle themes and qualities.

The most important of these episodes occurs early in the opening passages of the story. In these passages, Steinbeck describes the main character, Kino, awakening and going about his morning routine. In the midst of this routine, Kino looks down at the dirt floor of his hut and watches, in Steinbeck's words, "with the detachment of God," as an ant struggles to escape the sand trap of an ant lion. The image of this trap comes to mind readily: a small crater in the sand with the ant lion occupying a hole in the center and the ant desperately attempting to climb up the sides. Each time the ant nears the lip of the crater, the ant lion pushes more sand into his hole, causing both sand and ant to cascade back toward the center. Although the reader does not yet understand the analogy, this scene represents the theme of the story. Kino, like the ant, is trying to escape a trap; in Kino's case this trap is poverty.

Under normal circumstances, Kino would have no hope of climbing out of his trap. In the story, however, Kino is suddenly given an opportunity; he finds a giant pearl. If he can sell the pearl, he can buy his family the things needed for a better life. He is on the brink of escaping, on the lip of the crater. However, the society in which Kino lives does not allow people to run. It prevents Kino from being able to protect himself against others who wish the wealth of the pearl for themselves. Consequently, he is unable to sell the pearl, and his family never realizes the dream of a better life that the pearl puts within reach. Kino, like the ant, makes it only to the lip of the crater; society, like the ant lion, pulls the sand out from under him just before he makes it all the way. Thus, the eventual hopelessness of Kino's struggle is expressed beforehand through the struggle of the ant.

Anthony Steimle, Leland High School
San Jose, California

Continuing Assignment   Look over your preliminary thesis statement and the notes that you took for the Continuing Assignments on pages 444 and 449. Revise your thesis statement if necessary. Then prepare a sentence outline for your essay. If you prefer, prepare a topic outline—an outline in which the headings are not expressed in complete sentences.

Assignment Checklist

Check your assignment for the following points:

✔ 1. Did you identify the thesis statement and copy it at the top of your outline?

✔ 2. Did you prepare a sentence outline that shows the relationships of the ideas in the second and third paragraphs?

Check your Continuing Assignment for the following points:

✔ 3. Did you write a final thesis statement that can be adequately supported by the evidence gathered from the literary work?

✔ 4. Did you sort your note cards by their subject headings?

✔ 5. Did you prepare a logically organized outline that includes all the important points?

10.5 Writing the First Draft

Follow your outline as you write your first draft, making adjustments as you write. Your task is to work your evidence into the essay in such a way that the sequence of ideas is logical and the writing is smooth. As you compose the essay, remember that your purpose is to interpret the literary work, not to explain your own philosophy to the reader.

The Title

Give your essay a specific title. The title must indicate the aspect of the work with which your essay deals: for example, "Symbolism in Steinbeck's *The Pearl*" *or* "The Theme of D. H. Lawrence's 'The Rocking-Horse Winner.'"

The Introductory Paragraph

Your introductory paragraph is an overview of the essay. In it include the author and the title of the work, any brief description of the work that will help the reader understand your interpretation, and the thesis statement. At the same time, you should also attempt to interest the reader in what you have to say. The following introductory paragraph meets all of these requirements.

Model

From the beginning to the end of his novel *The Grapes of Wrath*, John Steinbeck paints a portrait of a dispossessed people. Beginning in the dusty Oklahoma fields and finishing in the rain-sodden California farm lands, Steinbeck's novel portrays a people who are stripped and cheated of their belongings, who set out and search for a new life, who are unwanted and harassed by society, and who endure and never give up. Throughout the book human lives are constantly being tested by the hostilities and **Thesis** hardships imposed on them. However, Steinbeck **statement** shows that human life will persist despite the hostilities of nature and of society so long as people unite in their struggles and help one another.

Jim Labrenz, Thousand Oaks High School
Thousand Oaks, California

The Body Paragraphs

As you write the body paragraphs, you should consult your outline as you incorporate the specific evidence from your note cards into the body of the essay. Be careful not to use too many quotations. An excessive use of quotations may suggest that you have not thought enough about the ideas in the work to be able to put them into your own words. The body paragraphs should consist primarily of summarized and paraphrased evidence that is clearly related to your thesis statement.

The Concluding Paragraph

In a concluding paragraph, you close the essay by summarizing what has been shown. You also establish how and why the aspect of the work that you have discussed is important to the work as a whole. The following paragraph concludes an essay in which the writer discusses the theme of a short story.

Model

> "The Garden Party," by Katherine Mansfield, deals with the recognition that frocks, pastries, garden parties, and—on a larger scale—class distinctions are made meaningless by death. Mansfield portrays a great awakening in this young woman. Realizing that life is not always a garden party for everyone, Laura Sheridan gains a clearer perspective on class relations. Her earlier ideas are changed during her experience down the lane; Laura perceives that class distinctions are absurd at a final point—in death.

> *Lisa Foderaro, Rumson-Fair Haven Regional High School*
> *Rumson, New Jersey*

Quotations

Short Prose Quotations.   When you decide to quote a particularly memorable passage, you should copy it in your essay exactly as it appears in the work. The proper way of incorporating a quotation in an essay depends on its length. Short quotations of no more than four lines are written or typed as part of the paragraph. They are enclosed in quotation marks and followed by the number of the page on which the quoted passage appears in the original work. In the following example, from an essay about *Pride and Prejudice,* notice that the final punctuation mark comes after the page reference.

> When Lady Catherine tries to dissuade Elizabeth from marrying Mr. Darcy, Elizabeth replies that even if the Darcy family resented the marriage, "it would not give me a moment's concern" (267–268).

Long Prose Quotations.   Quotations of five or more lines are made easier to read by setting them off from the text: they are indented five spaces on both sides and single-spaced. For quotations that are set off in this manner, it is not necessary to use quotation marks. The following quotation from *Pride and Prejudice* is long enough to be set off from the text of the essay in which it appears. In this kind of quotation, the page reference follows the final punctuation mark.

The fact is, that you were sick of civility, of deference, of officious attention. You were disgusted with the women who were always speaking and looking, and thinking for *your* approbation alone. I . . . interested you, because I was so unlike *them*. Had you not been really amiable you would have hated me for it; but in spite of the pains you took to disguise yourself, your feelings were noble and just. . . . (284)

The preceding quotation illustrates the way in which a long quotation may be shortened by the use of ellipsis points (. . .) to indicate the omitted words. Use three points in the middle of a sentence, and use three points plus a period at the end of a sentence. When you shorten a quotation, you sometimes need to supply words that are not part of the original text but are needed for sense. Enclose such words and phrases in brackets.

Poetry Quotations.   Quotations of up to three lines may be enclosed in quotation marks and run in with the text. The end of a line is indicated by a slash (/) with a space before and after it.

Coleridge's lines "It is an ancient Mariner, / And he stoppeth one of three" are among the most famous opening lines in British poetry.

When four or more lines of a poem are quoted, they are single-spaced and set off from the text just as a prose quotation is. No quotation marks are used.

Documentation

To **document** an essay is to supply information about the original works from which you copied the quotations in the essay. As you have seen, you must follow each quotation with a reference, in parentheses, to the page on which it appears in the original work. In an essay about a long poem, use line numbers instead; in an essay about a Shakespearean play, use the numbers of the act, scene, and line (such as III.i.56–65). Then, in a bibliography page at the end of the essay, list the complete information in a standard entry. For a full-length prose work, the following form is correct.

Woolf, Virginia. *A Room of One's Own*. New York: Harcourt Brace, 1963.

The forms vary for other kinds of works, such as a collected edition of an author's works. For additional information about bibliographies, see Section 11.5 in Unit 11.

Your teacher may prefer that you use another way of citing the work from which your quotations come. The first time you quote from the work, place an explanatory footnote at the bottom of the page or on a separate footnotes page. In either case, the correct form is as follows.

> [1] Virginia Woolf, *A Room of One's Own* (New York: Harcourt Brace, 1963), p. 45. Subsequent references are to this edition.

The remaining quotations in the essay are followed by page numbers in parentheses; the standard bibliography page is optional.

The preceding information applies only to literary essays that are based entirely on the original work. If an essay also includes references to secondary sources (*pages 447–448*), you must give a footnote for the first reference to the original work; you may include with the text other references to the work. References to quotations or ideas from secondary sources appear as footnotes, and the bibliography includes entries for each secondary source and for the original work. For additional information about documenting a paper, see Section 11.5 in Unit 11.

A Model Literary Essay

The literary essay referred to in this unit is given on the following pages as a model for reference and study.

Model

The Theme of "Rappaccini's Daughter," by Hawthorne

The short story can achieve many ends; a short story may reveal human character, illustrate the society in which the author lives, or illuminate a timeless universal truth. Nathaniel Hawthorne often uses his short stories to reveal some idea about humankind, and such is the case with "Rappaccini's Daughter." This story is filled with symbols and allusions. The main theme of "Rappaccini's Daughter," however, is that when human beings, in their assumed cleverness, tamper with nature, the result is disastrous.

An example of nature that has been made terrible through human intervention is Signor Rappaccini and his garden. The garden is resplendent with vegetation, much of which is beautiful, and it is this beauty that initially attracts Signor Giovanni Guasconti, a student at the University of Padua, whose lodgings overlook the garden. The flowers that flourish within the walls of Rappaccini's garden are, however, actually poisons "more horribly deleterious than Nature, without the assistance of this learned person, would ever have plagued the world withal" (1048). Signor Rappaccini, a physician, distills the plants to create potent medicines, and he administers these medicines to patients of his, sometimes with ill results—a fact alluded to by Professor Baglioni in a discussion between Giovanni and the professor.

Thus, Rappaccini has managed to modify nature; yet despite his knowledge of botany, his patients pay a penalty. Rappaccini has enough knowledge to influence nature, but not enough to understand it fully. The only thing in the garden that Rappaccini has not changed is the water in the fountain—the water that "continued to gush and sparkle into the sunbeams as cheerfully as ever . . . as if the fountain were an immortal spirit that sung its song unceasingly and without heeding the vicissitudes around it . . . " (1045). While the fountain, once a great work of human art, now crumbles, the pure water, nature's creation, continues to flow.

Perhaps the best example of humans doing harm to nature is Rappaccini's daughter, Beatrice. To Giovanni, she is strikingly similar to the flowers in the garden:

> for the impression which the fair stranger made upon him was as if here were another flower, the human sister of those vegetable ones, as beautiful as they, more beautiful than the richest of them, but still to be touched only with a glove, nor to be approached without a mask. (1046)

Beatrice is like a certain flowering shrub that, according to Giovanni, is the most beautiful of all the plants in the garden. Beatrice says that this plant germinated on the day she was born; although different in physical form, the shrub and the young woman share a common essence. Both the shrub and Beatrice are physically beautiful, and yet both are highly poisonous. The plant is so lethal that even Signor Rappaccini dares not touch it. Instead, the plant must be cared for by Beatrice, who suffers no harm. Beatrice's powers are revealed to Giovanni when Beatrice prevents him from touching the poisonous shrub. Earlier observations by Giovanni have suggested that Beatrice may possess terrible powers, but the fact that her mere touch sears the hand of Giovanni is concrete evidence that Rappaccini's daughter is indeed endowed with an extraordinary potency. Remarkably, Giovanni's burned hand is a deep purple color, similar to the color of the blossoms of the powerful shrub.

Yet, despite their power, neither the shrub nor the woman is naturally evil; rather, they have become dangerous through the constant effort of Signor Rappaccini. Indeed, both are innocuous by nature. The shrub, which grows in the midst of the fountain, draws its nourishment from the pure, clear water therein, and Beatrice, isolated from the world by her physical malady, has remained as innocent as a child, without acquiring the cynicism or the evil of humankind. Like the garden in which she lives, Beatrice is naturally wholesome, yet she has been corrupted through the knowledge—not the wisdom—of Rappaccini.

The relationship between Giovanni and Beatrice is still another testimony to the results of human interference with natural processes. There can be little doubt that Beatrice loves Giovanni. She tells him, "I dreamed only to love thee, and be with thee . . ." (1063). Whether Giovanni really loves Beatrice is less clear, and herein lies the impediment that determines the ultimate fate of their romance. Although Giovanni is enthralled by her beauty, he will not completely surrender his heart to Beatrice. He cannot decide whether she is lovely and innocent or horribly powerful. His doubt comes from the displays of Beatrice's powers that he has witnessed, as well as from his talks with Professor Baglioni, who tries to dissuade Giovanni from seeing her.

When Giovanni discovers that he himself now has awful powers of death, he immediately accuses Beatrice of poisoning him. Once Giovanni has made this accusation, their relationship is irreparably damaged. Beatrice dies soon thereafter. She tellingly places the blame for their failure in love when she says to Giovanni as she is dying, "Oh, was there not, from the first, more poison in thy nature than in mine?" (1065).

Ironically, "Rappaccini's Daughter" could easily have been a pleasant story: a beautiful girl who lives in a verdant garden meets a handsome boy, and they fall in love. However, Hawthorne conveys a meaning in "Rappaccini's Daughter" beyond the actual story he relates: human beings often bring harm to themselves by the ill use of their knowledge and intelligence. Indeed, all three male characters—Dr. Rappaccini, Professor Baglioni, and Giovanni—are very intelligent, yet they all lack the wisdom to use their intelligence beneficially. The only character who uses her heart more than her mind is, sadly, the one who suffers most from the misdirected efforts of human beings to outwit nature.

Bibliography

Hawthorne, Nathaniel. "Rappaccini's Daughter." In *The Novels and Tales of Nathaniel Hawthorne.* Ed. Norman Holmes Pearson. New York: Random House, 1937, pp. 1043-1065.

(Adapted)
Jay Geistlinger, Glenbrook South High School
Glenview, Illinois

Exercise   Prewriting: The Bibliography Entry   Given the following information about a book, write a bibliography entry for it. Use the bibliography entry on page 457 as a guide.

Title: *Summoned by Bells*
Author: John Betjeman
Date of publication: 1960
Publisher: Houghton Mifflin
Place of publication: Boston

Assignment   Writing   Take out the paper on which you wrote a topic and a thesis statement for a literary essay about a short story or poem (*page 444*). Write an introductory paragraph for the essay. Be sure to give the author and title of the work and to include your thesis statement. Save your paper.

Continuing Assignment   Writing   Using the note cards and the outline that you prepared for the Continuing Assignments on pages 449 and 453, write the first draft of your literary essay.

Assignment Checklist

Check your assignments for the following points:

   ✔ 1. Did you include the author and title of the work that you are discussing?

✔ 2. Did you include a clear thesis statement in your introductory paragraph?

Check your Continuing Assignment for these additional points:

✔ 3. Did you give your essay a title that indicates the aspect of the work that you are analyzing?

✔ 4. Did you present your evidence clearly in the body of the essay?

✔ 5. Did you write a concluding paragraph that summarizes what you have shown?

✔ 6. Did you use the proper form for quotations, and did you document them correctly?

10.6   Revising and Finishing Your Essay

If possible, begin your revision a day or so after you have finished writing your first draft. In this way you will have a more objective view of your writing. Revision is far more than proofreading. It is the reworking and polishing of the entire essay, both the content and the style. You will probably need to rewrite some passages and attach them to the appropriate portion of the first draft. In a thorough revision, you should observe the following guidelines.

Strategies

1. *Check the draft against the outline.* Be sure that you covered all of the points in the right order. Add any sentences that seem needed.

2. *Make sure that each piece of evidence supports your thesis statement.* Eliminate any sentences that give unnecessary information.

3. *Make sure that the ideas flow coherently.* Rearrange them if they do not, using transitional words as needed.

4. *Change wording where necessary* to make your choice of words more precise or to make the sentence structure smoother.

5. *Make sure that the tone of your essay is consistent.* It should be serious and formal.

6. *Make sure that you have used the third-person point of view consistently.*

7. *Make sure that you have used the present tense* when you refer to the characters, the action, and the author's techniques or subject matter.

8. *Proofread the essay.* Correct errors in grammar, usage, spelling, and punctuation. Make sure that you copied the quotations and page references accurately.

For more information about revising an essay, see pages 425–427. For general information about revision, see Unit 6, which begins on page 276.

When you are satisfied that your essay is as good as you can make it, you have a final draft. Copy it on 8½-by-11-inch paper, following accepted manuscript guidelines (*pages 208–209*) with any alterations that your teacher recommends. Proofread the finished paper carefully.

Exercise   Revising: The Literary Essay   Revise the following portion of a first draft. Pay special attention to tense, point of view, and the form used for quotations.

> In *The House of Mirth,* Edith Wharton wrote about a young woman's struggle to keep her place in the elite society of New York at the beginning of the century. Lily Bart, the heroine, had little money of her own. I think she believed that she could keep her social position if she married a wealthy man, however. The principal conflict in the novel is between Lily's pride and her awareness of her precarious position.
>
> At the beginning of the novel, Lily Bart was portrayed as an attractive, well-dressed young woman who was spending the weekend at the country estate of wealthy friends:
>
> > Everything about her was at once vigorous and
> > exquisite, at once strong and fine. (47)
>
> Apparently, she maintained her friendship with these people and with others as a way of living fashionably and searching for a

husband. I think that Lily worried about the future: "Under her dark hat and veil she regained the girlish smoothness, the purity of tint, that she was beginning to lose after eleven years of late hours and indefatigable dancing. . . . Had she indeed reached the nine-and-twentieth birthday with which her rivals credited her?" (4).

Assignment   Revising   Revise the introductory paragraph that you wrote for the Assignment on page 461.

Continuing Assignment   Revising   Revise the first draft that you prepared for the Continuing Assignment on page 461. Before you make revisions, review all of the information in this section. Then copy or type the finished paper and proofread it carefully. Submit your outline with the finished paper.

Assignment Checklist

Check your assignments for the following points:

  ✔ 1. Did you revise the first draft to make the tense, tone, and point of view consistent?

  ✔ 2. When necessary, did you correct the form used for quotations?

  ✔ 3. Did you add any needed sentences?

  ✔ 4. Did you eliminate any unnecessary sentences?

  ✔ 5. Did you revise the draft to make it more coherent?

  ✔ 6. Did you revise the draft to improve word choices and the phrasing of sentences?

  ✔ 7. Did you proofread the final draft for correct grammar, usage, spelling, and punctuation?

  ✔ 8. Did you prepare the finished paper according to your teacher's quidelines and proofread it carefully?

10.7   Writing an Explication of a Poem

Robert Frost observed that "poetry provides the one permissible way of saying one thing and meaning another." A poem is compressed communication and, as such, offers the reader layers of meaning that lie beneath the surface of the poem's words. In fact, it sometimes takes several paragraphs of prose to explain fully just a few lines of poetry.

The depth and richness of poetic meaning make writing about poetry somewhat different from writing about novels and short stories. Like a prose work, a poem should be read several times, but at least one reading should be aloud, so that you can experience the sound of the poem as well as the meaning.

In this section you will consider one form of writing about poetry: the explication. An **explication** of a poem is a detailed explanation of the work. An explication includes a line-by-line investigation of the poem and shows how the various aspects of the poet's craft contribute to the total meaning. Poetic techniques include imagery, figurative language (including similes, metaphors, and personification), and symbolism. They include, in addition, the various aspects of poetic sound: rhyme, repetition, alliteration, assonance, meter, and rhythm. When appropriate, an explication also includes some commentary about the form of the poem: whether it is a sonnet or a villanelle, for example. In your literature courses, you have probably examined both the forms and the techniques of poetry. If you need to review any of the preceding terms, consult a literature textbook, a literary handbook, or a book about poetry.

As you prepare an explication of a poem, analyze the techniques in the work as well as its form. Look up the definitions of unfamiliar words, historical and mythological references, and literary allusions.

This sonnet by William Wordsworth is followed by an explication. Notice that in each paragraph the writer discusses an aspect of the poem. The quotations and references to particular lines make the explication specific.

Composed upon Westminster Bridge

Earth has not anything to show more fair:
Dull would he be of soul who could pass by
A sight so touching in its majesty:
This City now doth, like a garment, wear
The beauty of the morning; silent, bare,   5
Ships, towers, domes, theatres, and temples lie
Open unto the fields, and to the sky;

All bright and glittering in the smokeless air.
Never did sun more beautifully steep
In his first splendour, valley, rock, or hill;   10
Ne'er saw I, never felt, a calm so deep!
The river glideth at his own sweet will:
Dear God! the very houses seem asleep;
And all that mighty heart is lying still!

William Wordsworth

Model

Situation described in poem

    "Composed upon Westminster Bridge," by William Wordsworth, presents a view of the majesty of London in the early morning. The city, seen from Westminster Bridge, is described as if glimpsed for the first time. In lines 1–3 the persona feels that few people could ignore such a view and that nothing else the earth possesses is more beautiful. Struck with awe at the sight, the persona exclaims in line 9, "Never did sun more beautifully steep," or bathe, the features of the city. This scene produces a sense of calm in the persona.

Figurative language and imagery

    Although London usually bustles with activity, the quiet city now appears vulnerable, approachable, and more human. The persona describes London wearing a cloak of beauty in the simile in line 4. The image of a garment spread across the city makes London seem like a sleeping person. The persona conveys a sharp impression of the "Ships, towers, domes, theatres, and temples" of London in line 8. This imagery suggests London's beautiful skyline, which is "bright and glittering." In line 12 the image of the river further illustrates the calm of the scene. The river glides rather than rushes by, at "his own . . . will." In line 13 the persona personifies the houses of London sleeping. Finally, in line 14 the persona's unique view is expressed through the main metaphor of the "mighty heart" of the city. At sunrise its heart is still. This figurative language and imagery

Form of poem

illustrate how London sleeps, almost like a giant, "Open unto the fields, and to the sky."

"Composed upon Westminster Bridge" is an Italian, or Petrarchan, sonnet. The first eight lines make up one sentence, with a rhyme scheme of *abba- abba.* This section describes London and its features, the dawn, and the feelings this sight evokes. The final six lines, with a rhyme scheme of *cdcdcd,* form a resolution, or final statement. The persona compares the beauty of London with the natural beauty of "valley, rock, or hill" and states that the city at this hour is more lovely.

Poet's use of sound

There is some alliteration in lines 9–10 (*sun, steep, splendour*) and some assonance in line 12 (*river, his, will*). However, the sense of calm, quiet, and beauty in the poem comes principally from the rhyme. The rhyming words sound simple and soothing—*steep, deep, asleep; hill, will, still.*

Overall meaning of poem

This striking sonnet by Wordsworth suggests that even a busy, crowded, and dirty city can be as beautiful as anything viewed in nature. London, "All bright and glittering in the smokeless air," captured by the poet in a meditative moment, exhibits serenity and loveliness.

Like all explications, the model begins with a consideration of the situation described in the poem and concludes with a paragraph about the overall meaning of the poem. In the concluding paragraph, the writer summarizes the total meaning in light of the various aspects of the poem that have been analyzed: the figurative language and imagery, the form of the poem, and the way in which sound reinforces meaning.

There is no set sequence for the paragraphs about these three aspects of a poem. You may use any order that seems appropriate for the work that you explicate.

Writing an explication is an excellent way of examining and appreciating a poem fully. It is also an excellent preparation for writing other kinds of literary essays about poetry.

Exercise 1   Prewriting: Analyzing Poetry   Read the following poem. Look up any words that you do not understand. Then, on your paper, list the poem's images, giving the line number of each.

SAMPLE   Ivory, line 3

Cargoes

Quinquireme of Nineveh from distant Ophir
Rowing home to haven in sunny Palestine,
With a cargo of ivory,
And apes and peacocks,
Sandalwood, cedarwood, and sweet white wine.   5

Stately Spanish galleon coming from the Isthmus,
Dipping through the Tropics by the palm-green shores,
With a cargo of diamonds,
Emeralds, amethysts,
Topazes, and cinnamon, and gold moidores.   10

Dirty British coaster with a salt-caked smoke stack
Butting through the Channel in the mad March days,
With a cargo of Tyne coal,
Road-rails, pig-lead,
Firewood, iron-ware, and cheap tin trays.   15

John Masefield

Exercise 2   Prewriting: Analyzing Poetry   Read the following poem. On your paper, give the rhyme scheme of the poem and list each instance of alliteration, assonance, and repetition. Give line numbers.

Sonnet 30

When to the sessions of sweet silent thought
I summon up remembrance of things past,
I sigh the lack of many a thing I sought,
And with old woes new wail my dear time's waste;
Then can I drown an eye (unus'd to flow)   5
For precious friends hid in death's dateless night,
And weep afresh love's long since cancell'd woe,

And moan th' expense of many a vanish'd sight;
Then can I grieve at grievances foregone,
And heavily from woe to woe tell o'er   10
The sad account of fore-bemoaned moan,
Which I new pay as if not paid before:
But if the while I think on thee, dear friend,
All losses are restor'd, and sorrows end.

William Shakespeare

Assignment 1   Writing/Revising   Write an explication of one of the poems in the preceding exercises. Using the Assignment Checklist, revise your work.

Assignment 2   Writing/Revising   Write an explication of one of the following poems: "Ozymandias," by Percy Bysshe Shelley; Sonnet XIX ("When I consider how my light is spent"), by John Milton; "A narrow Fellow in the Grass," by Emily Dickinson; "A Noiseless Patient Spider," by Walt Whitman. Revise your work before making a final copy.

Assignment Checklist

Check your assignments for the following points:

✔ 1. Did you explain the situation described in the poem?
✔ 2. Did you examine the poem's imagery (and symbols, if any)?
✔ 3. Did you examine the poem's figurative language?
✔ 4. Did you examine the poet's use of sound?
✔ 5. Did you examine the form of the poem?
✔ 6. Did you explain the total meaning of the poem?
✔ 7. Did you proofread your explication for correct grammar, usage, spelling, and punctuation?

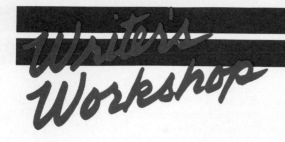

Personification: Writing About Poetry

Situation: You are a member of the Emerson Club, a club devoted to studying the life and works of Ralph Waldo Emerson. You have been asked to write an essay about one of Emerson's poems. The essay will appear in *The Emersonian,* a bulletin that all members of the club receive. You have decided to write about Emerson's use of personification in "The Snow-Storm." As you write your essay, you will keep in mind the following information.

Writer: you as a contributor to *The Emersonian*
Audience: members of the Emerson Club
Topic: Emerson's use of personification in "The Snow-Storm"
Purpose: to analyze the poem in a literary essay of no more than six hundred words

Directions: To plan and write your essay, follow these steps.

Step 1. Read the poem on the facing page, consulting a dictionary for the meanings of any unfamiliar words. Be certain that you understand the meaning of each line.

Step 2. Reread the poem, paying special attention to Emerson's use of personification. Notice the figure of the storm as a driver in the first stanza, the figure of the north wind in the second stanza, and, at the end, the figure of Art. Observe how these figures develop the meaning of the poem.

Step 3. Take notes on each instance of personification

(Continue on page 472.)

The Snow-Storm

Announced by all the trumpets of the sky,
Arrives the snow, and, driving o'er the fields,
Seems nowhere to alight: the whited air
Hides hills and woods, the river, and the heaven,
And veils the farm-house at the garden's end.   5
The sled and traveller stopped, the courier's feet
Delayed, all friends shut out, the housemates sit
Around the radiant fireplace, enclosed
In a tumultuous privacy of storm.

   Come see the north wind's masonry.   10
Out of an unseen quarry evermore
Furnished with tile, the fierce artificer
Curves his white bastions with projected roof
Round every windward stake, or tree, or door.
Speeding, the myriad-handed, his wild work   15
So fanciful, so savage, nought cares he
For number or proportion. Mockingly,
On coop or kennel he hangs Parian wreaths;
A swan-like form invests the hidden thorn;
Fills up the farmer's lane from wall to wall,   20
Maugre the farmer's sighs; and at the gate
A tapering turret overtops the work.
And when his hours are numbered, and the world
Is all his own, retiring, as he were not,
Leaves, when the sun appears, astonished Art   25
To mimic in slow structures, stone by stone,
Built in an age, the mad wind's night-work,
The frolic architecture of the snow.

                          Ralph Waldo Emerson

and select quotations that you will want to include in your essay.

Step 4. Write a thesis statement. Then, using your notes, prepare an outline of your essay.

Step 5. Write the first draft of your essay: an introductory paragraph, one or more body paragraphs, and a concluding paragraph. Be sure to write in the third person, to use the present tense, and to cite quotations correctly.

Step 6. Read over your first draft and make any necessary revisions.

Step 7. Make a final copy of your essay and proofread it carefully.

Unit Assignments

Assignment 1 Discuss the importance of setting in one of the following short stories.

1. "The Three Strangers," by Thomas Hardy
2. "The Return of Imray," by Rudyard Kipling
3. "The Lagoon," by Joseph Conrad

Assignment 2 Write an explication of one of the following poems.

1. "A Valediction: Forbidding Mourning," by John Donne
2. Sonnet XLIII ("How do I love thee? Let me count the ways"), by Elizabeth Barrett Browning
3. Sonnet 18 ("Shall I compare thee to a summer's day?"), by William Shakespeare

Assignment 3 Discuss the conflict experienced by the main character in one of the following works.

1. "Guests of the Nation," by Frank O'Connor
2. *A Doll's House,* by Henrik Ibsen
3. *Portrait of the Artist as a Young Man,* by James Joyce

Assignment 4 Discuss the relation of poetic sound and meaning in one of the following poems.

1. "Kubla Khan," by Samuel Taylor Coleridge
2. "Break, Break, Break," by Alfred, Lord Tennyson
3. "All Day I Hear," by James Joyce

Assignment 5 Compare and contrast two of the following Shakespearean heroes. Consider how their actions, words, and feelings are similar or different.

1. Macbeth
2. Hamlet
3. Othello
4. Shylock
5. Lear
6. Richard III

(Continue on the next page.)

Assignment 6   Discuss one of the following topics.

1. The theme of "The Unknown Citizen," by W. H. Auden
2. The character of the persona as it emerges in "Ulysses," by Alfred, Lord Tennyson
3. The use of metaphor in "Ode: Intimations of Immortality," by William Wordsworth

Assignment 7   Discuss an aspect of one of the following literary works.

1. *The Canterbury Tales,* by Geoffrey Chaucer
2. *Riders to the Sea,* by John Millington Synge
3. *The Diary,* by Samuel Pepys

Assignment 8   Discuss the imagery in one of the following poems.

1. "The Tiger," by William Blake
2. "Dover Beach," by Matthew Arnold
3. "Ode to the West Wind," by Percy Bysshe Shelly

Assignment 9   Discuss one of the following characters in *Pygmalion,* by George Bernard Shaw. Consider whether the character changes.

1. Liza
2. Higgins
3. Doolittle

Assignment 10   Discuss one of the following topics.

1. The use of symbolism in "The Metamorphosis," by Franz Kafka
2. The use of irony in "The Verger," by Somerset Maugham
3. The theme of "The Rocking-Horse Winner," by D. H. Lawrence

Assignment 11   Analyze a character in one of the following works.

1. A novel by Charles Dickens
2. A novel by Jane Austen
3. A novel by George Eliot

Assignment 12   Discuss an aspect of one of the following works.

1. *Antigone,* by Sophocles
2. *Medea,* by Euripides
3. *Murder in the Cathedral,* by T. S. Eliot

Revising Your Assignments

For help in revising a literary essay or an explication, consult the Checklist for Revision on the last page of this book.

Unit Tests

Test 1

A. Number your paper from 1 to 5. Next to each number, write *True* if the sentence is true or *False* if it is false.

1. When used in a literary essay, prose quotations of five or more lines are written or typed as part of a paragraph.
2. In writing a literary essay, you should use the third-person point of view.
3. Direct quotations, paraphrases, and summaries are different types of notes.
4. A suitable topic for a literary essay is an examination of some aspect of a literary period.
5. Your reading of secondary sources should be the basis of a literary essay.

B. Number your paper from 6 to 10. Next to each number, write the letter of the term that correctly completes the sentence. You will use all but one of the items.

    a. documentation   d. explication
    b. tone   e. bibliography
    c. thesis statement   f. point of view

6. A(n) __?__ is a detailed explanation of a poem.
7. Information about the works from which you copied quotations is known as __?__.
8. You must include your __?__ in the introductory paragraph of a literary essay.
9. If you use secondary sources in writing a literary essay, you must list them in a separate __?__.
10. The __?__ of a literary essay should be serious, in keeping with your approach to the work that you are discussing.

C. Number your paper from 11 to 15. Next to each number, write the letter of the item that correctly answers the question.

11. Which of the following topics would be suitable for an essay focusing primarily on interpreting the meaning of a literary work?

a. The view of mortality in "Thanatopsis"

b. Mood in Katherine Mansfield's "The Voyage"

c. The character of Othello

d. How Oscar Wilde created suspense in *The Picture of Dorian Gray*

12. With which of the following should you begin an explication of a poem?

a. A summary of the total meaning of the poem

b. An explanation of the situation in the poem

c. An analysis of the figurative language and imagery

d. An analysis of the poet's use of sound

13. Which of the following is a suitable topic for a literary essay?

a. Joseph Conrad's life

b. The plot of "The Secret Sharer," by Joseph Conrad

c. Naturalism in literature

d. The character of Leggatt in "The Secret Sharer"

14. Which of the following topics would be appropriate for an essay that compares elements in a literary work?

a. Fate in *Romeo and Juliet*

b. The theme of *Romeo and Juliet*

c. The roles of the Nurse and Friar Laurence in *Romeo and Juliet*

d. The character of Tybalt in *Romeo and Juliet*

15. Which of the following is *not* an appropriate question to ask about a prose work that you plan to write about?

a. From what point of view is the story told?

b. What is the central conflict?

c. What other books has the author written?

d. What is the setting?

Test 2

Choose one of the Unit Assignments. Write the assignment as directed and hand it in to your teacher.

Writing a Research Paper

Unit Preview

A research paper is a formal written presentation, in twenty-five hundred to three thousand words, of information gathered and conclusions reached through your research. In your introductory paragraph include a **thesis statement,** a statement that points out what you intend to prove in your paper. The body of your paper is coherent, well-organized evidence that supports your thesis statement.

The following paragraphs are from the beginning of a research paper on alternative sources of energy.

Introduction	As the world's supply of fossil fuels diminishes, there is increasing interest on both national and local levels in the feasibility of using renewable energy sources. The use of such renewable energy sources as solar energy, wind power, and geothermal energy can avert a worldwide energy shortage.
Thesis statement	
Body	Solar energy, currently the most widely used of the renewable sources, is energy given off by the sun. Scientists assert that approximately 47 percent of the sun's energy reaches the earth's surface. Using the unit of measure known as a kilowatt, scientists have also determined that in approximately forty minutes the earth receives as much solar energy as humans will use in a year.

For Analysis   Write answers to the following questions about the preceding paragraphs.

1. What does the writer intend to prove in this research paper?
2. What is the topic of the second paragraph?

In this unit you will follow the development of a research paper about the increasing use of biomechanics, from selecting and limiting the topic, through research and note taking, to preparation of the final paper. In addition, you will work through the steps of researching, planning, and writing your own paper, following the three steps of prewriting, writing, and revising.

11.1 Planning Your Research Paper

11.1a Selecting and Limiting a Topic

Your first task in writing a research paper is selecting and limiting a topic. Choose a topic that interests you and that you can research in the facilities available to you.

Make sure also that your topic is one that you can adequately explore in a research paper. A general topic, such as the practice of medicine in the twentieth century, is too broad, but it can be limited to a variety of narrower topics. Look at the following examples.

Internal medicine	Sports medicine	Geriatrics
Out-patient clinics	Health-care training	Surgery
Preventive medicine	Medical research	Pediatrics

These subjects are still too broad to be used as topics for a research paper. They can be narrowed even further, however, as the following examples show.

SUBJECT   Surgery

TOPICS   Corrective surgery, Cosmetic surgery, Surgical procedures

SUBJECT	Sports medicine
TOPICS	Sports counseling, Biomechanics, Sports injuries
SUBJECT	Preventive medicine
TOPICS	Holistic health, Nutrition, Weight control
SUBJECT	Out-patient clinics
TOPICS	Clinic locations, Cost factors, Quality care

Exercise 1   Prewriting: Research-Paper Topics   On your paper, write three possible research-paper topics for five of the following subjects.

SAMPLE	American Revolution
ANSWER	Economic factors leading to the American Revolution, Important Revolutionary leaders, France's role in the American Revolution

1. Art
2. Astronomy
3. Automobiles
4. Botany
5. Childhood
6. Colonial days
7. Communications
8. Criminology
9. Electricity
10. Environment
11. Furniture
12. Industry
13. Mathematics
14. Money
15. Movies
16. Music
17. Mythology
18. Nutrition
19. Photography
20. Physics
21. Psychology
22. Railroads
23. Television
24. Voting

11.1b Writing a Preliminary Thesis Statement

After you have selected a topic for your research paper, you must write a preliminary thesis statement. The **thesis statement** is a sentence in which you express your position on the topic; it summarizes what you intend to prove in your paper. Your preliminary thesis statement will serve as a guide for selecting the most useful information for supporting your position. As your research progresses, you will probably change your preliminary thesis statement to reflect additional information.

The following list demonstrates how to move from a general subject to a preliminary thesis statement.

Subject: Surgery

Topic: Cosmetic surgery

Thesis statement: Victims of disfiguring accidents can find new hope through cosmetic surgery.

Subject: Sports medicine

Topic: Biomechanics

Thesis statement: Biomechanics will soon become an important aspect of our daily lives.

Subject: Out-patient clinics

Topic: Cost factors

Thesis statement: Wider use of out-patient clinics can dramatically reduce the costs of health care.

Use the following procedure to develop a preliminary thesis statement for your research paper.

Procedure

1. *Read a few articles on your topic.* Skim several books, or try to discuss the topic with someone who is knowledgeable about it.

2. *Write down ideas, questions, suggestions, or comparisons that you find or that come to mind as you investigate the topic.*

3. *Use the ideas to develop a position that you can support through your research.* Write a preliminary thesis statement that summarizes your position.

Keep the following points in mind as you develop your preliminary thesis statement.

1. The thesis statement establishes your position on the topic.
2. The position in your thesis statement must be one that can be supported by research. Because the evidence in your

research paper must support your position, your thesis statement cannot be one of the following.

a. A well-known fact that is unarguable and is generally known to be true, such as "Public games, forerunners of the modern Olympics, were played in ancient Greece and Rome."

b. A biographical statement, such as "John Adams and Thomas Jefferson, important figures in American history, both died on July 4, 1826."

c. A biased opinion that can have no proof, such as "There will never be a more popular sport than baseball."

d. A personal statement that can be supported only from your own knowledge, such as "All of my recollections of our neighbor Ezra Peterson prove that he was a remarkably good-humored man."

Exercise 2   Prewriting: Thesis Statements   On your paper, explain why each of the following sentences is not a satisfactory thesis statement. Revise five of them to make them good thesis statements.

SAMPLE   Benjamin Franklin was a famous American.

ANSWER   Statement is simply a well-known fact.

Revised: Although Benjamin Franklin is best known as a printer and inventor, his most significant contributions to this country were his political and diplomatic accomplishments.

1. Fossils are petrified remnants of ancient life.
2. Outer space is the last frontier.
3. I have found interesting old tools in the attic in our house.
4. The Industrial Revolution was an important event.
5. Paul Bunyan is a favorite character in American folklore.
6. Julius Caesar was a famous Roman.
7. There is too much violence on daytime television.
8. My father runs a successful small business.
9. Some people are model-railroad enthusiasts.
10. Water pollution is a serious problem.

Exercise 3 Prewriting: Thesis Statements On your paper, limit five of the following subjects so that they are suitable topics for research papers. Then write a thesis statement for each of the five topics.

> **SAMPLE** Industry
>
> **ANSWER** *Topic:* Recent developments in the printing industry
> *Thesis statement:* Modern printing practices are being revolutionized by the introduction of electronic equipment.

1. History of science
2. Lasers
3. Mass media
4. Modern sculptors
5. Photography

6. Cartoons
7. American history
8. Shopping malls
9. Space program
10. Women artists

11.1c Making a Rough Outline

As you do your research, prepare a rough outline to guide you. This outline will be your research plan and will help you to identify the research findings that you can use to support your thesis statement.

Prepare your rough outline from the main ideas that you have gathered from your research. These main ideas will serve as the main headings in your outline. Later, when you have completed all of your research, you may change the order or contents of your rough outline, as well as your preliminary thesis statement. You will also develop a complete outline later, before you begin to write your paper.

The rough outline that follows is the research plan for the paper developed in this unit on the growing use of biomechanics in our daily lives.

> I. Biomechanics in athletic training
> II. Technology involved
> III. Medical uses
> IV. Business and industrial uses

Exercise 4   Prewriting: Rough Outline   On your paper, copy the following three thesis statements, allowing space for several headings under each. Under each, list the headings that belong with it. Then arrange the headings so that they form a rough outline for each topic.

1. To safeguard life on Earth, we must observe ecological principles.
2. Although the science of ecology is relatively new, some basic laws of ecology have been discovered.
3. Ecologists are often asked to help solve environmental problems.

> Ecologists suggested preventing flooding in Ohio with dams and planting
> Climate should not be changed accidentally
> Vegetation patterns are influenced by soil and climate
> Rangeland must be preserved
> Members of ecological communities sometimes cooperate
> Ecologists stopped building of airport in Everglades
> Natural communities of wildlife must be preserved
> Plants and animals live only where certain environmental conditions prevail
> Wastes from technology should not be allowed to destroy environment
> Ecologists restored Dust Bowl by stabilizing dunes
> Ecologists move endangered animals to new environments
> Land should be classified and used appropriately
> Plants and animals live in communities
> Ponds and lakes must be protected from silt build-up
> Competition is part of life in all communities
> Communities change over time
> Ecologists helped stop use of DDT
> Ecologists suggest laws for hunting
> Overused land should be restored
> An ecosystem is a system of living and nonliving things
> Ecologists suggest changes in land use to control pests

Assignment   Prewriting   Make a list of five subjects that interest you and that are suitable for research. Limit three of them to manageable topics, and write preliminary thesis statements for those three.

Continuing Assignment Prewriting *Step 1:* Select and limit a topic for your research paper. *Step 2:* Write a preliminary thesis statement that tells what you plan to prove. *Step 3:* Make a rough outline of the major points that you plan to cover. Save your preliminary thesis statement and your rough outline.

Assignment Checklist

Check your assignments for the following points:

✔ 1. Did you select topics that you can research?
✔ 2. Did you limit the topics so that you can cover them thoroughly in twenty-five hundred to three thousand words?
✔ 3. Did you write preliminary thesis statements in which you establish your position on the topics?

Check your Continuing Assignment for this additional point:

✔ 4. Did you make a rough outline of the ideas that you think you will use to support your thesis statement?

11.2 Doing the Research

11.2a Using a Library

You will do most of the research for your paper in a library. Because libraries differ in the resources that they have available, it is important for you to use the best library to which you have access.

Now that you have a rough outline to direct your research, your task is to find the books, magazine and newspaper articles, and other materials that will provide support for your thesis statement.

The Card Catalog

Start your search for information by consulting the card catalog. Books are alphabetically indexed in the card catalog in three ways: by author, by title, and by subject. Each card records the name(s) of the author(s), the complete title, the subject, the publisher, the publication date, the number of pages, and the call number—the number that tells you where to find the book on the library shelves. Illustrations, maps, bibliographies, and any special features are also listed on the card.

The following are examples of catalog cards.

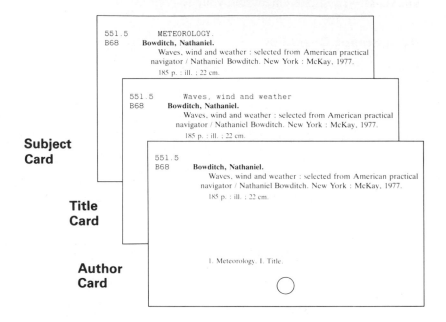

Subject Card

Title Card

Author Card

If you know the author or the title of a book, you can easily find out if the library has that book by looking up the author or title card. In doing research on your topic, however, you will probably find subject cards more useful. For common subjects such as radio, geology, railroads, and medicine, you will find subject cards when you look in the card catalog. For other subjects, you may find a cross-reference card directing you to another subject heading in the catalog. For example, the cross-reference for "Timber" directs you to "See Forestry." Sometimes you will see a "See also" reference directing you to other subject headings for additional books related to the topic. You may need to try several key words in your topic before you find references in the card catalog.

To find books on a library shelf, you need the call numbers. Nonfiction books are arranged on the shelves according to their call numbers. The call numbers follow the classification system used by the library, either the Dewey decimal system or the Library of Congress classification. The Dewey decimal system divides all branches of knowledge into ten parts numbered 000 through 999.

The Dewey Decimal System

000–099	General Works	500–599	Science
100–199	Philosophy	600–699	Technology
200–299	Religion	700–799	Fine Arts
300–399	Social Sciences	800–899	Literature
400–499	Language	900–999	History

The Library of Congress System divides all branches of knowledge into twenty lettered groups.

The Library of Congress Classification

A	General Works	M	Music
B	Philosophy, Psychology, and Religion	N	Fine Arts
		P	Language and Literature
C	History—Auxiliary Sciences		
D	History (except American)	Q	Science
E, F	American History	R	Medicine
G	Geography, Anthropology, and Sports	S	Agriculture
		T	Technology
H	Social Sciences	U	Military Science
J	Political Science	V	Naval Science
K	Law	Z	Bibliography
L	Education		

General Reference Works

Your research will be easier and more efficient if you know how to use general reference works. Some reference works give you information, while others direct you to other sources.

For a general overview of your topic, consult an encyclopedia. Within a given article or in the index volume, you may find useful cross-references to related topics; some articles will also provide short bibliographies. Most libraries have general encyclopedias such as *The New Encyclopaedia Britannica*, *The Encyclopedia Americana*, and *The World Book Encyclopedia*.

Specialized encyclopedias may also be useful to you. Most large libraries will have several specialized encyclopedias including the *Encyclopedia of World Art, Van Nostrand's Scientific Encyclopedia,* and *Grzimek's Animal Life Encyclopedia.*

Other references that you should be aware of are almanacs and yearbooks, atlases, and gazetteers. When you need biographical information, consult biographical references, such as *Who's Who in America, Who's Who in the World,* and *Current Biography.*

Periodical Indexes

Periodical indexes list articles in magazines, newspapers, journals, and other publications. You will often find the most current ideas and research about a subject in a periodical rather than in reference books. If your paper requires up-to-date information, begin your research by using periodical indexes. Most indexes are issued monthly or quarterly, with cumulative volumes published each year. At the front of each index is a list of abbreviations for the periodicals listed in that index. Authors and subjects are arranged in one alphabetical listing.

The most commonly used periodical index is the *Readers' Guide to Periodical Literature,* an index of popular and nontechnical magazines. There are other indexes that list articles in scholarly publications and specialized magazines. Other periodical indexes found in most large libraries include *The New York Times Index, General Science Index,* and the *Art Index.*

All periodical index entries are similar to the following one from the *Readers' Guide.*

JEROME, J.
The biomechanical effect. il Esquire 93:116-117
Ap '80

This entry contains the following information:

TITLE	"The Biomechanical Effect"
AUTHOR	J. Jerome
PERIODICAL	*Esquire*, volume 93
PAGES	116–117
DATE	April 1980

Exercise 1   Prewriting: Library Resources   On your paper, list which of the following sources you could use to find general information on each topic that follows the list.

a. *The New York Times Index*
b. *The New Encyclopaedia Britannica*
c. *Van Nostrand's Scientific Encyclopedia*
d. *Readers' Guide to Periodical Literature*
e. *Information Please Almanac*
f. *General Science Index*
g. *Encyclopedia of World Art*

> **SAMPLE**   Accomplishments of the French artist Georges Braque
>
> **ANSWER**   a, b, d, g

1. Discovery of subatomic particles
2. Marco Polo's travels
3. Diabetes research
4. Aztec pyramids
5. Indira Gandhi's political life
6. Work of Albert Schweitzer
7. Exploration of the Nile in the nineteenth century
8. Irrigation techniques

11.2b Making a Working Bibliography

Begin your research by preparing a working bibliography. A **bibliography** is a list of books, magazines, and other sources used in preparing a research paper. A **working bibliography** is the list you make at the beginning of your research of the sources that you intend to use. A working bibliography will help you to determine whether the library that you plan to use has sufficient information on your topic. Prepare your working bibliography by consulting the card catalog, indexes to periodical literature, and other references. If you find insufficient information on your topic, you will need to choose another topic.

Bibliography Cards

Use three-by-five-inch index cards to record information about books, articles, pamphlets, and other sources that you select. These cards will help you in two ways. First, when you are ready to take notes, you will be able to locate the source more easily. Second, when you prepare the footnotes and the bibliography for your research paper, you will have all the necessary information already recorded on the cards. On each card, include the call number of the source and the library where you found it, if you are using more than one library. Record the author, title, and publication information, using the following forms:

BOOK WITH ONE AUTHOR
> Thompson, Clem W. *Manual of Structural Kinesiology.* 8th ed. St. Louis: C.V. Mosby Company, 1977.

BOOK WITH TWO AUTHORS
> Logan, Gene A., and Wayne C. McKinney. *Kinesiology.* Illus. Philip J. Van Voorst. Dubuque, Iowa: Wm. C. Brown Company Publishers, 1970.

BOOK COMPILED BY AN EDITOR
> Burke, Edmund J., ed. *Toward an Understanding of Human Performance.* Ithaca, N.Y.: Mouvement Publications, 1977.

ARTICLE IN A COLLECTION
> Lockhart, Aileene S. "The Motor Learning of Children." In *A Textbook of Motor Development.* Ed. Charles B. Corbin. Dubuque, Iowa: Wm C. Brown Company Publishers, 1973, pp. 151-157.

ARTICLE IN A MAGAZINE
> Stuller, Jay. "Sports Scientists Train Athletes to Defy Old Limits." *Smithsonian,* July 1980, pp. 66-70.

UNATTRIBUTED NEWSPAPER ARTICLE
> "Bill Rodgers Wins 10-Kilometer Atlanta Regional Race." *New York Times,* 3 May 1981, Sec. 5, p. 16, col. 4.

INTERVIEW
> Humez, Alex. Personal interview. 9 April 1982.

TELEVISION TRANSCRIPT

"Race for Gold." Narr. Hal Douglas. Writ., prod., and dir. Paula S. Apsell. *Nova.* 1979.

ARTICLE IN AN ENCYCLOPEDIA

"Biomechanics." *McGraw-Hill Encyclopedia of Science and Technology.* 1977 ed.

PAMPHLET

U.S. Bureau of the Census, Department of Commerce. *Current Population Reports: Demographic Aspects of Aging and the Older Population in the United States.* (Special Studies, Series P 22, No. 59) Washington, D.C.: GPO, 1976.

The following is a sample bibliography card.

Bibliography Card

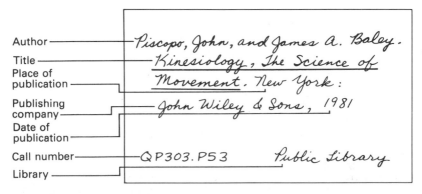

Author ——— Piscopo, John, and James A. Baley.
Title ——— Kinesiology, The Science of
Place of publication ——— Movement. New York :
Publishing company ——— John Wiley & Sons, 1981
Date of publication ———
Call number ——— QP303.P53   Public Library
Library ———

Exercise 2   Prewriting: Bibliography Entries   On your paper, write bibliography listings on the following information.

AUTHOR	TITLE	PUBLICATION FACTS
Books		
1. Alfred Leslie Rowse	*Windsor Castle in the History of England*	Putnam New York, New York 1974
2. Richard Ellman, editor	*The New Oxford Book of American Verse*	Oxford University Press New York, New York 1976

Articles

3. Samuel Eliot Morison — "Abigail Adams" — *The Patriots*
Virginius Dabney, editor
Atheneum
New York, New York
1975, pp. 66–67

4. J. Wierzbicki — "Contemporary Experimental Music" — *High Fidelity and Musical America*
November 1979
pp. 28–29

5. Not given — "Tapping Heavy Crude: A Forgotten Resource" — *Science News*
June 16, 1979
pp. 387–388

6. J. Castro — "The Battle in Network News" — *Time*
March 15, 1982
pp. 52–53

7. Not given — "Various Artists Comment on Reactions to Picasso and Retrospective of His Art" — *New York Times*
June 22, 1980
Sec. 2, p. 1, col. 3

8. Bill Barnhart — "Tax Bill Means Changes in Pension Strategy" — *Boston Globe*
September 6, 1982
p. 41, cols. 2–5
p. 42, cols. 1–2

Reference Books

9. Not given — "Benjamin Disraeli" — *Encyclopaedia Britannica,* 1975 ed.

Television Transcript

10. Cecil Avery, author and producer — *Westward Ho!* — Public Broadcasting System
January 8, 1980

Assignment   Prewriting   Prepare a working bibliography of at least five sources for research on one of the following topics.

Meteorology   History of flight
Cable television   Computers in medicine

Continuing Assignment Prewriting Prepare a working bibliography for the topic that you selected and limited in the Continuing Assignment on page 485. Use the card catalog, periodical indexes, and other reference works. Make a bibliography card for each source that you can consult for your research. Save your working bibliography.

Assignment Checklist

Check your assignments for the following points:

✔ 1. Did you use the card catalog, reference works, and periodical indexes to prepare your working bibliographies?

✔ 2. Did you make a separate card for each source?

✔ 3. Does each card contain complete bibliographical information as well as the call number, if the source is a book, and the name of the library where you found the source?

✔ 4. Did you write the bibliographical information in the correct form?

11.3 Taking Notes

You are now ready to locate the sources on your working bibliography, to evaluate each source, and to take notes on information that will help you to support your thesis statement.

11.3a Evaluating Sources

Evaluate each source carefully. Sometimes a source is not as helpful in providing useful information as you expected it to be. Follow the strategies listed below to evaluate a source before deciding whether to read it.

Strategies

1. *Examine the table of contents and the index* of each book to see whether it contains information directly related to your topic.

2. *Check the publication dates of books and articles.* If you plan to discuss recent developments, your sources should be up to date.

3. *Skim chapters or articles for information that supports your preliminary thesis statement.* Examine headings, subheadings, illustrations, charts, and tables as well as the text.

4. *Choose sources by authors who are well known and highly regarded in their fields.* If you do not know enough about an author to make such a decision, ask your teacher or librarian.

Exercise 1   Prewriting: Evaluating Sources   On your paper, indicate whether each source would provide useful information in support of the given thesis statement. Give a reason for each answer.

SAMPLE   *Thesis statement:* Two hundred years ago, the United States was a wilderness, and pioneer life was very difficult.

Sources:

a. *Heroines of the American Frontier,* 1969

b. "America Becomes an Industrial Nation," in *Modern History*

ANSWER   a. Useful. The book deals with the relevant period in United States history and probably describes some of the hardships faced by the pioneers.

b. Not useful. This chapter concerns a later period in history and a subject that is not relevant to the thesis statement.

1. *Thesis statement:* Although Johann Gutenberg usually receives credit for inventing the printing press in the fifteenth century, neither movable type nor printing was actually invented by Gutenberg.

Sources:

a. "Eleventh-Century Chinese Printing," in *History of Printing*

b. *Johann Gutenberg: Fifteenth-Century Printer*

c. "Modern Typesetting Trends," in *Graphic Arts Monthly*

d. *Incunabula: Books Printed Before 1500*

   e. "Japanese Wood-Block Printing Before A.D. 1200," article in *Japanese Art News*

   f. "A Study of Egyptian Hieroglyphics," in *Archaeology Today*

   g. "How to Make Intaglio Prints," article in *Modern Arts and Crafts*

2. *Thesis statement:* Much of the religious and political life of the ancient Aztecs of Mexico was characterized by sun worship.

   Sources:

   a. "Mexico City: A Modern Metropolis," in *Life* magazine

   b. "Pre-Columbian Archaeological Finds," Chapter 6 in *Mexico: A Social History*

   c. "Excavation of Tenochtitlan, Seat of the Aztec Empire," in *National Geographic*

   d. "Economics and Politics in Transition," Chapter 7 in *Native North Americans: The Nineteenth Century*

   e. "Early Rulers," Chapter 2 in *The Aztecs*

   f. "Crisis in Mexico," article in *The Wall Street Journal*

   g. "On the Government of the Ancient Mexicans," an article in a professional journal

11.3b How to Take Notes

Once you have decided that a source contains useful information, you are ready to take notes on its contents. Record your notes on three-by-five-inch or four-by-six-inch index cards. Use the following strategies for your note taking. These strategies will make it easier for you to record the information that you need as you are writing your paper.

Strategies

1. *Refer to your preliminary thesis statement and your rough outline as you work.* Read each source all the way through for understanding. Then read it a second time, taking notes on the ideas, facts, statistics, quotations, or other information that will help to support your thesis statement.

2. *Write a subject heading on the top line of each card,* as a way of identifying the subject of the note. Refer to headings of your rough outline. Some of the subject headings on your note cards will be the same as your outline headings; others will be more specific. These subject headings will be useful when you prepare a detailed outline for your paper. You will use many of them as the headings and subheadings.

3. *Write the last name of the author and an abbreviated title* to the right of the subject heading.

4. *Write only on the front of the card.* It is easy to overlook information that is written on the back. If necessary, use a second card to complete your record.

5. *Write only one idea on each card.* This strategy will allow you to arrange the cards later so that you can organize ideas and information that belong together into useful groups in preparation for outlining and writing your paper.

6. *Write on the bottom of the card the numbers of the pages from which you took the information.* You will need to record these page numbers in your footnotes.

There are several methods of taking notes: recording direct quotations, writing a paraphrase, writing a summary, or using a combination of these methods. Choose the method that is best suited to the source from which you are taking notes.

Direct Quotation

A **direct quotation** is the exact words of your source. Record a direct quotation when the author has made a point in an unusual or significant way and when the exact wording gives the best support to your thesis statement. When you want to record a direct quotation, copy the exact words from the source and enclose the passage in quotation marks. You may leave out some words from a quoted passage, if you wish. In that case, use ellipsis points (three spaced periods) to show that words have been omitted.

Direct Quotation

Subject heading

Author and abbreviated title

Note

Page reference

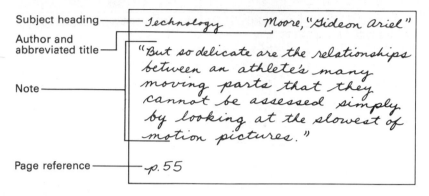

Technology   Moore, "Gideon Ariel"

"But so delicate are the relationships between an athlete's many moving parts that they cannot be assessed simply by looking at the slowest of motion pictures."

p. 55

Paraphrase

A **paraphrase** restates in your own words the ideas in a passage. Write a paraphrase note when you want to use material from a source but do not need to quote the exact words of the author. When you write a paraphrase, be careful to retain the author's intended meaning even though you are not quoting his or her words directly.

One method for writing a paraphrase note is to read the material carefully and then write the information or ideas in your own words without looking at the source. Check the source again to make sure that your paraphrase is accurate and that it still retains the author's meaning.

The following passage from a magazine article is the basis of the paraphrase note on the following page.

> Muscles are composed of two kinds of fibers—sprint and endurance fibers. No individual is all one or the other but rather a combination of types. The greater the precentage of sprint fibers, the better you are at stop-and-start sports. The greater the percentage of endurance fibers, the better you are at sports requiring a sustained level of activity.
>
> Use the Vertical Jump Test to determine your predominant muscle-fiber type. The higher you can jump, the more sprint fibers you have.
>
> "Does Your Sport Suit Your Body?" *Glamour*, p. 94

Paraphrase

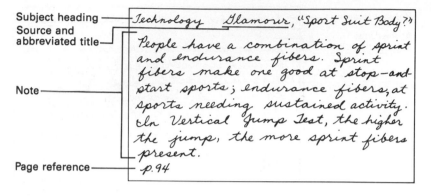

Subject heading — *Technology*   Glamour, "Sport Suit Body?"

Source and abbreviated title —

Note —

People have a combination of sprint and endurance fibers. Sprint fibers make one good at stop-and-start sports; endurance fibers, at sports needing sustained activity. In Vertical Jump Test, the higher the jump, the more sprint fibers present.

Page reference — p. 94

Summary

A **summary** is a condensed form of a passage. Write a summary in your own words, including only the main points and the most important supporting details. Writing a summary is a good way of taking notes when you are doing research for a paper. A summary is especially useful when you are recording ideas, facts, statistics, and other information from long passages. When you write a summary, look for key words in the passage and include them in your summary.

The following passage is the basis of the summary note on the following page.

> "We see the body as a mechanical system," says mechanical engineer Ali Seireg. "Therefore we should be able to describe human motions as a series of equations, feed those equations into a computer, and get useful information about how humans move and how to help them when they cannot move correctly." Dr. Seireg is most enthusiastic, however, about the simulated surgery he can perform using the model. Sitting at a video terminal, he is able to alter hypothetical bones and muscles and then see how such tinkering affects a patient's walk. This will aid surgeons when they remove pieces of bone to correct such conditions as knock-knees. In fact, Seireg has already conducted predictive surgery for a physician preparing to perform a difficult operation on a child in Milwaukee.
>
> "A Study in Motion," *Science Digest,* p. 97

Summary

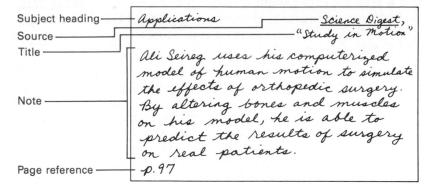

Subject heading —— *Applications*

Source ——

Title ——

Science Digest, "*Study in Motion*"

Note ——

Ali Seireg uses his computerized model of human motion to simulate the effects of orthopedic surgery. By altering bones and muscles on his model, he is able to predict the results of surgery on real patients.

Page reference —— *p. 97*

Exercise 2   Prewriting: Taking Notes   You are writing a research paper about customs in ancient Greek theater. You want to take notes on the information in the following passage. Using the subject heading "Audience response," write on your paper one note that is a direct quotation. Using the same subject heading, write another note that is a paraphrase.

> Performances began at dawn, and wealthy citizens often sent their slaves ahead of them to hold seats. The less wealthy members of the audience came, often in the hours of darkness before dawn, and milled about the entrances for vantage points from which to get the seats they wished when they were allowed to enter the theater. Everyone was in a festive mood, and there was much quarreling over particularly advantageous locations. The spectators wore garlands on their heads and brought lunch, and sometimes sunhats and cushions, for it would be a long day. The audience was critical and was not slow in letting its opinion be known. Unpopular plays were often hooted from the theater, and unpopular actors pelted with figs, olives, nuts, and even stones. The actor Aeschines nearly lost his life in such a stone barrage, it is said, and thereafter retired from the theater permanently. Applause was as much in order then as now, and it is difficult to conceive that the judges were not influenced by the public reception of the various productions.
>
> Vera Mowry Roberts, *On Stage,* p. 25

Exercise 3   Prewriting: Writing a Summary   You are writing a research paper about modern agriculture. You want to take notes on the information in the following passage. Using the heading "Potato—industrial uses," write on your paper a note that summarizes the following passage.

> The potato is one of the most important crops grown in the world today. On a yearly basis, over 10 billion bushels are produced by the potato-growing regions around the world. Most potatoes are grown as food, and while potatoes are not as nutritious as rice, they do have substantial food value. Almost 20 percent of the potato is carbohydrate, 2 percent is protein, and 78 percent is water. In Europe potatoes are grown for human and animal consumption both, while in America, only a small percentage of the potato crop is used for animal feed. In both Europe and America, potatoes are used in industry. Potato starch is used as sizing on paper and textiles. Dextrin, a product made from potato starch, is used as a coating for photographic film and as a paste. Potato starch can also be chemically converted into butyl and ethyl alcohols valuable to industry.

> Fillmore, *Agriculture*, pp. 23–24

Assignment   Prewriting   Find a short article in a magazine or newspaper. Read the article and write four note cards based on it. Make one note a direct quotation, one a paraphrase, one a summary, and one a combination by using a direct quotation in either a summary or a paraphrase. Give each note card a subject heading.

Continuing Assignment   Prewriting   In the Continuing Assignment on page 493, you prepared a working bibliography. Using those sources, take notes for each part of your rough outline. Use the type of note that is most appropriate for the information that you are recording. Save your note cards.

Assignment Checklist

Check your assignments for the following points:

    ✔ 1. Did you record information from your sources on note cards, using direct quotations, paraphrases, and summaries?

✔ 2. Did you include on each card a subject heading, the author's last name, an abbreviated title, and a page reference?

✔ 3. Did you copy quotations exactly?

✔ 4. Did you put quotation marks around *all* direct quotations?

✔ 5. Did you write the paraphrases entirely in your own words?

✔ 6. Did you write summaries that cover the key points that interest you?

11.4 Organizing Your Information

Revising Your Preliminary Thesis Statement

Now that you have gathered information from your sources, you may need to revise your preliminary thesis statement so that it accurately reflects the information and the conclusions that you are about to present. Review your notes carefully and compare your preliminary thesis statement with your research findings.

Your thesis statement must be expressed precisely because your entire paper will be developed from it. The following example shows the revision of the preliminary thesis statement for the research paper on biomechanics.

Preliminary thesis statement: Biomechanics will soon become an important aspect of our daily lives.

Revised thesis statement: Because of the rapid advances made in this science, biomechanics will someday affect the lives of everyone, athlete and nonathlete alike.

Making a Detailed Outline

The next step in preparing to write your research paper is to organize your ideas into a detailed outline such as the one on page 503. Use the following procedure in preparing your detailed outline.

Procedure

1. *Sort your cards according to their subject headings.* Keep together the cards having the same or similar subject headings.

2. *Use the subject headings on your groups of note cards to determine the main headings of your outline.* Review your rough outline. If some of the headings on your rough outline do not support your revised thesis statement, eliminate them. Using your note-card headings, add new main headings that support your thesis statement. Then arrange your headings in chronological order, in order of importance, or by cause and effect. Choose the arrangement that is best suited to your topic and your thesis statement.

3. *Add subheadings under each main heading,* using the information on your note cards. Note that you may not be able to use all the notes that you have taken. Use only the ones that support your thesis statement, and eliminate the others.

4. *Assign a Roman numeral to each main heading.* Use *I* for the introduction, and number the conclusion as well. Assign a capital letter to each subheading. If the outline contains further details under the subheading, assign Arabic numerals to those details. If the details in Arabic numerals require subheadings, assign small letters to them.

5. *Write all corresponding headings in parallel grammatical form.* For example, in a topic outline, such as the one on the facing page, if the heading for *A* is a phrase, the headings for *B, C,* and *D* should be the same kind of phrase. If you are preparing a sentence outline, write each heading as a complete sentence.

6. *Subdivide a topic into at least two sections,* or else eliminate it or make it part of another group. Do not have an *A* without a *B,* or a *1* without a *2.*

After you have organized your research findings, you should have a thesis statement and a detailed outline similar to those on the facing page. The outline is a plan for the model research paper on pages 521–534.

Thesis statement: Because of the rapid advances made in this science, biomechanics will someday affect the lives of everyone, athlete and nonathlete alike.

    I. Introduction
   II. Uses of biomechanics in sports training
      A. Traditional approach to training
        1. Exercises for long jumpers
        2. Training for baseball players
      B. Biomechanical discoveries about training
      C. Implications for training
  III. Technology involved in biomechanics
      A. Tests that measure performance and efficiency
        1. Oxygen consumption
        2. Weight distribution
        3. Traits for running
      B. Photography and light technology
      C. Computers for diagnosis and prediction
        1. Mac Wilkins's improved performance
        2. Terry Albritton's improved performance
  IV. Medical uses of biomechanics
      A. Recreational counseling
      B. Rehabilitative programs
        1. Surgery
        2. Medical products
   V. Business and industrial uses
      A. Sports equipment and clothing
      B. Industrial robots
  VI. Conclusion

Taking Additional Notes

Your outline enables you to check the sequence of your ideas and to rearrange the order, if necessary. Your outline also shows you the amount of support that you have for each major point. It is not necessary to give equal support to each heading, but if some topics need additional development, continue your research until you have enough information. It will be easier for you to write your paper once you have adequate support and a clear outline of your ideas.

Exercise 1   Prewriting: Outlining   Prepare an outline for each thesis statement and set of note-card headings. Arrange the subheadings under the appropriate main headings. Arrange the main headings and subheadings in a logical order.

1. *Thesis statement:* Methods of trying persons accused of crimes have changed drastically through the centuries.

   HEADINGS

   How trial by jury is different now
   Trials in the eleventh and twelfth centuries
   Other forms of Anglo-Saxon trials

   SUBHEADINGS

   Anglo-Saxon trial by ordeal
   Jury a step in formation of representative government
   Norman "inquests," or trials, after 1066
   Anglo-Saxon trial by compurgation (neighbors swear to a person's innocence)
   In jury trial evidence, reason replaces superstition, force, luck
   Twelfth-century trials—case decided by testimony of witnesses
   Anglo-Saxon trial by combat

2. *Thesis statement:* Thousands of years before steel was invented, people learned to make useful tools and weapons from iron.

   HEADINGS

   End of Iron Age, 1500–1850
   Iron-making in the Middle Ages, 500–1500
   Iron-making before A.D. 500

   SUBHEADINGS

   Production of iron in China 4500 years ago
   Steel Age begins mid-nineteenth century
   Middle Ages iron used for nails, tools, plows, armor
   Better furnaces developed A.D. 1200
   Iron from meteorites used in making tools 6000 years ago
   Catalan furnace invented 400 B.C.
   Roman legions used iron weapons 2000 years ago

Exercise 2   Prewriting: Outlining   Prepare a topic outline that develops the thesis statement. Use the note cards provided. The outline following the thesis statement shows the number of main headings, subheadings, and details that you will need. Provide for an introduction and a conclusion. Notice the subject headings of the note cards (Major parts of the eye, Eye and brain, The mind's eye); these are the three main headings II through IV. Supply the subheadings and details from the information in the notes.

Thesis statement: Our sense of sight depends as much on the brain as on the eye.

I. Introduction
II. ?
   A. ?
      1. ?
      2. ?
   B. ?
      1. ?
      2. ?
   C. ?
      1. ?
      2. ?
      3. ?
III. ?
   A. ?
      1. ?
      2. ?
   B. ?
IV. ?
   A. ?
   B. ?
      1. ?
      2. ?
V. Conclusion

NOTE 1

Major parts of the eye   Henderson, *Anatomy*
The outer layers of the eyeball are the *cornea* and the *aqueous humor:* together they form an outer lens through which light passes.
p. 45

(Continue on the next page.)

NOTE 2

Major parts of the eye   Mackey and Janson, *Vision*
A colored ring (*iris*) and a black center spot (*pupil*) lie just behind
the aqueous humor in the human eye. Light passes through the pupil
(but not the iris) to the lens. These are middle structures in the eye.
p. 78

NOTE 3

Major parts of the eye   G. Peterson, *Visual Perception*
The *lens* and *ciliary muscle* act together. The lens is a double convex
lens that acts like a magnifying glass. The ciliary muscle holds the
lens in place and changes its shape to make it possible to *focus* on
objects at different distances from the viewer. "Young children can
see objects clearly at 2½ inches, but older people must hold objects
farther and farther from the eye in order to see them clearly because the lens becomes less elastic as one gets older."
p. 329

NOTE 4

Eye and brain   Forman, *Eye Disorders*
The act of seeing begins with the multi-layered *retina,* which covers
the inner back part of the eyeball.
p. 56

NOTE 5

Eye and brain   G. Peterson, *Visual Perception*
One layer in the retina is the layer of *rods* and *cones.* Cones (about
6 million) detect fine lines and points and possibly color. Rods
(about 115 million) detect light and dark shades. Rods and cones
transmit impulses (not light) to the optic nerve.
p. 128

NOTE 6

> Eye and brain   Franklin, *The Nervous System*
> The *optic nerve* transmits nerve impulses to the "visual center" of
> the brain where the image is perceived. The brain also sends signals
> back to the muscles that control eye movement.
> p. 92

NOTE 7

> The mind's eye   L. Peterson, *Visual Disorders*
> It is in the brain that the image of what is seen is perceived. "The
> brain must learn to interpret the impulses received from the eye."
> This is *visual perception*.
> p. 34

NOTE 8

> The mind's eye   Mackey and Janson, *Vision*
> *Images* are received by the brain *upside-down*. The brain must learn
> that what appears to be at the lower part of the retina is actually the
> upper part of the object. The brain interprets *distance* of an object
> by comparing the images received from each eye. If the object is
> very close to the eye, the images are quite different. If the object is
> far away, the images are similar.
> p. 106

Assignment   Prewriting   Write five factors that contributed to
a historical event with which you are familiar. Outline those factors in
a logical order, using related data, such as causes, effects, major
leaders, and so on, as subheadings. Write a thesis statement and
place it at the top of your outline.

Continuing Assignment   Prewriting   *Step 1:* Read through
the note cards that you prepared for the Continuing Assignment on
page 500. If necessary, revise your thesis statement. *Step 2:* Separate
your note cards according to subject headings. Use your rough
outline and your note cards to write a detailed topic outline for your

paper. *Step 3:* Examine your note cards and your revised outline. If any parts of the outline do not have sufficient support, find additional sources and take notes to complete your research.

Assignment Checklist

Check your assignment for the following points:

  ✔ 1. Did you arrange the headings in a logical order?

  ✔ 2. Did you fully consider causes, effects, and other elements that could be listed as subheadings on your outline?

  ✔ 3. Did you write a thesis statement and place it at the beginning of your outline?

Check your Continuing Assignment for these points:

  ✔ 4. Did you revise your thesis statement if your new information helped you to focus it?

  ✔ 5. Did you separate your note cards by subject headings?

  ✔ 6. Did you write a topic outline that is well organized and includes all major and supporting points?

  ✔ 7. Did you take additional notes if you did not have enough supporting information for a point?

11.5 Drafting and Documenting Your Paper

11.5a Writing Your First Draft

    Once you have prepared the detailed outline and have arranged your note cards in an order corresponding to your outline, you are ready to write the first draft of your paper. Plan to write the paragraphs for each Roman numeral section in one sitting. Doing so will help you to focus on the topic of that section.

    Your main purpose in your first draft is to write down all of your major points and supporting information in a logical order. Write the first draft carefully, but remember that it is only a first draft. You can improve your word choice and sentence structure when you revise the paper.

Write your draft on every other line and only on one side of the paper. This procedure will make it easier for you to revise. Number each page.

The Introduction.   Write one or two paragraphs of introduction to explain the purpose and the scope of the paper. Include the thesis statement and enough background information to make it clear. Use the introduction also to capture your reader's interest, to explain the significance of the topic, to define terms, and to tell how the paper is organized.

The Body.   In the body of the paper, develop each heading on the outline, using the information on your note cards. Keep in mind that your objective is to support or prove your thesis statement by setting out in a logical way the information that you have gathered.

Where direct words from a source are important in making a point, use direct quotations, being careful to copy the words exactly. Use transitional words to incorporate the quotations into your paper.

The Conclusion.   Write a concluding paragraph that reviews all of your main points and shows that you have proved your thesis statement.

11.5b Documentation

You have included in your first draft the ideas and direct quotations that you recorded on your note cards. You must now document this information. **Documentation** is the process by which you acknowledge the sources of the information used in your research. Documentation includes footnotes and a bibliography.

Footnotes

A **footnote** gives the author and publication from which you have taken information. Whenever you use information that is not your own, footnote it. To do so, place a **superscript,** or raised number, in the text above the line at the end of the information. In the corresponding footnote, give the author and publication information. The following rules will help you to know when to use footnotes.

Rule   Footnote your source when you quote an author's exact words. Use direct quotations only when the author's wording is important or when the exact phrasing strengthens the point that you are making.

> "Before the model, we really had no way to determine what kinds of stresses were put on an injured joint," explains Dr. Murray. "Now we'll be able to develop rehabilitative exercises."[1]

Rule   Footnote your source when you use an author's idea, even though you have not used the author's exact words.

> Ariel also showed that, for baseball pitchers, training the wrist is useless, since the speed of the wrist movement is a result of a whip action of the legs, back, and shoulders, not a muscle contraction of the forearm.[2]

Rule   Footnote your source when you give figures or statistics.

> By following Ariel's advice, Wilkins increased his throw from 219 feet 1 inch to 232 feet 6 inches, broke the world record in discus throwing, and won an Olympic gold medal.[3]

You do not need to footnote information that is commonly known even though you did not previously know that information yourself. Information is considered to be commonly known if it appears in several sources. Try to avoid having too many footnotes in your paper. Remember to document all of your sources in order to avoid **plagiarism,** which is using someone else's words or ideas as if they were your own.

Footnote Forms.   Use the following forms to footnote various types of sources, unless your teacher suggests other styles of acknowledgment. Notice that you do not include the word *The* at the beginning of the title of a magazine, a newspaper, or an encyclopedia. Notice also that subtitles are not included in footnotes.

BOOK WITH ONE AUTHOR
[1]C. W. Thompson, *Manual of Structural Kinesiology,* 8th ed. (St. Louis: C. V. Mosby Company, 1977), p. 87.

BOOK WITH TWO AUTHORS

[2]John Piscopo and James A. Baley, *Kinesiology* (New York: John Wiley and Sons, 1981), p. 274.

BOOK COMPILED BY AN EDITOR

[3]Edmund J. Burke, ed., *Toward an Understanding of Human Performance* (Ithaca, N.Y.: Mouvement Publications, 1977), p. 17.

ARTICLE IN A COLLECTION

[4]Aileene S. Lockhart, "The Motor Learning of Children," in *A Textbook of Motor Development,* ed. Charles B. Corgin (Dubuque, Iowa: William C. Brown, 1973), pp. 96–97.

UNATTRIBUTED NEWSPAPER ARTICLE

[5]"Bill Rodgers Wins 10-Kilometer Atlanta Regional Race," *New York Times,* 3 May 1981, Sec. 5, p. 16, col. 4.

PERSONAL INTERVIEW

[6]Personal interview with Alex Humez, 9 April 1982.

MAGAZINE ARTICLE

[7]Jay Stuller, "Sports Scientists Train Athletes to Defy Old Limits," *Smithsonian,* July 1980, p. 67.

TELEVISION TRANSCRIPT

[8]"Race for Gold," narr. Hal Douglas; writ., prod., and dir. Paula S. Aspell, *Nova,* 1979.

ENCYCLOPEDIA ARTICLE

[9]"Biomechanics," *McGraw-Hill Encyclopedia of Science and Technology,* 1977 ed.

PAMPHLET

[10]U.S. Bureau of the Census, Department of Commerce, *Current Population Reports,* Special Studies, Series P 22, No. 59 (Washington D.C.: GPO, 1976), p. 1.

You may have to refer to a particular source more than once in your paper. Give complete information in the footnote for the first reference. In later references, called subsequent references, you need only identify the author (or the title if no author is given) and the page number, as shown here:

[5]Thompson, p. 106.

If you refer to more than one work by the same author, use a shortened form of the title to identify the particular work.

[10]Piscopo, *Clues to Safety,* p. 52.

Footnote Placement.   You may place your footnotes in either of the following positions. First, you may place the footnotes that go with the material on a particular page at the bottom of that page. Leave three blank lines between the text and the footnotes and single-space the footnotes. Second, you may place all the footnotes for the paper on a separate page at the end. Put *Notes* at the top of the page, and place the page before the bibliography. Double-space the footnotes and indent the first line of each one. Your teacher will tell you which placement to use.

Bibliography

The last page of your paper is the **bibliography.** It includes all the works listed in the footnotes. It may include the works that you read as general background before the writing but did not use as sources of specific ideas, facts, or direct quotations. Check with your teacher to see if you are to include such works in your bibliography. Arrange in alphabetical order the bibliography cards that you prepared when you were planning and researching your paper. (See page 490.) Make an entry for each card, using the following procedure.

Procedure

1. *Alphabetize bibliography entries by the authors' last names.* If a source does not have an author, alphabetize the entry by the first word in the title, omitting *A, An,* and *The.*

2. *Begin the first line of each entry at the left margin.* Indent the succeeding lines five spaces.

3. *Separate the parts of the entry with periods.*

4. *Include the subtitle if a source has one.*

5. *Give the author's name only in the first entry if there are two or more works by the same author.* In subsequent entries, use ten hyphens instead of the author's name, put a period after the last hyphen, and continue with the rest of the entry.

> Fulmer, Robert M. *Management and Organization.*
> New York: Harper and Row, 1980.
> ----------. *The New Management.* New York:
> Macmillan, 1982.

6. *Do not number the entries.*

7. *Alphabetize the entries by book titles when you are using more than one book by an author.*

Exercise 1 Writing: Footnotes On your paper, write footnotes for the following information. Use the item numbers as footnote numbers. Be sure to use correct punctuation.

AUTHOR	TITLE	PUBLICATION FACTS
Books		
1. Pierre Cabanne	*Pablo Picasso*	New York, New York Morrow 1977
2. Francoise Gilot and Carlton Lake	*Life with Picasso*	New York, New York McGraw-Hill 1964, p. 231
Article in a Book		
3. Meyer Shapiro	"Picasso's 'Woman with a Fan'"	*Modern Art: 19th & 20th Centuries: Selected Papers* New York, New York George Braziller 1979, pp.114–115

Periodicals

4. M. Stevens	"Picasso's Picassos"	*Newsweek* Oct. 22, 1979 pp. 126–127
5. Not given	"Nine Gatherings in a Mind"	*New Yorker* June 2, 1980 pp. 32–33
6. D. Trustman	"Ordeal of Picasso's Heirs"	*New York Times Magazine* April 20, 1980 pp. 42–46

Reference Book

7. Not given	"Pablo Picasso"	*Oxford Companion to Art* pp. 866–867

Exercise 2   Writing: Subsequent Footnotes   On your paper, write subsequent footnote entries using the information in Sources 1 through 5 in Exercise 1.

Exercise 3   Writing: Bibliography   On your paper, prepare a bibliography from the information in Exercise 1. Be sure to use correct punctuation and to alphabetize the entries.

Assignment   Writing   Using the note cards given and the outline that you prepared for Exercise 2 on page 504, write a first draft of two paragraphs for the body of a paper. Include one direct quotation.

Continuing Assignment   Writing   *Step 1:* Using the outline and the note cards that you prepared for the Continuing Assignments on pages 500 and 507, write a first draft of your research paper. Begin with an introduction that includes your thesis statement. Then write one section of your paper at a time. Write a conclusion that summarizes your main points. *Step 2:* Write your footnotes on a separate page, unless your teacher tells you to do otherwise. *Step 3:* Prepare a bibliography.

Assignment Checklist

Check your assignment for the following points:

- ✔ 1. Is the main idea of each paragraph clear?
- ✔ 2. Did you follow your outline, using the supporting information listed under each heading?
- ✔ 3. Did you correctly use direct quotations as needed?
- ✔ 4. Did you place a raised number after direct quotations?
- ✔ 5. Did you place a raised number after other information that you needed to footnote?

Check your Continuing Assignment for these additional points:

- ✔ 6. Did you write an introduction that includes your thesis statement?
- ✔ 7. Did you follow your outline, presenting your ideas in a logical way?
- ✔ 8. Did you write accurate footnotes for all of the quotations and ideas that you borrowed from sources?
- ✔ 9. Did you write a conclusion that summarizes the main points in the body of your paper?
- ✔ 10. Did you prepare the bibliography correctly?

11.6 Revising and Finishing Your Paper

After you have finished the first draft of your paper, put it aside for a while before beginning your revision. Doing so will make it easier for you to see where you need to improve organization, word choice, and sentence structure; to correct errors; and, in general, to make your paper more convincing and readable.

11.6a A Guide to Revising

Read through your draft carefully several times. Concentrate on one of the following points each time that you read, and make the necessary changes.

Organization. Refer to your outline and check to see that you have all of its points in correct order. It is not too late to reorganize or change sequence if doing so would improve your paper. If you do move a section, check to see that you have also moved any footnotes for that section. You must also change your outline to reflect the change in the paper.

Unity and Completeness.   Check each section for unity. Each supporting detail should clearly relate to the point being made in the section. In turn, each point being made should support or prove the thesis statement. Delete or rewrite any section that does not clearly relate to the point being made.

Be sure that there is enough information in each section to support each point. Use facts, examples, and quotations to show the reader what you mean.

Transitions.   Make your paper coherent by using transitional words and phrases. When you wrote the first draft, you concentrated on writing one section at a time. As you revise the paper, add appropriate transitions to lead the reader from one idea to the next. Use the following strategies to make smooth transitions.

Strategies

1. *Use transitional words and phrases.*

    TO SHOW TIME RELATIONSHIPS
    > *after, at the same time, finally, later, meanwhile, next, soon, then, until*

    TO PRESENT EXAMPLES
    > *for example, for instance, one, another, to illustrate*

    TO SHOW RESULTS
    > *as a result, consequently, for this reason, therefore*

    TO SHOW LOGICAL RELATIONSHIPS
    > *accordingly, also, because, however, in addition to, in fact, nevertheless, yet*

2. *Use a pronoun that refers to a person or an idea just mentioned in the preceding sentence or paragraph.*

    > *Long jumpers* appear to rise on their toes as they push off from the board. Traditionally *they* have trained by carrying heavy weights while rising on their toes.

3. *Repeat a key word or an idea from the last sentence of a paragraph in the first sentence of the next paragraph.*

> Indeed, the more we know about biomechanics and the more sophisticated the technology, the more possibilities for its *application* occur to us.
> Perhaps the *application* most closely allied to sports is in the field of recreational counseling.

Words and Sentences. Check to see that you have chosen the best words to express your ideas. Define any specialized terms that you have used.

To make your sentences effective, avoid wordiness. Combine short, choppy sentences into a single clear sentence. Separate long, confusing sentences into shorter, clearer ones. Use a variety of sentence structures and lengths to make your writing interesting. Check to see that you are consistent in point of view and in use of verb tense.

Proofreading. Read your paper once more to correct any errors in grammar, usage, spelling, punctuation, and capitalization. Make sure that your footnotes and bibliography are correct.

When you have completed all of the revisions and corrections, you will have a final draft. Choose a title that reflects the topic of your paper and will attract your readers' interest. Now you are ready to write or type your finished paper. The next section tells you how to do that.

Exercise 1 Revising: Sentences The following excerpt from a research paper needs revision. On your paper, write the letter of the suggested revision for the numbered sentence that you think would best improve the draft. If you think that a sentence is effective as it stands, write the letter that indicates *Make no change.*

(1) The material on which the ancient Egyptian scribes wrote was papyrus. (2) Papyrus was made from a sedge (a grasslike herb) native to the Nile River region. (3) Papyrus was once available in great quantities but is now almost extinct.

(4) Pliny, the Roman historian, describes the manufacture of papyrus sheets. (5) First the stalks were cut into lengths of about sixteen inches. (6) Then the marrow (inner part of the stalk) was

cut into strips.   (7) The strips were laid down in a row side by
side.   (8) Another layer of strips was placed on top of the first,
perpendicular to it.   (9) Both layers were saturated with a gum
solution and pressed and pounded until a smooth surface was
formed.   (10) The resulting sheets were about twelve inches long
and sixteen inches wide.   (11) These were glued together at the
sides to form a scroll.   (12) Sometimes the scrolls were cut in half
lengthwise (making a scroll six inches high), and sometimes they
were cut into quarters (making a scroll three inches high).   (13) Of
course, the smaller scrolls were easier to carry, so they were less
likely to be damaged.[1]

   (14)   Papyrus was a good material for paper-making because
the surface could be made smooth and it was available in large
quantities.   (15) When papyrus dried out, it was also easily damaged
by rain or dampness.   (16) Most papyrus scrolls that have been
found by archaeologists were preserved in dry, airtight Egyptian
tombs.

[1]Nancy Amanda Kellerman, *History of Printing* (New York:
Mark David Publishing Company, 1982), pp. 32–33.

1. Sentences 1 and 2
   a. Make no change.
   b. Combine the sentences to read: "The material on which the ancient
      Egyptian scribes wrote was made of papyrus, a sedge (grasslike
      herb) native to the Nile River region."
   c. Eliminate Sentence 2.

2. Sentence 3
   a. Eliminate the sentence.
   b. Make no change.
   c. Eliminate the sentence and the paragraph break.

3. Sentences 4 and 5
   a. Replace with "The manufacture of papyrus sheets began when the
      stalks were cut into lengths of about sixteen inches."
   b. Eliminate "First" at the beginning of Sentence 5.
   c. Make no change.

4. Sentences 6 and 7
   a. Make no change.
   b. Combine the sentences.
   c. Eliminate the parenthetical phrase in Sentence 6.

5. Sentences 8 and 9
   a. Add "Next" at the beginning of Sentence 8.
   b. Combine the sentences.
   c. Make no change.

6. Sentences 10 and 11
   a. Replace with "The resulting sheets, twelve inches high and sixteen inches wide, were glued together at the sides to form a scroll."
   b. Make no change.
   c. Replace with "The resulting sheets were twelve inches high and sixteen inches wide, and were glued together to form a scroll."

7. Sentences 12 and 13
   a. Make no change.
   b. Replace with "Since shorter scrolls were easier to handle and less likely to be damaged, the twelve-inch high scrolls were sometimes halved or quartered.[1]"
   c. Eliminate the footnote number.

8. Sentence 14
   a. Replace with "Papyrus was available in large quantities, so it was a good material for paper-making."
   b. Make no change.
   c. Add a footnote number.

9. Sentence 15
   a. Add "However," after the introductory clause.
   b. Combine with Sentence 14, using a comma and "and."
   c. Make no change.

10. Sentence 16
    a. Add the phrase "It is not surprising that" at the beginning.
    b. Eliminate the sentence.
    c. Make no change.

Exercise 2   Revising: Footnotes   Number your paper from 1 to 5. For each number, tell what is wrong with the corresponding footnote. Each footnote has one error or omission.

> **SAMPLE**   [1]Georges Duthuit and Madeleine Carson, *Twentieth-Century Painting* (New York: 1982), p. 29.
>
> **ANSWER**   Name of publishing company is missing.

[1]Katherine Bethune and Wanda Hopkins, eds., *A Pictorial History of Railroading* (Chicago: Mandrake Publishers, Inc.), pp. 56–59.

[2]Frank Lester, "Stocks and Bonds," 9 November 1982, Sec. C, p. 3, col. 3.

[3]*Piet Mondrian: Life and Work* (Boston: Houghton Mifflin Company, 1981), p. 67.

[4]Bruce Berenstein, "Vincent van Gogh: A Retrospective," *Burlington Magazine,* June 1974.

[5]*The Changing Universe,* dir. Marcy Davids, NBC Special.

Exercise 3 Revising: Bibliography Entries On your paper, tell what is wrong with the following bibliography entries. Each entry has one error or omission.

> **SAMPLE**   Wheeler, Michael. *French Graphic Art.* New York: 1978, Dover Publications, Inc.
>
> **ANSWER**   Date and name of publishing company are reversed.

1. Peter Legros. "Looking at the Economy." *Atlantic Monthly,* February 1968, pp. 92–100.
2. Wilson, Edward, and Abigail Schuster. *Higher Education in the United States.* New York: Harcourt.
3. *Mathematical Theory* by Henry Meyer. Washington, D.C.: Mt. Vernon Press, 1979.
4. Thule, Maria, and Robert Vasta, eds. *A Critical Anthology of Short Stories.* Chicago, 1980.
5. Gelfand, Margaret. *African Heritage.* 2nd ed. Paris: Lomat, 1970, pp. 34–56.

11.6b The Finished Paper

Your finished paper should include the following parts arranged in this order, unless your teacher has suggested an alternate format:

1. Title page
2. Outline
3. The written or typed paper
4. Notes (if you put your footnotes on a separate page)
5. Bibliography

Type your paper, if possible. If not, write it legibly, following the guidelines in Unit 3, "Mechanics," pages 208–209.

To prepare a title page, center the title halfway down the page. Capitalize the first word and all other words except articles, conjunctions, and prepositions of fewer than five letters. Do not underline the title or put quotation marks around it. Center the word *by* under the title and center your name under that. In the lower right section of the page, write your teacher's name, the name of the course, and the date.

A model research paper follows. (The outline is on page 503.)

```
              The Increasing Use of Biomechanics

                            by

                       Joyce Wilson




                                          Mr. Casey

                                          English IV

                                          May 3, 19__
```

In recent years many athletes and their coaches have used the principles of biomechanics to increase the quality of athletic performance. Biomechanics, a science that explores athletic movement, is not widely known outside the world of athletics. Soon, however, the term should be known to everyone. Because of the rapid advances made in this science, biomechanics will someday affect the lives of everyone, athlete and nonathlete alike.

One of the pioneers in the study of biomechanics is Peter Cavanagh, of the Biomechanics Laboratory at

Pennsylvania State University. He defines biomechanics as "the use of objective techniques to analyze patterns of body movement, the timing of body movements, and the forces that create or result from movement."[1] Mr. Cavanagh's studies and the studies of many of his colleagues have done much to advance athletic training and to improve performance.

In the past, coaches planned training and exercise programs based solely on the type of skill and the amount of strength required for a particular sport. As a result, all athletes engaged in the same sport followed the same program. The programs used for training in different sports were based on coaches' and sports physicians' best judgment about what produces excellent performance.[2]

Training programs were also frequently based on tradition. For example, long jumpers trained by rising on their toes while holding heavy weights. The purpose of this exercise was to strengthen the calf muscles, thereby giving the jumper a better push from the board.[3] It was believed that the stronger the push, the greater the distance that the jumper could cover.

Similarly, baseball pitchers traditionally trained to increase the strength of their forearm muscles on the assumption that a stronger forearm would mean a stronger wrist, which would enable the pitcher to throw harder. Biomechanics now shows that both the long jumper and the baseball pitcher were using ineffective training techniques.

Studies performed by Dr. Gideon Ariel of the University of Massachusetts, Amherst, proved the ineffectiveness of these and other training methods. Dr. Ariel, professor of exercise science, is a leading expert in the field of biomechanics. He showed that long jumpers do not point their toes until the pushing foot is already two feet off the ground. Therefore the exercise to strengthen the calf muscles is probably irrelevant to a successful jump. Dr. Ariel further showed that for baseball pitchers, training the wrist is useless, since the force of the wrist movement is a result of a whip action of the legs, back, and shoulders, not a muscle contraction in the forearm.[4]

These and other findings have greatly influenced the training of athletes. Since the early 1970s, when biomechanics began to grow as a science, coaches have stressed individual training programs for athletes. Since the human eye alone cannot determine how well an athlete performs or what errors he or she makes, coaches are using the technology of biomechanics to plan training programs that will lead to athletic excellence.

The technology used in biomechanics involves three major types of apparatus. First are the treadmill and other endurance-test mechanisms that measure performance and efficiency. Second are still cameras and movie cameras that record movement. Third are computers that aid in analysis and prediction.

The treadmill and other endurance—test mechanisms are
used to test and measure lung capacity, heart—lung
efficiency, motor ability, and flexibility. The purpose of
these tests is to determine whether an athlete has the
physical traits and the abilities needed for success in a
given sport.

A few years ago, Dr. David Costill, a sports
physiologist at Ball State University, was asked to perform
a series of tests on Bill Rodgers, the famous marathon
runner from Boston. Dr. Costill used the treadmill to test
Rodgers's suitability for long—distance running. The
treadmill measures an athlete's oxygen consumption, a
crucial factor in endurance sports. Rodgers's test results
showed an unusually high capacity for taking in oxygen.[5]

Another simple testing device, used by Peter Cavanagh
at Penn State, assesses weight distribution on the feet,
indicating potential problems in posture and balance that
could lead to inappropriate reactions in an athlete's
movements. Cavanagh, too, tested Bill Rodgers, who had
been told that a swinging motion of one of his arms was an
energy—wasting motion. However, tests showed that the arm
motion was necessary to offset an imbalance caused by a
slight difference in the length of Rodgers's legs. Without
that test, Rodgers might have been persuaded to do away with
this awkward arm movement, with possibly disastrous effects
on his running style.[6]

At the University of Denver, Dr. Marvin Clein, head of the Physical Education and Sports Science Department, uses a variety of simple tests and machines to evaluate the performance level of athletes. Dr. Clein looks not only at biomechanical traits, but also at the muscle—nerve and heart—blood vessel functions, as well as the psychological factors needed to make a successful athlete. One of his most interesting stories concerns Leslie Covillo, a fourteen—year—old girl who wanted desperately to be a track star. Except for her long legs, however, Leslie appeared to have few of the physical traits needed for success in track. After careful testing of balance, reflex time, and body proportion, Dr. Clein discovered that "she had the things that give her a mechanical advantage on the track: a great nervous system and the perfect body build for running."[7] Further testing showed that Leslie also had good psychological traits, as well as physiological ones, that could be developed through a carefully prescribed training program. All of the testing paid off; in her first year on the junior high track team, Leslie Covillo set five records and qualified for the Junior Olympics in three events.[8]

The technology of biomechanics also includes still cameras, movie cameras, and other uses of light. In the nineteenth century, it was discovered that cameras with fast—acting shutters could freeze the image of small segments of motion on film. Later, new high—speed cameras produced slow-motion action that showed the patterns of motion in successful athletic activity. These and other advances in light technology were important forerunners in biomechanical technology because they made possible the first study of individual movement.

In addition to slow-motion photography, there are special cameras, called photocyclographs, that can record a panoramic view of a course of motion. There are also stroboscopes, electronic flashes that light up a moving object on a screen with frequent flashes of light and have the effect of extending the time over which a particular motion can be seen.

Finally, when lights are attached to a hand, an arm, a leg, or a foot, a camera can be used to make a light trace of a motion. In other words, the track of the movement is recorded, or traced, by the camera. 9 All of these uses of the camera make it possible to see individual movements with great clarity and detail.

The relationships between an athlete's many moving parts are so complex that they cannot be adequately analyzed simply by looking at the slowest of motion pictures. 10 Nor can they be assessed by closely examining still photographs. Computer analyses of photographs provide detailed outlines of an athlete's strengths and weaknesses, suggesting ways in which he or she can improve. Dr. Ariel often uses a

digitizer pen to trace joints that appear as stick figures
on a computer display terminal.[11]   The computer can show how
an action as minor as moving a foot a few inches can
drastically alter an athlete's performance.

Mac Wilkins, a discus thrower, is one of several
athletes who have benefited from Dr. Ariel's analysis. Dr.
Ariel studied photographs of Wilkins in action and then fed
that visual record into a computer. At the time, Wilkins's
record for discus throwing was 219'9''. The world record
was 226'8''. According to Dr. Ariel's analysis, not only
could Wilkins match the world record, but he could even
surpass it. The analysis showed that by altering a leg
movement that was limiting his throw, Wilkins was capable of
throwing the discus two hundred and fifty feet. By altering
his stance, Wilkins went on to reach 232'6'', breaking the
world record and winning an Olympic gold medal.[12]

Gideon Ariel, Marvin Clein, and Peter Cavanagh are only
three of a fast-growing number of scientists and coaches
throughout the world who are devoting their professional
lives to the study and application of biomechanics. Their
work is directly responsible for improved performances by
both amateur and professional athletes. The application of
biomechanics is not limited to achievement in athletic
performance, however. As knowledge of biomechanics
increases, so do the possibilities for its use.

One increasing use of biomechanics is in the field of recreational counseling. Many people interested in physical fitness like to engage in recreational sports but may not know the sports for which they are best suited. Although a person's choice of recreational sport does not have to be determined solely by the potential for success, participating in a sport at which a person is successful makes exercising more pleasant and rewarding.

Dr. Robert Arnot, a sports physiologist, has created a set of tests simple enough to be performed at home. The results can be used to indicate which sports are compatible with a person's body traits. One test shows whether muscle fibers indicate success in sprint or endurance sports. A person having more sprint fibers is better suited to the hundred-yard dash, high jumping, or a game such as volleyball, all of which require short bursts of activity. A person with more endurance fibers is better suited to a sport such as distance running or cross-country biking. According to Dr. Arnot, the higher one can jump vertically, the better one should be at stop-and-start sports requiring sprint fibers.[13]

The medical profession is also making use of the science of biomechanics. Dr. Ali Seireg and his students at the University of Wisconsin worked for over ten years on finding ways to improve physical rehabilitation. As a

result of their efforts, they now have a computerized model
of every human movement, from walking to chewing.[14]

Using these models, Dr. Patricia Murray of the Veterans
Administration Hospital in Milwaukee has been able to
identify the best way to help a patient with an injured hip
learn to walk again. From data on the patient's size,
weight, and injury, the computer produces information,
including the best way for the patient to use a cane.
"Before, we really had no way to determine what kinds of
stress were put on an injured joint," explains Dr. Murray.
"Now we'll be able to develop the most advantageous
rehabilitative exercises."[15] Dr. Seireg has also used his
computerized models to simulate the effects of orthopedic
surgery. By altering the placement of bones and muscles on
his computer model, he is able to predict the results of
surgery on real patients.

There is growing evidence that biomechanics will soon
be applied to an increasing number of commonplace activities
in daily life. Popular and specialized magazines frequently
contain articles informing readers about the potential role
of biomechanics in achieving grace, efficiency, and comfort
in such activities as dancing, sitting, carrying groceries,
preparing meals, and dressing. One such article, in
Mademoiselle magazine, shows how to put on shoes while
standing, without losing one's balance. The key is to lean
forward slightly and to bring the knee straight up. Doing

so places one's weight on the ball of the other foot and
reduces the chance of falling.
16

Business and industry also reflect the increasing interest in biomechanics. A natural outgrowth of the study of athletic performance has been the development of sports equipment and clothing designed to enhance athletic performance. Track shoes, tennis balls, tennis racquets, javelins, poles used in pole vaulting, and exercise machines designed for home use are examples of the many items that have been redesigned as a result of increased knowledge of biomechanics.
17

In industry, knowledge in the field of the science of motion has also fostered significant improvements in the construction of industrial robots that have begun to take over some of the work of humans. For example, engineers who design robots have studied how muscles work to make the fingers move. They can now construct robots that move their "fingers" in the same way. Engineers simply use rods, wires, pulleys, motors, and a microprocessor in place of bones, muscles, and brains.
18

Clearly the science of biomechanics has had increasing influence on many aspects of daily life. Its possible uses seem endless. With further studies and further advances in technology, biomechanics may someday influence every move a person makes.

Notes

1
John Jerome, "The Biomechanical Effect," Esquire,

April 1980, p. 116.
2
Kenny Moore, "Gideon Ariel and His Magic Machine,"

Sports Illustrated, 22 August 1977, pp. 56–57.
3
Moore, p. 56.
4
"Race for Gold," narr. Hal Douglas; writ., prod., and

dir. Paula S. Aspell, Nova, 1979, pp. 8–12.
5
"Race for Gold," p. 14.
6
Jay Stuller, "Sports Scientists Train Athletes to Defy

Old Limits," Smithsonian, July 1980, p. 69.
7
Stuller, pp. 69–70.
8
J. Wartenweiler, "Status Report on Biomechanics," in

Medicine and Sport: Vol. 8, Biomechanics III, (Basel:

Karger, 1973), p. 67.
9
Moore, p. 55.
10
"Shape-up Now," Vogue, February 1980, p. 135.
11
Moore, p. 56.
12
Moore, p. 56.
13
"Does Your Sport Suit Your Body?" Glamour, May 1982,

p. 94.
14
John Piscopo and James A. Baley, Kinesiology (New

York: John Wiley and Sons, 1981), pp. 94–105.
15
"A Study in Motion," Science Digest, March 1982, p. 97.

16

"The Right Way to Move," <u>Mademoiselle,</u> October 1979,

p. 165.

17

"A Study in Motion," p. 97.

18

Moore, pp. 56–57, 59.

Bibliography

Ariel, G. "Use of Computers to Analyze Human Movement."

People, 24 September 1979, pp. 80–82.

"Bill Rodgers Wins 10–Kilometer Atlanta Regional Race." <u>New</u>

<u>York Times,</u> 3 May 1981, Sec. 5, p. 16, col. 4.

"Biomechanics." <u>McGraw–Hill Encyclopedia of Science and</u>

<u>Technology.</u> 1977 ed.

Burke, Edmund, J., ed. <u>Toward an Understanding of Human</u>

<u>Performance.</u> Ithaca, N.Y.: Mouvement Publications,

1977.

"Does Your Sport Suit Your Body?" <u>Glamour,</u> May 1982, pp.

94–95.

Frolich, Cliff. "The Physics of Somersaulting and

Twisting." <u>Scientific American,</u> March 1980, pp.

154–158.

Garfinkel, Perry. "Computer Readout Translates Body

Language into Skills." <u>Science Digest,</u> March 1977,

pp. 12–14.

Humez, Alex. Personal interview. 9 April 1982.

Jerome, John. "The Biomechanical Effect." <u>Esquire,</u> April

1980, pp. 116–117.

Lockhart, Aileene S. "The Motor Learning of Children." In

    A Textbook of Motor Development. Ed. Charles B.

    Corbin. Dubuque, Iowa: Wm. C. Brown Company

    Publishers, 1973, pp. 151–157.

Logan, Gene A., and Wayne C. McKinney. Kinesiology.

    Dubuque, Iowa: Wm. C. Brown Company Publishers, 1970.

Moore, Kenny. "Gideon Ariel and His Magic Machine."

    Sports Illustrated, 22 August 1977, pp. 52–60.

Muybridge, Eadweard. Animals in Motion. Ed. Lewis S.

    Brown. New York: Dover Publications, 1957.

Piscopo, John, and James A. Baley. Kinesiology: The

    Science of Movement. New York: John Wiley and Sons,

    1981.

"Race for Gold." Narr. Hal Douglas. Writ., prod., and dir.

    Paula S. Aspell, Nova. 1979.

Rasch, Philip J., and Roger K. Burke. Kinesiology and

    Applied Anatomy: The Science of Human Movement, 5th

    ed. Philadelphia: Lea & Feibiger, 1975.

"The Right Way to Move." Mademoiselle, October 1979, pp.

    164–169.

"Shape–up Now." Vogue, February 1980, p. 135.

"A Study in Motion." Science Digest, March 1982, p. 97.

Stuller, Jay. "Sports Scientists Train Athletes to Defy Old

    Limits." Smithsonian, July 1980, pp. 66–75.

Thompson, Clem W. Manual of Structural Kinesiology. 8th

    ed. St. Louis: C. V. Mosby Company, 1979.

U.S. Bureau of the Census, Department of Commerce. <u>Current</u>
   <u>Population Reports:</u> <u>Demographic Aspects of Aging and</u>
   <u>the Older Population in the United States,</u> (Special
   Studies, Series P 22, No. 59) Washington, D.C.: GPO, 1976.

Walker, Jearl. "The Amateur Scientists: In Judo and Aikido
   Application of the Physics of Forces Makes the Weak
   Equal the Strong." <u>Scientific American,</u> July 1980,
   pp. 150–159.

Wartenweiler, J. "Status Report on Biomechanics." In
   <u>Medicine and Sport: Volume 8, Biomechanics III.</u>
   Basel: Karger, 1973, pp. 65–72.

Wells, Katharine F. <u>Kinesiology,</u> 4th ed. Philadelphia:
   W.B. Saunders Company, 1966.

Welsh, Raymond. "The Limits of Movement: What Kinesiology
   Can Teach the Dancer." <u>Dance Magazine,</u> January 1980,
   p. 86.

Exercise 4   Revising: Analyzing a Research Paper   Write
answers to the following questions about the model research paper.

1. In the thesis statement, the writer says that biomechanics has had
   increasing influence in many aspects of daily life. In what aspects of
   daily life, outside of athletics, are those influences seen?
2. Copy the topic sentences of two paragraphs that contain examples.
3. What point in the introduction is reinforced in the conclusion?
4. List five examples of transitional words or phrases used to relate
   sentences.
5. List five examples of transitional words or phrases used to relate
   paragraphs.

Assignment   Revising   Revise the first draft of the paragraphs that you wrote for the Assignment on page 514. Be sure that the paragraphs are clear and complete and that you have made a transition between them.

Continuing Assignment   Revising   *Step 1:* Revise the draft that you prepared for the Continuing Assignment on page 514. Go over your draft as many times as you need to in order to improve your paper as much as you can. *Step 2:* Prepare your finished research paper. Follow the manuscript form given on pages 208–209, or follow your teacher's specific guidelines. Make a final copy of your notes page and bibliography page. Be sure to proofread your finished paper for correct spelling, punctuation, and capitalization.

Assignment Checklist

Check your assignment for the following points:

- ✔ 1. Did you develop each paragraph sufficiently?
- ✔ 2. Did you revise your paper to make all paragraphs unified?
- ✔ 3. Did you make clear transitions between paragraphs?

Check your Continuing Assignment for these additional points:

- ✔ 4. Did you check the organization of your draft against your outline?
- ✔ 5. Do all the points in your paper support the thesis statement?
- ✔ 6. Is each point clearly stated and developed?
- ✔ 7. Is your paper unified?
- ✔ 8. Did you connect your ideas with transitions?
- ✔ 9. Is your finished paper neat and free of errors?

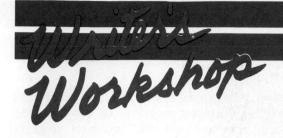

Puritans and Progress: A Research Paper

Situation: *Colonial Heritage Quarterly* is preparing a special issue on factors in America's heritage that have had a great impact on American life. As a staff writer, you have been asked to answer the question, "What effect did the Puritans have on the cultural life of New England?" You want to give the editor a thesis statement and two sample paragraphs from the article that you are preparing. As you write, you will keep in mind the following information.

Writer: you as a magazine staff writer

Audience: editor and readers of the magazine

Topic: the Puritans' effect on the cultural life of New England

Purpose: to investigate the topic and to present your findings

Directions: To plan and write your paper, follow these steps.

Step 1. Read the memo from your editor and the notes from your preliminary research in the library, which are on the following pages.

Step 2. Use the following model to construct a thesis statement:

The Puritans influenced (*what areas? literature? art?*) and were a (*major/minor*) factor in the cultural life of New England.

Step 3. Expand in outline form the first topic (literature) mentioned in the editor's memo. Use your library notes to find three main points and the supporting details that fully illustrate them.

(Continue on page 538.)

Notes from Library Sources

"Puritanism, A Factor in Colonial America," by Frank Weber, in
Liberty Magazine, Vol. X, No. 2, Sept. 1982.

—Puritanism: "that philosophy of life, that code of values, that
   religious point of view carried to New England from Great
   Britain in the first part of the seventeenth century."
—Force of Puritanism inspired traits that have persisted until
   today.
—Any discussion of the elements that went into the making of the
   mind of the early New Englander must begin with Puritanism.
—Puritans contributed greatly to moral codes, social modes,
   education, speech, and literature.
—Puritan "zeal" for recording everything.
—Great number of histories, journals, diaries, from the colonial
   period.
—Their language had a "clarity, directness, and grace that became
   the basis for all American literature." (p. 12)
—Puritans emphasized "the fruitfulness of the land and the
   goodness of God's protection." (p. 12)
—Books include William Wood's New England's Prospect, John
   Winthrop's Journal, William Bradford's Of Plimouth Plantation,
   and Cotton Mather's The Ecclesiastical History of New England.
—Puritans produced more poetry than other colonists.
—Like their prose, the Puritans' poetry was dedicated to serious
   matters (instructing people how to live a purposeful life).
—Poetry volumes were popular and abundant, including The Whole
   Book of Psalms (written by the ministers Richard Mather, John
   Eliot, Thomas Welde); Anne Bradstreet's The Tenth Muse Lately
   Sprung Up in America; Michael Wigglesworth's Day of Doom.

Main Currents in American Thought, Vernon Louis Parrington, New
York, 1954, Vol. 1.

—Puritan New England was the source of "such ideals and
   institutions as have come to be regarded as traditionally
   American." (p. 3)

(continued on the next page)

Memo from Editor
RE: Article on the Puritans
Include the following areas in your article, and
let me see your introductory paragraph and a
paragraph developing one of the items below.

   I. Overall effect of Puritans on cultural life
      in New England
  II. Notable areas of contribution
      A. Literature   D. Science
      B. Education   E. Government
      C. Art and architecture

537

Step 4. Write an introductory paragraph that explains the purpose and scope of your article. Include your thesis statement. Capture the reader's interest with a quotation that emphasizes the significance of the topic. Define Puritanism, and cite the areas that you will discuss. Footnote direct quotations.

Step 5. Using your outline, write the paragraph on the first topic. Footnote direct quotations. Use such transitional words and phrases as *in fact* or *also.*

Step 6. Read over the two paragraphs. Are they well organized? Does each sentence flow smoothly into the next? Proofread for errors in spelling, punctuation, and grammar.

Perry Miller and Thomas H. Johnson, eds. The Puritans: A Sourcebook of Their Writers, New York, 1963, Vol. 1.

—Miller: "Prose was the vehicle for their finest thought" and promoted "the spread of the powerful idiom for all men to use."

The Cultural Life of the American Colonies, by Louis B. Wright, New York, 1957.

—Puritan New England "produced more histories . . . and personal journals than all the rest of British America." (p. 164)
—The Puritans emphasized "the importance of writing history to record God's particular favor to his people of New England. This attitude helps to explain the Puritans' zeal for recording every act and deed that concerned them, and it lies behind a succession of histories written during the colonial period." (p. 159)

Unit Assignments

Assignment 1 Write a research paper on a significant period in the history of art, music, or dance. For example, you might discuss the growth, development, and importance of modern dance. You may want to include persons who have made significant contributions to modern dance.

Assignment 2 Write a research paper on a topic related to medical science. For example, you might prepare a paper on human sleep patterns. Narrow your topic to some aspect of sleep, such as dreaming or sleepwalking. Include up-to-date sources in your research.

Assignment 3 Write a research paper on an issue of current political interest. Consider, for example, possible changes in the electoral college system of electing the President and Vice President or in the primary election system of choosing presidential candidates.

Assignment 4 Write a research paper on a historic or contemporary person whose accomplishments you admire. You might choose Frederick Law Olmstead, for example, and prepare a paper on his contributions to modern landscape architecture.

Assignment 5 Prepare a research paper on a topic of particular interest to high-school students. For example, you might discuss strategies for choosing a career, how to start a small business, or a law that affects teen-agers. Be sure that your paper is well organized and properly documented.

Revising Your Assignments

For help in revising a research paper, consult the Checklist for Revision on the last page of this book.

Unit Tests

Test 1

A.   Number your paper from 1 to 5. Next to each number, write *True* if the sentence is true or *False* if it is false.

1. The thesis statement for a research paper is a sentence that states what you intend to prove in the paper.
2. You should prepare a working bibliography for your research after you have written a topic outline of your ideas.
3. Only the most important direct quotations need to be enclosed in quotation marks.
4. After you have completed your rough outline, you should write a first draft of your paper.
5. In your bibliography you need not include sources that you acknowledge in footnotes.

B.   Number your paper from 6 to 10. Next to each number, write the letter of the term that correctly completes the sentence. You will use all but one of the items.

        a. bibliography   d. Dewey decimal system
        b. footnote   e. thesis statement
        c. card catalog   f. periodical indexes

6. You can find sources of information in newspapers and magazines in __?__.
7. An alphabetical list of the books, magazines, and other sources used in preparing a research paper is called a __?__.
8. You should begin your research by consulting the __?__ to see what works are available on your topic.
9. In some libraries, books are arranged according to the __?__.
10. When you borrow information from a source, as in a direct quotation, you must document that information by writing a __?__.

C.   Number your paper from 11 to 15. Next to each number, write the letter of the item that correctly answers the question.

11. Which of the following is specific enough for a research-paper topic?

        a. Modern art   c. How people paint
        b. Museums   d. Van Gogh's style of painting

12. Which of the following is a satisfactory thesis statement for a research paper?
    a. Le Corbusier designed Chandigarh, a famous building in India.
    b. My visit to Ronchamp, a chapel designed by Le Corbusier, was one of the most important experiences of my life.
    c. All of Le Corbusier's work shows his concern with the human, as opposed to the technological, aspects of modern society.
    d. In the Venice Hospital, constructed in 1965, Le Corbusier created a building in which each patient bed was in a separate cell, or cubicle.

13. Which of the following information should *not* be included in a footnote?
    a. Author's name   c. Page reference
    b. Publication facts   d. Subject heading

14. Which of the following references would you not consult for information on veterinary medicine?
    a. The *Readers' Guide*
    b. *Current Biography*
    c. *The New York Times Index*
    d. *Van Nostrand's Scientific Encyclopedia*

15. Which of the following is *not* part of revising a research paper?
    a. Checking for errors in spelling, capitalization, and punctuation
    b. Checking for errors in grammar, usage, and sentence structure
    c. Checking footnotes and bibliography for proper form
    d. Checking your note cards against your outline to make sure that you have sufficient information to support your thesis statement

Test 2

Choose one of the Unit Assignments or a topic suggested by your teacher. Write the assignment as directed and hand it in to your teacher.

Unit 12

Technical Writing

Unit Preview

If you have ever described an object, written instructions, or reported, with or without diagrams, the results of a scientific experiment, you are familiar with technical writing. The purpose of technical writing is to present facts, data, or other information to describe and explain a mechanical operation or scientific process. Technical writing can vary from an explanation of one or two paragraphs based on your own observations to a carefully researched paper of several pages or more.

The following paragraphs are an example of technical writing.

> The cooling system of a car is designed to dispel the heat generated by the internal-combustion engine. Although some cars have air-cooled engines, most have water-cooled engines.
>
> The water-cooled system consists of a radiator, a fan and a fan belt, radiator hoses, a water pump, a thermostat, and water jacks around each cylinder in the engine block. Propelled by the water pump, water mixed with antifreeze circulates through the engine block and flows through hoses to the radiator, where it is cooled. In the radiator, water flows through tubes cooled by air drawn through the radiator by the fan. A fan belt passes through pulleys on the crankshaft and the fan, rotating the fan, which in turn operates the water pump. The thermostat controls the water temperature; it opens a valve that lets water pass through the cooling system once the water in the engine block has reached a set temperature.

The Cooling System

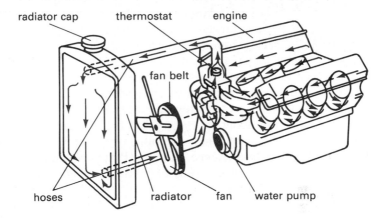

For Analysis On your paper, answer the following questions about the example.

1. What is the topic of the example?
2. What is the writer's purpose?
3. How would you describe the tone of the example?
4. In what way does the diagram clarify the description of the cooling system?

Analyzing the topic, the purpose, and the tone of the example will help you to understand what technical writing is and how it differs from other forms of writing. As you learn how to write about technical subjects, you will follow the three steps of the writing process: prewriting, writing, and revising.

12.1 The Nature of Technical Writing

Technical writing, which uses description and exposition to present factual information, has characteristics that distinguish it from other forms of writing. One distinguishing feature of technical writing is its objectivity, or total emphasis on its subject. Unlike types of writing that may include the author's thoughts and experiences, technical writing is devoid of the author's opinions and experiences.

Topics for Technical Writing

Another important distinguishing feature of technical writing is its subject matter, which includes the sciences, engineering, the mechanical arts, and all branches of technology. Any topic that is not scientific or technical is inappropriate. However, not all topics related to science or technology are suitable for technical writing. Only those topics about which you can write objectively are appropriate. For example, if you were writing about computers, you could write a technical explanation of a computer language. You would not write a technical explanation about why you want a home computer. The latter explanation is subjective, not objective, because it reflects personal opinions and experience. Suppose that you wanted to write a report on some aspect of the study of birds. You might write about the aerodynamics of bird flight, the construction of a bird's wing, or migration patterns. You could also explain how to build a birdhouse. You would not use technical writing to write about your pet canary, the time that you watched a bird learn to fly, or the reason that bird watching is your hobby.

The following lists should guide you in determining what topics are suitable for technical writing.

Suitable Topics:
   1. An explanation of how a camera lens works
   2. How to read a navigational chart
   3. The function of enzymes in human digestion
   4. The purpose and function of a fish's gills
   5. The use of robots in industry

Unsuitable Topics:
   1. How to do a swan dive
   2. Painting a portrait
   3. Raising orchids as a hobby
   4. Why we should vote in every election
   5. Raising money for a worthy cause

Writing a Technical Explanation

Use technical writing to present facts that your audience will need in order to solve a technical problem, perform a mechanical task, or understand an operation or a scientific process. Consider all of the following elements before beginning any piece of technical writing.

Audience.   As with any kind of writing, you need to think about who your audience is and how much your readers need to know about your topic. Adjust your writing to suit your audience, whether the audience is your classmates, members of your family, or someone else who needs the information that you are providing.

Occasionally, your readers may have specialized knowledge. For example, you may write for an audience with some knowledge of auto mechanics and its specialized vocabulary. Usually, however, you should assume that your readers have little or no specialized knowledge of the mechanism or the process that you are explaining. Consequently, define all necessary words, including technical terms. For instance, you can assume that your readers know what a computer is; however, you should not assume that they know what a byte is.

Tone and Point of View.   The tone (*page 406*) of all technical writing should be serious and impersonal. Remember that you are not expressing an opinion or attempting to persuade your reader to adopt some belief or to take some action; nor are you attempting to be humorous or entertaining. You are simply relating facts in an unbiased and unembellished way.

Use the third-person point of view (*pages 342–343*) in order to maintain an impersonal tone. Use of the third person focuses on the subject, not on the writer.

APPROPRIATE	Use a tripod to steady the camera when using a slow shutter speed.
INAPPROPRIATE	I have always found a tripod useful when I am using a slow shutter speed.

The second sentence is inappropriate because it shifts the reader's attention from the use of the tripod to the author's experience as a photographer.

Style.   Style (*pages 408–410*) is the manner in which you express your ideas. In technical writing your style should be formal. Avoid using colloquial expressions, slang, and contractions.

APPROPRIATE	For photographing sunsets, a clean lens reduces the chance of lens flare.
INAPPROPRIATE	When you are photographing sunsets, there's a pretty good chance you won't get any lens flare if your lens is clean.

The second sentence is inappropriate for technical writing because the slang, informal language, and contractions detract from the importance of the information. The sentence sounds conversational, rather than formal.

Technical writing requires precise, specific language. Imprecise words and expressions such as *some, later,* and *a few* can mislead or confuse the reader. Use precise language such as *one liter, three hours,* or *6½ pounds.*

Technical writing must also be concise and straightforward. Avoid words and phrases that detract from the clarity and fluency of your writing. For example, do not say "after no less than fifteen minutes" when you mean "after fifteen minutes." See Unit 6, "Revising" for further guidelines in writing concisely.

Writing Numbers.   Technical writing often requires the use of numbers. The following guidelines will help you to know when to write out numbers and when to express them in Arabic numerals.

Write out numbers that can be expressed in one or two words, such as *fourteen, sixty-three,* and *ten million.* Use Arabic numerals for all others, including fractions. Use numerals also to express percents, decimals, page numbers, monetary units, and exact measurements, as in the following examples: *11 percent, 51.6, page 109, $355,* and *45 acres.*

Using Abbreviations.   Although not accepted in most forms of writing, some abbreviations are permitted in technical writing, especially for expressing units of measurement. When referring to units of measurement, always spell the word out the first time it appears and use abbreviations, without periods (except for *in.*), in subsequent references. Use the same abbreviation for both singular and plural references. Consult the following chart for correct abbreviations of units of measurement.

A	ampere	km	kilometer
bbl	barrel	km/h	kilometers per hour
C	Celsius	kw	kilowatt
cal	calorie	kW·h	kilowatt hour
cm	centimeter	L	liter
dB	decibel	lb	pound
doz	dozen	m	meter
F	Fahrenheit	mL	milliliter
fl oz	fluid ounce	mm	millimeter
ft	foot	oz	ounce
ft²	square foot	qt	quart
ft³	cubic foot	s	second
gal	gallon	t	ton
g	gram	temp	temperature
h	hour	tol	tolerance
hp	horsepower	v	volt
in.	inch	W	watt
kg	kilogram	yd	yard

Using Illustrations.   Unlike other forms of writing, technical writing sometimes needs detailed diagrams or sketches or numbered steps to assist the reader in understanding complex explanations or instructions. However, with or without accompanying diagrams, you must present a clear, verbal picture of what an object looks like and how it operates. Diagrams are only an aid; they should not be a substitute for clear writing.

Exercise 1   Prewriting: Technical Writing Topics   Read the following list of topics. On your paper, write *Suitable* if the topic is suitable for technical writing. Write *Unsuitable* for each topic that is unsuitable, and explain why it is unsuitable.

1. How to install a home intercom system
2. Features of the newest calculators
3. Why I do not like to develop film
4. The beauty of the Painted Desert at sunset
5. How to provide good nutrition for pets
6. The adventure of traveling in Peru
7. How to operate a video camera

8. My experiences using a compass
9. One way to measure the depth of a lake
10. How I fixed my car when it broke down

Exercise 2 Writing: Style and Tone Read the following sentences. On your paper, write *Suitable* for those sentences that are suitable for technical writing and *Unsuitable* for those that are not suitable.

1. First, whatever else you do, cut off the electric current at its source; don't you dare forget that.
2. To reduce air resistance, most gliders have smooth surfaces of aluminum, fiber glass, or wood.
3. I think that making exact drawings of discoveries is the most important task for an archeologist.
4. Mold may begin to grow when a spore lands on a damp surface.
5. The first step in making glass is mixing a bunch of powders in a gigantic container.
6. Vitamins cause important chemical reactions to take place in the body.
7. I can tell you all sorts of things about the operation of a hydrophone.
8. To clear a hurdle, a runner must approach it correctly.
9. Although blood usually clots within seven minutes, the clotting process is complicated.
10. A stereo system is made of a lot of parts that do different things.

Assignment Prewriting On your paper, list ten topics that are suitable for technical writing.

Assignment Checklist

Check your assignment for the following points:

✔ 1. Did you choose scientific or technical topics?
✔ 2. Did you choose topics about which you can write objectively?
✔ 3. Did you choose topics for which you can provide factual information?
✔ 4. Did you choose topics for which you can provide illustrations if necessary?

12.2 Writing About a Mechanism

A **mechanism** is any device designed to accomplish a certain task or to serve a particular function. Some familiar mechanisms are elevators, television antennas, calculators, cash registers, faucets, and so forth.

In this section you will learn to do two kinds of technical writing: describing a mechanism and explaining how a mechanism works. You will present facts, interpret information, and give instructions. You will use description (*pages 332–339*) to communicate to your reader what a mechanism is. For example, if writing about an abacus, you will describe it before explaining its operation through the use of exposition (*pages 324–327*).

12.2a Describing a Mechanism

Your purpose in describing a mechanism is to make it and its operation clear to your readers.

Defining Terms

Begin your description by defining the mechanism that you are about to describe. Your definition should consist of three parts: (1) the name of the item defined, (2) the specific group or class to which it belongs, and (3) the features that distinguish it from other items in its class. Study the following chart.

ITEM	SPECIFIC GROUP	FEATURES
piton	a metal spike	fitted at one end with a ring through which to pass a rope; used in mountain climbing
dew point	a temperature	at which air becomes saturated and produces dew
asthma	a respiratory disease	often caused by allergies and accompanied by coughing and labored breathing
subpoena	a legal document	requiring one's presence in court to give testimony

Even with all three parts, a definition can still be inaccurate or confusing. Avoid writing circular definitions, in which you define a word by repeating it in a different form. For example, if you define *thrombosis* as "the presence or formation of a thrombus," your reader will need further explanation.

Also avoid using one specialized word to define another. Do not, for instance, define a *logic branch* as a "binary option" unless you are certain that your reader will know what a binary option is.

Organizing Your Description

After you have defined the mechanism, you are ready to describe it, concentrating on its individual parts. Spatial order is the best method to describe most mechanisms; it allows you to describe from top to bottom, left to right, outside to inside, or inside to outside. Choose the spatial order best suited to the mechanism. Conclude your description by naming the function of the mechanism. The following questions will help you to plan your description.

1. What is the mechanism? (definition)
2. What are its appearance, size, and weight? (description)
3. What parts does it have? (description)
4. What is it used for? (function)

The following description of a claw hammer is based on the preceding questions.

Model

Definition
Description

A claw hammer is a tool used to drive nails or to remove them. Measuring 10 to 14 inches in length and weighing 12 to 16 ounces, it is made of steel and wood, plastic, or fiber glass. A claw hammer has two parts: a handle approximately 12 inches long and made of either a wood, such as ash, or plastic or fiber glass, and a head made of hardened steel and attached to one end of the handle. At one end of the

Function

head is a striking force (called a *face*) for driving nails. At the other end is a claw shaped like a V for removing nails.

Use the following strategies when describing a mechanism.

Strategies

1. *Define all the necessary terms.* Unless you are sure that your reader has specialized knowledge, provide clear definitions of all technical or scientific terms.

2. *Use the third-person point of view and maintain a serious formal tone.* Avoid personal experiences and opinions.

3. *Use precise, clear, and straightforward language.* Avoid words and phrases that detract from the clarity and precision of your explanation.

4. *Use spatial order to develop your description.*

5. *Use words that indicate direction or relative position.* Such words as *above, below, behind, left, right, adjacent, abutting, overlapping, horizontal, vertical, lateral,* and *parallel* help your reader to visualize the mechanism.

Exercise 1   Writing: Definitions   On your paper, define each of the following terms. Be sure that your definition consists of three parts: the item, its class, and its distinguishing features. Use a dictionary to check your answers.

> **SAMPLE**   Combine
>
> **ANSWER**   A combine is a harvesting machine that cuts and thrashes grain.

1. Barometer
2. Pestle
3. Radar
4. Contact lens
5. Circuit breaker
6. Hearing aid
7. Meteorite
8. Pedometer
9. Derrick
10. Parachute

Exercise 2   Revising: Definitions   On your paper, rewrite the definitions on the following page making corrections and adding any missing parts. Make sure that your definition includes the three necessary parts.

SAMPLE	Malachite is green.
ANSWER	Malachite is a green mineral that is used to make copper.

1. A seismograph is an instrument that makes seismograms.
2. A cipher is a cryptogram.
3. A beaker is used in a laboratory.
4. A synthesizer is a machine that synthesizes music.
5. An antenna can be found on a car.
6. A lathe is a thing on which an item is spun while being shaped by a cutting or abrading tool.
7. Crampons are worn on the shoes of mountain climbers.
8. A crow's nest is a small platform.
9. A blueprint is a thing that shows the design of a building or a machine.
10. A spark plug is an engine part that makes a spark.

12.2b Explaining How a Mechanism Works

Technical writing also includes explaining how a particular mechanism operates. In writing this type of explanation, you will use some of the steps that you used in describing a mechanism.

Defining and Describing

Before explaining how a mechanism operates, explain what it is. If, for example, you are explaining how a stethoscope works, do not assume that your reader already knows what a stethoscope is. First, define it as follows:

> A stethoscope is a medical instrument used for listening to sounds produced in the body's chest cavity.

Next, include a brief physical description of the mechanism. Because the emphasis in this kind of technical writing is on how a mechanism operates, do not make either the definition or the description any longer than necessary. Your description of a stethoscope can be as brief as the following:

The stethoscope is Y-shaped, with a flat disc at the bottom of the Y attached to rubber-and-metal tubing that branches and joins two ear pieces.

Method of Development

The best method to describe the operation of most mechanisms is a combination of chronological order and cause-and-effect order. Chronological order allows you to explain in sequence the individual steps in an operation. However, in most operations, one step is the cause of a subsequent step or steps; thus you will need to use cause-and-effect development as well. The following model combines chronological order and cause-and-effect development to explain the operation of a spirit level.

Model

Definition and
Description

Development

A spirit level is an instrument used to determine whether a surface is level. It is a glass tube filled with a liquid, usually alcohol, that contains an air bubble.

The center of the glass tube, marked by a vertical line, has a slight upward curve. Holding the spirit level horizontally causes the center of the glass tube to become the highest point, making the air bubble rise to the center of the tube. Placing the spirit level on a surface that is not horizontal causes the air bubble to move to the left or the right of the center line.

Exercise 3   Revising: Explaining an Operation   On your paper, revise the following explanation of the operation of a smoke detector. Place all the sentences in correct sequence and add transitional words where needed. Delete or revise any sentences that are inappropriate in technical writing.

I want to tell you about an ionization smoke detector, a small device that warns people of the presence of smoke from a fire. The detector is housed in a small plastic box that usually is attached to the ceiling, the place where smoke first collects. Most alarms that I have seen are white.

When smoke reaches the alarm, particles in the smoke break that electrical current. An ionization detector contains a small amount of a radioactive substance, usually americium 241. The radioactive material is used to create an electrical current between two electrodes. The broken circuit causes a battery-powered buzzer to sound, warning people about the smoke. The detector is a simple mechanism that performs a valuable service.

Exercise 4   Writing: Explaining an Operation   On your paper, write an explanation of the operation of a dry-chemical fire extinguisher. Use the following information to write your explanation. Begin with a definition; then place all the sentences of the explanation in sequential order. Revise your sentences as necessary.

The extinguisher is used to put out fires started with gasoline, grease, or electrical equipment.

The gas is forced out of the nozzle in the container.

The extinguisher contains a container of gas and a chemical powder.

When a valve is opened by a fire fighter, the container of gas is punctured.

The dry chemical reacts with the heat of the fire to become carbon dioxide.

The gas is put into the container of the extinguisher under pressure.

The carbon dioxide smothers the fire.

As the gas is forced out of the nozzle, it pushes the dry chemical out with it.

Assignment 1   Writing   On your paper, write a description of a mechanism. Begin your description with a definition of the mechanism; then add as many descriptive sentences as necessary. Conclude with a sentence that states the purpose of the mechanism.

Assignment 2   Writing   On your paper, write an explanation of the operation of a mechanism. Begin by defining and describing the mechanism. Then explain its operation, using chronological order and cause-and-effect development.

Assignment Checklist

Check your assignments for the following points:

✔ 1. Did you define the mechanism?
✔ 2. Did you explain how the mechanism works?
✔ 3. Did you combine chronological order and cause-and-effect development in your explanation?
✔ 4. Did you use appropriate words to indicate location?
✔ 5. Did you use the third-person point of view?
✔ 6. Did you avoid colloquial expressions, slang, and contractions?
✔ 7. Did you maintain a serious tone and a formal style?
✔ 8. Did you proofread your paragraphs for correct grammar, usage, spelling, and punctuation?

12.3 Writing About a Process

A **process** is a series of actions, changes, or operations that bring about a product or a result. In technical writing you will describe processes that need an operator and processes that do not.

12.3a A Process with an Operator

A process that requires an operator is one in which a person must carry out a series of steps. Such a process may be as simple as changing a fuse or as complex as performing a scientific experiment. In this kind of technical writing, you explain causes and effects. Such writing must permit your reader to follow a series of steps (causes) and thereby achieve a result (effect) that matches the one described.

Considering Your Audience

A person reads an explanation of a process with an operator to learn how to make or do something. Your responsibility as writer is to include all the needed information in a clear sequence.

In explaining a process that is unfamiliar to your audience, put yourself in your reader's position. Ask yourself, "What do I, the reader, *need* to know?" Then supply only that information, using clear, precise, and straightforward language.

Organizing Your Explanation

Begin your explanation with a list of any materials that your reader needs. Then write your explanation of the process in chronological order. To complete a process, your reader needs to know the exact sequence of steps to follow. Therefore, if you were explaining how to change a light switch, for example, you would begin with "First, shut off the electric current at the main fuse box or circuit breaker."

If the process is complex or has more than five steps, writing the explanation as a numbered list, rather than as a series of paragraphs, will assist your reader in following the sequence.

Study the following example that explains a process that needs an operator.

Model

How to Repair a Bicycle Tire

To repair a punctured tube in a bicycle tire, you will need the following equipment:

wrench
set of tire irons
pen
talc
hand air pump

tire patch kit (containing
perforated metal strip or
sandpaper, patches, and
vulcanizing fluid)

1. First, examine the tire carefully to locate the puncture. It may be necessary to remove the wheel from the bicycle to repair the flat. If so, free the wheel from the bicycle, using the wrench.
2. When you have found the puncture, remove the valve cap from the valve core on the rim of the wheel, and push down on the core to release the air from the tire. Then insert the tire irons under the rim of the tire near the punctured part to free that portion of the tire from the rim. Pull out the punctured part of the tube from the tire.
3. Inflate the tube slightly, using the hand pump to locate the point where the air is escaping from the tube. Make an X on the spot with the pen.
4. Before proceeding further, choose a patch of an appropriate size to cover the puncture. Then roughen the area around the punc-

ture with either the perforated metal strip or the sandpaper. Remove the dust created by the abrasive.

5. Next, apply the vulcanizing fluid to the surface, spreading it slightly beyond the area to be covered by the patch. Let the fluid dry until it is no longer tacky.

6. Remove the metal foil from the patch and center the patch over the puncture, pressing firmly for five to ten seconds. Pull off the cover foil from the patch, and sprinkle talc over the area to absorb any remaining fluid.

7. With the puncture now repaired, replace the tube inside the tire and carefully work the tire back into the rim with your hands. Inflate the tire and reattach the wheel to the bicycle if necessary.

Use the following strategies when explaining a process with an operator.

Strategies

1. *Use the active voice and the imperative mood* to give authority and clarity to your explanation.

   APPROPRIATE   Sand the wood until it is smooth.

   INAPPROPRIATE   The wood should be sanded until it is smooth.

2. *List the steps of the process in chronological order.*

3. *Define all necessary terms for an audience lacking a technical background.* For example, a reader unfamiliar with carpentry might need a definition of *joist.* However, you could assume that the same reader would not need an explanation of the difference between hand tools and power tools, a difference that is common knowledge.

4. *List any special equipment necessary for the process.*

5. *Use transitional words and phrases* to make the chronology clear. Examples of such words include *first, then, next, the next day, after,* and so forth.

6. *Use numbered steps to explain a lengthy or a complex process.*

7. *Avoid personal opinions, experiences, and other extraneous wording.*

As a final check to see that your explanation is clear, complete the steps in the process yourself. If you have any difficulty, revise your explanation.

Exercise 1   Writing: Process with an Operator   On your paper, explain how to take a person's blood pressure by placing the following steps in correct chronological order. Add transitional words, where necessary. Include any necessary definitions.

Many people must have their blood pressure checked regularly. Checking someone's blood pressure requires only two pieces of equipment: a sphygmomanometer and a stethoscope. Mastering the process, however, does require practice.

Wrap the cuff around the person's arm just above the elbow. Inflate the cuff by gently squeezing the hollow rubber ball attached to the cuff. Slowly release air from the cuff and listen for the sound to start again. Place the stethoscope below the cuff on the person's arm. You will hear the sound of the blood pulsing. When you first hear the noise, note the number shown on the glass meter attached to the cuff. That is the person's systolic blood pressure. Note the number on the meter. That second number is the person's diastolic pressure. Keep listening until the sound becomes muffled. With practice, you can perform the process easily and accurately.

Exercise 2   Revising: Process with an Operator   On your paper, revise the following explanation of how to replace a washer. Using appropriate transitional words, place the steps in correct chronological order. Add any necessary definitions. Revise any sentences containing personal opinions or unnecessary wording.

If a faucet drips when it is tightly turned off, the washer probably needs to be replaced. If you follow my directions, you will need only a new washer, a screwdriver, a wrench, and a knife to do the task. Once the faucet handle is off, you will see a nut, which must be loosened with a wrench and taken off. Loosen the screw on the top of the faucet handle and remove the handle. Under the nut, there is a stem assembly, a metal cylinder. Remove it by firmly pulling it up. You will see a screw on the bottom of the assembly. Use a screwdriver to loosen it. I recommend that if the top of the screw is too worn to use a screwdriver on it, you should use a pair of pliers to loosen the screw. Use an old knife to pry out the washer, which is right under the screw. The flat side of the new washer should be next to the assembly. Once the old washer is out, use the knife to push in the new washer. Replace the screw in the stem assembly. Put the stem assembly back on the faucet, and reassemble the rest of the handle. If you did exactly what I have directed, the leak should be fixed.

12.3b A Process Without an Operator

If you were to write an explanation of how spontaneous combustion occurs or how coal is formed, you would be explaining a process without an operator. In this type of technical writing, sometimes called **process analysis,** you show how something happens by breaking down a process into its separate steps. Your analysis of a process will be clear to your reader if you divide your analysis into two parts: an introduction and a body.

Introduction.　Begin your process analysis with a brief introduction in which you define the process and explain where it occurs. Include any other background information that will help your reader. If your topic is photosynthesis, for example, your reader will better understand your analysis if you explain what photosynthesis is before telling how it happens.

Body.　The body of your analysis is a step-by-step explanation of the process. Depending on the complexity of your topic, you may need to explain each major step in a separate paragraph.

Include diagrams whenever they will help your reader. Remember, however, that diagrams are not a substitute for clear writing.

The following example explains a process without an operator.

Model

Crystallization is a process by which nonliving matter grows into crystals, solid compounds of atoms arranged in an orderly pattern. Crystals can form from vapors, solutions, or molten materials called melts. Lowered temperature or pressure or evaporation cause certain atoms in such substances to grow close together and join. Most often they do so on a crystallization nucleus, an impurity made up of a particle or a cluster of atoms. The atoms collect on the nucleus in structural units called unit cells to form a crystalline solid. Additional atoms forming on an expanding network of cells causes the crystals to increase in size.

Use the following strategies when explaining a process without an operator.

Strategies

1. *Define the process in your introduction.*

2. *Define additional key terms in the body of your explanation.*

3. *Use chronological order to explain the steps* that occur in the process.

4. *Use transitional words and phrases* to indicate time sequence. Examples are *next, meanwhile, finally, before,* and so forth.

5. *Use directional words when necessary.* Examples include *left, right, up, down,* and *parallel.*

Exercise 3   Prewriting: A Process   Read the following list of processes. On your paper, write *Operator* beside the number of each process requiring an operator. Write *No operator* next to those processes that do not require an operator.

1. Turning an old television set into a computer terminal
2. How a cell subdivides
3. How a desert forms
4. How an electric eye works
5. Implanting an artificial hip
6. How to analyze the chemicals in drinking water
7. How volcanic ash causes changes in the weather
8. Replacing a frayed cord on a lamp

Exercise 4 Writing/Revising: A Process On your paper, revise the following explanation of the use of windmills to pump water by placing the sentences in correct sequence. Include transitional words and definitions where they are needed. Eliminate personal opinions and unnecessary sentences.

> For years, windmills have been used to supply water for farms. Wind turns a large wheel of blades at the top of a windmill. My grandparents' farm has a windmill. As the wheel turns, it causes small gears to turn with it. The large gears are attached to long rods that move up and down as the gears turn. The small gears mesh with large gears and cause them to turn too. Those rods go into a cylinder in a pump. Each time that the rods move down, they push air out of the cylinder. When the rods move back up, a vacuum is created. The downward stroke of the rods pushes the water out of the pump. The vacuum pulls water up from the ground to fill the cylinder. Thus, I think that it is amazing that water is pumped without using expensive electricity or human labor.

Assignment 1 Writing On your paper, write one or two paragraphs explaining a process with an operator. If possible, write about a process that you already know about. If not, consult library sources. Use chronological order to explain the process. Include a diagram if it will aid your readers.

Assignment 2 Writing On your paper, write an explanation in at least two paragraphs of a process without an operator. You may have to do library research before you begin to write. Include diagrams as needed.

Assignment Checklist

Check your assignments for the following points:

✔ 1. Did you explain one process with an operator and one without an operator?
✔ 2. Did you define all important or unfamiliar terms?
✔ 3. Did you use chronological order?
✔ 4. Did you use transitional words and phrases?
✔ 5. Did you use the third-person point of view?
✔ 6. Did you maintain a serious tone and a formal style?
✔ 7. Did you proofread your explanations for correct grammar, usage, spelling, and punctuation?

12.4 Writing a Technical Report

Sometimes you have to combine the kinds of technical writing that you have just learned when you write a technical report.

12.4a The Purpose of a Technical Report

A **technical report** is an analysis of data about a product, a process, or a proposal; it is an analysis undertaken to answer a question or solve a problem. A technical report differs in purpose from other types of writing. For instance, in an essay (*Unit 9*), you present your own point of view on a subject to inform or to entertain your reader. In a research paper (*Unit 11*), you inform or enlighten your reader with the results of your investigation. In neither case do you expect the reader to take any action based solely on what you have written. In a technical report, however, your purpose is to provide the information to help the reader solve a problem or make a decision leading to an action.

In other forms of technical writing, you use your own knowledge and observation as a basis for your writing. In describing a mechanism, for example, often you need only to observe the mechanism closely in order to describe it. In writing a technical report, you cannot rely entirely on your own knowledge and observation; instead, you must rely on facts that you discover through research.

Suppose you were asked to provide information to be used in deciding which copying machine to purchase. The steps that you would follow are the same that you would follow in preparing any technical report: gather data, interpret the data, and make recommendations.

Gathering Data.   Data include facts, figures, statistics, and endorsements. Before starting to gather data, you must decide what to include in your report. Prepare a list of questions based on your reader's needs to guide your research. Suppose that preparing a report on copying machines, the choices had been narrowed to the Belle XIII, the Nathan-Jervis BX, and the Whitney 600. What, besides the initial cost, would your reader need to know? The following list of questions should guide your research.

1. What is the initial cost of each machine?
2. What are the basic features of each, including size?
3. What optional features are available? At what cost?
4. What is the cost of repairs?
5. What is the availability of service personnel?
6. What has been consumer response to each machine?

Once you have compiled a list of questions, begin your research by consulting any library references, including periodicals, that have information on your topic. (See pages 485–488 for a review of library sources and how to use them.) Your research will not end in the library. Gather data by interviewing persons who have information that you need. For a report on copying machines, for example, you could interview persons who have used each machine over a long time. Request brochures and other related information directly from manufacturers or sales representatives.

Interpreting Data. A technical report requires that you do more than simply list the data that you have gathered; often you will need to interpret the data for your reader. For example, suppose that you found that the purchase price of the Nathan-Jervis copier is significantly higher than the price of the other two. Suppose also that the Nathan-Jervis costs considerably less per year to operate. You must interpret for your reader the fact that the Nathan-Jervis may ultimately be the least expensive of the three.

Making Recommendations. When you have gathered and interpreted all data, make a recommendation in the conclusion of your technical report. Make sure that your recommendation is consistent with the facts that you have presented. Your recommendation should be one that, given the same data, anyone else would have made. Remember to write in the third person. Do not write "I recommend that we purchase the Nathan-Jervis BX"; instead, write "The facts suggest that the Nathan-Jervis BX is the most economical purchase."

Exercise 1 Prewriting: Technical-Report Topics On your paper, write *Suitable* for each topic on the following page that is appropriate for a technical report and *Unsuitable* for each topic that is inappropriate.

1. Why a helicopter stays in the air
2. The best way to improve the acoustics of an auditorium
3. Procedures that should be used to transport gasoline safely
4. The types of microscopes that exist
5. The most efficient locations for heating vents in a house
6. How recent changes in the inflation rate have affected me
7. An exercise program that is helpful for people with arthritis
8. How highways are resurfaced
9. A comfortable type of office chair
10. A method to decrease air pollution in a city

12.4b Parts of a Technical Report

A technical report contains parts arranged as follows: a title page, a table of contents, an abstract, a list of illustrations, an introduction, the body of the report, a conclusion, a glossary, an appendix, a list of footnotes, and a bibliography. You will study the parts of a technical report in the order in which you will write them.

Major Parts of the Report

Once you have gathered and analyzed data, you are ready to write the major parts of the report: the body, the conclusion, the abstract, and the introduction.

The Body.   The body of your report contains the results of your research. Because it is also the source of information to be included in the other major parts, you must write the body first.

Read the following portion of the body of a technical report on natural breads. Notice the objective presentation of the material.

```
CHOICE OF FLOURS

      Until 1874 flour was milled by grinding wheat between

   rotating stone discs; friction thereby reduced the grain to

   a fine powder.  In 1874, however, the milling process
```

changed radically with the introduction of the steel rolling

mill, which crushed, rather than ground, the wheat. The

wheat germ and bran were then sifted from the flour to

produce a highly stable product that could be stored for

long periods without spoiling. Modern analysis reveals that

the removal of the wheat germ and bran also removes as many
                                                         5
as twenty-two nutrients.

    Sidney Margoulius, author of <u>Health Foods: Facts and

Fakes,</u> concedes that "criticism of white bread and other

products baked from white flour is one issue that finds
                                                        6
orthodox nutritionists and health foodists in agreement."

There is no question that steel-roller milling of flour

removes high-quality proteins, such as lysine and

tryptophan, as well as unsaturated fatty acids and vitamin

E. In addition, minerals are removed from the wheat in

approximately the following percentages: manganese, 89

percent; iron, 80 percent; magnesium, 75 percent; and

phosphorus, 70 percent.

Illustrations. Illustrations help your reader to understand complex material that may require several paragraphs of explanation. Use diagrams to illustrate technical data or to show a cross section of a mechanism. Use a table to present statistical data and other types of numerical information in tabular form. Use graphs to present data that extend over a period or to show comparisons.

    The table on the following page shows a comparison of the nutrients in honey and molasses.

FIGURE 1

NUTRIENTS IN HONEY AND MOLASSES [1]

Nutrient	Honey (mg)	Molasses (mg)
Riboflavin	0.04	0.12
Niacin	0.3	1.2
Iron	0.5	6.0
Calcium	5.0	290.0
Vitamin B	0.02	0.2
Pantothenic acid	0.2	0.35

[1]
Adapted from R. S. Harris and E. Karmas, eds., Nutritional Evaluation of Food Processing, second edition (Westport, Connecticut: The Avi Publishing Company, Inc., 1975), p.382.

Use the following strategies when preparing illustrations.

Strategies

1. *Refer to all illustrations as* Figure 1, Figure 2, *and so forth,* consecutively throughout your report.

2. *Include a brief explanation of the illustration* in the body of your report.

3. *Include a footnote at the bottom of each illustration,* unless the illustration is one that you devised yourself.

4. *Make your illustrations large enough to be legible and label them clearly.*

5. *Make sure that all illustrations are relevant and necessary.*

Conclusion.   The conclusion is a succinct presentation of your findings, with a recommendation for any action that the facts warrant. To prepare your conclusion, look again at the findings that you detailed in the body of your report. Restate them briefly, but be sure to include enough information to make them clear. Make sure that your conclusion is an accurate reflection of the contents of your report. Also make sure that any recommendations that you make are consistent with the facts that you have reported.

Read the following example conclusion. Notice the conciseness and objectivity.

```
CONCLUSION

     Although the analysis of ingredients used in four

brands of new natural breads shows that these breads are

overall more nutritious than white bread, the consumer

should be aware that natural breads can be improved.  Of the

four brands whose ingredients were analyzed, Willson Mills'

Sprouted Wheat proved to be the consumer's best choice

because it is made of 100-percent stone-ground whole-wheat

flour and many added nutrients.

     All four of the brands analyzed would be improved if

they were made with stone-ground flour and unhydrogenated

vegetable oil.
```

Introduction. The purposes of an introduction are to provide background for your reader and to explain what you intend to do in your report. State clearly the subject and the purpose of your report. By writing the introduction after you have completed the body of your report, you will not inadvertently refer to material that you have deleted or changed.

Read the introduction from the technical report on natural breads that appears on the next page. Notice that the objectives of the report are itemized to make them more easily seen.

INTRODUCTION

Since the early 1900s, consumer dissatisfaction with

commercially prepared bread made of white flour has been

widespread. In 1911, referring to methods of milling flour,

the British medical journal The Lancet commented that "real

bread has been taken out of our mouths by modern methods of

impoverishment."[1] During World War I and at intervals

thereafter, the governments of the United States and Great

Britain tried to improve the low nutritional value of white

bread. Their efforts were not entirely successful. In 1951

Food and Drug Commissioner Paul B. Dunbar agreed that

commercial bread had degraded to the point of resembling

"cotton fluff wrapped up in a skin."[2]

In recent years, however, the food industry has begun

to respond to consumer demand by introducing natural breads

into the market. The purpose of this paper is to examine

the nutritional benefits of these new products.

This report has three objectives:

1. To explore recent improvements in mass-marketed

   commercial breads

2. To analyze ingredients common to the new natural loaves

3. To suggest further modifications in current bread-making

   processes and practices

The report uses examples of four widely available wheat

breads recommended by a best-selling natural-foods guide.

Choice of basic ingredients such as flours, sweeteners,

shortenings, and yeast are discussed, as well as the use of optional ingredients such as monoglycerides and diglycerides and yeast nutrients.

Information in this report is from a variety of sources, including works by nutritionists, microbiologists, and members of government regulatory agencies, as well as from interviews with consumer representatives and natural-food advocates.

Abstract.   An **abstract** is a brief summary of the main points in your report. Its purpose is to provide an overview for the reader who wants to know only the key points or who may not have time to read the full report. Therefore, to be effective, an abstract should be able to stand on its own as a separate document. In it, define any terms that you think necessary, even if they are later defined in the body or the glossary (*page 570*). Do not use illustrations and do not use any information that you have not included in your report.

Writing an abstract is one way to check the accuracy and completeness of your report. If you cannot summarize your report briefly, you may need to do more research or revising.

Read the following example from the abstract for the technical report on natural bread. Notice how it differs in content from the conclusion and the introduction.

ABSTRACT

Four examples of the new natural mass-marketed breads were analyzed for nutritional value. The samples were Real Grain's Natural; Real Grain's Bran Country Oat; Willson Mills' Sprouted Wheat; and Willson Mills' Cracked Wheat. Choices of flours, fats, sweeteners, and other ingredients were examined.

Findings show that the new natural loaves are more

nutritious than the mass-marketed white bread. Two major

faults were found in natural loaves. The first is the use

of unbleached enriched wheat flour as a main ingredient.

The second is the use of partially hydrogenated vegetable oil.

The report concludes with the recommendation that the

consumer buy Willson Mills' Sprouted Wheat. Its

ingredients--100-percent stone-ground whole-wheat flour,

honey, wheat germ, wheat kernels, sesame seeds, and sunflower

seeds--make it the most nutritious of the loaves analyzed.

Concluding Parts of the Report

The concluding parts of a technical report include the glossary, an appendix, footnotes, and the bibliography.

Glossary. A **glossary** is an alphabetical list of terms with their definitions; its purpose is to explain technical or specialized terms for nontechnical readers. Place the glossary at the end of your report, just after the conclusion. To determine whether you need a glossary, make note of all technical or specialized terms that you think should be defined. If you have over five such terms, prepare a glossary. If you have fewer than five, define each term when it first appears in the body of the report.

Whether in the glossary or in the body of the report, define a term by giving its class and features (*pages 549–550*). When a term from the glossary first appears in the text, use a parenthetical note to refer your reader to the glossary, such as (See "Glossary," page 17).

The following example is a portion of the glossary for the technical report on natural bread.

Glyceride: a compound that occurs naturally as fat or fatty
    oil; can also be made synthetically.

Hydrogenation: the process of adding hydrogen to harden an
    oil into a fat.

Lysine: a basic amino acid essential in human nutrition.

An Appendix.   An appendix provides further information on points discussed in your report. Not all technical reports require the kinds of information found in appendixes: sample questionnaires and responses, maps, photographs, formulas, statistical data, details of an experiment, and so forth.

If you must include an appendix, refer to it in the introduction and at appropriate places in the body of your report; use a parenthetical reference such as (See Appendix A). Label each appendix separately with a title such as "Appendix A: A Chart Showing Population Shifts in Essex County, 1965 – 1980."

Footnotes.   Use footnotes to document all references that you consulted in gathering data for your report. Place footnotes on a separate page after the glossary, instead of at the bottom of each page, unless you have other instructions. For correct footnote forms, see pages 509 – 512 in Unit 11, "Writing a Research Paper."

Bibliography.   The last section of your report is the bibliography. Use the format presented in Unit 11, "Writing a Research Paper," pages 512 – 513.

Introductory Parts of the Report

Once the major and concluding parts of your report are complete, you are ready to write the introductory parts: the list of illustrations, the table of contents, and the title page.

List of Illustrations.   On a page that will follow the abstract, list each numbered illustration in order with a brief description and a page reference. Study the following example that refers to the figure shown on page 566.

```
LIST OF ILLUSTRATIONS                                      page

Figure 1:  Nutrients in Honey and Molasses. . . . . . .    4
```

Table of Contents.   The table of contents lists in sequence all parts of your report. Study the example of a portion of a table of contents that appears on the following page.

```
TABLE OF CONTENTS

Abstract . . . . . . . . . . . . . . . . . . . . . . . iii

List of Illustrations. . . . . . . . . . . . . . . . . vii

INTRODUCTION . . . . . . . . . . . . . . . . . . . . . 1

CHOICE OF FLOURS . . . . . . . . . . . . . . . . . . . 3

CHOICE OF FATS . . . . . . . . . . . . . . . . . . . . 6
```

Follow this procedure when preparing a table of contents.

Procedure

1. *Type "Table of Contents" in all capital letters.*

2. *List the abstract and the list of illustrations with lower-case Roman numerals to identify their page numbers.* The title page, although not numbered, is considered page i. The table of contents is page ii, the abstract, page iii.

3. *List all other items with Arabic numerals for page numbers.*

4. *Write "Abstract" and "List of Illustrations" using capital and lower-case letters* as shown in the example. Write the remaining sections in all capital letters.

5. *Use a horizontal row of dots to connect section titles with their page numbers,* unless you receive other instructions.

Title Page.   After completing all other sections of your technical report, prepare the title page. Include the following information: the report title, the reader's name, your name, and the date. Center the report title on the page. Leave two lines; then center your teacher's name below the report title. Center your name two lines below your teacher's name, and place the date on the line immediately below your name. Study the following example.

```
               Commercial Breads of the 1980s:
       An Analysis of Ingredients in the New Natural Loaves


                       J. R. Samuels


                       Denise Kolek
                       December 4, 19__
```

Exercise 2 Writing: The Body of the Report Read the following notes for a technical report on an analysis of sites for a new shopping center. On your paper, write two paragraphs using the notes for the body of the report.

Two sites are available for a shopping center: one in Gilbert's field and one in the old Taft schoolyard

GILBERT'S FIELD

No gas lines in immediate area

One grocery store within one-mile radius

Two ponds on land—would have to be filled in

Room for large parking area

Would have to install sewage system

Low taxes

Would have to enlarge road to property

Residents want stores nearby but are worried about increased traffic in area.

Electric lines run next to property.

SCHOOLYARD

Flat, dry land

Residents want center if a small park is built outside of it.

Limited parking space

Gas lines and electric wires nearby

Blacktop must be torn up.

Two grocery stores, three clothing stores, and a dry-cleaning store in a six-block area

Moderately high taxes

Town sewage lines on property

Residents upset about noise and dirt during construction

Exercise 3 Writing: The Glossary Read the following paragraphs from a technical report on an analysis of computers. On your paper, list and define words to be included in a glossary. Select words that are likely to be unfamiliar to readers without a technical background.

The next factor to consider in deciding whether to buy a large computer or to rent computer time from another company is the cost of employees. In either case programmers will be needed. If buying a computer, consider the need to hire an operator and enter into a contract with a service engineer. If renting computer time, the cost of the services of those people will be included in the rental fee.

In addition, consider the cost of the special facilities that are needed for a large computer. First, in order to ensure a proper working environment and to maintain the necessary security, the computer must be installed in a separate room. Because the central processing unit generates heat, air conditioning must run in the computer room at all times. Also, a raised floor must be installed to cover the many cables that join the components of the computer. Finally, the electrical wiring to the computer room may have to be changed to ensure that it can provide the necessary voltage and current for the machine to operate.

Exercise 4   Writing/Revising: The Conclusion   On your paper, rewrite the following paragraphs from the conclusion of a technical report, omitting those sentences that are inappropriate. Revise the remaining sentences for correct style and tone.

When excess water must be released from the river to prevent it from flooding all along its banks, I don't think that there is any good place to drain the water. Releasing the water in the farmlands at the top of the river will destroy valuable crops and may even cause some farmers to go out of business. My Uncle Bill would not like that. Releasing the water in the valley would cause parts of five towns to be flooded, damaging thousands of houses and businesses. There sure aren't many people who would go for that. Further downstream, the excess water would flood parts of the O'Brien Wildlife Refuge and destroy the habitat of many wild animals. There are many beautiful animals in the refuge, and you can see them there on any weekend. The effects of the third option would be less devastating and less long-term than the effects of the first two. Therefore, I think that you had better accept that solution.

It is important, however, that the communities along the river join together to help the animals in the refuge. Before the water is released, the animals should be fenced away from the lowland, and food should be provided to replace the food covered by the water. In fact, if you are really interested in animals, you should become a member of one of the many organizations devoted to the preservation of wildlife.

12.4c Revising the Technical Report

When you have completed the first draft of your technical report, review each section of it carefully. Base your revision on the following points.

Contents.   Revise the body, the conclusion, the introduction, and the abstract to see that each contains only necessary information. Use these strategies to help you revise.

Strategies

1. *Make sure that the body presents your findings accurately, concisely, and objectively.*

2. *Make certain that the conclusion summarizes your findings and gives your recommendations clearly.*

3. *Be certain that the introduction contains all the necessary background information.*

4. *Make sure that the abstract contains only the major points from the introduction, the body, and the conclusion.* Do not include information not found in other sections of your report.

Style and Tone.   Review all parts of your report to see that your style and tone are appropriate. Remove any references to personal experiences and opinions. Make sure that you have used the third-person point of view throughout.

Words and Sentences.   Review your report again for vague or imprecise language. Substitute precise, specific words for vague expressions; delete any unnecessary words and sentences. Make sure that you have included appropriate transitional words and phrases where needed.

Proofreading.   Conclude your revision by proofreading all the parts of your technical report. Check for errors in grammar, usage, spelling, and punctuation.

Exercise 5   Revising: Sentences   The following excerpt from a technical report needs revision. On your paper, write the letter of the suggested revisions that you think would best improve the excerpt. If a sentence is effective as it stands, write the letter that indicates *Make no change.*

(1) The cost of heating fuel has gone up a lot.   (2) Therefore, people in many communities like Shavertown are trying to find ways to conserve fuel.   (3) I want to tell you how to decrease the amount of heating fuel that you use.   (4) There are several ways to do that.   (5) There are also many ways to conserve the amount of water that you use.   (6) The objectives of this report are to present those methods and to evaluate which are the most effective.

(7) Large amounts of heat can be lost from your house.   (8) The easiest way to detect those leaks is to check areas where you can feel a draft on a windy day.   (9) I want to tell you that a utility company can provide a more scientific check.   (10) For just a few bucks, they will take an infrared snapshot of the outside of your building.   (11) Heat escaping from the building shows up on an infrared photograph.   (12) Ultraviolet photographs also show things that normal photographs do not.   (13) Once you have determined where the leaks are, you must decide how to repair them.

1. Sentence 1
   a. Make no change.
   b. Rewrite the sentence: *Within the past five years, the cost of heating fuels has more than doubled.*
   c. Rewrite the sentence: *The cost of heating fuels is out of sight.*

2. Sentence 3
   a. Rewrite the sentence: *There are several ways to decrease the amount of heating fuel that is used each month.*
   b. Make no change.
   c. Remove sentence.

3. Sentence 4
   a. Make no change.
   b. Rewrite the sentence: *The most effective methods are eliminating heat leaks, improving the efficiency of heating systems, installing energy-saving devices, and using alternative sources of energy.*
   c. Rewrite the sentence: *If you use a combination of four methods, your conservation process will be effective.*

4. Sentence 5
   a. Rewrite the sentence: *Conserving water is not hard either.*
   b. Remove the sentence.
   c. Make no change.

5. Sentence 6
   a. Make no change.
   b. Rewrite the sentence: *This report will be very helpful.*
   c. Rewrite the sentence: *I hope that you will enjoy this report.*

6. Sentence 7
   a. Rewrite the sentence: *Heat generated by your furnace can be lost from leaks in your house.*
   b. Rewrite the sentence: *Large amounts of heat can be lost through cracks in the windows, the doors, the vents, and the roof of your house.*
   c. Make no change.

7. Sentence 8
   a. Rewrite the sentence: *Finding those spots yourself is no problem.*
   b. Remove the sentence.
   c. Make no change.

8. Sentence 9
   a. Rewrite the sentence: *You should know that a utility company can provide a more scientific check.*
   b. Make no change.
   c. Rewrite the sentence: *A utility company can provide a more scientific check.*

9. Sentence 10
   a. Rewrite the sentence: *For a low price, the company will take an infrared photograph of the outside of your building.*
   b. Rewrite the sentence: *It doesn't cost much to have an infrared photograph taken.*
   c. Make no change.

10. Sentence 12
   a. Rewrite the sentence: *If you take an ultraviolet photograph of an object, it will not look like a normal photograph.*
   b. Make no change.
   c. Remove the sentence.

Assignment 1 Prewriting *Step 1:* Select one of the following topics for a technical report, or choose another topic that interests you and about which you can find sufficient information. *Step 2:* Using the library and other sources, research your topic and make notes.

1. The use of wood-burning stoves as an alternative source of heat
2. Practical water-conservation methods for this community
3. The advantages and disadvantages of opening a fast-food shop in this neighborhood
4. Effective fire-prevention methods in the home

Assignment 2 Writing *Step 1:* Using the notes from your research in Assignment 1, write a technical report. Include numbered lists in the body of your report, if necessary. *Step 2:* Write a conclusion for your report, based on the recommendations that your research indicates. *Step 3:* Write an introduction that provides background information and explains the purpose of the report. *Step 4:* Prepare an abstract that covers the main points made in your report.

Assignment 3 Writing *Step 1:* Using your notes from Assignment 1, prepare footnotes to accompany your technical report. *Step 2:* If you have five or more terms to define, write a glossary for your report. *Step 3:* Prepare a bibliography from the references that you used in researching your topic.

Assignment 4 Writing *Step 1:* Prepare a list of illustrations if you included charts and diagrams in the body of your report. *Step 2:* Prepare a table of contents for the entire technical report. Double-check to see that all page references are correct. *Step 3:* Prepare the title page for your report.

Assignment 5 Revising Reread and revise all parts of your technical report before handing it in.

Assignment Checklist

Check your assignments for the following points:

✔ 1. Did you choose a topic that is appropriate for a technical report?

✔ 2. Did you do research to find information on your topic?

✔ 3. Did you write an abstract that covers the main points of your report?

✔ 4. Did you prepare a title page and a table of contents?

✔ 5. Did you write an introduction that explains the purpose of your report?

✔ 6. Did you write a body that accurately reports the findings of your research?

✔ 7. Did you write a conclusion that presents your recommendations?

✔ 8. Did you include footnotes in your report?

✔ 9. Did you write a glossary that defines the difficult terms in your report if you have five or more such terms?

✔ 10. Did you list the references that you used to research your report?

✔ 11. Did you list any illustrations that you used, including those that you made?

✔ 12. Did you revise your report?

✔ 13. Did you check your report for correct grammar, usage, spelling, and punctuation?

Miro-Weld Solar Panels: Writing a Technical Description

Situation: You are a copywriter for a catalogue of solar home-heating products. For a catalogue entry about Miro-Weld solar panels, you need to describe the panels and to explain how they work. As you write, keep in mind the following information.

Writer: you as a catalogue copywriter

Audience: potential buyers of solar home-heating systems

Topic: Miro-Weld solar panels

Purpose: to describe the product and to explain how it works

Directions: To write your copy, follow these steps.

Step 1. Read the notes and study the diagrams provided by Miro-Weld shown on the facing page.

Step 2. Using the notes labeled "Description and Function," write a paragraph that describes and explains the Miro-Weld panels. Remember that you are providing information about an object to readers who may know little about solar heating. Present your information in a logical sequence and refer to the diagrams as necessary.

Step 3. Using the information labeled "Panel Installation," write a second paragraph that explains how to install the panels.

Step 4. Write a concluding paragraph that explains how to order the panels.

Miro-Weld

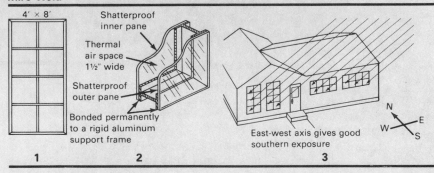

1

4' × 8'

2

Shatterproof
inner pane

Thermal
air space
1½" wide

Shatterproof
outer pane

Bonded permanently
to a rigid aluminum
support frame

3

East-west axis gives good
southern exposure

N
E
W
S

Description and Function
—A simple method of passive heat collection: The sun's rays pass
   through the panels and are absorbed by a thermal mass such as a
   stone floor or dark wall; double-layer panels keep the heat in the
   room.
—Panels measure 4 ft. by 8 ft.
—Panels transmit maximum solar radiation.
—Southern exposure provides maximum heat in the winter, minimum
   heat in summer.
—Panels collect all the energy (*direct* from the sun or *diffuse* on cloudy
   days) that passes through the panel.
—Panels are lightweight, unbreakable, shatterproof, economical
—Panels are made of 2 flat sheets of fiber glass bonded to a rigid
   aluminum support frame.
—Panels can withstand 2 days' exposure to temperatures of 300° F.
—Weigh only 1½ lb per sq ft.

Panel Installation
—Follow detailed instructions for home installation included with every
   order.
—Miro-Weld guarantees customer satisfaction.
—Lay panels out in horizontal rows.
—Allow ½ in. space between panels.
—Be sure to provide support on all four sides of panels when they are
   mounted.
—Panels are factory-assembled for easy installation.
—For waterproof installation use Miro-Weld sealant.
—Mount panels on south-facing wall or southern roof exposure for
   maximum heat again.

Ordering Information
—Order by mail, prepaid, from Miro-Weld Inc., P. O. Box 185, Chicago, Il
   60606
—Price, $200 per panel, including shipping.
—Allow six weeks for delivery.

Unit Assignments

Assignment 1   Define the following words, using a three-part definition: the item, its class, and its distinguishing features.

1. ligament   3. grafting   5. longitude
2. quasar   4. triceps   6. retina

Assignment 2   Select two of the following mechanisms; define each and explain how it operates.

1. binoculars   4. lever   7. spark plug
2. prism   5. pulley   8. sextant
3. block and tackle   6. fulcrum   9. calipers

Assignment 3   On your paper, write an explanation of one of the following processes requiring an operator. Include diagrams, if necessary. Use library sources and other references to obtain the necessary information.

1. how to operate a 16-mm movie projector
2. how to assemble, operate, and care for a stereo tone arm and turntable
3. how to develop film
4. how to draw a blueprint
5. how to change the oil in a car

Assignment 4   On your paper, write an explanation of one of the following processes not requiring an operator. Include diagrams, if necessary. Use library sources and other references to obtain the necessary information.

1. how stalagmites and stalactites are formed
2. how the human ear transmits sound
3. how a television picture is formed
4. how acid corrodes metal
5. how an electric clock works

Assignment 5   Write a technical report in which you analyze two types of cameras: a single-lens reflex and a camera that produces instant photographs. Using the library and other sources, compare the cost, size, and weight of both cameras. Include the cost of film for each and the cost of developing for the single-lens reflex camera. Discuss the practicality of using each indoors and outdoors. Conclude your report with recommendations.

Revising Your Assignments

For help in revising technical writing, consult the Checklist for Revision on the last page of this book.

Unit Tests

Test 1

A. Number your paper from 1 to 5. Next to each number, write *True* if the sentence is true or *False* if it is false.

1. In technical writing the opinions and experience of the author are not emphasized.
2. You may use slang and contractions in technical writing.
3. If you cannot explain a point clearly, you may substitute a diagram for an explanation.
4. Use spatial order when you describe a process.
5. Once you have gathered data for a technical report, you must interpret it and make a recommendation.

B. Number your paper from 6 to 10. Next to each number, write the letter of the term that correctly completes the sentence. You will use all but one of the items.

a. process   d. table of contents
b. glossary   e. technical report
c. mechanism   f. abstract

6. A(n) __?__ is any object or tool that is used for a specific purpose.
7. A(n) __?__ is a series of actions, changes, or functions that bring about a product or a result.
8. In a(n) __?__ your purpose is to help the reader solve a problem or to make a decision leading to an action.
9. A(n) __?__ is a brief summary of main points.
10. A(n) __?__ is an alphabetical listing of terms with their definitions.

C. Number your paper from 11 to 15. Next to each number, write the letter of the item that correctly answers the question.

11. Which of the following is *not* true about technical writing?
    a. It should be humorous.
    b. It should be impersonal.
    c. It should present facts in an unbiased way.
    d. It should be written from the third-person point of view.

12. Which of the following is *not* part of a definition of a mechanism?
    a. The name of the item.
    b. The group to which the item belongs.
    c. Features that distinguish the item from other items in its group.
    d. Examples of other items in its group.
13. Which of the following is a good strategy for explaining a process requiring an operator?
    a. Use the passive voice.
    b. Assume that your audience will know all the technical terms.
    c. List any special equipment necessary to work through the process.
    d. Include personal observations about the process.
14. Which of the following is *not* a part of a technical report?
    a. A title page
    b. A table of contents
    c. A glossary
    d. An index
15. Which of the following is a good strategy for writing the abstract of a technical report?
    a. Write it before you complete your report.
    b. Follow the same organization in it that you followed in your report.
    c. Place it at the end of your report.
    d. Include important informtion that is not included in your report.

Test 2

Choose one of the Unit Assignments. Write the assignment as directed and hand it in to your teacher.

Writing Business Letters

Unit Preview

Whenever you have occasion to write a business letter, make sure that your letter contains all the necessary information, presented concisely and courteously.

The letter on the following page contains all of the information necessary to the person who will receive it.

For Analysis   On your paper, answer the following questions about the letter from Kevin Kinnaly.

1. What is the purpose of the letter?
2. What information is being requested?
3. Why is the information needed?
4. Where should the information be sent?

In this unit you will learn how to write standard business letters: the order letter, the request letter, and the adjustment letter. In addition, you will learn how to write a letter applying for a job, how to write a résumé, and how to write a letter expressing your opinion. In writing these letters, you will practice the three steps of the writing process: prewriting, writing, and revising.

```
1502 Highland Terrace
Sacramento, California 95828
March 28, 19__

Dr. Nancy Christopher
Superintendent of Schools
Sacramento School District
842 Washington Avenue
Sacramento, California 95816

Dear Dr. Christopher:

On behalf of Valley High School's senior class,
I would like to invite you, as newly appointed
superintendent of schools, to participate in our
graduation ceremony in the Sacramento Civic
Center at 6:00 P.M., June 6.

It has been traditional for the superintendent
of schools to deliver a brief address of
approximately fifteen minutes to Valley High
School's graduating class.  We would be pleased
if you would continue the tradition.

In order to complete our plans, we hope to
receive your response to our invitation by
April 15. We would also like to ask you to
attend a reception with officers of the senior
class and the Valley High School administration.

Thank you very much.

Sincerely yours,
Kevin Kinnaly
Kevin Kinnaly
Senior Class President
```

13.1 Standard Business Letters

Parts of a Business Letter

All business letters, regardless of their purpose, consist of the following parts.

Heading.   The heading is your address and the date. Place it at the upper right or upper left of your stationery, depending on which letter style you are using (*page 588*). Spell out the name of your state, or abbreviate it by using the standard abbreviation or the Postal

Service abbreviation. In the date, give the month, the day, and the year.

Inside Address.   The inside address is the name and address of the person or organization to whom you are writing. Include such titles as *Dr., Mr.,* or *Ms.* with a person's name. In the last line of the inside address, use the same form for the state as you used in the heading.

Salutation.   Capitalize the first word and all the nouns in the salutation. Place a colon after the salutation. Use *Dear Sir, Dear Madam,* or *Dear Sir or Madam* when addressing someone whose name you do not know.

Body.   The body consists of the paragraphs that state your business. Leave an extra line of space between the salutation and the first paragraph and between all other paragraphs.

Complimentary Close.   Capitalize only the first word of the complimentary close. Place a comma at the end of the close. *Yours truly, Very truly yours, Sincerely yours,* and *Yours sincerely* are acceptable complimentary closes.

Signature.   Write your full name below the complimentary close. If your letter is handwritten, print your name under your signature. If it is typed, type your name under your signature.

Styles of Business Letters

The two styles of business letters are the block style and the modified block style. In the **block style,** all parts of the letter start at the left margin. Paragraphs are not indented. Use the block style only when you are typing a letter. The letter on page 587 is written in block style.

In the **modified block style,** place the heading, the complimentary close, and the signature to the right. You may either indent paragraphs or start them at the left margin, as in the block style. You may use the modified block style for either handwritten or typed letters.

Regardless of the style that you use, be sure to leave sufficient margins on all sides of your letter by centering your letter on the paper.

Follow these general strategies for writing brief, clear, and accurate business letters.

Strategies

1. *Use unlined paper measuring 8½ inches by 11 inches.*

2. *Type your letter, if possible.* If you cannot, use black or blue ink. Do not use pencil.

3. *Make sure that the heading and the inside address are complete and accurate.*

4. *Include in the body of the letter all the information necessary to achieve your purpose.*

5. *Avoid slang and contractions.* Do not write in a tone that is too casual or informal.

6. *Avoid using clichés and wordy expressions* in an effort to sound formal and businesslike. Note the substitutions in following examples.

AVOID	USE
in the amount of	for
enclosed please find	enclosed is
herein enclosed	enclosed
at the earliest possible date	as early as possible
at the present time	now
I wish to express my gratitude	thank you
in accordance with your request	as you requested
as per your request	as you requested

7. *Do not end your letter with a participial phrase,* such as "thanking you in advance" or "hoping to hear from you soon."

8. *Reread your letter carefully for errors in typing, spelling, grammar, and punctuation.* If you find errors, rewrite or retype your letter.

The Request Letter

Write a request, or inquiry, letter when you need information on a specific subject, or when you need a brochure or a catalogue. Like all business letters, the request letter should be brief, but it should also contain all the necessary information. Study the following example.

```
330 Owens Avenue
South Bend, Indiana 46605
October 10, 19__

Director of Admissions
Indiana State University
Terre Haute, Indiana 47809

Dear Sir or Madam:

I am a senior at Franklin High School in South
Bend.  In the fall I plan to attend college,
taking courses leading to a degree in marine
biology.  I would like to know if Indiana State
University offers a degree in marine biology.

Would you please also send the following:

     1. a current catalogue
     2. information on scholarships,
        particularly in the science department
     3. information on student loans and
        student work programs

If there is a charge for this service, please
let me know.  Thank you very much.

Sincerely yours,

Max Nelson

Max Nelson
```

When writing a request letter, follow the general strategies for business letters on page 589. In addition, follow these specific strategies.

Strategies

1. *Make your requests reasonable and specific.* For example, do not request from the National Park Service all the available information on parks. Instead, you could ask for information about one or two particular parks.

2. *Offer to pay for printed material if you are not certain that it is free.*

3. *Allow sufficient time for your request to be filled.* If you need information for a class report, for example, write at least three weeks before your report is due.

The Order Letter

When ordering merchandise through the mail, you must sometimes write an order letter. Make sure that your letter contains complete and accurate information about quantity, size, color, cost, and catalogue number. Study the letter on the following page.

When writing an order letter, follow the general strategies for writing business letters on page 589. In addition, follow these strategies.

Strategies

1. *Give the source of the advertisement or the catalogue year, season, or number from which you are ordering.*

2. *Double-check your arithmetic.* Also, make sure that you have included postage and handling costs, if necessary.

3. *Explain how you intend to pay for the merchandise.* Do not send cash through the mail. Use a money order or a check instead.

4. *Explain if you must have the merchandise by a certain date.*

5. *Type or write the word* Enclosure *in the bottom left corner of your letter* if you have enclosed a check or a money order.

617 Depot Road
Omaha, Nebraska 68123
September 23, 19__

Griffin Bros. Stationers
1122 Broad Street
Pittsburgh, Pennsylvania 15211

Dear Sir or Madam:

    I would like to order the following items from
your fall sale catalogue.

Code	Quantity	Description	Price
B-128	1	Calligraphy for Beginners	$8.95
P-900	1	St. Pierre pen	7.98
C-006	1	Extra-fine nib	1.00
C-009	1	B-2 nib	1.00
C-105	1	bottle black india ink	3.00
C-309	1	sheet 36" x 30" ivory parchment	3.00
			24.93
		Shipping and handling	2.50
		Total	$27.43

    Please send the items to me at my home address.

    If my order cannot be filled in full within six
weeks, please let me know; I may wish to cancel all
or part of it.

    I have enclosed a check for twenty-seven dollars
and forty-three cents ($27.43).

Sincerely yours,

Margaret Rogers

Margaret Rogers

Enclosure: check #157

The Adjustment Letter

Write an adjustment letter whenever an order that you place is not filled correctly or when merchandise that you purchase is defective. Explain the problem clearly and courteously and suggest a solution. Study the example letter.

911 Webster Avenue
St. Paul, Minnesota 55115
November 2, 19__

Western Trading Company
1172 Harbor Drive
Portland, Oregon 97267

Dear Sir or Madam:

On September 23, I ordered a pair of blue gloves, a cable-knit cardigan, and a red down vest from your company's winter preview catalogue. All the merchandise arrived promptly three weeks later; however, you mistakenly sent a navy blue vest instead of the red one I requested.

I am returning the blue vest to you in a separate package. In exchange please send me a red vest, size large (item number W-179).

Also, I would appreciate being reimbursed the $2.35 in postage charges incurred in returning the wrong vest to you.

Thank you.

Sincerely,

Marcus Hopkins

Marcus Hopkins

When writing an adjustment letter, follow the general strategies on page 589. In addition, follow the strategies on the following page.

Strategies

1. *State the problem accurately and clearly.* Try to explain the problem in the first paragraph of your letter.

2. *Suggest a solution.* Ask politely for a refund or a replacement.

3. *Keep a copy of your letter until the adjustment that you request has been made.*

Exercise 1   Writing: An Adjustment Letter   Use the following information to write an adjustment letter in modified block style.

Your name is Maryanne Bonica; you live at 811 Mountain View Drive, Memphis, Tennessee 38112. You ordered two tickets for *The Pirates of Penzance.* You asked for seats in the first balcony for the evening performance on February 9. You have received two tickets for February 9, but only one is for a seat in the first balcony; the other is for the second balcony. Because it is only January 28, there is still time to get the correct ticket. Write to the Majestic Theater, Box Office, 801 South Street, Memphis, Tennessee 38102, and request an adjustment.

Exercise 2   Revising: A Request Letter   Rewrite the following letter, making all necessary changes in form, tone, and content. Eliminate and revise sentences as needed.

April 20, 19—
Dover, Delaware
12 Prospect Lane 19901

Ms. Marlene Chu, Manager
16 Lancaster Road
Dover, Delaware
Bijou Theater

Dear Marlene,

Last summer my family, friends, and I attended all of the movies in the Humphrey Bogart Film Festival that you held last July. Boy, like Bogart was really something! I think it was really neat of you to give Bogart fans, both old ones and new ones, the opportunity to see his films in a theater instead of just on late-night television. You are also to be commended for providing worthwhile entertainment at a time when many young people have little to do.

This summer, how about having a Greta Garbo Film Festival? I know many young people, as well as adults, who would welcome the opportunity to see all of her movies. She was so beautiful. Did you see her in *Camille*? If you do not have another festival planned yet, I would appreciate your giving consideration to a Garbo Film Festival.

Thanking you in advance, I am

Yours truly,

Edward Sansone

Assignment 1 Writing On an unlined sheet of paper, write an adjustment letter in modified block style to the publisher of a photography magazine to which you recently subscribed at regular rates. Now you have discovered that student rates are available. Write to the magazine publisher and ask for an adjustment. Make up a name for the magazine and its publisher, but use your own name and return address.

Assignment 2 Writing On an unlined sheet of paper, write a letter in modified block style to a major airline requesting information on careers in air travel. Ask for descriptions and requirements for the position of flight attendant, as well as for other positions not requiring travel. Make up a name for the airline, but use your own name and return address.

Assignment Checklist

Check your assignments for the following points:

1. Did you include all of the necessary parts of the business letter?
2. Does the body of your letter contain all of the necessary information?
3. Did you use the modified block style?
4. Did you state your request briefly, clearly, and courteously?
5. Did you proofread your letter for correct grammar, usage, spelling, and punctuation?

13.2 Applying for a Job

When applying for a job, you need to write a letter of application and a résumé. Both are necessary to give a prospective employer an accurate impression of you and your qualifications.

Application Letter

The purpose of an application letter is to get an appointment for an interview. Be certain that your letter contains the following information.

Position Sought.   In the first paragraph, state what position you are seeking and tell how you learned of it. Do not merely say that you are interested in any position that happens to be open.

Experience.   In the second paragraph, make a brief reference to whatever experience that you have that qualifies you for the job. This information need not be presented in detail here. You will be more explicit in your résumé (*pages 597–598*).

Conclusion.   State courteously that you would like to have a personal interview at the employer's convenience. Tell where and when you can be reached to arrange an appointment.

Study the letter of application that appears on the next page.

When writing a job application letter, follow the general strategies for business letters on page 589. In addition, follow these specific strategies.

Strategies

1. *Express confidence in your ability to do the job, but do not boast.*

2. *Read your letter aloud for tone* to make sure that you do not sound arrogant, flippant, or too casual. If you wish, have a family member or a teacher read your letter.

3. *Include additional information about yourself in an attached résumé.*

```
                              227 West Pine Street
                              Flagstaff, Arizona 86001
                              May 8, 19__
Mr. David Stewart
1907 Central Avenue
Flagstaff, Arizona 86001

Dear Mr. Stewart:

        I am responding to your May 6
advertisement in the Review Journal for a
summer assistant in your law office. I would
like to be considered for that position.

        I understand from your advertisement that
your office needs an assistant to file, to
deliver material to the courthouse, and to do
occasional research. You will note from my
enclosed résumé that I have assisted in the
counseling offices of my high school and worked
at the public library. Through my library job,
I have become familiar with research work.

        I believe that my background, interests,
and experience qualify me for the position
advertised; furthermore, I am interested in law
as a career. I would be pleased to meet with
you for an interview at your convenience. My
home phone number is 555-0901, and I can be
reached there any afternoon after 3:15.

        Thank you for your consideration.

                              Very truly yours,

                              Elizabeth K. Knox
                              Elizabeth K. Knox
```

Writing a Résumé

With your letter of application, enclose a résumé. A **résumé,** sometimes called a data sheet, is a summary of your qualifications. Its purpose is to present your qualifications in a clear, well-organized manner. Include the following information in your résumé: position wanted, experience, education, personal interests and special skills, and references.

Begin work on your résumé before you start applying for a job. You need time to collect all the data and to write, organize, and revise your résumé until it represents your best effort. An early start will also allow you time to contact those persons whom you wish to use as references.

The sample résumé on the facing page has side headings to point out the categories of information contained.

Use the following strategies when writing a résumé.

Strategies

1. *Type your résumé.* It should be neat and free of errors.

2. *Limit your résumé to one or two pages.*

3. *List your most recent work experience first.* Include the dates that you were employed, the places where you were employed, and the responsibilities that you had.

4. *Do not include personal data* such as age, height, weight, religion, and so forth.

5. *List two, preferably three, references, with an address or telephone number for each.* One of your references should be a character reference, someone who knows you well. Do not include family members or friends your own age. Do not list anyone without first obtaining his or her permission.

Exercise 1   Writing: An Application Letter   Write a letter of application from Clark Masur, 11 Ridge Road, New Haven, Connecticut 06523, in response to the following advertisement. Supply all information needed.

ASSISTANT WANTED
Local landscape architectural firm needs assistant for major project. Must have knowledge of botany and be able to read plans. Mechanical drawing helpful but not required. Some light clerical duties involved. Reply by letter only to Mr. Gerry Travers, Tomasini Landscaping Inc., New Haven, CT 06525

Elizabeth K. Knox
227 West Pine Street
Flagstaff, Arizona 86001
Telephone: 555-0901

Position Wanted   Assistant in law office

Experience   Flagstaff Public Library, June-August
19__. Checked books in and out;
shelved books; assisted library
patrons in locating books and nonprint
materials; performed research
assignments

Mountainview High School, Counseling
Office September-May, 19__. Office
Assistant: typed and filed letters;
made telephone calls

Education   Will graduate with honors from
Mountainview High School, June 2, 19__

Skills and   Skills
Interests   Speak Spanish
Type 50 wpm
Have driver's license

Interests
Member of the Mountainview High School
debating team
Member of All-City Youth Choir
Participant in local amateur
theatricals

Award
Mountainview High School Debater of
the Year, 19__

References   Mr. Mark Anderson, Director
Flagstaff Public Library
548 Charleston Avenue
Flagstaff, Arizona 86002
Telephone: 876-9453

Mr. Robert Harney, Government Teacher
Mountainview High School
1702 Valley View Drive
Flagstaff, Arizona 86002
Telephone: 878-9720

Exercise 2   Writing: A Résumé   Using the following information, write a résumé for Clark Masur in the preceding exercise. Use
side headings to categorize the information. Proofread the finished
résumé and correct any mistakes.

Clark will graduate this year from Lincoln High School.
Among the courses he has taken are botany, biology, and mathematics. His hobbies include sketching and photography. He has a
driver's license and can drive both automatic and stick-shift vehicles.
He knows first aid.

Last summer from June through August, Clark worked for
Harvey Nursery and Gardeners in New Haven. His job included
watering and fertilizing flowers and shrubs, hauling soil, planting
flower bulbs, and checking plants for signs of insects or disease.

Clark is currently employed by the New Haven Botanical
Society, where he conducts Saturday-morning nature walks on which
he helps youngsters to identify and draw or photograph leaves and
wildflowers.

Clark's references are the following:

Mr. Robert Harney, Botany Teacher, Lincoln High School, New
Haven, CT 06514   Telephone: 555-0847

Mr. Mark Anderson, Manager, Harvey Nursery and Gardeners,
Wedgewood Road, New Haven, CT 06514
Telephone: 555-6211

Ms. Donna Schaeffer, New Haven Botanical Society, 60 Bellview
Avenue, New Haven, CT 06514   Telephone: 555-1145

Assignment   Writing   Find a help-wanted advertisement that
interests you in the classified section of your local newspaper. Write a
letter applying for the job. Prepare a résumé to accompany your
letter.

Assignment Checklist

Check your assignment for the following points:

✔ 1. Did you begin your letter by stating what position you are
seeking?
✔ 2. Did you tell where and when you can be reached?

✔ 3. Did you read your letter for appropriate tone?
✔ 4. Did you include side headings in your résumé?
✔ 5. Did you list your most recent work experience first in your résumé?
✔ 6. Did you list at least two references, with addresses and phone numbers, in your résumé?
✔ 7. Did your proofread your letter and résumé for correct grammar, usage, spelling, and punctuation?

13.3 Expressing an Opinion

Occasionally there may be local or national issues on which you wish to express your opinion. One effective way to express opinions is to write a letter to a newspaper, a national magazine, a television or radio network, or an elected official, such as a mayor or a senator.

Your letter of opinion will be more likely to achieve the result that you wish if you maintain a reasonable tone throughout. Anger, sarcasm, and accusations offend readers and will diminish your persuasiveness. If your letter is restrained, logical, courteous, and tactful, you may persuade others to accept your opinion.

Parts of an Opinion Letter

To be well organized, your letter of opinion should contain the following parts.

Summary and Opinion. Begin your letter by giving a brief summary of the situation or issue about which you are writing. Then state your opinion briefly and clearly.

Support. Support your opinions with logical and factual statements. Once you have made your point, do not wander from it; do not include irrelevant statements. See Unit 8, "Persuasive Writing," for help in writing persuasive arguments.

Conclusion. Conclude your letter by summarizing your main points or, when appropriate, by suggesting a course of action that you think should be followed.

Forms of Address

When writing to elected officials, use conventional forms of address. Consult the following chart.

PERSON AND ADDRESS	SALUTATION
The President	
The President The White House Washington, DC 20500	Dear Mr. President: Sir:
United States Senator	
The Honorable Justin Hale The United States Senate Washington, DC 20510	Dear Senator Hale: Dear Sir (or Madam):
United States Representative	
The Honorable Joan Weitz House of Representatives Washington, DC 20515	Dear Representative Weitz: Dear Congresswoman (or Congressman) Weitz: Dear Sir (or Madam):
Governor	
The Honorable Clyde Doyle Governor of Utah Salt Lake City, UT 84100	Dear Governor Doyle: Dear Sir (or Madam):
State Senator	
The Honorable Mary O'Brien The State Senate Jefferson City, MO 65101	Dear Senator O'Brien Dear Madam (or Sir):
State Legislator	
The Honorable César Ruiz The General Assembly Richmond, VA 21900	Dear Representative Ruiz Dear Mr. Ruiz: Dear Sir (or Madam):
Mayor	
The Honorable Lynn Venable Mayor of the City of Green Bay City Hall Green Bay, WI 54301	Dear Mayor Venable: Dear Madam (or Mr.) Mayor:

Study the letter of opinion that appears on the facing page.

542 Black Mountain Way
Aberdeen, South Dakota 57401
February 9, 19__

The Honorable Glenn Reid
Mayor of the City of Aberdeen
City Hall
Aberdeen, South Dakota 57401

Dear Mayor Reid:

    I am writing in response to a recent proposal
that the city build a parking garage on the downtown
lot formerly occupied by the Wentworth estate, at the
corner of Main Street and Marlboro Avenue. Since the
city of Aberdeen acquired the land from the Wentworth
heirs after the estate was demolished by fire two
years ago, several proposals for its use have been
discussed; yet only the latest has received serious,
though perhaps unjustified, attention.

    The city has built two parking garages in the
downtown area within the past decade; a third would
seem unnecessary. Certainly a feasibility study
should be completed before discussion of the parking
garage proposal proceeds further. Should such a study
forecast little demand for additional parking
facilities in the downtown area, perhaps the vacant
lot could be converted into a park/rest area for
downtown workers and shoppers. The Downtown Merchants
Association might even be willing to provide the
minimal upkeep necessary for a small park.

    If it is found that parking facilities are truly
needed, I would support the current proposal.
However, I suspect that a third parking garage would
prove superfluous, while a small park might be better
appreciated and enhance the appeal of Aberdeen's
downtown district.

                   Respectfully,

                   Joseph Albertson

                   Joseph Albertson

Writing the Opinion Letter

Use the following strategies to write an effective opinion letter.

Strategies

1. *Keep your letter brief.* Many newspapers and magazines indicate the preferred length for letters, usually two hundred words or less.

2. *Use the salutation* To the Editor: *in letters to newspapers and magazines.*

3. *Sign your letter.* Also include your address and telephone number so that the newspaper can verify that you wrote the letter.

4. *Write promptly.* Editors often will not publish letters on subjects that are no longer current.

5. *Address your query or suggestion to the public official who is best able to respond to it.* For example, do not write to the governor about matters that pertain to your community only, and do not write to your mayor about an issue to be decided in the United States Senate.

Exercise   Writing: An Opinion Letter   Using the following information, write a letter of opinion in modified block style. Then proofread your letter and revise it.

Your name is Scott Ames, and you live at 331 North Avenue, Brunswick, Maine 04011. Every Tuesday evening for the past three weeks, you have watched *American Classics Revisited,* a television series featuring dramatizations of famous American short stories. You are enjoying the series very much because of the quality of the acting and also because of the choice of stories, especially Eudora Welty's "A Visit of Charity." However, the program airs from 9:30 to 11:00, a time that you think is inappropriate for younger viewers. Write to Mr. Edward L. Reynolds, President, American Television Network, 7 Rockefeller Plaza, New York, NY 10020. Suggest that the program be switched to Friday night at the same time or to 8:00 to 9:30 on Tuesday nights.

Assignment 1 Writing Find a letter to the editor on the editorial page of your local newspaper. Write a letter to the editor in which you offer support for or arguments against the points it contains.

Assignment 2 Writing Think of an unresolved issue that affects your community or state. Write a letter to your governor or mayor in which you suggest a solution. Be specific.

Assignment Checklist

Check your assignments for the following points:

✔ 1. Did you state your opinion briefly, clearly, and courteously?
✔ 2. Did you make a unified and coherent argument?
✔ 3. Did you summarize your main points or suggest a course of action?
✔ 4. Did you maintain a reasonable tone?
✔ 5. Did you include your name, address, and telephone number?
✔ 6. Did you proofread your letter for correct grammar, usage, spelling, and punctuation?

A Model Senate Program: Writing a Business Letter

Situation: You have read a newspaper article about a program in another state that enables high school seniors to act as state legislators for a day. Students in the program discuss policy issues and follow the agenda of a regular legislative session. You are going to write a letter in which you explain to your state senator why you think this program should be made available to students in your state.

Writer: you as a high school senior
Audience: your state senator
Topic: the Model Senate Program
Purpose: to inform and persuade in a letter

Directions: To write your letter, follow these steps.

Step 1. Read the newspaper article on the facing page about the Model Senate Program in Moline.

Step 2. Write a letter in modified block style to your state senator. In the first paragraph, state who you are and tell why you are writing. In the next paragraph, tell what the Model Senate Program is and explain how it works. In the third paragraph, explain the benefits of the program and tell why you feel that your state should have a Model Senate Program. In the concluding paragraph, urge your senator to institute a Model Senate Program in your state. Thank the senator for considering your request and indicate courteously that you would appreciate a response.

Local Students Go to Senate

MOLINE—Eighteen high school seniors from Moline attended a Model Senate yesterday at the state capitol. The students, elected by their classmates and accompanied by a teacher, participated in a day-long session of legislative decision making. They participated in a lively debate and roll-call vote on a current issue.

The Model Senate Program, begun in 1980, gives students firsthand experience of the state's legislative processes. The students accompany their senator on a round of activities that begins in the senator's office and ends in the state senate chamber. As part of their activities, student "senators" greet constituents, read legislative briefs, and lunch in the Senate dining room. Both the students and their teacher are encouraged to ask questions of legislators about problems facing the state.

Legislators, educators, and students have praised the program for its ability to stimulate interest in government. State Senator Roberta Avedon comments, "I think it's a marvelous opportunity both for us and for the students. They have a genuine interest in how government works, and I wouldn't be surprised if some of these students went on to become legislators themselves." Jonathan Baccus, social studies teacher at Moline Senior High School, has accompanied students to the state capital every year since the program began. "The benefits are many," he says. "Students have a better grasp of how a bill becomes a law. We discuss and vote on these same issues in the classroom, and students are more involved than ever in how our government works to serve the people." The words of Bob Blanque, a student from Kendall High in Kendall County, capture it best: "For the first time, I feel that I'm really a part of the democratic process."

Unit Assignments

Assignment 1   You are interested in a certain occupation, and a relative has given you the name of someone in that field. Write a letter requesting an interview with that person and a tour of the job site. Make sure that your letter is brief, yet specific. Proofread and revise your letter to correct any errors.

Assignment 2   After you graduate you would like to work and continue your education at the same time. Write a letter of application to a prospective employer explaining your situation and your job needs. Include a résumé of your education and previous job experience. Proofread and revise your letter and résumé.

Assignment 3   There is a historic one-room schoolhouse in your community that is to be razed to make way for an access road to a new shopping mall. It has been maintained by a local civic group, and it is used for small community gatherings. Write a letter to the editor of your local paper explaining why you feel that the schoolhouse should not be demolished. Proofread and revise your letter to correct any errors in content, spelling, punctuation, and tone.

Assignment 4   Your state legislature is considering enacting a bottle bill. Write a letter to your local representative urging him or her to support or not to support the legislation. Explain the reasons that you feel the bill would or would not be good for your state. Proofread and revise your letter to correct any errors in spelling, punctuation, and tone.

Assignment 5   You ordered a number of items of camping equipment from C. M. Peterson's summer catalogue. When the package arrived, one item was missing. There was no notice that it would be sent at a later date. Write an adjustment letter to the company explaining the problem. Proofread your letter and eliminate any errors.

Assignment 6   While you were looking through Kaplan's catalogue of posters, you saw a poster of Mt. Everest that you would like to put on the wall of your room. Write an order letter to the Kaplan company. The poster is item 5603 in the fall catalogue, and its price is $5.99. Then proofread and revise your letter to eliminate any errors.

Assignment 7   You and several of your friends are interested in the sport of windsurfing. Write to the branch of the National Windsurfing Association in a city near your home. Ask where windsurfing can be done in your area, when lessons are given, and what equipment is needed. Proofread and revise your letter to correct any errors in content, spelling, punctuation, and tone.

Assignment 8   You believe that your school should present a career day in which local business people explain what types of jobs are available and what qualifications are necessary for those jobs. Express your opinion in a letter to the principal of your school. Explain why you think that the career day would be valuable to students. Then proofread and revise your letter to eliminate any errors.

Revising Your Assignments

For help in revising letters, consult the Checklist for Revision on the last page of this book.

Unit Tests

Test 1

A. Number your paper from 1 to 5. Next to each number, write *True* if the sentence is true or *False* if it is false.

1. In a résumé you should list your most recent work experience first.
2. Letters to the editor do not have to be signed.
3. A job-application letter is meant to secure an appointment for an interview.
4. If you cannot type a business letter, you should write it in blue or black ink.
5. Your résumé should include a minimum of four references.

B. Number your paper from 6 to 10. Next to each number, write the letter of the term that correctly completes the sentence. You will use all but one of the terms.

a. adjustment letter   d. opinion letter
b. block style   e. inside address
c. résumé   f. modified block style

6. The __?__ is the name and address of the person to whom you are writing.
7. In the __?__, all parts of the letter start at the left margin.
8. You write a(n) __?__ when an order that you place is not filled correctly or when merchandise that you purchase is defective.
9. A(n) __?__ is a summary of your qualifications for a job.
10. A(n) __?__ expresses your view of a local or national issue.

C. Number your paper from 11 to 15. Next to each number, write the letter of the item that correctly answers the question.

11. Which of the following statements would be appropriate in a request letter?
    a. Hoping to hear from you soon.
    b. I'm sure your catalogue will take some of the hassle out of trying to decide which college to apply to.
    c. Please let me know if there is any charge for this service.
    d. Send the information to the above address right away.
    e. As per your request, I am enclosing a stamped, self-addressed envelope.

12. Which of the following does *not* belong in a job application letter?
   a. I feel that I am qualified for the position.
   b. I am 5 feet 11 inches tall and weigh 142 pounds.
   c. I will be happy to come for an interview at your convenience.
   d. From my enclosed résumé you will note that I have studied accounting.
   e. Thank you for your consideration.

13. Which of the following is an appropriate reason for writing an opinion letter to your United States senator?
   a. You feel that your community should continue to sponsor the Spring Kite Festival, as it has done in the past.
   b. You disagree with those people who feel that your city is not large enough to support a professional basketball team.
   c. Although you realize that no one welcomes an increase in the state sales tax, you think that your state should raise the tax rate.
   d. You would like to see a national holiday in honor of Benjamin Franklin, whom you consider to be unjustly ignored.
   e. You think that Saturday morning television should offer a wider choice of programming.

14. Which of the following points should *not* be mentioned in a résumé?
   a. You can write a computer program.
   b. You speak and write French.
   c. You participated in an after-school tutorial program for non-English speaking students.
   d. You are nineteen years old.
   e. You know standard first-aid procedures.

15. Which of the following statements about résumés is *not* true?
   a. Résumés should have side headings to categorize information.
   b. Résumés should not be handwritten.
   c. Listed references should always contain telephone numbers.
   d. The résumé should begin with a description of the position sought.
   e. The place and date of one's birth belong at the top of the résumé.

Test 2

Choose one of the Unit Assignments. Write the assignment as directed and hand it in to your teacher.

Part Three

Related Skills

As you complete assignments and other projects now and in the future, you will need skills that are related to writing. By studying the units in Part Three, you will learn skills that you can use to present your ideas better in either writing or speaking. Techniques for improving your spelling and your vocabulary will aid you in all of your work, and they will also help you to present yourself well to prospective employers and other people in your community. Test-taking skills, too, can be useful to you when you take tests to apply for a job or to be admitted to a college. You may use public speaking skills to address a class or to present information to the members of an organization to which you belong.

Unit 14

Spelling Skills

14.1 How to Study Spelling Words

Following these five steps will help you to improve your spelling skills and will enable you to learn to spell new words as you increase your vocabulary.

Procedure

1. *Look at the word and study its letters.*

2. *Pronounce the word* to yourself and think about the letters in it and the sounds that they have.

3. *Write the word.* As you write it, think about any difficult letter combinations in the word.

4. *Check your spelling* to see whether it is correct.

5. *Study the word* until you have memorized its spelling.

14.2 Spelling Rules

14.2a Making Nouns Plural

The following rules will help you to form correctly the plurals of nouns when you write.

Regular Plurals

Most noun plurals are formed according to the following rules.

Rule Form the plural of most common nouns and proper nouns by adding *-s* to the noun.

alibi	Celt	omelet	Paquette
alibis	the Celts	omelets	the Paquettes

Rule Form the plural of common nouns and proper nouns that end with *s, x, z, ch,* or *sh* by adding *-es* to the noun.

abyss	tax	crutch	Ruiz
abysses	taxes	crutches	the Ruizes

Rule Form the plural of a common noun that ends with *y* preceded by a consonant by changing the *y* to *i* and adding *-es*.

commodity	intricacy	observatory	promontory
commodities	intricacies	observatories	promontories

Rule Form the plural of a common noun that ends with *y* preceded by a vowel by adding *-s*.

buoy	fray	replay	valley
buoys	frays	replays	valleys

Rule Form the plurals of most nouns that end with *f* or *fe* by changing the *f* to *v* and adding *-es*.

	wolf	loaf	thief
	wolves	loaves	thieves
BUT	spoof	waif	
	spoofs	waifs	

Rule Form the plural of nouns that end with *ff* by adding *-s*.

bluff	cuff	sheriff	staff
bluffs	cuffs	sheriffs	staffs

Rule Form the plural of nouns that end with *o* preceded by a vowel by adding *-s*.

cameo	kazoo	radio	scenario
cameos	kazoos	radios	scenarios

Rule   Form the plural of nouns that end with *o* preceded by a consonant in one of three ways: for some nouns, add *-s*; for others, add *-es*. For a few nouns, add either *-s* or *-es*; both spellings are correct. Check your dictionary when you are uncertain.

dynamo	virtuoso	innuendo	memento
dynamos	virtuosos	innuendoes	mementos
			mementoes

Rule   Form the plural of a letter, a symbol, a number, or a word that is in italic type (underlined) (*pages 201–202*) by adding an apostrophe and *-s* (*'s*). Do not underline (italicize) the plural ending.

J	*20*	*yes*	*
J's	*20*'s	*yes*'s	*'s

Irregular Plurals

Some nouns do not follow the preceding rules for forming plurals. The following are two examples of irregular plurals. Check your dictionary when you are uncertain of how to form a plural.

Certain nouns change their form when they are plural.

crisis	die	mouse	tooth
crises	dice	mice	teeth

Some common nouns and many proper nouns have the same form for both singular and plural.

aircraft	chassis	grouse	Japanese

Compound Nouns

Rule   Form the plural of a compound noun that is written as one word by changing the last word in the compound to its correct plural form. Form the plural of a compound noun that is hyphenated or written as two or more words by making the most important word plural.

onlooker	hanger-on	bill of sale
onlookers	hangers-on	bills of sale

14.2b Adding Endings

The following rules will help you to remember how to spell words when you add endings other than the plural (-*s* and -*es*).

Doubling the Final Consonant

Double the final consonant *only when you add an ending that begins with a vowel.* Then follow these rules:

Rule Double the final consonant when you are adding an ending to a one-syllable word that ends with a single consonant preceded by a single vowel.

flip	peg	skim
flipping	pegged	skimmed

Rule Double the final consonant when you add an ending to a word that has more than one syllable and ends with a single consonant preceded by a single vowel and has the primary stress on the last syllable.

allot	regret	prefer
allotted	regrettable	preferred

Rule To words that end in *c* preceded by a single vowel, add -*k* before endings that begin with *e* or *i* to keep the hard *c* sound.

picnic	mimic	shellac
picnicking	mimicking	shellacked

Keeping or Dropping the Final *e*

Rule When you add an ending that begins with a consonant to most words that end with silent *e,* keep the final *e.*

	blithe	contrite	loathe
	blithely	contriteness	loathesome
BUT	argue	acknowledge	
	argument	acknowledgment	

Rule When you add an ending that begins with a vowel to most words that end with silent *e,* drop the final *e.*

contrive	cringe	disparage
contrivance	cringing	disparaging

BUT   singe
          singeing

Rule When you add an ending that begins with *a* or *o* to most words that end with *ce* or *ge,* keep the final *e* to preserve the soft sound of the *c* or *g.*

enforce	advantage	notice
enforceable	advantageous	noticeable

BUT   mortgage
          mortgagor

Changing Final *y* to *i*

Rule For most words that end with *y* preceded by a consonant, change the *y* to *i* before adding any ending except *-ing.*

levy	luxury	liquefy
levied	luxurious	liquefy**ing**

BUT   wry
          wryly

Rule For most words that end with *y* preceded by a vowel, do not change the *y* to *i* before adding an ending.

alloy	enjoy	journey
alloyed	enjoyable	journeying

BUT   day
          daily

Assignment   Adding Endings On your paper, write the correct spelling of each word with the ending indicated in parentheses. When adding plural endings, you must choose the correct plural form (*-s, -es, -'s*). Use your dictionary if you need help. Then write a sentence using each new word form.

1. colony (*-al*)
2. head of state (plural)
3. collate (*-ed*)
4. courtesy (plural)
5. codify (*-ing*)
6. convey (*-ed*)
7. industry (*-ous*)
8. notice (*-able*)
9. crescendo (plural)
10. harmony (*-ous*)
11. cup (*-ful*)
12. guide (*-ance*)
13. reflex (plural)
14. tradesman (plural)
15. polite (*-ness*)
16. leaf (plural)
17. passer-by (plural)
18. double-header (plural)

14.3 Spelling Patterns

The *ie/ei* Pattern

The following rules will help you to decide whether to spell a word with *ie* or with *ei*.

Rule   Use *ie* if the vowel combination has a long *e* sound (as in *fiend*) unless the letter *c* immediately precedes the pair of vowels.

	chief	liege	siege
	grieve	shield	perceive
BUT	neither	leisure	

Rule   Use *ei* after *c* or when the sound is not long *e*.

	receipt	meiosis	foreign
BUT	lie	efficient	

Rule   If the vowel combination has a long *a* sound (as in *sleigh*) use *ei*.

neighbor   feint   veil   weight

Rule   If the two vowels are pronounced separately in the word, spell them in the order of their pronunciation.

diet   piety   reimburse

The "Seed" Sound Pattern

The "seed" ending sound has three spellings: *-sede, -ceed,* and *-cede.* The spelling *s-e-e-d* does not occur as a suffix in any word.

1. Only one word ends in *-sede*: *supersede.*
2. Three words end in *-ceed*: *exceed, proceed,* and *succeed.*
3. All other such words end in *-cede*: *accede, intercede, secede,* and so on.

14.4 Pronunciation and Spelling

Certain kinds of pronunciation errors commonly cause spelling problems. Check your dictionary for the pronunciation of words that you are unsure of, and note the letters that spell the sounds.

Extra Sounds or Omitted Sounds.   Words are often misspelled because they are pronounced with extra sounds or with sounds left out. Study the words in the following list. Pay special attention to the underlined letters to make sure that you neither add nor omit sounds when you spell or pronounce the words.

different	leverage	surprise
foliage	recognize	temperament

Transposed Letters.   Sometimes people write letters in the wrong order because they think of them in the wrong order. Such errors often occur in the words in the following list. Pay special attention to the underlined letters to make sure that you pronounce them and spell them in the correct order.

amateur	pervade	tragedy
hundred	prevalent	unanimous

Homophones and Commonly Confused Words.   Words that have the same pronunciation but different origins, spellings, and meanings are called **homophones.** Some other sets of words are not homophones, but they are similar enough in sound and spelling to create confusion. Learn the spellings and meanings of the words in the following list so that you will use them correctly in your writing.

acclamation, acclimation
aesthetic, ascetic
air, heir
callous, callus
chili, chilly
cite, sight, site
cooperation, corporation
discus, discuss

envelop, envelope
flaunt, flout
hew, hue
ingenious, ingenuous
knead, need
later, latter
pray, prey
verses, versus

14.5 Other Spelling Aids

In addition to learning the preceding spelling rules and patterns, use the following strategies to help you to improve your spelling.

Strategies

1. *Develop your own methods of word study.* Make sure that you know the rules and patterns of spelling.

2. *Keep a list of troublesome words.* Study your list frequently, and use the words in your writing.

3. *Create your own memory aids,* called mnemonic (nĭ-MŎN′ĭk) devices, for difficult words. For example:

   Something that is **extraordinary** is *extra ordinary.*

   History tells a *story.*

   An **island** *is land.*

   There are no *a*'s buried in *cemetery.*

4. *Think carefully about how words sound and look.*

5. *Always consult a dictionary if you are unsure of the spelling of a word.*

Alternate Spellings of Sounds

If you do not know how to spell a word, you may have difficulty locating it in your dictionary. You may have to guess the spelling of the word and then check other possible spellings until you find the correct one. You already know which letters usually stand for the various sounds in English, but some sounds can be spelled in more than one way. The following list suggests where to look for a word when it does not begin in the way that you expect.

CONSONANT SOUNDS	ALTERNATE SPELLINGS
f, as in *f*east	*ph*, as in *ph*ysical
j, as in *j*ustice	*g*, as in *g*enerate
k, as in *k*eep	*c* and *ch*, as in *c*onfirm and *ch*orus
n, as in *n*est	*gn*, *kn*, and *pn*, as in *gn*arl, *kn*ow, and *pn*eumonia
r, as in *r*ight	*wr*, as in *wr*ing
s, as in *s*ip	*ps* and *c*, as in *ps*eudo and *c*ircus

VOWEL SOUNDS	ALTERNATE SPELLINGS
a, as in *a*che	*ei*, as in *ei*ghteen
i, as in *i*dea	*ei*, as in *Ei*nstein
u, as in *u*rban	*e* and *ea*, as in *e*rmine and *ea*rly

14.6   Frequently Misspelled Words

Certain words are misspelled so often that many writers consider them problem words. You have studied some troublesome words earlier in this unit. The following list gives fifty more words for you to master.

academically	hypocrisy	prominent
accessible	immense	questionnaire
accumulation	incessant	rehearsal
aggressive	inevitable	reminisce
apparatus	inimitable	requisition
buoyancy	inoculate	rhythm
clientele	intellectual	ridiculous
competent	irrelevant	scissors
coupon	irritable	schism
criticism	laboratory	severely
curriculum	livelihood	suppress
exhibition	miscellaneous	suspicion
exhilaration	mucilage	sympathize
ecstasy	ordinarily	tyranny
exaggerate	parallel	vacillate
embarrass	pastime	vengeance
facile	phenomenon	

Assignment 1 Improving Your Spelling On your paper, list ten words that you want to learn to spell from the preceding list. Create a mnemonic device (*page 621*) for each of the words on your list; write each device next to its word. Use the mnemonic devices to study the words.

Assignment 2 Learning New Words On your paper, list three pairs or sets of words from the list of homophones and other commonly confused words on page 621. Write one or two paragraphs that include all of the words that you chose. Underline the words. Consult your dictionary to check your spelling and usage of each word.

Unit 15

Vocabulary Skills

The words that you use when you speak or write can add to or detract from what you have to say. The words that you recognize when you listen or read can increase your comprehension of what other people have to say. Developing a good vocabulary can add to your ability to use and recognize words.

In this unit you will discover how to learn new words, how certain words have become part of our language, how to choose the words that will carry the meaning that you wish to convey, and how to use your dictionary most effectively.

15.1 How to Learn New Words

In your notebook, make a list of words that you want to add to your vocabulary. Look up the meanings in your dictionary, and add them to your list. Study each word and its meaning frequently. Use at least one of these words every day in your writing or in your conversation.

Once you are confident in using these new words, add more words to your list and use the same approach to learn them. In this way, you can build a reliable and effective vocabulary.

15.2 Using Context to Get Meaning

When you come across an unfamiliar word in your reading, you may be able to determine its meaning by examining the **context,** the words that precede and follow it and the general meaning of the passage in which the word appears. The following strategies suggest ways in which context can help you determine meaning.

Strategies

1. *Use the general sense of the passage* along with your existing knowledge of what is described to infer a meaning.

2. *Look for synonyms or restated definitions of the unfamiliar word.*

3. *Look for examples in the passage* that may help you to determine the meaning of the unfamiliar word.

4. *See whether the unfamiliar word is compared or contrasted with a familiar word or idea.* If it is, use that known idea to help you determine the meaning of the unfamiliar word.

Assignment Context Read the following paragraph, paying special attention to the words in italic type. Write those words in your notebook. Beside each word write the meaning that you think the word has in the paragraph. Then find each word in your dictionary, and make sure that the dictionary definition is similar to the one that you got from the context. If not, write the correct definition in your notebook.

> Farmers who live in *arid* areas have developed *ingenious* ways to provide water for their crops. A simple method that they use is to leave half their land *fallow,* or unplanted, each year. That land *accumulates* moisture during the year and is suitable for growing crops the next year. Farmers who want to *utilize* all of their land use *irrigation;* that is, they send water from lakes or wells to the crops through canals. These canals are lined with fine soil to prevent *seepage.* If the soil is fine enough, little water can pass through it. These two methods allow crops to *flourish* in areas that would otherwise be *barren.*

15.3 Getting Meanings from Word Parts

If you know the meanings of some common roots, prefixes, and suffixes, you can often use them to determine the meanings of unfamiliar words.

Roots. Many words in English have Latin or Greek origins; therefore, you can expand your vocabulary by learning the meanings of some Latin and Greek roots. If you recognize a **root,** the central or basic element of a word, you can use this clue to figure out the meaning of an unfamiliar word. For example, you may recognize the common root *-magn-* (meaning "great," "grand," "large") in the words *magnificent, magnify,* and *magnitude.* If you read the sentence "All agreed that the contribution was a *magnanimous* gesture on his part," you can use your knowledge of the root *-magn-* to conclude that *magnanimous* means "grand" or "generous."

Keep in mind that the spelling of a root may change slightly when it is combined with a prefix, a suffix, or another word root.

You should also remember that two different word roots can have the same meaning even if they have different origins. For example, in the following list of roots, the Latin root *-circ-* and the Greek root *-cycl-* both mean "circle"; the Latin root *-aqua-* and the Greek root *-hydr-* both mean "water"; and the Latin root *-equ-* and the Greek root *-iso-* both mean "equal."

The hyphens before and after each root in the following lists indicate that the root may appear at the beginning, in the middle, or at the end of a word.

COMMON LATIN ROOTS

	Root	Meaning(s)	Examples
1.	-ag- (-act-)	do, drive, lead	agent, action
2.	-am- (-amic-)	love, friend	amorous, amicable
3.	-aqua-	water	aquarium, aquatic
4.	-cent-	hundred	centimeter, century
5.	-circ-	circle	circus, circulate
6.	-equ-	equal	equidistant, equation
7.	-jur- (-jud-, -jus-)	law, justice	jury, judge, justify
8.	-rupt-	break	abrupt, interrupt
9.	-seq- (-sec-)	follow	sequel, consecutive
10.	-sol-	alone	isolate, solitude

COMMON GREEK ROOTS

	Root	Meaning(s)	Examples
1.	-cycl-	circle	bicycle, cyclone
2.	-hydr-	water	hydraulic, hydroplane
3.	-iso-	equal	isosceles, isotope
4.	-micro-	small	microbe, microscope
5.	-morph-	form	amorphous, metamorphosis

6. -neo-	new	Neolithic, neophyte
7. -nom-	divide	astronomy, binomial
8. -proto-	first	protocol, prototype
9. -soph-	wise	philosophy, sophisticated
10. -zo-	animal	zoology, protozoan

Prefixes and Suffixes. A **prefix** is a letter or a group of letters placed before a word or a root to create a different word. A **suffix** is a letter or a group of letters placed at the end of a word or a root to change its function and, sometimes, to change its meaning. The spelling of a root word does not change when you add a prefix. The spelling may change, however, when you add a suffix. Two or more suffixes may be added to a base word to make another word; for example, *residentially* is made up of *reside* plus *-ent* plus *-ial* plus *-ly*.

If you know the meanings of several prefixes, suffixes, and roots, you can use this knowledge to determine the meanings of unfamiliar words. For example, if you know that *con-* means "together," that the root *-junct-* means "to join," and that *-ion* means "state of," you can figure out that *conjunction* means "the state of being joined together."

PREFIXES

Prefix	Meaning(s)	Examples
1. ambi-	both, around	ambiguous, ambivalent
amphi-	both, around	amphibious, amphitheater
2. bi- (bin-)	two, twice	bicycle, binocular
3. contra-	against, contrary	contradict, contrary
4. hyper-	over, beyond	hyperbole, hypersensitive
5. inter-	between, among	intercede, intermission
6. intra-	in, within	intramural, intravenous
7. intro-	in, into	introspective, introvert
8. retro-	back, backward	retroactive, retrospect
9. super-	above, over	superfluous, superimpose

SUFFIXES

Suffix	Meaning(s)	Examples
These suffixes are used to make verbs:		
1. -ate	make, apply, do	fascinate, radiate
2. -en	cause to be, become	brighten, lengthen
3. -fy	make, form into	amplify, qualify
4. -ize	make into, have the quality of	realize, sterilize

These suffixes are used to make nouns:

1. -ee	recipient of action, in condition of	addressee, employee
2. -ian	of or belonging to, skilled in	civilian, physician
3. -ion	result of act or process, state of being	evolution, adhesion
4. -ment	result of act or process, state of being	advertisement, cnvironment

These suffixes are used to make adjectives out of nouns or verbs:

1. -able (-ible)	inclined to, capable of	adaptable, collapsible
2. -ic	of, pertaining to, characteristic of	angelic, scenic
3. -ish	suggesting, like	impish, stylish
4. -less	lacking, without	aimless, sleepless

This suffix is used to make adverbs out of adjectives:

-ly	in a way that is	carefully, joyously

Assignment   Roots, Prefixes, and Suffixes   Choose one word root, one prefix, and one suffix from the lists on pages 626–628. For each of these three word parts, write three words that contain the part. Write these nine words in your notebook; then write a sentence for each of the nine words.

15.4 Word Origins

Words come into our language in one of the following ways: they are borrowed from other languages, or they are coined (created) from new or existing words.

Borrowing. The following words have been incorporated into our language directly from other languages.

Word	Language Origin
mesa	Spanish
soprano	Italian
résumé	French

Coining. The following words and expressions have been created from existing words or ideas.

These are *conversions* from one part of speech to another.

Word	Origin
a commute (n.)	to commute (v.)
to diagnose (v.)	a diagnosis (n.)

The following words are *combinations* of two or more existing words.

spacecraft	space, craft
backwoodsman	back, woods, man

These are words taken from the *name* of a person or a place.

cardigan	after the Seventh Earl of Cardigan
jovial	from the Roman god Jupiter, also called Jove

The following words *sound* like the action that they denote. This process of word-making is known as onomatopoeia.

crackle	crunch

These words are *shortened* forms of other words.

bus	omnibus
hi-fi	high fidelity

These are *specialized* or *technical* words from certain trades, professions, or industries.

CAT scan	Computed Axial Tomography (medicine)
bit	a binary digit (computer technology)

Assignment   Word Origins   In your notebook, make a list of six words that have come directly into our language from other languages. Use words other than those in the preceding list. Next to the six words, write the language from which they were borrowed. Use your dictionary to find this information. For each word, write a sentence that clearly conveys its meaning.

15.5 How to Choose the Best Word

Learning about synonyms and about denotation and connotation can help you to choose the best word for the context with which you are working.

Synonyms

Words that have similar meanings are called **synonyms.** Although many words have similar meanings, no two words have the same meaning. There is always a slight difference that separates one from another. These differences are often referred to as shades of meaning. Recognizing shades of meaning can help you to make the most appropriate word choices.

Notice the shades of meaning that differentiate the words in the following sets of synonyms.

> **steady,** even, equable, uniform, constant
>
> **habit,** practice, custom, usage, fashion

Now, look carefully at the word *courage* and three of its synonyms.

> *Courage* means strength that can be used to face danger. *Fortitude* stresses endurance during difficulty. *Mettle* emphasizes the capacity to rise to a challenge. *Tenacity* stresses persistence in resisting adversity.

You can see from the preceding examples that it is important to choose the right synonym to convey precise meaning. Most dictionaries list synonyms for certain entry words (*page 632*).

Denotation and Connotation

Many words have a denotative meaning and a connotative meaning. **Denotation** refers to the definitions listed in a dictionary.

Connotation refers to the ideas and feelings associated with words. In the following examples, note the stronger connotation of the word *staunch* when compared with the connotation of the word *loyal.*

> Frederick was a **staunch** supporter of the cause; he devoted all of his free time to it.
> Christine has been a **loyal** fan of the basketball team for years.

Also, the same word can have different connotations in different contexts. Notice the different connotations of the word *friends* when it is used in different contexts.

> Janice said that Beth and Roberta were her best **friends.**
> Ron said, "With **friends** like you, who needs enemies?"

Make sure that the connotations of the words that you use convey your intended meanings.

Assignment Synonyms Choose five words from the following list and write them in your notebook. Use your dictionary to find at least two synonyms for each word. Write the synonyms next to the words. Then, for each set of synonyms, write a sentence using one of the synonyms. Make sure that your sentences show the correct use of the synonyms in context.

SAMPLE	indifferent
ANSWER	indifferent, uninterested, apathetic
	The witness showed no emotion; he appeared to be quite apathetic.

1. miniature	4. obvious	7. sequence
2. fatigued	5. candid	8. objective
3. assert	6. tranquil	9. inquire

15.6 Using the Dictionary

If you wish to find the meaning, the pronunciation, or other information about a word, you need to know how to use your dictionary.

Locating a Word

Use the **guide words** at the tops of the pages to find the page that the word is on. Then look for the **entry word,** listed in alphabetical order on that page.

The **entry** includes the following information about the word: syllabication, pronunciation, part(s) of speech, definitions, and etymology. Entry words of more than one syllable are divided by dots or hyphens. This syllabication indicates where to divide the word at the end of a line of writing.

Using a Pronunciation Key

Pronunciations.   The pronunciation of a word usually follows the entry word and is printed inside brackets, parentheses, or bars. Most dictionaries contain a complete **pronunciation key** near the front of the dictionary and a shorter key at the bottom of each page or each pair of facing pages. Use these keys to interpret the pronunciation symbols.

Parts of a Dictionary Entry

Definitions.   The most important information in a dictionary is the definitions of words. When an entry word has multiple definitions, each definition is numbered. You should read all of the definitions to make sure that you select the one that is most appropriate to the context in which the word is used.

Parts of Speech.   Dictionaries identify the part(s) of speech of a word. The following abbreviations are used in most dictionaries and usually appear after the pronunciation.

n.—noun	*adj.*—adjective
pron.—pronoun	*adv.*—adverb
v. or *vb.*—verb	*prep.*—preposition
tv. or *tr. v.*—transitive verb	*conj.*—conjunction
iv. or *intr. v.*—intransitive verb	*interj.*—interjection

Labels.   When appropriate, dictionary entries include usage labels, such as Nonstandard, Informal or Colloquial, Regional or Dialect, or Slang. Such labels are a guide to the correct use of words.

632

Synonyms. Dictionaries often list synonyms for an entry word and explain their connotations. Some dictionaries list **antonyms,** words that mean the opposite of the entry word.

Homographs. Words that are spelled alike but have different origins and different meanings are called **homographs.** Homographs may also have different pronunciations and syllabications. In most dictionaries homographs are listed as separate entry words and are identified by **superscripts,** small raised numerals placed before or after the entry word. When homographs are listed in your dictionary, read all of the definitions for each entry to find the meaning that is most suitable to a given context. For example, for the entry word *present* you might find the following definitions: **present**[1] "a period in time between the present and the future," and **present**[2] "to introduce or make a gift of."

Etymologies. The **etymology** of a word is the origin and the history of that word. The etymology is usually given in brackets or parentheses after the pronunciation or at the end of the entry. The etymology usually gives information about or insight into the meaning of the word. For example, the word *recreant,* meaning "cowardly or disloyal," comes from words that mean "to yield in a contest."

Assignment **Improving Your Vocabulary** From the following list, choose ten words that you would like to add to your vocabulary. Write the words in alphabetical order in your notebook, leaving room for a definition and a sentence after each word. Using your dictionary, learn the meaning and the pronunciation of each word. Then, in your notebook, write a brief definition and a sentence for each word. Review the words at least once a week, and use them in your speaking and writing. When you have learned these words, make a new list of the remaining ten words and study them in the same way.

1. dormant	6. benevolent	11. insinuate
2. perplex	7. heterogeneous	12. permutation
3. whimsical	8. subtlety	13. cache
4. corroborate	9. attrition	14. affiliated
5. renown	10. rebuke	15. ultimatum

Unit 16

Public
Speaking
Skills

16.1 Uses of Public Speaking Skills

As a student, you engage in public speaking every time you speak in class. You probably speak before groups of listeners in other situations as well. Whether your audience is large or small, friends or strangers, your objective as a speaker is to convey a message to your listeners. In this unit you will study and apply principles that will help you to be a more effective public speaker.

Kinds of Speeches

Speeches may vary from formal to informal, depending on the occasion, the purpose, and the audience. An address to Congress, for example, is a very formal speech. A committee report at a club meeting, on the other hand, is relatively informal.

In addition to being formal or informal, a speech may be either prepared or impromptu. A prepared speech is planned carefully before it is delivered. If you were giving a speech to your English class on the life of Shakespeare, for instance, you would do the needed research, organize your material, write your note cards, rehearse, and then deliver your prepared speech.

On the other hand, if you were asked in class to summarize the first act of *Othello,* your answer would be an impromptu speech. Other examples of impromptu speeches include unscheduled announcements, speeches accepting unexpected awards, and other talks that you give on the spur of the moment, without preparation.

Purposes of Speaking

When you make a speech, your purpose may be to inform your listeners, to persuade them, or to entertain them. Sometimes you may combine purposes in a single speech, as you would if you wanted to inform your listeners about an issue and persuade them to support your position on that issue.

Your purpose in giving an informative speech is to convey new and interesting information to your listeners. An informative speech may explain, define, report, describe, or demonstrate. For example, when you define for a government class the concept of justice under different legal systems, your purpose is to inform your audience.

Your purpose in giving a persuasive speech is to form or change your listeners' attitudes or opinions. You may also want your audience to take some action. For example, when you encourage the members of your physics class to plan a trip to the science museum, your purpose is to persuade.

In giving an entertaining speech, your purpose is to provide your listeners with a pleasant diversion. Personal experiences, interesting events, human-interest stories, or amusing anecdotes may form the basis of an entertaining speech. As the welcoming speaker at the class dinner, for instance, your purpose would be to entertain.

Considering Purpose, Audience, and Topic

In deciding on a speech topic, you should consider who your audience is, what subjects might interest them, and what would be appropriate for the occasion. A group of students new to your school, for example, would probably be interested in an informative talk about the layout of the school and the activities and services available to them. The same talk would not be very interesting to students who had already been attending your school for several years.

Besides considering appropriate topics for your listeners, think also about the purpose of your speech. If you decide to make a speech on camping, you have several possibilities. You can inform your listeners about some aspect of camping, persuade them to try a particular camping method, or entertain them with a funny story about camping. You must always consider your purpose, your audience, and your topic in relation to one another.

16.2   Planning Your Speech

The key to making a successful speech is good planning. Adequate attention to each step in the preparation process makes the next step that much easier. These are the steps to follow:

1. Selecting and limiting your topic
2. Gathering information and developing ideas
3. Organizing your speech
4. Preparing and rehearsing your speech
5. Delivering your speech

16.2a   Selecting and Limiting a Topic

Any subject that interests you can be the source of a good speech topic. In choosing a topic, you should think about your own experiences, knowledge, observations, work, hobbies, or special interests. You may also find a topic by talking to friends and family members or by getting ideas from radio, television, films, books, newspapers, or magazines.

Sometimes you will be assigned a general subject, such as solar energy, the English novel, or computer technology. At other times you will choose your own topic. In both situations you must limit your topic so that it will be narrow enough for you to cover well and also be appropriate for your audience and the occasion.

Factors to take into account in limiting your topic are the general and specific purposes of your speech, your thesis statement, your audience, and your time limit.

General and Specific Purposes

The **general purpose** of your speech is to inform, to persuade, to entertain, or perhaps some combination of these purposes. Your **specific purpose** is a more exact statement of what you want your listeners to know, to feel, to think, or to do.

GENERAL PURPOSE	SPECIFIC PURPOSE
To inform	I want my audience to learn how a scuba tank operates.
To persuade	I want my audience to support educational television.
To entertain	I want my audience to be amused by my experiences when I worked as a supermarket checker.

Your Thesis Statement

After you have determined your general and specific purposes, you are ready to write a thesis statement (*page 435*). In clear, specific language, the thesis statement tells your audience what you are going to talk about. Study how the preceding statements of specific purpose are incorporated into thesis statements in these examples.

GENERAL PURPOSE	THESIS STATEMENT
To inform	Today we will look at the parts of a scuba tank and see how they function.
To persuade	Educational television can benefit us as students; we should all support it.
To entertain	Let me tell you from my own experience some of the funny things that can happen to a supermarket checker.

Your Audience

For your speech to be successful, your limited topic must hold your listeners' interest. When you are selecting and limiting your topic, ask yourself the following questions about your audience:

1. Who are my listeners? (Are they teen-agers? Adults? What are their interests, experiences, attitudes?)
2. Will they be interested in my topic?
3. How much do they already know about my topic?
4. How do I want to affect my audience?

Analyzing your audience in relation to your topic and purpose will help you to gain their attention and to get a favorable response to your speech.

Your Time Limit

The amount of time allotted for your speech is another factor for you to consider when you are limiting your topic. Knowing how long you will be speaking will also help you as you gather information and organize your speech. If you have not been given a time limit for your speech, discuss the matter with the person in charge.

16.2b Gathering Information

Sources of Information

Information for your speech may come from many sources. List briefly some of the information you need to meet your specific purpose and to support your thesis statement. Depending on your topic, any of the following sources may provide the information you need.

1. Personal knowledge, observations, and experiences
2. Books, newspapers, magazines, pamphlets, encyclopedias, and other reference materials
3. Radio, television, and films
4. Speeches, lectures, and public meetings
5. Interviews with friends, family members, or experts on the topic

Your librarian can help you to locate some of the printed materials. Use the card catalog and appropriate indexes. Take careful notes, and keep track of the sources you use.

Kinds of Information

The material you present in your speech may be facts, your own opinions, someone else's opinions, or opinions supported by facts. All of these kinds of information may be appropriate, depending on the topic and the purpose of your speech. You should, however, be sure to distinguish between fact and opinion and to use them appropriately (*page 357*).

An informative speech focuses primarily on factual, objective information. A persuasive speech is necessarily an expression of your opinion. The more strongly you can support your position with facts and other evidence, however, the more likely your audience is to accept it.

You may need to include any of the following kinds of information in your speech.

1. *Explanations.* You may need to explain unfamiliar concepts to your listeners, telling what something is, how something functions, or why something happens as it does.
2. *Definitions.* When you include an unfamiliar term or use a word in an unusual way, you need to define it for your listeners.
3. *Examples and illustrations.* You can clarify what you are saying by giving examples of general categories or by using illustrations, which are extended and detailed examples.
4. *Statistics.* Use statistics—facts in the form of numbers— only sparingly, so that they interest your listeners and give authority to your points.
5. *Quotations.* The statement of another person, cited exactly as originally spoken or written, can add variety and impact if chosen carefully.
6. *Anecdotes.* You can use a brief account of an incident to amuse, inspire, or enlighten your audience. Be sure that any anecdote you use relates directly to the ideas in your speech and is appropriate for your audience and the occasion.

Use the following strategies in planning your speech.

Strategies

1. *Keep your audience and purpose in mind* when you select and limit your topic.
2. *Gather information that is appropriate* to your topic and purpose.
3. *Take notes* and indicate your sources of information.
4. *Distinguish fact from opinion.*

Assignment 1   Speech Topics   On your paper, list a speech topic for each of the following categories. For each of your topics, write a general purpose and a specific purpose. Save your paper.

1. An interesting experience that you have had
2. A subject that you already know about or that you want to know about
3. An issue that you feel strongly about

Assignment 2   Thesis Statements   For each of your speech topics from Assignment 1, write three thesis statements, one for each of these situations: a five-minute talk to a seventh-grade class; a ten-minute speech to your English class; a twenty-minute speech to a group of adults. Make your thesis statements consistent with your specific purposes. Save your papers.

Assignment 3   Gathering Information   Select from Assignment 2 one of your speech topics and its thesis statement that you wrote for a ten-minute speech to your English class. *Step 1:* Gather and list the information and supporting material that you already have about your topic. *Step 2:* List the specific kinds of additional information that you need. Also list questions that you need to have answered. *Step 3:* List all the sources you can think of that might provide the material and the answers that you need. *Step 4:* Find the needed information. Take accurate notes and record your sources. Save your notes.

16.3   Organizing Your Speech

Organize your material into a speech with an introduction, a body, and a conclusion. Because the body of the speech contains most of the material, it is the part that you should develop first.

The major points that you plan to cover in your speech are the main headings under which you organize your material into subheadings. Choose an organizational pattern that will best help your audience to understand your main ideas and the information that supports them.

16.3a The Parts of Your Speech

The Body of Your Speech

There are various ways to organize a speech so that your ideas are clear and in an order appropriate to your topic and purpose. Note the following methods:

1. Use **topical order** when you can divide your topic into distinct parts.
2. Use **chronological order** when your topic involves a step-by-step process or a historical progression.
3. Use **spatial order** when your topic involves physical or geographical relationships.
4. Use **order of importance** when you can rank your headings from least to most important or from most to least important.
5. Arrange your material by **cause and effect** when your speech topic deals with the reasons behind an event or with the results of an event.
6. Organize your speech by **comparison and contrast** when you point out similarities and differences between situations, persons, or concepts.
7. Organize a speech by the **problem-solving method** when you define a problem and evaluate alternate solutions, as in many persuasive speeches.

The Introduction to Your Speech

The purpose of the introduction is to create interest in your topic, to show why it is important, to establish common ground with your listeners, and to lead them into the body of your speech. You present your thesis statement in the introduction and give your audience some indication of how the speech will be organized.

To make your introduction effective and to arouse your listeners' interest, you may want to include a rhetorical question, a quotation or a startling statement, a moving or humorous anecdote, or a piece of little-known information. Keep in mind that any material you use in your introduction should relate directly to what you will say in the rest of your speech.

The Conclusion of Your Speech

Your conclusion should sum up your speech and leave a strong impression in your listeners' minds. In an informative speech, this is your last chance to help your listeners understand and remember the information that you have presented. In a persuasive speech, it is your last chance to influence their opinions or actions.

Different kinds of conclusions are appropriate for different kinds of speeches. An informative speech may end with a summary of major points. A persuasive speech may end with a restatement of your position, a striking statement, a challenging question, or a call for action. An entertaining speech may end with an anecdote, a quotation, a startling statement, or a question.

16.3b Unity, Coherence, and Conciseness

Three elements that contribute to the effectiveness of a speech are unity, coherence, and conciseness.

Unity.   A unified speech includes only material that relates directly to the topic. Be sure that everything you include supports your thesis statement or your position and fulfills your specific purpose.

In planning your speech, strive for unity in the introduction, the body, and the conclusion.

Coherence.   When a speech has a logical relationship among its ideas, it is coherent. A coherent speech is easy for your listeners to follow and to understand. Remember these points to make your speech coherent.

Strategies

1. *Keep related ideas together*. Do not jump from idea to idea.

2. *Present your ideas in a logical order*. One idea must follow another for a particular reason.

3. *Use transitional words and phrases* to link the parts of your

speech and to connect the ideas within your speech. You will learn more about transitions later in this unit.

Conciseness.   A concise speech does not have wasted words. Say clearly what you mean, using as few words as possible. Concise statements are easier for your listeners to understand and to remember, and they will make it easier for you to cover all your information within your time limit.

WORDY STATEMENT
> Frequently a chapter title reveals to the reader the main point that the author desires to bring out during the course of the chapter.

CONCISE STATEMENT
> The title of a chapter often reveals its main idea.

Complicated expressions of your thoughts can become tiresome to your audience. Simple, direct words that say exactly what you mean not only save time, but also maintain your listeners' interest by keeping your speech moving. For example, say *because* rather than *due to the fact that.*

16.3c The Wording of Your Speech

A reader can examine written material at leisure, pausing to think about the ideas and to absorb them at a comfortable rate. A reader can reread a passage any number of times.

The listening audience does not have the opportunity to consider at leisure the ideas of the speech. If listeners pause to reflect on a point, they will miss the next point in the speech and be left behind. They cannot go back and hear over again a sentence that they did not quite understand. Therefore, the words of a speech must be easily and completely understandable to the audience.

Style is the manner of using language. Spoken style is more forceful, more informal, and more personal than written style. It may also be simpler in the use of vocabulary and sentence structure, signals and transitional words, repetition, and summary.

Sentence Structure for Speeches

Since your audience must grasp and remember the words of a sentence in just one hearing, spoken sentences should not be too long or complex. Keep in mind the following points:

1. A simple sentence with a clear sequence of subject and verb is easy for your audience to understand. A compound sentence, one that has two or more independent clauses, is also easy to follow. (*See pages 67–68.*)

   > Every game has its humorous incidents.
   > Wages continue to go up, but prices keep on rising faster.

2. A complex sentence (*page 68*) is easier to understand when the subordinate clause follows the main clause.

   > The next decade will require new ideas, new approaches, and new concepts because you cannot approach the future with yesterday's tools.

3. As a speaker, you need not avoid ending sentences with prepositions if the effect is natural.

   > This is the first issue for us to be concerned with.

4. You can use commands, exclamations, and questions as effective ways to awaken interest.

   > Never underestimate your own creative power.
   > The results were amazing!

5. You may occasionally use partial sentences in a speech to achieve a certain effect.

   > Today, not tomorrow.
   > More courses, more options, more knowledge.

6. By using parallel structure, you can lend a rhythmical quality to parts of your speech, making your message both pleasant to listen to and easy to understand.

   > We get Vitamin A from carrots and spinach, Vitamin C from oranges and tomatoes, and Vitamin D from fish oils and sunshine.

Signals and Transitional Words

Signals are words or phrases that alert your listeners to what is coming next in your speech. You insert signals to tell them what to listen for or to indicate key points or shifts in focus.

SIGNAL OF PURPOSE
"I would like to tell you about . . ."
"I will present evidence to show . . ."

SIGNAL OF BACKGROUND INFORMATION
"Let us see how this situation came about."

SIGNAL OF KEY POINTS
"There are three basic types of . . ."

SIGNAL OF SUPPORTING MATERIAL
"An example of this is . . ."
"In a recent survey . . ."

Transitional words and phrases contribute to coherence by establishing the connections between your basic ideas and your supporting material and between the parts of your speech. Note the following kinds of transitional words and phrases:

LIKENESS	moreover, in addition, and, similarly, likewise
CONTRAST	but, on the other hand, however, nevertheless, although, conversely
EMPHASIS	even more important, chiefly, significantly, indeed
EXAMPLE	for instance, as an example, specifically, such as, that is
CONSEQUENCE	thus, it follows, as a result, therefore, so, then, hence
CHRONOLOGY	finally, next, then, at last, later, as soon as, until, prior to, before
RESTATEMENT	in other words, that is, in short, in effect
CONCLUSION	finally, to sum up, in closing

Repetition and Summary ▬▬▬▬▬▬▬▬▬▬▬▬▬▬▬

You sometimes need to repeat for your listeners. Repeating the same idea in the same words ensures that your listeners take note of it, remember it, and realize that it is important.

If repetition of the same words threatens to become tiresome, you can relate the same information in different words. This technique is also helpful if you think your listeners may not have understood the idea as you phrased it originally.

STATEMENT   During the Gilded Age, the economy of the United States experienced rapid growth.

REPETITION   Remember that we saw earlier that the economy of the United States experienced rapid growth during the Gilded Age.

RESTATEMENT   The economy of this country expanded at a remarkable rate during the late 1800s.

A summary is a general repetition or restatement of points made in your speech. The summary forms a total picture of the parts under discussion. You may summarize one section of your speech before continuing with the next section, as well as summarizing the entire speech in your conclusion.

As you recall, the three characters in the novel had similar backgrounds, experiences, and expectations, but each was a distinct individual.

I have presented to you the advantages of joining the hiking club and have shown you how hiking can be fun and educational.

Effective Vocabulary ▬▬▬▬▬▬▬▬▬▬▬▬▬▬▬

Spoken language must be understood instantly. Your audience has no dictionaries, maps, reference books, or explanatory notes to refer to; therefore, each word that you use must express your exact meaning and be easily understood. Your listeners will understand you best when you choose words that are short, familiar, concrete, specific, and vivid.

Short Words.   Short words are usually preferable to longer words in public speaking. Short words are convenient and economical, easier to pronounce and to comprehend.

> *keen judgment* instead of *perspicacity*
> *water cycle* instead of *hydrologic cycle*
> *green* instead of *verdurous*

In choosing words, you need to consider your listeners' level of understanding. In talking to a class of sixth-graders, you would use short, simple words in almost every instance. In speaking to a group of college professors, you could vary your speech by using some longer and more complex words where they would truly add a dimension to your speech.

Familiar Words.   In general, shorter words tend to be more familiar to most people. There are some exceptions to this rule, however, and in these cases the more familiar word is usually the preferable one. In the following examples, the longer words would probably be more easily understood by your listeners.

> *widespread* instead of *rife*
> *relatives* instead of *kin*
> *meadow* instead of *lea*

Concrete Words.   A concrete word refers to something that can actually be seen and touched rather than to an abstract concept. The definition of a concrete word is less open to question than the definition of an abstract word. Therefore, concrete words are more likely to present to your listeners the same idea or mental picture that is in your own mind.

> ABSTRACT TERMS   means of access for the disabled
>
> CONCRETE TERMS   ramps, wide doorways, low door handles

Specific Words.   Use specific words that tell exactly what you mean. Give your listeners as much information as you can by substituting specific words for those that are general and vague.

> VAGUE WORDS   trees, birds, nice
>
> SPECIFIC WORDS   oaks, robins, friendly

Vivid Words. Some words create images in your listeners' minds by invoking the five senses: taste, touch, smell, sight, and hearing. Such words make your speech more lively and more interesting.

His hands were hard, rough, and scarred.

The cool, damp cave was pleasant after the heat of the sun.

The waving fields of grain shimmered in the hazy sunshine.

Muffled rolls of thunder boomed across the sky.

The sharp, salty taste made my tongue tingle.

Pitfalls to Avoid

When you are thinking about the words you want to use in your speech, keep in mind the following pitfalls that can weaken your presentation.

Generalizations. A generalization is a statement that includes every member of a category or every occurrence of an event.

GENERALIZATIONS   All artists live unconventional lives.

Gossip always leads to trouble.

A generalization can be disproved by finding just one exception. If one artist leads a conventional life, the generalization in the preceding example is not valid. You can usually limit a generalization by changing or inserting a word or a brief phrase. You can say, for instance, "*Some* artists live unconventional lives," or "Gossip *frequently* leads to trouble."

Other words that appear in generalizations are *everyone, never, anytime, completely, constantly, every, invariably, no,* and *none,* as well as *all* and *always.* Words and phrases to replace them include *many, often, some, few, usually, sometimes, frequently, in most cases,* and *for the most part.*

Keep in mind that not all statements containing such words as *all* and *always* need to be changed. The statement "All triangles have three sides" has no exceptions and is a valid statement.

Jargon. Many occupations and areas of interest such as sports and hobbies have their own special vocabularies or expressions. In a speech, avoid using this special language, called jargon, unless your audience is also familiar with the terms. (See page 88.)

If you are giving a talk to the chess club, you can include specialized terms that other chess players would know. If you give a talk on chess to another audience, though, you should limit your use of jargon and explain those terms that you do use.

Clichés. Some words and expressions have been used so often that they have lost their impact. Avoid using these clichés, or trite expressions; they do not stimulate audience interest or contribute to understanding.

Examples of trite expressions include *nice, great, terrific, awful, few and far between, last but not least, nervous as a cat,* and so on.

Assignment   Organizing Your Speech   Use your notes from Assignment 3 on page 640. Select a suitable method of organizing your speech. Then make an outline, organizing your material into main headings, subheadings, and supporting details. Write an introduction and a conclusion for your speech. Save your papers.

16.4 Preparing and Delivering Your Speech

Having outlined your speech, you are ready to plan for delivering it to your audience. With good preparation, your presentation is likely to be successful.

16.4a Preparing Yourself to Speak

You can use certain techniques to help you prepare for an effective delivery. Depending on how you plan to deliver your speech, you will need to know how to make and use note cards or how to write out your manuscript. You should consider also the use of visual aids, rehearsing your speech, and your setting.

Using Note Cards

You can use note cards as a guide when you deliver your speech. You should have a card for the introduction, another for the conclusion, and a varying number for the body, depending on the length and complexity of your speech. Each card for the body of your speech should contain no more than one main idea with its subheadings and supporting information. Write key words and phrases on the cards to help you remember your points.

Write out in full any material that you must present in exact form, such as quotations and statistics. Include names, dates, and other important information. You may want to use different colored inks for main ideas, subheadings, and supporting material.

Write on only one side of your note cards. Do not crowd your notes, and write clearly so that you will be able to read them at a glance. Number your cards so that you can keep them in order.

Writing Out Your Speech

On certain occasions, particularly formal ones, it is sometimes preferable to write out your speech word for word and read it to your audience. When you use a written speech, your language can be more precise and polished than when you speak from notes.

Write marginal notes on the pages to remind yourself when to pause, to be emphatic, to speed up or slow down, or to build to a climax. You should be careful to make frequent eye contact with your audience, for the chief drawback of delivery from a written speech is the barrier that seems to exist between the speaker and the listeners. The speaker must make a conscious attempt to break down that barrier.

Using Visual Aids and Props

Visual aids and props can add interest to your speech and enhance understanding and retention. If you decide to use aids, plan exactly what materials are needed and precisely where in the speech they will be used. Keep visual aids clear and simple, and be sure that they can be seen by all members of your audience. Practice with the aids until you are sure that you can manage them skillfully.

Include a visual aid in your speech only when it is so important that the speech would be incomplete without it. The aid should enable you to present information more quickly and effectively than you could with words alone.

Rehearsing Your Speech

The best way to improve your delivery is to practice. You will give your speech with more ease, confidence, and authority if you rehearse it well.

Using your note cards, practice your speech aloud. Use a tape recorder if one is available, or ask family members and friends to listen and comment. Practice your speech standing as you will when you actually deliver it. Remember to practice with your visual aids if you are using any.

Knowing Your Setting

The more you know in advance about the setting in which you will deliver your speech, the better you will be able to plan your delivery. These are some of the questions you may have about the setting:

1. Is the room large or small?
2. Will there be a desk, a lectern, a microphone?
3. Does the setting lend itself to any visual aids that I might use?

16.4b Speaking Before a Group

Your delivery is a significant factor in how your listeners respond to your speech and how well you achieve your purpose. Your voice, posture, gestures, and use of eye contact are all important.

Using Your Voice Effectively

Variety in the rate, loudness, pitch, and quality of your voice helps you to express your thoughts and feelings. In addition, vocal variety keeps your audience interested.

The quickness or slowness with which you speak and the length of pauses between words and phrases constitute the rate. You will want to vary your rate enough to heighten interest without sacrificing clarity.

Your voice should be loud enough to be heard easily, yet not so loud that your audience finds it unpleasant. Try lowering or raising your voice for emphasis. Also try not to pitch your voice too high or too low. Let your pitch vary, however, within a comfortable range.

The quality of your voice should be pleasing, full, rich, vibrant, and alive. Work to overcome such problems as harshness, breathiness, or nasality.

Posture, Gestures, and Eye Contact

Stand straight, but not stiffly, as you deliver your speech. Avoid leaning on a desk or lectern. Feel free to move about, provided your movements are natural and do not detract attention from what you are saying.

Gestures can be effective in reinforcing your meaning. Use gestures as you would in everyday conversation. If you relax and concentrate on your topic, your gestures will be more natural.

Avoid the following distracting gestures and movements: locking hands and arms behind or in front of your body, covering your mouth with your hand, pacing nervously, leaning, jingling objects in your pockets, twisting your hair or a ring, standing in a frozen posture, and rocking or swaying.

Remember to make eye contact with your audience. Look at your listeners, not at the back wall, the floor, or the ceiling. Let your eyes move from face to face, establishing personal contact.

Avoiding Nervousness

Almost everyone is nervous about making a speech. If you have prepared your speech well and rehearsed until you know the material thoroughly, you will be more confident. Concentrate on what you are saying and remember that the message is what is most important.

The more you practice before others, the more easily you will be able to speak in public. Many speakers never completely conquer nervousness, but by selecting a topic you care about, preparing carefully, and taking time to rehearse and refine your techniques, you will feel more comfortable. You will reduce your nervousness and increase your confidence.

16.4c Extemporaneous and Impromptu Speeches

Sometimes you make a speech with little or no preparation. When you prepare your topic in advance and then speak without notes, or with a few brief notes, your speech is **extemporaneous.** When you speak on the spur of the moment, with no preparation, your speech is **impromptu.**

Impromptu speaking requires thinking on your feet. So does extemporaneous speaking, for it involves delivering a planned message in the language of the moment. You can practice by reading a short story or an article; when you finish it, summarize aloud what you have read. Use a tape recorder or have a friend listen.

Another way to practice is to have a friend suggest topics for you to speak on without preparation. The more you practice thinking on your feet, the more you will develop self-confidence and ease.

Even if you do not yet feel completely confident, you can help yourself and convince your audience by standing straight, using a strong voice, avoiding nervous mannerisms, and looking directly at your audience. Pause when you think about what to say next, rather than filling in with such expressions as "you know," "well," "um," and so on.

When you speak extemporaneously, give special thought to how you will open and close your speech. A strong opening will catch the attention of your listeners, and a strong closing will get your point across and leave no doubt about your purpose. In impromptu speaking, try to apply the same principles. Take a deep breath before you begin and think of a good opening. Ask yourself, "What is my thesis statement?"

Before concluding your speech, pause and ask yourself, "What are the main points I need to summarize? What idea or feeling do I want to leave with my audience?" If you concentrate on your message and not on yourself, your speech is likely to be effective.

Assignment   Delivering Your Speech   Use the material you prepared for the Assignment on page 649. Prepare note cards and rehearse your speech, making any needed improvements in your notes. Then deliver your ten-minute speech to your English class.

▰ Unit 17 ▰

Test-Taking Skills

No matter what your future plans are, you will probably have to take a standardized test at some point in order to achieve your educational or career goals. Most colleges and many technical and vocational schools use scores on standardized tests as a basis for admission or placement. The United States military services also use test scores to determine placement for volunteers. This unit offers suggestions on how you can improve your performance on standardized tests.

Preparing for any standardized test takes time. Last-minute cramming is not helpful. The best way to prepare for a test is to complete your class assignments conscientiously and to read widely. Through reading you can enlarge your vocabulary and develop your ability to comprehend what you read.

17.1 Verbal Skills

Most standardized tests have at least one section designed to measure the extent of your vocabulary and your ability to understand what you read. This section may include test items covering antonyms, analogies, sentence completion, and reading comprehension. In this unit you will learn how to answer each kind of test item.

17.1a Antonyms

In a test of antonyms you must select the word most nearly opposite in meaning to a given word. Most antonym items follow the format shown here.

AFFLUENT: (A) afflicted (B) effluent (C) indigent (D) fluid (E) wealthy

The word most nearly opposite in meaning to *affluent* is *(C) indigent.*
Use the following strategies when taking a test on antonyms.

Strategies

1. *Consider all of the choices* before deciding which one is the best possible answer. Do not choose the first answer that appears to be correct; there may be a better answer.

2. *Bear in mind that many words have more than one meaning.* If you do not realize that *impress* means "to confiscate property" as well as "to affect or influence greatly," you may miss a test item.

3. *Use your knowledge of prefixes, suffixes, and Greek and Latin roots* to help you understand the meaning of unfamiliar words. Refer to Unit 15, "Vocabulary Skills."

Assignment 1 Antonyms Write the letter of the antonym of each word given in capital letters. Use a dictionary, if necessary, to check your choices after you have finished.

1. MOROSELY: (A) gloomily (B) happily (C) modestly (D) morbidly (E) sincerely
2. HETEROGENEOUS: (A) conscious (B) dissimilar (C) homogeneous (D) indigenous (E) redundant
3. QUESTIONABLE: (A) declarative (B) doubtful (C) indubitable (D) pardonable (E) querulous
4. ITINERANT: (A) incumbent (B) migratory (C) repentant (D) sedentary (E) traveler

5. ABATE: (A) debate   (B) discuss   (C) increase   (D) inundate
   (E) saturate
6. DORMANT: (A) awake   (B) dreary   (C) hibernating
   (D) latent   (E) portable
7. VILIFY: (A) citify   (B) debase   (C) degrade   (D) glorify
   (E) unveil
8. DISCORD: (A) concord   (B) record   (C) ripcord
   (D) stationery   (E) tied

17.1b Analogies

A test of analogies challenges your ability to understand the relationship between two words and your ability to recognize a similar or parallel relationship between two other words. In an analogies test, you must first establish the relationship that exists between two given words. Then, from a list of choices, you select another pair of words with a similar or parallel relationship.

Most analogies test items follow the format shown in the example. When reading such an item, substitute "is to" for the single colon. Substitute "as" for the double colon. You should read the following example this way: "Smallest *is to* small *as* best *is to* well, larger *is to* large" and so forth.

> SMALLEST : SMALL :: (A) best : well   (B) larger : large
> (C) lest : less   (D) long : longest   (E) more : less

If you look carefully at the first two words in the example, you see that the relationship between them is that the first word is the superlative form of the second. Among the answer choices, that same relationship exists only in *(A) best : well*. In answers (B) and (E), the first word is the comparative of the second. In answer (C), *lest* is meant to distract the reader, who may be thinking of *least*. In answer (D), the superlative form appears, but it is the second word, not the first. To be correct, the second word pair must follow the same sequence as the first two words.

Use the following strategies when taking an analogies test.

Strategies

1. *Determine the relationship that exists between the first pair of words.* In a sentence or a phrase, say to yourself what that relationship is.

2. *Read all of the answer choices before selecting one.*

3. *Make sure that the words you choose are in the same sequence as the first pair of words.*

Assignment 2 Analogies On your paper, write the letter of the pair of words having the same relationship as the words in capital letters.

1. SYNONYM : ANTONYM :: (A) active : passive
   (B) same : similar   (C) symphony : chorus   (D) synagogue : church
   (E) word : symbol

2. NOVEL : WRITER :: (A) song : choir   (B) editor : book
   (C) law : judge   (D) poet : poem   (E) symphony : composer

3. EDAM : MADE :: (A) green : go   (B) lame : male
   (C) mail : stamp   (D) red : stop   (E) war : raw

4. CANINE : DOG :: (A) bovine : cow   (B) feline : deer
   (C) tiger : cat   (D) mammal : elephant   (E) whine : bark

5. CONFLAGRATION : FLAME :: (A) hose : water
   (B) fire : ash   (C) hurricane : breeze   (D) log : kindling
   (E) mishap : catastrophe

6. FLY : FLIES :: (A) bye : buys   (B) pry : prize   (C) sigh : size
   (D) try : tries   (E) why : wise

7. SLIGHT : SLEIGHT :: (A) light : dark   (B) right : write
   (C) sly : slay   (D) slender : frail   (E) tricky : skillful

8. FRANCE : PARIS :: (A) Montana : America   (B) London :
   England   (C) Switzerland : Bern   (D) Albany : New York
   (E) Quebec: Canada

17.1c Sentence Completion

Sentence-completion test items require you to supply a missing word or words that fit in the context of the sentence. To do so, you

657

must first understand the ideas in the sentence. Sentence-completion items do not require any knowledge beyond an understanding of the words in the sentence and in the answer choices. Your skill in determining meaning from context is very important (*pages 624–625*).

Study the following example.

Hypocrites portray emotions that they do not __?__, but which they feel that they should __?__.
(A) condone..suspend   (B) respect..motivate   (C) tolerate..improvise   (D) possess..display   (E) exemplify..repress

Only the words in answer (D) make sense in both blanks; in the other choices, the first word makes sense, but the second one does not.

Follow these strategies when answering sentence-completion test items.

Strategies

1. *Read the entire sentence through before trying to supply the missing word or words.*

2. *Make sure that both answers make sense in a sentence that has two blanks.*

3. *Check your answers by reading the complete sentence silently with the word(s) in place.*

Assignment 3   Sentence Completion   On your paper, write the letter of the word or words that complete the sentence. Use a dictionary, if necessary.

1. Mr. Wiggins displays __?__ by writing a paragraph when a sentence is sufficient.
   (A) brevity   (B) verbosity   (C) animosity   (D) intolerence
   (E) attentiveness

2. A fresh, new group of volunteers __?__ the weary group who had been stacking sandbags in an effort to __?__ the flood waters.
   (A) rebuked..placate   (B) depressed..preserve
   (C) replaced..halt   (D) admired..avoid
   (E) cheered..sanitize

3. It is __?__ to accept the __?__ and foolish to combat it.

(A) cowardly..deterioration   (B) hopeless..cheating

(C) silly..untenable   (D) wise..inevitable

(E) cynical..apparent

4. Both crocuses and robins are considered by many to be __?__ of approaching __?__.

(A) harbingers..spring   (B) symbols..storms

(C) reminders..disasters   (D) omens..peace

(E) prototypes..joy

5. Millions of voters __?__ guerilla threats to __?__ the presidential elections in the small South American country.

(A) forgot..win   (B) defied..sabotage   (C) made..cancel

(D) heard..defeat   (E) exacerbated..defraud

17.1d Reading Comprehension

Reading-comprehension items test your ability to understand what is stated directly. They also test your ability to interpret, analyze, and make inferences about what you have read. The reading passages given contain all of the information that you need to answer the questions that follow them.

Follow these strategies when answering reading-comprehension test items.

Strategies

1. *Read the passage closely and attentively.* Try to get a sense of the ideas and the organization of the passage, but do not waste time underlining or making marginal notes.

2. *Read the questions first if the passage is on a subject unfamiliar to you.* For example, if the passage is on astronomy, about which you may know little, reading the questions first may help you to follow the information more easily and to look for important points.

3. *Read all possible answers before selecting one.*

4. *Select your answer solely on the basis of the material that is in the passage,* not on your personal knowledge or opinion.

5. *Skip a passage that is too difficult for you and go on to the next one.* Come back to it if you have time after you have answered the rest of the questions.

Read the following passage and then study the comprehension items that come after it.

In his first dive in the bathyscaph FNRS-3, Jacques-Ives Cousteau planned to descend 4500 hundred feet into the ocean. The FNRS-3 was a sphere with an interior diameter of two meters. Its walls were lined with navigational instruments. Even though feelings of anxiety were natural under the circumstances, Cousteau had confidence in his pilot, Commander Georges Houot, who had previously taken the bathyscaph to a depth of 6890 feet.

Cousteau kept a constant watch at the porthole to observe changes during the descent. Just below three hundred feet, he noted, "The pellucid sea darkened quickly from nile green to blue. I was already deeper than I had ever been before."

Below five hundred feet, Cousteau observed a "snowstorm of tiny organisms glaring out of the darkness." Then he noted a living transparent organism with filaments two feet long. Darkness increased with the depth, with only a tinge of blue left at 1200 feet. At 1500 feet, no evidence of the sun remained.

After passing the three-thousand-foot level, Cousteau began to see many things that he never knew existed. He saw a fish twenty inches long and shaped like a drafting triangle, with the color and thinness of aluminum foil and a "ridiculous little tail." Red squid, about eighteen inches long, dispensed, to Cousteau's surprise, white ink. He saw several sharks, different in size and shape from their more familiar cousins in the heights of the ocean. Finally, with the bathyscaph's light shining full on the ocean floor, Cousteau saw the most incredible sight of all—a legible newspaper.

1. The "snowstorm" that was observed by Cousteau was made of
   (A) sand   (B) hailstones   (C) snowflakes   (D) salt crystals
   (E) living things

2. The water was completely dark between the depths of
   (A) 6 and 300 feet   (B) 300 and 500 feet   (C) 500 and 1200 feet
   (D) 1200 and 1500 feet   (E) 1500 and 4500 feet
3. Before his dive in the bathyscaph FNRS-3, Cousteau's record dive had
   been at a depth
   (A) less than 300 feet   (B) about 500 feet   (C) about 750 feet
   (D) about 920 feet   (E) more than 1200 feet

If you read the passage carefully, following the strategies on pages 659–660, you should be able to answer the questions easily. The answer to question 1 is (E). Cousteau refers to a "snowstorm of tiny organisms"; organisms are living things. For question 2, the answer also is (E). Notice the sentence "At 1500 feet, no evidence of the sun remained." To answer question 3, note the second paragraph. When the sphere had descended just below three hundred feet, Cousteau observed, "I was already deeper than I had ever been before." The correct answer is (A).

Assignment 4 Reading Comprehension   Read the paragraphs about legal assistants on pages 326–327 in Unit 7, "Three Modes of Writing." Then, on your paper, write the letter of the correct answers to the following items.

1. Legal assistants are persons who
   (A) run errands for judges   (B) find lawyers for people with low incomes   (C) serve as court stenographers during trials   (D) perform a variety of tasks for lawyers   (E) cover courtroom proceedings for newspapers, radio, or television
2. The most important trait that a legal assistant should have is
   (A) an excellent memory   (B) an interest in working with people
   (C) a desire to see criminals punished   (D) superior stenographic skills   (E) good public-speaking skills
3. In the course of their work, legal assistants may find themselves
   (A) serving subpoenas to witnesses   (B) preparing simple contracts
   (C) conducting television interviews   (D) testifying in court
   (E) representing clients in court

17.2 Standard Written English

Some standardized tests also have a section designed to test your knowledge of standard written English. You will be expected to recognize errors in usage and in sentence structure.

Usage.   In usage test items you must identify examples of incorrect use of idiomatic expressions and slang; the incorrect use of verbs, pronouns, and other parts of speech; the incorrect use of punctuation marks, and so forth. Items on usage usually follow the format shown here. You are to identify the lettered sentence part, if any, that contains an error.

> In his letter Uncle Tim promised to take Dad, Mother,
>   A
>
> Rick, and I to the theater when we visit him in New York.
>   B   C   D
>
> No error.
>   E

Read the sentence, looking carefully at each lettered choice. Sometimes a sentence has no error. No sentence has more than one error. This example does have an error: Choice C. The correct form is *and me.*

Sentence Structure.   Some items in a standardized test reflect errors in logic or in sentence structure. You must choose the best way of stating an underlined portion of a sentence or an entire sentence. If more than one answer seems correct, choose the one that is most effective in the context. In this kind of test, choice (A) is always the same as the underlined portion and means "Make no change." Study the following example.

> Because the crop is smaller this year, less persons will be needed for the harvest.
> (A) less persons will be needed for the harvest.
> (B) for the harvest less persons will be needed.
> (C) not as many persons will be needed for the harvest as were needed last year.
> (D) few persons will be needed for the harvest.
> (E) fewer persons will be needed for the harvest.

Read the sentence; then study closely the underlined portion to determine if it is incorrect and, if so, why. In the example the underlined portion is incorrect because it uses *less* to refer to items (persons) that can be counted individually (*page 150*). Choice (B) is incorrect for that same reason and also because the inverted clause is awkward. Choice (C) is too wordy. Choice (D) uses *few* instead of its comparative form. Choice (E) is the correct answer.

Assignment 1 Usage On your paper, write the letter of the usage error in each of the following sentences. Write (E) if there is no error.

1. I would go with you to the exhibit this evening if I was free. No error.
   <u>A</u> ... <u>B</u> ... <u>C</u> <u>D</u> ... <u>E</u>

2. After putting the dogs into the back of Father's truck, we climbed into
   <u>A</u> ... <u>B</u> ... <u>C</u> ... <u>D</u>
   the cab. No error.
   ... <u>E</u>

3. One section of the grocery store was devoted to mangoes, papayas,
   <u>A</u> ... <u>B</u> ... <u>C</u>
   and bananas—those kind of fruit that comes from tropical climates.
   ... <u>D</u>
   No error.
   <u>E</u>

4. The huge Wawona sequoia, felled by a storm in the winter of 1969,
   ... <u>A</u> ... <u>B</u>
   now lays in the national park. No error.
   <u>C</u> ... <u>D</u> ... <u>E</u>

5. Boasting of nonexistent accomplishments is usually a symptom of an
   inferiority complex; furthermore, those who boast some times come to
   <u>A</u> ... <u>B</u> ... <u>C</u>
   believe their own boasting. No error.
   ... <u>D</u> ... <u>E</u>

6. In the critics' reviews in the morning papers, we saw that everybody
   <u>A</u> ... <u>B</u> <u>C</u>
   but Walter and her received unfavorable notices. No error.
   <u>D</u> ... <u>E</u>

7. "I appreciate you lending me extra dining chairs when the McLeans
   <u>A</u> ... <u>B</u> <u>C</u>
   were here last week," Grant told us. No error.
   <u>D</u> ... <u>E</u>

8. Whomever planned the interior decor of this building should have
    ——————   ——   ——
   A   B   C

known that light carpet gets dirty quickly. No error.
                               —————— ————
                                   D   E

Assignment 2   Sentence Correction   On your paper, write
the letter of the error in each of the following sentences. Write (E) if
there is no error.

1. Roger won first place in the shot-put; however, he won second place
   in the javelin.
   (A) put; however,   (B) put, unless   (C) put, for instance,
   (D) put, however,   (E) put; nevertheless

2. If he had handled the baton more carefully and run faster, the relay
   team would have won.
   (A) had handled the baton more carefully and run   (B) had handled
   the baton more carefully and ran   (C) had handled the baton carefully and had run   (D) handled the baton more carefully and ran
   (E) handled the baton carefully and had ran

3. Mr. Trumbull supposed I to be she.
   (A) I to be she.   (B) I to be her.   (C) me to be her.   (D) me to
   be she.   (E) I was her.

4. The state income tax laws in California are different than those in
   other states.
   (A) different than those   (B) different to those   (C) different to the
   ones   (D) different than the ones   (E) different from those

5. The League of Women Voters invited the two candidates for governor, Long and him, to participate in a debate.
   (A) the two candidates for governor, Long and him,   (B) the two
   candidates for governor, Long and he,   (C) the two candidates for
   governor, he and Long,   (D) Long and he, the two candidates for
   governor,   (E) he and Long, the two candidates for governor,

6. Swimming in her aquarium, Margie saw seven baby guppies.
   (A) Swimming in her aquarium, Margie saw seven baby guppies.
   (B) In her aquarium swimming, Margie saw seven baby
   guppies.   (C) Swimming in her aquarium, seven guppies that were
   babies were seen by Margie.   (D) Margie saw seven baby guppies
   swimming in her aquarium.   (E) Margie saw seven guppies, which
   were babies, in the aquarium that belonged to her.

7. Being as how it was almost dark, we decided to walk back to the cottage where we were staying.

(A) Being as how it was almost dark,   (B) Almost dark,   (C) Being that it was almost dark,   (D) Being almost dark,   (E) Because it was almost dark,

8. Charles might have come in first in the annual Three Oaks Marathon if he would have trained harder.

(A) if he would have trained harder.   (B) if he would train harder.   (C) if he had trained harder.   (D) should he have trained harder.   (E) with harder training on his part.

9. Glenda is one of those gifted musicians who is able to play many instruments.

(A) who is   (B) who are   (C) whom are   (D) whom is (E) whose

10. To prepare for the race, I plan to get up early, to eat a light breakfast, and will do some stretching exercises.

(A) and will do some stretching exercises.   (B) and doing some stretching exercises.   (C) and to do some stretching exercises. (D) and do some stretching exercises.   (E) and will do some exercises to stretch my muscles.

Index

with, 118–122; defined, 7; reference of pronoun to, 131–132

Antonyms: defined, 633; in tests, 655

Apostrophe: in contractions, 193; in plural forms, 193–194, 616; in possessives, 192–193

Appendix, for technical report, 571

Application letter, 596–597

Appositive phrases: defined, 48; essential, 48–49; nonessential, 48–49, 183; pronouns in, 129

Appositives: defined, 48; essential, 48–49, 183; nonessential, 49, 183

Archaic language, 87

Argument: clarifying remarks in, 375–377; concluding sentences in, 382; defined, 373; fallacies in, 388–391; moderation in, 384–386; reasons in, 378, 379; rebuttals in, 380–381; revising, 384–391; supporting sentences in, 377–378, 379, 380–381

Articles: defined, 18; in titles, 174

Atlases, 488

Audience: considering, 322; defined, 233–234; for essay, 405–406; for literary essay, 438; for persuasive writing, 360–361; for speech, 635, 637; for technical writing, 545, 555

Author card, 486

Auxiliary verbs: agreement with subjects, 109; definition of, 13; list, 13; modals, 99–100; with past participle, 91, 92; with present participle, 91, 92; with verbals, 51, 55; in verb phrases, 13, 109

Balanced sentences, 307–308

Be: as auxiliary verb, 91, 92; as linking verb, 13, 43; partial conjugation of, 106

Bibliography: for literary essay, 457–458, 461; for research paper, 489–491, 512–513; for technical report, 571

Bibliography cards, 490–491

Body: of business letter, 588; of

essay, 420–421, 425; of literary essay, 455; of paragraph, 246–252; of research paper, 509; of speech, 641

Brackets, 200

Business letters, 586–604: adjustment letter, 593–594; application letter, 596–597; block style, 587, 588; body, 588; complimentary close, 184, 588; heading, 587–588; inside address, 588; modified block style, 588; opinion letter, 601–604; order letter, 591–592; request letter, 590–591; salutation, 188, 588; signature, 588; strategies for writing, 589, 591, 594, 596, 604

Call number, 486–487

Capitalization: of the abbreviations *A.D., B.C., A.M., P.M.*, 175; of abbreviations after names of people, 173; of compass points, 173; of family-relationship words, 172; of first word of direct quotation, 171; of first word of line of poem, 172; of first word of sentence, 171; of initials, 172; of interrupted quotation, 171; of names of awards and documents, 174; of names of days, months, etc., 174; of names of gods of mythology, 173; of names of heavenly bodies, 174; of names of historical events and periods, 174; of names of languages, 174; of names of nationalities and peoples, 174; of names of organizations, 175; of names of people, 172; of names of school subjects, 174–175; of names of structures, 175; of names of trains, ships, etc., 175; of personal and official titles, 172–173; of place names, 173; of Postal Service abbreviations, 176; of proper adjectives, 19, 175; of proper nouns, 4, 172–175; of titles of books, newspapers, etc., 174; of trade names, 175

placement of, 51
Participles, as adjectives: auxiliaries with, 51; defined, 50; past, 50–51; present, 50; tenses of, 97
Part-of-speech labels, in dictionary, 632
Parts of speech, 3–33. *See also* Adjectives, Adverbs, Conjunctions, Interjections, Nouns, Prepositions, Pronouns, Verbs.
Passive voice, 15, 103–104, 308–309
Past perfect tense, 96
Past tense, 96
Period, 35, 178–179
Periodical indexes, 488
Periodic sentences, 307
Personal pronouns: agreement with antecedents, 118–122; case, 123–126; chart, 8; defined, 8; gender, 8, 121; number, 8, 119–121; person, 8, 121–122; plural, 8, 119; possessive, 8, 20, 125–126; singular, 8, 119
Person of pronouns: agreement of pronouns and antecedents in, 121–122; defined, 8
Persuasive writing, 356–391
Phrases, 46–56: absolute, 51–52; appositive, 48–49, 129, 183; defined, 46; essential, 48–49; gerund, 53–54; infinitive, 55–56; nonessential, 48–49, 183; participial, 51–52; placement of, 137–139; prepositional, 27–28, 46–48; verb, 13–14; verbal, 50–52, 53–56
Plagiarism, 510
Point of view: in literary essay, 439; in narratives, 342–343; in technical writing, 545
Position statement: in argument, 374–375; in persuasive writing, 363; strategies for clarifying, 376–377
Positive degree, 134–135
Possessive case, 123, 125–126
Possessive nouns, 20, 192–193
Possessive pronouns: as adjectives, 20, 126; defined, 8; referring to or replacing nouns, 125

Postal Service abbreviations, 176, 178, 587–588
Predicate: complete, 38; compound, 37; placement of, 38–39; simple, 36–37
Predicate adjective: defined, 44; placement of, 44
Predicate nominative: defined, 43; and subject-verb agreement, 115–116
Prefixes: defined, 627; hyphen after, 196; list of common, 627; and meaning, 627
Prepositional phrases: as adjectives, 27–28, 47–48; as adverbs, 27–28, 47; defined, 27, 46
Prepositions: compound, 27; defined, 26; distinguishing from adverbs, 28; lists, 26, 27; objects of, 27; placement of, 27; in titles, 174
Present perfect tense, 96
Present tense, 95
Prewriting, 218–234: analyzing and interpreting information, 224–225; defined, 218; developing ideas, 227–230; exploring subject, 229; finding ideas, 219–224; focusing ideas, 232–234; lists, 227–228; notes, 225, 229–230; questions, 224, 229
Principal parts: defined, 15, 90; of irregular verbs, 91–93; of regular verbs, 91
Problem-solving method, in speeches, 641
Process, in technical writing: analysis, 559–560; defined, 555; describing a, 555–558, 559–560
Progressive forms, of verb, 98–99
Pronominal adjectives. *See* Possessive pronouns.
Pronoun case: in appositive phrases, 129; in comparisons, 130; defined, 123; of interrogative pronouns, 127–128; nominative, 123, 124; objective, 123, 124–125; of personal pronouns, 123–126; possessive, 123, 125–126; of relative pronouns, 128

Pronoun reference, 131–132
Pronouns: as adjectives, 20–21, 126; agreement with antecedents, 118–122; antecedents, defined, 7; in appositive phrases, 129; case, 123–126, 127–128, 129–130; in comparisons, 130; in compound constructions, 126; consistency in use of, 281–282; correct use of, 118–132; defined, 7; demonstrative, 8–9; indefinite, 10, 20, 111–112, 119–120, 122; intensive, 9, 122; interrogative, 9, 127–128; personal, 8, 118–122; plural, 119; possessive, 8, 20, 125–126; reference to antecedents, 131–132; reflexive, 9, 122; relative, 10, 128; singular, 119
Pronunciation: in dictionary, 632; key, 622, 632; spelling and, 620–621, 622
Proofreading: defined, 310; an essay, 426–427; a research paper, 517; symbols, 207–208; a technical report, 575
Proper adjectives: capitalization of, 19, 175; creating with suffixes, 19; defined, 19
Proper nouns: capitalization of, 4, 172–175; defined, 4
Public speaking, 634–653. *See also* Speeches.
Punctuation, 177–200: apostrophe, 192–194; brackets, 200; colon, 187–188; comma, 180–184; dash, 197; ellipsis points, 198; exclamation point, 35, 179; hyphen, 195–197; parentheses, 199–200; period, 35, 178–179; question mark, 35, 179; quotation marks, 189–190; semicolon, 185–186
Purpose, in speaking, 635, 636–637
Purpose, in writing: considering, 321–322; defined, 233; of descriptive writing, 320, 332; of essay, 402–403; of expository writing, 320, 324; of literary essay, 437–438; of narrative writing, 320; of persuasive

writing, 320, 356

Question mark, 35, 179
Questions: for literary essay, 441–442; prewriting, 224, 229; for understanding audience, 233
Quotation marks, 189–191
Quotations. *See* Direct quotations.

Readers' Guide to Periodical Literature, 488
Reading-comprehension tests, 659–661
Reading, for literary essay, 440–442
Reasoning, in persuasive writing, 370–371
Reasons: in argument, 378, 379; in paragraph development, 246–247
Rebuttal, in argument, 380–381
Reduction, revising by, 300–302
Redundancy, 89, 300
Reference works, general, 487–488
Reflexive pronouns: agreement with antecedents, 122; defined, 9
Regular verbs, 91
Relative adverbs, 60
Relative pronouns: as adjectives, 20; case, 128; defined, 10; introducing adjective clauses, 10; in subordinate clauses, 59, 60, 66
Repetition, in speech, 646
Request letter, 590–591
Research paper, 478–534: bibliography for, 489–491; defined, 478; direct quotations in, 496–497; documentation of, 509–512; drafting, 508–509; finished form for, 521–534; footnotes in, 509–512; organizing information for, 501–503; proofreading, 517; research for, 485–491; revising, 515–517; selecting and limiting topic for, 479–480; taking notes for, 493–499, 503; thesis statement for, 478, 480–482, 501
Résumé, writing a, 597–598
Retained object: defined, 104
Review, writing a, 328–330

Acknowledgments (continued)

The Publisher also wishes to thank all the students whose names appear in this textbook for granting permission to use their writing as models. The editors and the Publisher have been solely responsible for selecting the student writing used as models.

The editors have made every effort to obtain permission to use student writing. In three instances, however, it was not possible to locate student writers.

From *The Norton Anthology of English Literature* edited by M. H. Abrams et al. Reprinted by permission of W.W. Norton & Company, Inc.   From *The Wild Inside* by Linda Allison. Copyright © 1979 by Linda Allison. Reprinted with the permission of Sierra Club Books and Charles Scribner's Sons.   From "A Study in Motion" by Joseph Alper. First appeared in *Science Digest*, © 1982 by The Hearst Corporation. Reprinted by permission of the author.   From *A Glimpse of Eden* by Evelyn Ames. Copyright © 1967 by Evelyn Ames. Reprinted by permission of Houghton Mifflin Company, and Russell & Volkening, Inc. as agents for the author.   From *Fundamentals of Meteorology* by Louis J. Battan. Copyright © 1979. Reprinted by permission of Prentice-Hall, Inc.   From *Get 'em and Go Travel Guide: Mexico 1982* by Stephen Birnbaum. Copyright © 1981 by Houghton Mifflin Company. Reprinted by permission of Houghton Mifflin Company, and Penguin Books Ltd.   From *The Prairie World* by David F. Costello. Published by University of Minnesota Press, copyright © 1980. Reprinted by permission of the author.   From "Sailing Through Space on Sunlight" by Eric Drexler. First published in *Smithsonian*, February 1982. Reprinted by permission of the author. From "The Snail That's Too Good for Its Own Good" by Carrol Fleming. First published in *Smithsonian*, March 1982. Reprinted by permission of the author. From "Does Your Sport Suit Your Body?" Courtesy *Glamour*. Copyright © 1982 by The Condé Nast Publications Inc.   From page 382, Table 13.8, *Nutritional Evaluation of Food Processing* by R.S. Harris and E. Karmas, 1975. Reprinted by permission of The AVI Publishing Company, Inc., P.O. Box 831, Westport, CT 06881.   From "The Snows of Kilimanjaro," in *The Short Stories of Ernest Hemingway*, by Ernest Hemingway. Copyright 1936 Ernest Hemingway, copyright renewed 1964 Mary Hemingway. Used with the permission of Charles Scribner's Sons, and Jonathan Cape Ltd.   From "A Sunrise on the Veld" from *African Stories* by Doris Lessing. Copyright © 1951, 1953, 1954, 1957, 1958, 1962, 1963, 1964, 1965 by Doris Lessing. Reprinted by permission of Simon & Schuster, and Curtis Brown Group Ltd.   From "Bat Quest" from *All Creatures Great and Small* by Daniel P. Mannix. Copyright © 1963 by Daniel P. Mannix. Reprinted by permission of the Harold Matson Company, Inc.   "Cargoes" by John Masefield from *Collected Poems* by John Masefield. Published by Macmillan Publishing Company, Inc., © 1953. Reprinted by permission of Macmillan Publishing Company, Inc., and The Society of Authors as the literary representative of the Estate of John Masefield.   From "The Duke's Children" by Frank O'Connor from *Domestic Relations* by Frank O'Connor. Copyright 1956 by Frank O'Connor. Published by Alfred A. Knopf, Inc. Reprinted by permission of Joan Daves.   From *Readers' Guide to Periodical Literature*. Copyright © 1980, 1981 by The H.W. Wilson Company. Material reproduced by permission of the publisher. From *On Stage: A History of Theater*, 2nd edition, by Vera Mowry Roberts.

Credits

Checklist for Revision

As a guide in revising your writing, consider the following questions:

✔ 1. Did you cover your topic thoroughly?

✔ 2. Did you remove any information not directly related to your topic?

✔ 3. Did you include a topic sentence or a thesis statement?

✔ 4. Did you present your information in a logical order?

✔ 5. Did you use transitional words and phrases to emphasize the order of your ideas?

✔ 6. Did you write an appropriate conclusion?

✔ 7. Did you use words and details that are suitable for your audience?

✔ 8. Did you achieve your purpose for writing?

✔ 9. Did you vary the length and structure of your sentences?

✔10. Did you use accurate and precise words?

✔11. Did you use the correct forms for research papers, technical reports, and letters?

✔12. Did you avoid using sentence fragments, run-on sentences, and other incorrect sentence structures?

✔13. Did you use correct usage, spelling, punctuation, and capitalization?

✔14. Did you carefully proofread your finished copy?